71588

D1241099

HOW THE FAR EAST WAS LOST

*American Policy and the Creation of
Communist China, 1941-1949*

HOW THE FAR EAST WAS LOST

American Policy and the Creation of Communist China, 1941-1949

by

Dr. Anthony Kubek

Chairman, Department of Political Science
University of Dallas

071588

HENRY REGNERY COMPANY
Chicago: 1963

LIBRARY OF CONGRESS CATALOG CARD NUMBER: 63-12892
Copyright © 1963 by Henry Regnery Company, Chicago 4, Illinois.
Manufactured in the United States of America

For
Mrs. Aurelia DeHart
and
Michael Kubek, Sr.

PREFACE AND ACKNOWLEDGMENTS

The Far Eastern policy pursued during the Roosevelt-Truman administrations has long been the subject of spirited controversy among historians. This volume is the result of seven years of intensive research into a mass of documentary data dealing with the Communist conquest of China. As I have read these documents, both published and unpublished, it has become apparent that there was a connecting thread drawing them all together. Both a friendly attitude towards Communism on the part of many prominent officials in the Roosevelt-Truman administrations and a belief that in the future, the Soviet and American systems could abide in friendly fashion, led to an American commitment to a futile partnership with the U.S.S.R. in the building of a postwar "one world" organization. In the pursuit of such an aim, grave sacrifices of vital American interests were made, the war was unnecessarily prolonged and nuclear warfare was needlessly initiated.

As one reviews the actions of Harry Dexter White, Alger Hiss, Owen Lattimore and Lauchlin Currie, it becomes obvious that their interest in Soviet expansion was not merely academic. The threats of Soviet statesmen have weight today primarily because President Franklin D. Roosevelt extended to a badly beaten and disorganized Russia the Lend-Lease help that transformed that nation-in-retreat into a conquering power, which was to move across the map of Europe in giant steps, not halting until it had drawn the new frontiers that now menace world peace. Roosevelt, not Stalin, shaped the growth of modern Russia, and General George C. Marshall achieved an unenviable reputation for guessing wrong in almost every crisis.

In preparing this book I have been particularly fortunate in having access to the private papers of General Patrick J. Hurley, our former Ambassador to Nationalist China. They shed a great deal of significant light upon the China policy of the Roosevelt administration.

At the Hoover War Memorial Library at Stanford University I was able to examine in detail the private diaries and correspondence of General Joseph Stilwell and to learn the exact role played by "Vinegar Joe" in the China tragedy. Transcripts from the Harry Dexter White Papers in Princeton University library helped me to understand the real meaning of the dubious activities of this financial expert and highly influential official in the Roosevelt administration.

Of great assistance and inspiration to me in the preparation of this monograph has been my friend Professor Charles Callan Tansill. It would be impossible for me to acknowledge more than a fraction of my debt to him. He has advised me throughout the period of writing the manuscript of this book.

I wish to acknowledge my deep gratitude to Mr. George W. DeArmond, Jr., who has generously assisted me in the preparation and editing of the manuscript.

I have been most fortunate in being able to turn to my highly esteemed friend, Dr. Robert Morris, former Chief Counsel of the Internal Security Sub-Committee, for valuable advice concerning the extent of the Communist conspiracy and its influence upon American policy.

I am happy to record my indebtedness to Dr. Stephen Johnsson for his kindness in sending to me some very pertinent transcripts from the Harry Dexter White Papers in the Princeton University library.

To young aspiring professors of history and political science who are interested in a revisionist brand of history, Professor Harry Elmer Barnes has long been an inspiration and a real friend. He not only read chapters of my manuscript but gave me innumerable suggestions that were of great value.

To Professor David Nelson Rowe who was kind enough to read the manuscript.

In particular I wish to express my indebtedness to Professor John A. Carroll, Admiral Maynard Cooke, Mr. Robert McManus, Mr. Bryton Barron, Professor Donald Dozer, Reverend Joseph Costanzo, S.J., Professor Kenneth Colegrove, and General Albert C. Wedemeyer. Their intimate knowledge of many aspects of American policy in the Far East was of great assistance to me.

At the University of Dallas my good friend and colleague, Reverend Edward Maher, has often extended to me wise counsel and friendly encouragement meaning a good deal to me.

There are many personal friends who have helped me at every turn: Congressman Walter Judd, Mr. Lester DeHart, Mrs. Aurelia DeHart, Mr. Michael Kubek, Reverend John Wang, Mr. James Landrum, Mrs. Margaret Wasko, Dr. William Bining, Mr. Thomas Thalken, Mr. Don Lohbeck, Mr. Maurice Rubenstein, Mr. John Kubek, Mr. Peter O'Donnell, Jr., Mrs. Joanne Rogers, Mrs. Joan DeArmond, Mrs. Barbara Nunlist, Mr. Gene Glazier, Miss Rosemary Tichy, Mr. Nelson B. Hunt, Mr.

Peter Gifford, Mr. Richard D. Bass, Mr. Herbert Hunt, Prof. Robert Wood, and David Kubek.

Last, but certainly not least, I wish to record the assistance of my dutiful wife, Naomi, who has helped me tremendously in every way in the preparation of this book.

ANTHONY KUBEK

University of Dallas
December, 1962

FOREWORD

In this important book Professor Kubek discusses American foreign policy in the Far East during the eventful decade from 1941 to 1949. It was in many ways the most significant period in our long diplomatic history. America is now engaged in a protracted and perilous "cold war" with the Soviet Union. The background of this war was formed in 1940 when President Roosevelt began to exert upon Japan the economic pressure which produced a climate of opinion that led to war in the Far East. During the decade of the thirties, when America was slowly emerging from a serious depression, our foreign trade with Japan constantly expanded until, by 1938, our exports to that country were as large as our exports to the entire continent of South America. Japan had become our third largest export market.

Under ordinary circumstances, these expanding economic ties would have drawn Japan and the United States close together. But there were other factors that helped to unbalance this uneasy international equation. When Japan purchased increasing amounts of American cotton and thus conferred a boon upon anxious cotton producers in the South, she also increased her volume of manufactured cotton goods and began to push British manufacturers out of the Far Eastern market. This, in part, accounts for a new note of hostility that became manifest in the British attitude towards Japan. It should also be noted that the large American missionary establishment in China was ardently pro-Chinese with reference to the troubled situation in the Far East. The anti-Japanese reports that poured into missionary headquarters in America helped to color American opinion and exerted pressure upon the sensitive Department of State.

From the late months of 1931, when Secretary Stimson began to bedevil the Far Eastern situation, a basic ignorance prevailed in this Department. Stimson had closed his eyes to the fact of Soviet expansion in North China. By 1930, both Sinkiang and Outer Mongolia had fallen under Soviet control. Under the famous American circular note of July 3, 1900, the American Government had gone on record as supporting the preservation of Chinese territorial integrity. The rapid Soviet absorption of large areas of China did not disturb Stimson, and no notes of protest were sent to Russia. Japanese statesmen watched with growing apprehension the movement of this Red tide across north China, and they moved their armies into Manchuria and Inner Mongolia to serve as dikes to restrain this menacing Soviet advance. Secretaries Stimson and Hull refused to face the plain realities of the Far Eastern situation, and they entered upon a policy of the destruction of the Japanese Empire. With the fall of Japan, the last barrier to Russian domination of the Far East was removed.

Professor Kubek discusses with unusual candor and clear vision the many mistakes of the Roosevelt and Truman Administrations with reference to the Far East. There are new data and fresh interpretations that lend additional evidence to support the contentions of earlier writers that the diplomacy of the Administrations of Roosevelt and Truman was disastrous in the extreme. The strange actions of General Marshall in China, and his blind policy while Secretary of State, were chief factors in the loss of China to the Communists. In a noteworthy chapter that all Americans should read, Professor Kubek traces in damning detail the tragic role that Marshall played in the fall of Nationalist China.

This is a volume that will earn the sharpest criticisms of the motley hordes that crowded the Roosevelt and Truman bandwagons, but it is a *must book* for any American who wants to know why the present sawdust Caesar, Khrushchev, can insult at will the President of the United States and can hurl continual threats to "bury" all Americans. Soviet military might is the direct product of billions of Democratic Lend-Lease aid, coddling of Communists in high places in the American Government, and failure to understand the basic drives of world Communism. Never before in our history was Presidential leadership so devoid of vision, and never before had the mistakes of our Chief Executives been so fraught with peril to our nation. Read this book and then begin to worry about how Americans will fare in the next decade.

CHARLES CALLAN TANSILL
Professor Emeritus of
Diplomatic History,
Georgetown University

CONTENTS

PROSPECTUS

On July 19, 1935, the United States Ambassador in Moscow, William C. Bullitt, sent a dispatch to Secretary of State Cordell Hull. Included was this prophetic observation:

It is . . . the heartiest hope of the Soviet Government that the United States will become involved in war with Japan. . . . To think of the Soviet Union as a possible ally of the United States in case of war with Japan is to allow the wish to be father to the thought. The Soviet Union would certainly attempt to avoid becoming an ally until Japan had been thoroughly defeated and would then merely use the opportunity to acquire Manchuria and Sovietize China.[1]

So was it planned. And so it was to be.

The Soviet leaders planned, too, to set up a Communist government in defeated Japan. But this was not to be. Their agent in the American Government, Harry Dexter White, and his cohorts, worked brilliantly to secure this end. They reckoned without the greater brilliance of one man of incorruptible integrity. The conqueror of Japan became her savior—General of the Army Douglas MacArthur.

There was no one to save China. Some tried.

---

1 Department of State, *Foreign Relations of the United States, The Soviet Union, 1933-1939* (Washington: Government Printing Office, 1952), p. 227.

PART ONE

Destroying the Balance of Power in the Pacific

CHAPTER I

WAR IN THE PACIFIC:
A MAJOR SOVIET OBJECTIVE

The road to Pearl Harbor unfolds with all the certainty of a Greek tragedy. Since the announcement of the Open Door Policy at the turn of the century, the United States had attempted to "preserve the territorial and administrative integrity" of China. But Far Eastern power politics and sixty years of chaos in China had made it difficult for the United States to pursue this policy.

After the close of the First World War, Communism became a growing threat to the stability of the Far East. The successful *coup d'etat* led by Lenin in 1917, not only ushered in a new regime in Russia, but was also destined to bring the most powerful challenge to humanistic civilization in Asia since the coming of the Mongols. In China, Russian Communists found fertile soil for the reception of their ideas, and thus the way was prepared for infiltration. In 1920, the Communist movement in Asia was organized after Lenin sent his secretary, Marin, to establish secretly a Chinese Communist Party as a branch of the Communist International.

Then, in 1922, the Soviet government sent Adolf Joffe to China on the delicate mission of establishing official diplomatic relations with the internationally recognized Chinese government in Peking, while at the same time arranging for Soviet support of the revolutionary movement of the Kuomintang, which aimed at overthrowing the Peking government. Joffe did not meet with immediate success in Peking, but during a meeting with Sun Yat-sen at Shanghai in January, 1923, he was able to arrange an entente between Soviet Russia and the Kuomintang.[1]

Joffe returned to Russia and was succeeded by Leo Karakhan, the foremost Soviet expert in Oriental diplomacy. In 1924 he obtained official recognition of the Soviet Union from the Peking government.[2] Mean-

---

[1] Allen S. Whiting, *Soviet Policies in China* (New York: Columbia University Press, 1954), pp. 202-203.
[2] *Ibid.*, p. 221.

1

while, Sun Yat-sen wrote to Karakhan in Peking, requesting him to send a representative with whom Sun might discuss mutual relations. Karakhan sent Michael Borodin, who arrived in 1923 in Canton, where Sun had established the Kuomintang government. Soviet agents dealt with the legitimate government in Peking on the basis of normal diplomatic relations, while the Communist International dealt with the Kuomintang. "On the one hand, the Soviet Foreign Office carried on diplomatic negotiations with the Chinese government. On the other, the Communist International proceeded to set up a Chinese Communist party." [3]

Borodin's task was to pump new life into the Kuomintang. Soon the Soviet Union began to spread communistic philosophy in China, and this eventually affected the position of Japan as well. A vital issue, as far as Japan was concerned, was whether Communism would triumph in China and bring this vast domain with its teeming millions under the domination of Moscow. The Comintern spared neither effort nor money to create a Chinese Soviet Republic. From the first, their program in Asia was supported actively and ceaselessly.

In October, 1927, in a major speech before the Chamber of Commerce of the United States, George Bronson Rea outlined the picture of Bolshevism spreading over China: "If we admit that Soviet Russia has a right to intervene in the internal affairs of China and use the Chinese armies . . . to carry forward its warfare against the interests of other powers, then the powers . . . have the same right to intervene in the internal affairs of China for the protection of its interests." [4]

Friction between China and Russia developed chiefly out of conflicting claims concerning the administration of the Chinese Eastern Railway. The Sino-Soviet agreements of 1924 provided for the joint administration of the railway as a commercial enterprise. There was also a clause forbidding the dissemination of propaganda inimical to the political and social institutions of either country. In the spring of 1927, Chang Tso-lin, lord of Manchuria, was informed that the Russians were breaking the agreement of 1924 by spreading propaganda favorable to Bolshevism. On April 6, 1927, his troops raided the Soviet Embassy in Peking and discovered documents that "abundantly proved that members of the Embassy staff" were distributing Communist literature in violation of treaty obligations.[5] On May 27, 1928, Chang's troops raided the Soviet Consulate in Harbin and arrested forty-two consular officials.

These incidents indicated that Soviet Russia was moving vigorously to establish Communism in China. The Japanese saw this situation very

---

[3] Chiang Kai-shek, *Soviet Russia in China* (New York: Farrar, Strauss and Cudahy, 1957), p. 15.

[4] Dorothy Borg, *American Policy and the Chinese Revolution, 1925-1928* (New York: The Macmillan Company, 1947), p. 351.

[5] Robert T. Pollard, *China's Foreign Relations, 1917-1931* (New York: The Macmillan Company, 1933), p. 391.

clearly, and Japan, to protect her own security, began to take measures to check the flow of the Red tide. Japan understood the Communist threat in the Far East far better than any other nation could have. The outcome of the conflict between China and Soviet Russia in 1929 had important implications for Japan. First of all, it was clear that Russia had violated the provisions of the Sino-Russian agreement of 1924. The vast amount of data seized by Chinese police in the Harbin Consulate left no doubt on this point. It was apparent to Japanese statesmen that unless bastions of defense were built in Manchuria and Inner Mongolia, Communism would spread through all of North China and seriously threaten the security of Japan. To the Japanese, expansion in Manchuria was a national imperative.

The United States had its danger zone in the Caribbean, and since the era of Thomas Jefferson, every effort had been made to strengthen the American position and to keep foreign nations from establishing naval and military bases that would threaten American security. So Japan regarded Manchuria. Japan followed this natural policy and attempted to practice it with reference to the lands that bordered upon the China Sea. Korea, Manchuria, and Inner Mongolia were essential pillars of her defense structure, and she could not permit them to be undermined by Communism—which grew more menacing each year. But this fact was not recognized by the American Government after the close of World War I.

After the Manchurian Incident in 1931, Secretary of State Henry L. Stimson directed a long verbal barrage against the Japanese. He believed that intervention in Manchuria could save the whole structure of the peace treaties, and he urged the League of Nations to impose economic sanctions on Japan. Owing to the opposition of President Herbert Hoover, who feared that such measures would be "roads to war," [6] the Stimson policy did not succeed. However, Stimson went as fast and as far as Hoover would permit him to go. It was his non-recognition policy that helped drive the Japanese out of the League of Nations. The American government would not recognize the validity of territorial acquisitions that were obtained through force. This policy was severely criticized by the American minister, Hugh Wilson, who watched the dramatic proceedings at Geneva: "I began to question the non-recognition policy," he said, and "more and more as I thought it over, I became conscious that we had entered a dead-end street." [7]

When Franklin Roosevelt became President in 1933, he supported the "Stimson Doctrine" without reservation. But it was apparent to seasoned

---

[6] Ray L. Wilbur and Arthur M. Hyde, *The Hoover Policies* (New York: Charles Scribner's Sons, 1937) , p. 603.

[7] Hugh Wilson, *Diplomat Between Wars* (New York: Longmans, Green and Company, 1941), pp. 279-281.

diplomats that the manner in which Stimson endeavored to apply the
non-recognition formula was so provocative that war with Japan became
a possibility. It is significant that during the first Cabinet meeting of the
Roosevelt Administration, March 7, 1933, the eventuality of war with
Japan was carefully considered.[8] Already the shadows of conflict were
beginning to cloud the Far Eastern picture.

On October 5, 1937, the President made a famous address at Chicago,
in which he advocated a "quarantine" against aggressor nations.[9] His
words of sharp criticism were directed chiefly at Japan, and it is evident
that his challenging words marked a tragic turning-point in U. S. relations with Japan. He had inaugurated a new policy of pressure that
helped drive Americans down the road to war.

On July 26, 1939, notice was given to Japan that after six months the
Commercial Treaty of February 21, 1911 would expire.[10] This action
was a blow to the national pride of the Japanese. The big question for
the Roosevelt Administration was whether to employ economic sanctions
against Japan. Concerning this campaign of economic pressure, Ambassador Joseph C. Grew remarked: "I have pointed out that once started
on a policy of sanctions, we must see them through and that such a policy may conceivably lead to eventual war." [11] However, in order to see
sanctions through, Roosevelt brought into his Cabinet on June 20, 1940,
as Secretary of War, Henry L. Stimson who had convinced him of the
efficacy of that policy back in January, 1933. [12]

With the arrival of Stimson in the Cabinet, the Roosevelt Administration began to forge an economic chain around Japan that foreclosed
any hope of understanding between the two countries. Japan's steel industry was small compared to that of the United States. In 1940 the total
production of ingot steel in Japan and Korea was about 7.5 million tons;
in the same year, American production was about ten times greater. It
became doubtful whether there would be enough raw materials to keep
this small industry in full production. Therefore, the American iron and
steel embargo, plus the restraints which were imposed later on exports
of iron ore to Japan, severely hurt her and threatened the entire Japanese
economic structure. It forced the Japanese steel industry to operate during

---

8 James F. Farley, *Jim Farley's Story: The Roosevelt Years* (New York: Whittlesey
House, 1948), p. 39.

9 Department of State, *Peace and War: United States Foreign Policy, 1931-1941*
(Washington: Government Printing Office, 1943), pp. 383-387.

10 Secretary Hull to the Japanese Ambassador (Horinouchi) July 26, 1939, *Peace and
War: United States Foreign Policy, 1931-1941*, p. 475.

11 Joseph C. Grew, *Ten Years in Japan: A Contemporary Record Drawn from his
Diaries and Private and Official Papers, 1932-1942* (New York: Simon and Schuster,
1944), p. 295.

12 Richard Current, *Secretary Stimson* (New Jersey: Rutgers University Press, 1954),
Chapter 6.

the next critical year well below capacity, and it prevented any program of expansion.[13]

Under these circumstances, Japan was compelled to adopt a new policy. She began to expand to the south in order to control those areas which would supply not only the necessities of life, but also the products essential to the Japanese war effort—notably oil, rubber, tin, and adequate foodstuffs.[14]

On July 25, 1941, Roosevelt issued from Hyde Park an executive order, effective the next day, freezing all Japanese assets in the United States. This order brought under government control all financial and import-and-export trade transactions in which Japanese interests were involved. In effect, it created an economic blockade of Japan.[15] Our highest military and naval authorities—among them Admiral Harold R. Stark, Chief of Naval Operations and General George C. Marshall, Army Chief of Staff—believed that the freezing order would cause Japan to take last-ditch counter measures. Six days before the order was issued, the War Plans Division warned that an embargo on Japan would possibly involve the United States in early war in the Pacific. Dr. Stanley K. Hornbeck, Advisor on Political Relations to the State Department, and Secretaries Morgenthau and Stimson strongly advocated the order.[16]

When the Japanese Ambassador, Admiral Kichisaburo Nomura, called at the Department of State to inquire as to the meaning of the executive order, he was coolly received by Undersecretary of State Sumner Welles.[17] This attitude was discouraging to Nomura, who felt that Japanese-American relations had reached an impasse which held dangerous implications. In Tokyo, Japanese officials held a series of urgent conferences to review the situation and to prepare for war if it should come. "We are convinced," these officials said, "that we have reached the most impor-

---

[13] Herbert Feis, *The Road to Pearl Harbor* (New Jersey: Princeton University Press, 1950), pp. 108-109.

[14] Joseph C. Grew, *Turbulent Era: A Diplomatic Record of Forty Years* (Cambridge Riverside Press, 1952), II, 1263.

[15] U. S. Department of State, *Papers Relating to the Foreign Relations of the United States: Japan: 1931-1941* (Washington: Government Printing Office, 1943), II, 266-267.

[16] U. S. Congress, Joint Committee on the Investigation of the Pearl Harbor Attack. *Hearings Before the Joint Committee on the Investigation of the Pearl Harbor Attack,* 79th Cong., 2d Sess., (Washington: Government Printing Office, 1946), Part 5, pp. 2382-84. On July 21, Admiral Stark submitted to the President a memorandum recommending against a trade embargo, on the grounds that such a step "would probably result in a fairly early attack by Japan on Malaya and the Netherlands East Indies, and possibly would involve the United States in early war in the Pacific. If war in the Pacific is to be accepted by the United States, actions leading up to it should, if practicable, be postponed until Japan is engaged in war in Siberia." *Ibid.,* Part 5, 2382, ff.; see also testimony of Admiral Turner, *Ibid.,* Part 4, 2013-14.

[17] Memorandum of conversation between Sumner Welles and Ambassador Nomura, July 28, 1941. *Japan: 1931-1941,* II, pp. 537-539.

tant, and at the same time, the most critical moment in Japanese-U. S. relations." [18]

The picture was not encouraging. The powerful Japanese Planning Board, which co-ordinated the complex structure of Japan's war economy, found the country's resources meager and only enough, in view of the blockade, for a quick and decisive war. "If the present condition is left unchecked," asserted Teuchi Suzuke, President of the Board, "Japan will find herself totally exhausted and unable to rise in the future." The blockade, he believed, would bring about Japan's collapse within two years, and he urged that a final decision on war or peace be made "without hesitation." [19]

Tojo, then Minister of War, regarded the "freezing order" by the United States as driving Japan "into a tight corner." [20] Oil was vital to Japan, and from now on each fall of the level on oil brought the hour of decision closer. Marquis Kido, the Lord Keeper of the Privy Seal, came to the conclusion that "Japan's lack of oil was so critical that there would be an acute national crisis if there is a mistake in diplomacy." [21] In case of war, he said, "we would have enough only for one and a half years," and a conflict "would be a hopeless one." [22] Fleet Admiral Nagano, supreme naval advisor to the Emperor, declared:

I think one of the large causes of this war was the question of oil. . . . Not only the two services but the civilian elements were extremely interested, because after the U. S., Great Britain and the Netherlands refused to sell any more oil, our country was seriously threatened by the oil shortage; consequently, every element in Japan was keenly interested in the southern regions.[23]

Historian Louis Morton, Chief of the Pacific Section, Department of the Army, wrote that America, by adopting a program of unrestricted economic warfare, left Japan the embarrassing choice of humiliating surrender or resistance by whatever means lay at hand. He termed the American order of July 26 "the Japanese Pearl Harbor," suggesting a degree of provocation in excess of what many have been willing to con-

---

18 Intercepted message from Japanese Foreign Office to Ambassador Nomura, August 5, 1941, *Pearl Harbor Attack*, Part 12, pp. 10-11. Kenneth Scott Latourette, the noted missionary and church historian, argues against an embargo in early 1940. He said it would not stop Japan, but would only involve the United States in a useless and disastrous war. Kenneth Scott Latourette, "A Church-made War with Japan?" *Christian Century*, LVII, No. 5, (January 31, 1940), 140-142.

19 Louis Morton, "The Japanese Decision for War," *U. S. Naval Institute Proceedings*, Vol. 80, No. 12 (December 1954), p. 1328.

20 Interrogation of Tojo, *Far Eastern Military Tribunal*, Document No. 4169 (Alexandria, Virginia: Federal Records Bureau, 1946-1948), (Mimeographed), Exhibit No. 3441, pp. 32979-85.

21 "Kido's Diary," *Ibid.*, Document No. 1632, p. 73.

22 *Ibid.*, p. 78.

23 *Interrogations of Japanese Officials*, Naval Analysis Division, United States Strategic Bombing Survey, Vol. II, Interrogations No. 392. November 20, 1945, p. 353.

cede.[24] To Japanese officials it seemed obvious that this constant economic pressure by the Roosevelt Administration was a design to provoke war.

While the President was preparing the new economic offensive against Japan, Foreign Minister Yosuke Matsuoka was prepared to discuss Japan's position in China. He asked Bishop James E. Walsh, Superior General of the Catholic Foreign Mission Society of Maryknoll, New York, and Father J. M. Drought, of the same order, to undertake a special mission to Washington in order to impress upon the President the fact that the Japanese Government "wished to negotiate a peace agreement: (1) An agreement to nullify their participation in the Axis Pact. . . . (2) A guarantee to recall all military forces from China and to restore to China its geographical and political integrity." Other conditions bearing upon the relations of Japan and the United States were to be explored and agreed upon "in the conversations that it was hoped would ensue."

Bishop Walsh and Father Drought then had a conference with General Muto, the director of the General Bureau of Military Affairs, who assured them that "he and his associates in the Japanese Army were in accord with the efforts to reach a peace agreement." Bishop Walsh and Father Drought hurried to Washington where on January 23, 1941, they placed the whole matter before President Roosevelt and Secretary Hull in a conference of more than two hours. They were told that the matter would be "taken under advisement," [25] and thus ended the anxious effort of the Japanese Government to find a path to peace even though this path led to a renunciation of Japan's objectives in China and a tremendous loss of face.

President Roosevelt and his advisers seemed unable to understand the realities in the Far Eastern situation. They never understood the fact that Manchuria and Inner Mongolia were danger zones for Japan. Japanese statesmen of every party had realized for years the significance of the Russian menace to Japanese security.

After 1923, the tide of Communism was rolling across the plains of North China, and national defense became the principal factor in Japanese relations with both China and Russia. The military leaders in Japan read the situation with the expert eyes of men who knew that Russia was determined to exploit her tremendous advantages in Siberia to their full power. Since 1934, the Soviets had infiltrated and practically taken over

---

[24] *Washington Times-Herald*, January 4, 1954. Admiral Stark testified that high officials in Washington had known the embargo meant ultimate war. He stated that if he were Japanese, he would "go down and take" oil where he could find it. *Pearl Harbor Attack*, Part 5, pp. 2379-80.

[25] *Far Eastern Military Tribunal:* Record of Proceedings (Mimeographed), Exhibit No. 3441, pp. 32979-85.

two large provinces of China, Sinkiang and Outer Mongolia. After 1935, she had on the border of Outer Mongolia a large army of Chinese Communists that would act as an advance guard of Russian interests. The future of Japan was seriously imperiled by the Chinese thrust. It had to be countered. Yet Japan was willing, in order to secure peace with the United States, to withdraw her military forces from China.

The German invasion of Russia on June 22, 1941, was to have important repercussions in Japan. Foreign Minister Matsuoka felt deeply committed to the Germans and was much impressed by the new vistas opened for Japan by the Nazi-Soviet conflict. Early in May, 1941, he had assured the German Ambassador in Japan that "no Japanese Premier or Foreign Minister would ever be able to keep Japan neutral in the event of a German-Russian conflict. In this case, Japan would be driven, by the force of necessity, to attack Russia at Germany's side. No neutrality pact would change that at all." [26] The Japanese Foreign Ministry now told the Soviet Ambassador in Japan that if the Tripartite Axis Pact and Japan's Neutrality Agreement with the Soviet Union should prove at variance with each other, the latter would have to be dropped.[27]

The German invasion of Russia presented Japan with a golden opportunity to launch an assault on Soviet Siberia, which would eliminate once and for all the threat of Communist power.[28] Germany began to apply pressure to obtain Japan's declaration of war against the Soviet Union. The German Ambassador to Tokyo, Eugene Ott, was instructed to advise the Japanese that they had a "unique opportunity for the new order in East Asia by going to war with the Soviet Union. After the elimination of Soviet power in Asia, the solution of the China question would have no difficulty." [29] Ott handed the message to Matsuoka, who was in full agreement with it and said that he would bring it to the attention of the army and navy officials and the Emperor. [30]

Bypassing the Prime Minister, Matsuoka hurried to the Imperial Palace to expound his grand design, but was coolly received. [31]

Japan wanted to be ready to take full advantage of the eventual collapse of Soviet Russia. A decision had been made to hasten the reinforce-

---

26 Ambassador Ott to Foreign Minister Ribbentrop, *Ibid.*, Document No. 4074.

27 Ambassador Ott to German Foreign Ministry, May 6, 1941 *Ibid.*, Exhibit No. 1068; Defense Document No. 1580; excerpts from diary of K. A. Smetanin, the Soviet Ambassador, April 25, 1941, *Ibid.*, Document No. 1886.

28 *Ibid.*, p. 7955; Document No. 879, p. 52; For an excellent analysis of Matsuoka's policy over the German-Russian War, see Interrogation of Kido, *Ibid.*, pp. 494-499.

29 "American and British Phase: Summary of Proof," *Ibid.*, p. 61. Also Ribbentrop to Ott, Berlin, June 28, 1941, *Ibid.*, Document No. 4097.

30 Ambassador Ott to Foreign Minister Ribbentrop, Tokyo, July 3, 1941, *Ibid.*, Document No. 4062.

31 "Matsuoka was opposed to the 'southern advance' on the ground that it would jeopardize relations with Great Britain and the United States." Toshikazu Kase, *Journey to the "Missouri"*, (New Haven: Yale University Press, 1950), p. 48.

ment of Japanese troops in Manchuria. If the Kremlin should be obliged to withdraw part of her army from the Far East, Japan would be in a superior military position if it became necessary to strike.[32]

On July 2, an Imperial Conference was held in Tokyo. It was decided not to move against the Soviet Union through Siberia, but to prosecute, instead, a plan of advance into Indo-China and Siam at the risk of war with the United States and Great Britain. With respect to the German-Soviet conflict, Japan would continue to observe her Neutrality Pact with the Soviet Union. Should the war go in Germany's favor, however, Japan would then intervene "to secure stability in the northern regions." [33]

The possibility of a Japanese attack, or of a joint German-Japanese invasion through Siberia, was a specter that haunted Soviet officials. Invasion of Siberia, however, offered no material advantage to Japan, other than a purely military one. Japan needed oil, and, with the United States constantly applying economic pressure, it was to Japanese advantage to move in the direction of Southeast Asia, where oil was available. This was the view strongly advocated by the Japanese naval officials, who opposed simultaneous war with the Anglo-Saxon powers and the Soviet Union.[34]

The significance of Japan's decision to move south instead of against the Soviet Union cannot be overestimated. V. Kravchenko, a high Soviet official before he defected to the United States, describes how Soviet Far Eastern troops were able to stem the tide against the German advance into Russia. He wrote: "Beginning with the nineteenth [October 1941], the situation improved The first seasoned Siberian and Far Eastern forces began to arrive. . . . Far East troops, hardened in border struggle with the Japanese, and Siberian forces inured to winter warfare were rushing westward across a continent to hold the invaders." [35]

The Kremlin had been promptly informed by its master spy, Richard Sorge, of the Japanese decision of July 2, and especially of the postponement of the military operations into Siberia.

---

[32] "Kido's Diary," *Far Eastern Military Tribunal* (Manuscript). Document No. 1632; intercepted message from Tokyo to Nomura, August 20, 1941, *Pearl Harbor Attack*, Part 12, pp. 18-19.

[33] *Far Eastern Military Tribunal*, Defense Document No. 1652: "Tojo Memorandum," *Ibid.*, Record pp. 36254-58; "Konoye's Memoirs," Appendix III, *Pearl Harbor Attack*, Part 20, pp. 4018-19. A neutrality pact between the Soviet Union and Japan was signed in Moscow on April 13, 1941; for text, cf. Department of State *Bulletin*, April 29, 1945, p. 812.

[34] President Roosevelt followed the debate through the medium of "Magic"—a name applied to intercepted and decoded Japanese messages. He described the Imperial Conference as "a real dragdown and knockout fight . . . to decide which way they are going to jump—attack Russia, attack the South Seas (or) sit on the fence and be more friendly with us." President Roosevelt to Secretary Ickes, July 1, 1941 cited in William L. Langer and S. Everett Gleason, *The Undeclared War, 1940-41* (New York: Harper and Brothers, 1953), p. 464.

[35] V. Kravchenko, *I Chose Freedom* (New York: Charles Scribner and Sons, 1950), p. 377-378.

Sorge's primary duty when he was sent to Tokyo in 1933 was "to observe most closely Japan's policy toward the U.S.S.R. . . . and at the same time, to give very careful study to the question of whether or not Japan was planning to attack the U.S.S.R." [36]

Sorge had originally been in the Shanghai spy ring with Agnes Smedley. In preparation for his assignment in Tokyo, the Soviet Fourth Bureau somehow managed to get him a Nazi party card. After establishing himself as a correspondent for the Frankfurter Zeitung, Sorge proceeded from Germany to Tokyo, where he presented himself at the German Embassy. And he immediately began organizing a Soviet spy ring in Tokyo.

His assistant was Hotsumi Ozaki, an adviser to the Japanese Premier. Ozaki was aided by Kinkazu Saionji, Secretary of the Japanese Council of the Institute of Pacific Relations.[37] Sorge developed a close friendship with Colonel Eugene Ott, later to be Germany's wartime ambassador in Tokyo.

Sorge became a close friend of Mrs. Ott. She was a source of information that enabled Sorge to report to the Kremlin the dialogues exchanged between Premier Konoye and Ambassador Ott on relations with the Soviet Union and Japan.[38]

In 1936, when Japan became a member of the Rome-Berlin Axis by signing the Anti-Comintern Pact, Sorge was able to reassure alarmed officials in the Kremlin. The Japanese had refused to agree to a military alliance and had merely declared that they were against World Communism. In 1937, he informed the Kremlin that there was no need to be concerned about the China Incident. Ozaki's estimate showed that the Japanese forces would bog down in North China and that the struggle would be indecisive.[39]

In the summer of 1939, the Red Army and the Japanese Kwantung Army clashed on the Manchukuo-Mongolian border. The Red Army was in no condition to fight a major war, and there was considerable alarm in Moscow. Sorge was able to supply detailed information on Japanese troop dispositions and reinforcements. He notified the Kremlin also that the Japanese had no intention of provoking a major war—this was just a feeler operation, local in character.[40]

The Tripartite Pact, establishing a German-Italian-Japanese military

---

[36] Ralph de Tolendano, Spies, Dupes and Diplomats (New York: Duell, Sloan and Pearce; Boston: Little, Brown and Company, 1952), p. 80 (Quoting from Sorge's confession.)

[37] U. S. Congress, Senate Committee on the Judiciary, Internal Security Subcommittee, Institute of Pacific Relations, Hearings, 82nd Cong. 1st Sess. (Washington: Government Printing Office, 1951), Part 2, pp. 363-364; p. 505.

[38] Far Eastern Military Tribunal, Defense Document No. 1486.

[39] de Toledano, Spies, Dupes and Diplomats. p. 97.

[40] Ibid, p. 98.

alliance, was signed in Berlin on September 27, 1940. The signatory nations agreed to go to war with any nation which attacked one of the parties, either in Europe or in the Pacific. Nations already involved in the war in Europe were excepted.

Sorge could not prevent the pact. But he was there when the preliminary negotiations began. Ralph de Toledano has commented: "Sorge was in effect the 'primary architect' of that pact. Any military alliance is a loaded pistol, and Sorge saw to it that the gun pointed at the United States rather than at Russia." [41]

On May 20, 1941, Sorge chalked up one of his greatest achievements. On that date he warned the Kremlin that the Germans were concentrating 170 to 190 divisions along the German-Soviet border in partitioned Poland. The attack, he predicted, would be launched on June 20. Sorge missed by two days; it came on the morning of June 22. Although warned in time, the Red Army fell back in disorder, due primarily to an error in strategy by Marshal Stalin.[42]

Sorge was ordered to drop all other intelligence work and to give his attention exclusively to two questions: "Would Japan take advantage of the rout and launch the long-threatened war on Russia? Or could the Red Army pull out its Far Eastern garrisons and throw them into the battle for Moscow?" [43]

A secondary mission was assumed by Sorge. He had long worked to turn the Japanese southward—away from Siberia and toward a possible war with the United States. This effort was now intensified. Mitsusada Yoshikawa, Director of the Special Investigation Bureau of the Attorney General's Office of the Japanese Government, testified before the Senate Internal Security Sub-committee that Sorge, working through Ozaki and Saionji, sought to impress on the Japanese officials that, if they struck north, their forces would encounter powerful Red Armies. There would be little of value in Siberia, and Japan would probably meet greater difficulties than in her war with China. But if she struck south, it was pointed out, she would find many useful resources. Besides, Japan historically had always failed in any military mission toward the north. [44]

The stage was set for Sorge's last and, perhaps, greatest achievement. His last report to Moscow before his discovery and arrest in mid-October,

---

41 *Ibid*, p. 99.

42 *Ibid.*, p. 100.

43 *Ibid.*, pp. 100-101.

44 Testimony of Mitsusada Yoshikawa, August 20, 1951, *Institute of Pacific Relations, Hearings*, Part 2, p. 504. Ozaki was unofficial adviser to the Konoye Cabinet, 1938-39. As a friend of Konoye and of Konoye's private secretaries, Ushiba and Kishi, Ozaki knew all about the decisions of the Japanese Cabinet and Liaison Conferences. Therefore, especially from 1938 to October 1941, Moscow knew fully and accurately about Japanese political decisions and intentions; it also received a wealth of military and economic data. See Charles A. Willoughby, *Shanghai Conspiracy: The Sorge Spy Ring* (New York: E. P. Dutton and Company, Inc., 1952), pp. 33-39; 102-117.

stated that there was no serious danger of an attack from Manchuria. The Japanese, he said, would move south, and war· with the United States and Britain was probable before the end of the year.[45] Far Eastern forces were rushed to the western front. A year later the tide of war changed at Stalingrad. Japanese prison records show that Sorge was hanged on the morning of November 7, 1944.[46]

Even as Japanese military intentions were being projected southward, President Roosevelt and Prime Minister Churchill met at Newfoundland from August 9 to 13, 1941. The Atlantic Conference provided Churchill with sufficiently strong assurances of United States military support in the Far East to enable him to base important wartime military decisions on those assurances.[47] These facts and the complete understandings with which the two leaders parted are attested by Churchill's speech in the House of Commons as set forth in the *Private Papers of Senator Vandenberg*. The Senator's reaction to the speech was recorded on January 27, 1942:

Churchill spoke to the British Commons today. *And we learned something of very great importance over here in the U.S.A.* In discussing events leading up to the war in the Far Pacific he said: '. . . the probability since the Atlantic Conference, at which *I discussed these matters with President Roosevelt, that the United States, even if not herself attacked, would come into the war in the Far East* and thus make the final victory assured, seemed to allay some of these anxieties, and that expectation has not been falsified by the events.'

In other words, Churchill said that when he met Roosevelt the first time—and wrote 'The Atlantic Charter'—he talked with the President about the fact that Britain must not fight alone in the Far East, and got some sort of an assurance . . . that the U.S. would go to war with Japan *regardless of whether* Japan attacked us or not. In still other words, *we were slated for this war by the President before Pearl Harbor.* Pearl Harbor merely precipitated what was 'in the cards.' To whatever extent this is true, it indicates how both Congress and the Country were in total ignorance of the American war-commitments made by the President and never disclosed.[48]

---

[45] U.S. Congress, House of Representatives, Committee on Un-American Activities, *Hearings on American Aspects of the Richard Sorge Spy Case*, 82nd Cong., 1st Sess. (Washington: Government Printing Office, 1951), pp. 1198-99.

[46] de Toledano, *op. cit.*, pp. 9-10. It is barely possible that Stalin, intending to stay out of the Pacific war until Japan had been defeated, extracted from Japan some concessions for his assurance of Soviet neutrality. But the best of Soviet agents seem to have nine lives. In 1949, a German career diplomat who had talked with Sorge in his last days stopped off in New York while on a mission to Washington. "If Sorge walked into the execution chamber," he told friends, "he walked out on his own feet. Sorge is not dead. Stalin made a deal with the Japanese. After the war, I heard reports that Sorge was still alive. I believe those reports. The prison records? Every Bolshevik knows that records are kept only to be falsified."

[47] That we were in a "shooting war" with Germany long before Pearl Harbor is purely academic. According to the Canadian navy history, strategic control operations of Canadian and British warships on the western side of the Atlantic were placed under American command by agreement of Roosevelt and Churchill in their "Atlantic Charter" meeting. The American Navy's convoy role in "one of the most active theaters" of World War II was made under orders of Roosevelt before the United States was officially at war. Cf. *Times Herald* (Washington, D.C.), April 1, 1953.

[48] Arthur H. Vandenberg, Jr. (ed.), *The Private Papers of Senator Vandenberg*

What stronger evidence can there be that President Roosevelt did make positive commitments of support to Churchill?

In August, 1941, Prime Minister Fumimaro Konoye, realizing the situation with the United States was getting worse, made a proposal to meet with President Roosevelt at Honolulu. Ambassador Joseph C. Grew was so deeply impressed with the sincerity of Konoye's plea that he immediately sent a dispatch to Secretary Hull and urged, "with all the force at his command, for the sake of avoiding the obviously growing possibility of an utterly futile war between Japan and the United States, that this Japanese proposal not be turned aside without very prayerful consideration. . . . The opportunity is here presented . . . for an act of the highest statesmanship . . . with the possible overcoming thereby of apparently insurmountable obstacles to peace hereafter in the Pacific." [49]

There was "little doubt" that Konoye "would appeal for American cooperation," Grew's communication continued, "in bringing the China affair to a close and would probably be prepared to give far-reaching undertakings in that connection, involving also the eventual withdrawal of Japanese forces from Indochina." The "time element" was "important because the rapid acceleration given by recent American economic measures to the deterioration of Japan's economic life will tend progressively to weaken rather than to strengthen the moderate elements in the country and the hand of the present Cabinet and to reinforce the extremists." In Grew's opinion the "most important aspect of the proposed meeting" was that if the results were "not wholly favorable," there would, nonetheless, be "a definite opportunity to prevent the situation in the Far East from getting rapidly worse." [50]

On August 26, Ambassador Nomura received an urgent message which expressed an almost frantic desire to arrange a meeting between the leaders of the two countries. The instruction stated: "Now the international situation as well as our internal situation is strained in the extreme and we have reached the point where we will pin our last hopes on an inter-

---

(Boston: Houghton Mifflin Co., 1952), p. 27. (Emphasis in original) On February 23, 1941, the *New York Times* reported that although a Gallup poll showed 56 percent of those polled were in favor of an effort to keep Japan from seizing the Dutch East Indies and Singapore, only 39 percent supported going to war to do it. Another poll made in August, 1941, by *Fortune* showed that 33.7 percent of those polled were in favor of defending the Philippines, East Indies, and Australia, and only 22.3 percent favored the defense of an unspecified portion of this area.

[49] Ambassador Grew to Secretary Hull, Tokyo, August 18, 1941. *Japan: 1931-1941*, II, p. 565.

[50] Ambassador Grew to Secretary Hull, August 19, 1941. *Foreign Relations, 1941*, IV, pp. 382-383.

The imposition of the embargo on exports of oil in the previous month was looked upon by the Japanese as a "severance of economic relations." Former Ambassador Nomura has characterized the action as "a step just short of war." Admiral Kichisaburo Nomura, "Stepping-Stones to War," *United States Naval Institute Proceedings*, LXXVII (September, 1951), No. 9, p. 930.

view between the Premier and the President." [51] Two days later the Japanese Ambassador handed President Roosevelt Konoye's proposal for a meeting to "take place as soon as possible." [52] It was rejected.[53]

Since the end of 1940 our Ambassador in Tokyo had pressed for a "thorough re-examination of our approach to the problems of the Far East and a redefinition of the main immediate objectives to be pursued by American diplomacy." [54] Both he and the entire embassy staff were convinced the problem "could never be solved by formulas drawn up in the exploratory conversations." They believed the problem "could and would be solved if the proposed meeting between Prince Konoye and the President should take place." [55] When Ambassador Grew urged President Roosevelt to make a speech at the earliest possible moment in order that the Japanese public would gain knowledge of our true intentions, his "recommendation was not carried out." "Why?" Grew asked: "History will wish to know." In his opinion this gesture "might well have turned the whole trend in Japan at this critical time." [56]

Following the outbreak of war, Grew asked Hull why Konoye's important proposal had not been accepted. Hull answered: "If you thought so strongly, why didn't you board a plane and come to tell us?" The Ambassador reminded him of the urgent telegrams he had repeatedly sent the Department. Suddenly, he "wondered whether Mr. Hull had been given and had read all of the dispatches from Tokyo." [57] There is "no evidence" in the official correspondence, of either a "desire or of efforts on the part of our Government to simplify Prince Konoye's difficult task or to meet him even part way." [58] Ambassador Grew assured the President that Konoye was willing to "go as far as is possible, without incurring open rebellion in Japan, to reach a reasonable understanding with us." [59] He pleaded his case with courage and determination:

It seems to me highly unlikely that this chance will come again or that any Japanese statesman other than Prince Konoye could succeed in controlling the military extremists in carrying through a policy which they, in their ignorance of international affairs and economic laws, resent and oppose. The alternative

---

[51] The Japanese Foreign Office to Ambassador Nomura, August 26, 1941. *Pearl Harbor Attack*, Part 12, p. 20.

[52] The Japanese Prime Minister (Prince Konoye) to President Roosevelt, August 27, 1941. *Japan: 1931-1941*, II, 573.

[53] President Roosevelt's reply to the Japanese Prime Minister (Prince Konoye), handed to the Japanese Ambassador (Nomura) on September 3, 1941. *Ibid.*, p. 591.

[54] Grew, *Turbulent Era: A Diplomatic Record of Forty Years, 1904-1945*, II, 1255.

[55] *Ibid.*, p. 1264.

[56] *Ibid.*, p. 1343.

[57] *Ibid.*, p. 1330.

[58] *Ibid.*, p. 1334.

[59] Ambassador Grew to President Roosevelt, September 22, 1941. *Foreign Relations, 1941*, IV, 468. The risk to Prince Konoye's life was real, not imaginary. On Septem-

to reaching a settlement now would be the greatly increased probability of war
—*Facillis descensus Averno est*—and while we would undoubtedly win in the
end, I question whether it is in our own interest to see an impoverished Japan
reduced to the position of a third-rate Power.[60]

A memorandum was prepared in the Far Eastern Division of the
Department of State, which attempted to evaluate the arguments, pro
and con, regarding the proposed Roosevelt-Konoye meeting. Joseph Ballantine arrived at the conclusion that the arguments against the meeting
outweighed those in favor of it. It was feared that if we entered into
negotiations with Japan, Chinese morale might be "seriously impaired."
In this event "it would probably be most difficult to revive in China the
psychology necessary to continue effective resistance against Japan."[61]
Lauchlin Currie, Administrative Assistant to the President, strongly emphasized this viewpoint. He was opposed to an American agreement with
Japan because it "would do irreparable damage to the good will we have
built up in China."[62] Moreover, it was pointed out that the British,
Dutch and other governments would entertain "misgivings" about America's will to resist. This could result in a "breakdown in their efforts to
maintain a firm front against Japan." Ballantine expressed the view
that "such a meeting would create illusions for the Japanese people and
would operate as a factor to hide from the Japanese people the wide
discrepancy between the viewpoints of the American and the Japanese
Governments."[63]

Ambassador Grew seemed to be of the opinion such a meeting would,
on the contrary, dispel such illusions. What he thought necessary "was
a dramatic gesture, something that would electrify the people both in
Japan and the United States and would give impetus to an entirely new

---

ber 18, "an attempt on Prince Konoye's life was made by four men who jumped on
the running-board of his car with daggers and short swords as he was about to leave
his private residence at Ogikubo. Fortunately the doors of the car were locked inside
and the would-be assassins were quickly overpowered by plainclothes police." Grew,
Turbulent Era, II, 1332.

[60] Ambassador Grew to President Roosevelt, September 22, 1941. *Foreign Relations,
1941*, IV, 469.

[61] Memorandum by Mr. Joseph W. Ballantine, September 25, 1941. *Ibid.*, p. 479.
The pro arguments were summarized, as follows: A Roosevelt-Konoye meeting would
indicate that Japan was drawing away from the Axis and that she questioned Germany's ability to win the war in Europe. The war-weary people of Japan would
welcome a normalization of relations between the two countries. The result might
strengthen the hands of those who seek to lead Japan in the way of peace and co-
operation with the democratic nations. The meeting would give an evidence that the
United States bore no hostility toward the Japanese Government or people. The
President would be able to explain his views and purposes face to face with the Japanese Prime Minister. *Ibid.*, pp. 478-479.

[62] Memorandum by Lauchlin Currie to President Roosevelt, September 13, 1941, as
quoted in Langer and Gleason, *The Undeclared War, 1940-1941*, p. 710.

[63] Memorandum by Joseph W. Ballantine, September 25, 1941, *Foreign Relations,
1941*, IV, 479-480.

trend of thought and policy." [64] Finally, the Ballantine memorandum stated: "The effect of such a meeting upon the American public would in all probability be unfavorable, particularly among those groups which have exhibited an uncompromising stand on the question of stopping Japanese aggression." [65]

Secretary Hull rejected the idea of a Konoye-Roosevelt meeting and remarked to Ambassador Nomura that, before there could be a meeting between the President and Prince Konoye, there would first have to be an agreement upon basic principles of policy.[66] He knew that such an agreement was not possible. In other circumstances, Hull's reason might have had validity; in the unique circumstances of the Konoye offer, it had none. The meat of the Konoye offer was that the Emperor would act; preliminary negotiations would serve only to make the Emperor's action doubtful.

The British attitude was generally affirmative with regards to the Konoye offer. They presumed it would serve their interest of securing Singapore and maintaining the stabilization of Southeast Asia. Actually, of course, war did result in the loss of Singapore. However, the record indicates that Sir Robert Craigie, British Ambassador in Tokyo, was "firmly of the opinion" that the Roosevelt-Konoye meeting should be held. In his view "it would be a foolish policy if this superb opportunity is permitted to slip by assuming an unduly suspicious attitude." [67] According to Duff Cooper, Ambassador Craigie stated to the Foreign Office shortly before the fall of Konoye Cabinet, "Time now suitable for real peace with Japan. Hope this time American cynicism will not be allowed to interfere with realistic statesmanship." [68]

The hard-pressed Chinese stood to benefit from failure of the conference and from involvement of Japan in war with the United States. China could win only in a peace following the war. Clarence Gauss, then Ambassador to China, believed it was "indeed vital" to "give China all the support we can in her fight against Japanese aggression." In a message which was received in Washington following the outbreak of war, he wrote:

At the same time I believe that it is important that we bear in mind that the defeat of Japanese aggression does not necessarily entail as many Chinese think,

---

64 Grew, *Turbulent Era*, II, 1350.

65 Memorandum by Joseph W. Ballantine, September 25, 1941, *Foreign Relations, 1941*, IV, 480.

66 Oral statement handed by Secretary Hull to Ambassador Nomura, October 2, 1941, *Japan: 1931-1941*, pp. 656-661.

67 The Japanese Foreign Office to Ambassador Nomura, October 3, 1941, *Pearl Harbor Attack*, Part 12, p. 51.

68 Owen Lattimore, American Political Advisor to Generalissimo Chiang Kai-shek, to Mr. Lauchlin Currie, Administrative Assistant to President Roosevelt, November 2, 1941, *Foreign Relations, 1941*, V, p. 747.

our crushing Japan militarily. The complete elimination of Japan as a force in the Far East would not be conducive either to order or prosperity in this area.[69]

Major General Charles A. Willoughby, who was formerly American Intelligence Chief in the Far East, has testified that Prince Konoye "was desperately serious in effecting a last-minute understanding with the United States." [70]

Sentiment within the Department of State was generally unfavorable to the proposed Roosevelt-Konoye meeting. The Treasury Department —which was to play an increasingly formative role in the development of American Far Eastern policy—voiced its firm opposition to any agreement with Japan. The President was warned of the hidden perils of "a new Munich." Harry Dexter White submitted a spirited appeal for bolder action in the Far East:

Mr. President, word was brought to me yesterday evening that persons in our country's government are hoping to betray the cause of the heroic Chinese people and strike a deadly blow at all your plans for a world-wide democratic victory. I was told that the Japanese Embassy staff is openly boasting of a great triumph for the "New Order." Oil—rivers of oil—will soon be flowing to the Japanese war machines. A humiliated democracy in the Far East, China, Holland, Great Britain will soon be facing a Fascist coalition emboldened and strengthened by diplomatic victory—So the Japanese are saying.

Mr. President, I am aware that many honest individuals argue that a Far East Munich is necessary at the moment. But I write this letter because millions of human beings everywhere in the world share with me the profound conviction that you will lead a suffering world to victory over the menace to all our lives and all of our liberties. To sell China to her enemies for the thirty blood-stained coins of gold will not only weaken our national policy in Europe as well as in the Far East, but will dim the bright lustre of America's world leadership in the great democratic fight against Fascism.

On this day, Mr. President, the whole country looks to you to save America's power as well as her sacred honor. I know—I have, the most perfect confidence—that should these stories be true, should there be Americans who seek to destroy your declared policy in world affairs, that you will succeed in circumventing these plotters of a new Munich.[71]

Although tension was mounting in Tokyo, Japanese officials did not lose hope that an agreement could be made to avert war. Ambassador Nomura was instructed to present a *modus vivendi* to the Secretary of State, but this was rejected when it became certain the Chinese and the British would not agree. However, Hull went ahead and drafted a *modus vivendi* of his own which President Roosevelt regarded as a "fair proposition" but he was "not very hopeful" of its success.[72]

---

[69] Ambassador Gauss to President Roosevelt, November 19, 1941, *Ibid.*, p. 550.

[70] Testimony of General Charles A. Willoughby, August 9, 1951. *Institute of Pacific Relations, Hearings*, Part 2, p. 382.

[71] *Harry Dexter White Papers*, Princeton University MSS., [Undated].

[72] *Pearl Harbor Attack*, Part 14, p. 1142. Paul W. Schroeder in his interesting analysis of our relations with Japan for the year 1941, says until "the middle of July,

At noon on November 25, Secretaries Stimson and Knox met at the White House together with General Marshall and Admiral Stark. The discussion dealt mainly with the Japanese situation concerning the intercepted message fixing the November 29 deadline.[73] The President "brought up the event that we were likely to be attacked perhaps (as soon as) next Monday, for the Japanese are notorious for making an attack without warning." The main question was *"how we should maneuver them into the position of firing the first shot without allowing too much danger* to ourselves. It was a difficult proposition." This took place before Hull sent his ultimatum on November 26.

The next morning Stimson heard from Hull over the telephone that Hull had "about made up his mind" not to go through with his plan for a three months' truce, but, instead, to "kick the whole thing over" and tell the Japanese that he had no proposition at all. The decision for a *modus vivendi* was thus dropped and the President gave his blessing to the shelving of it in his morning interview with Hull on November 26.[74]

The proposed *modus vivendi* provided for a truce of three months

---

1941, the policy of Japan was unmistakably aggressive in nature." The American position in this same period was definitely defensive. After July, 1941, America went on a diplomatic offensive with constant economic pressure being used as a weapon to push Japan back, to compel her to withdraw from her conquests. On the other hand, Japan, after freezing orders, was hesitant, worried and in retreat. Her main objective was "somehow to extricate herself from the desperate position in which she was entangled, to get relief from the inexorable economic pressure of the embargo, and to avoid what seemed to be inevitable war." *The Axis Alliance and Japanese-American Relations, 1941,* (Ithaca, New York: Cornell University Press, 1958), pp. 173-176.

73 On November 22, 1941, Washington officials intercepted a message from Tokyo to the Japanese Embassy. It extended Japan's deadline from November 25 to November 29, but warned that thereafter "things are automatically going to happen." *Pearl Harbor Attack,* Part 12, p. 165.

74 Italics mine. Henry L. Stimson's *Diary,* November 25, 1941, *Ibid.,* Part II, pp. 5433-34. Richard Current in "How Stimson Meant to 'Maneuver' the Japanese" says, "The fact that the President and his advisers on November 25 did *not* expect the Japanese soon to strike at American territory was precisely the reason why the question 'how we should maneuver them into the position of firing the first shot' was such a 'difficult proposition.' Since the Japanese were not thought likely to initiate hostilities against the United States itself, the problem was how to put them in a position of *seeming* to fire the 'first shot' at this country." *Mississippi Valley Historical Review* (June 1953), p. 74. Dr. Harry Elmer Barnes, in his review of Current's book, *Secretary Stimson: A Study in Statecraft* points out the fallacy in Current's argument. "The only weak spot in Professor Current's book lies in his treatment of the attitude of Roosevelt and his entourage in the days immediately preceding Pearl Harbor. . . . There is no doubt that the White House and the warmongering strategists in the Cabinet were panic-stricken for a time over this possibility of having to make war without any Japanese attack. . . . But this alarm passed away with the receipt of the welcome news (decoded Japanese messages) which revealed, as clearly as daylight, that the Japanese could attack Pearl Harbor. . . . By the evening of December 6th, the Japanese' reply to Hull's ultimatum of November 26th convinced Roosevelt that war with Japan was about to break out." *Facts Forum News,* February 1956, p. 50. For other interpretations of Stimson's statement Cf. Charles Beard, *President Roosevelt and the Coming of the War, 1941,* (New Haven: Yale University Press, 1948), Chapter XVII; Charles C. Tansill, *Back Door to War* (Chicago: Henry Regnery, 1952), pp. 645-652; George Morgenstern, *Pearl Harbor* (New York: Devin-Adair Company, 1947), Chapter XIX.

during which time the United States and Japan would agree not to "advance by force or threat of force" in Southeastern and Northeastern Asia or in the southern and northern Pacific area. The Japanese would agree to withdraw their troops from Indochina and to relax their freezing and export restrictions, permitting the resumption of trade in embargoed articles. The United States would modify its restrictions in the same way. The draft of the proposal declared: "The Government of the United States is earnestly desirous to contribute to the promotion and maintenance of peace in the Pacific area and to afford every opportunity for the continuance of discussions with the Japanese Government directed towards working out a broad-gauge program of peace throughout the Pacific area." There had been "some progress" made in regard to "the general principles which constitute the basis of a peaceful settlement covering the entire Pacific area." [75] This proposal was never submitted to the Japanese Government.

Had a *modus vivendi* with Japan been reached—and it could have been reached with far fewer concessions at the expense of China than were later to be made to Soviet Russia at Yalta—almost certainly the war with Japan would thereby have been averted, particularly in view of the German reverses in Russia in the winter of 1941-1942. A growing conviction existed in Japanese military circles that Germany was in a death struggle in her war with Russia. In his testimony before the Congressional Committee investigating the attack on Pearl Harbor, General Marshall said that if the 90-day truce had been effected, the United States might never have become involved in the war at all; that a delay by the Japanese from December, 1941, into January, 1942, might have resulted in a change of Japanese opinion as to the wisdom of the attack because of the collapse of the German front before Moscow in December, 1941.[76]

Why did Secretary Hull change his mind about a *modus vivendi*? It is difficult to get a precise sequence of events which led to the final decision. However, factors which must have influenced the decision were the strong protest from the Chinese, and Churchill's views which were received during the night of November 25.[77]

Another factor which cannot be dismissed was the pressure exerted by Harry Dexter White. As soon as word of Secretary Hull's offer of a *modus vivendi* became known, White took precipitate action. A letter signed "Henry Morgenthau, Jr." was dispatched to President Roosevelt

75 Final Draft of Proposed "Modus Vivendi" with Japan, November 25, 1941, *Foreign Relations, 1941*, IV, pp. 662-664.

76 *Pearl Harbor Attack, Final Report*, Part 39, p. 502; Part 3, p. 1149.

77 Prime Minister Churchill to President Roosevelt, November 26, 1941, *Pearl Harbor Attack*, Part 14, p. 1300. See also Mr. Churchill's views in *The Grand Alliance*, (Boston: Houghton-Mifflin Company, 1950), pp. 595-597. For a description of the attitude of Congress see Admiral Stark's testimony in *Pearl Harbor Attack*, Part 5, pp. 2327 ff. For complaints by Chinese officials see *Ibid.*, Part 14, p. 1161; 1167-1170.

on the 24th or 25th of November. Its words told of the dire consequences that would come in the wake of any agreement with Japan.
"After our long association, I need not tell you that this is not written
in any doubt of your objectives, but I feel and fear that if the people,
our people, and all the oppressed people of the earth, interpret your
move as an appeasement of repressive forces, as a move that savors strongly of 'selling out China' for a temporary respite, a terrible blow will have
struck against those very objectives." The President was reminded of the
"supreme part" he was "to play in world affairs." This role could be
played "with complete effectiveness if only [he] retain [ed] the people's
confidence in [his] courage and steadfastness in the face of aggression,
and in the face of the blandishments of temporary advantages." The
letter continued:

It is because of your forthright and unyielding stand, it is because you are the
one statesman whose record has never been besmirched by even a trace of appeasement that the United States holds its unique and supreme position in
world affairs today. Not the potential power of our great country, but your
record, Mr. President, has placed the United States and you, its titular head and
spokesman. in a position to exercise the leading force which will bring ultimate
victory over aggression and Fascism.

Mr. President, I want to explain in language as strong as I can command, my
feeling that the need is for iron firmness. No settlement with Japan that in any
way seems to the American people, or to the rest of the world, to be a retreat,
no matter how temporary, from our increasingly clear policy of opposition to
aggressors, will be viewed as consistent with the position of our government or
with the leadership that you have established. Certainly the independence of
the millions of brave people in China who have been carrying on their fight for
four long, hard years against Japanese aggression is of no less concern to us and
to the world than the independence of Thailand or French Indochina. No
matter what explanation is offered the public of a "truce" with Japan the
American people, the Chinese people, and the oppressed peoples of Europe, as
well as those forces in Britain and Russia who are with us in this fight, will
regard it as a confession of American weakness and vacillation. How else can
the world possibly interpret a relaxation of the economic pressure which you
have so painstakingly built up in order to force Japan to abandon her policy
of aggression when that relaxation is undertaken not because Japan actually
abandoned it, but only because she promises not to extend her aggressive acts
to other countries? The parallel with Munich is inescapable.

The continuation and further intensification of our economic pressure against
Japan seems, in the light of all the opinions I have sounded out, to be the
touchstone of our pledge to China and the world that the United States will
oppose Japanese aggression in the Pacific.[78]

78 Secretary Morgenthau to President Roosevelt [Ca. November 24, 1941] *Harry
Dexter White Papers,* Princeton University, MSS, File I, China 3. From the files of
White is a diary of "Conferences and Committee Meetings Attended by Mr. White"
which discloses the following appointments and in some instances the nature of the
business transacted with Emile Despres:

"January 7, 1946, 9:30 to 10:20: Mr. Emile Despres (at Mr. Morgenthau's request,
regarding Japanese memo in fall of 1941).

Pressure exerted by Communist sympathizers in the Institute of Pacific Relations must also be taken into account when analyzing the reasons for the rejection of a truce with Japan. On November 25, Professor Owen Lattimore of Johns Hopkins University, the United States' special adviser to Chiang Kai-shek, dispatched an anxious cable to Presidential Assistant Lauchlin Currie arguing against any agreement between the United States and Japan on a *modus vivendi*.

On the same day Harry Dexter White sent "an urgent telegram" to Edward C. Carter, Secretary General of the Institute of Pacific Relations, asking him to "come to Washington." When Carter arrived the following morning White assured him that everything was all right and "that every friend of China could be satisfied." [79] On that day Secretary Hull changed his mind and decided to "kick the whole thing over" because Chiang Kai-shek felt that the *modus vivendi* proposal "would make a terrifically bad impression in China." [80]

Hull declared later that he dropped the *modus vivendi* proposal largely because "the Chinese Government violently opposed the idea." He testified: "It developed that the conclusion with Japan of such an arrangement would have been a major blow to Chinese morale." There was a "serious risk of collapse of Chinese morale and resistance, and even of disintegration of China." In light of this fact it "became perfectly evident that the *modus vivendi* aspect would not be feasible." The cable from Owen Lattimore to Lauchlin Currie, dated November 25, was the only documentary evidence which Cordell Hull presented in defense of his rejection of the *modus vivendi*.[81] The cable read as follows:

After discussing with the Generalissimo the Chinese Ambassador's conference with the Secretary of State, I feel you should urgently advise the President of the Generalissimo's very strong reaction. I have never seen him really agitated before. Loosening of economic pressure or unfreezing would dangerously increase Japan's military advantages in China. A relaxation of American pressure while Japan has its forces in China would dismay the Chinese. Any *modus vivendi* now arrived at with China (sic) would be disastrous to Chinese belief in America and analogous to the closing of the Burma Road, which permanently destroyed British prestige. Japan and Chinese defeatists would instantly exploit the resulting disillusionment and urge oriental solidarity against occidental

---

"Jan. 7, 1946 (no time): Mr. White called Mr. Morgenthau (in New York) after talking to Mr. Despres for a while, with regard to background of memorandum to the President, in the fall of 1941, on policy toward Japan. Mr. White said he would tell Mr. Despres all the details and Despres will prepare a memo for Mr. Morgenthau." U.S. Congress, Senate, Committee on the Judiciary, *Interlocking Subversion in Government Departments* (The Harry Dexter White Papers), 84th Cong., 1st Sess. (Washington: Government Printing Office, 1956), Part 30, p. XXVIII.

79 Testimony of E. C. Carter, July 25, 1951. *Institute of Pacific Relations, Hearings,* Part I, pp. 153-154.

80 "The Stimson Diary," November 26, 1941. *Pearl Harbor Attack,* Part 11, p. 5434.

81 Testimony of Cordell Hull, November 23, 1915. *Ibid.,* Part 2, 434-435 and Unnumbered Volume, pp. 36-37.

treachery. It is doubtful whether either past assistance or increasing aid could compensate for the feeling of being deserted at this hour. The Generalissimo has deep confidence in the President's fidelity to his consistent policy but I must warn you that even the Generalissimo questions his ability to hold the situation together if the Chinese national trust in America is undermined by reports of Japan's escaping military defeat by diplomatic victory.[82]

The question arises here as to whether the Chinese did reject this proposal. The Chinese Ambassador denied his Government was blocking the putting into effect of a temporary arrangement which might afford a cooling-off spell in the Far Eastern situation.[83]

There may be grounds for doubt that Lattimore correctly reported Chiang Kai-shek's position. But it is hardly conceivable that he presented the *modus vivendi* to the Generalissimo in a manner designed to gain his acceptance.

Lauchlin Currie may have been one of the key figures in the rejection of a truce with the Japanese. He is reported as having been agitated over the *modus vivendi* until Secretary Hull finally decided to abandon the idea. On November 28, when Currie lunched with Edward C. Carter, he was no longer worried. In place of the *modus vivendi,* Hull had, on November 26, submitted to the Japanese Ambassador ten conditions which Japan found too stiff a price for peace and war was now a foregone conclusion.

"I should think," Carter noted on November 29, "that Currie probably had a terribly anxious time for the past week. For a few days it looked as though Hull was in danger of selling China and America and Britain down the river." [84] But now everything was all right. What Ambassador Grew had called "an utterly futile war" with Japan was now directly ahead.

On the afternoon of November 26, 1941, Secretary Hull abandoned all thought of a truce with Japan and put in final shape the ten-point ultimatum to Japan. The Japanese Ambassadors were given an ultimatum

82 Owen Lattimore to Lauchlin Currie, November 25, 1941, *Foreign Relations, 1941,* Vol. IV, p. 652.

83 Memorandum of Conversation by the Chief of the Division of Far Eastern Affairs (Hamilton), December 1, 1941. *Foreign Relations, 1941,* IV, 702. Chiang Kai-shek did urge the American Government not to "relax the economic blockade and freezing of Japanese assets" until the question of Japanese evacuation was settled. The telegram was sent to T. V. Soong on November 25, but was not transmitted to the Department of State until December 2. *Foreign Relations, 1941,* IV, 660-661.

84 *Institute of Pacific Relations, Hearings,* Part 1, p. 157. In August, 1941, Carter wrote Currie asking if letters to Lattimore in China could be transmitted so that "they are not read by others before reaching him." Currie promptly replied on a White House letterhead that "I will be glad to get the letters you mentioned to Lattimore uncensored." Currie's assistant in the White House was a Michael Greenberg, a British alien, who later became an American citizen and supplied information to a spy ring. Washington *Times-Herald,* April 15, 1951, p. 5. See also Elizabeth Bentley's testimony in *Institute of Pacific Relations, Hearings,* Part 2, Exhibit No. 111, 112, pp. 433-434. Currie has established residence in South America after spy disclosures in 1948 placed him in the Silvermaster espionage cell.

reading: "The Government of Japan will withdraw all military, naval, air and police forces from China and from Indochina." [85] Both Ambassadors were aghast at the "sudden change of attitude." [86]

Admiral Stark and General Marshall had reviewed the Far Eastern situation. They had recommended that "no ultimatum be delivered to Japan." [87] But Hull went ahead with it. Then he told Secretary of War Stimson: "I have washed my hands of it and it is now in the hands of you and Knox—the Army and the Navy." [88]

It is significant that the ultimatum presented by Hull to the Japanese was based upon an explosive memorandum written by Harry Dexter White, a Soviet agent.[89] White had first drafted a memorandum embodying his views in May, 1941. This document with its lavish bounty to the Japanese business class, would have made a certain bizarre sense at its writing, but by November the business class no longer had political power, and the United States was dealing with the military, which was oblivious to the yen's international value. As the Hull-Nomura negotiations moved towards a climax. White twice redrafted his May, 1941, document.

On November 18, 1941, Secretary Morgenthau sent to Secretary Hull a long memorandum, drafted by White, with reference to the terms for peace that should be presented to Japan.[90] These terms were so stiff that White knew that Japan could not accept them. He was apparently anxious for war between Japan and the United States because such a conflict would relieve Japanese pressure upon Russia's Far Eastern flank. Russia had over 200,000 men facing Japan in the Far East. These troops were desperately needed in the war against Germany.

On November 19, Maxwell Hamilton, Chief of the Far Eastern Division of the Department of State, revised the White memorandum slightly. He found the memorandum "the most constructive one which I have yet seen." [91] Secretary Hull had both the White memorandum and the

85 Oral statement handed by Secretary Hull to Ambassador Nomura and Kurusu, November 26, 1941, *Japan: 1931-1941*, II, 766-770.

86 *Far Eastern Military Tribunal*, Document No. 3105.

87 *Pearl Harbor Attack*, Part 14, pp. 1061-1062; Part 16, pp. 2222-2223.

88 *Ibid.*, Part 11, p. 5422 ff.

89 Robert Morris, *No Wonder We Are Losing* (New York: The Bookmailer, 1958), p. 133.

90 Memorandum by Secretary Morgenthau, November 17, 1941, *Foreign Relations, 1941*, IV, pp. 606-613. In view of White's known relation with Currie and one of the Hiss brothers at this time, it is altogether improbable that he would have acted except in collaboration with them. White had heard his draft was being tampered with in the State Department, as indeed it was, and wished to have the tampering stopped.

91 Maxwell Hamilton to Secretary Hull, November 19, 1941, *Ibid.*, pp. 622-625. Admiral Stark considered the White memorandum acceptable to the Navy and Lee Gerow, acting in General Marshall's absence, said the White plan would attain "one of our present major objectives—the avoidance of war with Japan." Alexander Deconde, *Isolation and Security* (Durham: Duke University Press, 1957), p. 153.

Maxwell revision before him when he drafted the ultimatum of November 26. It is significant that in this ultimatum eight of the drastic demands of the White memorandum found a place. In other words, Harry Dexter White, a Soviet agent, helped in an important way to draft the ultimatum that provoked war between Japan and the United States. This was a primary Soviet aim in the Far East.[92]

Secretary of the Treasury Morgenthau was fearful that the American public would not like the way he had helped to precipitate war between the United States and Japan, and it may be significant that he refused to permit investigators to look at his diary for December 7, 1941.[93]

With reference to the Communist drive to involve the United States and Japan in a war, the following remarks by Benjamin Gitlow, a devoted Communist before breaking with the Party, are pertinent:

As far back as 1927 when I was in Moscow, the attitude toward the United States in the event of war was discussed. Privately, it was the opinion of all the Russian leaders to whom I spoke that the rivalry between the United States and Japan must actually break out into war between these two.

The Russians were hopeful that the war would break out soon, because that would greatly secure the safety of Russia's Siberian borders and would so weaken Japan that Russia would no longer have to fear an attack from her in the East. Stalin hopes through the activities of the American Communist Party, to create a public opinion in the United States that would favor a war, presumably in defense of democracy against the encroachment of Fascism, but actually against Japan. Stalin is perfectly willing to let Americans die in defense of the Soviet Union even if they are not members of the Communist Party. . . ."[94]

Neither Roosevelt nor Hull believed that the Japanese would accept the terms embodied in the American note of November 26. Why, then, did they proffer it? Could it be that they meant to provoke Japan to attack the United States so that the latter might get into war with Germany by the "back door"? This is the thesis followed by a number of reputable historians today.[95]

Vice Admiral Frank E. Beatty, who was an aide to Secretary of the

92 The thesis is this: Since 1933 one of the main objectives in Soviet policy had been to maneuver America into war with Japan. Japan was a serious threat to Soviet desires in the Far East. If her power were broken, there would be no difficulty in realizing Soviet objectives in Asia. The Roosevelt Administration, wittingly or unwittingly followed the Soviet line, and Harry Dexter White, an important and trusted official in the Administration, drafted a note to Japan that produced the war for which Roosevelt had long been looking.

93 New Yorker, October 26, 1946, p. 24.

94 Benjamin Gitlow, I Confess (New York: E. P. Dutton, Inc., 1940), pp. 485-486

95 Among them are Tansill, Morgenstern, Beard, Grenfell, Sanborn, and Barnes. Harold Ickes, Secretary of Interior, wrote in his diary in October 1941: "For a long time I have believed that our best entrance into the war would be by way of Japan. . . . Japan has no friends in this country, but China has. And, of course, if we go to war against Japan, it will inevitably lead us into war against Germany." The Secret Diary of Harold L. Ickes (New York: Simon and Schuster, 1954), III, p. 630. For an excellent analysis of Roosevelt's Foreign policy, see Perpetual War for Perpetual Peace, Edited by Harry Elmer Barnes (Caldwell, Idaho: Caxton Printers, 1953).

Navy Frank Knox and close to the inner circle in the White House, remarked:

Prior to December 7, it was evident even to me . . . that we were pushing Japan into a corner. I believed that it was the desire of President Roosevelt, and Prime Minister Churchill that we get into the war, as they felt the Allies could not win without us and all our efforts to cause the Germans to declare war on us had failed: the conditions we imposed upon Japan—to get out of China, for example—were so severe that we knew that nation could not accept. We were forcing her so severely that we should have known that she would react toward the United States. All her preparations in a military way—and we knew their overall import—pointed that way.[96]

Secretary Hull certainly made it clear that unless Japan accepted his ten-point ultimation, economic pressure upon her would continue. Japan was faced with an alternative of making a public surrender of all she had for years been building in the Far East. At this time, Japan was deeply committed in China. Her expenditures for carrying out the war in China had been high. The bulk of her national wealth was tied up in the China effort. As Captain J. C. Wylie has noted:

If they had chosen to get out of China, I do not see how they could have avoided an internal revolution. No power clique such as the one that ruled Japan will ever abdicate (and that would have been the result of getting out of China); and even if they had done so, their successor would have come to power in opposition to any such course.[97]

If Japan had withdrawn her troops from China as Hull's note demanded, Japan would have lost her position as a stabilizing power against Russia.[98] The Red tide had begun to flow rapidly over the plains of Manchuria, and Japan was the only power that was able to build bastions of defense to stop it. But the Department of State seemed not to regard Japan as a bulwark against Soviet expansion in North China. As a matter of fact, not one word of protest was sent by the Department of State to the Soviet Union, despite her absorption of Sinkiang and Outer Mongolia, while at the same time Japan was censured for stationing troops in China.[99]

On the 25th of November, Stimson had stated the problem as one of "how we should maneuver them into the position of firing the first

---

[96] Vice Admiral Frank E. Beatty, "Another Version of What Started the War with Japan," *U.S. News and World Report* (May 28, 1954), p. 48.

[97] Captain J. C. Wylie, Jr., "Reflections on the War in the Pacific," *United States Naval Institute Proceedings*, 78 (April, 1952), 352.

[98] "The Explanation of the Foreign Minister at Imperial Conference," December 1, 1941, *Far Eastern Military Tribunal*, Record p. 26092.

[99] *Ibid.*, p. 26101. According to Alexander Barmine, who was in charge of the supply of Soviet arms, by 1935, Sinkiang had become "a Soviet colony in all but name." *One Who Survived* (New York: G. P. Putnam's Sons, 1945), pp. 231-232.

shot." [100] Secretary Hull had solved the problem the very next day. This was the conclusion of the Army Pearl Harbor Board when it reported that the Hull note "touched the button that started the war." [101]

When the American note arrived in Tokyo on November 27, high Japanese officials were "dumbfounded" at its severity and agreed that it indicated America's determination to go to war with Japan. In the words of Foreign Minister Togo Shigenori, one of the most moderate members of the Government: "I was utterly disheartened, and felt like one groping in darkness. The uncompromising tone was no more than I had looked for; but I was greatly astonished at the extreme nature of the contents." [102] It was obvious that the next step was war.

Moves on the diplomatic front kept pace with Japan's military preparations. President Roosevelt and all key administration officials were able to observe Japan's preparations for war through the eyes of "magic." Since 1940, sixteen months prior to the Pearl Harbor attack, the Army Signal Corps had broken the Japanese diplomatic code known as "Purple." American officials were thus able to decipher and read all diplomatic messages between Tokyo and Japanese officials all over the world, including Washington. It is still a mystery why a Purple machine was not supplied to the Hawaiian commanders. The concentration of the Fleet in that area made a decoding machine highly desirable militarily. On December 4, Army Intelligence made available to high officials in Washington an ominous message from the Japanese Government to its embassies in Washington and in Havana, ordering the destruction of certain code machines.[103] According to Admiral Richard R. Turner, the message could have only one meaning—war.[104] This was also the opinion of Admiral John R. Beardall, naval aide to the President, who called Roosevelt's particular attention to the important message. The gist of his conversation was as follows:

> I said, "Mr. President, this is a very significant dispatch," which he read very carefully, and he said, "Well, when do you think it will happen?" I said, "Most any time."[105]

---

100 As Stimson explained: "In spite of the risk involved . . . in letting the Japanese fire the first shot, we realized that in order to have the full support of the American people, it was desirable to make sure that the Japanese be the ones to do this so that there should remain no doubt in anyone's mind as to who were the aggressors." Stimson's Testimony quoted in Basil Rauch, *Roosevelt from Munich to Pearl Harbor* (New York: Creative Age, 1950), p. 473.

101 *Pearl Harbor Attack*, Part 39, p. 137. Churchill has since written that the Hull ultimatum "not only met our wishes and those of the associated governments, but indeed went beyond anything we had ventured to ask." Churchill, *The Grand Alliance*, p. 597.

102 Togo Shigenori, *The Cause of Japan* (New York: Simon and Schuster, 1956), p. 176

103 *Pearl Harbor Attack*, Part 12, pp. 215 ff.

104 Testimony of Admiral Richard R. Turner, April 14, 1946, *Ibid.*, Part 26, p. 283.

105 Testimony of Admiral John R. Beardall, April 11, 1946, *Ibid.*, Part 11, p. 5284.

None of this information was sent to the commanders in Hawaii. Another important interception that gave American officials important data occurred when the Japanese consulate in Hawaii was making numerous reports giving the exact location of carriers, battleships, and cruisers in Pearl Harbor. As the diplomatic situation grew more tense, Tokyo's interest in Pearl Harbor intensified until the consul increased the frequency of his "ships-in-the-harbor report" to two a week. On November 29, the dispatch said: "We have been receiving reports from you on ship movements, but in the future will you also report even where there are no movements." [106] Not the slightest hint of this was sent to the Hawaiian commanders. "Had I learned . . . the 'ships in harbor' messages," wrote Admiral H. E. Kimmel, who was charged with protecting the U. S. fleet at Pearl Harbor, "I would have gone to sea with the fleet and endeavored to keep it in an intercepting position at sea." [107] Why was Admiral Kimmel not informed of these important data?[108]

Another strange episode in the Pearl Harbor debacle was the so-called "Winds" signal intercepted on December 4 by the Navy radio receiving station at Cheltenham, Maryland. On November 19 the Japanese Government set up a system for informing its representatives throughout the world of the time when Japan would go to war with the United States. This was to be done in a false weather report—"east wind rain." The American armed forces were on the alert for this message. As soon as it was translated, Lieutenant-Commander Kramer handed it to Captain Laurence F. Safford with the explanation: "This is it." Safford got in touch immediately with Rear Admiral Noyes, who had telephoned the substance of the intercepted message to the naval aide to the President, Admiral Beardall.[109]

As a witness before the Joint Committee on Pearl Harbor, Captain Safford was subjected to a humiliating examination because he adhered to his story, first to last, that the "winds execute" message had been received.[110] He testified that the

106 *Pearl Harbor Attack, Final Report*, p. 517.

107 Husband E. Kimmel, *Admiral Kimmel's Story* (Chicago: Henry Regnery Co., 1955), pp. 109-110.

108 According to Captain T. B. Kittredge, naval historian, "No definite information available in Washington concerning German and Japanese (as well as Soviet and British) action, intentions, and capabilities were ever withheld from the Commands in the Pacific." "The Muddle Before Pearl Harbor," *U. S. News and World Report*, (December 3, 1954), p. 137. This hardly squares with the known facts concerning intercepted Japanese messages. To cite one example, the intercepted "bomb plot" message which meant an attack on our fleet at Pearl Harbor, was distributed to the President, Secretary of the Navy, Chief of Naval Operations, Chief of War Plans Division, Director of Naval Intelligence. This information was not available to Admiral Kimmel or General Short. *Pearl Harbor Attack*, Part 39, pp. 518-521; 524-525; 531-532.

109 Testimony of Captain Laurence F. Safford, February 1, 1946, *Ibid.*, Part 8, pp. 3586-3587.

110 *Ibid.*, Part 8, pp. 3555-3814.

'Winds' message and the change of the [Japanese] naval operations code came in the middle of the week: two days to Saturday and three days to Sunday. It was unthinkable that the Japanese would surrender their hopes of surprise by delaying until the week-end of December 13-14. This was not crystal-gazing or 'intuition'—it was just the plain, common sense acceptance of a self-evident proposition. Col. Sadtler saw it, and so did Capt. Joseph R. Redman, U.S.N., according to Col. Sadtler's testimony in 1944. . . . The Japanese were going to start the war on Saturday, December 6, 1941, or Sunday, December 7, 1941.[111]

Both Captain Safford and Lieutenant-Commander Kramer tried in vain to get some action out of their superior officers with regard to the implications of the "east wind rain" message. Thanks to the intercepted messages, the main steps in Tokyo's preparations for war were known in Washington shortly after they were taken. There was no doubt whatever that the ax was about to fall, but Washington officers certainly manifested no interest in informing the commanders at Hawaii.[112]

By 2:00 P.M. on December 6, Army Intelligence intercepted a secret message from the Japanese Foreign Minister to Ambassador Nomura, which stated that the Japanese reply to Hull's memorandum of November 26 would be sent shortly in thirteen parts and that a later dispatch would inform the ambassador as to the time the reply would be handed to Hull. This "pilot message'" was available to Hull, Stimson, and various military personalities by 3:00 P.M.

As the zero hour approached for the attack on Pearl Harbor, the problem grew more complicated. Captain Arthur N. McCollum, who headed the Far Eastern section of naval intelligence in the Navy Department, testified that "by late Saturday night, we had, if I remember correctly, thirteen of the parts. They were transmitted almost as soon as received, to the Secretary of State, to the President, to the Chief of Naval Operations, and to people over here in the War Department." [113]

When the thirteen parts were taken to the White House about 9:00 P.M. on the night of the 6th, Roosevelt turned to Hopkins and exclaimed: "This means war." [114] Roosevelt then tried to get in touch with Admiral Stark, who was at the National Theatre. Unable to establish contact, the President said "that he would reach the Admiral later, that he did not want to cause public alarm by having the Admiral paged." [115]

One would think that the Chief Executive would surely want to meet with the heads of his Army and Navy. But the most critical days were

---

111 George Morgenstern, *Pearl Harbor: The Story of the Secret War* (New York: The Devin-Adair Co., 1947), p. 211.

112 Kimmel, *op. cit.*, Chapter IV.

113 Testimony of Captain Arthur N. McCollum, January 30, 1946, *Pearl Harbor Attack*, Part 8, pp. 3424-3426.

114 Testimony of Lieutenant L. R. Schulz, February 15, 1946, *Ibid.*, Part 10, pp. 4660-4664. Cf. John Chamberlain "The Man Who Pushed Pearl Harbor," *Life*, April 1, 1946, p. 85.

115 *Ibid.*

passed and no word was sent to the Hawaiian commanders. On the morning of December 7, in view of overnight developments, one would have expected General Marshall and Admiral Stark to arrive at their offices early. But Marshall did not vary from his normal Sunday routine of a horseback ride through Rock Creek Park. He did not reach his office until 11:25 A.M.—two hours before the impending surprise attack at Pearl Harbor.

On the morning of December 7, when Colonel Rufus S. Bratton saw the last part of the Japanese instruction to Nomura, he realized at once that "Japan planned to attack the United States at some point at or near 1:00 o'clock that day." [116] Another officer concerned with bringing the important Japanese message to the attention of high Washington officials was Captain McCollum, who testified:

Early, Sunday morning, when I arrived to take over the duty of my office, where we had a special watch set since early November, the fourteenth part was coming in; and while Admiral Wilkinson and I were discussing the situation about 9:00 o'clock Sunday morning, or possibly earlier, nearer 8:30, with Admiral Stark, the instruction which directed the delivery of the note to the Secretary of State was brought in, shown .to Admiral Stark, who immediately called the White House on the telephone, and the draft was taken over to the Secretary of State and to the White House. At the time, the possible significance of the time of delivery was pointed out to all hands—In other words it was pointed out that 1 P.M. Washington time would mean about 8 o'clock in the morning Honolulu time.

ADMIRAL HEWITT: 7:30

CAPTAIN McCOLLUM: 7:30, yes sir, and very early in the morning out in the Far East, that is, out in the Philippines and those places; and that we did not know what this signified, but that if an attack were coming, it looked that the timing was such that it was timed for operations out in the Far East, and possibly on Hawaii at the time. We had no way of knowing, but because of the fact that the exact time for the delivery of this note had been stressed to the Ambassadors, we felt that there were important things which would move at that time, and that was pointed out not only to Admiral Stark, but I know it was pointed out to the Secretary of State. I was present and assisted in pointing out to Admiral Stark and it was taken over, with instructions to point out to the Secretary of State.[117]

---

116 Morgenstern, *Pearl Harbor*, p. 275; See also the testimony of Rufus S. Bratton in *Pearl Harbor Attack*, Parts 9-10, pp. 4508-4628.

117 Testimony of Capt. McCollum, *op. cit.*, pp. 3427-3428. Compare with Admiral Stark's own testimony: "I usually got down to the office Sunday mornings around 10:30 and I just assumed that I had gotten there somewhere around 10:30 or 11 o'clock. I was lazy on Sunday mornings unless there was some special reason for getting up early. I usually took a walk around the grounds and greenhouse at the Chief of Naval Operations' quarters and didn't hurry about getting down and my usual time, as I recall, was about 10:30 or 11. What time it was on this particular Sunday morning I couldn't go beyond that." When asked when he received the 1 p.m. message, Admiral Stark said: "My remembrance, as I said, was 10:40." Testimony of Admiral Stark, January 2, 1946. *Ibid.*, Part 5, pp. 2183-84. Also compare Stark's testimony with that of Lieutenant-Commander Kramer who said that at 9:00 A.M. on December 7, he

Everything pointed toward a dawn attack on Pearl Harbor. There was ample time in which a message could have been sent to the Pearl Harbor commanders. The dispatch fixing the hour for the delivery of the Japanese ultimatum to the United States as 1:00 P.M. (Washington time) was intercepted and decoded by the Navy Department by 7:00 A.M., December 7 (Washington time) and 1:30 A.M. (Hawaiian time). This was nearly six and a half hours before the attack.[118] The delay has not been explained satisfactorily by any apologist for President Roosevelt's administration.

Another confusing factor in the Pearl Harbor equation was the last minute attitude of General Marshall. When Colonel Bratton saw the last part of the Japanese message, he immediately tried to contact Marshall, but was unable to do so. Marshall had slipped out of his office on the 6th as soon as he learned that the pilot message (which indicated war at any moment) was coming in. He did not return to his office—occupied by General Gerow Miles and Colonel Bratton—until 11:25 A.M. December 7. He immediately began reading the fourteenth part of the message lying on his desk. Bratton tried to show him the significance of the time-of-delivery message, but the General insisted on reading the entire message even though time was a critical factor.[119] Finally, when Marshall saw the other message, all the officers present agreed that it indicated a Japanese attack upon U. S. forces somewhere in the Pacific, at or about 1:00 P.M.

The General then wrote out a longhand message to the various commanders and it was ready for encoding at 11:58, which still left ample time to contact Honolulu. But Marshall did not use the scrambler telephone on his desk, or the Navy radio, or the FBI radio any of which could have reached General Short and Admiral Kimmel thirty or forty minutes before the attack began. Instead, the message was sent by Western Union to San Francisco and by RCA commercial radio to Honolulu and not marked "priority." It reached Short's headquarters six hours after the attack, and Kimmel had it two hours later.[120]

General Marshall seems to have deliberately held up his message and sent it by means he knew would get it there too late. The Army Pearl Harbor Board saw no reason for this blunder. The investigators remarked: "We find no justification for a failure to send this message by multiple secret means either through the Navy radio or the FBI radio

---

delivered to Admiral Stark the 1 P.M. message, that Stark cried out in great alarm: "My God! This means war. I must get word to Kimmel at once." Morgenstern, *op. cit.*, p. 269.

118 *Pearl Harbor Attack*, Part 12, p. 248; Part 39, p. 449.

119 Testimony of Colonel Bratton, *Ibid.*, pp. 4514-4518.

120 *Ibid.*, Part 14, p. 1334; Testimony of Admiral Stark, *op. cit.*, p. 2184; Part 39, p. 94; *Pearl Harbor Attack, Final Report*, p. 530.

or the scrambler telephone or all three." [121] There has never been a satisfactory explanation why on the morning of December 7, Washington officials refused to send one short message to Hawaii in time to anticipate the Japanese attack.[122] No officer could make such a grave error of omission and retain his office unless he were acting under orders. Such orders could have come only from Roosevelt. He was the only common commander for all concerned. Admiral Kimmel sums it up:

> When the information available in Washington prior to the attack was finally disclosed to me, I was appalled. Nothing in my experience of nearly forty-two years service in the Navy had prepared me for the actions of the highest officials in our government which denied this vital information to the Pearl Harbor commanders.
>
> If those in authority wished to engage in power politics, the least they should have done was to advise their naval and military commanders what they were endeavoring to accomplish. To utilize the Pacific Fleet and the Army forces at Pearl Harbor as a lure for a Japanese attack without advising the commander-in-chief of the fleet and the commander of the Army base at Hawaii is something I am wholly unable to comprehend.[123]

Roosevelt's "Back Door to War" was Stalin's open door to conquest of China.

---

121 *Pearl Harbor Attack*, Part 39, p. 95. Marshall's own explanation was that he refrained from using it because of the "possibility that the Japanese could construe the fact that the Army was alerting its garrisons in Hawaii was a hostile act." *Ibid.*, *Final Report, Minority Views*, p. 520.

122 The only logical explanation is that given by Admiral Theobald: " . . . the possibility of causing the cancellation of the surprise attack must have been the sole reason for not sending word to Hawaii on that Sunday morning." Rear Admiral Robert A. Theobald, *The Final Secret of Pearl Harbor* (New York: The Devin-Adair Company, 1954), p. 119. A postwar disclosure by a member of the Japanese attacking force confirmed a logical assumption that the Task Force was under orders to turn back if the American military forces at Pearl Harbor were alerted to repel the attack. *Pearl Harbor Attack, Final Report*, p. 54.

123 Kimmel, *op. cit.*, p. 186. Roosevelt was insistent on keeping the Pacific Fleet in its exposed position in Hawaii. Admiral Richardson was relieved of his command on February 1, 1941, because of his opposition to concentrating the Fleet at Hawaii.

CHAPTER II

CHARMING THE REDS:
ROOSEVELT WOOS STALIN

The United States was at war. And in this war she found herself allied with the Soviet Union. For many Americans this was a situation to which they could not easily become accustomed. Retaliation against Japan, who had delivered the Pearl· Harbor attack, was one thing, but any feeling of comradeship with the Soviets was quite another.

A large number of the American people were still deeply suspicious of the nation that had carried on its conflict with Finland in such a barbarous manner that it had been expelled from the League of Nations in 1939. Archbishop Curley of Baltimore expressed the view of most Catholics when he stated in his usual fashion: "I have no more confidence in Stalin than I have in Hitler." [1] Catholic opinion was so strongly anti-Communist because of religious persecution by the Soviet regime that Roosevelt became seriously perturbed by the extensive press campaign in the autumn of 1941. After he established diplomatic contact with the Vatican, the campaign died down.[2] A few days after Hitler's invasion of Russia, Senator Robert A. Taft, in a radio address, correctly observed: "But the victory of Communism in the world would be far more dangerous to the United States than the victory of Fascism." [3]

There is no doubt that those officials who made policy had ample

---

[1] T. A. Baily, *A Diplomatic History of the American People* (New York: Appleton-Century-Crofts, 1958), p. 727. But opinon was by no means unanimous. *The Christian Science Monitor* said, "Much as we dislike Communism, it is necessary to recognize that Russia has in twenty years shown neither the disposition nor the ability to assail the free peoples." (July 5, 1941). Langer & Gleason, *The Undeclared War, 1940-1941* (New York: Harper & Brothers, 1953), p. 544.

[2] Robert Sherwood, *Roosevelt and Hopkins: An Intimate History* (New York: Harper & Brothers, 1948), p. 384, 398. *Wartime Correspondence by President Roosevelt and Pope Pius XII* (New York: Macmillan Co., 1947), pp. 57-64. The *Catholic World* was particularly critical of our aid to Russia. James M. Gillis wrote: "To defend democracy with the help of Stalin would be like calling on Jesse James or John Dillinger to maintain law and order. Collaboration with Communism against Nazism is as indefensible as collaboration with Nazism against Communism." (August 1941), p. 513.

[3] *Human Events* (March 28, 1951).

warnings not to trust the Russians too far. All through the early period of World War II, when Americans and Russians were closest allies, the U.S. was being warned by its own men in Moscow to look for double-dealing—that the Russians regarded Americans more as enemies than as friends. For example, on June 17, 1941, Laurence Steinhardt, then U.S. Ambassador to Moscow, sent a message to Washington on the subject of doing business with the Soviets. At that moment, just five days before the German attack on the Soviet Union, when it was obvious that the U.S. and Russia would soon be allies, Steinhardt advised that "it is not possible to create 'international' good will" with the Russians, that "they will always sacrifice the future in favor of an immediate gain, and they are not affected by ethical or moral considerations. . . . Their psychology recognizes only firmness, power and force. . . . I am of the opinion they must be dealt with on this basis and on this basis alone." The Ambassador continued to warn our officials that any "friendly co-operation or good will . . . have been received by the Soviet authorities with marked suspicion. . . ." [4]

Earlier, on May 17, 1941, the U.S. Embassy in Moscow warned the Department of State that the United States was honeycombed with Red spies. Discussing an all-inclusive Soviet ban on foreigners traveling inside the Soviet Union, Ambassador Steinhardt said this in a telegram to Washington:

Should the Department consider it expedient to establish a similar prohibition with respect to travel in the United States I would recommend that the prohibition be not limited to diplomatic and consular representatives of the Soviet Union and their employees but apply as well to all Soviet citizens who have arrived in the United States since the outbreak of the war, inasmuch as any Soviet citizen who has been permitted to travel abroad since then is of course an agent of the Soviet Government.[5]

Inside the Department of State, too, there were some officials who were alarmed about Russian espionage in the United States. For example, on July 10, 1941, three weeks after Germany attacked Russia, Adolf A. Berle, Jr., Assistant Secretary of State, sent this memorandum to FBI Director, J. Edgar Hoover:

Considerations of expediency have led the Russian policy from one of hostility to the United States to one of friendship. Like considerations may change the policy back again to one of hostility at any moment, and perhaps without previous warning. . . .
For this reason the Department feels that it would be unwise to abandon surveillance over the activities of the Russian and Communist agencies in the

[4] Ambassador Steinhardt to Secretary Hull, Moscow, June 17, 1941, *Foreign Relations, 1941*, I, pp. 764-766.
[5] Ambassador Steinhardt to Secretary Hull, Moscow, May 17, 1941, *Ibid.*, p. 882.

United States and in the Western Hemisphere; and that it would be unwise to permit agents to these groups to establish themselves in strategic or influential positions.

Furthermore, freedom of this country from subversive activities of these units should rest, not on the attitude of the Russian Government, but on the ability of the United States to protect itself against such activities whenever necessary.[6]

The Communist device of using American hostages to pry favors out of the United States won freedom in 1941 for Mikhail Gorin, a Russian travel agent who had been convicted of espionage in Los Angeles in 1939. Undersecretary Sumner Welles outlined the Kremlin's proposition in a memorandum of January 21, 1941: "The Soviet Union desires to obtain, through a Presidential pardon, the release of Mr. Gorin. If the United States will agree to permit the deportation of Mr. Gorin to the Soviet Union, the Soviet Union will agree to the deportation of two American citizens now in jail in the Soviet Union . . . Roszkowsky and Jarsky." [7]

The United States agreed to Russia's terms. Ambassador Steinhardt's idea had been to get six people—three U.S. citizens and three Russian wives of Americans—out of Russia in exchange for Mr. Gorin. When Steinhardt heard of the Gorin deal, on March 23, he telegraphed: "I am stunned by the Department's action in releasing Gorin without affording me the slightest opportunity of capitalizing on the Soviet Government's intense desire for his release." [8]

Some U.S. officials continued to look with suspicion upon possible Soviet agents endeavoring to come to America. Loy Henderson, the Assistant Chief of European Affairs, warned that the Soviets "have not . . . relaxed" their close supervision over American citizens in Russia. They continue to "prevent American officials in the Soviet Union from traveling throughout the country." They do not in general "desire" the presence of American citizens in the Soviet Union. The American Communist Party has not "ceased to work for the eventual overthrow by force of this Government." Henderson concluded: "In these circumstances the American authorities would be derelict if they should fail to take adequate precautions to prevent secret Soviet or Communist International agents from entering, and carrying on activities in, the United States." [9]

The Americans were not the only ones who had trouble getting along with the Soviet officials. Repeated messages from the U.S. Embassy told how other Western diplomats discovered that the best way to handle the

6 Assistant Secretary of State (Berle) to J. Edgar Hoover, July 10, 1941, *Ibid.*, pp. 789-790.

7 *Ibid.*, p. 930.

8 Ambassador Steinhardt to Secretary Hull, Moscow, March 23, 1941, *Ibid.*, p. 945.

9 Memorandum by Loy Henderson to Undersecretary of State Welles, April 9, 1942, *Foreign Relations, 1942*, III, p. 436.

Russians was to get tough.[10] These frequent warnings by American officials apparently did not modify the appeasement policy toward the Soviet Union.

Roosevelt had always been extremely naive about Communism. When Congressman Martin Dies, Chairman of the House Committee on Un-American Activities, became insistent on digging Reds out of the Administration, he was summoned to the White House, where Roosevelt, in fury, told him, "several of the best friends I've got are Communists. You're all wrong about this thing. . . ."[11]

Roosevelt, indeed, acted as if some of them were. After Earl Browder, the head of the Communist Party in the United States, had been sent to the penitentiary for passport fraud in making a clandestine trip to Moscow, Roosevelt pardoned him as a contribution to "national unity," now that Russia was our ally. Browder boasted, in his testimony before the Tydings Committee in 1950, that in 1942 and 1943 he reported to Roosevelt, and that the information he relayed to the White House had an important part in reshaping American policy in China.[12]

Besides, Roosevelt seems to have had an exalted opinion of himself as a diplomat. Frequently his ambassadors were by-passed by his direct personal diplomacy. During the Beaverbrook-Harriman Mission in October, 1941, Harriman said to Marshal Stalin, "I hope you will feel free to cable President Roosevelt directly on any matters that you consider of importance. President Roosevelt would welcome such messages."[13] So the groundwork was laid for the personal negotiations between Roosevelt and Stalin that were to cause so much difficulty later on.

It is true that the staff of the State Department consoled itself by writing memos, but it is doubtful whether the men who went to Cairo

---

10 Ambassador Steinhardt to Secretary Hull, Moscow, February 8, 1941, *Ibid.*, I pp. 160-161.

11 *U.S. News and World Report* (August 20, 1954), p. 59. As an example of Roosevelt's naiveté, Dies remarked that the President and his key aides "told me quite frankly and definitely that they did not believe the findings and the conclusions of the Dies Committee with reference to the criminal and aggressive plans, tactics and methods of Communists at home and abroad, and that they believed that the future of America depended upon close collaboration with Russia and a tolerant if not protective attitude towards Communists in the United States." Martin Dies to David Lawrence, *Evening Star* (Washington, D.C.), April 11, 1955.

12 President Roosevelt intervened also, in behalf of Mrs. Raissa Irene Browder, wife of Earl Browder. She had entered the U.S. illegally in 1939. Roosevelt urged the legalization of her stay in the U.S. because he wanted to avoid the "embarrassment" of a personal demand for such action by Marshal Stalin at a forthcoming conference. On January 3, 1944, he wrote Attorney General Biddle asking for statements on Mrs. Browder's case. Biddle replied that the case was too "controversial" to cancel the deportation. But on January 19, 1944, the Board of Immigration Appeals permitted her to leave the United States voluntarily. Mrs. Browder went to Montreal, Canada, and applied for an immigration visa. The State Department notified the American Consul at Montreal that it had no objection to issuance of the visa. *Times Herald* (Washington, D.C.), March 22, 1953.

13 William H. Standley and Arthur A. Ageton, *Admiral Ambassador to Russia*, (Chicago: Henry Regnery Co., 1955), p. 202.

and Teheran read them. These two important conferences were arranged directly and secretly by the White House. "I am very anxious to have a talk with you," Roosevelt wrote to Stalin, "My suggestion would be that we meet secretly in some secure place in Africa that is convenient to all three of us." [14]

Though Secretary Hull knew the meetings were being planned, he did not actively share in the determination of American aims and decisions. Later, he was to remark: "I learned from other sources than the President what had occurred at the Casablanca, Cairo, and Teheran Conferences. I had no special occasion to interrogate Mr. Roosevelt on the developments at these conferences. . . ." [15]

The President had no doubt that he could enroll Stalin as a member of his circle and could lead the Soviet leader along new paths of accommodation. As early as March, 1942, the President in writing to Churchill had said: "I tell you that I think I can handle Stalin personally better than either your Foreign Office or my State Department." [16] Later Roosevelt told Ross McIntire, his private physician, "If I can convince him [Stalin] that our offer of co-operation is on the square, and that we want to be comrades rather than enemies, I'm betting that he'll come in. And," the President added with a grin, "what helps a lot is that Stalin is the only man I have to convince. Joe doesn't worry about a Congress or a Parliament. He's the whole works." [17]

The President had little patience with diplomats who were well acquainted with Soviet policy and who warned him against any optimism about establishing cordial Russian-American relations.[18] And he was capable of being ruthless toward critics of the Soviets. One such case is particularly noteworthy. Former Governor George H. Earle of Pennsylvania was a Lieutenant Commander in the Navy serving as assistant naval attaché in Turkey. Earle sent frantic dispatches to Washington concerning the alarming situation in that country in regard to Russia. In May, 1944, he flew to Washington to see the President. While waiting in an

14 Charge d'Affaires Henderson to Foreign Minister Molotov, December 5, 1942, *Foreign Relations, 1942*, III, p. 665.

15 Cordell Hull, *The Memoirs of Cordell Hull* (New York: The Macmillan Company, 1948), II, p. 1110.

16 Quoted by Chester Wilmot, *The Struggle for Europe* (New York: Harper and Brothers Publishers, 1952), p. 138. But General Deane wrote of Teheran: "Stalin appeared to know exactly what he wanted at the Conference. This was also true of Churchill, but not so of Roosevelt." John R. Deane, *The Strange Alliance*, (New York: The Viking Press, 1946), p. 43.

17 Ross T. McIntire, *White House Physician* (New York: G. P. Putnam's Sons, 1946), p. 171.

18 William Henry Chamberlain, *America's Second Crusade* (Chicago: Henry Regnery Co., 1950), pp. 183-186. "His deep-rooted prejudice against . . . the permanent officials of the Department of State" and "At Yalta also such advice was lacking" are words of a critical summary in Sumner Welles, *Seven Decisions that Shaped History* (New York: Harper and Brothers, 1950), p. 216.

ante-room in the White House, he met Secretary Forrestal and conveyed his fears of Russia. Within the shadow of the President's desk, Forrestal told him: "My God, I think this is dreadful. We were all alone over here. Russia can do no wrong. It is perfectly dreadful. They just simply are blind to the whole situation." [19] When Earle saw Roosevelt, he said: "Mr. President, the real menace is not Germany, it is Russia." FDR gave Earle a smile and said: "George, Russia is a nation of 180 million people speaking 120 different dialects. When the war is over she will fly to pieces like a centrifugal machine at high speed." [20]

A short time later, Roosevelt wrote a letter to Earle forbidding him to publish an article concerning his critical views of Russia. Commander Earle was exiled as Governor of Samoa, a remote island in the Pacific, "so I could not talk." There he literally was forgotten until after the war when it took the personal intervention of a Pennsylvania congressman with President Truman to release him from his Samoan exile.[21]

During the first two years of World War II, the Soviet Union had been able to absorb Latvia, Lithuania and Estonia, plus large portions of Poland and Finland. In the Far East, Russia's relations with Japan had been governed by the concept of watchful waiting. The basis of these relations had been the Soviet-Japanese neutrality pact of April 13, 1941. Obviously, it was to her interest to keep the Japanese forces occupied in areas remote from the Soviet border, just as later it became American policy to induce Russia to intervene in the Far East and thus help bear some of the burden in that zone.

The Pearl Harbor attack precipitated a crisis in the American attitude towards Russia. After Pearl Harbor, the problem of Russian military co-operation loomed larger in the minds of American military and political planners than did political considerations. "Let us win the war first and talk about politics thereafter" became the oft-heard political slogan. It had generally been assumed that in the event of war with Japan, Russia would intervene, at least to the extent of allowing American forces to use bases in eastern Siberia. This was suggested indirectly by President Roosevelt to Ambassador Maxim Litvinov on December 8, 1941.[22] On the same day, Secretary Hull, on instructions from the Pres-

19 Testimony of George H. Earle, November 13, 1952, U. S. Congress, House of Representatives, Select Committee, *The Katyn Forest Massacre, Hearings,* 82nd Cong. 2d Sess. (Washington: Government Printing Office, 1952). Part 7, p. 2197.

20 George H. Earle, "Roosevelt's Fatal Error," *Human Events* (March 24, 1960); cf. *Katyn Forest Massacre, Hearings,* Part 7, p. 2204.

21 In a special article written for the *Philadelphia Inquirer,* February 9, 1947. See also "FDR's Tragic Mistake," by George H. Earle in *Confidential* (August 1958), pp. 57-58.

22 Department of Defense, *The Entry of the Soviet Union Into the War Against Japan: Military Plans, 1941-1945* (Washington: Department of Defense Office of Public Information, 1955), p. 1.

ident, asked Litvinov about a Russian declaration of war and brought
up the possibility of basing American planes in the Maritime Provinces.[23]
However, when Stalin instructed Litvinov for the time being to preserve
strict neutrality, Hull became provoked and argued with the Soviet Ambassador about the wisdom of Stalin's decision. He even went so far as
to hint that Lend-Lease supplies might be curtailed should the Soviet
decision stand. But Litvinov remained firm, and Hull did not press the
case.[24] On January 19, 1942, Hull told the Australian Minister to the
U.S., Richard G. Casey, that the Soviet Union "would not give us bases
in the Far East . . . . nor does Russia intend to fight Japan at present." [25]

Many Americans expected the Soviet Union to participate in the eventual defeat of Japan and looked forward hopefully to this event. Public
opinion polls showed that an overwhelming majority of the American
people believed that Russia "owes it to the United States" to enter the
Far Eastern conflict, sooner or later.[26] Strategic bombing advocates were
particularly keen on having Russia as an ally, since bombers based in
Siberia could easily reach Japanese home islands. Although we had been
attacked by Japan, the top strategists of the United States, the Joint Chiefs
of Staff, felt that Germany was "still the prime enemy" and that "her
defeat is the key to victory." Therefore, "only the minimum of force necessary for the safeguarding of vital interests in other theatres should be
diverted from operations against Germany." [27] This curious view taken
by these officers coincided with the views expressed to Prime Minister
Churchill by the British Chiefs of Staff Committee: "Russian declaration
of war on Japan would be greatly to our advantage, provided, but only
provided, that the Russians are confident that it would not impair their
Western front either now or next spring." [28]

Early in June, 1942, the discussion of Russia's participation in the
Pacific war assumed new significance when Germany launched a great
offensive against European Russia, and an attack by Japan on the Russian rear seemed all the more likely. Stalin told U.S. Ambassador William Standley that Germany "had demanded that the Japanese attack
Soviet Siberia," but that Japan said if Germany would supply them with
"one million tons of steel, five hundred thousand tons of shipping" and
other material, Japan "would consider" the German request.[29] Where-

23 Hull, *Memoirs*, II, pp. 1111-1112.

24 *Ibid.*, p. 1112.

25 Memorandum of Conversation, by Secretary Hull, January 19, 1942, *Foreign Relations, 1942*, III, 410.

26 *Public Opinion Quarterly*, IX, 249 (Summer, 1945).

27 American-British Grand Strategy, approved December 31, 1941, *Entry of Soviet Union Into War Against Japan*, p. 4.

28 Churchill, *The Grand Alliance*, III, 627.

29 Memorandum by Ambassador in the Soviet Union (Standley), undated, *Foreign Relations, 1942*, III, 644.

upon Roosevelt dispatched, on June 15, 1942, an immediate warning to Stalin:

We are ready in case of such an attack to assist you with our air power, providing there are available in Siberia landing fields which are adequate. To permit the prompt effectuation of such an operation, there must be careful coordination between the Soviet Union and the United States. . . . This matter is to be considered to be of such great urgency that our conferees should have the power to make definite plans and begin action. I propose that such representatives appointed by you and me meet in Moscow and Washington at once.[30]

When no reply was received by June 24, 1942, Roosevelt sent a second message to Stalin. He hoped for a change in the Soviet attitude—in particular, that arrangements for Lend-Lease deliveries in Siberia might result in some Soviet-American co-operation in the Far East. The President believed American officials might survey aircraft delivery routes, and that some pilots might fly lend-lease aircraft across Siberia. If so, the United States would be better prepared to aid the U.S.S.R. in case of a Japanese attack. At least, the groundwork would have been laid for action against Japan, and the United States would have obtained some additional information about Soviet military requirements in the Far East.[31]

In reply, Stalin "addressed himself only to the question of a lend-lease air route from Alaska, avoiding discussion of the possibility that the Japanese would attack Siberia. . . . "[32] In spite of this partial acceptance of his proposal, Roosevelt informed Stalin on July 6, 1942, that he had decided to send Major General Follett Bradley of the Army Air Forces to Moscow "to discuss and arrange co-operative action against Japan if the question should be raised by Soviet officials."[33] The hope that General Bradley would make some progress soon proved unfounded. He could neither arrange for American pilots to fly the Siberian route nor draw from the Soviets any information about their capabilities and intentions in the Far East.[34]

Attributing his failure to Soviet fear of Japan, Bradley suggested a new message to Stalin. If the President would pledge three heavy bomber groups to the defense of Soviet Asia, then Moscow's unco-operativeness might disappear. Since other experts told him that Bradley's advice was sound, Roosevelt accepted the suggestion. Cabling Stalin on December

30 President Roosevelt to Marshal Stalin, June 17, 1942, *Entry of Soviet Union Into War Against Japan*, pp. 10-11.

31 President Roosevelt to Marshal Stalin, June 24, 1942, *Foreign Relations, 1942*, III, pp. 599-600.

32 Ambassador Standley to Secretary Hull, July 2, 1942, *Entry of Soviet Union Into War Against Japan*, p. 12.

33 *Ibid.*, p. 13.

34 For a clear description of the difficulties Bradley encountered with Russian officials, see Standley and Ageton, *Admiral Ambassador to Russia*, Chapter XV; cf. *Foreign Relations, 1942*, III, p. 662.

30, 1942, he declared that one-hundred four-engine bombers from the American Pacific air forces would be dispatched to Siberia at the first news of Japanese attack. Airfields would have to be ready for them, of course, and bombs, lubricants and so on stockpiled for their use. A survey of Siberia should, therefore, be undertaken by Americans, with Soviet and American officers meeting at once to discuss all phases of operations in the Far East. In this manner, the President repeated the offer to help secure the U.S.S.R. against Japan. He raised again the question of Siberian bases, and he requested once more that the Soviets reveal their intentions in Asia.[35] The offer of one hundred bombers fared no better than his earlier proposals. Stalin replied obliquely, and, when Roosevelt repeated his offer, making it even clearer that he was talking only about the Far East, Stalin made the same evasive reply. One hundred bombers, the Soviet leader declared both times, would be received with gratitude; they were badly needed in the war against Germany.[36]

Earlier, the buildup of Russian strength against Germany had already become the main interest of American top officials. "As you can well recognize," Roosevelt informed Stalin, "I have had a problem in persuading the people of Australia and New Zealand that the menace of Japan can be most effectively met by destroying the Nazis first." [37]

Russian funds in the United States were unfrozen, and goods began to flow from the United States within the first two weeks of the Russo-German war.[38] As early as July 21, 1941, Roosevelt had ordered "immediate and substantial shipments of assistance to the Union of Soviet Socialist Republics." [39] The first purchases in the United States were paid for in cash, but, on September 11, 1941, the Russian Ambassador Constantine Oumansky began negotiations for some form of credit.[40] The outcome of the negotiations was a declaration by the President, issued

---

35 President Roosevelt to Marshal Stalin, December 30, 1942, Ministry of Foreign Affairs of the U.S.S.R., *Stalin's Correspondence with Churchill, Atlee, Roosevelt and Truman, 1941-1945* (London: Lawrence and Wishart, 1958) , II, pp. 47-48.

36 Marshal Stalin to President Roosevelt, January 5, 1943, *Entry of Soviet Union Into War Against Japan*, p. 14. One of the reasons why Russia did not permit the use of bases in Siberia was fear that this action might provoke a conflict with Japan. The Chief of the U.S. Military Missions to Moscow during the war, Major General John R. Deane, has written that the Japanese Kwantung Army at this time was close to a million men and considerably stronger than the Red Siberian Army. By 1943, however, Russia felt reasonably sure of her defensive strength in the Far East. *The Strange Alliance*, pp. 223-224. Herbert Feis says that U.S. was "trying to get Russians— to fight on a second front—in the Far East." *Churchill, Roosevelt, and Stalin* (New Jersey: Princeton University Press, 1957), p. 117.

37 Charge d'Affaires Loy Henderson to Foreign Minister Molotov, November 21, 1942, *Foreign Relations, 1942*, III, p. 662.

38 Edward R. Stettinius, Jr., *Lend-Lease* (New York: The Macmillan Co., 1944), p. 122.

39 *Ibid.*

40 Donald F. Drummond, *The Passing of American Neutrality, 1937-1941* (Ann Arbor: The University of Michigan Press, 1955), pp. 294-295.

on November 7, 1941—the anniversary of the Bolshevik Revolution—in which he proclaimed: "The defense of the Union of Soviet Socialist Republics is vital to the defense of the United States." He ordered the Lend-Lease Administrator Edward R. Stettinius, Jr. "to transfer defense supplies to the Union of Soviet Socialist Republics under the Lend-Lease Act. . . . " [41]

Roosevelt was particularly insistent upon lavish aid to Soviet Russia. At a Cabinet meeting on August 1, he spoke for some forty-five minutes on the Soviet aid program. Secretary Morgenthau was at the meeting and recorded that the President "went to town in a way I never heard him go to town before. He was terrific. He said he didn't want to hear what was on order; he said he wanted to hear what was on the water." [42] Secretary Ickes wrote: "The President started in by giving the State Department and the War Department one of the most complete dressings down that I have witnessed. He said that these departments had been giving Russia a 'run-around'." [43]

On August 2, Roosevelt sent a strong directive to Wayne S. Coy, a special assistant to the President, to expedite matters in getting materials delivered to the Russians.

I raised the point in Cabinet on Friday that nearly six weeks have elapsed since the Russian war began and that we have done practically nothing to get any of the materials they asked for on their actual way to delivery to Siberia. Frankly, if I were a Russian, I would feel that I had been given the run around in the United States.

Please get out the list and please, with my full authority, use a heavy hand—act as a burr under the saddle and get things moving![44]

The admission of Communist Russia to the benefits of Lend-Lease reflects the rapid shift of public and official opinion in the United States. Roosevelt framed his policy of "charming" Stalin into good will and good behavior through his personal intermediary, Harry Hopkins. Hopkins had been appointed to administer Lend-Lease. In late July, 1941, he was sent to Moscow to report on the Russian front and to discuss with Stalin the problem of supplying American aid to the Soviet war effort.[45] In a message to the President on July 25, he requested authorization of aid and made this personal observation:

41 Directive of the President (Roosevelt) to the Lend-Lease Administrator (Stettinius), November 7, 1941, World Peace Foundation, *Documents on Foreign Relations, 1941,* (ed.) S. Shepard Jones and Denys P. Meyers (Boston: World Peace Foundation), p. 607.

42 Langer and Gleason, *The Undeclared War,* p. 560.

43 Ickes, *Secret Diary,* III, p. 592.

44 Elliot Roosevelt (ed.), *F.D.R.: His Personal Letters* (New York: Duell, Sloane, and Pearce, 1950), II, pp. 1195-96.

45 *Survey of International Affairs, 1939-1946: America. Britain, and Russia, Their Cooperation and Conflict: 1941-1946* (London: Oxford University Press, 1953) , p. 23.

I have a feeling that everything possible should be done to make certain the Russians maintain a permanent front even though they be defeated in this immediate battle. If Stalin could in any way be influenced at this critical time I think it would be worth doing by a direct communication from you through a personal envoy. I think the stakes are so great that it should be done. Stalin would then know in an unmistakable way that we mean business on a long-term supply job.[46]

Hopkins was warmly received by Foreign Minister V. M. Molotov, who reported of him: "Mr. Hopkins will demand no concessions whatever. His desire is to ask nothing and give everything. What he wants is to keep us in the fighting—and that is all. Mr. Hopkins is completely on our side and may be trusted absolutely." [47]

When Hopkins met Stalin at the first meeting, they discussed the subject of Soviet needs and American supplies. He told the Red dictator that the United States was "willing to do everything that they possibly could during the succeeding weeks to send materiel to Russia." [48] Stalin was, of course, delighted to hear these fervid promises of Lend-Lease assistance, and he had no doubt that they would be fulfilled. That afternoon, Hopkins and Ambassador Laurence A. Steinhardt met with Molotov to discuss the Far East. Hopkins said the United States "could not look with complacency" upon a possible Japanese invasion of Siberia. Molotov suggested that a "warning" to Tokyo by President Roosevelt might prevent such a development. This impressed Hopkins and he agreed to convey the request to the President.[49]

During their final meeting, Hopkins told Stalin that the President would like his personal analysis of the military situation. Stalin assured him that the Russian front would hold, and he requested substantial aid from the U. S. Before Hopkins left the Kremlin, Stalin, with his unerring judgment of men, said that Britain and Russia could not alone defeat Germany. America would inevitably "come to grips with Hitler," and the "one thing" that could make his defeat certain—"perhaps without ever firing a shot"—was for the United States to declare war upon Germany.[50] This remark was aimed at the receptive ear of Roosevelt.

These meetings with Stalin made a profound impression on Harry Hopkins. Ambassador Steinhardt reported to the Department of State that Stalin had talked to Hopkins "with a frankness unparalleled in my

46 *Pearl Harbor Attack*, Part 20, pp. 4384 ff.

47 Richard L. Stokes, "A Tragic Tale of Lend-Lease," *Human Events* (April 1, 1953). For Hopkins' reception in Moscow, see "The Inside Story of My Meeting with Stalin," *American Magazine*, CXXXII (December, 1941) : Referring to previous Nazi-Soviet relations, Hopkins remarked that "whatever your personal feelings about the U.S.S.R. may be, it is to Russia's credit that she has observed her commitments and treaties to the letter."

48 Sherwood, *Roosevelt and Hopkins: An Intimate History*, p. 341.

49 *Ibid.*, pp. 331-332.

50 *Ibid.*, p. 342.

knowledge in recent Soviet history [on] the subject of his mission and the Soviet position." [51]

The Hopkins mission is significant as a prelude to a series of important policy decisions relating to World War II. Aid to Russia, thereafter, became an important factor in our foreign policy.

Hopkins returned to Britain and joined Churchill aboard the *Prince of Wales* for a meeting with Roosevelt at Argentia, Newfoundland.[52] At the Atlantic Conference, he gave the President and the Prime Minister an account of his meetings with Stalin. The reports of his conversations with Stalin greatly impressed Roosevelt. Soviet resistance to Hitler was to be sustained regardless of the cost and commitments involved. The President's attitude was clearly reflected in his directive to Secretary Stimson ordering immediate preparation of a list of supplies that could be committed to Russia for delivery by June 30, 1942. Roosevelt said: "I deem it to be of paramount importance for the safety and security of America that all reasonable munitions help be provided for Russia, not only immediately, but as long as she continues to fight the Axis powers effectively. I am convinced that substantial and comprehensive commitments of such character must be made to Russia by Great Britain and the United States at the proposed conference." [53]

Shortly after the Atlantic meeting, Hopkins became concerned over the persistent public opposition to aid to Russia, particularly by religious groups in America. He wrote to Brendan Bracken, British Minister of Information, that "We are having some difficulty with our public opinion with regard to Russia. The American people don't take aid to Russia easily. The whole Catholic population is opposed to it, all the Nazis, all the Italians and a lot of people who sincerely believe that Stalin is a great menace to the world." [54]

With reference to the operations conducted by Hopkins, General John R. Deane wryly remarked that this Roosevelt agent administered Russian Lend-Lease "with a zeal which approached fanaticism." [55] He later wrote in an article in the *American Mercury*: "There can be no doubt that the attitude of the President was reflected throughout the government, and there can be no doubt that his confidante, Harry Hopkins, encouraged the President in this attitude." [56]

The influence of Hopkins upon the President, particularly in the mat-

---

[51] *Ibid.*, pp. 346-347.

[52] *Ibid.*, p. 349.

[53] President Roosevelt to Secretary Stimson, August 30, 1941, *F.D.R.: His Personal Letters*, II, pp. 1201-3.

[54] Sherwood, *op. cit.*, p. 372. For opinions of religious groups concerning aid to Communist Russia, cf. Raymond Dawson, *The Decision to Aid Russia, 1941* (Chapel Hill: University of North Carolina Press, 1959), pp. 86-96.

[55] Deane, *The Strange Alliance*, p. 90.

[56] Deane, "From Washington to Moscow," *American Mercury*, 75 (December, 1952), p. 107.

ter of unconditional aid to the Russians, provides a baffling question
whose proper dimension historians have not accurately measured. In the
summer of 1941, Hopkins was a stranger to the Russians, who looked
upon his advent with a little suspicion and dread. But at the Teheran
Conference, two years and four months later, when he met Stalin for a
second time, the ardor of cordial friendship was apparent. "In greeting
Hopkins," remarked Ambassador Averell Harriman, "Stalin displayed
more open and warm cordiality than he had been known to show to any
foreigner." [57] Roosevelt was enchanted. To Jan Ciechanowski he exclaimed: "Harry gets on with Stalin like a house afire. In fact, they seem
to have become buddies." [58] Hopkins was not a Communist or a fellow
traveller. His constant appeasement of the Soviet Union was not a result
of any fanatical devotion to Marxist dogma, but of his insistence on the
complete destruction of Germany and Japan. He sincerely believed he
could get along with Stalin by giving him everything he wanted and asking
nothing in return. When Ambassador Standley complained to him that
General Philip Faymonville was bypassing his superiors in Lend-Lease
negotiations with the Russians, Hopkins refused to dismiss him. This
prompted Ambassador Standley to say: "Harry Hopkins was independent of everyone in Government except the President." [59]

The power to help Stalin, which Hopkins enjoyed, is beyond popular
conception. He entrenched himself in a fortress commanding all ap-
proaches to Soviet affairs—diplomatic, military, and economic.[60] As a
striking display of such complete and unrestrained power, let us recall
the incident at the Newark Airport. An American passenger plane, while
leaving the runway, accidentally brushed a medium bomber donated to
Russia through Lend-Lease. Colonel Kotikov, the head of the Soviet
mission at the airfield, became so enraged he threatened to "call Mr.
Hopkins" if both the pilot and American Airlines were not expelled
from the airfield. When Major George R. Jordan refused to comply with
this alien dictation, an order came from Washington several days later
"not ordering American Airlines off the field, but directing every aviation company to cease activities at Newark forthwith." "The order was
not for a day or a week," says Major Jordan. "It held for the duration
of the war." [61]

57 Sherwood, *Roosevelt and Hopkins*, p. 781.

58 Jan Ciechanowski, *Defeat in Victory* (New York: Doubleday and Company, 1947),
p. 231.

59 Standley and Ageton, *Admiral Ambassador to Russia*, p. 360. Admiral Standley
observed in his diary for April 24, "He [Faymonville] gives Russian desires priority
above all else."

60 Leahy, *I Was There*, p. 138. Mr. Sherwood writes that Hopkins was "the second
most important individual in the United States Government during the most critical
period" of the war. *Roosevelt and Hopkins*, p. 212.

61 George Racey Jordan, *From Major Jordan's Diaries* (New York: Harcourt, Brace,
and Company, 1952), p. 25.

At the very time American materials poured across the Soviet borders, it was Hopkins again who insisted that the United States fulfill its broad pledge to Russia. In mid-January, 1942, he wrote to Admiral Emory S. Land, Chairman of the U.S. Maritime Commission:

I am still terribly disturbed about the fact that an adequate number of ships are not available for Russia. . . . This government has made a firm pledge to Russia and we simply cannot go back on it. . . . You simply must find some ships that can be diverted at once for this Russian business.[62]

Because the Russian requirements for Lend-Lease supplies in some respects conflicted with those of the American armed forces, and because of the limited availability of shipping, delivery of supplies to Russia in the latter part of 1941 and the early months of 1942 was slow. This prompted the President to send letters on March 7, 1942, to all U.S. agencies, stating that he wished all material promised to the Soviet Union shipped immediately regardless of the effect of these shipments on any other part of the war program.[63] "I am convinced," wrote General Deane, "that the measure taken by the President was one of the most important decisions of the war . . . . it was the beginning of a policy of appeasement of Russia from which we have never fully recovered and from which we are still suffering." [64]

On the eve of General Follett Bradley's departure for Moscow, Roosevelt turned to him and remarked: "the important thing to impress on the Russians is that we are wholly realistic about shipments to Russia." Every effort will be made "to make deliveries by any and all practical means." Our position should be to say to the Russians that *"we can let them have almost everything they want."* [65]

A flood of American Lend-Lease goods began to pour into Russia. Over fifteen million tons of cargo, in more than twenty-five hundred ships, were delivered. Hundreds of thousands of trucks, motorcycles, and combat vehicles, plus millions of tons of industrial goods and foodstuffs, bolstered the Soviet armies. "Our policy," writes General Deane, "was to make any of our new inventions in electronics and other fields available to the Russians. . . . " [66] Each month the General received a revised list of secret American equipment about which Russia could be informed.

In addition, with the enthusiastic help of Harry Hopkins, the United

---

[62] Robert Sherwood, "The Secret Papers of Harry L. Hopkins," *Collier's* (July 17, 1948), p. 23.

[63] President Roosevelt to Donald Nelson, March 7, 1942, War Production Board Files, *MS.* National Archives.

[64] Deane, *The Strange Alliance*, p. 89. Deane tells of the delivery of a tire factory from Detroit, p. 100.

[65] Memorandum by President Roosevelt, July 23, 1942, *Foreign Relations, 1942* III, p. 715. Italics mine.

[66] Deane, *The Strange Alliance*, pp. 49-50.

States shipped, year after year, millions of pounds of atomic bomb material.[67] "Every possible effort will be made to meet all Protocol commitments at the earliest possible date," said Hopkins. "The United States remains firm in the belief that material aid" to the Soviet Union is of "highest strategical importance." [68] In 1943, the U.S. government issued export licenses for the delivery of atomic bomb materials to the U.S.S.R.[69] Restricted orders of the Manhattan Project were bypassed by the Canadian Radium and Uranium Corporation, an American firm with the "right" contacts in Washington.[70]

The Russians grew so bold that soon they exported baggage without passengers, in batches of fifty suitcases at a time. Every two or three weeks another batch of fifty, guarded by armed Soviet couriers, passed through our assembly and transit base at Great Falls, Montana. One single batch of fifty, later in the war, contained thirty-eight hundred pounds of oil refinery maps.[71] Everything—from the blueprints of the B-36 Super- Fortress to photostats of our confidential reports from the embassy in Moscow—was speeded on to the U.S.S.R.[72]

Ambassador Standley held an interview with correspondents just before his return to Washington for consultations. Among the comments Ambassador Standley was reported to have made was "the astounding admission that he did not know what commitments the U.S. had made to Russia, or to what degree they had been met. He said he believed that General Philip R. Faymonville, head of the U.S. Supply Missions in Moscow, had such information." [73]

The cost in American lives and ships to satisfy Stalin's desires sometimes went to extremes. Our ships carrying supplies and munitions to Russia through the "Murmansk run" met with some terrible disasters at the hands of the German fleet and land-based bombers. The risks involved were "out of proportion to the aid which such . . . ships could render the Soviet Union." [74] Our losses amounted to one out of every

---

67 Testimony of George Racey Jordan, March 3, 1950, U.S. Congress, House of Representatives, Committee on Un-American Activities, *Hearings Regarding Shipment of Atomic Material to the Soviet Union During World War II*, 81st Cong. 2d Sess. (Washington: Government Printing Office, 1950), p. 1156.

68 Harry Hopkins to General Philip R. Faymonville, *Foreign Relations, 1942*, III, p. 697. In contradiction of most sources, the 1952 *Register of Graduates*, USMA, shows General Faymonvilles first name to be spelled with only one "l" (p. 254).

69 *New York Times*, December 8, 1949.

70 Testimony of Lawrence C. Burman, January 23, 1950, *Hearings on Atomic Material to the Soviet Union*, p. 967.

71 *Ibid.*, p. 922. Jordan, *From Major Jordan's Diaries*, pp. 77-81.

72 *Ibid.*, p. 1160. Isaac Don Levine, "Stalin's Spy Ring in the U.S.A.," *Plain Talk* (December, 1947), p. 3.

73 *Foreign Relations, 1942*, Volume III, p. 740, fn. 54.

74 *Foreign Relations, 1942*, III, p. 701, fn. 84. Robert J. Scovell, American Red Cross representative in the Soviet Union reported the existence of serious conditions and privations for American shipwrecked merchant seamen at northern ports of the Soviet Union. *Ibid.*, p. 600, fn. 78.

three ships. Hopkins was distressed over these figures because it meant our ships were being sunk faster than we could build them.

For a short time the Murmansk run was abandoned. Although Stalin was well informed of our untenable losses, neither Hopkins nor Roosevelt dared to tell him the last convoy had been canceled. Finally, on October 5, 1942, Roosevelt cabled Churchill: "I think it is better under any circumstances that we run this risk rather than endanger our whole relations with Russia at this time." [75]

This zeal to help Russia raises several important questions. What were the real objectives behind this stream of Lend-Lease goods that poured into Russia, and what terms of eventual world peace were aimed at in this program?

Nicholas J. Spykman, of Yale University, published a book in 1942 wherein he posed these questions and supplied answers revealing a judicious estimate of the tensions of political forces in time of war. "If the foreign policy of a state is to be practical," he wrote, "it should be designed not in terms of some dream world, but in terms of the realities of international relations, in terms of power politics." [76] He maintained that the continuing objectives of U.S. policy should be, in Europe and Asia, a balance of power. We found ourselves at war because the balance on the opposite shores of both the Atlantic and the Pacific had been upset. Our war aim should be to restore the balance.[77] We should not annihilate either Germany or Japan, lest we leave Europe or the Far East open to domination by Russia. As for Europe: "A Russian state from the Urals to the North Sea can be no great improvement over a German state from the North Sea to the Urals." He thought similarly about the Far East: "The danger of another conquest of Asia must be removed, but this inevitably means the elimination of the military strength of Japan and the surrender of the Western Pacific to China or Russia." [78] So reasoned Professor Spykman in 1942.

On January 14, 1943, at the Casablanca Conference, President Roosevelt announced to the world the Allied objective of "unconditional surrender" of Germany and Japan. According to Hull, the President's announcement came as a surprise to the Department of State. He declared that the President's promotion of the unconditional surrender formula also took Churchill by surprise.[79] Elliot Roosevelt, who was present at

---

[75] Sherwood, *Roosevelt and Hopkins*, pp. 639.

[76] Nicholas J. Spykman, *America's Strategy in World Politics: The United States and the Balance of Power* (New York: Harcourt, Brace and Company, 1942). p. 446.

[77] *Ibid.*, p. 461.

[78] *Ibid.*, p. 460.

[79] Hull, *Memoirs*, II, pp. 1570-71. However, Churchill eagerly fell in with the notion. He was so obsessed with the idea of total military victory that he lost the customary British concern for postwar problems of balances of power.

the time, claims that the President thought up the phrase "unconditional surrender" one day while having lunch. The President remarked: " 'Of course, it's just the thing for the Russians. They couldn't want anything better. Unconditional surrender,' he repeated, thoughtfully sucking his tooth. 'Uncle Joe might have made it up himself. . . .' " [80] There was no intention to restore the European or Asian balance of power. This fatal shortsightedness contributed to the loss of Eastern Europe and much of Asia to Soviet imperialism.

Secretary of the Navy James V. Forrestal was dissatisfied with the Allied formula for victory: " . . . he was aware that a policy of 'unconditional surrender' which could lead merely to the destruction of Germany and Japan would seriously unbalance the international system in the face of Soviet power." [81]

The implications of this policy are exceedingly interesting. It enabled Hitler to convince the great majority of Germans that they had to fight to the bitter end or see their country destroyed; it hardened the firm resolve of the Japanese to continue the struggle.[82] Roosevelt's policy unquestionably meant prolongation of the war and caused unnecessary loss of American lives. Only one country was to benefit by this formula—Soviet Russia.[83]

In the summer of 1942, General James H. Burns, who had an important role in the Lend-Lease program, prepared an important memorandum for Hopkins, foreshadowing the policy of appeasement of the Soviet Union established at the Quebec Conference in August, 1943. He said: "We not only need Russia as a powerful fighting ally in order to defeat Japan . . . we [also] need her as a real friend and customer in the post-war world." Among his suggestions for improving relationships were: "Agree to assist, in every proper and friendly way, to formulate a peace that will meet Russia's legitimate aspirations." But the most fantastic statement of the entire memorandum was the establishment of the general policy of the U.S. government towards Russia. General Burns said: "Establish the general policy throughout all U.S. departments and agencies that Russia must be considered as a real friend and be treated accordingly and that personnel must be assigned to Russian contacts that are loyal to this

---

80 Elliot Roosevelt, *As He Saw It*, (New York: Duell, Sloane, Pearce, 1948), p. 117.

81 Walter Millis (ed.), *The Forrestal Diaries* (New York: The Viking Press, 1951), p. 24. Hanson Baldwin has said that it was "perhaps the biggest political mistake of the war." *Great Mistakes of the War* (New York: Harper and Brothers, 1950), p. 14.

82 Allan Dulles wrote: "Goebbels quickly twisted it (unconditional surrender) into the formula 'total slavery,' and very largely succeeded in making the German people believe that was what unconditional surrender meant . . . The Gobbelses and Bormanns were able to use 'unconditional surrender' to prolong a totally hopeless war for many months." *Germany's Underground* (New York: The Macmillan and Company, 1947), pp. 132-133.

83 Lord Hankey said that the Unconditional Surrender "removed the barriers against Communism in Europe and the Far East and greatly decreased the security of the whole world." *Politics: Trials and Errors* (Chicago: Henry Regnery, 1950), p. 48.

concept." [84] This extraordinary paragraph implies that only pro-Soviet Americans in our government service were to be selected to make contacts with Russian officials, the latter, of course, being trained spies.

The significance of the Burns memorandum comes to light at the Quebec Conference in August, 1943, when Hopkins presented this same memorandum as the basis for American-Russian relations after the war. In all probability it was endorsed by General Marshall. This "defeatist" memorandum pointed out that

> . . . Russia's post-war position in Europe will be a dominant one. . . . Since Russia is a decisive factor in the war, she must be given every assistance and every effort must be made to obtain her friendship. Likewise, since without question she will dominate Europe on the defeat of the Axis, it is even more essential to develop and maintain the most friendly relations with Russia.
>
> *Finally, the most important factor the United States has to consider in relation to Russia is the prosecution of the war in the Pacific.* With Russia as an ally in the war against Japan, the war can be terminated in less time and at less expense in life and resources than if the reverse were the case. Should the war in the Pacific have to be carried on with an unfriendly or a negative attitude on the part of Russia, the difficulties will be immeasurably increased and operations might become abortive.[85]

Robert Sherwood understood the memorandum's significance. He remarked: "This estimate was obviously of great importance as indicating the policy which guided the making of decisions at Teheran and, much later, at Yalta." [86] It is obvious that the influence of General Marshall went very deep and spread very far in shaping American policy in Europe and the Far East. Harry Hopkins was not a thinker and he never posed as one. But he carried out the viewpoints of other persons who did a lot of thinking. General Marshall, always eager to please the inner circle around Roosevelt, stayed pretty much in step with Hopkins. However, he in turn undoubtedly had some influence on Hopkins.

Many prominent officers in the Navy did not agree with the reasoning in the Hopkins memorandum. Indeed, upon many occasions, the viewpoints of Army and Navy officials were sharply at variance. To officers in the Navy, it seemed evident that Stalin would push to the limit the American desire to extend assistance, and they doubted the importance of Russian assistance to the American war effort in the Far East.[87] In his instructions to General Deane on September 18, 1943, General Marshall pointed out the "great importance to the United States of Russia's full participation in the war against Japan after the defeat of Germany as

---

[84] Sherwood, *Roosevelt and Hopkins,* pp. 641-643.
[85] *Ibid.,* pp. 748-749. (Emphasis in original)
[86] *Ibid.,* p. 749.
[87] Capt. W. D. Puleston, *The Influence of Force in Foreign Relations* (New York: D. Van Nostrand Co., 1955) , pp. 167-168.

essential to the prompt and crushing defeat of Japan at far less cost to
the United States and Great Britain." [88] However, General Deane warned
General Marshall not to trust the Russians too far. At least two months
before Yalta, he told General Marshall:

> Everyone will agree on the importance of collaboration with Russia—now and
> in the future. It won't be worth a hoot, however, unless it is based on mutual
> respect and made to work both ways. I have sat at innumerable Russian banquets
> and become gradually nauseated by Russian food, vodka and protestation of
> friendship. . . . It is amazing how these [vodka] toasts go down past the tongues
> in cheeks. After the banquets we send the Soviets another thousand airplanes
> and they approve a visa that has been hanging fire for months. We then scratch
> our heads to see what other gifts we can send and they scratch theirs to see what
> they can ask for.[89]

As a result of this American generosity as expressed in Lend-Lease operations, Stalin made a bow in the direction of American objectives in the
Far East. In October, 1943, he asked Secretary Hull, who was in Moscow
attending a Foreign Minister's Conference, to tell President Roosevelt
that the Soviet Union would enter the Pacific war and help defeat Japan
as soon as the Germans were beaten. Stalin had previously mentioned
this to General Patrick J. Hurley on November 15, 1942. Hull writes that
on October 30, Stalin repeated:

> . . . clearly and unequivocally that, when the allies succeeded in defeating
> Germany, the Soviet Union would then join in defeating Japan. . . . The
> Marshal's statement of his decision was forthright. He made it emphatically, it
> was entirely unsolicited, and he asked nothing in return. . . . When Stalin made
> his promise, for transmission to the President, it had no strings attached to it.[90]

It is significant to note that Stalin asked for nothing in return.

Marshal Stalin made a great impression upon Secretary Hull when,
after saying good-bye and walking away a few steps, he walked back and
shook hands again. "I thought to myself," Hull writes in retrospect, "that
any American having Stalin's personality and approach might well reach
high public office in my own country." [91]

The Moscow conference was a curtain-raiser for the first meeting of
the Big Three in Teheran later in the year. In the meantime, a separate
conference was held at Cairo between Chiang Kai-shek, Churchill, and
Roosevelt. Here it was agreed that Japan was to be deprived "of all the
islands in the Pacific, which she has seized or occupied since the begin-

---

88 *Entry of Soviet Union Into War Against Japan*, p. 21.

89 Major General Deane to General Marshall, Moscow, December 2, 1944, U.S.
Department of State (ed.), *The Conference at Malta and Yalta, 1945* (Washington:
Government Printing Office, 1955), pp. 447-448. (Hereafter cited as *Yalta Documents*)

90 Hull, *Memoirs*, II, pp. 1309-1310.

91 *Ibid.*, p. 1311.

ning of the First World War in 1914, and that all the territories Japan has stolen from the Chinese, such as Manchuria, Formosa and the Pescadores, shall be restored to the Republic of China." [92] Thus, Japan was to be expelled from the continent of Asia and reduced to the status of 1894. Since that date the population of Japan had increased from 35,-000,000 to 70,000,000 people. The Cairo declaration may have seemed like an invitation to millions of Japanese to commit suicide. It was a sharp challenge to Japanese statesmen and it helped to prolong the war and destroy American lives.[93] The promise made to Chiang Kai-shek at Cairo is very significant because it was later broken at Yalta in February, 1945, when Roosevelt gave the Soviet Union much of the territory pledged to Nationalist China.[94]

The Cairo Conference is important for another reason. Roosevelt notified Chiang Kai-shek that he must take the Communists into his cabinet. He told his son Elliot how he had complained to Chiang about the character of his government: "I'd told him it was hardly the modern democracy that ideally it should be. I'd told him he would have to form a unity government, *while the war was still being fought,* with the Communists in Yenan." [95] This was a foreshadow of the Wallace mission in 1944 and of the later fateful efforts of General Marshall to force a coalition government in China.

President Roosevelt's attitude towards Churchill was very cordial before and at the beginning of the war. However, as the time approached for the Teheran Conference, his attitude towards Great Britain changed perceptibly under the influence of several factors. Wartime strains and tensions had levied a terrific toll on his mental and physical strength. The demand for unity among the allies precluded a public discussion of the problem, and in this enforced silence he began to exhibit a definite anti-English bias. This state of mind explains in part the President's apparent presumption that the threat to world security lay in British imperialism rather than Russia or international Communism.[96]

When, at the Casablanca Conference, Winston Churchill began to insist upon an invasion of Europe through its "soft underbelly," and per-

---

[92] U.S. Congress, Senate Committee on Foreign Relations, *A Decade of American Policy 1941-1949* (Washington: Government Printing Office, 1950), p. 22.

[93] Robert Butow, *Japan's Decision to Surrender,* (Stanford, California: Stanford University Press, 1954), p. 40.

[94] Testimony of General Albert C. Wedemeyer, June 11, 1951, U.S. Congress, Senate, Hearings Before the Committee on Armed Forces and the Committee on Foreign Relations. *Military Situation in the Far East,* 82nd Cong., 1st Sess. (Washington: Government Printing Office, 1951), Part 3, p. 2416. The recently published Cairo-Teheran documents reveal that Roosevelt broke his pledge to Chiang seven days later, at the Teheran Conference. See Chap. III.

[95] Elliot Roosevelt, *As He Saw It,* p. 164. (Emphasis in original)

[96] Puleston, "Blunders of World War II," *U.S. News and World Report* (February 4, 1955), pp. 121-123.

sisted in his plan, his motives became suspect to some Americans who felt that his military proposals were designed to extend the British sphere of influence in the Mediterranean area.[97] As Churchill steadfastly pursued his objectives, Roosevelt strove for the rejection of imperialism as an instrument of national policy. Unfortunately, subsequent events began to distort his perspective. In the President's mind, the Prime Minister and the English nation became one and inseparable. The attributes and deficiencies of Churchill became those of the English nation. As Roosevelt understood it, Britain's imperial policy, approved by her people, would continue to threaten world peace. As a result, he became increasingly susceptible to the blandishments of Russia and her disciples. America's role in the future would be that of the arbiter between Great Britain and the Soviet Union. In the words of Bernard M. Baruch:

> Roosevelt strove constantly to prevent suspicion from interfering with the prosecution of the war. 'We must treat Russia as an equal and give her our full confidence,' he often remarked. Only with difficulty was he able to convince Churchill this was the course to follow. The President asked me to 'speak to Winston about his attitude towards the Russians.' This I did, in Roosevelt's presence, shortly after the Quebec Conference.[98]

To some extent Churchill was merely following the time-honored idea of regarding war as an instrument of national policy. He felt that nations did not usually fight merely for the fun of fighting. There were certainly clearly defined objectives behind every conflict, and wars were successful only if these objectives were obtained. He was constantly looking at postwar conditions, and he knew that if Russia gained a dominant position in the Balkans she would be a most serious menace to peace in Europe.[99] Churchill was a statesman who was deeply concerned with the results of World War II. English blood, sweat, and tears would have been spent in vain if Russia were to emerge from the conflict so strongly entrenched in Europe and in the Far East that capitalistic countries would cower under the shadow of her power. At the Teheran Conference, Roosevelt remarked to his son Elliot: "Trouble is, the P.M. is thinking too much of the *post*-war, and where England will be. He's scared of letting the Russians get too strong." [100]

Roosevelt had more sympathy than Churchill, to say nothing of most

---

[97] Elliot Roosevelt, *As He Saw It*, p. 93. President Roosevelt pointed out that although the United States was Britain's ally, America was not in the conflict in order to help Britain's "hang on to the archaic, medieval, Empire ideas." *Ibid.*, pp. 121-122.

[98] Bernard M. Baruch, "A Few Kind Words for Uncle Sam," *The Saturday Evening Post* (June 12, 1948), p. 16.

[99] The secret papers in the Department of State, however, show that Churchill was not so convincing in pointing up the menace of U.S.S.R. in the Balkans as he represents in his writings.

[100] Elliot Roosevelt, *As He Saw It*, p. 185.

Americans, for the Bolshevik experiment. He regarded the Communist threat as less grave and certainly less immediate than the Nazi menace. He fancied that over the years the Soviet and American systems would appreciate each other.[101] In a letter to Admiral William D. Leahy he wrote that after Europe is liberated from Nazi domination, "I do not think we need worry about any possibility of Russian domination." [102]

Roosevelt's correspondence and conversations are filled with his emphasis upon winning the war. To a considerable extent, this was also true of Churchill.[103] This appalling lack of vision is partly responsible for some of the tragic conditions of the world today. Roosevelt was long on war plans with grandiose visions but amazingly short on practical plans for a just and durable peace. His estimate of Stalin and of Soviet intentions shows that he was tragically naïve about international politics. Numerous forces, events, and pressures made him look with favor upon Russia. The past errors of that country had been explained away as "growing-pains," and Russian victories over the Nazis were acclaimed in press and pulpit. The pro-Russian attitude in Washington was intense according to one official.[104] "Of all the United States government agencies," says Jan Ciechanowski, "the office of War Information, under its new director Mr. Elmer Davis, had very definitely adopted a line of unqualified praise of Soviet Russia. . . . " [105] American propaganda broadcasts to occupied Poland offered proofs of this new line. Ambassador Ciechanowski protested repeatedly against the pro-Soviet character of the propaganda broadcasts to occupied Poland. "When I finally appealed to the Secretary of State and to divisional heads of the State Department . . . I was told that the State Department was aware of these facts but could not control this agency, which boasted that it received its directives straight from the White House." [106]

The Soviet Union encouraged this pro-Russian state of mind with a number of superficial concessions, including the dissolution of the Third International, the reopening of a number of churches, and some lessen-

101 Sumner Welles, *Where Are We Heading* (New York: Harper and Brothers, 1946), pp. 36-37.

102 President Roosevelt to Admiral Leahy, June 26, 1941, quoted in *I Was There*, pp. 37-38.

103 Some individuals question what Churchill's war aims actually were. According to Russell Grenfell, the motives of Churchill were primarily "winning the war." In the House of Commons on May 13, 1940, the Prime Minister said: "You ask what is our policy? I will say: 'It is to wage war, war by sea, land and air, with all our might and with all our strength that God can give us; to wage war against the monstrous tyranny, never surpassed in the dark lamentable catalogue of human crime.' That is our policy. You ask, what is our aim: I can answer in one word: 'Victory—victory at all cost.'" *Unconditional Hatred* (New York: Devin-Adair Co., 1954), pp. 102-103. See also Chapters 7 and 8.

104 Puleston, "Blunders of World War II," *op. cit.*, p. 121.

105 Jan Ciechanowski, *Defeat in Victory*, pp. 115-116.

106 *Ibid.*, pp. 130-131.

ing of control over certain countries incorporated into the Soviet Union. America magnified these acts until they were out of proportion to their importance. Many persons who were close to the President were prompt to defend Soviet actions.[107] Roosevelt, himself, was ever ready to assign the most favorable interpretation to Soviet actions.

To William Bullitt, the former ambassador to Moscow, Roosevelt declared: "I have just a hunch that Stalin . . . doesn't want anything but security for his country, and I think that if I give him everything I possibly can, and ask nothing in return . . . he won't try to annex anything and will work for a world of democracy and peace." [108] To the Polish leader Stanislaw Mikolajczk, he remarked: "Stalin is a realist, and we mustn't forget, when we judge Russian actions, that the Soviet regime has had only two years of experience in international relations. But of one thing I am certain, Stalin is not an Imperialist." [109]

Roosevelt could not have been more wrong either in his estimate of Soviet political inexperience or of her imperialistic intentions.[110] He had sought to avoid any action which might make Stalin suspicious of Anglo-American intentions. He had opposed Western attempts to set up a *"cordon sanitaire* of satellite states." [111] Roosevelt's naiveté was in sharp and unfortunate contrast to the astute moves of Stalin. They had hardly met at Teheran when Stalin, in a display of solicitation, invited Roosevelt to stay with him in the Russian Embassy. Stalin himself moved to a small cottage on the Embassy grounds to make room for his guest.[112] At first the President was discouraged when it appeared that he had not immediately attracted the favorable notice of the Russian dictator:

I thought it over all night and made up my mind I had to do something desperate. Then . . . I began to tease Churchill about British news . . . about his cigars, about his habits. It began to register with Stalin. . . . Finally, Stalin broke out into a deep hearty guffaw, and for the first time in three days, I saw the light, I kept it up until Stalin was laughing with me, and it was then that I called him "Uncle Joe". . . . From that time on our relations were personal.[113]

The belief that he had won Stalin's friendship exercised a most impor-

107 Puleston, "Blunders of World War II," *op. cit.*, p. 122.

108 William C. Bullitt, "How We Won the War and Lost the Peace," *Life* (August 30, 1948), p. 94.

109 Stanislaw Mikoljczk, *The Rape of Poland: Pattern of Soviet Aggression* (New York: Whittlesey House, McGraw Hill Book Co., Inc., 1948), p. 59.

110 Arthur Bliss Lane, former Ambassador to Poland, remarked: "Roosevelt had been unable to gain . . . the principal decisions over Stalin." Arthur Bliss Lane, *I Saw Poland Betrayed* (Indianapolis: Bobbs-Merrill Company, 1948), p. 78. "I was disturbed by President Roosevelt's exaggerated confidence in the power of his charm to persuade diplomatic and political adversaries to his point of view. He seemed to feel that this charm was particularly effective on Stalin." *Ibid.*

111 Chester Wilmot, *The Struggle for Europe*, p. 447.

112 Sherwood, *Roosevelt and Hopkins*, p. 776.

113 Frances Perkins, *The Roosevelt I Knew*, (New York: Viking Press, 1947), pp. 83-84.

tant influence on the policy which Roosevelt pursued between Teheran and his next meeting with Stalin at Yalta.

Elliot Roosevelt, who was at his father's side at the Teheran Conference, gives an important view of the President's feelings toward Stalin. When he asked his father whether he liked the Russian dictator, Roosevelt "nodded an emphatic affirmative . . . 'I'm sure we'll hit it off, Stalin and I,' Father said. 'A great deal of the misunderstandings and the mistrusts of the past are going to get cleared up during the next few days . . . I hope once and for all.' " [114] And in one of his private conversations with Stalin, the President discussed the question of a common front against the British. He proposed that he and Stalin would back Chiang Kai-shek against Churchill on the question of Hong Kong and Shanghai. Elliot Roosevelt's explanation of this is that "the biggest thing was" to make "clear to Stalin that the United States and Great Britain were not allied in one common bloc against the Soviet Union." [115]

It was significant that at Teheran Stalin reaffirmed what he had said to General Hurley on November 15, 1942—the Soviet Union planned to join in the Pacific war against Japan. Roosevelt and Churchill, as well as their military staffs, were well pleased with the Soviet affirmation.[116] However, Stalin was extremely cautious about revealing any Soviet objectives. Roosevelt, on his own initiative, suggested that Russia might have access to Dairen, which would be a free port under international supervision, and added that the Chinese would not, as Stalin suggested, object to this, provided the Soviet Union cooperated with China and the Chinese sovereignty was not impaired.[117] The arrangement was finally confirmed at Yalta and written into the Soviet-Chinese treaty of August, 1945. Years have passed and Dairen is far removed from the status of a free port.

Defenders of Roosevelt have constantly used two arguments regarding his decisions at the Yalta Conference in February, 1945. They say that he was a sick man and not responsible for his acts and that by February, 1945, at the time of the Conference, the Soviet Union had acquired such a strong military position that the West had to submit to Stalin's demands. These arguments, however, do not stand up with the facts. First of all, Roosevelt was in good health and in command of his faculties when he bargained with Stalin at Teheran in 1943. It was at this conference that Stalin agreed to enter the Pacific war against the Japanese. The Yalta Conference merely confirms what took place at Teheran. As a

[114] Elliot Roosevelt, *As He Saw It*, pp. 176-177.

[115] *Ibid.*, p. 206.

[116] *Entry of Soviet Union Into War Against Japan*, pp. 25-27. cf. *Foreign Relations, 1942*, III, 656.

[117] Department of State, *United States Relations with China* (Washington: Government Printing Office, 1949), p. 558.

matter of fact, the Teheran Conference is the most important meeting of
the war because it was here that Roosevelt first generously appeased the
Russian dictator. Moreover, at the time of the Teheran Conference in
November, 1943, Russia had not yet gained a military position of strength
to make her a commanding factor in the Pacific war. According to Bullitt, the American bargaining power could have been used more effectively at Teheran:

> President Roosevelt could have faced up to Stalin's demands at Teheran.
> Hitler's armies were still on Soviet soil, and Stalin needed the full flood of our
> Lend-Lease supplies to regain even the frontiers he had held when he made his
> pact with Hitler in August, 1939. And the bugaboo which haunted our chiefs
> of staff—that unless we give Stalin everything he wanted he would make a
> separate peace with Hitler—was the creation of military imagination functioning
> in political ignorance. It takes one to make war; but two to make peace. . . .
> The only result of a serious attempt by Stalin to get together with Hitler would
> have been that Hitler would have informed the British and ourselves of Stalin's
> overtures and tried to make a separate peace with us. The President, therefore,
> could safely have stood up to Stalin at Teheran.[118]

At the airport as Roosevelt was preparing to depart on the return trip
to Cairo, he and General Hurley had a final, private talk. Hurley warned
the President that we could not afford to make to the Russians and the
British any concessions that would force the abandonment of the principles for which we claimed to be fighting. Roosevelt replied that he
had to go far enough to keep our allies in the war, but that he would
not make any concessions that would prevent the building of the postwar peace on the principles enunciated in the Atlantic Charter. Hurley
then said that any encouragement to the imperialists might make it difficult to sustain these principles when peace had been achieved. Roosevelt and Hurley were seated in the President's limousine during this conversation, the President having his arm extended along the arm rest
between them, his palm down. He said, "Why, Pat, I can change all that,
at the proper time, as easily as this," slowly turning his hand palm up.
"It is sad for America," Hurley adds, "that when the time came to change
the situation, the President seemed to have lost his perspective—and,
eventually, was not able to move his hands the way he wanted." [119]

Roosevelt left Teheran believing that he had won the confidence and
friendship of Stalin. He announced in a broadcast on December 24, 1943:

> To use an American and ungrammatical colloquialism, I may say that I got
> along fine with Marshal Stalin. . . . I believe that we are going to get on well
> with him and the Russian people, very well indeed. . . . The rights of every

---

118 William C. Bullitt, "How We Won the War and Lost the Peace," *Life* (September 6, 1948), p. 86.
119 Don Lohbeck, *Patrick J. Hurley* (Chicago: Henry Regnery, 1956), p. 219.

nation, large and small, must be respected and guarded as jealously as are the rights of every individual in our republic. The doctrine that the strong shall dominate the weak is the doctrine of our enemies, and we reject it.[120]

Considering Russia's earlier domination over Latvians, Lithuanians, Estonians, and other peoples of Eastern Europe, this was an unrealistic statement. It is difficult to believe that Roosevelt could have been so tragically naive about Russian history and Communist philosophy. He could scarcely have been altogether ignorant of the vast network of slave labor camps in the Soviet Union. The horrors of Soviet mass deportations from eastern Poland and the Baltic states during the period of the Stalin-Hitler pact should have been well known to him. Perhaps the best exposition of Roosevelt's idea of getting along with the Russians is to be found in a memorandum which Hopkins wrote six months after Yalta. "We know or believe," he said, "that Russia's interests, so far as we can anticipate them, do not afford an opportunity for a major difference with us in foreign affairs. We believe we are mutually dependent upon each other for economic reasons. We find the Russians as individuals easy to deal with. The Russians undoubtedly like the American people. They like the United States. They trust the United States more than they trust any other power in the world . . . . above all, they want to maintain friendly relations with us. . . . They are tenacious, determined people who think and act just like you and I do." [121]

At the Quebec Conference in September, 1944, the British Chiefs of Staff approved the over-all plan for the defeat of Japan. The intention of invading the Japanese home islands received the endorsement of the President and the Prime Minister.[122] The planning date for the end of the war against Japan was decided at the same conference. When on September 23, 1944, American Ambassador Harriman and British Ambassador Clark-Kerr had called on Marshal Stalin to tell him of the plans, the Soviet leader seemed puzzled because the program did not appear to take more account of the part Russia was to take in the fighting. He remarked: " . . . there had been no change in the Russian attitude, but if the United States and Great Britain preferred to bring Japan to her knees without Russian participation, he was ready to agree." [123]

President Roosevelt was deeply concerned about Stalin's attitude for fear that Russia might not join in the war against Japan. On September 28, 1944, he wrote to Ambassador Harriman: "I have at no time entertained any doubts whatever in regard to the Teheran agreement about

---

120 *America's Second Crusade*, p. 202.

121 This memorandum, written on August 1st, 1945, is quoted by Sherwood, *Roosevelt and Hopkins*, pp. 922-923.

122 *Entry of Soviet Union Into War Against Japan*, p. 30.

123 Deane, *The Strange Alliance*, p. 240.

[the] Pacific campaign." [124] Two days later he cabled to Prime Minister Churchill that "Stalin is at the present time sensitive about any doubt as to his intention to help us in the Orient." [125]

To Marshal Stalin, the President, on October 4, sent the following message:

> . . . I want to reiterate to you how completely I accept the assurances which you have given us on this point [the war against Japan]. Our three countries are waging a successful war against Germany and we can surely join together with no less success in crushing a nation that I am sure in my heart is as great an enemy of Russia as she is of ours.[126]

Actually, the question of Russia's participation in the war against Japan had been agreed to in general terms at the Teheran Conference when Stalin promised Roosevelt he would fight the Japanese as soon as the war ended with Germany. However, when it came to definite arrangements, the Russians placed many obstacles in the way of anxious American planners. As a result, little progress had been made toward settling in detail what Russia's share in the Japanese war would be.[127]

General Deane noticed at firsthand the signs of disintegration of the war-time alliance with Russia. He emphasized that it was time for a changed policy, that all relations should be on a *quid pro quo* basis. His final specific recommendation for a new policy was that "we should stop pushing ourselves on them and make the Soviet authorities come to us. We should be friendly and co-operative when they do so." [128] The prevailing attitude in Washington *vis-à-vis* Russia was expressed by Secretary of the Navy Forrestal in a letter to Palmer Hoyt of the *Denver Post* on September 2, 1944:

> I find that whenever any American suggests that we act in accordance with the needs of our own security he is apt to be called a god-damned fascist or imperialist, while if Uncle Joe suggests that he needs the Baltic Provinces, half of Poland, all of Bessarabia and access to the Mediterranean, all hands agree that he is a fine, frank, candid and generally delightful fellow who is very easy to deal with because he is so explicit in what he wants.[129]

The visit of Prime Minister Churchill to Moscow in October, 1944 provided a new opportunity for the discussion of Soviet participation in the war against Japan. Stalin presented a list of supplies the Soviet Army needed in the Far East, and, at the same time, accepted the American

---

124 President Roosevelt to Ambassador Harriman, September 28, 1944, *Entry of Soviet Union Into War Against Japan*, p. 35.
125 President Roosevelt to Prime Minister Churchill, September 30, 1944, *Ibid.*
126 President Roosevelt to Ambassador Harriman, October 4, 1944, *Ibid.*, pp. 35-36.
127 *Ibid.*, p. 31.
128 Deane, *op. cit.*, pp. 84-86.
129 *The Forrestal Diaries*, p. 14.

request for air bases in the Siberian area.[130] But in spite of this promise, says General Deane, "the end result was that the Russians got their supplies and the United States got nothing except a belated and last minute Russian attack against the Japanese." [131] Field-Marshal Lord Alanbrooke, who was Churchill's military adviser at the conference, sums up Russia's attitude very well:

I still feel . . . that we started off on the wrong leg in our first negotiations with Moscow. We gave everything unconditionally and never asked for anything. We were dealing with a semi-Asiatic race with innate bargaining instincts. The supplies of equipment, etc., should have been counter-balanced by greater co-operation. During the whole of the war I never received a Russian order of battle showing their dispositions. . . .[132]

Russia's refusal to indicate any enthusiastic co-operation with American military officials did not prevent Soviet armies from receiving ever-increasing amounts of trucks, telephone equipment, canned food, and other Lend-Lease supplies. The Roosevelt Administration had decided to build up the Soviet Air Force to a considerable strength in long range bombers. Fortunately, the plan had not been carried very far along before the war ended and Soviet-American relations cooled. Two messages to Roosevelt and the Joint Chiefs of Staff, one from General Deane, and one from Ambassador Harriman, contain the references to this proposal to build up a long-range Soviet bomber air force. Both messages are dated October 15, 1944. Harriman cabled the President that "Stalin said he would be glad to receive four-engined bombers and instructors to train a strategic air force for Soviet use in the war against Japan." [133] General Deane's message described a meeting with Russians and stated:

I then gave them the strategic objectives which you authorized me to suggest to them as coming from you. This of course included the part they might play in securing the lines of communications across the north Pacific. I told them that the United States was prepared to assist the Soviet Union to the extent consistent with our commitments in the war against Germany by supplying munitions and particularly B-24 aircraft for building up of a Soviet air force.[134]

When General Deane pressed Soviet authorities for certain commit-

---

130 For these discussions see the following memoranda: Ambassador Harriman to President Roosevelt, October 10, 1944; Ambassador Harriman to President Roosevelt, October 11, 1944; President Roosevelt to Ambassador Harriman, October 11, 1944; Ambassador Harriman to President Roosevelt, October 15, 1944; Major General Deane to Joint Chiefs of Staff, October 15, 1944; Ambassador Harriman to President Roosevelt, October 17, 1944; Major General Deane to Joint Chiefs of Staff, October 17, 1944. All printed in Department of State, Yalta Documents, pp. 362-374.

131 Deane, The Strange Alliance, p. 249.

132 Arthur Bryant, The Turn of the Tide: Diaries of Field-Marshal Lord Alanbrooke, Chief of the Imperial General Staff. (New York: Doubleday and Company, 1957), p. 374.

133 Ambassador Harriman to President Roosevelt, Moscow, October 15, 1944, Yalta Documents, p. 369.

134 General Deane to the Joint Chiefs of Staff, Moscow, October 15, 1944, Ibid., p. 367.

ments, the Russian General Staff decided to forego our proposal to create a strategic air force. However, during the late 1944 months, and during 1945, five U.S. B-29's made emergency landings on Russian fields in Siberia. Russia took these planes over and refused to give them up. Instead, our then-ally made copies of the planes, designating the Soviet model the TU-4. No mention was made by Roosevelt of this strange fact when he met Stalin at Yalta. Roosevelt apparently did not entertain any suspicion of Russia's motives, but went ahead and dealt generously with Stalin.

A two-motored American bomber which had taken part in the air raid on Japan on April 18, 1942, had been forced to land, because of insufficient fuel, at a Soviet air field in the Maritime kray (region). The crew of five was interned. Secretary Hull was disturbed over Soviet behavior. In a dispatch to Standley, he said: "It is hoped that you will be able to prevail upon the Soviet authorities to permit a member of your staff to visit the interned persons in the near future." [135]

As our military leaders increased their urging that Soviet participation in the war against Japan was essential to American victory, so did Stalin increase his price for such participation. To Ambassador Averell Harriman, he "expressed his opinion that the Japanese war would be of short duration after Russia attacked, and if stores could be built up now, the attack could be made two or three months after Germany's collapse. He said he was not ready to give a definite date but that planning should begin at once. Furthermore, there were political aspects which would have to be given consideration. . . ." [136]

On December 14, 1944, Marshal Stalin spelled out to Ambassador Harriman the political requirements for Soviet participation, including the annexation of the Kuriles and lower Sakhalin, the restoration of former Russian holdings in Manchuria, and the recognition of the *status quo* in Outer Mongolia.[137] Meanwhile, a major setback was experienced on the military level when General Deane was informed by General A. I. Antonov on December 16 that the United States' request for air bases in the Maritime Provinces could not be granted, since all the available facilities would be needed by the Soviet forces. United States protests against this reversal of Marshal Stalin's previous assurances failed to alter the decision.[188]

Between the Japanese attack on Pearl Harbor and the closing months of 1944, the U.S. Air Force continually demanded from Russia the use of

135 *Foreign Relations, 1942*, III, p. 550.
136 Ambassador Harriman to President Roosevelt, October 15, 1944, in *Patrick J. Hurley*, p. 356.
137 Ambassador Harriman to President Roosevelt, December 15, 1944, *Yalta Documents*, pp. 378-379.
188 Major General Deane to Joint Chiefs of Staff, December 16, 1944, *Entry of Soviet Union Into War Against Japan*, p. 38.

bases in Siberia to strike at the heart of Japan.[139] Had this been arranged, it might have shortened the war and saved many American lives. But the Russians deliberately vacillated after making many promises to our military observers in Moscow. Time and again General Deane complained to officials in Washington about this Russian perfidy. But Russian discourtesy failed to lessen the ardor of Americans who were devoted to the idea of helping Russia in a significant manner. She must have not only large amounts of Lend-Lease help, but should also receive assistance in the form of impressive loans of money. Both Harriman and Secretary Morgenthau were strongly in favor of a Russian loan that would run into billions of dollars.[140] In a typical note to Secretary Stettinius, Harriman observed:

It is my basic conviction that we should do everything we can to assist the Soviet Union through credits in developing a sound economy. I feel strongly that the sooner the Soviet Union can develop a decent life for its people, the more tolerant they will become.[141]

In view of later disclosures, it is disturbing to recall that a top Morgenthau aide in the Russian loan talks was Harry Dexter White.[142]

A telegram from Harriman to Stettinius early in January, 1945, reports that Soviet Foreign Minister V. M. Molotov, handed the American Ambassador a note suggesting the kind of loan that interested Russia. It was to be a six billion dollar credit to be repaid in thirty years at annual interest of 2.5 per cent. The Molotov note was so detailed that Harriman was surprised. But the Russians, he reminded Washington, were ignorant of normal business procedures.[143] Within six days after receipt of this telegram from Harriman, Secretary Morgenthau sent President Roosevelt a memorandum proposing a ten billion dollar reconstruction credit for Russia at only 2 per cent for a period of thirty-five years.[144] The Morgenthau proposal was shelved "because of legislative restrictions" which had to be lifted by Congress and because the offer seemed ill-timed. Harriman agreed.[145] The whole idea of a U.S. loan to Russia finally was abandoned.

139 *Stalin's Correspondence with Roosevelt*, II, p. 110.

140 This loan of six billion dollars to Russia was discussed backstage in the Roosevelt Administration for nearly a year before the Yalta Conference. Secretary Hull says that "Morgenthau . . . often interfered in foreign affairs, and sometimes took steps directly at variance with those of the State Department." Hull, *Memoirs*, II, p. 1379.

141 Ambassador Harriman to Secretary Stettinius, Jr., Moscow, January 6, 1945, *Yalta Documents*, p. 314.

142 It is significant to point out the tremendous influence White had in foreign affairs. See Chapter VIII.

143 Ambassador Harriman to Secretary Stettinius, Moscow, January 4, *Yalta Documents*, pp. 310-312.

144 Secretary Morgenthau to President Roosevelt, January 10, 1945, *Ibid.*, p. 315.

145 Assistant Secretary of State (Clayton) to Secretary Stettinius, January 20, 1945, *Ibid.*, pp. 318-319.

Nevertheless, our policy-makers seemed to have been bent on saving "Mother Russia," and American supplies continued to pour into that country with no strings attached. "I know," says Admiral Standley, former Ambassador to Russia, "that the Kremlin 'took us for all the traffic would bear' while I was in Moscow, and even more so after I left. . . . For long months, I saw Special Representative after Big Dignitary come to Russia, leapfrog over my top-hatted head, and follow out the Rooseveltian policy —do not antagonize the Russians, give them everything they want, for, after all, they are killing Germans, they are fighting our battles for us." [146]

At the same time, General "Hap" Arnold writes that in Alaska: "We gave them everything it was possible to give them, even turning over to them the houses of our own officers and enlisted men and their families. . . . They never gave us any thanks. . . ." [147]

Former Ambassador Bullitt once stated in substance that the great tragedy of our time was the total inability of Western leadership to grasp and understand Communist mentality. He summarized our disastrous errors as follows:

When our government began in 1941 to treat the Soviet Union as a 'peace loving democracy' instead of as a predatory totalitarian tyranny, it made one of the most disastrous errors in the history of the United States. We based our foreign policy on the exact reverse of the truth. While our soldiers, sailors and aviators were fighting with superb skill and courage, our foreign policy was being handled with ignorant and reckless disregard of the vital interests of the American people. We did nothing whatsoever to guarantee ourselves against the possibility—which was in fact a certainty—that Stalin's totalitarian dictatorship would turn out to have the same aim of world conquest as Hitler's totalitarian dictatorship . . . [and a lot better chance of achieving it—the author].[148]

As a result of Roosevelt's "Alice in Wonderland" outlook, Stalin was enabled to carve out a mightier empire than any Tsar had ever ruled.

---

146 Standley and Ageton, *Admiral Ambassador to Russia*, p. 195.

147 H. H. Arnold, *Global Mission* (New York: Harper and Brothers, 1949), p. 471.

148 William C. Bullitt, "Can Truman Avoid World War III?" *The American Mercury* (June, 1947), p. 646.

CHAPTER III

PERSONAL DIPLOMACY AT CAIRO AND TEHERAN

The dangers to responsible government which are inherent in one-man diplomacy have never been better illustrated than by the Department of State's "records" of the Cairo-Teheran Conferences of November, 1943. At these conferences, post-war American policy in Asia was explored and developed in consultation between President Roosevelt, Prime Minister Churchill, Chiang Kai-shek, Marshal Stalin and their top military and political advisers. Yet, apart from some preliminary papers and some memoranda of the Joint Chiefs of Staff, there is virtually no official published record of the numerous conversations held on the subject of the future of Asia.

Again and again, in noting the round of diplomatic lunches, dinners, meetings, sessions and discussions during the five fateful days, the Department of State reports: "No records of these conversations have been found," "No minutes. . . . ," "No Memoranda. . . . ," "No official American record," "No record," "No record," "No record." However, since a large amount of Teheran material is still unpublished by the State Department, the reported paucity of material must be accepted with some degree of skepticism.

Here was an occasion when the future of the United States and of the world was being shaped, yet the American Department of State was compelled to request, in 1956, that the Chinese Government make available to us their summary record of the Roosevelt-Chiang Dinner Meeting at the President's villa on November 24, 1943. So, for an account of what the President agreed on as to China's future role as one of the "Big Four" and leading power in the Far East, we have only the version of a foreign government.

Prior to Teheran, Roosevelt and Churchill had invited Soviet participation at such meetings as the Atlantic Charter conference and Casablanca, but they had accepted Stalin's excuses and had kept him informed of developments. Throughout 1942, Russia was still a "junior partner" in the opinion of Roosevelt and Churchill. Their main anxiety had been to keep the Russians from surrendering. The situation changed dramatically after the Soviet victory at Stalingrad. By February, 1943, the German advance had been halted. Russia then began to shape her part of the postwar world by unilateral moves.[1]

As early as December 14, 1941, President Roosevelt wrote Marshal Stalin about the possibility of meeting him personally: "I very much wish that you and I could meet to talk this [common action] over personally." But the President indicated that he realized the impossibility of initiating a meeting at this time.[2]

In April, 1942, the President corresponded with Stalin inconclusively about getting together sometime during the summer of that year, perhaps somewhere near Alaska. Again in November and December of the same year he wrote to Stalin about the possibility of their meeting with Churchill in January, 1943—at or near Khartoum or in southern Algeria, or perhaps early in March, 1943, in North Africa.[3] Roosevelt had enjoyed a close personal relationship with Churchill. The President was confident that he could establish the same sort of relationship with Stalin if he could meet the Soviet leader face to face.

Finally, on May 5, 1943, Roosevelt wrote Stalin that he was sending him a personal note through his old friend, Joseph E. Davies. He wrote: "It is my thought that neither of us would want to bring any Staff. I would be accompanied by Harry Hopkins, an interpreter and a stenographer—and that you and I would talk very informally and get what we call 'a meeting of the minds.' I do not believe that any official agreements or declarations are in the least bit necessary. You and I would, of course, talk over the military and naval situation, but I think we can both do that without staffs being present." [4]

Davies presented the President's personal letter to Stalin on May 20. It was read by an interpreter and was "cordially received." This was followed by two and a half hours of discussions with Stalin and Molotov in the "most friendly atmosphere." [5] In his official reply to the President's

---

1 Edna R. Fluegel, "Are We Ready for the Summit?" *Free World Forum* (May, 1959).

2 *Foreign Relations*, 1941, IV, p. 752.

3 *Ibid.*, 1942, III, pp. 545, 665-666, 675.

4 President Roosevelt to Marshal Stalin, May 5, 1943. Department of State, *Foreign Relations of the United States: Conferences at Cairo and Teheran, 1943* (Washington: Government Printing Office, 1961), p. 4. Hereafter cited as *Cairo-Teheran Papers*. Speaking before the Senate and House of Representatives on May 19, 1943, Churchill said: "We (the President and I), both of us, earnestly hope that at no distant date we may be able to achieve what we have so long sought—namely, a meeting with Marshal Stalin and if possible with Generalissimo Chiang Kai-shek. But how, when and where this is to be accomplished is not a matter upon which I am able to shed any clear ray of light at the present time, and if I were I should certainly not shed it." *Congressional Record*, Vol. 89, Part 4, p. 4621.

5 The President's Special Representative (Davies) to President Roosevelt and Secretary Hull, May 21, 1943, *Cairo-Teheran Papers*, p. 5.

letter, Stalin agreed "our meeting" should be arranged in July or August, and concluded with words of thanks "for sending Mr. Davies who had a knowledge of the Soviet Union and can [sic] unbiassedly judge of things." [6]

Roosevelt felt that a small staff meeting with Stalin offered certain advantages. He told Churchill that perhaps the Russian leader would be "more frank in giving his views on the offensive against Japan now and later," and that Stalin would also be "more frank" in regard to China. He was anxious to "explore" Stalin's thinking "as fully as possible" concerning Russia's "post-war hopes and ambitions." [7]

Stalin was interested in meeting the American President, but could not agree on a place for the conference. In memoranda to both Churchill and Roosevelt he explained why he could not go farther than Teheran, or to any of the locations suggested by the President.[8]

Roosevelt was disappointed. He explained to Stalin that he could not "risk" being away from Washington for "constitutional reasons." Congress would be in session. New laws and resolutions "must be acted on by me after their receipt and must be returned to the Congress physically before ten days have elapsed." After suggesting Cairo, Bagdad, and other sites more accessible by air, Roosevelt added further inducements to an early meeting:

In any event, I think the Press should be entirely banished, and the whole place surrounded by a cordon so that we would not be disturbed in any way. . . .
I am placing a very great importance on the personal and intimate conversations which you and Churchill and I will have, for on them the hopes of the future world will greatly depend.[9]

But Stalin was "adamant," and insisted that "not one of the places proposed by you for the meeting instead of Tegeran [Teheran] is acceptable for me." [10] Secretary of State Hull reported from Moscow that "I fear that Stalin will continue immovable on the question." [11] The President then suggested Basra and again reminded the Russian leader that "constitutional requirements" made Teheran impossible as a meeting place. "I would gladly go ten times the distance to meet you," he said, "were it not for the fact that I must carry on a constitutional government more than one hundred and fifty years old." [12] For the moment, at least, the President held out against Teheran as a meeting place.

---

6 Marshal Stalin to President Roosevelt, May 26, 1943, *Ibid.*, p. 6.

7 President Roosevelt to Prime Minister Churchill, June 28, 1943, *Ibid.*, p. 11.

8 Marshal Stalin to President Roosevelt and Prime Minister Churchill, September 12, 1943, *Ibid.*, pp. 22, 25.

9 President Roosevelt to Marshal Stalin, October 14, 1943, *Ibid.*, pp. 31-32.

10 Marshal Stalin to President Roosevelt, October 19, 1943, *Ibid.*, p. 33.

11 Secretary Hull to President Roosevelt, October 21, 1943, *Ibid.*, p. 35.

12 President Roosevelt to Secretary Hull, October 21, 1943, *Ibid.*, p. 36.

In August, 1943, a meeting in the White House reviewed a memorandum which advanced the thesis that Russia would be the dominant power in postwar Europe and must be appeased. It was decided that the United Nations must be established before war's end and must include Russia. Otherwise one war would merge into the next. The conclusion was reached that we must meet with the Russians and fashion binding agreements while the war was in progress in order to provide the "cement" for allied unity. This was our main reason for holding the first foreign ministers meeting at Moscow, preceding the summit meeting at Teheran.[13]

On October 25, 1943, General Marshall suggested to Admiral Leahy the possibility of Russian participation in the Combined Chiefs of Staff conferences. "My view is," said Marshall, ". . . we are not asking for anything from the Russians in the way of information but are offering them virtually a complete insight into all of our strategical and logistical doings." [14] Since Stalin had insisted he would not go beyond Teheran, Roosevelt thought Marshall's suggestion might be a fine way of getting him or possibly Molotov to come the President's way. He felt it was appropriate to ask Churchill what he thought of the idea.

Churchill was vigorously opposed to Russian participation in Joint Staff meetings. He explained:

I deprecate the idea of inviting a Russian military representative to sit in at the meetings of our joint staffs. Unless he understood and spoke English, the delays would be intolerable. I do not know of any really high officer of the Russian Army who can speak English. Such a representative would have no authority or power to speak except as instructed. He would simply say [bay] for an earlier second front and block all other discussions. Considering they tell us nothing of their own movements, I do not think we should open this door to them as it would probably mean that they would want to have observers at all future meetings and all discussions between us would be paralyzed.[15]

Meanwhile Ambassador Winant reported to Roosevelt from London on November 4 that the Prime Minister was "deeply disturbed" at the President's suggestion to introduce a "Russian military representative" in the projected Anglo-American Staff meetings. "He is absolutely set against it." [16] As a result, Roosevelt was faced with the choice of seeing Stalin at Teheran or not at all. He tried to coax Stalin to fly down to Basra, if only for a day but this did not develop.

The President finally gave in. He wrote to Stalin on November 8 that he was "especially happy" to inform the Russian leader that Teheran would be acceptable. Roosevelt explained to Churchill: "I have just

13 Edna R. Fluegel, "Are We Ready for the Summit?" *Free World Forum* (May, 1959).
14 General Marshall to Admiral Leahy, October 25, 1943, *Cairo-Teheran Papers*, p. 41.
15 Prime Minister Churchill to President Roosevelt, October 27, 1943, *Ibid.*, pp. 47-48.
16 Ambassador Winant to President Roosevelt, November 4, 1943, *Ibid.*, pp. 64-65.

heard that U. J. [Uncle Joe] will come to Teheran. I received a telegram from him five days ago which made me think he would not come even to that place—this because his advisors did not wish him to leave Russian soil. I wired him at once that I had arranged the Constitutional matter here, and therefore that I could go to Teheran for a short meeting with him and told him I was very happy. Even then I was in doubt as to whether he would go through with his former offer to go to Teheran. His latest message has clinched the matter . . . !" [17]

Apparently Churchill wanted the British and American staffs to have "many meetings" before being joined by the Russians and the Chinese. But Roosevelt disagreed. He wrote the Prime Minister that "it would be a terrible mistake if U. J. thought we had ganged up on him on military action. During the preliminary meetings in Cairo the Combined Staffs will, as you know, be in the planning stage. That is all. It will not hurt you or me if Molotov and a Russian military representative are in Cairo too. They will not feel that they are being given the 'run around.' They will have no staff and no planners. Let us take them in on the high spots." [18]

Churchill still did not like the President's idea of having the Soviets sit in on military conversations before the big meeting at Teheran. ". . . the presence of a Soviet military observer so early in the conference," he said, "may cause grave embarrassment". [The British] ". . . cannot abandon their rights to full and frank discussions with you and your officers about the vital business of our intermingled armies. A Soviet observer cannot possibly be admitted to the intimate conversations which our own Chiefs of Staff must have and his exclusion may easily cause offense." [19]

The problem was finally resolved when Stalin informed Roosevelt and Churchill that Molotov could not attend the meeting at Cairo. Apparently Stalin was disturbed to learn from Churchill that Chiang Kai-shek would be in Cairo at the same time as Molotov and that Chinese military representatives were expected to be at the Cairo Conference. [20]

On November 20, the President's Personal Representative, General Hurley, sent an important memorandum to Roosevelt regarding several conferences he had with Generalissimo Chiang Kai-shek. He reported that the Generalissimo questioned whether he could meet with Stalin at Teheran "on terms of amity." Chiang related to Hurley his "suspicions" concerning Russia's desires to "communize China." Hurley recalled to Chiang Stalin's renunciation of world conquest as a funda-

17 President Roosevelt to Prime Minister Churchill, November 11, 1943, *Ibid.*, pp. 79-80.
18 *Ibid.*, p. 80.
19 Prime Minister Churchill to President Roosevelt, November 12, 1943, *Ibid.*, pp. 81-82.
20 Marshal Stalin to President Roosevelt, November 12, 1943, *Ibid.*, p. 82.

mental policy of Communism, and expressed the opinion that Stalin was "now committed to the proposition that Communism can succeed in Russia alone without an attempt being made to force it on the rest of the world. I said also that in my opinion Russia is no longer subsidizing or directing Communist activities in other nations." [21]

Chiang was not persuaded by these observations and appeared to entertain grave doubts of any friendly intentions of the Soviet Government toward China. General Hurley would soon become convinced as to the correctness of Chiang's original estimate.

One of the principle purposes of the conferences at Cairo and Teheran was that of co-ordinating and strengthening the war effort on the part of the Allies. During the months of arranging for these conferences it was understood that President Roosevelt would be accompanied by the U.S. Chiefs of Staff, and that his talks with Prime Minister Churchill, Generalissimo Chiang, and Marshal Stalin would center primarily on military problems.

In view of the military nature of all these proposed discussions President Roosevelt relied primarily on the Joint Chiefs of Staff to make necessary substantive preparations. Acting Secretary of State Stettinius was informed of the President's projected trip, and a few memoranda on political subjects were submitted to the President in response to his requests. But the Department of State was not asked to draft any policy recommendations or "position papers" of the type that were prepared and organized into comprehensive "briefing books" for the later conferences at Yalta and Potsdam. The Joint Chiefs of Staff prepared an agenda for the military discussions, but there was no agenda for any of the political discussions at Cairo and Teheran.[22]

In this connection it is worth noting that Secretary Hull was at the Moscow Conference of Foreign Ministers during the latter half of October. This conference was regarded as being preparatory for the forthcoming meeting of the Heads of Government. By delimiting major areas of agreement and disagreement, the Foreign Ministers at Moscow did, in effect, identify certain subjects which would need to be referred for further consideration by the Big Three. For this reason Roosevelt postponed his departure for North Africa until after Hull had returned to Washington and had personally briefed him on the highlights of the Moscow Conference.[23]

For many of the subjects touched upon at Cairo and Teheran there were no preparatory papers or special negotiations in anticipation of the meeting of the Heads of Government. The Cairo-Teheran Papers are filled with military estimates and plans for future campaigns against the

21 General Hurley to President Roosevelt, November 20, 1943, *Ibid.*, pp. 102-103.
22 See "Editorial Note," *Ibid.*, p. 108.
23 *Ibid.*, See also Hull, *Memoirs*, II, p. 1313.

Axis. Political agreements are lacking in description. Yet the political agreements were the ones which would so profoundly affect the postwar world situation.

On November 6, 1943, the Combined Chiefs of Staff had prepared a memorandum on basic military policy. It recommended helping Russia to bring about at the earliest possible date the unconditional surrender of the Axis Powers and application of "unremitting" pressure against Japan. Upon the defeat of the Axis in Europe, the memorandum recommended, the full resources of the United States and Great Britain, in co-operation with other Pacific Powers and, *if possible, with Russia,* should be utilized to bring about the earliest possible unconditional surrender of Japan.[24]

In another memorandum by the U.S. Chiefs of Staff, dated November 18, 1943, an estimate of Japan's strength for the year 1944 was specifically noted: ". . . real power in Japan," the report stated, "rests in the hands of small groups of leaders capable of manipulating the symbols of emperor-worship for their own self-interest. An early collapse of Germany would have a tremendously depressing effect upon such leaders. This, combined with ever increasing United Nations pressure and approach to the homeland, might conceivably bring about a re-shuffle of the ruling cliques followed by an attempt to secure a negotiated peace." [25] As will be seen later, this memorandum was most prophetic. But the Japanese pleas for a negotiated peace were to be ignored.

The Joint Chiefs stated that "the Japanese shipping situation has become acute, with her total tonnage being further reduced by sinkings in excess of total new construction." Japan's rate of building "cannot keep pace even with the present rate of sinkings . . . the . . . shipping position is becoming increasingly difficult and may well become precarious in 1944." [26] Her heavy industrial production as a whole "is not expected to show great gains in 1944. . . ." [27]

As for Soviet capabilities in the Far East, the following estimate was made: "Offensively, the U.S.S.R. could scarcely hope for any success until her forces in the west have been released by the defeat of Germany." A realistic estimate of Soviet intentions was made:

The U.S.S.R. is likely to intervene in the war against Japan at some stage, but not before the German menace to her has been removed. After that, she would be likely to intervene only when she reckoned that Japan could be defeated at small cost to her. It is unlikely that any arguments that we might

---

[24] Memorandum by the Combined Chiefs of Staff, November 6, 1943, *Cairo-Teheran Papers*, pp. 157-158. Emphasis added.

[25] Memorandum by the United States Chiefs of Staff, November 18, 1943, *Ibid.*, pp. 235-236.

[26] *Ibid.*, p. 237.

[27] *Ibid.*, p. 240.

bring forward, except substantial progress in our war against Japan, would greatly affect the timing of the Soviet intervention.[28]

Had the clear logic of this memorandum been followed during the next two years, the postwar situation would have been much improved.

The Combined Chiefs of Staff met on November 22, 1943, in the Mena House to discuss operations in the Far East. General Marshall read a memorandum prepared by General Stilwell giving the Generalissimo's views of future operations in the Chinese Theater. It was agreed that the Generalissimo and his principal advisers should be invited to be present at the Combined Chiefs meeting at 2:30 P.M. on November 23. General Marshall said that he felt the Combined Chiefs of Staff should consider the question of their relationship, both during the Conference and in the future, with the military representatives of the U.S.S.R. and China. There had already been an intimation from Generalissimo Chiang Kai-shek that he would welcome an invitation for a Chinese military representative to sit with the Combined Chiefs of Staff. It might facilitate the development of good faith and mutual understanding with the U.S.S.R. and China if each were invited to have a representative present with the Combined Chiefs of Staff. Marshall thought there might be certain advantages in having the Soviet representatives attend at least some conferences in order that they could appreciate the difficulties of a world-wide war on every front, in comparison with their own and China's highly localized operations.[29]

It was pointed out that it would be "impossible for the Chinese and the Soviet representatives to sit at the same table" since they were not engaging the same enemies. Nor should the Soviet representatives attend deliberations of the Combined Chiefs of Staff dealing with the war against Japan. Admiral Leahy suggested that they should be invited to be present only when the Combined Chiefs of Staff were discussing the problems of the particular fronts in which each was interested.[30]

Two days previously, after a six hour conference with Generalissimo Chiang Kai-shek, General Hurley reported to the President these conclusions: "The Generalissimo and the Chinese people are opposed to the principles of imperialism and communism. He believes that you, of course, favor democracy and liberty. He understands, however, that you may temporarily have to temporize with imperialism and communism in the interests of the joint war effort. He is aware that the future cooperation and unity of the United Nations must depend upon your ability to assimilate rather than eliminate divergent ideologies. He is convinced that you must find principles on which the Big Four nations

---

28 *Ibid.,* pp. 241-242.
29 Minutes of the Combined Chiefs of Staff, November 22, 1943, *Ibid.,* pp. 305-306.
30 *Ibid.,* p. 306.

can agree. In seeking these principles he feels that you must have extensive freedom of action." [31]

It was generally recognized that China's manpower and air bases must play an important role in the defeat of Japan. But it required the sustained personal attention of President Roosevelt to build up a sufficient air transport system to China to keep her in the war. China demanded a campaign in Burma to reopen the Burma Road. Naval, air and land action around the fringes of the Pacific had whittled away Japanese naval and air strength to the point where she was distinctly on the defensive. Through our submarine and air action we had reduced the Japanese merchant marine so much that an early abandonment of some of her outposts seemed probable.

The British did not consider China's war effort essential enough to warrant serious conferences. There was the notion that Roosevelt might make excessive promises to Chiang which might upset British plans in Europe. "The talks of the British and American Staffs were sadly distracted by the Chinese story," Churchill wrote, "which was lengthy, complicated and minor. Moreover . . . the President, who took an exaggerated view of the Indian-Chinese sphere, was soon closeted in long conferences with the Generalissimo. All hope of persuading Chiang and his wife to go and see the Pyramids and enjoy themselves till we returned from Teheran fell to the ground, with the result that Chinese business occupied first instead of last place at Cairo." [32]

Regarding China's part in the over-all Allied strategy, the President was particularly concerned whether Chiang Kai-shek could continue active resistance to Japan. As early as June 30, he had informed Chiang "it is very important that we get together." [33] In reply the Generalissimo said that he would be very happy to meet with the President before the latter's conference with Stalin. Stalin was curious to know the real purpose of Roosevelt's forthcoming meeting with Generalissimo Chiang Kai-shek. Molotov was particularly "anxious to find out what military subjects would be discussed." [34] But Stalin did not attend the Cairo Conference.

The first plenary meeting at Cairo was held at Roosevelt's villa on November 23, at 11:00 A.M. The President, extending a warm welcome to the Generalissimo and Madame Chiang Kai-shek, and to the Chinese Delegation, said that this was an historic meeting. He hoped it would bear fruit not only today and in the immediate future, but for decades to come. There was, he felt sure, unanimous agreement that every effort should be made to send more equipment to China, with a view to accelerating the

---

31 General Hurley to President Roosevelt, November 20, 1943, *Ibid.*, p. 264.

32 Churchill, *Closing the Ring*, p. 328.

33 President Roosevelt to Generalissimo Chiang Kai-shek, June 30, 1943, *Cairo-Teheran Papers*, p. 13.

34 Ambassador Harriman to President Roosevelt, November 9, 1943, *Ibid.*, p. 76.

process by which we could launch an air offensive against the heart of Japan itself.

Roosevelt and Chiang Kai-shek agreed upon a plan for a ground offensive in north Burma by Chinese, British and American troops. The plan was to drive the Japanese out of Burma and open the Burma Road. The plan (code name operation BUCCANEER) was to be a co-ordinated amphibious operation south of Burma supported by the British navy in the Indian Ocean. This operation was very important to Chiang Kai-shek. At the first Plenary meeting he said that the success of the operations in Burma depended, in his opinion, "not only on the strength of the naval forces established in the Indian Ocean, but on the simultaneous co-ordination of naval action with the land operations." [35]

But Churchill observed that any naval operations south of Burma would not necessarily be co-ordinated with and linked to the land campaign. Britain's naval superiority in this area, he said, should ensure the security of her communications and present a threat to those of the enemy. He disagreed with Chiang Kai-shek that the operation was essential to winning the land campaign in Burma.

The Generalissimo observed that the enemy would reinforce Burma troops and supplies through South Burma ports and that this could be stopped only by vigorous naval support.[36] Churchill's disagreement on this issue is recorded in his memoirs: "The President, in spite of my arguments, gave the Chinese the promise of a considerable amphibious operation across the Bay of Bengal within the next few months. . . . On November 29, I wrote to the [British] Chiefs of Staff: 'The Prime Minister wishes to put on record the fact that he specifically refused the Generalissimo's request that we should undertake an amphibious operation simultaneously with the land operations in Burma.'" [37]

Churchill reasoned that a Burma operation at the time would not be feasible. It would mean a drain on naval forces and land troops needed for more vital theaters of war. The President, however, continued his support of Chiang for his Burma campaign. These differences remained unchanged until after Roosevelt and Churchill returned to Cairo from their talks with Stalin. At Teheran the decision to carry out the Burma campaign was postponed for reasons that supplies were essential for landings in Europe. Moreover, at Teheran, Stalin reiterated his promise to enter the war against Japan. This apparently convinced Churchill that there was no need to speed-up a land route through Burma into China.

The President eventually came around to the Prime Minister's views. He felt that unless Britain would supply the necessary naval support

---

[35] Plenary Meeting, November 23, 1943, *Ibid.*, p. 314.
[36] *Ibid.*
[37] Churchill, *Closing the Ring*, p. 328.

needed for the operation, the whole effort would not be practicable. As a result he informed Churchill that "BUCCANEER is off." [38]

At a dinner meeting with Chiang on November 23, held at the President's villa, Roosevelt expressed the view that China should take her place with the Big Four and participate on an equal footing with them in all the decisions. Generalissimo Chiang, of course, responded favorably to these remarks.[39]

Roosevelt then asked Chiang his views as to whether the institution of the Emperor of Japan should be abolished after the war. The Generalissimo said that this would involve the question of the form of government of Japan and should be left for the Japanese people themselves to decide after the war, so as not to precipitate any error which might perpetuate itself in international relations.

The President was of the opinion that China should play the leading role in the post-war military occupation of Japan. Chiang, however, did not believe that China was ready to shoulder this considerable responsibility. He thought the task should be carried out under the leadership of the United States and that China could participate only if it was deemed necessary. The Generalissimo took the position that the final decision on the matter could await further development of the actual situation.

Chiang proposed that a part of the reparation Japan was to pay China after the war could be paid in the form of actual properties. Much of Japan's industrial machinery and equipment, war and merchant ships, rolling stock, etc., could be transferred to China. Roosevelt expressed his concurrence in the proposal.

Both leaders agreed that the Northeastern provinces of China, Taiwan and the Pescadores—all of which Japan had taken from China—must be restored to China after the war. It was understood that the Liaotung Peninsula and its two ports, Port Arthur and Dairen, must be included. The President then referred to the question of the Ryuku Islands and inquired more than once whether China would want the Ryukyus. The Generalissimo replied that China would be agreeable to joint occupation of the Ryukyus by China and the United States and, eventually, joint administration by the two countries under the trusteeship of an international organization. President Roosevelt raised also the question of Hong Kong. The Generalissimo suggested that the President discuss the matter with the British authorities before further deliberation.

Roosevelt proposed a postwar alliance between China and the United States. The two countries would come to each other's assistance in the event of foreign aggression. The United States should maintain adequate

---

[38] *Cairo-Teheran Papers*, p. 725.

[39] This account of the Roosevelt-Chiang Dinner Meeting is based entirely on a summary record made available by the Chinese Government at the request of the Department of State, *Cairo-Teheran Papers*, pp. 323-325.

military forces on various bases in the Pacific in order that it could effectively share the responsibility of preventing aggression. Chiang agreed to both proposals. He expressed his hope that the United States would be in a position to extend necessary aid to China for equipping its land, naval and air forces for the purpose of strengthening her national defense and enabling her to carry out her international obligations. Chiang proposed, also, that China would be prepared to place Lushun (Port Arthur) at the joint disposal of China and the United States. Roosevelt, on his part, proposed that China and the United States should consult with each other before any decision was to be reached on matters concerning Asia. The Generalissimo indicated agreement.

Generalissimo Chiang pointed out that China's post-war economic reconstruction would be a tremendously difficult task which would require United States financial aid in the form of loans, etc., and also various types of technical assistance. Roosevelt indicated that close and practical consideration would be given to the matter.

President Roosevelt inquired especially as to the present status of Tannu Tuva and its historical relations with its neighbors. Generalissimo Chiang pointed out that the area had been an integral part of China's Outer Mongolia until it was forcibly taken and annexed by Russia. He said that the question of Tannu Tuva, together with that of Outer Mongolia, must be settled in time to come through negotiations with Soviet Russia. At Cairo, Roosevelt, Chiang Kai-shek and Churchill expressed their political agreements in a statement known as the Cairo Declaration. A paragraph of great importance read:

The three great Allies are fighting this war to restrain and punish the aggression of Japan. They covet no gain for themselves and have no thought of territorial expansion. It is their purpose that Japan shall be stripped of all the islands in the Pacific which she has seized or occupied since the beginning of the first World War in 1914, and that all the territories Japan has stolen from the Chinese, such as Manchuria, Formosa, and the Pescadores, shall be restored to the Republic of China. Japan will also be expelled from all other territories which she has taken by violence and greed.[40]

The significance of this declaration comes to light at Yalta where Roosevelt, without consulting Chiang Kai-shek, ceded territory to Soviet Russia which gave her a dominant position in China.

At a meeting of the Joint Chiefs of Staff, on November 24, 1943, Ambassador Harriman reported that he thought that "the Soviets had every intention of joining the U.S. and the British in the war against Japan as soon as Germany had capitulated. They fear, however, a premature break with Japan and placed great value on the substantial amount of supplies which they are now receiving through Vladivostok. . . . He hoped that the

---

[40] *A Decade of American Foreign Policy: Basic Documents*, p. 22.

question of Russian participation in the Japanese war would be raised either by the President or by the Chiefs of Staff and indicated that it would be well to point out and to emphasize any advantages which the Soviets would receive from such participation. One difficulty which he foresaw was the Soviet fear that information of the discussions might reach the Japanese and thus provoke a break with them before the Soviets are ready." [41]

In preparation for the Teheran Conference Marshal Stalin sent word through Ambassador Harriman that he was concerned about the distance that separated the American Legation from the Russian Embassy compound. It was well known that the city of Teheran was filled with Axis sympathizers and he found that an unhappy incident might occur to one of the Heads of State driving through the city to visit each other. In his letter of May 25, 1954, to the Historical Division of the Department of State, Harriman discussed the question of Roosevelt's moving with Hopkins, Hurley, and others on the morning of November 28, 1943. "All but one favored the move. When we told the President he was pleased. Churchill, when consulted, was much relieved. He and his colleagues explained that they would have been glad to have the President stay in the British Embassy, but if he went there he would only have a bedroom and sitting room and could not have the privacy with visitors which he would wish." [42] Ambassador Harriman pointed out that if we persisted in our refusal to accept quarters in the Russian compound, we would be responsible for any injury that Marshal Stalin might suffer in driving through the town to consult with President Roosevelt. Harriman emphasized that the city of Teheran had been under complete German control only a few months before and that the risk of assassination of Churchill or Stalin while coming to visit President Roosevelt was very real. He said that the Russians offered a part of their Embassy that would be under a separate roof and that the President's party would have complete independence. It would bring the three Heads of State so close together that there would be no need for any of them to drive about town. The President accepted the Russian invitation and announced that he would make the move to the Russian Embassy, taking with him his own servants.

The President, Admiral Leahy, Mr. Hopkins and Major Boettiger left the American Legation by auto for the Russian Embassy to live there as guests of the Russian Government. While the President and his party occupied the main building of the Embassy, Marshal Stalin and his party lived on one of the smaller houses within the Russian Embassy Compound. The British Legation was just one block distant.

41 Meeting of the Joint Chiefs of Staff, November 24, 1943, *Cairo-Teheran Papers*, p. 328.

42 *Ibid.*, p. 463, fn. 11.

After seeing the President comfortably quartered at the Russian Embassy, Admirals Brown and McIntire and General Watson returned to the American Legation so as to continue the impression of occupancy of those quarters by the President and his party.[43]

Immediately following the President's arrival at the Russian Embassy, Marshal Stalin, accompanied by Mr. Pavlov (his interpreter), called on Roosevelt. They had a long private talk—without Mr. Churchill present. The President greeted Marshal Stalin when he entered with "I am glad to see you. I have tried for a long time to bring this about." [44]

Marshal Stalin, after suitable expression of pleasure at meeting the President, said that he was to blame for the delay in this meeting; that he had been very occupied because of military matters.[45]

Following these pleasantries, the President broached the possibility that after the war a part of the American-British merchant fleet could be made available to the Soviet Union. Marshal Stalin replied that an adequate merchant fleet would be of great value, not only to the Soviet Union, but for the development of relations between the Soviet Union and the United States after the war. He hoped that such relations would be greatly expanded. He said, in reply to the President's question, that if equipment were sent to the Soviet Union from the United States, a plentiful supply of raw materials from that country could be made available to the United States.

The Conference then turned to the Far East. The President said that he had had an interesting conversation with Chiang Kai-shek in Cairo, on the general subject of China. Stalin remarked that the Chinese had fought very badly because of poor leadership.

The President said that we were now supplying and training 30 Chinese divisions for operations in Southern China and were proposing to continue the same process for 30 additional divisions. He added that there was a new prospect of an offensive operation through North Burma to link up with China in Southern Yunnan (sic) and that these operations would be under command of Lord Louis Mountbatten.

After Stalin departed, Molotov called on the President. No record has been found of the remarks exchanged by Roosevelt and Molotov during this visit. That the visit was short, and may have been limited to an exchange of courtesies, is suggested by the fact that Roosevelt's conversation with Stalin, which preceded it, is stated in the Bohlen minutes to have ended at 4 o'clock and the Big Three meeting which followed it is stated to have begun at that same time.[46]

---

[43] The President's Log at Teheran, November 27-December 2, 1943, *Ibid.*, pp. 463-464.

[44] This account of the Roosevelt-Stalin Meeting is based on the Bohlen Minutes, *Ibid.*, pp. 483-484.

[45] *Ibid.*, p. 483.

[46] Editorial Note, *Ibid.*, p. 486.

The President, Prime Minister Churchill and Marshal Stalin, with their respective military staffs and other delegates, met at the Russian Embassy on November 28 at 4:00 P.M. This was the first joint meeting of these gentlemen.[47]

The President said, as the youngest of the three present, he ventured to welcome his elders. He said he wished to welcome the new members to the family circle and tell them that meetings of this character were conducted as between friends with complete frankness on all sides and with nothing that was said to be made public. He added that he was confident that this meeting would be successful and that our three great nations would not only work in close co-operation for the prosecution of the war but would also remain in close touch to preserve the peace.

Marshal Stalin welcomed the delegations of Great Britain and the United States. He said that history had given to us here a great opportunity and it was up to the representatives here to use wisely the power which their respective peoples had given to them and to take full advantage of this fraternal meeting.

The President then gave a general survey of the war and the necessary equipment needed to win it. Before turning to the war in the Pacific, the President said he desired to emphasize that the United States shared equally with the Soviet Union and Great Britain the desire to hasten in every way possible the day of victory. He then said that the United States was more directly affected by the war in the Pacific and that the American forces were bearing the chief burden in that theater with, of course, help from the Australian and British forces. The greater part of the U.S. naval establishment was in the Pacific and over a million men were being maintained there. He pointed out as evidence of the immense distances in the Pacific that one supply ship operating from the United States could make only three round trips a year. The allied strategy in the Pacific was based on the doctrine of attrition. It was proving successful. We were sinking more Japanese tonnage than the Japanese were able to replace. He said that the allies were moving forward against the Japanese.

Although the operations extended over vast expanses of the Pacific, the number of ships and men allocated for the purpose were being held down to a minimum. He summed up the aims of these operations as follows: (1) to open the road to China and supply that country in order to keep it in the war, and (2) by opening the road to China and through increased use of transport planes, to put ourselves in position to bomb Japan proper.

Marshal Stalin stated that in regard to the Pacific war the Soviet Government welcomed the successes of the Anglo-American forces against the Japanese. But up to the present and to their regret, they had not been

---

[47] First Plenary Meeting, November 28, 1943, based on Bohlen Minutes, *Ibid.*, pp. 487-488.

able to join the effort of the Soviet Union to that of the United States and England against the Japanese. The Soviet armies were too deeply engaged in the west. He added that the Soviet forces in Siberia were sufficient for defensive purposes but would have to be trebled before they could take the offensive. But, he continued, once Germany was finally defeated, the Soviet Union could transfer the necessary reinforcements to Siberia and then we should be able by our common front to defeat Japan.

Roosevelt, Churchill, and their military staffs were apparently satisfied with Stalin's estimate of the situation. Soviet entry into the war against Japan, promised at this early date, must have been welcome news for President Roosevelt. It is significant, however, that Stalin was not asking his price for coming in. His claims were later negotiated at Yalta. He was fully occupied with the military defeat of Germany and may have felt that his claims would get closer attention after victory in Europe. Stalin was primarily concerned at Teheran with getting increased military support and supplies for the European operation. He was quite willing to give President Roosevelt assurances of future Soviet help against Japan.

Another Roosevelt-Stalin meeting was held on November 29 at 2:45 P.M. in the President's quarters at the Soviet Embassy. Roosevelt reminded Stalin that, during the Moscow Conference, the American officials had requested the use of air bases in the Soviet Union for the primary purpose of the shuttle-bombing between Great Britain and Russia. He gave Stalin a memorandum on the subject and expressed his personal hope that the Marshal would give the project his immediate support. He said this was very important and he wished to hear personally the Soviet leader's consent in regard to the defeat of Japanese forces and victory over Germany.

Roosevelt observed that we must be prepared for their eventual defeat and do some advance planning. He gave the Marshal two papers showing the interest our military organizations have in a joint operation with the Soviets in the Far East. The papers proposed: (1) the desirability of establishing American air bases in the Maritime Provinces of the Soviet Union; (2) that planning begin at once for the air operations against Japan; (3) preliminary planning for naval operations against Japan. In handling these papers to Marshal Stalin, the President emphasized that the entire matter would be held in the strictest security and any contacts between Soviet and American officers on the subject would be strictly secret. Stalin promised to study these proposals later with Harriman. But his answers were evasive. Either he feared the Japanese might learn about them despite the secrecy promised by the President, or the Soviet government did not want American air and naval personnel operating from Soviet territory.[48]

---

48 Roosevelt-Stalin Meeting, November 29, 1943, based on Bohlen Minutes, *Ibid.*, p. 529; see also pp. 618-619.

On November 30, Roosevelt, Churchill and Stalin had a luncheon meeting at the President's quarters in the Russian Embassy. Stalin wanted to know what could be done for Russia in the Far East. Churchill asked what he had in mind. Stalin remarked that of course the Russians had their desires, but that it would perhaps be better to await the time when the Russians would be taking an active part in the Far East war. He added, however, the Soviet Union had only one port in the Far East that was not closed off, that Vladivostok was only partly ice-free, besides being encircled by a Japanese controlled Straits.

Roosevelt thought Soviet needs in this area could be met by establishing a free port and mentioned Dairen as a possibility. Stalin thought the Chinese would not like such a scheme. To which the President replied that they might like the idea of a free port under an international guarantee. Stalin said that sounded like a good idea.[49] This arrangement was actually confirmed at Yalta and written into the Soviet-Chinese treaty of August, 1945.

On his return from his meeting with Marshal Stalin at Teheran, President Roosevelt held a second Cairo Conference with Winston Churchill. The President and the Prime Minister wished to compare their reactions to Stalin and review the military and political discussions they had held with the Soviet Union.

On December 4, 1943, the Combined Chiefs of Staff met with Roosevelt and Churchill. The President said that he must leave Cairo on Monday morning. It was therefore necessary that all reports of the Conference should be signed by Sunday night.

The Prime Minister said that he did not wish to leave any doubt that the British viewed the early termination of the Cairo Conference with great apprehension. There were still many important questions to be settled. Two decisive events had taken place in the last few days. In the first place, Marshal Stalin had voluntarily proclaimed that the Soviet would make war on Japan the moment Germany was defeated. This would give us better bases than we could ever find in China. The Prime Minister said that Chiang Kai-shek had left Cairo under the impression that we were going to do BUCCANEER [the amphibious operations against the Andaman Island south of Burma]. The new facts now were: the Soviet Union had declared themselves ready to go to war with Japan immediately after Germany's collapse; it had been decided to do OVERLORD [cross-channel] in May; and ANVIL [southern France] was also to be undertaken. He added that he was very anxious lest the Russian promise should leak out.

The President agreed and added that it would be unwise to tell the Chinese. Continuing, he said that 18 to 20 additional landing craft must

49 Roosevelt-Churchill-Stalin Luncheon Meeting, November 30, 1943, based on Bohlen Minutes, *Ibid.*, pp. 565-568.

be provided by hook or by crook. As for the BUCCANEER assault, he thought that 14,000 instead of 58,000 men would be ample. The Supreme Commander in the Far East must be told that he must do his best with the resources which had already been allocated to him. It should be possible for the staffs to settle their problems in principle, leaving the details to be worked out afterwards.[50] The Burma campaign promised to Chiang Kai-shek at the first Cairo Conference was to be postponed. This change of policy marked the beginning of our diminishing support of Nationalist China.

Roosevelt met with the Joint Chiefs of Staff on December 4 to inform them of his decision to concentrate on OVERLORD and ANVIL and to stop further argumentation in favor of Operation BUCCANEER as scheduled for the spring of 1944. According to Leahy and King, President Roosevelt expressed to the Joint Chiefs of Staff his reluctance in making this decision and indicated his intent to offer a substitute to Chiang Kai-shek. The alternative offer to Chiang was drafted by Roosevelt and Hopkins, presumably at the conclusion of Roosevelt's meeting with the Joint Chiefs of Staff. It was submitted to Churchill in the form of a memorandum.

In explaining his decision to General Stilwell and John P. Davies on the following day, Roosevelt is reported by Stilwell to have said: "I've been stubborn as a mule for four days but we can't get anywhere, and it won't do for a conference to end that way. The British just won't do the operation, and I can't get them to agree to it." The Davies notes on this conversation indicate that Roosevelt also emphasized in this connection that he had fought at Teheran, with Stalin's support, and that Churchill had finally given in. This was presumably a reference to the argument about fixing the date of OVERLORD.[51]

On December 2, an over-all plan for the defeat of Japan was reported by the Combined Staff Planners. It reported the following significant points: (1) It was possible that invasion of the principal Japanese islands might not be necessary and the defeat of Japan might be accomplished by sea and air blockade, with intensive air bombardment from progressively advanced bases. The plan must, however, be capable of expansion to meet the contingency of invasion. (2) The U.S.S.R. might enter the war against Japan early after the defeat of Germany. The plan proposed that all possible preparations should be made to take advantage of such development. Further progress was dependent upon staff conversations with the Soviets.

The report recommended preparations that should be made for possible Russian entry into the war and suggested the following:

---

50 Meeting of the Combined Chiefs of Staff with Roosevelt and Churchill, December 4, 1943, *Ibid.*, pp. 675-681.

51 Editorial Note, *Ibid.*, pp. 725-726.

It is most desirable to examine as early as practicable with the Soviets the problems involved in establishing and maintaining a U.S.-British air force in the Maritime Provinces of the U.S.S.R., leading to conclusions as to the size of force that may be achieved and the effort required to maintain it by sea, land and air routes. This will depend upon staff conversations with the Soviets.[52]

Shortly after Roosevelt returned to Washington, he spoke at a meeting of the Pacific War Council, held in the Cabinet Room of the Executive Offices at the White House. Added insight into the Cairo and Teheran Conference was revealed. The President informed the Council that his discussions with Generalissimo Chiang Kai-shek and with Marshal Stalin were highly satisfactory—in that both had agreed that Japan should be stripped of her island possessions. Marshal Stalin has specifically agreed to the idea that Manchuria, Formosa and the Pescadores should be returned to China. The Soviet Union, having no ice-free port in Siberia, was desirous of getting one, and Marshal Stalin looked with favor upon making Dairen a free port for all the world. Russian exports and imports could be sent through the port of Dairen and carried to Siberian territory over the Manchurian Railroad in bond. He had agreed that the Manchurian Railway should become the property of the Chinese Government. He wished all of Sakhalin to be returned to Russia and he wanted the Kurile Islands turned over to Russia in order that she might exercise control of the straits leading to Siberia.

President Roosevelt stated that it was extremely gratifying to him to find that the Generalissimo and Marshal Stalin saw "eye to eye" with him on all major problems of the Pacific and that he felt that there would be no difficulty in reaching agreements about the control of the Pacific once Japan had been completely conquered.[53]

Roosevelt and his advisers left Teheran with a feeling that they had gained an appreciable insight into the attitudes and intentions of the Soviet Union towards Nationalist China. Stalin had given every indication he would respect the sovereignty of China and give his support to Chiang Kai-shek.

At the first Cairo Conference the President had assured Chiang Kai-shek that U.S. and Britain would provide him with massive help—both land and sea—in clearing Burma of Japanese. Roosevelt's promise to the Generalisimo, however, had been broken at the Teheran meeting.

When Roosevelt and Churchill got together again at Cairo, after the Teheran meeting, Churchill argued strongly against the Burma venture. He is quoted in the record as arguing: "In the face of Marshal Stalin's

---

[52] Report by the Combined Staff Planner, December 2, 1943, *Ibid.*, p. 765, and p. 772.
[53] Minutes of a Meeting of the Pacific War Council, January 12, 1944, *Ibid.*, pp. 868-870.

promise that Russia would come into the war, operations in the Southeast
Asia Command had lost a good deal of their value." [54]

It was at Teheran that Stalin promised to attack Japan *after* the surrender of Germany. The United States and Britain made the fatal decision to scrap the Cairo agreement to equip Nationalist China and pledged
to build up Soviet Russia forces in Asia instead. These decisions made
Russia—and later Communist China—dominant in Asia.

The second meeting between Roosevelt and Stalin was held at Yalta
in February, 1945, when the defeat of Germany was imminent and after
the successful invasion of the Philippines. The participants and purposes
were the same, but the negotiating position of Soviet Russia was greatly
strengthened.[55]

Some added light was later thrown on the Far Eastern implications of
the Cairo-Teheran Conferences.

At a weekly press conference of September 23, 1948, Dr. Hollington K.
Tong, Director of Chinese Government Information Office, replied as
follows to questions:

QUESTION: Have you any comment to make on Harry L. Hopkin's article in
August 28 *Colliers,* which has been commented on editorially by *Shanghai Eve-
ning Post and Mercury,* stating that President Roosevelt discussed disposal of
Dairen with Generalissimo at Cairo, long before Yalta agreement?

ANSWER: "Now it happens that I was present at Cairo on occasion of meeting
which Mr. Hopkins cites.

Accord to my recollection President Roosevelt, in one of his conversations
with President Chiang at Cairo, inquired about possibility of conversion of
Dairen into free port at end of war. The reply of President Chiang was that
he might give consideration to such a proposal when time came, provided there
was no [infringement?] of the sovereignty of China.

The nature of the commitment later made by President Roosevelt at Yalta
differed from what President Roosevelt himself had suggested to President
Chiang at Cairo. The Yalta commitment was not known to the Government of
China at the time it was made.

Dr. Tong was later asked if he was personally present during the conversation referred to between President Roosevelt and the Generalissimo.
He evaded the question by replying that Madame Chiang had acted as
interpreter for the Generalissimo.[56]

On September 3, 1945, T. V. Soong had inquired whether the U.S. prepared to complete its commitment to equip 100 Chinese divisions. This

54 Meeting of the Combined Chiefs of Staff with Roosevelt and Churchill, December
4, 1943, *Ibid.,* p. 676.

55 Edna R. Fluegel, "Afro-Asian Presence at the Summit," *Trinity Alumnae Journal,*
June, 1959.

56 Ambassador Stuart to Secretary Marshall, September 24, 1948; *Cairo-Teheran
Papers,* p. 881.

commitment is said to have been made to Chiang by President Roosevelt at Cairo and apparently was not in writing. Mr. Hopkins affirms that some such commitment was made at Cairo when action in the Chinese theater was agreed upon. After the Teheran Conference, Chiang, who was disturbed by the postponement of action planned for the Chinese theater, was apparently assured that the commitment would be kept.[57]

The Cairo-Teheran Conferences are very significant in their bearing upon our wartime attitudes and policies towards Nationalist China and the Soviet Union. Decisions were made that had far-reaching effects upon the preservation of China's "territorial and administrative" integrity.

But of perhaps greater import than the decisions reached were the attitudes displayed. Here we can see the postwar world dimly taking shape, not so much by design as through the vanity of men in their political dealings.

President Roosevelt was overly eager to please Marshal Stalin. The President wanted a strong assurance of Soviet participation in the war with Japan. And he wanted Stalin's co-operation in a postwar organization of the world. To secure these ends, the President was willing to go very far to win the Marshal's approval and good will.

At the Teheran Conference, Roosevelt sided more often with Stalin than with Churchill—going so far, even, as to join Stalin in subjecting the Prime Minister to some ridicule and embarrassment. It is to Churchill's credit as a diplomat that the British-American alliance did not suffer as a result.

On November 29, 1943, Stalin was host to the President and the Prime Minister and their top aides at a dinner. From the Bohlen minutes we have the following interesting account: "The most notable feature of the dinner was the attitude of Marshal Stalin toward the Prime Minister. Marshal Stalin lost no opportunity to get in a dig at Mr. Churchill. Almost every remark that he addressed to the Prime Minister contained some sharp edge. . . . In the discussion in regard to future treatment of Germans, Marshal Stalin strongly implied on several occasions that Mr. Churchill nursed a secret affection for Germany and desired to see a soft peace. . . . In regard to the future treatment of Germany, Marshal Stalin . . . said . . . at least 50,000 and perhaps 100,000 of the German Commanding Staff must be physically liquidated. . . ."

"The President jokingly said that he would put the figure of the German Commanding Staff which should be executed at 49,000 or more. The Prime Minister took strong exception to what he termed the cold-blooded execution of soldiers who had fought for their country." [58]

[57] Secretary Byrnes, to President Truman, September 3, 1945, *Ibid.*, p. 889.

[58] Tripartite Dinner Meeting, November 29, 1943, based on Bohlen Minutes, *Ibid.*, pp. 553-555.

Elliott Roosevelt has reported the reaction to his father's proposal: "Americans and Russians laughed. The British, taking their cue from their Prime Minister's mounting fury, sat quiet and straight-faced." [59]

But, at Teheran, President Roosevelt did far more than contribute to Churchill's discomfiture. The Prime Minister had to go along with post-war political arrangements contrived by Roosevelt and Stalin. Perhaps the most significant of these political concessions made at Teheran dealt with the whole of Eastern Europe. It was at the Teheran Conference that Stalin received what he considered to be acceptance by the West of his plan to grab the Baltic states and part of Poland for Russia after the war, and to give Poland a slice of Germany. It was also at this conference that Stalin won what amounted to a free hand in the Balkans and Eastern Europe. (Churchill, of course, had been repeatedly rebuffed in his attempts to win support for a Balkan Campaign through the "soft underbelly of Europe".) The western allies also committed themselves to a D-Day invasion in the spring of 1944. The U.S. and Britain then remained out of the Balkans, and, in fact, agreed to increase their aid to the Communist Partisans in Yugoslavia led by Joseph Broz Tito. Thus the postwar era found the Communists in control of the entire strategic area. President Roosevelt had made it abundantly clear to Marshal Stalin at Teheran that U.S. troops would not be on hand to interfere with any postwar ambitions that Russia might have in Eastern Europe.

The record shows that President Roosevelt discussed the Polish question during his second private conversation with Marshal Stalin at Teheran on December 1, but there is no record that President Roosevelt ever expressed an intention to "make" Stalin live up to the Atlantic Charter in his treatment of Poland and the Baltic states. Instead, the President agreed in principle to let Soviet ideas prevail in regard to the future of Poland. According to minutes kept by translator Charles E. Bohlen, Roosevelt told Stalin that personally he agreed with his views, but he had some "political considerations for not going into details." The President added that "there were in the United States from six to seven million Americans of Polish extraction, and *as a practical man, he did not wish to lose their vote. . . .* He would like to see the Eastern border [of Poland] moved further to the west and the Western border moved even to the River Oder. He hoped, however, that Marshal [Stalin] would understand that *for political reasons outlined above,* he could not participate in any decision here in Teheran . . . and that he could not *publicly* take part in any such arrangement at the present time." [60]

Approval of Soviet expansion across Eastern Europe was momentous in itself. But it was merely symptomatic of the world outlook that was

---

[59] Elliott Roosevelt, *As He Saw It,* p. 189.

[60] Roosevelt-Stalin Meeting, December 1, 1943, based on Bohlen Minutes, *Cairo-Teheran Papers,* pp. 594-596. Emphasis is added.

to affect America for years to come. Coming events cast long shadows at Teheran.

President Roosevelt's determination to destroy colonialism in general, and to cause dismemberment of the British Empire in particular, was evidenced. There is more than just a hint of a vision of a "One World" of Soviet-type nations.

This vision of the world of the future became most clearly revealed in the private conversations between President Roosevelt and Marshal Stalin. Here it is that we find the prophetic "meeting of minds" that the Teheran Conference produced. The President said he "would like to talk with Marshal Stalin on the question of India; that he felt that the best solution would be reform from the bottom, *somewhat on the Soviet line,*" translator Bohlen reported in his official minutes.

Stalin replied that the "India question was a complicated one, with different levels of culture and the absence of relationship in the caste." He added that *"reform from the bottom would mean revolution."* The President said "he felt it would be better not to discuss the question of India with Mr. Churchill" and Marshal Stalin "agreed that this was a sore spot with the British." [61]

Roosevelt also volunteered secretly to Stalin that the French should give up Indochina. Bohlen officially reported that Roosevelt was in "100 per cent in agreement with Marshal Stalin" that *France should not get back Indochina* (then occupied militarily by Japan)." The President's reason was his further secret agreement with Stalin that the *"French must pay for their criminal collaboration with Germany."* As an added opinion he agreed "that after 100 years of French rule in Indochina, the inhabitants were worse off than they had been before." [62]

The Teheran Conference was marked by considerable elation on the part of the participants. A tripartite dinner meeting was held in the British legation at 8:30 P.M., November 30. Thirty-three members of the American, British and Soviet representatives at Teheran gathered with Mr. Churchill for dinner on the occasion of his 69th birthday. There was a strong feeling of optimism that appeared to be based on the view that if the three nations went forward together in war, there was real hope for a better world in the future. President Roosevelt sat on the Prime Minister's right, and Marshal Stalin on his left. All speeches took the form of toasts—a custom established at a Russian dinner the day before.

Even Prime Minister Churchill got into the act of making remarks calculated to please Stalin. In one toast he observed that he had heard the suggestions concerning changing political complexions in the world. He said that he could not speak with authority concerning the political

---

[61] *Ibid.,* p. 486. Emphasis is added.
[62] *Ibid.,* p. 485. Emphasis is added.

view which might be expressed by the American people in the coming year's elections, and that he would not presume to discuss the changing political philosophy of the Russian nation. But he continued, so far as the British people were concerned, he could say very definitely that their "complexions are becoming a trifle pinker." Stalin spoke up instantly: "That is a sign of good health!"

In what he declared would be the concluding toast of the evening, Churchill referred to the great progress which had been made at Teheran toward solution of world problems, and he proposed a joint toast to the President and Marshal Stalin.

But before the dinner could break up, Stalin requested of his host the privilege of delivering one more toast. Churchill nodded assent and Stalin then said he wished to speak of the importance of "the 'machine" in the present war, and to express his great admiration for the productive capacity of the United States. He had been advised, he said, that the United States would very soon be producing 10,000 planes every month. This compared, he said, with 2,500 to 3,000 planes which the Soviet Union was able to produce.

Without these planes from America the war would have been lost, said Stalin with emphasis. He expressed his gratitude and that of the Russian people for the great leadership of President Roosevelt which had developed the great production of war machines and made possible their delivery to Russia. He wound up with a warm toast to the President.

The great pragmatist, Stalin, wanted "guns now." The world could wait.

Then Roosevelt sought the privilege of adding a last word. He said these meetings at Teheran had raised all hopes for a better world in the future. "There has been discussion here tonight of our varying colors of political complexion," he said. "I like to think of this in terms of the rainbow. In our country the rainbow is a symbol of good fortune and of hope. It has many varying colors, each individualistic, but blending into one glorious whole. Thus with our nations. We have differing customs and philosophies and ways of life. Each of us works our scheme of things according to the desires and ideas of our own peoples. But we have proved here at Teheran that the varying ideals of our nations can come together in a harmonious whole, moving unitedly for the common good of ourselves and of the world. So as we leave this historic gathering, we can see in the sky, for the first time, that traditional symbol of hope, the rainbow." [63]

The President reported briefly to Secretary Hull the results of the Teheran Conference: "My conferences with the Generalissimo" [Stalin] he said, "were very satisfactory and I liked him. He is delighted with the

---

[63] *Ibid.,* pp. 582-585.

results of the Moscow Conference. In Teheran things went on the whole very well and better than I expected. Marshal Stalin and I worked together toward objectives which turned out to be very similar. I will bring you the minutes of all that was said and done. Molotov sent you his very warm personal regards." [64]

To Marshal Stalin the President reported that he considered the conference was "a great success" and that it indicated the Big Three could work in the "utmost harmony for peace to come." The President said he enjoyed his personal talks and particularly the opportunity to meet the Russian leader face to face. "I view those momentous days of our meetings," he remarked, "with the greatest satisfaction as being an important milestone in the progress of human affairs." [65]

The geographical concessions President Roosevelt made at Teheran and the attitudes he expressed in his private talks with Marshal Stalin reveal that his "one world rainbow" featured exclusively one end of the spectrum, the red. "Hindsight" gives us, today, a good view of the resulting "progress of human affairs."

---

[64] President Roosevelt to Secretary Hull, December 3, 1943, *Ibid.*, p. 784.
[65] President Roosevelt to Marshal Stalin, December 3, 1943, *Ibid.*, p. 785.

CHAPTER IV

YALTA: PROLOGUE TO TRAGEDY

Excepting only the meeting at Teheran, the one at Yalta, in the Crimea, was the most important international parley since the peace conference at Paris in 1919. And judging by its results one may say that history has repeated itself. President Roosevelt was out-traded and out-maneuvered by Stalin, just as the pragmatic-minded statesmen of Europe dealt with President Wilson. Roosevelt pinned his hopes on the curative potentiality of the United Nations organization as Wilson did with his League of Nations. Europe, which at the Paris Peace Conference sold out idealism and principle for territorial greed and a punitive peace, finally produced an embittered Germany that accepted Hitler as a better alternative than the misery and chaos of economic ruin forced upon her by excessive reparations. The League proved powerless to correct the mistakes of the Versailles Treaty. The same thing has been in evolution now with the United Nations which has been powerless to correct the mistakes of World War II.

But the primary responsibility for the policies which characterized our wartime diplomacy must rest with Roosevelt who, far more than any other American President, directed the conduct of our foreign relations. Under the influence of Soviet sympathizers and reinforced by his own eagerness to please Stalin, no one in the country was more thoroughly deceived by Russian promises than Roosevelt. He was obsessed with the idea that through a personal meeting with Stalin he could mold the pattern of international relations in the form that was closest to his heart's desire.[1] This important factor of egotism is commented upon by Hanson Baldwin as follows:

---

[1] Roosevelt's conception about Communism was incredible. In a memorandum to the Secretary of the Navy, Frank Knox, on May 4, 1942, approving the employment of Communist radio operators on American ships, Roosevelt wrote: "The Soviet people in Moscow are said to have little liking for the American Communists and their methods—especially because it seems increasingly true that the communism of 20 years ago has practically ceased in Russia." U.S. Congress, Senate. *Report of the Subcom-*

The Presidential ego unavoidably became stronger in Roosevelt's closing years. His great wartime power, the record of victory, the high esteem in which he was held by the world, and the weakness of the State Department all combined to reinforce the President's tendency to depend upon himself.[2]

President Roosevelt's active interest in diplomatic arrangements was taken for granted. It has often been said he thought of himself as his own Secretary of State. As often as not Secretary of State Cordell Hull knew little or nothing of Roosevelt's diplomatic moves. The niceties of Constitutional law requiring the "advice and consent" of the Senate were largely evaded by means of "executive agreements." No President in the history of the United States occupied a position quite comparable to that of President Roosevelt during the years 1941-1945.

It is glibly asserted by many die-hard New Dealers that there was no alternative to the policy of Soviet appeasement. Regarding this assertion two questions may fairly be asked. First, did the Soviet record before the conferences at Teheran and Yalta suggest that a dominant position for the Soviet Government in Europe and Asia would promote the interest and security of the United States? Second, were voices of warning raised, pointing to the probably grave consequences of acquiescing in the annexationist ambitions of a regime with unlimited aspirations for world domination? The answer to the first question is an emphatic "No." The answer to the second question is an equally definite "Yes." Before the Yalta Conference, which took place early in February, 1945, there were no less than eight major actions of the Soviet Union, well known to official Washington, and which should have inspired grave doubts as to Soviet intentions and good faith.[3] Surely these "Stop, Look and Listen" signs should have been heeded by American negotiators at Yalta. But some of these advisers were strongly pro-Soviet, looking forward to a close association between Stalin and Roosevelt in determining the condition of the postwar world. They were eager to push Roosevelt into the hungry arms of Stalin who had his own ideas about world domination.

mittee to Investigate the Administration of the Internal Security Act and other Internal Security Laws, 83rd Cong., 2d Sess. (Washington: Government Printing Office, 1955), p. 24.

[2] Hanson Baldwin, Great Mistakes of the War, p. 8.

[3] These actions can be summarized as follows: (1) The Soviet Union, after posing as an irreconcilable enemy of Fascism, signed a pact with Nazi Germany on August 23, 1939, which cynically divided up eastern Europe between Communist and Nazi tyrannies. (2) In violation of a pact of non-aggression between the two countries, the Soviet Red Army invaded Poland in September 1939. The Soviet authorities behaved with the utmost brutality in the part of Poland which was annexed, deporting over a million men, women, and children to slave labor under such bad physical conditions that about a quarter of them perished. (3) In violations of similar treaties, the Soviet Union overran and annexed the small Baltic Republics, Latvia, Lithuania, and Estonia, in 1940. There was a repetition of the mass deportations which had been practiced in Poland. (4) Again in violation of a non-aggression treaty, the Soviet Union attacked Finland on November 30, 1939, fought an aggressive war for three and a half months, and annexed about one-tenth of Finland's territory—land that was historically and

The concessionary and conciliatory attitude of Roosevelt and many of his advisers toward Russia may explain in great part the large influence gained by Soviet agents and fellow-travelers, many of whom occupied offices of great power and made many grave decisions. For example, Admiral Adolphus Staton, who holds the Congressional Medal of Honor, the nation's highest award for devotion to our country, tried to obey the mandate of Congress during the war to clean Communists out of the communications rooms of American vessels. He was directly overruled by Roosevelt.[4] The war, with its security regulations, censorship, and military discipline, actually operated to cover up activities which protected Communists and furthered Communist objectives.

President Roosevelt took the initiative in seeking a conference with Stalin at Yalta in a top secret cable sent via Navy channels on July 17, 1944: "Things are moving so fast and so successfully that I feel there should be a meeting between you and Mr. Churchill and me in the reasonably near future." [5] This cablegram produced a series of cables, as the Big Three squabbled over a meeting place.

Roosevelt first suggested to Stalin that the "most central point for you and me would be the north of Scotland."[6] Stalin scotched that idea with the reply, through Ambassador Harriman, that he had suffered ear

---

ethnically Finnish. (5) The Soviet Union, even when it received increasing amounts of American and British aid after Hitler's attack in 1941, consistently refused to consider making good the wrongs that had been inflicted on Poland and the Baltic States. (6) The Soviet Union, with characteristic cynicism, took the exposure of one of its own most revolting "war crimes," the massacre of some 15,000 Polish officer war prisoners in the Katyn Forest, near Smolensk, and elsewhere as an excuse for breaking off diplomatic relations with the legitimate government of Poland. This occurred in the spring of 1943; from this time on the Soviet Union intensified its efforts to impose on Poland a Red Quisling regime, dominated by Communists. (7) When the Red Army approached the Polish capital, Warsaw, in the summer of 1944, the Soviet radio broadcast appealed in Polish for an uprising. When the Polish underground forces, nationalist in political sympathy, went into action against the German garrison, the Red Army stood still and the revolt was suppressed with frightful loss of life, accompanied by the complete destruction of the city of Warsaw. (8) After overrunning Bulgaria in 1944 the Soviet authorities took care to shut out the United States and the other Western powers from any effective voice in the negotiation of a Bulgarian peace settlement. This was in line with the general Soviet policy of setting up puppet Communist-dominated regimes in every country "liberated" by the Red Army. William Henry Chamberlain "Hindsight, Foresight, and Blind Sight," *Human Events* (July 23, 1955).

4 The implications of this order are extremely important, particularly when one ponders the following paragraph: "The Secretary (Knox) then spoke and said that he had no brief for the activities of the Communist Party, but that the President had stated that, considering the fact that the United States and Russia were allies at this time and that the Communist Party and the United States efforts were now bent toward our winning the war, the United States was bound not to oppose the activities of the Communist Party, and specifically, to not disapprove the employment of any radio operator for the sole reason that he was a member of the Communist Party or that he was active in Communist Party affairs. The Secretary further stated that this was an order and must be obeyed without mental reservation." *Senate Internal Security Subcommittee Report,* January 3, 1955, p. 22.

5 President Roosevelt to Marshal Stalin, July 17, 1944, *Yalta Documents,* p. 3.

6 *Ibid.*

trouble after his 1943 trip to Teheran, and thus his "doctors considered any change of climate would have a bad effect." [7] On July 27, 1944, Roosevelt asserted that a conference of the Big Three "would help me domestically." [8] Roosevelt also said that "we are approaching the time for further strategical decisions." [9] However, as weeks went by without an agreement being reached on a place for the conference, the closer came the date for the November elections. Roosevelt, assuming he would be re-elected, then sent a cable on October 4 to Churchill: "I am prepared for a meeting of the three of us any time after the election here. . . ." [10] Finally, a February date was agreed upon.

Two days before he left for the Yalta Conference, Roosevelt received from General MacArthur detailed terms of Japanese surrender overtures. These terms were virtually identical with those later accepted as the basis for Japanese surrender. General MacArthur urged that the President start immediate negotiations with the Japanese, warning against inviting the Soviets to enter the war in the Far East. President Roosevelt rejected MacArthur's advice with the contemptuous remark that "MacArthur is our greatest general and our poorest politician." [11]

Roosevelt went off to Yalta, there to buy Stalin's entry into the war we had already won. We are still paying the price. The needless and bloody battles on Iwo Jima and Okinawa were immediate costs. The dropping of atomic bombs on Asiatic civilian populations—acts which have so prejudiced the United States in the eyes of Asian people—was another. Sovietization of China and the Korean War were still others. And the end is not yet in sight.

The Japanese surrender terms were comprehensive and "came from responsible Japanese acting for Emperor Hirohito." They were made up of five separate proposals, two of which came through American channels and three through British. Itemized as to specific terms, they were as follows:

1. Full surrender of the Japanese forces on the sea, in the air, at home, on island possessions, and in occupied countries.
2. Surrender of all arms and munitions.
3. Occupation of the Japanese homeland and island possessions by Allied troops under American direction.
4. Japanese relinquishment of Manchuria, Korea and Formosa, as well as all territory seized during the war.

---

7 Ambassador Harriman to President Roosevelt, Moscow, September 24, 1944, *Ibid.*, p. 5.
8 President Roosevelt to Marshal Stalin, July 27, 1944, *Ibid.*, pp. 4-5.
9 *Ibid.*
10 President Roosevelt to Ambassador Harriman, October 4, 1944, *Ibid.*, p. 7.
11 Chamberlain, *America's Second Crusade*, p. 219: New York *Journal-American*, March 18, 1955: *Congressional Record*, March 22, 1955, pp. 2848-49.

5. Regulation of Japanese industry to halt present and future production of implements of war.

6. Surrender of designated war criminals.

7. Release of all prisoners of war and internees in Japan proper and in areas under Japanese control.[12]

Perhaps the strangest thing about the rejected Japanese surrender proposals is the manner in which they came to light. Our Government has never made this sensational episode public, and it is quite likely that the original document was quietly destroyed.

The story has been told by Harry Elmer Barnes:

It so happens that MacArthur's document passed over the desk of a high-ranking military officer in Washington who was greatly disturbed at what he feared might happen at Yalta. He wished to get MacArthur's communication on record so it could not be destroyed by Mr. Roosevelt or his associates or hidden away from the public for many years as "top secret" material. Hence, he called in his friend, Walter Trohan of the *Chicago Tribune,* and suggested that Trohan make an exact copy of the Japanese overtures. But he first bound Trohan to absolute secrecy and confidence until the end of the war. Trohan kept his promise, but on the Sunday after V-J Day (August 19, 1945) Trohan published the material in full in the *Chicago Tribune* and the *Washington Times-Herald.* Despite the very timely and sensational nature of the Trohan article, no prominent newspaper, so far as I know, noticed or republished it either then or at any time since.[13]

In 1951, former President Herbert Hoover took the Trohan article to General MacArthur. The General confirmed its accuracy in every detail and without qualification. Neither the White House nor the State Department has ever challenged the authenticity of the Trohan material.

It can now be revealed that the "high-ranking military officer" who gave Trohan the material was none other than Fleet Admiral William D. Leahy, Chief of Staff to the President—our highest ranking military officer.

The President did not appear to be in good health on his trip to the Crimea. He neither spent much time in conferring with his advisers, nor did he read the policy papers prepared for his guidance at the conference. Ever since the Teheran conference, Roosevelt's health had declined perceptibly. In December at the time of his return, Jim Farley remarked: "There were disturbing reports about Roosevelt's health. Hundreds of persons, high and low, reported to me that he looked bad, his mind wandered, his hands shook, his jaw sagged, and he tired easily. . . ."[14] John Gunther wrote of having seen the President at the time of the Foreign Policy Association speech on October 4, 1944, before his fourth inaugu-

---

12 Harry Elmer Barnes, "Hiroshima: Assault on a Beaten Foe," *National Review* (May 10, 1958) .

13 *Ibid.*

14 Farley, *Jim Farley's Story: The Roosevelt Years,* p. 363.

ral. He was shocked, he said, by the change in Roosevelt's physical appearance: his face was "gray, gaunt, and sagging and the muscles controlling the lips seemed to have lost part of their function. . . . I felt certain that he was going to die."[15] Merriman Smith said that he was shocked at Roosevelt's physical appearance on election night when he addressed his neighbors from the porch of his home at Hyde Park.[16] The day before his inauguration, following a brief cabinet meeting, Frances Perkins visited with him in a room at the White House. She was so horrified at the appearance of the President that she burst into tears.[17]

Three days later, secretly, this dying man was shipped aboard a heavy cruiser to Yalta, a port on the Black Sea. There he would face the rugged Stalin, to agree upon the fruits of victory. "In our evaluation of President Roosevelt," says Farley, "Cordell Hull and I agreed that he was a sick man at Yalta and should not have been called upon to make decisions affecting this country and the world. Physical illness, we knew, taxed his mind and left him in no shape to bargain with such hard bargainers as the Russians and such astute diplomats as the British." [18] The conclusions of most of the friends and close observers of the President show that before he went to the Yalta Conference his "health was visibly poor." [19] It must be emphasized, however, that Roosevelt was in fine health at the Teheran Conference where the important decisions were actually made. Yalta merely confirmed what took place at Teheran.

Stalin held out from beginning to end for a meeting in the Soviet Union. The location of the conference on Soviet soil was again due to Stalin's reluctance to travel far from Moscow. It clearly shows that Stalin intended to, or thought he would, dominate the conference. Roosevelt and Churchill let him call the shots right at the beginning, even though Yalta was about the most unhealthy and disease-ridden spot that could be selected, particularly for a man of Roosevelt's poor health. In the President's log of his trip to Yalta, aides recorded that "medical officers of the *U.S.S. Catoctin* had accomplished a very effective job of de-bugging at Yalta." [20] Churchill reluctantly agreed to the site, complaining that the

15 John Gunther, *Roosevelt in Retrospect: A Profile in History* (New York: Harper and Brothers, 1950), p. 28.

16 Merriman Smith, *Thank You, Mr. President* (New York: Harper and Brothers, 1946), pp. 158-159.

17 Perkins, *The Roosevelt I Knew*, pp. 388-390.

18 Farley, *Jim Farley's Story: The Roosevelt Years*, pp. 376-377. Churchill writes that at Yalta "the President was ailing. . . . His face had a transparency . . . and often there was a far-away look in his eyes" and that when they said good-by at the end of the conference, "the President seemed placid and frail. I felt that he had a slender contact with life." Churchill, *Triumph and Tragedy:* (Boston: Houghton Mifflin, Co. 1953), p. 397, 477.

19 Herman E. Batsman, "Observations on President Roosevelt's Health During World War II", *The Mississippi Valley Historical Review*, (June, 1956), p. 97.

20 *Yalta Documents*, p. 460.

climate was not warm enough and that the comforts would be too few. ". . . ten years of research," Churchill said, "could not have found a worse place in the world than Yalta. . . ."[21] The location is described in official reports as a dirty pest-hole of about thirty thousand in the Soviet Crimea. It had little to recommend it as a place for an important international conference.[22]

One may find some explanation for the Yalta give-away in a review of the men who made up Roosevelt's delegation. The most important of these advisers was General George Marshall, Chief of Staff. His name has been connected with several grave historical situations, and controversies are still raging as to the responsibility which should be imputed to him. He stood at Yalta urging the grim necessity of Russia's entry into war against Japan. He did nothing to deter Roosevelt from embarking on his ill-starred course which ended in disaster.[23]

The desire to have Russia's help in the Far East was constantly stressed by Marshall, and was embodied, as we know, in the fateful appeasement memorandum of the first Quebec Conference in August, 1943—the document which charted America's course at Teheran and Yalta thereafter. It was Marshall's mistaken estimate of Japan's capacity for continued military resistance, after all signs pointed to enemy collapse, that fortified Roosevelt in his determination to buy Soviet entry into the Pacific war at the price of vast strategic concessions in China.[24] This deal foreordained the loss of China to Communist control.

Another important delegate at the Yalta Conference was Charles E. Bohlen, who served as Roosevelt's interpreter. He also assisted President Roosevelt at Teheran and President Truman at Potsdam. On March 2, 1955, during the hearings on Bohlen's nomination as Ambassador to Russia, the members of the Committee on Foreign Relations put many questions to the nominee concerning the Teheran, Yalta, and Potsdam conferences, at all three of which Bohlen was officially present. He did not attend, he said, as a "policy-maker" because, as he explained to the Committee, "nobody is in a policy-making position in the Department of State except the Secretary of State or the Acting Secretary." [25] When, however, the friendly Senator Theodore Green of Rhode Island tried to help him out of a difficult spot during the questioning by urging that "he acted simply as interpreter" at Yalta, Bohlen was quick with his

21 *Ibid.*, p. 460.

22 *Ibid.*

23 Senator Joseph R. McCarthy, *America's Retreat from Victory: The Story of George Catlett Marshall* (New York: Devin-Adair Company, 1951) , p. 54.

24 Baldwin, *Great Mistakes of the War*, pp. 80-81.

25 U.S. Congress, Senate, *Hearings Before the Committee on Foreign Relations, the Nomination of Charles E. Bohlen to be United States Ambassador Extraordinary and Plenipotentiary to the Union of Soviet Socialist Republics.* 83d Cong., 1st Sess. (Washington: Government Printing Office, 1953), p. 116.

rejection: "Senator, might I say this, that I was also an assistant to the Secretary of State at Yalta, and I had a certain advisory capacity. . . ." [26]

With respect to the Yalta agreements, Bohlen found nothing wrong from a 1945 perspective. In 1953, by "hindsight" and in restrospect, he suggested two possible valid criticisms of the Far Eastern program. First, "it was unnecessary," and secondly, it was done without the participation of the Chinese Government.[27]

As for the European agreements at Yalta, Teheran, and Potsdam, Bohlen had no criticism of any kind, even by hindsight. In spite of Senator Homer Ferguson's almost begging him to put some qualifying phrase into the record, Bohlen declined to say a word against the treatment of Poland, for example, in the Yalta agreements, or the provisions for forcible repatriation of Soviet citizens:

SENATOR FERGUSON: As you say now, hindsight makes Yalta and these other agreements look like a great mistake.
MR. BOHLEN: I would not say that, sir, for the ones relating to Europe . . .
SENATOR FERGUSON: You claim now . . . that these agreements were correct governmental agreements so far as America was concerned, but that the interpretation put on them by Russia is what caused the . . .
MR. BOHLEN: I would say, sir, I would go further than that; saying . . . it is not so much interpretation as violation. . . .
SENATOR FERGUSON: Why did we have to surrender the rights of these people and be a party to the surrender?
MR. BOHLEN: I don't consider that the agreement at Yalta involved a surrender. It involved the opposite.[28]

Certainly Bohlen's defense of Yalta is contrary to the fundamental aims of the Atlantic Charter which seem to have been abandoned by Roosevelt.

Testifying before the MacArthur Hearings, Patrick Hurley, former Ambassador to China, disagreed with Bohlen's interpretation of the Yalta Agreement. He said: ". . . They talk about Stalin breaking his agreements, gentlemen. He never had to break one. We cowardly surrendered to him everything that he had signed and we did it in secret . . . at the time of Yalta the United States had unquestionable power to make Russia respect her solemn agreements, but instead we surrendered them in secret. Russia did not have to break her agreements or commitments. All of them were surrendered to her by American diplomats at Yalta and subsequently. . . ." [29]

Bohlen's testimony concerning the part Alger Hiss played at Yalta indicates either that the late Edward R. Stettinius, Jr., in his book on

---

[26] *Ibid.*, p. 3.
[27] *Ibid.*, pp. 20-21.
[28] *Ibid.*, p. 32; 60.
[29] *Military Situation in the Far East*, Part 4, pp. 2839-2840.

Yalta, made a faulty presentation, or that Bohlen is much more concerned with minimizing the part played by Hiss. At the outset of his testimony to the Senate Foreign Relations Committee, Bohlen said the Stettinius book "is a scrupulously accurate account of what actually transpired at Yalta." [30] But what Bohlen said later on is neither quite in accord with what the Stettinius book indicates nor with what the official Yalta documents reveal.

Thus, Bohlen says Hiss dealt with United Nations affairs at Yalta "and confined his activities to that," and he emphasized that Hiss was not present at the Roosevelt-Stalin-Churchill meetings. But he seems not to have recognized the powerful role Hiss played as adviser to the President through Secretary of State Stettinius, who in his book writes of the Yalta Conference: "The next morning at 10:30, Harriman, Matthews, Hiss, Bohlen and I met with the President on the sun porch overlooking the sea, to review our proposals for the conference agenda." [31]

How close an adviser Hiss was to Secretary Stettinius was brought out at a congressional hearing in 1953 by J. Anthony Panuch of the Department of State. He testified that Hiss exercised a "Svengali-like influence over the mental processes of Junior Stettinius." [32]

Senator William F. Knowland was sharply critical of Bohlen's remark that Hiss played an insignificant part at Yalta. Reading from Stettinius' book the Senator said there were many references to Hiss "that at least to me would seem to indicate that he did more than merely sit in on these large plenary meetings." [33] When Hiss had already become a controversial figure but before his conviction on a perjury charge at a second trial, Stettinius had this to say:

Hiss performed brilliantly throughout the Dumbarton Oaks conversations, the Yalta Conference, the San Francisco Conference, and the first meeting of the United Nations Assembly in London. I always had reason to believe that Hiss acted honorably and patriotically in the performance of his duties at these conferences. The following pages of this book reveal his contributions at the Yalta Conference.[34]

A glance at the index of Stettinius' book shows sixteen separate references to Hiss. An examination of the work credited Hiss in the book gives an impression of influence. Hiss often sat directly behind President

---

[30] *Hearings of the Nomination of Charles E. Bohlen*, p. 6.

[31] Stettinius, *Roosevelt and the Russians*, p. 84. James F. Byrnes, former Secretary of State, said: "It is plain that Hiss had easy access, for good or evil, to Stettinius and Hopkins, who were trusted advisers of the President." James F. Byrnes, "Yalta and Hiss and the Atom Bomb." *Look Magazine* (October 14, 1958), p. 79; see also his *All in One Lifetime*, (New York: Harper and Brothers, 1958), p. 260.

[32] U.S. Congress, Senate, *Interlocking Subversion in Government Departments, Hearings Before the Subcommittee to Investigate the Administration of the Internal Security Act and Other Internal Security Laws*. Part 13, 83d Cong., 1st Sess. (Washington: Government Printing Office, 1953) , p. 853.

[33] *Hearings on the Nomination of Charles E. Bohlen*, p. 41.

[34] Stettinius, *Roosevelt and the Russians*, pp. 30-31.

Roosevelt at the conference table, and he attended some private consultations with the President and Secretary of State Stettinius. Stettinius speaks of reviewing with Matthews, Hiss, and Foote on his way to Malta "the questions reserved for subsequent discussion with the President at Malta." [35] Hiss sat in on conferences which discussed: the establishment of a European high commission composed of representatives of Great Britain, the Soviet Union, France, and the United States; the dismemberment of Germany; the Polish question; relations between UNRRA and the Soviet government; the rights of American representatives on the Allied control commissions for Bulgaria, Romania, and Hungary; Iran; China; the Turkish Straits question; International Trusteeships.[36]

Writing about the consideration of the Polish boundary, Stettinius says:

During one adjournment that afternoon the President asked me to get a lawyer to consult with him over the wording of the Polish boundary statement. I called Alger Hiss and while the two of us were trying to work out a solution for the President, Roosevelt suddenly looked up at us and said, "I've got it."[37]

Stettinius speaks of asking "Hiss to do a quick summary of the State Department's memorandum on the trusteeship issue," which he showed to Churchill and "seemed to satisfy him." [38]

An interesting memorandum concerning Hiss is a letter of the executive secretary of the staff of Secretary Stettinius to Assistant Secretary Nelson A. Rockefeller which reads: "At the Secretary's and Staff Committee meeting on January 10, [1945] the Secretary [Stettinius] asked that all memoranda for the President on topics to be discussed at the Meeting of the Big Three [at Yalta] should be in the hands of Mr. Alger Hiss not later than Monday, January 15." [39] This related to top

35 Stettinius, *op. cit.*, p. 36. Dr. Edna Fluegel, who was in the Office of Special Political Affairs when Hiss joined it, testified: "Right before Dumbarton Oaks, when he first came, he immediately took a very active part. He was in charge of all of the arrangements. He was secretary to several of the top planning committees and attended Dumbarton Oaks in that capacity. I suppose you would describe his job as pretty much the job of a secretary general plus personal adviser to the delegates." *Institute of Pacific Relations, Hearings*, Part 8, p. 2838. Dr. Fluegel continued her testimony that after the Dumbarton Oaks conference Hiss participated "in all of the meetings, discussing plannings for Yalta, since a major part of the Yalta conference—as a matter of fact, the reason for the Yalta conference—was the failure to settle certain questions during the Dumbarton Oaks conference," *Ibid.*, p. 2838.

36 Stettinius, *op. cit.*, pp. 36-46. Dr. Fluegel, who had access to Hiss's original handwritten notes on Yalta, was asked what role he played in it. She replied: "Well, of course, he went to Yalta as the top international organization specialist, and a large part of the Yalta conference was to be devoted to that." *Institute of Pacific Relations, Hearings*, Part 8, p. 2843.

37 Stettinius, *op. cit.*, p. 270.

38 *Ibid.*, p. 238. The notes taken by Hiss related that James F. Byrnes, an adviser to President Roosevelt at Yalta, was very much upset by the President's agreement to give Russia three votes in the United Nations Assembly—including one for White Russia and one for the Ukraine.

39 *Yalta Documents*, p. 42.

secret documents the Department of State had compiled setting forth the pros and cons of all the problems to arise at Yalta, plus the Department's policy recommendations.

The secret briefing papers which Hiss saw in advance and which the President took with him to Yalta contained the Department of State's views on the Far East. These briefing papers clearly reflected an official apprehension about the future of Russian-American relations in that part of the world, but which Roosevelt's conversations at Yalta did not reflect in the least. Roosevelt may never have seen these briefing papers. He told Stalin that he blamed General Chiang Kai-shek more than "the so-called Communists" for the failure to gain a coalition government. Stalin replied that "new leaders" were needed around Chiang Kai-shek.[40]

If Hiss at the time of the Yalta Conference was still under orders of the Communist apparatus, which is entirely possible, it is not, then, logical to suspect that copies of our preparatory documents for the Yalta Conference might have been immediately channeled to Soviet representatives in Washington, to be forwarded to the Kremlin. Roosevelt was then a very tired and enfeebled man who before, during, and after the Yalta Conference seemed to be in a perpetual hurry to get things done no matter how (admittedly not even looking at the carefully prepared briefing papers). Is it not at least a strong possibility that, prior to the Yalta Conference, Stalin and Molotov familiarized themselves with our American background and program documents while the President of the United States neglected to do so? Is it not quite possible that our Soviet antagonists knew of our moves beforehand—that they knew what points of our program they would attack before Roosevelt knew that he was going to make those points?[41] If the Soviet Union had advance access to our positions and policies, we would be like a man playing poker with a mirror at his back. His opponent could see his hand before the play began.

How important was Alger Hiss at Yalta? Hiss himself answered that question when he testified before the House Committee on Un-American Activities. Here are some key questions by Congressman Karl Mundt of South Dakota and answers as they appear in the official record at the hearing:

MR. MUNDT: Did you participate in the Yalta Conference?
MR. HISS: I did, Mr. Chairman.
MR. MUNDT: Did you draft or participate in the drafting of parts of the Yalta agreement?

---

40 *Ibid.*, p. 771.
41 Felix Wittmer, "What Really Happened at Yalta?", *Facts Forum News*, May, 1955, pp. 50-51.

MR. HISS: I think it is accurate and not an immodest statement to say that I did to some extent, yes.[42]

A bit later in the hearing, Mundt asked Hiss if he had participated in drawing up the veto provisions that later were to appear in the United Nations charter. This colloquy developed:

MR. MUNDT: What I was trying to get to is whether you participated in the creation of the draft.
MR. HISS: I did participate in the creation of the draft that was sent by President Roosevelt to Churchill and Stalin, which was the draft actually adopted at San Francisco.
MR. MUNDT: Did you lend your influence in the direction of having the veto provision included in that draft?
MR. HISS: I did. That was practically the unanimous position of the American government, I might add.[43]

Why, after repeated disclosures concerning the Communist activities of Alger Hiss, did our top officials insist on including him in the delegation at Yalta? Whittaker Chambers in his book says he told about Hiss in 1939 to Assistant Secretary of State Adolph Berle, who talked to President Roosevelt about it.[44] In another instance, Martin Dies, former chairman of the House Committee on Un-American Activities, says that Roosevelt and his key aides in 1941 did not believe the list of about two thousand Communists on the federal payroll, including Alger Hiss.[45] But in spite of these grave revelations about Hiss, his name was placed in the list of delegates to the Yalta Conference.[46]

The role Hiss played at the conference was unquestionably an important one. Some of his notes appear in the *Yalta Documents* and some have been deleted.[47]

The deplorable results of the Yalta Conference can be ascribed to the weakness of the American delegation. It was Harry Hopkins who was instrumental in the appointment of Edward R. Stettinius, Jr., as Secretary of State. Considering the critical position America was facing in foreign relations, Stettinius was one of the most naive and inexperienced men in the field of foreign affairs who ever occupied that office. His lack of training was soon noticed by his associates in the Depart-

[42] U.S. Congress, House Committee on Un-American Activities, *Hearings Regarding Communist Espionage in the United States,* 80th Cong., 2d Sess. (Washington: Government Printing Office, 1948), p. 656.
[43] *Ibid.,* p. 657.
[44] Whittaker Chambers, *Witness* (New York: Random House, 1952), p. 470.
[45] *U.S. News and World Report* (August 20, 1954), p. 57.
[46] *Yalta Documents,* p. 439. Professor Donald D. Dozer was fired from the Department of State, he declares, because he protested the issuance of a "distorted" report given in the Yalta Documents. He charged that the Department of State deliberately suppressed data showing that President Roosevelt insisted upon taking Alger Hiss with him to Yalta. *Chicago Tribune,* October 22, 1955.
[47] Barron, *Inside the State Department,* Chapter 2.

ment of State. They felt that he was nothing more than a captive millionaire of the New Deal.

Former Ambassador to Poland, Arthur Bliss Lane, says the appointment was made to give the President and Hopkins "complete personal control over our foreign policy, especially as relating to the Soviet Union." [48] A witty person once remarked to William Henry Chamberlain that Stettinius "could not distinguish the Ukraine from a musical instrument. It required a battery of promoters at the San Francisco conference which inaugurated the United Nations to keep Stettinius from continually muffing his lines and making his country appear ridiculous." [49] Alger Hiss was Secretary General of the San Francisco Conference in April, 1945. Our chief economic adviser there was Harry Dexter White. Both were identified as Soviet agents in a November, 1945 FBI memorandum circulated to our top officials.

Also in the Yalta delegation was Averell Harriman, an intimate and confidential adviser to President Roosevelt throughout the war period. He holds the unique distinction of having attended almost every major political and military strategy conference between the Soviet Union and the United States. When he returned from his second trip to Moscow in 1941, he began singing praises of Stalin. "Whenever Stalin gets tough with us," he told Ambassador William H. Standley, "it's the Politburo attitude he's expressing, not his own views on the major subject at issue." [50] He was optimistic about a large postwar trade with Russia and advocated a huge loan which would rehabilitate Russia from the destruction by Germany.

Harriman was certain that the Russians had no designs against the United States. Ambassador Standley had reported the Soviet intention of setting up a belt of satellite states, but Harriman knew better. "The Russian attitude on the Polish question is influenced above all by determination to prevent the revival of the *cordon sanitaire*," he said. "Their neighbors must view them with a free eye." [51] He was "personally convinced" that the Katyn Forest massacre of Polish officers, in fact perpetrated by the Russians, was "a German job." [52] When Ambassador Standley returned from Russia after having resigned his post, Harriman was cool, and he would accept no part of the Admiral's diagnosis and prognosis—an analysis of present and future which, read today, is a blueprint of what has since occurred. Harriman has repeatedly defended the Yalta Conference and its agreements, putting the blame on Stalin

48 Lane, *I Saw Poland Betrayed*, p. 71.

49 Chamberlain, *America's Second Crusade*, p. 184.

50 Standley and Ageton, *Admiral Ambassador to Russia*, pp. 213-214.

51 Peter Minot, "Harriman: New Deal Reshuffled," *National Review*, December 14, 1955, p. 14.

52 *Ibid.*

for all the difficulties resulting from them.[53] According to Secretary of State Stettinius, Ambassador Harriman played an important confidential role in private discussions between the President and the Russians, which led to the signing of the top-secret agreement involving the sell-out of Outer Mongolia, the Kurile Islands, Southern Sakhalin, Dairen, and the Manchurian railroads to Russia in return for her belated entry into the Japanese war five days before it ended.[54]

Also in the Yalta delegation was James Byrnes, Admirals Leahy and King. Some social life was contributed to the conference by the presence of the Democratic boss, Edward Flynn, and the President's daughter, Anna Boettinger. Harriman's daughter and Churchill's daughter completed the female guest list.[55]

The President, accompanied by Admiral Leahy on the cruiser *Quincy*, had arrived at Malta on February 2, 1945. There they were met by General Marshall and Admiral King. Both Marshall and King felt that the President, despite his ten-day vacation on the journey, was "a very sick man." [56] Churchill met Roosevelt at Malta, and they conferred on the reports of the military staff and on the agenda for the forthcoming conference.

At Malta, Britain's Foreign Secretary, Anthony Eden, passed along to the President, through Stettinius, this advice on the way to meet the Russians at Yalta: "There was . . . no need for us to offer a high price for their participation, and if we were prepared to agree to their territorial demands in the Far East we should see to it that we obtained a good return in respect of the points on which we required concessions from them." [57] We know now Stalin's announced price was paid.

The background of the concessions made to the Russians at Yalta contains many items which perplex historians who are still eager to defend the role of Roosevelt at this disastrous conference.

One of the big arguments in explaining away Roosevelt's major political concessions to Stalin at Yalta is that there was no certainty about the atom bomb. However, it is now officially documented that Roosevelt, without a doubt, had information to the contrary. The atom bomb has been credited with helping to bring Japan to its knees to sue for peace on August 10, 1945, exactly six months from the week of the Yalta Conference. The end of hostilities (V-J Day) came four days later. Russia, whose help was not needed, entered the war against Japan only five days before the cease-fire.

---

[53] *Ibid.*, p. 15. See also statement of W. Averell Harriman in *Military Situation in the Far East*, Part 5, pp. 3328-3342.

[54] Stettinius, *op. cit.*, pp. 92-96.

[55] *Yalta Documents*, pp. 460-462.

[56] Ernest J. King and Walter Muir Whitehill, *Fleet Admiral King: A Naval Record* (New York: W. W. Norton & Co., Inc., 1952), pp. 585-586.

[57] *Yalta Documents*, February 1, 1945, p. 501.

At least a month before the conference at Yalta, Roosevelt had received "reasonably certain" assurance from top scientists that the A-bomb would be ready to drop in about seven months. These facts are revealed in a top secret memorandum written by Major General Leslie B. Groves, wartime head of the atomic bomb project, to General Marshall. The memorandum is dated December 30, 1944, and a notation on it shows that it was presented to Roosevelt by Secretary Stimson. The Groves note opens with these extraordinary words:

It is now reasonably certain that our operation plans should be based on the *gun type bomb* [atom bomb], which, it is estimated, will produce the equivalent of a 10,000-ton TNT explosion. The first bomb, without previous full-scale test which we do not believe will be necessary, *should be ready about 1 August, 1945*.[58]

A footnote to this memorandum adds that General Groves was certain the bomb would explode, that he had double-checked the scientists, and that the explosion would wreck a large city. General Groves said he had first hoped for the bomb to be ready in the spring, but difficulties prevented it from being ready until fall.

The Groves' note also disclosed that apparently everyone connected with the atomic bomb project and the Air Corps were so certain of the A-bomb's capability that they had already organized the 509th Composite Air Group, 20th Air Force, to deliver the bomb. As a matter of fact this Air Group was not only organized but in training before the Yalta Conference.

General Groves recommended that a start be made in informing the top air generals in the Pacific area so that "our operation plans" could be revised in order to take into account the atomic bomb. This memorandum carried a notation by General Marshall, as well as by General Groves, stating: "The Secretary of War and the President both read this paper and approved it." [59] Moreover, a Colonel William S. Considine of the Manhattan Engineer District flew to the island of Malta where he met with Secretary Stettinius and briefed him, immediately prior to Yalta, on the certainty of the atom bomb.[60]

---

[58] General Groves to General Marshall, December 30, 1944, *Ibid.*, pp. 383-384 (Emphasis in original). Stettinius indicates that he was given information about the atomic bomb by Roosevelt a few weeks before the trip to Crimea. Stettinius, *Roosevelt and the Russians*, pp. 33-34.

[59] *Yalta Documents*, p. 384.

[60] *Military Situation in the Far East*, Part 4, p. 3120. Admiral Ellis Zacharias believes that if the Japanese had been given a precise definition of what America understood by unconditional surrender as late as June, or even July, 1945, both Soviet intervention and the dropping of atomic bombs on Hiroshima and Nagasaki could have been averted. *Secret Missions* (New York: G. P. Putman's Sons, 1946), pp. 367-368. He also believes that intelligence reports indicated that the Japanese were on the verge of collapse, making it unnecessary for the Russians to intervene. These reports im-

Thus, there are two reasons why Roosevelt should not have sought Soviet entry into the Pacific War. First, the Japanese were already beaten and were seeking a way to surrender. Second, our possession of an effective atomic bomb assured almost immediate total victory.

On February 3, 1945, the American and British delegations flew from the island of Malta to the Crimea. Since the airfield was about ninety miles from the places appointed to receive the delegates, they did not arrive until evening, and the conference began on the next day.

One of Roosevelt's prime purposes in coming to Yalta was to pin down firmly and finally Stalin's promise, given at Teheran, to join in the Japanese war as soon as he could gather his forces together after victory had come in Europe. Details of the scale and timing of Russian intervention against Japan had largely been settled during discussions with Ambassador Harriman in December, 1944.[61] What had not been settled was the price to be paid for Stalin's intervention. The Soviet dictator had mentioned in October the political prerequisites for his intervention; in December, 1944 he explained to the American Ambassador, Averell Harriman, exactly what he wished to gain in the Far East. Thus Roosevelt arrived at Yalta with a clear knowledge of what would be demanded of him.[62] He came also, it is safe to surmise, with the definite intention of accepting Stalin's major demands in order to gain Russian military assistance which the United States Joint Chiefs of Staff assured him would be of vital importance for shortening the war against Japan.[63] Before going to Yalta, both Stalin and Soviet Minister Molotov knew that the Japanese were reeling under the impact of America's round-the-clock bombings and submarine attacks. The Soviets were in no position to drive a hard bargain. Roosevelt was.

At the opening session on Sunday, February 4, Stalin made a gesture which was very tactful. He proposed, as he had at Teheran, that Roosevelt should take the chair. Once again he brought the President halfway to his side.[64] Yet Stalin showed no early inclination to follow the

---

plied a willingness to surrender and were available at the time of the Yalta Conference. One in particular predicted the resignation of General Koiso as Premier in favor of the pacific Admiral Susuki. The Admiral, in turn, would turn over power to the Imperial Prince Higashi Kuni, who would possess sufficient authority and prestige, backed by a command from the Emperor, to arrange the surrender. "I am convinced," says Zacharias, "that had this document, later proven to be correct in every detail, been brought to the attention of President Roosevelt and his military advisers, the war might have been viewed in a different light, both Iwo Jima and Okinawa might have been avoided, and different decisions could have been reached at Yalta." *Ibid.,* p. 335.

[61] Statement of W. Averell Harriman, *Military Situation in the Far East,* Part 5, p. 3330.

[62] Louis Morton, "The Military Background of the Yalta Agreements," *The Reporter* (April 1945), p. 20.

[63] Stettinius, *Roosevelt and the Russians,* p. 90.

[64] *Ibid.,* p. 105.

chairman's lead, least of all with regard to the President's cherished plan for creating a world peace organization based on the recognition of the sovereign rights of all nations. The first time the subject was raised, "Stalin made it quite plain," says Stettinius, "that the three Great Powers which had borne the brunt of war should be the ones to preserve the peace." He declared, moreover, that he would "never agree to having any action of any of the Great Powers submitted to the judgment of the small powers." [65] In reply to this argument, Churchill spoke for all the Western World in saying, "The eagle should permit the small birds to sing, and care not wherefor they sang." [66] That evening, when Stettinius and Eden discussed the outlook they agreed that "the trend . . . seemed to be more toward a three-power alliance than anything else." [67]

The meeting on the afternoon of the fifth day of the Conference (February 8) is reported in minutes written by Charles E. Bohlen.[68] Roosevelt and Stalin discussed the military situation in the Pacific. The subject of American air bases in the Maritime Provinces of Siberia came up, and the President indicated he would like co-operation in the establishment of these bases. He hoped by intensive bombing to be able to destroy Japan and its army and thus save American lives. Once again Stalin promised the use of bases.

Following the discussions on the military aspects of the Far Eastern war, Stalin told the President he would like to bring up the subject of the political questions under which the U.S.S.R. would enter the war against Japan. He had already discussed the matter with Ambassador Harriman. Roosevelt said he had received a report from Harriman regarding this conversation, and felt that there would be no difficulty whatsoever in regard to the southern half of Sakhalin and the Kurile Islands going to Russia at the end of the war. He reminded Stalin, regarding a warm water port, that they had already discussed that point at Teheran. As far as the President was concerned he was in favor of the use of a warm water port at the end of the South Manchurian railroad, at possibly Dairen on the Kwantung Peninsula. This could be arranged in either one of two ways: (1) the port might be leased from the Chinese or, (2) Dairen might be made into a free port under some form of international control. Of the two the President said he preferred the latter method, because of the relation to the question of Hong Kong.[69]

---

65 *Ibid.*, p. 112.

66 *Ibid.*

67 *Ibid.*, p. 116.

68 *Yalta Documents*, pp. 766-771.

69 "When the matter of making Dairen a free port came up," wrote Leahy, "I leaned over to Roosevelt and said, 'Mr. President, you are going to lose out on Hong Kong if you agree to give the Russians half of Dairen . . .' He shook his head in resignation

Stalin remarked that there was another question. It involved the use by the Russians of the Manchurian railways. During the Czarist period Russia had use of a line running from Manchouli on the Siberian border to Harbin and from there southward to Dairen and Port Arthur, as well as a line running east from Harbin to connect with the line to Vladivostok.

Roosevelt assured him that, although he had not talked with Chiang Kai-shek on the subject, there were two possible methods whereby an arrangement could be made. The railways could be leased under direct Soviet operation, or they might be placed under a commission composed of one Chinese and one Russian.

Stalin brought up the subject of public opinion in the Soviet Union. He told Roosevelt that if the conditions they had discussed were not met, it would be difficult to explain to the Russian people that they must go to war against Japan. Roosevelt should have known that Russian public opinion was not an important factor in that country's foreign policy. But Roosevelt was quite lenient and remarked that he had not yet had an opportunity to discuss these problems with Chiang Kai-shek, and that he felt one of the difficulties in speaking to the Chinese was that anything said to them was known to the whole world in twenty-four hours. Stalin agreed and added that he thought it would be a good thing if the three powers, before leaving Yalta, would agree in writing on the conditions of the Soviet entry into the Pacific war. The President indicated that he thought this could be done.

The internal conditions in China were also discussed at the same meeting. Roosevelt pointed out that for some time the United States had been trying to keep China alive. Stalin replied that China would remain alive, and then added that new leaders were needed around Chiang Kai-shek. Although there were some good leaders in the Nationalist Government, he did not understand why they were not brought forward. Roosevelt said General Wedemeyer and Ambassador Hurley were having much more success than their predecessors, and were making more progress in bringing the Communists in the North together with the Chungking government. He then added that *"the fault lay more with the Kuomintang and the Chungking government than with the so-called Communists."* [70] Stalin remarked that he did not understand why they did not get together, since they should have a united front against the Japanese. He thought for this purpose Chiang Kai-shek should assume leadership.

---

and said, 'Well, I can't help it.' " Leahy, *I Was There*, p. 314. The President had "hoped that the British would give back the sovereignty of Hong Kong to China." He knew "Mr. Churchill would have strong objections to this suggestion." *Yalta Documents*, p. 769.

[70] *Ibid.*, p. 771. Italics mine.

On February 10 Molotov submitted a memorandum to Harriman concerning Stalin's conditions for Russia's entry into war against Japan. The price was high. Harriman at once said President Roosevelt would wish (1) to change Soviet leasehold of Port Arthur and Dairen to international free ports; (2) to put the Manchurian railways under the joint operation of a Chinese-Soviet commission; and (3) not to dispose finally of these two matters in which China was interested without the concurrence of the Generalissimo.[71]

At another meeting that afternoon, Stalin took up the matter with Roosevelt. He said he was willing to have Dairen a free port under international control, and for the Manchurian railways to be operated by a Chinese-Soviet Commission. But he insisted that since Port Arthur was to be a Soviet naval base, a lease was required. Stalin also agreed on the need for concurrence of the Generalissimo on matters of ports, railways and the *status quo* in Outer Mongolia.

Roosevelt and Stalin then discussed how and when the Generalissimo should be told of the agreement. The President asked Stalin whether Stalin wished to take these matters up with T.V. Soong when he came to Moscow or whether Stalin wished the President to take them up with the Generalissimo. Stalin replied that since he was an interested party he would prefer the President to do it. Roosevelt agreed to do so. Roosevelt then asked when, in view of the question of secrecy, Stalin thought the subject should be discussed with Chiang Kai-shek.[72]

All of this was kept secret from Chiang Kai-shek who was our ally in the Pacific. Stalin was afraid the Japanese would find out. He told Roosevelt that he intended to start the movement of twenty-five Russian divisions across Siberia to the Far East and this operation must be conducted in utmost secrecy.[73] It is questionable whether Japan could have done anything about such a movement of troops, for by late 1944 what remained of the Kwantung Army was largely composed of green conscripts and second-rate troops with virtually no air support, and incapable of a prolonged campaign.[74]

The stated purpose for Stalin's moving twenty-five divisions to the border of Manchuria was to help China defeat the Japanese. Stalin told Roosevelt that when it was possible to move twenty-five divisions to the Far East it would be possible to speak to Chiang Kai-shek about these matters.[75] The Russian dictator wanted to make sure he had a formi-

71 *Yalta Documents*, p. 894.
72 *Ibid.*, p. 895.
73 Sherwood, *Roosevelt and Hopkins*, p. 866.
74 Chalmers M. Roberts writing in the Washington *Post*, March 27, 1955, stated that Washington officials knew "through prisoner interrogations and other means during MacArthur's Philippines campaign that these troops, the Kwantung Army, had moved to the Philippines to be replaced in Manchuria by green manpower."
75 *Yalta Documents*, pp. 769-770.

dable force on the Chinese border before he would take up with Chiang the matter concerning the Chinese territory Russia was to get.

On February 11, the text defining the gains which Russia should have from Japan's defeat was shown to Churchill, and his concurrence was requested. Despite the fact that he had taken no active part in drawing it up, the Prime Minister decided to sign the document which accordingly took the form of a tripartite agreement.[76] Eden had tried to persuade him not to. Churchill answered that the whole position of the British Empire in the Far East might be at stake. "He was going to sign," he said, "in order that Great Britain might stay in the Far East," and added "that he had great faith in President Roosevelt and felt that he could rely completely on the President's judgment in this matter." [77]

Roosevelt negotiated the agreement for Russia's entry into the Pacific war not only without consulting Churchill, but also without the participation of his own Secretary of State. The exclusion of Stettinius from this transaction is an extraordinary feature of the whole Yalta Conference. The excuse was that the agreement for Russia's entry into war was purely a military matter in which the Department of State was not concerned. This was a specious reason, for Stalin had long since committed himself on the basic military issue; the main point to be decided at Yalta was the political price of his participation.[78] Stettinius him-

---

[76] In its final form the agreement read as follows: "The leaders of the three Great Powers—the Soviet Union, the United States of America and Great Britain—have agreed that in two or three months after Germany has surrendered and the war in Europe has terminated, the Soviet Union shall enter into the war against Japan on the side of the Allies on condition that:

"(1) The *status quo* in Outer Mongolia shall be preserved:

"(2) The former rights of Russia violated by the treacherous attack of Japan in 1904 shall be restored, viz.:

"(a) the southern part of Sakhalin, as well as all the islands adjacent to it shall be returned to the Soviet Union,

"(b) the commercial port of Dairen shall be internationalized, the preeminent interest of the Soviet Union in this port being safeguarded and the lease of Port Arthur as a naval base of the U.S.S.R. restored;

"(c) the Chinese-Eastern Railroad and the South-Manchurian Railroad which provided an outlet to Dairen shall be jointly operated by the establishment of a joint Soviet-Chinese Company, it being understood that the preeminent interests of the Soviet Union shall be safeguarded and that China shall retain full sovereignty in Manchuria;

"(3) The Kurile Islands shall be handed over to the Soviet Union. It is understood that the agreement concerning Outer Mongolia and the Ports and railroads referred to above will require concurrence of Generalissimo Chiang Kai-shek. The President will take measures in order to obtain this concurrence on advice from Marshal Stalin.

For its part the Soviet Union expresses its readiness to conclude with the National Government of China a pact of friendship and alliance between the U.S.S.R. and China in order to render assistance to China with its armed forces for the purpose of liberating China from the Japanese yoke." *Yalta Documents,* p. 984.

[77] Stettinius, *Roosevelt and the Russians,* pp. 94-95.

[78] Chester Wilmot, *The Struggle for Europe,* p. 651; Hull, *Memoirs,* II, p. 1309.

self in his memoirs, whether out of loyalty to Roosevelt or to cover up
his own humiliation, accepts the military version of the matter.[79]

But a treaty involving extensive postwar territorial changes and transfers of sovereign rights is obviously the proper concern of a country's
diplomats, not merely of its soldiers. Moreover, Hopkins and Harriman, who were not military men, were brought into the discussions,
though Stettinius and his team of advisers from the Department of State
were kept out of them. Roosevelt's failure to call on them for information and advice about the extremely complex Far Eastern problems
with which he had to deal is all the more strange because he had previously refrained from reading the memoranda which the Department of
State had prepared for his perusal on the journey to the conference.
Byrnes relates in *Speaking Frankly*:

> . . . not until the day before we landed at Malta did I learn that we had on
> board a very complete file of studies and recommendations prepared by the
> State Department. I asked the President if the Department had given him any
> material and he advised me it was all in the custody of Lieutenant William M.
> Ridgon. Later, when I saw some of these splendid studies, I greatly regretted
> they had not been considered on board ship. I am sure the failure to study them
> while en route was due to the President's illness. And I am sure that only
> President Roosevelt, with his intimate knowledge of the problems, could have
> handled the situation so well with so little preparation.[80]

Roosevelt's own knowledge of the problems, however, appears not to
have been as intimate as Byrnes would have one believe. The agreement on Manchuria stated that "the former rights of Russia violated by
the treacherous attack of Japan in 1904 shall be restored," and afterwards, in verbal justification of the pact, Roosevelt claimed that the
Russians were not getting anything new from China but only recovering what the Japanese had taken from them.[81] This indicates that he
was unaware that the original leases to Russia of Port Arthur, and Dairen were forced upon the Manchu Government in 1898 as a result of
aggressive action, and that the Soviet Government had renounced these
Tsarist privileges in its declarations of 1919 and 1920. Furthermore,
the Soviet Government had sold the Chinese Eastern railway to the puppet state of Manchukuo. The Soviet Union had no more right to hold
these ports and railways in Manchuria than did Japan.[82] The concessions in Manchuria were in reality a violation of the agreement of
Roosevelt with Chiang Kai-shek at Cairo in 1943.

These were historical facts not likely to be known to anyone who was

---

79 Stettinius, *Roosevelt and the Russians*, pp. 92-94.

80 Byrnes, *Speaking Frankly*, p. 23.

81 Leahy, *I Was There*, p. 318.

82 Tien-Fong Cheng. *A History of Sino-Russian Relations* (Washington, D.C. Public
Affairs Press, 1957), p. 267.

not a specialist in Far Eastern affairs. A President of the United States could not be expected to discover them by intuition, but if he had been willing to avail himself of the services of the Department of State, which kept files and archives for recording such facts, he would have been correctly informed about the past history of the properties which he made over to Stalin at China's expense. He would have been informed also that these leased territories and railways, whether held by Russia or Japan, had prevented the proper exercise of Chinese sovereignty in Manchuria for half a century. At best, he was perpetuating what had hitherto proved to be the most dangerous and intractable sources of conflict in Far Eastern affairs.[83]

On the evening of February 10, Churchill gave a dinner at which high spirits and a sense of relief and relaxation prevailed. On the next day, all that remained was to sign the documents which the Conference had produced.

The President's company in its passage back across the Atlantic was not a happy one. Hopkins, feeling desperately ill, left the ship in order to fly home, where he promptly went to a hospital. Roosevelt was annoyed at his departure, and the two men parted coolly, never to meet again. A similarly unhappy ending to a long companionship came when Roosevelt's military aide, General "Pa" Watson, died of a heart attack on board ship. Roosevelt was personally affected by this loss.[84]

The Yalta Documents show that on the eve of the Conference the U.S. Navy had advised Roosevelt it would like a base in the Kuriles. Instead, the Kuriles were handed over to Russia.[85] There is not a word about Roosevelt's considering the wishes, needs, or security of the United States Navy in this matter. Not once do the records show Roosevelt arguing on behalf of China's independence, or making the point of China's need for Manchuria's industrial production. There was no hint of the long American recognition of China's independence as the key to stability in Asia. Stalin, continuing the imperialism of the Czars, remembered Port Arthur; Roosevelt forgot John Hay and the Open Door.

It is to be emphasized that all who met at Yalta, whatever their exhilaration at impending victory, were tired and sick of the burdens of war. The entire question of the extent of the mental exhaustion of the negotiators needs extensive examination. Samuel Rosenman, meeting Roosevelt on his way home from Yalta, was disheartened by his physical

[83] In his book *Seven Decisions That Shaped History*, p. 216, Sumner Welles said: "At the Cairo conference . . . the President had at his side no expert adviser on Far Eastern affairs. At Yalta also such advice was lacking." If we had at those conferences an expert on Far Eastern affairs, "a number of defects in the Cairo and Yalta agreements on Asia might well have been avoided."

[84] Sherwood, *Roosevelt and Hopkins*, pp. 873-75.

[85] *Yalta Documents*, p. 382.

appearance. "I had never seen him look so tired . . . . he was listless and apparently uninterested in conversation—he was all burnt out." [86]

The myth that Russian participation in the Japanese war was a military necessity, has been refuted adequately. History will record that at Yalta the United States repudiated some of its solemn obligations, yielded to Russian imperialism, and gave way to appeasement, and all for mythical reasons. It will be regretted for decades.

The result of Yalta remains a triumph for Communist diplomacy. From John Hay to Cordell Hull, America maintained the "open door" in China. At Yalta, America slammed shut the "open door." "American diplomats," says Patrick J. Hurley, "surrendered the territorial integrity and the political independence of China, surrendered the principles of the Atlantic Charter, and wrote the blueprint for the Communist conquest of China in secret agreement at Yalta. . . . " [87]

On March 1, 1945, Roosevelt appeared before a joint session of Congress for the purpose of making a "personal report" on what had been accomplished at the Yalta Conference. It was significant that he resorted to mendacity in this report. He realized that the American people would not relish the news of a complete sellout to Stalin with reference to our Far Eastern policy. In his address before Congress he stated that the Yalta Conference had "concerned itself only with the European war and with the political problems of Europe and not with the Pacific war." [88] The principal work of the Conference had been particularly concerned with the problems of the Far East and he had solved those problems by giving the answers that had been suggested by Stalin.

Roosevelt had disliked the idea of having to give any accounting to Congress. Unlike President Wilson, he had not summoned any Peace Congress to find a path to a just and durable peace. He remembered clearly what had happened to the Treaty of Versailles when it came before a hostile Senate. There would be no Senate rejection of any treaty he made. Instead, he chose the system of making the peace through an executive agreement that did not have to be passed upon by the Senate. For the first time in American history an important war had been brought to a close, not by a treaty, but by an agreement made by the President with the rulers of a few countries that had been closely associated with the United States in the conduct of hostilities against the Axis Powers.

It seems evident that the President had a definite contempt for the democratic process as far as foreign relations was concerned. He grew

[86] Samuel I. Rosenman, *Working with Roosevelt* (New York: Harper and Brothers, 1952), p. 522.

[87] Testimony of Major-General Patrick J. Hurley, June 20, 1951, *Military Situation in the Far East*, Part 4, p. 2837.

[88] *Congressional Record*, Vol. 91, Part 2, pp. 1619-1622 (March 1, 1945).

more autocratic each year he remained in the White House. Only he could bend the bow of circumstance that the statesmen of the world in 1945 had placed before them. His strong desire for secret conferences was expressed on May 5, 1943, in a letter he wrote to Marshal Stalin:

> I am sending this personal note to you by the hand of my old friend, Joseph E. Davies. . . . I want to get away from the difficulties of large staff conferences or the red tape of diplomatic conversations. . . . The simplest and most practical method that I can think of would be an informal and completely simple visit for a few days between you and me.[89]

He was never able to arrange this "completely simple visit" with Stalin. At Yalta he had a typical large staff conference and he resented the constant flow of advice that poured into his reluctant ears. It was a tragedy that General Marshall was one of his closest advisers. The General seemed to have a penchant for guessing wrong on issues involving Communist ambitions. We have already referred to the dubious roles of Alger Hiss and "Chip" Bohlen at Yalta.

There is little doubt that Yalta marked the greatest diplomatic defeat in American history. With a naval base at Port Arthur, commercial preponderance in Dairen, and control over the South Manchuria railway, Soviet Russia could dominate North China. Control over the Kurile Islands took away from Japan her great fishing grounds and made her dependent upon Russian favors.[90]

No discussion of Yalta by those who were present at that conference, thus far, explains Roosevelt's generosity to Stalin, why he violated his own principles of the Atlantic Charter by transferring territory from one country to another without the consent of the deprived country, or why he reneged on his promises to Chiang Kai-shek at Cairo. It must be remembered he had promised the Generalissimo all the territory Japan had taken since 1914. Roosevelt gave to Stalin at Yalta effective control of the same territory over which the United States had gone to war with Japan, and by doing so set the stage for the Communist conquest of China, and it was a prelude to the war in Korea.

Churchill did not take part in the Far Eastern discussions. His memoirs for late 1944 show his curt dismissal of the importance of China. "This American obsession," he wrote, "that China is one of the world's four great powers is an absolute farce." [91] At Yalta Churchill was content to let Roosevelt and Stalin play out the farce themselves. He takes

---

[89] Franklin Delano Roosevelt, *F.D.R., His Personal Letters*, 1928-1945. Edited by Elliott Roosevelt, II, p. 1422.

[90] When the Senate ratified the Japanese Peace Treaty on March 20, 1952, special reference was made to the Yalta agreements. The Senate made it clear that it considered nothing in the ratification of the treaty implied recognition of the provisions of the Yalta agreements.

[91] Churchill, *Triumph and Tragedy*, p. 701.

pains to point out in *Triumph and Tragedy* that Roosevelt, not he, was the architect of the China sellout; "I must make it clear that, although on behalf of Great Britain I joined in the agreement, neither I nor Eden took any part in making it. It was regarded as an American affair. . . . We were not consulted but only asked to approve." [92] According to Robert Sherwood, President Roosevelt consented to the agreement because he was "tired out and anxious to end the negotiations relative to Russia's entry into war with Japan." [93]

T.F. Tsiang, chairman of the Chinese delegation to the United Nations, concluded sadly, "we must pronounce the Yalta Agreement a great mistake, a disastrous mistake." [94]

The postwar successes of Russia are not due to Soviet strength but to the weakness of American foreign policy. On January 30, 1949, shortly after the fall of the Chinese mainland, Representative John F. Kennedy commented on Yalta: "At the Yalta Conference in 1945 a sick Roosevelt, with the advice of General Marshall and other Chiefs of Staff, gave the Kurile Islands as well as the control of various strategic Chinese ports, such as Port Arthur and Dairen, to the Soviet Union." Then, in his speech at Salem, Massachusetts, Representative Kennedy continued, quoting from former Ambassador Bullitt's 1948 *Life* magazine article:

Whatever share of the responsibility was Roosevelt's and whatever share was Marshall's the vital interest of the United States in the independent integrity of China was sacrificed, and the foundation was laid for the present tragic situation in the Far East.[95]

Today President Kennedy, in Europe as well as in Asia, finds Roosevelt's Yalta mistakes still great handicaps.

---

[92] *Ibid.*, p. 390. James Byrnes said: "Later I was to learn that shortly after my departure Stalin requested the President to stay another day because he wished to discuss a very important matter with him. There is no doubt about the importance of the subject discussed, for it concerned Soviet requests for a warm water outlet on the China coast. These agreements were kept secret." Byrnes, *All in One Lifetime*, p. 266.

[93] Sherwood, *Roosevelt and Hopkins,* p. 854, 867.

[94] Werner Levi, *Modern China's Foreign Policy* (Minneapolis: University of Minnesota Press, 1953), p. 243.

[95] *Congressional Record*, February 21, 1949, p. A993.

CHAPTER V

THE UNNEEDED ALLY

In 1941, when Japan struck at Pearl Harbor, her economic potential was approximately ten per cent of that of the United States. The acreage of her arable land was no more than three per cent, yet it had to support a population more than half as large. Japan depended on Manchuria and Korea for most of her raw materials and large supplies of grain, which had to cross the Sea of Japan and the Yellow Sea. Because of this, the center of her economic existence was Japan's merchant navy, without which she could not survive.

We had a decisive superiority over Japan. In the battle of Midway the Japanese Navy lost the cream of its air force, and after that the change of tide in the war situation set in. Air, sea, and ground engagements preceding the bombardment of her home islands, had sealed Japan's doom. Our shipping losses could be replaced much more rapidly than could those of the Japanese. From the latter part of 1942, American submarines threatened the security of Japan's entire system of sea communications. The prime targets were tankers from the Indies: by 1944 only five per cent of the petroleum from Sumatra and Borneo reached Japan. Imports of bauxite and coal had fallen by ninety and ninety two per cent, respectively, before the war ended.[1]

Early in 1944, Rear Admiral Takagi, of the Japanese Naval General Staff, after he had analyzed the events of the war, came to the conclusion that Japan could not win it and should therefore seek a compromise peace.[2] But it was not until the loss of Saipan that the Japanese leaders definitely realized they faced defeat. Japan's inner defense line had been breached and the enemy had reached within striking distance of the Japanese homeland. Tojo's failure to prevent this was evidence

---

[1] Alfred Crofts and Percy Buchanan, *A History of the Far East* (New York: Longmans, Green and Co., Inc., 1958), p. 437.

[2] United States Navy, United States Strategic Bombing Survey, Naval Analysis Division, *Japan's Struggle to End the War* (Washington: Government Printing Office, 1946), p. 3.

of the bankruptcy of his policy; consequently the Diet and even his own Cabinet turned against him.[3] On July 18, 1944, he reluctantly resigned.

On July 29, 1944, President Roosevelt and General Douglas MacArthur ended a four-day visit in Honolulu. Present were Admirals Chester W. Nimitz, William Halsey, Jr., and William Leahy. The purpose of this conference was to discuss the Pacific war and its relationship to the entire picture. General MacArthur took the position that invasion of the Philippines would split the Japanese empire, that our naval activities would leave the Japanese homeland without an adequate supply of rice which is the essential food of the Japanese people. Conversely, it would deprive their forces of support from the homeland. Thus, the Japanese would be forced to surrender. In other words, an invasion of Japanese home islands by ground forces would not be necessary.[4]

A plan was evolved under Secretary of the Navy Forrestal and laid before Roosevelt early in 1945 to bring Japan to her knees without the use of the atom bomb and without Soviet intervention.[5] Admiral Ellis Zacharias, a Naval Intelligence Officer, writes that on December 16, 1944, he had outlined a plan to conduct an intensive campaign of psychological warfare against the enemy "on the basis of the information we had on the faltering Japanese will to fight." Secretary Forrestal accepted the plan and "did everything in his power to have our commitments to Russia canceled and to persuade our leaders to release Stalin from his 'obligation' to join us in the Pacific war." But the Joint Chiefs of Staff after Roosevelt's death urged President Truman to sustain the Yalta decisions, despite spirited opposition by Admiral King. After several recommendations as to how to negotiate had been considered, surrender terms to the Japanese were rejected by officials in Washington.

Admiral Zacharias then decided to "offer the Japanese an opportunity to surrender on the terms of the Atlantic Charter." This stirred up a hornet's nest in Washington. The Department of State told newsmen that Admiral Zacharias had "no authority to speak for the U.S.

---

3 Toshikazu Kase, *Journey to the "Missouri"* (New Haven: Yale University Press, 1950), pp. 73-80.

4 *Survey of International Affairs, 1939-1946: America, Britain and Russia. Their Co-operation and Conflict, 1941-1946*, pp. 400-401. General MacArthur stated before a Senate Committee in 1951: ". . . they had at least three million of as fine ground troops as I have ever known, that laid down their arms because they didn't have the materials to fight with. *Military Situation in the Far East, Hearings*, Part 1, p. 58. Admiral Leahy wrote that the invasion plans for Japan "presumed that defeat of the enemy's armed forces in the Japanese homeland would be prerequisite to the unconditional surrender of the enemy, a premise with which I did not agree." Leahy, *I Was There*, p. 414.

5 Hilary Grey, "In Memoriam: James V. Forrestal, American Patriot," *American Mercury* (June 1959), pp. 12-13.

Government." Officials in Tokyo announced an "open invitation to begin surrender negotiations on the terms we had proposed." Forrestal supported the plan and told Arthur Krock of the *New York Times* that Admiral Zacharias had "the authority to make the Statement" he did in the broadcast. Forrestal then flew to Potsdam to try to sell the American officials on the idea but, unfortunately, it was canceled out by the Potsdam Declaration. Admiral Zacharias concludes:

> The Potsdam Declaration, in short, wrecked everything we had been working for to prevent further bloodshed and insure our postwar strategic position. Just when the Japanese were ready to capitulate, we went ahead and introduced to the world the most devastating weapon it had ever seen and, in effect, gave the go-ahead to Russia to swarm over Eastern Asia. . . . I contend that the A-bombing of Japan is now known to have been a mistake. . . . It was wrong on strategic grounds. And it was wrong on humanitarian grounds. . . .[6]

The loss of the Marianas had been a disturbing factor in Japanese Pacific strategy. After that many Tokyo officials felt the war was hopeless. Prince Higashuni, Commander-in-Chief of Home Defense Headquarters, admitted defeat: "The war was lost," he said, "when we heard the B-29's were coming out. . . . We had nothing in Japan we could use against such a weapon. From the point of view of the Home Defense Command, we felt the war was lost and said so." [7]

The peace faction was becoming bolder in its attempts to bring the war to an end. Prince Takamatsu, the younger brother of the Emperor told Shigemitsu that he "felt it highly advisable to seek the termination of hostilities without delay, provided in the process the imperial house was left intact." Unfortunately, U. S. officials never gave this assurance. As a result the conflict continued—to the benefit of the Soviet Union. A negotiated peace might have relieved the United States from facing Communist troops later in Manchuria and Korea. "Politically the fall of Saipan," said Toshikazu Kase, "opened an avenue for peace, however dim and distant, for it facilitated the ousting of Tojo from the premiership; as the author of the war he would never have consented to abandon the struggle." [8]

---

6 Admiral Ellis M. Zacharias, "How We Bungled the Japanese Surrender," *Look*, (May 23, 1950) , pp. 13-21; see also memorandum from Acting Secretary of State (Grew) to Secretary of State (Byrnes), July 22, 1945, U.S. Department of State, *Foreign Relations of the United States: The Conference of Berlin, 1945* (The Potsdam Conference) (Washington: Government Printing Office, 1960), Vol. II, p. 1273. Hereafter cited as *Potsdam Papers*.

7 Michael Armine, *The Great Decision* (New York: G. P. Putman's Sons, 1949), p. 78. When questioned concerning the necessity for a land invasion of Japan scheduled for November 1, 1945, Major General Emmett O'Donnell, Jr. said: ". . . once we were in the Marianas (Saipan, July 1944) we were convinced it was over; because they were taking the most terrible pounding . . . I thought—we all thought—I thought personally in a couple of weeks it would be all over." *Military Situation in the Far East, Hearings*, Part 4, p. 3111.

8 Kase, *Journey to the "Missouri,"* p. 78.

One of the most decisive engagements in the Pacific war, the battle in Leyte Gulf in October, 1944, resulted in the destruction of the Japanese Navy. Except for the challenge of land-based aircraft, the United States had won undisputed command of the sea.[9] When Admiral Mitsumasa Yoni, Navy Minister of the Koiso Cabinet, was questioned after the war, he admitted that the defeat of Leyte "was tantamount to loss of the Philippines." As for the larger significance of the battle, he said, "I felt that that was the end." [10]

This "larger significance" was missed by President Roosevelt and his advisors, who failed to appreciate the political implications of their overwhelming victory. There is no question that the Japanese Navy virtually ceased to exist and that Japan could not win the war. Thus, the American problem was predominantly political—that is, how Japan's defeat could be brought about at the highest profit to the United States.

It was a far simpler problem than the one that faced President Roosevelt in Europe. There he had to consider his allies, but the war with Japan was ninety-five per cent an American war, and to win it at the highest profit it was essential that the United States should win it single-handed. Had this been understood, it would have been appreciated that, as Russia was the only power who could complicate the issue, it was highly desirable for the United States to bring the war with Japan to an end before or immediately after Germany collapsed—that is, while Russia was still deeply involved in Europe. This was quite feasible, provided the United States had taken advantage of the serious internal situation in Japan resulting from U.S. naval victories.

Loss of shipping was the dominant factor in Japan's economic decline; it was the shortage of coal, oil, food, and other raw materials that struck the deadliest blow at her economy. Loss of shipping limited the import of iron ore, and shortage of steel limited the building of ships; labor efficiency declined for lack of food, and food for want of ships. Japan was confronted with serious economic problems which became increasingly worse.[11]

The Emperor realized the critical situation. Evidence in the Tokyo War Criminal Trials reveal that he acted as a peace-maker at the various top-level conferences. He realized that a negotiated peace would at least save his country from total destruction. According to Admiral Zacharias, the Office of Strategic Services in Rome reported during the winter of 1944 that the Japanese Emperor had asked the Pope to act as mediator for peace. But "the State Department discouraged it on the

---

9 Andrieu d'Albas, *Death of a Navy: Japanese Naval Action in World War II* (New York: The Devin-Adair Company, 1957), p. 333.

10 James A. Field, Jr., *The Japanese at Leyte Gulf* (Princeton University Press, 1947), pp. 230-231.

11 *Japan's Struggle to End the War*, pp. 16-19.

ground that American public opinion might never approve of a peace negotiated with the aid of the Roman Catholic Church." [12]

Why then did the United States enlist the aid of the Soviet Union in the war in the Pacific? Roosevelt's intimates give two reasons. Admiral Leahy, who was Roosevelt's personal Chief of Staff, says that the President was actuated by the belief that "Soviet participation in the Far East Operation would insure Russia's sincere co-operation in his dream of a united, peaceful world." [13] On the other hand, his Secretary of State, Stettinius, reports that immense pressure was put on the President by our military leaders to bring Russia into the Far Eastern War. He adds that the American Chiefs of Staff had warned Roosevelt that "without Russia it might cost the United States a million casualties to conquer Japan" and that the Pacific War might not end until 1947.[14]

The chief advocate of this view was General Marshall, who submitted a memorandum to the President on January 23, 1945:

Russia's entry at as early a date as possible consistent with her ability to engage in offensive operations is necessary to provide maximum assistance to our Pacific operations. The U.S. will provide maximum support possible without our main effort against Japan.

The objective of Russia's military effort against Japan in the Far East should be the defeat of the Japanese forces in Manchuria, air operations against Japan proper in collaboration with U.S. air forces based in Eastern Siberia, and maximum interference with Japanese sea traffic between Japan and the mainland of Asia.[15]

This was an unrealistic view of the military situation. By late 1944 it should have been apparent to American military officials through intelligence that what remained of the Kwantung Army was largely composed of green conscripts and second-rate troops, with virtually no air support and incapable of a prolonged campaign; it had been bled white to provide reinforcements for other fronts. Lieutenant General Ija Kawabe, commander of the Japanese Air Force in Manchuria from

[12] Dorothy Thompson in the *Evening Star* (Washington D.C.) April 20, 1955.
[13] Leahy, *I Was There*, p. 2.
[14] Stettinius, Jr., *Roosevelt and the Russians*, p. 304. Admiral Leahy's interpretation was probably the correct one. He was far more astute in foreign affairs than Secretary Stettinius, and he was also much closer to Roosevelt. Admiral Leahy had read the Japanese surrender offer, transmitted to Roosevelt, before Yalta, by General MacArthur. Although the subject is somewhat beyond the scope of this volume, the primary purpose and obsession of the architects of Yalta aimed at the building of an international "One World" organization. In view of the clear actualities of the military situation, "military necessity" must have been the excuse rather than the reason for frantic urgings that the Soviet Union be brought into the Pacific war. All legitimate American interests, as well as those of many other countries, were prostituted to an incredible proposition that Stalin be made one of the chief helmsmen of a "One World" organization for "peace."
[15] General Marshall to President Roosevelt, January 23, 1945, *Yalta Documents*, p. 396.

May, 1943 to August, 1944, told interrogators of the Strategic Bombing
Survey that "in July or August of 1943 the bulk of [his] planes were
moved out of Manchuria. . . . For the last six months I was there, anyhow, the actual planes which would be considered operational were nil,
practically none." [16] General William J. Donovan's Office of Strategic
Services was reporting from China that the Kwantung Army had been
dissipated and depleted. In any case, said the OSS., what was left could
not be moved to Japanese home islands because of the lack of shipping.
Nor could the Japanese troops in China be moved.[17]

In September, 1944, Prince Konoye headed a group which was prepared to surrender the conquered territories and possibly Manchuria, in
an effort to end the war. The Swedish Minister to Japan, Mr. Widar
Bagge, reported everything to Stockholm, but the Allied demand for unconditional surrender was "one of the greatest obstacles to peace." In
Stockholm Mr. Bagge had a "long talk" with American Ambassador
Herschel V. Johnson, and gave him "a comprehensive account of the
whole peace problem." [18]

Admiral Ellis Zacharias has written that the American Joint Chiefs of
Staff persuaded the President to bring the Soviet Union into the war
against Japan on a wholly inaccurate and misleading intelligence report.
He asserts that at least two other—accurate—intelligence reports were
available, one prepared in the War Department and one prepared by
himself, but that both had been pigeonholed somewhere in the Pentagon.[19] Neither of them reached the Joint Chiefs of Staff, who acted
on the basis of an intelligence document which overestimated enemy
strength. No one has yet explained how these strange occurrences came
to pass.

Other important officers in the Navy were strongly opposed to this
movement to get Russia into the Pacific war as quickly as possible. They
continued to believe that Japan could be strangled into submission by
blockade. In October, 1944, the Japanese Navy had suffered such a crushing defeat that, well before Yalta, Admiral Leahy considered that the
war against Japan "had progressed to the point where her defeat was

16 The United States Strategic Bombing Survey, *Interrogations of Japanese Officials*,
p. 425.

17 McCarthy, *America's Retreat from Victory*, p. 60. General Yukio Kasahara, Chief
of Staff of the Kwantung Army between August 1942 and April 1945 said that by the
end of 1944 there were no highly trained divisions left, few tanks and aircraft, and
limited stocks of munitions and fuel. *Far Eastern Military Tribunal, Record*, p. 23201.

18 Butow, *Japan's Decision to Surrender*, pp. 40-44; 56, fn. 80.

19 Admiral Ellis Zacharias, "The Inside Story of Yalta," *United Nations World*
(January 1949), p. 16. Admiral Zacharias has explained in terms of poor intelligence
furnished to Roosevelt by the Chiefs of Staff, grossly exaggerating Japan's Army
strength at 5,000,000 effectives instead of 2,000,000 men of all kinds, *Ibid.*, pp. 12-16.
As late as July 1945, scarcely a month before V-J Day, Stimson believed that the U.S.
would need 5,000,000 men to defeat Japan in her own islands, Stimson and McBundy,
op. cit., pp. 618-619. This was after the Japanese Navy had been all but destroyed.

only a matter of time and attrition. Therefore, we did not need Stalin's help to defeat our enemy in the Pacific. The Army did not agree with me. . . . " [20] This was also the opinion of General Arnold, the Chief of Air Staff, whose Super-Fortresses were already bombing Japan from island airfields. There was no longer any great need for air bases in the Maritime Provinces of the Soviet Union, and, after the unhappy experiment of a "shuttle-bombing" in Europe, Arnold did not set much store by any facilities he might be granted in Asia.[21] Nevertheless, the advice of Marshall prevailed.

Admiral King, in command of the United States Naval forces in the Far East, was convinced that Japan would be defeated without any invasion of the home islands. He declared: "regardless of the desirability of the Russians entering the war they were not indispensable and he did not think we should go so far as to beg them to come in." He had no doubt "we could handle it alone." [22] But, upon Marshall's insistence, the Joint Chiefs of Staff went ahead and prepared plans for a landing. Neither King nor Leahy liked the idea; however, as "unanimous decisions were necessary in the Joint Chiefs meetings," they reluctantly acquiesced, feeling that in the end sea power would accomplish the defeat of Japan. This proved to be true.[23] The Joint Chiefs of Staff did not truly agree unanimously on the invasion of Japan, although it has been repeatedly stated that they did. In the summer of 1944, Admiral Chester W. Nimitz expressed the same opinion as Leahy and King that Japan could be strangled into submission by blockade.[24]

There were dissenters among Army officials also as to whether it was advisable to have Russia enter the war in the Far East. A group of veteran intelligence officers, most of them regular Army colonels, prepared a document known as the Colonels' Report before our leaders went to Yalta. From about September, 1944, and increasingly as the months went by, the Colonels felt that Japan was beaten and that the only practical course was to try to arrange an "unconditional surrender" or some other diplomatic means to take Japan out of the war. If they had been consulted by the "high level" leaders before Yalta, the following advice would surely have been given:

The entry of Soviet Russia into the Asiatic war would be a political event of world-shaking importance, the ill effect of which would be felt for decades to come. Its military significance at this stage of the war would be relatively unimportant. Many military experts believe that the United States and Great Britain

---

[20] Leahy, *I Was There*, p. 293.

[21] Arnold, *Global Mission*, pp. 470-471; 494-495; 540.

[22] Minutes of meeting held at the White House, June 18, 1945 at 3:30 P.M. *Potsdam Papers*, I, p. 910.

[23] King and Whitehill, *Fleet Admiral King: A Naval Record*, p. 598.

[24] New York *Times*, September 19, 1944, p. 14.

without further help possess the power to force unconditional surrender upon Japan, or to occupy the islands and mainland possessions. It may be expected that Soviet Russia will enter the Asiatic war, but at her own good time and probably only when the hard-fighting stage is over. The entry of Soviet Russia into the Asiatic war at so late a moment would shorten hostilities but little, and effect only a slight saving of American lives. . . . Strong enough to crush Japan ourselves, the United States should make no political or economic concession to Soviet Russia to bring about or prevent an action which she is fully determined to take anyway. . . . It should be reiterated that the United States Army is by no means united in believing it wise to encourage the Soviet Union into the Asiatic war. . . .[25]

Major General Charles A. Willoughby has gone on record that MacArthur's staff held before Yalta that there was not the slightest reason for permitting Russia to sneak into the war at the last moment. "Without Russia, even without the atom bomb, the Japanese were finished," declared Willoughby, and "it was only a matter of how soon they would quit." [26] General MacArthur was not consulted in advance of the Yalta Conference on the question of whether Russia should be offered inducements to enter the war against Japan: "Had my views been requested . . . " he said, "I would most emphatically have recommended against bringing the Soviet into the Pacific War at that late date. To have made vital concessions for such a purpose would have seemed to me fantastic." [27] General Willoughby said that MacArthur's staff could not explain or understand on what the Joint Chiefs of Staff based their estimate of the length of the Japanese war in their report to Roosevelt and Churchill. General MacArthur has commented: "I had urged Russian intervention in 1941 to draw the Japanese from their southward march and to keep them pinned down in Siberia. By 1945 such intervention had become superfluous." [28]

To Admirals King, Leahy, Nimitz, and naval officers in general, it had always seemed that the defeat of Japan "could be accomplished by sea and air power alone, without the necessity of actual invasion of the Japanese home islands by ground troops." [29]

The failure to appreciate fully the strategical position of Japan colored the military thinking at Yalta and helped to lead to indefensible political arrangements. "Certainly," as the *Washington Post* on September 9, 1948 has commented, "the Chiefs of Staff made a blunder to ad-

[25] *Military Situation in the Far East, Hearings*, Part 4, pp. 2916-2918. The Report also recommended that "General MacArthur should be summoned to Washington immediately. The President should consider the all-important matter of Soviet Russia's entry into the Asiatic war with General MacArthur eye to eye. All other political and military personages should be excluded from the conference."

[26] *Congressional Record*, March 22, 1955, p. 3374.

[27] *U.S. News and World Report* (October 28, 1955) , p. 32.

[28] Major General Charles A. Willoughby, *MacArthur: 1949-1951* (New York: McGraw-Hill Book Co., 1954), p. 285.

[29] King and Whitehill, *Fleet Admiral King*, p. 598.

vise Roosevelt and Churchill at Yalta that Japan would last eighteen months after V-E Day. Our military men underrated Japan at the beginning of the war, then overrated it, and refused to see the patent fact, obvious to the Navy, that Japan was through even while the brass hats were meeting at Yalta." [30]

Hanson Baldwin, a military expert, writing after the event, said: "At the time of Yalta, Japan was already beaten—not by the atomic bomb which had not yet been perfected, not by conventional bombing then just starting, but by attrition and blockade." [31] Further evidence in this regard was disclosed by the United States Strategic Bombing Survey after carrying out a series of interrogations of Japanese Officials immediately following the war. The conclusion was that "by January, 1945, Japan was in fact a defeated nation." [32]

Those who defend the Yalta Agreement have frequently stated that the Soviet Union was capable of "taking what it wanted with or without the Yalta Agreement." [33]

According to Chester Wilmot, the real issue at Yalta was:

What did the Soviet Union receive at Yalta which she could not have taken without flagrantly violating the fundamental principles of the Atlantic Charter and the United Nations to which she had subscribed? The real issue for the world and for the future was not what Stalin would or could have taken but what he was given the right to take. This agreement provided Stalin with a moral cloak for his aggressive designs in Asia, and, more important, with almost a legal title enforceable at the Peace Conference to the territories and privileges which he demanded.[34]

If the Soviet Union had decided to take what it wanted with or without the Yalta Agreement, our rapidly growing military power was capable of meeting any challenge provided by Russia in the Far East. The argument is further belied by the Soviet Union's extreme weakness in the Far East.

At the Yalta Conference, the Soviet Union agreed to enter the war against Japan three months after the defeat of Germany. Marshal Stalin was insistent, however, that Russia would have to be supplied and stockpiled with American material before any action was taken against the Japanese. All in all, Stalin said, the Russians would need more than

---

[30] *Washington Post*, September 9, 1948.

[31] Baldwin, *Great Mistakes of the War*, p. 79.

[32] United States Strategic Bombing Survey, *The Campaigns of the Pacific War*, (Washington: Government Printing Office, 1947), pp. 289-290.

[33] John L. Snell, *The Meaning of Yalta: Big Three Diplomacy and the New Balance of Power* (Baton Rouge: Louisiana State University, 1956), pp. 163-164; 202-203. This is also the argument of Secretary Acheson when he said: "the Soviet Union . . . could in any case have seized all the territory in question and considerably more regardless of what our attitude might have been." *Military Situation in the Far East, Hearings,* Part 4, p. 2840.

[34] Wilmot, *The Struggle for Europe,* p. 654.

1,000,000 tons of cargo, and they must be delivered by June 30, 1945, the deliveries to be in addition to those already being made under the Fourth Lend-Lease Protocol.

The new request created serious problems for the logistic as well as the strategic planners. Vice Admiral Oscar C. Badger testified at the MacArthur Hearings in 1951 that as far back as Teheran, Allied agencies, after careful study of their evidence and statistics, concluded that Russia was "so weak logistically in the Far East" as to be almost completely dependent for supplies coming from American ports. He also pointed out the important fact that once Russia declared war on Japan, Russian ships would no longer be free from Japanese attack, so that "the logistic staff recommended that the USSR be advised not to enter the war against Japan." In other words, Soviet weakness in the Far East was definitely recognized as a fact, and Russia's participation in the war against Japan at that time was undesirable.[35]

In spite of this important advice, by the time of the Potsdam Conference, the United States officials went ahead and supplied Russia with enough equipment to make her a major power in the Pacific, a gesture made at the expense of our own fighting forces in that part of the globe. General MacArthur protested bitterly when he received a directive from Washington upsetting at a critical time his timetable for the Philippines campaign. Major General Courtney Whitney tells the whole story, " . . . one hundred of his transport ships were to be withdrawn immediately," he said, "to be used to carry munitions and supplies across the North Pacific to the Soviet forces in Vladivostok. . . . Later, of course, they were the basis of Soviet military support of North Korea and Red China." [36]

During the period between the Yalta Conference in February, 1945, and the time when Soviet Russia entered the war against Japan in August, 1945, a number of important incidents indicated that Japan was definitely ready to surrender.[37] However, Washington officials failed to take advantage of them as a result of a conflict in the Administration regarding a surrender policy for Japan.

In March, 1945, General George C. Kenney arrived in Washington on a mission for General MacArthur. In a long talk with General Marshall he insisted that the war in the Pacific was over and that "there was no

35 Testimony of Admiral Oscar Charles Badger, June 19, 1951, *Military Situation in the Far East, Hearings,* Part 4, pp. 2730-31.

36 Major General Courtney Whitney, *MacArthur: His Rendezvous with History* (New York: Alfred A. Knopf Publishers, 1956), p. 186.

37 Shignenori Togo, former Foreign Minister, stated that Japan "wanted to make peace with the United States after the destructive March 10-11 air raids—Japan was pretty well devastated and in no position to carry on successful war." Chicago *Tribune,* October 22, 1955.

longer a necessity of holding back until . . . the Russians came in."
Marshall said he did not agree with this view and insisted Japan still
had a strong army and was full of fight. Likewise, Marshall "made it
clear that he had little faith in the Japanese overtures for peace." [38] Not
satisfied with this answer, General Kenney went directly to the White
House and told the same story of the rapid disintegration of Japan's
power, but Roosevelt did not seem to be much interested.

In March, Colonel Dana Johnson, Army Chief of psychological warfare in the Pacific, flew to Washington to confide to the highest circles
his conviction, based on exchanges with ranking prisoners of war, that
the Japanese Army was ready to quit if only the Emperor was spared.[39]
The Japanese believed, however, that "unconditional surrender" would
be equivalent of national extinction. The ideas of foreign occupation of
the Japanese homeland, foreign custody of the person of the Emperor,
and the loss of prestige entailed by the acceptance of "unconditional
surrender" were most revolting to the Japanese. The Emperor was the
godhead of the armed forces, and in the eyes of the people a divinity;
yet there was one thing he could not do, and that was to order his
people to surrender unconditionally and thereby acquiesce in his becoming a war criminal, to be placed on trial or shot at sight. Interrogations
of Japanese prisoners of high rank revealed "that the Japanese were on
the point of giving up but held back by a fear that the imperial institution would be abolished and the emperor himself punished as a war
criminal." [40]

The day before Christmas, 1944 (two months before the Yalta Conference), U.S. intelligence authorities in Washington had received a report from a confidential agent in Japan that a peace party was emerging and that the Koiso cabinet would soon be succeeded by a cabinet
headed by Admiral Baron Suzuki who would initiate surrender proceedings.[41] The Koiso cabinet was succeeded by a new government
headed by Suzuki in early April, 1945. This drastic move was a signal
to the world that the Emperor was in the saddle and that Japan might
be prepared to move towards peace talks.[42] However, to officials in

---

[38] George C. Kenney, *General Kenney Reports* (New York: Duell, Sloan and Pearce,
1949), p. 530. In the spring of 1945 Shigemitsu asked the Swedish Minister Bagge to
explore the chances of a negotiated peace when he returned home. Affidavit of Bagge,
Far Eastern Military Tribunal, Record, pp. 34561-62. Mamoru Shigemitsu, *Japan and
Her Destiny: My Struggle for Peace* (New York: E. P. Dutton and Company Inc.,
1958), p. 339.

[39] Testimony of Eugene Dooman, September 14, 1951, *Institute of Pacific Relations,
Hearings*, Part 3, p. 727-728.

[40] Current, *Secretary Stimson: A Study in Statecraft*, p. 224.

[41] Ellis M. Zacharias, "The Bomb Was Not Needed." *United Nations World* (August
1949). See also Wesley R. Fishel "A Japanese Peace Maneuver in 1944." *The Far
Eastern Quarterly*, VIII (1949), pp. 387-97.

[42] Kase, *Journey to the "Missouri"*, pp. 108-114.

Washington who had the power to take action, the change of administration in Japan apparently carried no real meaning.

Admiral Suzuki was "given to understand" from the Emperor to arrange an end to the war.[43] The stumbling block was the "unconditional
surrender" policy announced by Roosevelt at Casablanca in 1943. On
April 24, 1945, the Joint Chiefs again reviewed the war in the Pacific
and said that the "concept of 'unconditional surrender' is foreign to the
Japanese nature" and that "unless a definition of unconditional surrender can be given which is acceptable to the Japanese, there is no alternative to annihilation and no prospect that the threat of absolute defeat
will bring about capitulation." [44] Annihilation was, of course, the desire
of Soviet Russia.

There is no doubt that the unconditional surrender formula ensured
the continued dominance of the Army in Japan, even after the fall of
Tojo and of Koiso. Despite Allied statements that the destruction of
Japan was not intended, it was not clear, until the Potsdam Declaration and the subsequent exchanges of notes between Japan and the
Allies, just what was intended. Until then, the advocates of peace in
Japan could always be met with the reply that it was useless to talk of
peace when the Allies insisted that Japan must first lay down her arms
and put herself at their mercy. As Cordell Hull, who was at heart opposed to the formula, put it, "Japan surrendered . . . when she perceived that the principle of unconditional surrender could be applied
conditionally." [45]

In the middle of May, Henry Luce, *Time-Life* publisher, reported to
Acting Secretary Joseph C. Grew, that he was "very much aroused" over
his government's failure to procure the surrender of an enemy already
defeated. That failure, Luce advised Grew, was "doing great damage to
the morale of the American forces" who were "anticipating . . . the
losses that would have to be paid" in full-scale invasion of the Japanese
homeland.[46] Impressed with this testimony, Secretary Grew asked Eugene Dooman, a Far Eastern expert, to prepare a draft of peace proposals to the Japanese. On May 28, 1945, a draft was prepared guaranteeing the Japanese people a government of their own choice, including,
if they so elected, "a constitutional monarchy." [47]

Since V-E Day, Secretary Grew had believed that, in face of the heavy
air assault, the Japanese Government could be persuaded to surrender
by a declaration that our war aims did not envisage destruction of the

---

43 Butow, *Japan's Decision to Surrender*. p. 67.

44 *The Entry of the Soviet Union Into War Against Japan: Military Plans, 1941-1945,*
p. 63.

45 Hull, *Memoirs*, II, p. 1582.

46 *Institute of Pacific Relations, Hearings*, Part 3, p. 728.

47 *Ibid.*

Japanese nation or the Emperor's office.[48] Grew knew the depth of feeling in Japan, and he also knew the facts about the military clique that was in control in Japan. He laid the proposal before the State Department policy board, consisting of the assistant secretaries, where it met its first obstacle. The clause respecting the Emperor provoked "a violent reaction" from Assistant Secretaries Dean Acheson and Archibald MacLeish. Assuming full responsibilities, Grew went to the White House and submitted the paper to President Truman in the presence of Judge Samuel I. Rosenman. The President quickly gave his approval, subject only to the endorsement of the military.[49]

Also on May 28, Harry Hopkins, in Moscow, sent an important memorandum concerning peace with Japan. It read: "Japan is doomed and the Japanese know it. Peace feelers are being put out by certain elements in Japan and we should therefore consider together our joint attitude and act in concert about the surrender of Japan. Stalin expressed the fear that the Japanese will try to split the Allies." [50] Stalin did not want the Japanese to surrender before Russia had an opportunity to enter the war. He further suggested to Hopkins that the Allies outwit the Japanese by obtaining a surrender without using the words 'unconditional surrender' but give them the works once we got into Japan.[51]

On May 29, the President called a special meeting at the Pentagon. Those present were Secretary Grew, James Forrestal, John McCloy, Elmer Davis, Eugene Dooman, and joint staff officers headed by General Marshall. All those present agreed that an announcement should be made to the Japanese explaining our terms for surrender, providing that there was a fair chance it would bring the war to an end. However, General Marshall expressed the opinion that the paper was "premature" and the project was pigeonholed.[52]

It had been Marshall's desire since the famous Marshall memorandum at Quebec in August, 1943, to have the Soviet Union enter the war against Japan. The memoirs of the late Secretary Stettinius and Major John R. Deane make it explicit that Marshall alone and operating through Roosevelt sent Averell Harriman and Deane to Moscow in the fall of 1943 to bribe Stalin into the Asiatic war. A study of the sources leaves little doubt that Marshall, even more than Roosevelt, fathered the strange Yalta Agreement.

Shortly before the Potsdam Conference convened, there were those

---

48 Grew, *Turbulent Era*, Vol. II, Chapter XXXVI.

49 *Institute of Pacific Relations, Hearings*, Part 3, pp. 728-730.

50 Sherwood, *Roosevelt and Hopkins*, p. 903; *Potsdam Papers*, I, p. 44.

51 Sherwood, *Roosevelt and Hopkins*, pp. 903-904.

52 *Institute of Pacific Relations, Hearings*, Part 3, pp. 729-730. *The Turbulent Era*, Vol. II, Chapter XXXVI.

who felt that the United States could not afford to hold out to Japan any clarifications of terms that might be construed as an American desire to end the war before the Soviet Union had the opportunity to enter it. Eugene Dooman said that in the final weeks of World War II there existed two parties in the Administration: one earnestly seeking an early peace, the other bent upon delaying the end of the war until some ulterior purpose could be achieved.[53] Dooman placed in the peace party on May 29: Undersecretary Grew, President Truman, Secretary of the Navy Forrestal, Secretary of War Henry L. Stimson, and Assistant Secretary of War John J. McCloy. In the opposing faction, as disclosed by Dooman, were Dean Acheson, then Assistant Secretary of State, his colleague Archibald MacLeish, Elmer Davis, chief of the OWI, and the Army Chief of Staff, Marshall.[54]

Forrestal, Stimson, and Grew made persistent efforts to bring about an early peace. As June wore away, a note of urgency entered their deliberations. General Marshall seemed bent upon launching a frontal attack upon the Japanese homeland without first trying to secure peace. On June 19, Forrestal noted Stimson's "vigorous" agreement with Grew's contention at a State, War and Navy Conference that terms safeguarding the Emperor's status should be worked out as a means of averting the invasion. Forrestal wrote: "Both Stimson and Grew most emphatically asserted that this move ought to be done, and that if it were effective at all, it must be done before any attack was made upon the homeland of Japan. . . ."[55]

It was on June 20 that the Japanese Emperor in Tokyo called a meeting of the Supreme War Direction Council and told them it was necessary to have a plan to end the war at once.

Again, at the State, War and Navy meeting of June 27, Secretary Stimson read the paper he was to hand to the President on July 2. It was a reworking of the Dooman draft of May 28. Forrestal reported that "it was agreed by all present that such a statement should be made before the actual invasion of the homeland of Japan was begun." [56] On July 2, Secretary Stimson submitted to the President the conclusion of his discussions with Secretary Forrestal and Undersecretary Grew.

In his memorandum he stated, "We have the following enormously favorable factors on our side . . . :

Japan has no allies. Her navy is nearly destroyed and she is vulnerable to a surface and underwater blockade which can deprive her of sufficient food and supplies for her population. She is terribly vulnerable to our concentrated air attack upon her crowded cities, industrial and food resources. She has against

---

[53] *Institute of Pacific Relations, Hearings*, Part 3, pp. 728-731.
[54] *Ibid.*
[55] *The Forrestal Diaries*, p. 69.
[56] *Ibid.*, p. 71; *Potsdam Papers*, I, pp. 887-888.

her not only the Anglo-American forces but the rising forces of China and the ominous threat of Russia.

We have inexhaustible and untouched industrial resources to bring to bear against her diminishing potential. We have great moral superiority through being the victim of her first sneak attack.[57]

Stimson felt it useful to say:

Japan is not a nation composed wholly of mad fanatics of an entirely different mentality from ours. On the contrary, she has within the past century shown herself to possess extremely intelligent people, capable in an unprecedentedly short time of adopting . . . the complicated technique of Occidental civilization. . . . Her advance . . . has been one of the most astounding feats of national progress in history. . . . I believe Japan is susceptible to reason in such a crisis to a much greater extent than is indicated by our current press and other current comment.[58]

Stimson recommended issuance of an allied proclamation spelling out the terms of surrender before Japan could be driven to fanatical despair. He thought that acceptance was likely, thereby making the costly invasion of the home islands unnecessary. He believed that inclusion of an assurance that the Japanese Government could, if desired, continue as a constitutional monarchy under the present dynasty would substantially add to chances of acceptance.[59] These conclusions were submitted to the President for consideration at Potsdam.

On July 6, Grew expressed to Secretary Forrestal his apprehension that the peace overture: ". . . would be ditched on the way over (to the Potsdam Conference) by people who accompany the President—Bohlen [Charles E. "Chip" Bohlen] among others—who reflect the view that we cannot afford to hold out any clarification of terms to Japan which could be construed as a desire to get the Japanese war over with before Russia has an opportunity to enter." [60]

What Grew voiced was a suspicion that persons high in the Administration were holding a view that Bohlen could reflect—a view that placed Russia's interest in the Far East above the need and desire of the United States for an immediate peace. So actively did Forrestal share Grew's forebodings that he took off, "uninvited, to the Potsdam Conference," no doubt to urge his own views on the surrender demands.[61]

The issue of invasion *vs.* peace came to a head at a conference of the President and his military leaders at the White House on the eve of his departure for Potsdam. The military, paced by Marshall, assured the President that the invasion was necessary to obtain Japan's submission.

---

[57] Memorandum from Secretary Stimson to the President, July 2, 1945. *Potsdam Papers*, I, pp. 889-892.
[58] *Ibid.*
[59] *Ibid.*
[60] *The Forrestal Diaries*, p. 73-74.
[61] *Ibid.*, p. 76.

McCloy spoke up for a "political" offensive first, including a hint of the atomic bomb and a promise to preserve the Emperor. Although the "military leaders were somewhat annoyed at his interference," the President "welcomed" the idea.[62] The Office of War Information, headed by Elmer Davis, backed up by a certain element in the Department of State, were advising the President that the Japanese Emperor system should be abolished. Owen Lattimore even paid a call on Truman to convince him of this view.[63]

After the Potsdam Conference began, Forrestal arrived and told Secretary Byrnes in detail of the intercepted messages from the Japanese government to their Ambassador in Moscow, indicating Japan's willingness to negotiate surrender.[64]

Many of these intercepted Japanese messages are now published in the recent *Potsdam Papers,* and it is significant they were circulated among our delegates at the conference. In one such message Ambassador Sato expressed his estimate of the situation: "Our country is literally standing at the crossroads of destiny. If we were to continue the war under the present circumstances the citizens would die with the satisfaction of having truly served their country loyally and patriotically, but the country itself would be on the verge of ruin. Although it is possible to remain loyal to the great and just aims of the Greater East Asia War to the very end, it is meaningless to insist on them to the extent of destroying the state . . . we are at the mercy of the enemy and committed to whatever the enemy should will . . . continuing the war after our fighting strength has been destroyed should be considered impossible . . . . I only pray that we may quickly terminate the present situation, in which we can no longer hope to achieve our future objective and in which we continue to resist simply from past inertia." [65]

"The true question," said Secretary Stimson, "was not whether surrender could have been achieved without the use of the [atomic] bomb, but whether a different diplomatic and military course would have led to an earlier surrender. Here the question of intelligence became significant. Interviews after the war indicated clearly that a large element of the Japanese Cabinet was ready in the spring to accept substantially the same terms as those finally agreed on. Information of this general attitude was available to the American government. . . . It is possible, in light of the final surrender, that a clearer and earlier exposition of American willingness to retain the Emperor would have produced an

62 *Ibid.,* pp. 70-71.
63 *Institute of Pacific Relations, Hearings,* Part 3, pp. 729-731.
64 Byrnes, *All in One Lifetime,* p. 297.
65 Ambassador Sato to Foreign Minister Togo, July 20, 1945, *Potsdam Papers,* II, pp. 1252-1257.

earlier ending of the war; this course was earnestly advocated by Grew and his immediate associates during May, 1945." [66]

On August 6 the atomic bomb was dropped on Hiroshima, and on August 9 Russia entered the war.[67]

Had American officials attempted more earnestly to negotiate surrender terms with the Japanese in June, 1945, the Americans and Chinese and not the Red Army would have taken the surrender of the Kwantung army. That army's huge stores, the Mukden arsenal, and the industrial facilities of Manchuria would not then have been put at the disposal of the Chinese Reds. Without those munitions, or their equivalent from Russian sources, the Reds could scarcely have conquered China. Nor, with peace in June, would there have been an excuse for the War Department to partition Korea along the thirty-eighth parallel, the historic frontier between Russian and Japanese imperialistic ambitions.

As an ally in the Pacific war, the Soviet Union was as unneeded as she should have been unwanted. As noted previously, Japanese surrender could have been arranged before the Yalta Conference, and on the same terms as those of the final peace settlement. The bloody battles of Okinawa and Iwo Jima need not have been fought. The lives of countless noncombatant Japanese civilians would have been spared. The names of Hiroshima and Nagasaki would denote important Japanese cities and nothing more.

The final months of the Pacific war were militarily unnecessary and without any reasonable purpose. Soviet agents who had penetrated our government would, of course, have sought to prolong the war. But it can hardly be supposed that some of our highest civilian and military figures were motivated by a desire to expand Communist imperialism. It is difficult to understand how anyone could believe that a world organization, supposedly dedicated to peace, law, and humanity, could be built upon a foundation of senseless continuation of war, betrayal of reason, and inhumanity. But perpetuation of war was the price we paid for a vain hope that Stalin would co-operate in peace.

As in the past, the elation of the victors found expression in a vainglorious design for peace. The design took precedence over all reasonable and humane considerations, and war—senseless, continued war against a beaten foe—became the highroad toward a world where a placated Soviet government was supposed to lie down in peace and brotherhood with the united nations of the world.

As we have sown so have we reaped.

---

[66] Henry L. Stimson and McGeorge Bundy, *On Active Service in Peace and War* (New York: Harper and Brothers, 1947), p. 628.

[67] "Interrogation of the highest Japanese officials, following V-J day, indicated that Japan would have surrendered to the air attack even if no surface invasion had been planned, if Russia had not entered the war, and if the atomic bombs had not been dropped." United States Strategic Bombing Survey, *Air Campaigns of the Pacific War,* p. 53.

CHAPTER VI

POTSDAM, THE BOMB, AND
JAPANESE SURRENDER

After the Yalta Meeting serious rifts developed between the United States and the Soviet Union. Angered by Soviet intransigence and aggressiveness in Europe, President Truman and his advisers began to restudy the question of Soviet collaboration in the Far East. Truman's own inclination, at one point, is indicated in minutes of a White House conference. "The President said . . . that he felt our agreements with the Soviet Union so far had been a one-way street and that he could not continue . . . . if the Russians did not wish to join us they could go to hell." [1]

President Truman was more than justified in his attitude. It was well known that the Soviets had already been breaking their Yalta Agreements with respect to Poland and Rumania, clamping a Soviet type system on those unhappy peoples by means of mass murder and the spread of terror. Secretary Stettinius later indicated Washington's concern when he wrote that ". . . the military leaders and I discussed the failure of the Soviet Union to abide by the Yalta Agreement on the Balkans." [2]

On June 23, 1945, Maynard B. Barnes, U.S. representative in Bulgaria, telegraphed: "Now is the moment for maximum resistance to Russian designs in all areas of interest to U.S. with respect to the maintenance of peace and opposition to aggression. If we are in the poker game of world affairs, and I assume we are, then we should play the game to the best of our ability. I believe that we have more chips than any one at the table." [3]

From Rumania came a series of recommendations by Brigadier General C. T. Schuyler, U.S. representative on the Allied Control Commis-

---

[1] Minutes by Charles E. Bohlen in *Forrestal Diaries*, April 23, 1945, p. 50.

[2] Stettinius, *Roosevelt and the Russians*, p. 97.

[3] The Representative in Bulgaria (Barnes) to the Acting Secretary of State, June 23, 1945, *Potsdam Papers*, I, p. 383.

sion there. On June 28, he telegraphed: "There is of course an urgent need for the establishment of a truly tripartite Allied Control Commission. . . . There is also a basic need for establishment of a government in Rumania truly representative of all political parties. Such a government should not be made up of ministers hand picked by the Russians." [4]

From General Schuyler's counterpart in Bulgaria, Major General John A. Crane, came this report on July 10:

Complete control is still being exercised by the Russians over our plane and personnel entry into Bulgaria for no reason whatever. This includes officials and employees of our Government. We are still confined to Sofia unless under escort of a Russian officer.

Our position here is most embarrassing. People, Bulgarians and representatives of other governments, openly comment on our apparent helplessness before the power of Russia.

In view of our treatment it is difficult to explain the fact that we are still furnishing them with lend-lease supplies, and are apparently preparing to lend them $6,000,000,000. . . .

Can't we talk a little tough to the Russians in Moscow and avoid being kicked in the face every day?[5]

These reports were received by our government before the President met with Stalin at Potsdam. Moreover, our officials were well acquainted with the inexcusable treatment of American soldiers whom the Soviets "liberated" from Nazi prison camps but refused to give information as to their numbers, identification, or whereabouts. Admiral Standley, who was U.S. Ambassador to Moscow during the war, cites an incident in 1942 when our airmen had to escape from the prisons of our so-called ally and make their way to Iran. When Ambassador Standley had pleaded with Molotov for their release, Molotov replied, "To escape from the Soviet Union is impossible." [6]

In the Pacific the Soviets had, throughout the war, behaved like anything but allies when they confiscated our B-29's which were forced down in Siberia after bombing raids on Japan. General Arnold, who was in command of our air forces, wrote that our crews were interned and "treated almost like captured enemies" as late as 1944 and 1945. Our policy toward the Russians during the war seems to have been well summed up by General Arnold: "Don't do anything; it might make somebody mad at us!" [7]

[4] The Chief of the Military Representation on the Allied Control Commission for Rumania (Schuyler) to the War Department, June 28, 1945, *Potsdam Papers*, I, p. 397.

[5] The Representative on the Allied Control Commission for Bulgaria (Crane) to the Commanding General, United States Army Forces, Mediterranean Theater of Operations (McNarney), July 10, 1945, *Ibid.*, I, pp. 404-405.

[6] Standley and Ageton, *Admiral Ambassador to Russia*, pp. 232-234.

[7] Arnold, *Global Mission*, p. 482.

Concern was developing in Washington that Soviet power grabs, so evident in Europe, might be repeated in China. G-2, the Military Intelligence Division of the War Department, had an impressive report of the Chinese Communist movement. Several months of intensive research had gone into the project, the staff of military and civilian experts having examined over twenty-five hundred reports, pamphlets, and books covering a period from 1919 to 1945. The conclusions reached were prophetic: "The Chinese Communists are Communists. . . . The 'democracy'. . . which the Chinese Communists sponsor represents 'Soviet democracy'. . . ." The report concluded that "in order to prevent the separation of Manchuria and North China from China, it is essential that if Soviet Russia participates in the war, China not be divided (like Europe) into American-British and Russian zones of military operations." [8]

This report was presented in May, 1945, three months before the Potsdam Conference, and marked "secret." One hundred and ten copies of the report were made and distributed in July to government agencies and overseas military theaters. Fifteen copies went to the White House and three to the Department of State.[9]

Many of the most influential Kuomintang leaders had also been apprehensive about what might happen to China if Soviet Russia entered the war. The Chinese Communists would take over North China while the Russians were sweeping through Korea and Manchuria. Although the Nationalist Government expressed approval of Soviet denunciation of the Japanese pact, there was a question of when and how Russia would enter the war. The Chinese had hoped that the United States would be able to deal with Japan alone without the assistance of the Soviet Union, who might complicate Kuomintang-Chinese Communist relations and the future status of Manchuria and China.[10]

Meanwhile, Russia had not waited until the defeat of Germany to transport her troops from the European war to Siberia in preparation for the attack on Manchuria. Japanese intelligence knew about these troop movements and made efforts to request the Soviet Union for continued observance of the neutrality pact.[11]

When Harry Hopkins was in Moscow on May 28 Stalin told him that the Soviet government intended to carry out the Yalta Agreements. Speaking of Chiang Kai-shek, he said he was "the best of the lot." Stalin saw "no other possible leader and that for example he did not believe

8 *Institute of Pacific Relations, Hearings*, Part 7A, pp. 2305-2310.

9 Elizabeth Brown, *The Enemy At His Back* (New York: The Bookmailer, 1956), pp. 144-145.

10 *Institute of Pacific Relations, Hearings*, Part 7A, p. 2374.

11 Kase, *Journey to the "Missouri"*, p. 224.

that the Chinese Communist leaders were as good or would be able to bring about the unification of China." [12]

Stalin indicated that the Red Army would be ready to enter the war against Japan August 8, but he added that the actual date depended upon China's willingness to agree to the Yalta Agreement. He was willing to discuss these matters with T. V. Soong when the latter made his "expected visit to Moscow" not later than the first of July.

Actually, the Soviet dictator showed surprisingly little concern about the spoils he stood to gain in China. True, he might encounter some difficulty in collecting immediately all the promised loot if the Pacific war should end before the Red Army could move in. But he was playing for larger stakes: Soviet domination in the whole of Asia.

Stalin reiterated his support of the doctrine of "unconditional surrender." He went on to tell Hopkins that "Japan was doomed . . . and already so-called Republican movements were beginning to arise behind the scenes which were attempting to play up to the Soviet Union in the hope that they could split the Allies." Stalin remarked that "war such as the present could only happen once in a hundred years and it was better to take advantage of it and utterly defeat Japan and cope with the military potential and in that manner assure fifty to sixty years of peace." [13]

The continuing American and Japanese casualties meant nothing to the Soviet dictator. Stalin wanted a complete destruction of the balance of power in the Pacific.[14] And he wanted to make sure that it would be permanent.

During Hopkins' visit to Moscow, agreement had been reached for July 15 as the approximate date for the next Big Three Conference to be held at Potsdam, Germany. Hopkins reported that Stalin was very "anxious" to discuss problems concerning Japan at the forthcoming conference with the President. The Soviet leader, he said, expects that Russia "will share" in the actual occupation of Japan. There are "certain elements in Japan . . . putting out peace feelers" and as a result we should be thinking about acting "in concert" with the Soviets regarding the surrender of Japan.[15]

U. S. Naval officials were more and more convinced that Japan's capitulation could be brought about by the application of sea power. Admiral

---

[12] *Potsdam Papers,* I, p. 46.

[13] *Ibid.,* p. 44. In reply to a question by Hopkins, Stalin thought that Hirohito "was not a leader but merely a figurehead." But "he might be succeeded at some time in the future by an energetic and vigorous figure who could cause trouble."

[14] On May 11, 1945, Ambassador Harriman told Forrestal that the Russians feared a separate peace between the U. S. and Japan more than any American fear that Japan might come to some agreement with the Soviet Union. *Forrestal Diaries,* p. 55.

[15] President's Adviser and Assistant (Hopkins) to the President, May 30, 1945, *Potsdam Papers,* I, p. 160.

King, a member of the Joint Chiefs of Staff, went directly to the President on June 18, 1945, and "emphasized the point" that the Russians were not "indispensable" and we should not go so far as "to beg them to come in." While the cost of defeating Japan would be greater without Russian aid, there was no question in King's mind but that "we could handle it alone." He thought the realization of this fact should greatly strengthen the President's hand in the forthcoming conference in Potsdam.[16]

The officers of the Air Forces made no objections to the Navy's ability to blockade Japan into submission. Since recent studies had revealed that air bases in Siberia would add only one and a half per cent to the number of bombs that could be dropped on Japan, the Air Forces no longer championed the Siberian bases project.[17] Only the Army continued to argue vehemently the need for Russian assistance.

General George Marshall, the Army Chief of Staff, disapproved a tough policy toward Russia. He said he "hoped for Soviet participation in the war against Japan at a time when it would be useful to us. The Russians had it within their power to delay their entry into the Far Eastern war until we had done all the dirty work." [18]

General Marshall had estimated the strength of the Japanese troops in Japan proper to be approximately 1,800,000.[19] It was he who strongly recommended that the aid of the Soviet Union was necessary to take care of these troops. "I was for Russia entering the Pacific War," he stated in an interview. "We needed everything we could get to save American casualties." [20]

In preparation for the Potsdam meeting, the Joint Chiefs of Staff again re-examined the plans for "unconditional surrender" of Japan in light of recent developments. On June 14 Admiral Leahy informed the Joint Chiefs of Staff that the President desired to discuss the details of our campaign against Japan. Four days later, Secretary Stimson, Secretary Forrestal, and Assistant Secretary John McCloy, together with the Joint Chiefs of Staff, met with the President to discuss allied strategy for the "unconditional surrender" of Japan. It was the view of Admiral Leahy that he could "not agree with those who said to him that unless we obtain the unconditional surrender of the Japanese that we will have lost the war. He feared no menace from Japan in the foreseeable future, even if we were unsuccessful in forcing unconditional surrender.

---

16 *The Entry of the Soviet Union Into the War Against Japan: Military Plans, 1941-1945*, p. 85.

17 Deane, *The Strange Alliance*, p. 263.

18 *Forrestal Diaries*, p. 51.

19 Tripartite Military Meeting, July 24, 1945, at 2:30 P.M. *Potsdam Papers*, II, p. 346.

20 "The Story Marshall Told Me," *U.S. News and World Report* (November 2, 1959), p. 51.

What he did fear was that our insistence on unconditional surrender would result only in making the Japanese desperate and thereby increase our casualty lists. He did not think that this was at all necessary." [21] It was recognized that the war might come to a sensationally quick end, and messages were sent to MacArthur and Nimitz, warning them to take action within the near future on the basis of Japanese capitulation, possibly before Russian entry.[22]

On July 6 as President Truman was leaving for Potsdam, the U.S. Ministry in Sweden cabled the Department of State that Prince Carl Bernodotte, nephew of King Gustov, had been told by the Japanese military attaché in Sweden that Japan had lost the war and wanted to enter surrender negotiations through the King of Sweden.[23]

Two factors were operating to frustrate Japanese endeavors to surrender. One was our insistence upon Roosevelt's "unconditional surrender" slogan, reflected in a persistent refusal to spell out specific terms for Japanese surrender. In particular, our officials refused to give the Japanese any inkling as to the future status of the Emperor. The other factor was the Soviet Union's determination that the Pacific war should go on until the complete destruction of Japan had been achieved.

Both Secretary Byrnes and former Secretary of State Cordell Hull opposed efforts of Grew and Stimson to modify "unconditional surrender" to the extent of letting the Japanese keep their Emperor. Assistant Secretaries of State Archibald MacLeish and Dean Acheson supported Byrnes in opposition to Grew and Stimson. On July 6, 1945, MacLeish submitted a top secret memorandum to Byrnes with the following observation:

What has made Japan dangerous in the past and will make her dangerous in the future if we permit it, in large part, the Japanese cult of emperor worship which gives the ruling groups in Japan—the *Gumbatsu*—the current coalition of militarists, industrialists, large land owners and office holders—their control over the Japanese people.[24]

MacLeish pointed out that at one of the staff meetings Acheson had criticized the Emperor's throne as "an anachronistic, feudal institution, perfectly adapted to the manipulation and use of anachronistic, feudal-

21 Minutes of Meeting Held at the White House, June 18, 1945, at 3:30 p.m., *Potsdam Papers*, I, p. 903. On June 15, 1945, Secretary of State Stettinius sent a report to Acting Secretary Grew suggesting that "a demand for unconditional surrender" of Japan be contained in a tripartite demand to be issued "at or after the Big Three Meeting." Secretary of State, Stettinius, to Acting Secretary of State, Grew, June 15, 1945, *Potsdam Papers*, I, p. 173.

22 *The Entry of the Soviet Union Into the War Against Japan*, p. 106.

23 U.S. Minister to Sweden (Johnson) to Secretary Byrnes, July 6, 1945, *Potsdam Papers*, II, pp. 1589-1590.

24 Assistant Secretary of State MacLeish to Secretary Byrnes, July 6, 1945, *Ibid.*, I, p. 896.

minded groups" within Japan. And then MacLeish offered the same argument Stalin had presented to Hopkins two months earlier, in Moscow:

> . . . however useful the emperor may be to us now, he may be a source of the greatest danger a generation from now. The same consideration applied to the argument that lives will be saved now if the Japanese are allowed to keep their emperor. The lives already spent will have been sacrificed in vain, and lives will be lost again in the future in a new war, if the throne is employed in the future as it has been employed in the past by the Japanese Jingoes and industrial expansionists.[25]

At a meeting of the Secretary's Staff Committee on July 7, the subject as to whether or not to clarify the meaning of unconditional surrender was discussed. Acting Secretary Grew reviewed his arguments in favor of such a statement. It was his belief that it was "absolutely impossible to abolish the institution" and that the "military element and not the Emperor" has been responsible for the war. Acheson remarked that he "could not understand why, if the Emperor had no importance in Japanese war-making capacity, the military element in Japan should be so insistent on retaining the Emperor." [26]

On July 11, fifteen days before we issued the Potsdam Proclamation, peace attempts reached a clearly defined point. The Japanese Foreign Minister Togo sent new instructions to Japan's Ambassador in the Soviet Union:

> The foreign and domestic situation for the Empire is very serious, and even the termination of the war is now being considered privately. Therefore the conversations [between Koki Hirota and the Soviet Ambassador in Japan] are not being limited solely to the objective of closer relations between Japan and the U.S.S.R., but we are also sounding out the extent to which we might employ the U.S.S.R. in connection with the termination of the war.
>
> Our readiness to promise long-term mutual support for the maintenance of peace, as mentioned in our proposal, was also intended for the purpose of sounding out the Soviet attitude toward Japan with reference to the above. The Soviet Union should be interested in, and probably will greet with much satisfaction, an abandonment of our fishery rights as an amendment to the Treaty of Portsmouth. . . . Therefore, although we of course wish the completion of an agreement from the Malik-Hirota negotiations, on the other hand, sounding out the Soviets as to the manner in which they might be used to terminate the war is also desired. We would like to learn quickly the intentions of the Soviet Government regarding the above. As this point is a matter with which the Imperial Court is also greatly concerned, meet with Molotov immediately whether or not T. V. Soong is present in the U.S.S.R.[27]

On July 12, Prince Konoye was received by the Emperor and ordered

---

[25] *Ibid.*

[26] *Ibid.*, I, pp. 900-901.

[27] Foreign Minister Togo to Ambassador Sato, July 11, 1945, *Ibid.*, I, p. 874.

to Moscow as a peace plenipotentiary to "secure peace at any price." [28]
His Foreign Minister Togo sent the following message to Ambassador
Sato in Moscow: "His Majesty the Emperor is greatly concerned over
the daily increasing calamities and sacrifices faced by the citizens of the
various belligerent countries of this present war, and it is His Majesty's
heart's desire to see the swift termination of the war." [29] Sato was
unsuccessful in presenting this message to Molotov personally; the
Soviet Minister would not receive him. Sato informed Togo that the
possibility of employing the Soviet Union in connection with terminating the war "is next to nothing." The thinking of Soviet officials "is
realistic" and you cannot "move them with abstractions." [30] Unable to
see Molotov, who was departing for the Potsdam Conference, Sato
conveyed to the Deputy Minister for Foreign Affairs, Alexander Lozovsky, the Emperor's message regarding the proposed Konoye mission to
Moscow. Sato explained that this mission was "absolutely different in
nature from those special missions previously proposed to Molotov."
Prince Konoye in this case was being sent "in response to His Majesty's
personal wish." Moreover, if it was impossible to get an answer "prior
to Molotov's departure" then it would be desirable to establish communications directly with him in Berlin by "telephone" for an answer.
Lozovsky replied that he would convey the message to Molotov without
delay.[31]

At the same time Sato reminded his government that if Konoye was
coming with a proposal "lacking in concreteness" he would not get anywhere with the Soviets.[32]

On the night of July 14 Stalin and Molotov departed for the Potsdam
Conference without answering the request to receive Konoye. In a dispatch on July 15, Sato attempted to explain to his government the
possible reasons for "the Soviet's hesitation." He thought, perhaps, one
of the reasons was that the Russian government needed "to ascertain
the attitudes of England and America" before giving a definite reply.[33]

It is significant that these intercepted messages were known and circulated by our delegation before the Potsdam Conference began. President Truman even admitted to Department of State historians in a conference on January 24, 1956, that "he was familiar" with the contents
of these Japanese peace feelers.[34]

[28] Strategic Bombing Survey, *The Summary Report of the Pacific War* (Washington:
Government Printing Office, 1946), p. 26.
[29] Foreign Minister Togo to Ambassador Sato, July 12, 1945, *Potsdam Papers*, I, p.
876.
[30] Ambassador Sato to Foreign Minister Togo, July 12, 1945, *Ibid.*, I, pp. 877-878.
[31] Ambassador Sato to Foreign Minister Togo, July 13, 1945, *Ibid.*, I, pp. 879-880.
[32] Ambassador Sato to Foreign Minister Togo, July 13, 1945, *Ibid.*, I, pp. 880-881.
[33] Ambassador Sato to Foreign Minister Togo, July 15, 1945, *Ibid.*, I, pp. 882-883.
[34] *Potsdam Papers*, I, p. 873.

Secretary Stimson was also familiar with the Japanese intercepts, for in his diary entry for July 16, he recorded: ". . . I also received important paper *in re* [*sic* in regards] Japanese maneuverings for peace. . . ." [35] The importance of these Japanese peace maneuvers prompted Stimson to send a memorandum to President Truman urging him to deliver a warning to Japan, "designed to bring about her capitulation as quickly as possible." This was the "psychological moment," he said, "to commence our warnings to Japan," and these warnings should be announced during the course of the Potsdam Conference. If the Japanese should persist, the "full force of our newer weapons should be brought to bear." [36]

The Japanese Government continued its efforts to secure Soviet mediation for terminating the war. On July 17 in an intercepted dispatch to the Japanese Ambassador in Moscow, Foreign Minister Togo, stated: ". . . if only the United States and Great Britain would recognize Japan's honor and existence we would terminate the war and would like to save mankind from the ravages of war," but if they insist "on unconditional surrender to the very end, then our country . . . would unanimously resolve to fight a war of resistance to the bitter end." [37]

The proposed Konoye mission to Moscow was rejected by the Russian Government on July 19. Deputy Minister for Foreign Affairs Lozovsky informed Ambassador Sato that since the Emperor's message is "general in form and contained no concrete proposal,"[38] the Soviet Government was unable to give a definite reply. Lozovsky was stalling for time as instructed. Nothing was done.

It was not until the Potsdam Conference that Stalin officially informed President Truman of Japan's repeated requests for Moscow's good offices as mediator in settling the war.[39] What Stalin may not have known was that President Truman and Secretary Byrnes already knew, through intercepted messages decoded in Washington before the beginning of the Potsdam Conference, that officials in Tokyo were instructing their Ambassador in Moscow to obtain the aid of the Soviet Union in ending the war short of unconditional surrender.[40] The record indicates that Washington officials failed to take advantage of this vital intelligence data. The mere fact that the Japanese had approached the Soviet Union with a request for mediation should have suggested the possibility that

---

35 Stimson's Diary, July 16, 1945, *Potsdam Papers*, II, p. 1266, fn. 4.

36 Secretary Stimson to President Truman, Babelsberg, July 16, 1945, *Ibid.*, II, pp. 1265-66.

37 Foreign Minister Togo to Ambassador Sato, Tokyo, July 17, 1945, *Ibid.*, II, p. 1249.

38 Ambassador Sato to Foreign Minister Togo, Moscow, July 19, 1945, *Ibid.*, II, pp. 1250-1251.

39 Byrnes, *Speaking Frankly*, p. 205, 208; cf. Truman, *Memoirs: Year of Decisions*, p. 396; Churchill, *Triumph and Tragedy*, pp. 641-642.

40 *The Forrestal Diaries*, pp. 74-77; Byrnes, *All in One Lifetime*, p. 292.

Japan, for all of her talk about "death to the last man," might accept the allied demand for unconditional surrender if only it were explained in more specific terms.[41]

Just before the American delegation departed for Potsdam in July, the Operations Division of the Army completed its plans for Japan. In addition to adhering to the scheduled dates of invasion—Kyushu on November 1, 1945, and invasion of Honshu on March 1, 1946, they submitted this cogent analysis:

> There is much to be gained by defining as completely as possible, the detailed U. S. war aims toward Japan. . . . Japanese surrender could be advantageous for the U. S., both because of enormous reduction in the cost of the war and because it would give us a better chance to settle the affairs of the Western Pacific before too many of the allies are committed there and have made substantial contributions towards the defeat of Japan. . . .
> The present stand of the War Department is that Japanese surrender is just possible and is attractive enough to the U.S. to justify us making any concession which might be attractive to the Japanese, so long as our realistic aims for peace in the Pacific are not adversely affected.[42]

When President Truman arrived at Potsdam, however, he told General Eisenhower that one of his "primary objectives" was to get Russia into the Japanese war. Eisenhower begged him at that time not to assume that he had to give anything away to do this, that the Russians were desperately anxious to get into the Far Eastern war and that in Eisenhower's opinion there was no question but that Japan was already thoroughly beaten.[43] Admiral Leahy writes that he was also against making any concessions to the Russians. "I also had told the President of my jaundiced view of Russia's going into Manchuria. This also was discussed at length by the Joint Chiefs, but the Army already had won that argument and the decisions had been confirmed at Yalta."[44]

At a meeting of the Combined Chiefs of Staff on July 16, British officials agreed that there "might be some advantage" in explaining unconditional surrender, particularly concerning the position of the Emperor who would be in "a position to order the cease-fire in outlying areas whereas, if the dynasty were destroyed," the Japanese would continue to fight for many months.[45] When the American Joint Chiefs of Staff met on July 17, General Marshall stated that "the attitude of the Joint Chiefs of Staff" should be to do nothing "prior to the termination of hostilities," which would affect the status of the Emperor; his removal

41 Butow, *Japan's Decision to Surrender*, p. 131.

42 Ray S. Cline, *Washington Command Post: The Operations Division in the United States Army in World War II* (Washington: Department of the Army: Office of Chief of Military History, 1951) , p. 340.

43 Dwight D. Eisenhower, *Crusade in Europe* (New York: Doubleday and Company, Inc., 1948), pp. 441-442.

44 Leahy, *I Was There*, p. 385.

45 *Potsdam Papers*, II, p. 36.

from office might give the Japanese a stronger determination to resist.[46] As late as July 24, 1945, the British and American Combined Chiefs of Staff still planned to invade Japan, and recommended to President Truman and Prime Minister Churchill that Anglo-American policy should be "to encourage Russian entry in the war against Japan." [47] The planning date for the end of organized resistance by Japan was set at November 15, 1946—eighteen months after the defeat of Germany. This estimation was unrealistic in view of numerous intelligence reports indicating that Japan was on her last legs.

When Truman, Stalin, and Churchill met at Potsdam from July 17 to August 2, their primary concern was with the European problems following the defeat of Germany. However, the last phase of the war against Japan was discussed, as well as matters concerning China. At the first Truman-Stalin meeting on July 17, held at Truman's quarters in Babelsberg, Stalin called on the President at noon and stayed for lunch.[48] He apologized for being late and explained that he had been delayed because of discussions with T. V. Soong who was in Moscow for negotiations for a Sino-Soviet treaty. He also explained that his doctors had forbidden him to fly because of the condition of his lungs.

President Truman said he understood and had been looking forward to meeting the Soviet leader. The two leaders discussed various problems concerning the Far East. Stalin told the President that Russia would enter the war before the middle of August.

Stalin then gave a brief summary of negotiations with China. The major differences, he said, involved the railroads in Manchuria and the status of Dairen and Port Arthur. Soong was not optimistic about set-tling these differences and had asked for Soviet assurances recognizing Manchuria as part of China and subject to its sovereignty. These assurances were given, Stalin reported.

The Soviet leader also mentioned Soong's request for assurances that the Nationalist Government would be the only recognized authority in Manchuria—having in mind the Communist army. Stalin repeated his promise that the Soviet Union would give its complete assurances on these points. Then President Truman remarked he was pleased to hear these matters were near settlement.

Stalin repeated his promise that there would be one government and one army, and that this would be stated in the treaty, which was to last for thirty years. It would also provide for noninterference in Chinese internal affairs.

---

46 *Ibid.*, II, p. 40.

47 *The Entry of the Soviet Union Into War Against Japan*, p. 91.

48 The account of this meeting is based entirely upon a memorandum submitted by Charles E. Bohlen to the Secretary of State, March 1960, which appears in Appendix D, *Potsdam Papers*, II, pp. 1582-1587.

Secretary Byrnes asked Stalin what major differences still remained between the Soviet Union and China. Stalin replied that the Yalta Agreement provided that the railways should be jointly administered and that the pre-eminent interests of the Soviet Union were to be safeguarded not only concerning the railroads but also in Dairen and Port Arthur. The Chinese, however, did not recognize the Soviet pre-eminent interest in these areas. In answer to his own rhetorical question as to what the Soviet pre-eminent interests were, Stalin pointed out that they were asking no profit from the railroads, the administration of which would be equally divided, although they had been built by Russian money. Furthermore, he said, there would be no guards such as the Japanese had maintained, but Chinese would protect the railroads themselves. The previous treaty concerning the railroads had been for eighty years, after which time they would revert to China. The Soviet suggestion in the present instance was thirty years. He mentioned that the Russians wished to have a majority of one on the railroad board and a Russian director, but the Chinese wanted a Chinese director with no Russian majority. There was also the question of the Chinese administration of Dairen. At this point there was an exchange between Secretary Byrnes and Stalin relating to the question of joint administration and a Chinese majority. Stalin said that the Soviets had proposed a city council with a joint board in which the Russians would participate.

The President then asked what effect this arrangement would have on the rights of the United States. Stalin answered that it would be a free port open to the commerce of all nations, to which the President observed that it would follow, therefore, the Open Door policy.

Reverting to the question of Soviet entry into the Far Eastern war, Stalin repeated that the Soviets would be ready in mid-August, as was agreed at Yalta, and he said they would keep their word. The President expressed his confidence that the Soviets would keep their word.

Secretary Byrnes reverted to the negotiations with the Chinese and said that, if the arrangements were in strict accordance with the Yalta agreement, this would be all right, but that if at any point they were in excess of that agreement, this would create difficulties. Stalin stated that their desires were more liberal than the Yalta Agreement, which had provided for the restoration of Russian rights. This would have entitled them to station troops and to have the railroads run for eighty years exclusively by Russians. He said they would have had that formal right, but they had not insisted on it. The Soviets did not wish to add in any respect to the Yalta Agreement or to deceive the Chinese. However, he said that Chungking did not understand horse trading; they were very slow and tried to wangle every little thing. They did not seem to be aware of the big picture.

The President and Secretary Byrnes both indicated that the main interest of the United States was in a free port.

In reply to the Secretary's inquiry as to Soong's movements, Stalin stated that Soong expected to return to Moscow at the end of July to finish the negotiations.[49] Thus ended the first meeting between Truman and Stalin.

At the Potsdam Conference on July 18 Stalin and Truman met to consider Japanese peace overtures.[50] On hand were Secretary Byrnes, Foreign Minister Molotov, and their interpreters. They met at Stalin's lakeside villa in Babelsberg, Germany. The session opened with Stalin stating that he wished to make an important announcement: the Soviet Union received a communication from the Japanese. He handed the President a copy of the note from Sato, Japanese Ambassador to Moscow, with a message from the Emperor. Stalin then inquired whether is was worthwhile to answer this communication. The President replied that he had no respect for the good faith of the Japanese.

Stalin pointed out that the Soviet Union was not at war with Japan and that it might be desirable to lull the Japanese to sleep by returning a general and unspecified answer, pointing out that the exact character of the proposed Konoye mission was not clear. Alternatives would be that the USSR might ignore it completely and not answer, or send back a definite refusal. The President said that he thought the first course of action would be satisfactory.[51]

Molotov remarked that this would be wise since it was not quite clear what the Konoye mission would have to offer. Secretary Byrnes commented that it was possible this peace overture by the Japanese was inspired by fear of what the Soviet Union intended to do. Japanese officials knew through intelligence that Russian troops and equipment were moving towards the Far East. Stalin stated he was aware of that fact.

On July 18, Churchill lunched alone with President Truman. Both touched on the topic of the possibility of an early Japanese surrender. Churchill said that the "Japanese war might end much quicker than had been expected, and that the eighteen months period which we had

---

49 Stimson's *Diary* for July 17 includes the following entry relating to the Truman-Stalin meeting of that date: "The President, however, told me briefly of his first meeting with Stalin and said he thought that he had clinched the Open Door in Manchuria." *Potsdam Papers*, II, p. 43.

50 This account of the meeting is based entirely on Bohlen's memorandum to the Secretary of State, March 28, 1960, *Potsdam Papers*, II, pp. 1587-1588. Admiral Zacharias in *Behind Closed Doors* (New York: Putman and Co., 1950), states that as early as June 25, 1945, the Soviet Government refused "to transmit to the United States Government frantic Japanese requests for mediation with a view towards peace." p. 63.

51 Truman in his memoirs mentions the meeting on July 18th with Stalin, but does not say he advised Stalin to reject the Japanese peace offer. *Year of Decisions*, I, pp. 396-397.

taken as a working rule required to be reviewed. Also, Stage III might be upon us in a few months, or perhaps even earlier. I imparted to the President the disclosure about the offer from the Mikado, made to me by Marshal Stalin the night before; and I told him he was quite free to talk it over with the Marshal, as I had informed him at the Marshal's expressed desire. . . ."

The President also thought the war might come to a speedy end. "Here I explained," Churchill remarked, "that Marshal Stalin had not wished to transmit this information direct to him for fear he might think the Russians were trying to influence him towards peace. In the same way I would abstain from saying anything which would indicate that we were in anyway reluctant to go on with the war against Japan as long as the United States thought fit. However, I dwelt upon the tremendous cost in American life and, to a smaller extent, in British life which would be involved in forcing 'unconditional surrender' upon the Japanese. It was for him to consider whether this might not be expressed in some other way, so that we got all the essentials for future peace and security, and yet left the Japanese some show of saving their military honour and some assurance of their national existence, after they had complied with all safeguards necessary for the conqueror. The President countered by saying that he did not think that Japanese had any military honour after Pearl Harbour. I contented myself with saying that at any rate they had something for which they were ready to face certain death in very large numbers, and this might not be so important to us as to them. He then became quite sympathetic, and spoke, as Mr. Stimson had to me two days [one day?] earlier, of the terrible responsibilities that rested upon him in regard to the unlimited effusion of American blood." [52]

While the delegations of the great powers were gathered at Potsdam, came the final proof that Russian entry into the Pacific war was unnecessary and unwise—for on July 16 the atomic bomb was successfully tested on the New Mexico desert. Secretary Stimson received the news at Potsdam, Germany, where he had gone to counsel the President on atomic matters.

He writes that on July 21, at 11:35 A.M., he received a special report by courier from General Groves regarding the successful atomic test in New Mexico. "It was an immensely powerful document," he recorded, "clearly and well written and with supporting documents of the highest importance." After conferring with General Marshall, he went to the "Little White House" and asked President Truman to call in Secretary Byrnes. When Byrnes arrived, Stimson "read the report in its entirety."

---

[52] Truman-Churchill Luncheon meeting, July 18, 1945, *Potsdam Papers*, II, p. 81.

The President was "tremendously pepped up by it . . . and said it gave him an entirely new feeling of confidence." [53]

The next day Secretary Stimson talked with Prime Minister Churchill for an hour. Churchill had read the Groves report regarding the new atomic bomb. He told Stimson that he had noticed at a Big Three meeting yesterday that Truman was evidently much fortified for some reason and that he stood up to the Russians in a most emphatic and decisive manner, telling them that there were certain demands they absolutely could not have. "Now I know what happened to Truman yesterday. I couldn't understand it. When he got to the meeting after having read this report he was a changed man. He told the Russians just where they got on and off and generally bossed the whole meeting." [54]

As one reads the minutes of the Big Three meeting for July 21, there is hardly any indication that Truman stood up to the Russians as perceived by Churchill.

Churchill's first reaction upon learning the contents of the report of the first atomic test was a typically well-phrased exclamation: "Stimson, what was gunpower? Trivial. What was electricity? Meaningless. The atomic bomb is the Second Coming of Wrath." [55]

President Truman felt he was obligated to inform Marshal Stalin of the successful experiment with the A-bomb. He discussed ways and means with Churchill of sharing information about the bomb with Russia. The Prime Minister "felt the same way" as the President: he was in fact not only "not worried about giving the Russians" information about the new weapon, but was rather inclined to use it as an argument for our own benefit.[56] Finally the President decided to break the news on July 24, after a round table conference. But Stalin, whose intelligence services had known of the coming test and had full knowledge of the nuclear weapon, seemed only slightly interested.[57] All he said was "That's fine, I hope you make good use of it against the

[53] Stimson's *Diary* entry for July 21, 1945, *Potsdam Papers*, II, p. 1361, fn. I, Current, *Secretary Stimson*, pp. 231-232. Stimson's *Diary* entry for July 16, 1945, concludes: " . . . At 7:30 P.M. Harrison's first message concerning the test of the S-1 bomb arrived and I took it at once to the President's house and showed it to Truman and Byrnes who of course were greatly interested." *Potsdam Papers*, II, p. 1360, fn. 2.

[54] Stimson *Diary*, July 22, 1945. Minutes of the Stimson-Churchill conversation, July 22, *Potsdam Papers*, II, p. 225.

[55] Harvey Bundy, "Remembered Words" *The Atlantic* (March 1957), p. 57.

[56] Stimson *Diary*, July 22, 1945, *Potsdam Papers*, II, p. 225. Churchill reported that Stalin smiled. Charles Curran, "Stalin Merely Smiled." *The Spectator* (London: Sept. 18, 1959), p. 357.

[57] Alan Moorehead, "Traitor—Klaus Fuchs," *Saturday Evening Post*, May 31, 1952. See U.S. Congress *Report of Joint Committee on Atomic Energy*. Although Stalin knew about the bomb, our theater commanders did not. "We didn't want the theater commanders to get too optimistic about the new weapon," says General Marshall, "so we didn't tell them about the bomb until the last minute." *U.S. News and World Report* (November 2, 1959).

Japanese." [58] There is no indication throughout the conference that Truman's disclosure of the atom bomb affected Stalin's attitude during the rest of the conference. Nor was there any discernible change of mood or attitude on our part regarding our new military superiority *vis-a-vis* Soviet Union.

It was only the Soviet dictator who seemed to understand the military meaning of the new bomb. The bomb might have impressed Truman, but he was still "anxious for Russian entry into the Japanese war." He even wrote a letter inviting Stalin to join the war "on behalf of the community of nations and to maintain peace and security." [59] Later Truman found out that: "We didn't need Russia there and that the Russians·have been a headache to us ever since." [60]

On July 24, Stimson made a last unsuccessful effort with Truman to have the projected ultimatum to Japan indicate a continuance of the Emperor. The next day Stimson and Truman approved orders written in Washington to drop the first atomic bomb on Japan "after about 3 August 1945." Truman wrote: "With this order the wheels are set in motion for the first use of an atomic weapon against a military target. I had made the decision. I also instructed Stimson that the order would stand unless I notified him that the Japanese reply to our ultimatum was accepted." [61] That same day the Japanese Foreign Minister instructed Ambassador Sato in Moscow to see Molotov personally on plans for surrender. This was stressed as "urgent," although four days before Togo had reiterated to Sato that "we can not accept unconditional surrender." [62] The series of messages between Togo and Sato were intercepted and were circulated during the course of the Potsdam Conference.

President Truman wrote to Churchill that he would inform him as soon as Chiang Kai-shek replied, giving his consent to the Declaration that was to be sent to the Japanese Government. "We will issue the Proclamation jointly from here, if that is satisfactory to you." [63] Churchill returned the copy with amendments and a note saying, "I am willing to sign it on behalf of His Majesty's Government in its present form, and I hope you will issue it as you propose whenever you choose and as soon as possible." [64] On July 26, Ambassador Hurley

[58] Byrnes, *All in One Lifetime*, p. 300.

[59] Byrnes, *Speaking Frankly*, p. 209.

[60] Memorandum from President Truman to Secretary Byrnes, January 5, 1946, as quoted in *Mr. President* by William Hillman (New York: Farrar, Straus, and Young, 1952), p. 23.

[61] Truman, *Year of Decisions*, I, p. 421.

[62] Foreign Minister Togo to Ambassador Sato, July 21, 1945, *Potsdam Papers*, II, pp. 1258-59.

[63] President Truman to Prime Minister Churchill, July 25, 1945, *Ibid.*, II, p. 1279.

[64] Prime Minister Churchill to President Truman, July 25, 1945, *Ibid.*, II, p. 1279.

informed the President and Secretary of State that Chiang Kai-shek gave his "concurrence" to the proposed Declaration to Japan.[65]

On July 26, the Potsdam Declaration was issued, stating the terms offered Japan on surrender. The ultimate sentence read: "We call upon the Government of Japan to proclaim now the unconditional surrender of all Japanese armed forces. . . . The alternative for Japan is prompt and utter destruction." [66] The proclamation contained one notable omission—the Emperor. The terms were essentially the same as the original draft produced earlier by Eugene Dooman which was declared "premature" by General Marshall in May, 1945.

The terms left open one matter of deep concern to all patriotic Japanese—what would be the future status of the Emperor? Was he a war criminal? Or was he to be permitted to remain a figurehead in the Japanese Government? Before Secretary of State Byrnes left for Potsdam, Cordell Hull had advised him that any statement about the Imperial Institution not be made until "the climax of allied bombing and Russia's entry into the war." [67] Secretary Byrnes replied on July 17 that he agreed that issuance of a statement regarding Japanese surrender "should be delayed and, when made, should not contain commitment" concerning the Emperor.[68] The Declaration, therefore, did not refer specifically to the status of the Emperor nor did it contain any advance warning about the atomic bomb.[69]

The omission of any mention of the Emperor was interpreted by Japanese military officials as indicative of Allied intentions to destroy the Imperial Institution. It seems tragic that we never asked the Japanese whether they would surrender on certain conditions. This would have prevented a great deal of destruction and agony. We know that men like Grew, Admiral Zacharias, Stimson, and John McCloy felt that our "unconditional surrender" policy was in error when it did not provide negotiating about the Emperor.

---

65 Ambassador Hurley to the President and the Secretary, July 26, 1945, *Ibid.*, II, p. 1282; cf. Document No. 1252, pp. 1282-1283.

66 See text in Department of State, *A Decade of American Foreign Policy, 1941-1949* (Washington: Government Printing Office, 1958), pp. 49-50.

67 Acting Secretary of State Grew to Secretary Byrnes, July 16, 1945, *Potsdam Papers*, II, p. 1267.

68 Memorandum by Acting Secretary of State Grew, July 17, 1945, *Potsdam Papers*, II, p. 1268.

69 On July 26, the Joint Chiefs of Staff met with the Soviet officials to discuss more specifically the co-ordination of Allied operations. Ambassador Sato sent two other reports the same day to the Japanese Foreign Office concerning his talk with Lozovsky. Phrases in these reports described the urgency of Japan's military position. Before leaving, Sato concluded with this remark: "The intention of the Japanese Government, regarding Prince Konoye's mission, is to ask the Soviet Government's assistance in terminating the war. I am sure that the intention is good. Therefore, it is my hope that you will be able to make arrangements so that the Soviet Government will have an opportunity to hear directly from the Prince on this matter." Ambassador Sato to Foreign Minister Togo, July 25, 1945, *Ibid.*, II, p. 1264.

Secretary Stimson recorded in his diary for July 24, 1945, that he spoke to President Truman of the "importance" of reassuring the Japanese on the "continuance of their dynasty." He felt it was important that an "insertion" be made in any "formal warning" to the Japanese because that would "make or mar their acceptance." He had hoped the President would "watch carefully" that the Japanese might be assured verbally through diplomatic channels if they were "hanging fire" on the issue of the Emperor.[70]

Now that we had an atomic weapon, President Truman was "very anxious" to know how General Marshall felt about the need for Russian assistance against Japan. At a luncheon meeting on July 23, Stimson asked Marshall his views on this subject. Marshall pointed out that "even if we went ahead in the war without the Russians, and compelled the Japanese to surrender . . . that would not prevent the Russians from marching into Manchuria anyhow and striking, thus permitting them to get virtually what they wanted in the surrender terms." [71]

Marshall's point of view is generally accepted by those who defend the seeking of Russia's entry into war against Japan. But far more fundamental questions arise. Was our position at Potsdam so frozen that we could not have informed the Soviet Union her help was no longer necessary—that we could take care of Japan alone? Did the Yalta Agreement imply an obligation on our part to wait for the Soviet Union to enter the Pacific War? We knew the Soviet Union had been violating her solemn agreements under the Yalta Treaty. We could have said to Marshal Stalin that now with our new weapon we would not need his assistance to defeat Japan. At this time America was at the peak of her strength; we had amassed the most powerful striking force in the world, and, with the new atomic weapon, we had a superior military position vis-a-vis Soviet Union. At the Potsdam Conference, our officials had within their power an opportunity to negotiate from a superior position of strength. Our President could speak the only language the Soviets understand—the language of power. He did not do so.

At the Tenth Plenary meeting on July 28, Stalin told Truman and the newly elected British Prime Minister Clement Attlee, that although the Soviet Delegation had "not been informed" when the Declaration to Japan was drawn up, he wished to inform them now about the latest Japanese peace offer. A translator then read in English the communication from Ambassador Sato. It was another request for the Soviet Government to receive the mission of Prince Konoye and to apply her offices as mediator of the war. Stalin said there was "nothing new" in this latest overture, except that it was "more definite" than the earlier

---

70 *Ibid.*, II, p. 1272.

71 Stimson's Diary, July 23, 1945, *Potsdam Papers*, II, p. 1324.

one and since it was more definite the answer would be more definite. It was "no." Truman, without comment, thanked him for the information.[72] President Truman told Department of State historians in a conference on January 24, 1956, that he was familiar with the contents of the second Japanese peace offer before Stalin brought it to his attention.[73]

Two days after the release of the Potsdam Declaration Secretary Byrnes told Forrestal he was "most anxious to get the Japanese affair over with before the Russians got in, with particular reference to Dairen and Port Arthur. Once in there, he felt, it would not be easy to get them out. . . ." [74]

In Tokyo the Supreme War Council immediately began to consider the Potsdam Declaration. The majority of the members agreed that the terms should be rejected since they provided no basis for negotiations. Premier Suzuki and the Minister of Foreign Affairs and the Navy felt that it must be accepted at once, but the war minister and the two chiefs of staff objected that the terms were "too dishonorable." They insisted on discussing the fate of the Emperor, the disposition of "war criminals," and the future "national policy." [75] On July 28, Premier Suzuki rejected the Potsdam ultimatum by announcing that the Government "does not find any important value in it." [76]

"If the Suzuki government could have made up its mind promptly to accept the Potsdam Declaration as a basis for peace," says Samuel Morison, "there would have been no explosion of an atomic bomb over Japan." [77] Toshikazu Kase, the American affairs expert in the Japanese Foreign Office, says Suzuki's statement about the proclamation "should have meant simply that we refrained from commenting on it. To state expressly that we would ignore the proclamation was entirely contrary to the purpose of the decision. Such was the penalty of having an inexperienced man at the head of the government." [78]

This rejection had not been intended by the Supreme War Council since they were still hoping for some sort of negotiated peace that would save Japan from humiliation. The Japanese leaders were expectantly awaiting a Soviet agreement to mediate an end to the war. "To my

[72] Minutes of the Tenth Plenary Meeting, July 28, 1945, 10:30 p.m., *Potsdam Papers,* II, p. 460.

[73] See Editor's note in *Ibid.,* I, p. 873, and Document 1234, Vol. II, p. 1262. Byrnes says in *All in One Lifetime,* that Forrestal told him "in detail of the intercepted messages from the Japanese government.", p. 297.

[74] *The Forrestal Diaries,* p. 78.

[75] *Japan's Struggle to End the War,* p. 8.

[76] Press Conference Statement by Prime Minister Suzuki, July 28, 1945, *Potsdam Papers,* II, 1293.

[77] Samuel Eliot Morison, "Why Japan Surrendered," *The Atlantic* (October 1960), p. 44.

[78] Kase, *Journey to the "Missouri,"* p. 211.

amazement," commented Togo Shigenori, Foreign Minister, "the news-papers . . . reported that the government had decided to ignore the Potsdam Declaration. I protested without delay to the Cabinet . . . pointing out that the report was at variance with our decision of the preceding day." [79] Suzuki's reply was made in the hope of retaining a bargaining position until he knew precisely what the Potsdam Procla-mation meant. As yet the Japanese had received the news of the state-ment of Allied policy at Potsdam only through their radio listening post. It was not addressed to their government and the ultimatum had not yet reached them through official channels.

Long before the Potsdam Proclamation, civilian advisers close to the Emperor were toiling with the idea of surrender, but the stumbling block was the complete dominance of the Army. The Emperor needed all the support he could get. If a statement about the dynasty had been issued as early as May, 1945, the surrender-elements in the Government might have taken charge.[80] If surrender could have been brought about in May, June, or July, 1945, before the entrance of Soviet Russia into the war and the use of the atomic bomb, the United States would have seriously benefitted. Moreover, if the Japanese Kwantung Army had sur-rendered to the United States, it would mean our forces instead of the Soviets would occupy Manchuria. As General Deane cogently pointed out: "Russia had to buy her ticket to the Pacific peace conference, but she had to hurry or the show would have started and the seats would all be taken." [81] As Bullitt says, "We held the power to enforce our will throughout the earth." [82]

On July 30, the New York *Times* informed its readers, as did other papers elsewhere throughout the United States and the world at large, that Japan had dismissed the Potsdam Declaration with a contemptuous gesture.[83] "In face of this rejection," said Secretary Stimson, " we can only proceed to demonstrate that the ultimatum had meant exactly what it

---

[79] Shigenori, *The Cause of Japan*, p. 313; W. J. Coughlin in "The Great *Mokusatsu* Mistake," *Harpers,* (March 1953), states that the Japanese Cabinet had already decided in favor of the Potsdam Declaration, but Premier Suzuki "told the Japanese newsmen that his cabinet was holding to an attitude of *mokusatsu,* a word that is difficult to translate directly into English. He meant that the cabinet was withholding comment on the ultimatum, that a decision was not yet to be announced. But the Domei News Agency, in translating Suzuki's statment into English for shortwave broadcast to the West, put the wrong meaning on *mokusatsu* and mistranslated it as "ignore." p. 32.

[80] The Emperor, the Lord Privy Seal, the Prime Minister, the Foreign Minister, and the Navy Minister had decided as early as May of 1945 that the war should be ended even if it meant acceptance of defeat on Allied terms. The War Minister was deter-mined that the war should continue.

[81] Deane, *The Strange Alliance*, p. 275.

[82] "How We Won the War and Lost the Peace," *Life* (August 30, and September 6, 1948), p. 83.

[83] *New York Times,* July 30, 1945 and July 31, 1945 (editorials).

said . . . the inevitable and complete destruction of the Japanese armed forces . . . and utter devastation of the Japanese homeland." [84]

Shortly before the Potsdam Conference adjourned, final arrangements for Soviet entry into war against Japan were made. Molotov told Truman and Byrnes he would have to find an excuse for Russia's entry at this time because the neutrality pact with Japan had not expired. He asked the American and British governments to address a formal request to Russia to enter the war against Japan. He suggested this might be based on the grounds that Japan had rejected the Potsdam ultimatum.[85] Secretary Byrnes did not feel that the United States "should be placed in a position of asking another government to violate its agreement without good and sufficient reasons." [86] The Soviet Union had agreed at Yalta to enter the war in the Pacific within three months after the defeat of Germany, and now Marshal Stalin was anxious to enter the Far Eastern conflict before it ended. But he wanted some tricky justification for the act. Our diplomats were prompt to give him one.

On July 31, President Truman sent a letter to Stalin indicating that the Soviet Union might cite the Moscow Declaration of October 30, 1943, and certain Articles of the United Nations Charter as providing a proper basis for the Soviet action in co-operating ". . . with other great powers now at war with Japan with a view of joint action on behalf of the community of nations in maintaining peace and security." [87] Stalin expressed great appreciation for the American idea. In fact, within ten days after the arrival of the President's letter the Soviet Union commenced hostilities against Japan. One of the earliest applications of the United Nations Charter was ironic, if not prophetic. Sanction was taken for the Soviet Union's violation of her neutrality pact with Japan and her unprovoked attack on that nation. And her purpose was one of territorial aggrandizement at the expense of China.

Thus, when the Potsdam Conference adjourned at midnight August 1, it was settled that the war with Japan would go on until the ultimatum was accepted. It is interesting to note that Marshal Stalin made a great impression on President Truman just as he did on Roosevelt and many other American officials. "From the beginning," says Jonathan Daniels, "Truman liked Stalin, as he liked Churchill but in a different way . . . 'Stalin is as near like Tom Pendergast as any man I know. . . .' 'I got the impression,' Truman said later, 'that Stalin would stand by his agree-

---

84 Henry L. Stimson, "The Decision to Use the Atomic Bomb," *Harpers* (February, 1947) , p. 105.

85 Truman-Molotov Meeting, July 29, 1945, 12:00 P.M., *Potsdam Papers*, II, p. 476.

86 Byrnes, *Speaking Frankly*, p. 207.

87 Truman, *Year of Decisions*, I, p. 403.

ments, and also that he had a Politburo on his hands like the Eightieth Congress.' " [88]

Meanwhile, from Moscow, Ambassador Sato sent an urgent message to Togo on July 27 that he must promptly come out with "a concrete proposal" to end the war.[89] On July 30 Sato saw Vice Commissar Lozovsky and said that Japan found it difficult to accept the demand in the Potsdam Declaration for unconditional surrender, but that Japan was willing to terminate the war provided the Imperial Institution were preserved. "For this purpose we asked the Soviet Government for assistance," Sato reported. He begged Lozovsky to notify Molotov that the Japanese Government was still anxious to send Prince Konoye, and that he "will be empowered to discuss a wide range of subjects with the Soviet Government." Sato concluded with the hope that the Potsdam Declaration would not "obstruct the assistance from the Soviet Government" to mediate the war.[90]

The Soviet Government refused to make any commitment, and Sato reminded him again on August 2 of the extreme urgency of the situation.[91] While President Truman was at sea on board the U.S.S. *Augusta,* on August 2, he gave the final order to drop the bombs on two Japanese cities. On August 6, the first atomic bomb was dropped on Hiroshima, completely destroying four and a half square miles of the city and killing an estimated 71,379 people including the military. Another 19,691 were seriously injured and about 171,000 rendered homeless. The next morning every London newspaper published the news with horror—except one. The *Daily Worker* wanted more atom bombs on Japan: "The employment of the new weapon *on a substantial scale* should expedite the surrender of Japan." [92]

When Sato requested an interview with Molotov he received an appointment for five o'clock in the afternoon on August 8. At this meeting, without allowing Sato to state his case, Molotov abruptly notified him that the Soviet Union would be at war with Japan as from the following day.[93] And at the same time—on the eve of the atom bombing of Nagasaki—a cartoon in the London *Daily Worker* showed a bomber squadron labelled "Surrender or Die" dropping a swarm of missiles labelled "Atomic Bombs" on a blazing target labelled "Japan." [94]

---

[88] Jonathan Daniels, *The Man From Independence* (Philadelphia: J. B. Lippincott Company, 1950), p. 278.

[89] Ambassador Sato to Foreign Minister Togo, July 27, 1945, *Potsdam Papers*, II, p. 1291.

[90] Ambassador Sato to Foreign Minister Togo, July 30, 1945, *Ibid.*, II, pp. 1297-1298.

[91] Kase, *Journey to the "Missouri,"* p. 222.

[92] Charles Curran, "Stalin Merely Smiled," *The Spectator* (September 18, 1959), p. 369.

[93] Kase, *Journey to the "Missouri,"* p. 223.

[94] Curran, *op. cit.*

The Soviets declared war on the very next day, a week ahead of their timetable—and after having observed for four years an ostentatious neutrality which enabled Japanese divisions to move freely against New Guinea and the Philippines when they would otherwise have been immobilized along the Siberian border. The Soviet Union's entry neither defeated Japan nor materially hastened the acceptance of surrender. In order to lay claim to the territorial plums he had been promised at Yalta, Stalin had to enter the war before the Japanese empire crumbled of its own dead weight.

We know today that Stalin played a Machiavellian game. To Britain and America, at Potsdam he appeared as a defender of "unconditional surrender," but in reality he was deliberately forestalling any mediation between Japan and the United States. As Paul Kecskemeti pointed out in his incisive book *Strategic Surrender:* "There could be only one conceivable reason for a Japanese failure to surrender without delay on the terms proclaimed at Potsdam, namely, Japan's hope that prolonged resistance would force the allies to make further concessions. The Allies ruled out the possibility that the Japanese might refrain from bowing to the Potsdam ultimatum for a different reason. Actually, such a reason did exist; the Japanese expected last-minute diplomatic help from Soviet Russia." [95]

As Soviet troops moved into Manchuria, the second atomic bomb was dropped on Nagasaki; 45,000 people perished and an additional 60,000 were injured.[96] The Japanese Government expressed its willingness to surrender on August 10 provided her Imperial Institutions were preserved.[97] When the Japanese reply reached Washington, by the way of the Swiss Government, the American policy makers faced the question of accepting the surrender with the string attached. The President held a conference with the Secretaries of State, War, and the Navy. Admiral Leahy urged acceptance of the Japanese proposal to retain the Emperor. Secretary Byrnes objected to any retreat from unconditional surrender. The President agreed, and Byrnes drafted a reply which Truman and Stimson approved.[98]

On August 11, the Allies made their official reply which said: "From the moment of surrender the authority of the Emperor and the Japanese Government to rule the state shall be subject to the Supreme Commander of the Allied Powers. . . ." [99] The Japanese accepted the reply on August

---

[95] Paul Kecskemeti, *Strategic Surrender* (Stanford: Stanford University Press, 1958), pp. 187-188.

[96] United States Strategic Bombing Survey. *The Effects of Atomic Bombs on Health and Medical Services in Hiroshima and Nagasaki* (Washington: U.S. Government Printing Office, 1947), p. 84.

[97] For a full reply see Butow, *Japan's Decision to Surrender*, Appendix D, p. 244.

[98] Byrnes, *Speaking Frankly*, p. 209; Leahy, *I Was There*, pp. 434-435.

[99] For a full reply see Butow, *Japan's Decision to Surrender*, Appendix E, p. 245.

14, and on the same day military operations were supended, and General MacArthur was appointed Supreme Commander. On September 2, the formal surrender documents were signed aboard the U.S.S. *Missouri* in Tokyo Bay. World War II had ended.[100]

Almost immediately after the atomic bombs fell on Japan several questions arose: Was it a mistake to drop the bombs, and would the U.S. position in the world be different had this weapon not been used? A special committee known as the Interim Committee, more than any other group, made recommendations to President Truman, although the final decision was his.[101] This committee suggested that the bomb be used against Japan as soon as possible, that a military target be selected, and that no prior warning be given.

Ralph A. Bard, Undersecretary of the Navy, was the only member of the Interim Committee "to oppose use of the bomb without warning or efforts to secure Japan's surrender by diplomatic means." He submitted the following significant memorandum to the assistant chairman of the Interim Committee on June 27, 1945:

Ever since I have been in touch with this program I have had a feeling that before the bomb is actually used against Japan that Japan should have some preliminary warning for say two or three days in advance of use. The position of the United States as a great humanitarian nation and the fair play attitude of our people generally is responsible in the main for this feeling.

During recent weeks I have also had the feeling very definitely that the Japanese government may be searching for some opportunity which they could use as a medium for surrender. Following the three-power conference (at Potsdam) emissaries from this country could contact representatives from Japan somewhere on the China coast and make representations with regard to Russia's position and at the same time give them some information regarding the proposed use of atomic power, together with whatever assurances the President might care to make with regard to the Emperor of Japan and the treatment of the Japanese nation following unconditional surrender. It seems quite possible to me that this presents the opportunity which the Japanese are looking for.

I don't see that we have anything in particular to lose in following such a program. The stakes are so tremendous that it is my opinion very real consideration should be given to some plan of this kind. I do not believe under present circumstances existing that there is anyone in this country whose evaluation of the chances of success of such a program is worth a great deal. The only way to find out is to try it out.[102]

An argument advanced against preliminary warning was the possibility that the bomb might be a dud, and in that case chances for peace would

---

100 *The Entry of the Soviet Union into War Against Japan*, p. 107.

101 Members of the Committee were James F. Byrnes; Secretary of War Stimson; Assistant Secretary of State William L. Clayton; Undersecretary of the Navy Ralph A. Bard; and three scientists high in Government councils—Drs. Vannevar Bush, Karl T. Compton and James B. Conant.

102 *U.S. News and World Report*, (August 15, 1960), p. 74.

be worse. James F. Byrnes was President Truman's personal representative in early deliberations on use of the atomic bomb. He expressed the view that if the Japanese were warned of the atom bomb they might bring American prisoners to that area.[103] He shared the feeling that the U.S. had no alternative to dropping the bomb, in light of knowledge then available. He doubted that a concession to Japan on the question of the Emperor would have brought surrender much more quickly than it did.[104]

In Japan, Sokoh Tanemura, assistant to the Deputy Chief of Staff of the Japanese Army through World War II and now head of the Historical Facts Research Institute, says: "The Americans blundered in not guaranteeing the safety and status of the Emperor. Otherwise, the war would have ended before A-bombs were used. The American position in Japan and Asia would be much better now if the A-bomb had never been used." [105]

As two key scientists, Dr. Leo Szilard and Dr. Edward Teller explained in their interview with the *U.S. News and World Report,* many scientists had strong doubts about using the bomb. Even before the Interim Committee met, Szilard relates, he and two other atomic scientists visited Byrnes on May 28, 1945, to express their doubts. This meeting produced no results.

Seventy-two hours later, Byrnes and other members of the Interim Committee entered a two-day session to settle the question of using the bomb. Present at this meeting were four advisory scientists,[106] General Marshall, and Brigadier General Leslie R. Groves, chief of the atomic project.

In those two days, May 31 and June 1, the fourteen men thrashed out alternatives to unrestricted use of the bomb. Foremost of these was the idea of an explicit warning to Japan before using the bomb, or some kind of demonstration on an uninhabited area. Both suggestions were rejected. Byrnes states that the "decision makers" did not discuss the political consequences of using the bomb. Nor was it suggested that an effort might be made to negotiate Japan's surrender before the bomb was used.

On June 1, the Interim Committee suggested that the bomb be used against Japan as soon as possible, and that the target consist of a military installation and surrounding homes and buildings. This implied that civilians would be among the casualties. That same day, President

---

103 Byrnes, *Speaking Frankly,* p. 261.

104 *U.S. News and World Report* (August 15, 1960), pp. 65-68.

105 *Ibid.,* p. 65.

106 The Interim Committee was assisted by an advisory panel of four scientists then working on the atomic bomb. They were Drs. Arthur Compton, Enrico Fermi, Ernest O. Lawrence and Robert Oppenheimer.

Truman was told of the recommendations. He agreed with them. In his memoirs he writes: "The final decision of where and when to use the atomic bomb was up to me. Let there be no mistake about that. I regarded the bomb as a military weapon and never had any doubt that it should be used." [107]

Yet, outside the small circle of "decision makers," opposition to use of the bomb persisted. Lewis L. Strauss, then a Navy officer and later Chairman of the Atomic Energy Commission, had doubts about the use of the bomb. He wrote a memorandum to Undersecretary Bard that the bomb "be used in Japan over either an uninhabited area or, after a warning, over a sparsely inhabited area, preferably a forest near Kikko, where the effect of blast and heat would be demonstrable after the explosion. I thought that this would demonstrate the power of the bomb fully as well as the destruction of a city without leaving the aftermath of resentment and grief that the employment of so dreadful a weapon would entail." [108]

Dr. Szilard, employed in the Chicago branch of the bomb project, and six other scientists sent a report to Stimson urging a demonstration. The day after the bomb was tested in the desert of New Mexico, Szilard and more than sixty other scientists at Chicago petitioned the President not to use the bomb against Japan.[109] Szilard has gone on record as stating that "Truman did not understand what was involved. You can see that from the language he used." [110] Dr. Edward Teller, who was at the Los Alamos branch of the project, "believed that it was a mistake" to drop the bomb on Japan.[111]

The atomic bombing of Hiroshima and Nagasaki and the Soviet Union's declaration of war did not produce Japan's decision to surrender, for that decision had long been taking shape. At the time the Interim Committee submitted its recommendations on the use of the bomb, our military situation in the Pacific was very favorable. B-29's were pulverizing Japanese cities and factories. In one bombing mission on May 23, 520 B-29's dropped 3,729 tons of incendiary bombs on Tokyo. On May 29, 450 B-29's destroyed 6.9 square miles of Yokohama.[112] On top of this,

---

107 Truman, *Year of Decisions*, I, p. 419

108 *U.S. News and World Report*, (August 15, 1960), p. 72. Fletcher Knebel and Charles W. Bailey, II, "Hiroshima: the Decision That Changed the World," *Look* (June 7, 1960), p. 26-27.

109 On July 12, 1945, Dr. Farrington Daniels, the director of the Metallurgical Department of the University of Chicago, polled 150 scientists, then working on the atomic bomb, in order to get their views on how the bomb should be used. Results suggested that 124 scientists favored some kind of demonstration of the weapon's effectiveness before the bomb was actually used against Japan. *U.S. News and World Report* (August 15, 1960), p. 64.

110 *Ibid.*, p. 71.

111 *Ibid.*, p. 75.

112 USSBS, *Air Campaigns of the Pacific War*, p. 52.

the Japanese Army was disintegrating, her air force was just about wrecked, and her fleet was at the bottom of the sea. Japan was a defeated nation. "I was unable to see any justification," writes Admiral Leahy, "for an invasion of an already thoroughly defeated Japan. I feared that the cost would be enormous in both lives and treasure." [113] In a similar vein Admiral King remarked that "the defeat of Japan could be accomplished by sea and air power alone, without the necessity of actual invasion of the Japanese home islands by ground troops." [114]

There were some observers in the United States who wondered why, if the object was simply to bring Japan to an early defeat, the surrender terms were not fully clarified. If the war had ended in May, 1945, Russia, whatever she might eventually have done, would not have been given a free and coridal hand to expand her influence over the Far East. Equally important, the atomic bomb would not have been dropped by Americans. According to General Willoughby, who was in charge of intelligence under MacArthur:

Japan was ready for the *coup de grace* as early as October, 1944, and it could have been administered with conventional weapons. With Japan's weakness completely revealed, the employment of the atomic bomb had no justification. It is rare in military history that a nation obtains a monopoly on a hitherto secret weapon or technique of absolute supremacy. Had Truman kept the atomic bomb a secret, the American politico-military position today would be impregnable. Premature exposure led to intensified Russian espionage through a sinister element of modern decadence—the fifth column, the native traitor, the citizen saboteur.[115]

The United States Strategic Bombing Survey gave the opinion that "certainly prior to December 31, 1945, and in all probability prior to November 1, 1945, Japan would have surrendered even if the atomic bomb had not been dropped, even if Russia had not entered the war, and even if no invasion had been planned or contemplated." [116] Admiral Leahy wrote: "It is my opinion that the use of this barbarous weapon at Hiroshima and Nagasaki was of no material assistance in our war against Japan. The Japanese were already defeated and ready to surrender. . . ." [117]

Admiral Nimitz believed that the decisive factor in defeating Japan was "the complete impunity with which the Pacific Fleet pounded Japan."[118] The Secretary of the Navy, James Forrestal, wrote in his diary on August 10, 1945, that by using the atomic bomb, "we must remember

---

113 Leahy, *I Was There*, pp. 384-385.
114 King and Whitehill, *Fleet Admiral King*, p. 598.
115 *Congressional Record*, January 9, 1958, p. A133.
116 *Summary Report, Pacific War*, p. 26.
117 Leahy, *I Was There*, p. 441.
118 Quoted in Baldwin, *Great Mistakes of the War*, p. 93.

that this nation would have to bear the focus of the hatred of the Japanese." [119] General "Hap" Arnold, Chief of the Air Force, wrote that "it always appeared to us that, atomic bomb or no atomic bomb, the Japanese were already on the verge of collapse." [120] In his memoirs Admiral Halsey stated:

Japan capitulated so soon after the atomic bomb and Russia's declaration of war that the public may over-value these two factors. My own estimate of their importance—that they merely gave the Nips an excuse, and helped them save face—received authoritative support from Admiral Soemj Toyada, chief of the Japanese Naval General Staff, in a statement recently published by the Naval Analysis Division of the United States Strategic Bombing Survey: 'I do not think it would be accurate to look upon the use of the atomic bomb and entry and participation of Soviet Russia into the war as direct cause of the termination of the war, but I think (they) did enable us to bring the war to a termination without creating too great chaos in Japan.'[121]

President Truman sought to justify the atom bombing of Hiroshima and Nagasaki with his callous statement that "I think the sacrifice of Hiroshima and Nagasaki was urgent and necessary for the prospective welfare of both Japan and the allies." [122] Secretary Byrnes states: "We would have had more casualties" without the A-bomb.[123]

The historical record shows that the bombing of these Japanese cities was unnecessary to bring the war to a speedy end, eliminating the scheduled assault against the Japanese mainland. Then why did the U.S. decide to use the atom bomb? According to Norman Cousins and Thomas Finletter the main purpose was not military, but diplomatic, and the real target was not Japan but Russia. This was the same view held by General Leslie Groves who was in charge of the Manhattan Project. He told the board in the Oppenheimer hearings:

I think it important to state that there was never from about two weeks from the time I took charge of the project any illusion on my part that Russia was the enemy and that the project was conducted on that basis. I didn't go along with the attitude of the country as a whole that Russia was a gallant ally. I always had suspicions and the project was conducted on that basis. Of course, that was reported to the President.[124]

---

119 *Forrestal Diaries*, p. 83.

120 Arnold, *Global Mission*, p. 598.

121 William F. Halsey, *Admiral Halsey's Story* (New York: Whittlesey House, 1947), p. 271.

122 Harry Elmer Barnes, "Hiroshima: Assault on a Beaten Foe," *National Review* (May 10, 1958), p. 441. Dr. Compton stated that without the atomic bomb "the war would have continued for many months." Dr. Karl Compton, "If the Bomb Had Not Been Used," *Atlantic Monthly* (December 1946), p. 54.

123 *U.S. News and World Report* (August 15, 1960), pp. 65-67.

124 As quoted in Michael Armine, *The Great Decision: The Secret History of the Atom Bomb* (New York: G. P. Putman's Sons, 1959), p. 234.

Even Henry L. Stimson's *Memoirs* hinted that "Russia and not Japan was the real target of the atom bomb." The use of the bomb would "give democratic diplomacy a badly needed 'equalizer' as against the postwar power of the Communist colossus." [125] It is strange that an obvious and bloodless alternative did not occur to Washington officialdom: learning how to say "no" to the Soviet Union and refraining from building up her postwar power.

The war against Japan upset the whole structure of the international balance of power in the Far East. The United States destroyed the only power—other than a U.S.-China alliance—that was able to check the flow of that Red tide in the Far East. Deprived of her empire in China, and with her cities and industries destroyed, Japan was back where she started at the dawn of her modern era. All this was the result of the Stimson Nonrecognition Doctrine, the diplomacy of Pearl Harbor, the Yalta Agreement, "unconditional surrender," and the atom bomb. A negotiated peace with Japan in the summer of 1945 would have eliminated the necessity of invading the Japanese homeland and would certainly have spared us many lives. Sovereignty over Chinese soil could have been restored to China, rather than yielded to Red imperialism. Had the Allies given Suzuki more time in which to obtain his government's support for acceptance of the Potsdam Declaration, the war might have ended toward the latter part of July, or the very beginning of August without the atomic bomb and without Soviet participation in the conflict.

---

[125] Current, *Secretary Stimson*, p. 237.

CHAPTER VII

YALTA PLAGUES AMERICAN DIPLOMACY

At the Yalta Conference Roosevelt had told Stalin that he would send an American officer to Chungking via Moscow to inform Chiang Kai-shek of the agreement. Stalin knew the Generalissimo would be dissatisfied with this agreement once he was informed of it. He insisted, therefore, that these agreements must be put in writing and must contain the statement: "The heads of the three Great Powers have agreed that these claims of the Soviet Union shall be unquestionably fulfilled after Japan has been defeated." [1] Roosevelt involved himself in a firm commitment. Suppose China had refused to agree to any of the Soviet claims? Any objections China might have could be overridden; she was almost completely dependent upon the United States.

After the Yalta Conference the agreement regarding Japan was kept a closely guarded secret. Its text was guarded by Admiral Leahy in a special file in the White House, and probably only half a dozen men in the United States knew of its existence. When President Roosevelt made a report on the conference to Congress he did not mention it. He even went so far as to say that the Yalta Conference had "concerned itself with the European war and with the political problems of Europe, and not the Pacific war." Vice-President Truman knew nothing of the pact until after his succession to the presidency on April 12, 1945. Then he had to make a search for the text.

But Roosevelt did show Ambassador Hurley the text when the latter returned to Washington at the end of February, 1945. Hurley protested that the United States had surrendered the territorial integrity and political independence of China. This Roosevelt denied. Some days later Roosevelt admitted to Hurley that there were some features in the agreement which justified his fears. He wanted Hurley to talk with Churchill and Stalin to see if he could ameliorate it or set it aside.[2]

---

[1] Sherwood, *Roosevelt and Hopkins*, p. 867.
[2] Testimony of Major-General Patrick J. Hurley, June 30, 1951, *Military Situation in the Far East Hearings*, Part 4, pp. 2883-2888.

On April 5 Hurley met with Churchill and discussed Britain's responsibility under the Atlantic Charter. At one point the discussion became heated when Churchill called the long-range American policy towards China "the great American illusion." He also disapproved of the American withdrawal of resources in Burma and India for use in China. Hurley countered by saying this material was "necessary for the purpose of maintaining the American position in China."

Churchill was provoked when Hurley remarked that if Britain refused to adhere to the principles of the Atlantic Charter and continued to hold on to Hong Kong, the Soviet Union might find an excuse to make similar demands on North China. The Prime Minister responded bluntly, that England was not "bound by the principles of the Atlantic Charter; furthermore Hong Kong will be eliminated from the British Empire only over my dead body." At the end of the discussion Churchill made the statement that Britain would support U.S. policy in China.[3]

While Hurley's plane was on the way to Moscow, Ambassador Harriman notified Stalin of Roosevelt's death. On the night of April 15 Hurley had an interview with Stalin. He reminded Stalin that during his last visit in Moscow Molotov told him "the Chinese Communists were not real Communists but rather simple people who merely desired certain reforms," and that the Soviet Union was not supporting the Chinese Communist Party. Stalin declared that there was corruption among certain Nationalist officials, but that he approved of pursuing Chinese unification advocated by the United States.

Hurley was not to inform Chiang Kai-shek about the secret Yalta accord without first checking with the Soviet dictator. He was instructed by President Truman that when it is "appropriate, you will be advised." [4] Stalin brought up the subject of notifying Chiang and stated he would not be afraid to divulge the secret agreement after two or three months, when Russia had sufficient forces in the Far East.

Hurley informed Stalin that the U.S. was equipping and training thirty-six Chinese divisions. Our government "would also like to train and equip the Communist troops and combine them with the nationalist troops under the national government." Stalin was in complete agreement with this proposal.[5]

The optimism which this interview created in Hurley's mind was not shared by George Kennan, who was then serving in the Moscow Embassy. "It would be tragic," Kennan observed, "if our natural anxiety for sup-

---

[3] Ambassador Hurley to Secretary Stettinius, April 13, 1945, *Hurley Papers*. File 313, Document No. 67. *MSS.*, Santa Fe.

[4] President Truman to Ambassador Hurley, *Hurley Papers*, File 226, Document No. 15. *MSS.*, Santa Fe.

[5] This summary of the talk regarding the situation in China is based on a memorandum by Edward Page, Second Secretary of U.S. Embassy in Moscow, April 15, 1945, *Hurley Papers*, File 313, Document No. 69. *MSS.*, Santa Fe.

port of the Soviet Union at this juncture, coupled with Stalin's use of
words which mean all things to all people and his cautious affability,
were to lead us into an undue reliance on Soviet aid or even Soviet ac-
quiescence in the achievement of our long term objectives in China." [6]
This cautious attitude was shared by Averell Harriman, the American
Ambassador in Moscow, and was one which seemed most acceptable to
Washington.[7] Of course Harriman must have known that the Yalta
Agreement he helped to prepare hastened the end of Nationalist China.

The Yalta Agreement enabled Russia to realize her imperialistic ambitions in China. Hurley's vigorous attempt to change or have it set aside
was not successful.[8]

An opportunity for possibly modifying the Yalta Agreement had been
proffered Truman upon his succession to the presidency. He was "gravely concerned over the serious deterioration in the relations" with the
Soviets. It was essential for a meeting of minds clearly defining what the
past agreements were and clarifying the agreements as to situations which
had arisen since Yalta. As a result, he sent Joseph E. Davies, a Soviet
apologist, to see Churchill. At the same time, Harry Hopkins, a dying
man, was dispatched to Moscow. When Davies returned from London,
he reported that he had informed Churchill that Truman's "position was
that every agreement made by President Roosevelt would be scrupulously
supported. . . ." [9] He wrote the President the following about Churchill:
"His attitude placed not only the future, but possibly the immediate
peace in real danger. To assume that we could win through a 'tough'
approach, in my opinion, would involve a terrific risk. . . . I said that,
frankly, as I had listened to him inveigh so violently against the threat of
Soviet domination and the spread of Communism in Europe, and disclose
such a lack of confidence in the professions of good faith in Soviet leadership, I had wondered whether he, the Prime Minister, was not willing to
declare to the world that he and Britain had made a mistake in not supporting Hitler. . . ." The Davies report went on:

For such value as it might have, I wished to give my judgment as to the
Soviets. My opinion was that we could rely upon the good faith of the Soviet
leaders (1) to work for a practical Peace Structure; (2) to co-operate with
Western Europe as good neighbors and not seek to proselytize Europe, to the
degree that was consistent with her security as against a possible implacable
religious, economic or political hostility of Western neighbors.[10]

---

[6] *U.S. Relations with China,* pp. 96-97.

[7] *Ibid.,* pp. 97-98.

[8] Acting Secretary of State Joseph Grew instructed Hurley on June 18, 1945: "As you
know, the President is wholly committed to the fulfillment of the agreement made at
Yalta. . . ." Grew to Hurley, June 18, 1945, *Hurley Papers.* File 326, Document No. 29.
MSS., Santa Fe.

[9] The Chairman of the President's War Relief Control Board (Davies) to the President, June 12, 1945, *Potsdam Papers,* I, pp. 64-65.

[10] *Ibid.,* pp. 72-74.

Churchill was not persuaded. He became "vehement and violent" in his criticisms of the Soviet Union. He spoke with much feeling of the "steel curtain" of the Soviets being "clamped down" on Eastern Europe. He said that when Stalin asked him recently why he feared the Soviets in Europe, he replied that was it because they had sent in advance of the Red Army, Communist propagandists and leaders, "like locusts," to establish Communist cells.[11] Davies wound up his report to President Truman with a list of conclusions, including these:

He [Mr. Churchill] was bitterly disappointed by the President's decision and the fact that American troops were already being diverted from Europe to the Eastern [Pacific] Theatre, and would be withdrawn (retreat, as he called it) to the occupational zones agreed upon. . . .
It had been his purpose, and so avowedly stated, to employ the presence of American forces and their position in advance of their lines, as trading material to induce concessions from the Soviets. . . .[12]

In spite of his pleading, Churchill lost. President Truman refused to delay the withdrawal of American troops. On July 1, they began pulling back from the territory in Eastern Germany that they had won by force of arms. Soviet troops moved in to replace them—and the Iron Curtain moved west to the middle of Germany.

The bargaining power that Churchill wanted for the West was lost even before the Potsdam Conference began.

Of Hopkins' mission, President Truman writes: "I was assured to learn from Hopkins that Stalin had confirmed the understanding reached at Yalta. . . . Russian entry into the war against Japan was highly important to us." [13] From Hopkins came this worried report about a conversation with Stalin: "I told Stalin further that I personally felt that our relations were threatened and that I frankly had many misgivings about it and with my intimate knowledge of the situation, I was, frankly bewildered with some of the things that were going on." [14]

In the meantime, the war in the Pacific was taking a terrible turn for the Japanese. Since they had lost command of the sea and air, their Army, scattered for thousands of miles on the continent and over the Pacific Ocean, was considerably less effective than formerly. U.S. forces could pick their objectives and attack in overwhelming strength. During January and February, 1945, the American Army completed the conquest of Luzon and seized key points such as Palau. Iwo Jima was captured in March and was used along with Saipan as bases for the air bombardment of Japan. Japan was cut off from her own Army and her defenses

---

11 *Ibid.*, p. 67.
12 *Ibid.*, pp. 77-78.
13 Truman, *Memoirs*, I, p. 265.
14 *Potsdam Papers*, I, p. 58.

were destroyed. The invasion of Okinawa on April 1 was a prelude to an attack upon Japan. For the Japanese Navy, Okinawa was the climax. If it could not be defended, then the homeland itself was virtually defenseless. After 82 days of bloody fighting, Okinawa had fallen.

As Japanese power was gradually being crushed, it became increasingly evident to some officials in Washington that the Yalta Agreement should be reappraised. On May 12, Acting Secretary of State, Joseph C. Grew, submitted a memorandum to the War and Navy Departments in which he asked two important questions: (1) Is it of such vital importance to the United States that the Soviet enter the war against Japan at the earliest moment possible that we should not attempt to obtain Soviet agreement to certain desirable political objectives in the Far East before such entry? (2) Should the United States reconsider the secret Yalta Agreement in regard to Soviet political desires in the Far East, or should the Agreement be carried out in whole or in part? [15]

Stimson replied that Russian entry would "materially shorten the war and thus save American lives," that the Yalta concessions were "within the military power of Russia to obtain regardless of U.S. military action short of war," and that our experiences with the Russians in the occupation of Germany, "might" in the future lead to considerations which would point to the wisdom of exclusive occupation by our own forces." However, "The discussion of this subject prior to Russian entry into the Japanese war does not seem necessary at this time." [16]

The two questions submitted by Grew were extremely important in view of the Japanese attempt to obtain Soviet mediation to end the conflict with America. As early as February, 1945, the Japanese had been sending peace feelers, but this information was carefully concealed by Stalin from American officials until the Potsdam Conference, five months later. Stalin did not wish to see the Pacific War end "prematurely" without first exacting maximum concessions from the United States as his price to enter the war against Japan.

As Japan's combat potential was seriously weakened by January, 1945, due to our constant military pressure, it is questionable whether Soviet assistance was necessary in the Far East. We were not under any obligation after the conference at Yalta to wait for the Soviet Union to enter the war. Secretary Stimson was warned in an intelligence report, dated July 5, 1945, that "with the total defeat of Japan, Russia will again emerge as the sole military land power of any account in Asia. But she will be vastly stronger than at any time in the past." [17] With our military striking power and the constant diminution of Japan's potential, our diplomats were in a most excellent position at the time of the Yalta

---

[15] Grew, *Turbulent Era*, II, p. 1456.
[16] Current, *Secretary Stimson*, p. 228.
[17] *Ibid.*

Conference to negotiate to protect our interest in the Far East. America could speak the only language the Communists understand, the language of power. Roosevelt at the time of the Yalta Conference had at his command the most powerful land, sea, and air forces ever assembled on earth. He had unquestionable strength to make Russia respect her solemn agreements. He could have made use of this military strength as a power factor in negotiating with the Soviet Union, but the "Russophilism which possessed his mind at this time blinded him to all other considerations." [18]

The official explanation for not informing Chiang Kai-shek of the Yalta Agreement was "for reasons of military security, and for those only, it was considered too dangerous for the United States to consult with the National Government." [19] This is difficult to understand since China and not the Soviet Union was our ally in the Pacific. All those who were close to the Generalissimo have testified to his loyal support of our war effort against Japan.[20]

Why did Stalin want the Yalta Agreement kept secret? He indicated that he was afraid that information would leak from Chungking to Tokyo, thus provoking a Japanese attack on the Russian Far East. As reported earlier, he told Roosevelt that "when it was possible to . . . move twenty-five divisions to the Far East, he thought it would be possible to speak to Marshal Chiang Kai-shek about these matters." [21] "These matters," of course, were the Chinese territory Russia was to get. This secrecy denied Chiang the opportunity to initiate moves to prevent the seizure of Japanese arms and supplies by the Russians at the moment of surrender.

Stalin suggested that the time for a meeting with China's Foreign Minister T. V. Soong should be the end of April. The implication of Stalin's statement is that with twenty-five formidable Soviet divisions on the Chinese border, Chiang would "wholeheartedly" agree to giving up his territory to the Russians. How such troop movements could fail to be detected by the Japanese agents and observers is difficult to understand. And the Japanese did know it.[22]

Generalissimo Chiang Kai-shek was willing to have a rapprochement with the Soviet Union.[23] But before sending T. V. Soong to Moscow to negotiate, Chiang was eager to know what talks concerning China had

---

[18] George N. Crocker, *Roosevelt's Road to Russia* (Chicago: Henry Regnery Co., 1959), p. 270.

[19] *U.S. Relations with China*, p. IX.

[20] Testimony of General Albert C. Wedemeyer, June 11, 1951, *Military Situation in the Far East Hearings*, Part 3, pp. 2432-2433. Hurley testified that the Yalta Agreement was "well known" to the Russian and Chinese Communists and the Japanese, but "I learned of its existence through the Chinese armed Communists." *Ibid.*, Part 4, p. 2836.

[21] *Yalta Documents*, pp. 769-770.

[22] Kase, *Journey to the "Missouri,"* p. 224.

[23] Statement of W. Averell Harriman, *Military Situation in the Far East Hearings*, Part 5, pp. 3334-3335.

taken place between Roosevelt and Stalin at Yalta. Roosevelt did not tell Chiang anything about the secret agreement. Even during the San Francisco Conference, when T. V. Soong visited President Truman in Washington on May 14, Yalta was not mentioned.[24] Stalin told Hopkins and Harriman at Moscow at the beginning of June that Soviet troops would begin to attack the Japanese forces early in August if China had by then accepted the terms of the agreement. Finally, Truman divulged the secret pact to Soong on June 9.[25] Six days later Hurley officially informed the Generalissimo of the agreement and the latter expressed his disappointment.[26]

It is now evident that under duress, not only from the Soviet Union but also from the United States, China was forced to negotiate her treaty with Russia. It conceded vital rights in Manchuria and abandoned all China's rights in Mongolia. This action by our government towards an ally is unprecedented in the history of American Foreign Relations.

What would have happened if Generalissimo Chiang Kai-shek had rejected the Yalta Agreement? There is no record in the Yalta Papers indicating that Roosevelt and Stalin discussed this possibility. It can be assumed, however, that a rejection by the Generalissimo would have caused the antagonism of both Roosevelt and Stalin. Chiang's peril was so great that he had no alternative but to agree to it. He was in no position to challenge the Yalta Agreement. The whole affair was disappointing to him since Roosevelt had promised at the Cairo Conference that China would receive all the territory Japan had taken since 1914. Chiang was faced with a *fait accompli*.

There were "certain points" concerning the "implementation" of the Yalta Agreement that Chiang wanted cleared.[27] To make the best of a bad situation he made one last effort to persuade the United States to stand beside him. He made the suggestion that the United States and Britain should become parties to any agreement between China and the Soviet Union. At least this would assure the possibility of Russia fulfilling her terms in good faith. Chiang also advised that Port Arthur should be designated as a joint naval base for four powers: China, the Soviet Union, the United States, and Great Britain. These proposals were not accepted by the American Government.[28] Hurley was advised that our government "could not very well agree to participate in the joint use of

---

[24] Herbert Feis, *The China Tangle* (New Jersey: Princeton University Press, 1953), p. 306, 312.

[25] Grew, *Turbulent Era*, II, pp. 1465-1466.

[26] Ambassador Hurley to Acting Secretary of State Grew, June 15, 1945, *Hurley Papers*, File 315, Document No. 3. *MSS.*, Santa Fe.

[27] Memorandum by the Acting Secretary of State Grew, June 16, 1945, *Potsdam Papers*, I, p. 176.

[28] Memorandum from Dr. Wang Shih-chieh, Minister of Information, to Ambassador Hurley, June 15, 1945, *Hurley Papers*, File 326, Document No. 26. *MSS.*, Santa Fe.

Port Arthur as a naval base or become a party to China's agreement with the Soviet Union." [29]

Soong arrived at Moscow early in July to start negotiations with the Soviet Government. Actually, China was in a very weak bargaining position. Committed to the Yalta provisions, Chiang Kai-shek was anxious to arrive at some agreement with Stalin before Russia entered the Far Eastern War, so that Russia would be bound by a treaty negotiated with the Chinese Government, and not simply by the Yalta Agreement, to which China was not a signatory. The demands made by Stalin would, however, mean a dominating Soviet influence in Manchuria. First, Stalin wanted a controlling interest in the Chinese Eastern Railway and the South Manchurian Railway, insisting on a "majority of directors," which Soong resisted. Second, he demanded that the military zone under Russian control should include "Dairen as well as Port Arthur." Third, the Chinese should recognize the complete independence of the Mongolian People's Republic (Outer Mongolia). [30]

Stalin's insistence that China recognize the independence of Outer Mongolia came as a "complete surprise" to Chiang Kai-shek. His views were clearly stated in a critical message to Stalin, a copy of which was sent by Hurley to Truman and Byrnes at Potsdam. "It would be against the traditional convictions of our people," he wrote.

Chiang Kai-shek was willing to make "every possible concession" to satisfy Soviet desires, but he could not go "entirely beyond" what the Chinese people were ready to accept. As to the management of the two railroads, he held that this should be Chinese in accordance with respect for the sovereignty of China. The manager of the Chinese Eastern Railway should be Russian; the manager of the South Manchurian Railway should be Chinese. He declared that Dairen should be a "free port" under Chinese management, but offered it as a long-term commercial lease. As for Port Arthur as a naval base, Chiang was willing to accept the joint use of the port, but the civilian administration "should be Chinese." This was the substance of the message Chiang sent to Marshal Stalin. [31]

Soong saw Stalin again on the night of July 12 and offered the maximum concessions his government could make in return for full Soviet recognition of China's sovereignty in Manchuria. As to the management of the railroads, Soong proposed an equal number of directors with a Chinese to be chairman; the manager of the Chinese Eastern Railroad to be Russian and the assistant manager Chinese; the manager of the

29 Acting Secretary of State Grew to Ambassador Hurley, *Hurley Papers*, File 326, Document No. 29. *MSS.*, Santa Fe.

30 Ambassador Harriman to the President and Secretary of State, July 12, 1945, *Potsdam Papers*, I, p. 862.

31 Ambassador Hurley to the President and Secretary of State, July 20, 1945, *Potsdam Papers*, II, pp. 1225-27.

South Manchurian Railroad to be Chinese with a Russian as assistant manager. He proposed that Port Dairen should be a free port under Chinese management, but offered the Soviets docks and storage areas under commercial lease for their traffic. He said he could not agree on placing Port Dairen in a Soviet military zone or to be used as a Soviet naval base. Soong proposed Port Arthur as a naval base for joint use but under Soviet control. Stalin rejected these concessions.[32]

Soong complained to President Truman that Stalin's demands exceeded the terms of the Yalta Agreement, and in reply Secretary of State Byrnes telegraphed him not to go beyond them.[33] Soong later told Admiral Leahy that China could not accept the intended degree of control over Manchuria promised the Russians in the agreement. China, he said, would prefer to settle the controversy by military action during the "next five hundred years." [34] In a message to Ambassador Harriman, Soong stated that "I am convinced that we have gone as far as we possibly could in meeting Soviet demands." [35] Later General Albert C. Wedemeyer testified that Soong felt so strongly about the treaty that he "told me he would not sign such an agreement . . . ceding territory whose sovereignty had been recognized," and "he didn't." Wang Shih-chieh signed in his stead.[36] As the terms of the two sides were far apart, no agreement was reached in the talks. Finally Soong told Stalin that he must seek instructions in Chungking, but would be ready to return to Moscow when Stalin wished. Soong left Moscow on July 14 and Stalin also departed for the Potsdam Conference.

Regarding Soviet desires in Manchuria, Secretary Stimson recorded some pertinent passages in his personal diary. Sometime before July 14 he had several talks with President Truman and submitted a memorandum concerning our Open Door Policy and Soviet demands on Dairen. He warned the President to be "absolutely sure that the Russians did not block off our trade by their control over the Chinese Eastern Railway." [37] On July 15, Ambassador Harriman visited Stimson and was "much worked up over his fears of the Russian plans for Manchuria" and wanted advice. Stimson remarked that if the Russians carry out any such

---

[32] Ambassador Harriman to the President and Secretary of State, July 13, 1945, *Potsdam Papers*, I, p. 863.

[33] Byrnes, *Speaking Frankly*, p. 205.

[34] Leahy, *I Was There*, p. 381. T. F. Tsiang, Chairman of the Chinese delegation at the United Nations, explained in 1952 that the "Chinese Government and people were not blind to the meaning of the Yalta Agreement" and that "we must pronounce the Yalta Agreement a great mistake, a disastrous mistake," Aitchen K. Wu, *China and the Soviet Union* (London: Metheum Company, 1950), pp. 289-292; J. Patrick White, "New Light on Yalta," *Far Eastern Survey*, XIX, (1950), pp. 105-112.

[35] *Hurley Papers*, File 326, Document No. 42. *MSS.*, Santa Fe.

[36] *Military Situation in the Far East*, Part 3, p. 2432.

[37] Stimson *Diary*, Undated entry inserted before July 14, 1945, *Potsdam Papers*, II, p. 1224, fn. 4.

plan to "monopolize trade in Manchuria," this would be a violation of our Open Door Policy. The next day Stimson went to the White House for a conference with Byrnes and "impressed upon him" the importance of the Open Door Policy and advised that "any claim" by Stalin should be opposed.[38]

In the meantime Chiang Kai-shek sent an urgent appeal to President Truman while the latter was attending the Potsdam Conference. He said: "Although China was not represented at the Yalta Conference, you, Mr. President, will realize that we have gone to the limit to fulfill the Yalta formula. We have even gone beyond it in the case of Outer Mongolia. We have gone as far as the public opinion of China will stand. We may even have already gone beyond the limit that the Chinese people will support. I trust in your conversations with Generalissimo Stalin, you will impress upon him the (sic) eminently reasonable stand we have taken, so that he will not insist on the impossible." [39]

Following their interruption by the Potsdam Conference, negotiations were resumed on August 7 with Dr. Wang Shih-chieh, the new Chinese Foreign Minister, replacing Soong as chief Chinese plenipotentiary. At the outset the United States informed the participants that it expected to be consulted prior to the signing of any Sino-Soviet agreement, in view of its role at Yalta. Each night around midnight the meetings began in Stalin's office in the Kremlin, and they lasted until four or five o'clock in the morning. During the day the meetings would continue with Molotov.

Difficulties over the interpretation of the provisions of the Yalta Agreement arose from the very beginning, with the Soviet Union interpreting the agreement to suit its own purposes. As Soviet sordid views of the Yalta Agreement became increasingly apparent, the United States finally felt compelled to inform both parties that certain Soviet proposals exceeded the Yalta provisions.

Finally, on August 14, a series of agreements between the Soviet Union and China, including a Treaty of Friendship and Alliance, were concluded. They were ratified by the Chinese Government on August 24, 1945, and were made public at that time. The first of the agreements was a treaty of friendship and alliance directed against the possibility of a renewal of Japanese aggression.[40] In an exchange of notes relative to the treaty, the Soviet Government pledged itself "to render to China moral support and aid in military supplies and other material resources, such support and aid to be entirely given to the National Government

---

[38] Entry for July 15, 1945, *Ibid.*

[39] Chiang's message was sent by Ambassador Hurley to the President, July 19, 1945, *Hurley Papers,* File 326, Document No. 43. *MSS.,* Santa Fe.

[40] *U.S. Relations with China,* p. 586.

as the central government of China." [41] The Soviet Union agreed to recognize Chinese sovereignty in Manchuria, and China agreed to recognize the independence of Outer Mongolia if a plebiscite after the defeat of Japan confirmed that that was the desire of the Outer Mongolian people.[42] The agreement on Dairen committed China to declare Dairen a free port "open to the commerce and shipping of all nations," and provided for Chinese administration of the port; but it exceeded Yalta by granting the Soviet Union a lease of half of the port facilities, free of charge.[43] A special clause provided for complete Soviet domination of Dairen in the event of war with Japan. It is on the basis of this provision that the Soviet Union refused to open up Dairen to international shipping after the war, as no peace treaty with Japan had been signed.

The agreement on Port Arthur provided for the "joint use" of the naval base by the two powers. The commission consisted of three Soviet and only two Chinese members, with a Soviet representative as chairman. The Civil Administration of the area "will be Chinese," but must "take into account the interest of U.S.S.R." in making appointments to responsible positions. The Soviet Union had the right to maintain in the area of Port Arthur "its army, naval, and air forces and determine their location." [44]

The guarding of the railways was to remain China's responsibility. The Sino-Soviet agreement provided for joint ownership and operation of the Chinese Eastern and South Manchurian Railways. The Treaty and the agreements regarding Dairen, Port Arthur, and the railroad were to run for thirty years.[45]

From Chungking Ambassador Hurley informed Secretary Byrnes on August 16 that Chiang Kai-shek was "generally satisfied with the treaty." [46] The Nationalist Government had reasoned that if its policy satisfied the Soviet government, there would be no excuse for Moscow to support the Chinese Communists; civil war might be avoided in China, and Stalin would be the main force in preventing a Communist victory. But the Kuomintang was hardly deceived by the assurance provided by the agreement of August, 1945. They had a deep distrust of the Russians.[47] They were not naive enough to expect that Stalin would become the grave digger of Chinese Communism. Trying to make the best of an inevitable

---

[41] Commissar for Foreign Affairs, Molotov to the Chinese Minister for Foreign Affairs, Wang, August 14, 1945, *Ibid.*, p. 587.

[42] Foreign Minister Wang, to Commissar for Foreign Affairs, Molotov, August 14, 1945. *Ibid.*, p. 588.

[43] *Ibid.*, p. 589.

[44] *Ibid.*, pp. 590-591.

[45] *Ibid.*, p. 118.

[46] *Ibid.*, p. 120.

[47] Carsun Chang, *The Third Force in China* (New York: Bookman Associates, 1953), p. 162.

situation, Chiang calculated that by giving the Russians what they wanted, he could quickly execute his part of the treaty and then have his hands free to deal with the Communists.

Eventually the treaty was to create friction between the Soviet Union on the one side and China and the United States on the other, over the withdrawal of Russian troops from the port of Dairen. While Port Arthur was claimed by and given to the Soviet Government for defense purposes, Dairen was to remain under Chinese administration in spite of the fact that it was to be surrounded by Soviet-leased territory. The Russians argued that since no peace treaty with Japan had been signed, they could stay in Dairen. When they finally agreed to let Nationalist civil administrators into the city, the Chinese Communists had surrounded it and were running its administration under Russian protection.[48]

The Chinese Communists cut rail lines over which troops could be moved into liberated territory and repeatedly without provocation attacked troops of the Nationalist Government.

Russia's entry into war against Japan in August encouraged the Chinese Communists to increase their efforts to exploit the situation. Chaing Kai-shek was much concerned about this and ordered the Communist armies to refrain from taking further actions, but General Chu Teh remained resolute in his refusal. The Soviet officials did not object to the entry of the Chinese Communist forces in Manchuria. It is estimated that within a month after V-J Day there were over 100,000 Communist troops in Manchuria alone.

Soviet authorities co-operated in setting up control of local governments under Communist rule. The Russian Commander, Malinevsky, for example, told the Nationalist leaders that as regards to areas north of Changchun the Soviet army could not wait for the arrival of Nationalist troops and therefore "local forces," meaning Communists, had to take over where the Russians left.[49]

The admission of Chinese Communists into Manchuria enhanced their power and encouraged their ambition. Moreover, it gave them a strong military position adversely affecting the possibility of a compromise with the Kuomintang and increasing the probability of a civil war. When Chiang Kai-shek tried to occupy Manchuria to bring that area under Chinese sovereignty as provided under the Cairo declaration and the Sino-Soviet Treaty, he encountered Communist obstruction and Soviet refusal to permit government troops to land in Dairen.

Soviet officials delayed on numerous occasions the withdrawal of her forces and prevented the peaceful occupation of Manchuria by the

---

48 David Dallin, *Soviet Russia and the Far East* (New Haven: Yale University Press, 1948), pp. 333-338.
49 Chang, *The Third Force in China*, p. 171.

Nationalist armies. Soviet evacuation did not take place until spring of 1946, when a race began between Nationalist Government and Communist troops for cities about to be evacuated by Russian forces.

It was meaningless for China to sign agreements with the Soviet Union at great sacrifice of China's territorial and administrative integrity to bring Russia into war against an already defeated Japan. It was equally meaningless for the United States to go to war against Japan to preserve the "Open Door" policy and then sacrifice it at the altar of Yalta. The territorial and administrative integrity of China had been the cardinal plank in our Asiatic platform since John Hay's day. The Yalta concessions placed Stalin in a position from which he could dominate China and communize vast portions of Asia.

Immediately after its declaration of war on Japan, 700,000 Soviet troops moved into Manchuria ahead of Nationalist forces. In October, 1945, Vice-Admiral Daniel Barbey was ordered to escort Nationalist troops to Manchuria, but found all seaports closed to him. He was forced to retreat from the Manchurian port of Hulutao, after Communist troops had fired at his launch.[50] Manchuria's two main ports, Dairen and Port Arthur, were under Russian control, thanks to the Yalta Agreement.

The Red Army's refusal to allow the Chinese Nationalists to use Dairen constituted a violation of the Sino-Soviet Treaty of August, 1945, according to which Dairen was supposed to be an international port. Thus Chinese Nationalists forces could not be transported by sea to Manchuria and were landed instead in North China. Thence they marched north, overland, being also denied the use of railways by the Russians. As they reached Manchuria, they were met by the Chinese Communist forces armed by Russia and in prepared positions.

Stalin had pledged to Soong that Soviet troops would completely withdraw from Manchuria, at the latest, three months from the day of Japanese surrender. But the Russians postponed the withdrawal time and again.[51] The presence of American Marines in Manchuria annoyed the Soviet Government, and the matter was broached by Molotov at a meeting of the Moscow Conference of Foreign Ministers on December 16, 1945. Secretary Byrnes pointed out most emphatically that American Marines were there at the request of the Nationalist Government to help disarm Japanese troops. Molotov replied "it was intolerable that there were still Japanese forces which had not yet been disarmed."

---

[50] George Moorad, *Lost Peace in China* (New York: E. P. Dutton and Company, 1949), pp. 91-92. Dallin, *Soviet Russia and the Far East*, p. 252. The Soviet Union had permitted landings at Hulutao and Yengkuo, neither of which is as good a harbor as that of Dairen. Communist troops were concentrated near Hulutao. Statement by Wang Shih-chieh, Minister of Foreign Affairs, October 31, 1945, *Hurley Papers*, File 315, Document No. 9. *MSS.*, Santa Fe.

[51] Ambassador Harriman to Ambassador Hurley, August 30, 1945, *Hurley Papers*, File 326, Document No. 50. *MSS.*, Santa Fe.

In a subsequent conversation with Secretary Byrnes, Stalin also objected to the use of American troops in the demobilization of Japanese troops in China. The communique issued at the close of the Moscow Conference contained the following statement regarding China: "The Three Foreign Secretaries . . . were in agreement as to the need of a unified and democratic China under the National Government . . . and for a cessation of civil strife. . . . The two Foreign Secretaries (Byrnes and Molotov) were in complete accord as to the desirability of withdrawal of Soviet and American forces from China at the earliest practical moment consistent with the discharge of their obligations and responsibilities." [52] The wording of this agreement indicates a superficial arrangement on this issue.

When Senator Owen Brewster of Maine returned after an inspection tour in the Far East, he remarked that American Marines were in China to make sure that "China will not be in America tomorrow under the spur of a Soviet dictatorship as ruthless as Genghis Khan's," and that "a Sovietized China in the next quarter of a century would mean the certain end of America and everything for which it stands." [53]

It soon became clear that the Soviet Government intended to secure important economic concessions as a result of the presence of her troops in Manchuria, particularly declaring that all industrial enterprise in Manchuria could be regarded as war booty.[54]

In May and June, 1946, a reparations commission, under the chairmanship of Edwin Pauley, investigated industrial conditions in Manchuria on behalf of the United States. His report stated: "Upon their arrival, the Soviets began a systematic confiscation of food and stock piles and in early September started the selective removal of industrial machinery." It was, Pauley believed, intended to complete these removals by December 3, 1945—the date originally fixed for the withdrawal of Soviet military forces. Pauley estimated the damage to Manchurian industry at $858 million and the cost of replacement at $2,000 million.[55]

Large numbers of Chinese Communists troops were in control in important areas of Manchuria within two or three months after the Russians withdrew, and many of them were armed and equipped from the materials left by the Japanese after their surrender. Russian withdrawals were timed in such a way as to facilitate the Chinese Communists' advances and their seizures of materials. American and British newspapermen visiting parts of Manchuria brought back lurid stories of Russian occupation, of terrorism, of wholesale destruction of property and

52 A Decade of American Foreign Policy, pp. 63-64.
53 New York Times, August 9, 1946.
54 Daniel S. Law, "Manchurian Booty and International Law," American Journal of International Law (Volume 40, July 1946), pp. 584-591.
55 Department of State Bulletin, December 22, 1946.

removal of machinery and supplies, and of Russian and Red Chinese co-operation.

On October 17 the Soviet Government had announced that its troops would begin withdrawing from Manchuria and that the evacuation would be completed by the end of November. After numerous delays and excuses the final evacuation of Soviet troops was not completed until May 31, 1946. This withdrawal did not include Port Arthur and Dairen.

Stalin had collected, in full, his Yalta concessions. A friendly Chinese government has since been pushed into a last stand on Formosa. But we helped make possible the birth of the antagonistic new force in the world—Red China. We ignored repeated surrender overtures of a defeated Japan and helped build in Asia a far greater menace—Communist Russia.

Admiral Leahy warned President Roosevelt about Russian entry into war against Japan. General MacArthur, as early as January, 1945, advised President Roosevelt to negotiate Japanese surrender. Admiral King told President Truman that the Russians were "not indispensable" and we should not "beg them to come in." General Eisenhower begged Truman not to give "anything away" because "there was no question but that Japan was already thoroughly beaten."

All such advice fell on deaf ears, and Stalin had his way. The balance of power in the Far East shifted from Japan to the Soviet Union. The way had been prepared for Communist conquest. And soon, an incredible new art of conquest would be revealed to the world—conquest by subversion, intrigue, policy sabotage, propaganda, and "brainwash."

PART TWO

Undermining an Ally

CHAPTER VIII

THE TREASURY TAKES A HAND

In 1919, John Maynard Keynes, the British economist, observed:

Lenin is said to have declared that the best way to destroy the capitalist system was to debauch the currency. . . . Lenin certainly was right. There is no subtler, no surer means of overturning the existing basis of society than to debauch the currency. The process engages all the hidden forces of economic law on the side of destruction, and it does it in a manner which not one man in a million can diagnose.[1]

In the 1930's, during the early years of the Roosevelt administration, Communist infiltration centered mainly in the government agencies concerned with economic recovery. In such areas the Communists could see the largest hopes for immediate success in instituting programs based upon their philosophy of government, which was socialism.

With the gathering of war clouds in Europe, U. S. government agencies concerned with domestic economy became greatly reduced in importance to the Communist apparatus in the United States. There was a dramatic shift in the direction of infiltration. Agencies concerned with foreign affairs, Lend Lease, and the like had now become the prime targets for infiltration. Communist agents placed in these agencies could be of maximum usefulness to the Soviet Union. The war-time agencies became infiltrated to a degree sufficient to give Communists decisive influence.

Significantly, and beginning in the 1930's, the United States Treasury Department became one of the most heavily and decisively infiltrated of all departments of the U. S. Government. This group exercised almost complete control in the Treasury Department during the early 1940's. During the period of 1944-1946, another shift in direction of Communist infiltration occurred. The United Nations, its Specialized Agencies, and organizations such as the International Monetary Fund became gather-

---

[1] Paul Bakewell, Jr., *What Are We Using For Money* (New York: D. Van Nostrand, Inc., 1952) , p. 201.

ing points for Communist agents who flocked from various agencies of the U. S. Government. Most of the key agents in the Treasury Department moved to the International Monetary Fund and to various agencies of the United Nations. Apparently they felt that the monetary and economic affairs of the United States had become so enmeshed in the workings of international organizations that the most decisive influence could be exercised at the international level. Also, in view of Congressional investigations and other exposures of Communist activity, international agencies offered a far safer haven than agencies of the United States Government. However, it would be naive to suppose that the Communist apparatus would put all its eggs in one basket. Indeed, more recent disclosures have shown that the Soviets by no means abandoned infiltration of our government agencies.

During the war years—a period in which monetary matters were of critical importance to the government of China—a group of Soviet agents in the Treasury Department enjoyed dominant influence in monetary matters of the United States and also over economic aspects of the prosecution of the war. Heading this group was Dr. Harry Dexter White. White was a brilliant intellect, an outstanding economist, an expert in monetary matters, and an exceptionally gifted organizer. He joined the Treasury Department on June 30, 1934. His rise was rapid, and he soon became the dominant influence in that department. On March 25, 1938, he became Director of Monetary Research. On August 30, 1941, White was appointed Assistant Secretary of Treasury, in charge of all monetary affairs. In 1945, the Director of Monetary Research under White was V. Frank Coe, identified by Elizabeth Bentley as a member of the Silvermaster group. Coe's assistant was Dr. Harold Glasser, identified by Elizabeth Bentley as a member of the Perlo group. Thus, by the end of the war, the monetary affairs of the United States were virtually in the control of the Communist apparatus.[2]

It was this group of men that made the decisions bearing on the financial stability of the Chinese Government. They had the power and the resources to stabilize the Chinese currency and preserve the Government of China— or to debauch the currency and overthrow that government. In line with Soviet policy, they took the latter course.

Much light has been cast upon the manner in which these Soviet agents in the Treasury Department established policies designed to insure economic collapse of the Nationalist Government of China. It should be pointed out that these people, in many instances, operated directly con-

2 In view of the present gold situation in the United States, some thoughtful Americans are concerned that our government may still be following monetary policies originally set up by White and his Communist associates. White's concern with foreign aid of all sorts and his expressed desire to spread our gold all over the world lend credence to such a belief.

trary to the policies and orders of President Roosevelt. They so misled and befuddled Secretary of the Treasury Henry Morgenthau, Jr., as to render him totally ineffectual. In the case of President Roosevelt, he was often led to believe that the course of action being taken was the opposite of that actually taken by White and his associates. Congress was in much the same position. Nothing indicates any personal responsibility of President Roosevelt with regard to the contrived economic collapse of the Chinese Government.

Extensive testimony has been given by Dr. Arthur N. Young, financial adviser to the Chinese Government from 1929 to 1946. Young, in the 1920's had been an economic adviser to the State Department. In 1951 and 1952, he was head of the financial mission to Saudi Arabia. Young traced the background of the monetary problem in China:

When the Nationalist Government became the Government of China in 1928, they faced a chaotic situation. The currency was in a very confused state, with a variety of silver, copper, and paper money which bore no relation to each other. The revenues had been so inadequate that no previous Peiping government could survive for very long. The debts were in default to a very large extent.

When the Nationalist Government took over, they set out on a program of financial rehabilitation. During the period from 1928 to 1937 they succeeded in unifying and stabilizing the currency. They developed quite promptly very large revenues, sources of revenue, from the customs and internal revenue with the result that the Government had a large degree of financial stability by 1937. Also the greater part of these defaulted debts had been settled.

In fact, the situation was so promising in 1937 that China's economy was going ahead by leaps and bounds. Foreign capital was coming into the country. The outlook was really very good.

I agree with the appraisal made by former Ambassador Dr. Hu Shih, Chinese Ambassador in Washington, who said that, during this period in the 1930's, China had the best government it has ever had. I think one of the reasons why the Japanese attacked in 1937 was that China was getting ahead so rapidly that they had reached the conclusion that it was now or never.

The result of the Japanese attack was, of course, to disrupt, to tear down a great deal of good work which the Nationalist Government had done during this period. . . .

When the war came, the Japanese rapidly overran the principal cities and destroyed the sources of revenue. They also, of course, drove the Chinese out of the areas where the most modern developments had taken place, and it was not possible at that time for the Chinese Government to derive adequate revenues from the sources at its command.

The Chinese Government, therefore, was forced to rely on paper money, inflation, as the main financial resource available for the purpose of fighting the war.[3]

---

[3] Testimony of Arthur N. Young, July 13, 1956, U. S. Congress, Senate, Committee on the Judiciary, Internal Security Subcommittee, *Scope of Soviet Activity in the United States, Hearings,* 84th Cong., 2nd Sess. (Washington: Government Printing Office, 1957), Part 35, p. 1956.

This was the situation in 1941 when the United States became allied with China in the war against Japan. Our ally had, for four years, been fighting a protracted war against the now common enemy. Certainly, China needed military aid. But far more important, she needed help in averting imminent economic collapse that faced her solely as a result of the protracted war she had been fighting.

As early as 1939, Young had discussed China's grave financial situation with Dr. Stanley Hornbeck and Secretary Hull of the State Department, pointing out that "China, because of its difficult financial situation, was in fully as much danger from financial disintegration as it was from the Japanese, from the war." [4] At the same time, Young discussed the matter with Secretary of the Treasury and with White.

> I explained to all of these people that it was very urgent that China should have additional financial resources for the purpose of maintaining stability of the currency, and that was the policy that was carried out, that was followed up by Dr. T. V. Soong when he came here in 1940, and I came back from China with him to help conduct certain negotiations. He was seeking financial help because of the great need in China to try to hold that situation together financially. And that led up to this stabilization matter of 1941.[5]

Young told how the Treasury Department—that is, the office of Harry Dexter White—took over the whole matter of Chinese currency stabilization:

> . . . the document . . . that Dr. Soong submitted, proposed a continuation of the type of stabilization operations that we had conducted up to 1941. That is, the stabilization of the open market and the maintenance of confidence through support of the rate of exchange, and in my discussions with the State Department in 1939 and also in my discussions with Mr. Morgenthau, I had supported that same policy which we thought had worked reasonably well, considering the resources that we had, and so far as I could judge, the State Department was convinced of the merits of that policy. . . .
> Then in 1940, when this matter got into the hands of the Treasury, they shifted the base. The Treasury supported the idea of introducing an exchange control into China at this period. That was an idea that we had played with from the very beginning. We considered it at the very outbreak of the Japanese —the Sino-Japanese War.
> We rejected it on the grounds that the Japanese would have control of the ports and that the Chinese Government would have no means to administer an exchange control and also lacked the administrative experience at that time to do it.
> But the Treasury nevertheless took up the idea of exchange control and, when they introduced this stabilization plan in 1941, it was based on the idea of an exchange control. So they took the ball away from those of us who had been

4 *Ibid.,* p. 1957.
5 *Ibid.,* p. 1957.

handling it before and, when the stabilization plan of 1941 was put into operation, it was done on the basis of an exchange control.[6]

Secretary Morgenthau submitted this stabilization plan to the Congress and received its approval. Young testified that Harry Dexter White had been anxious to get control of the Stabilization Board and to devise his own plan. This he did, the plan being that submitted to Congress by Secretary Morgenthau. Young had, in 1939, given the State Department an estimate of the cost of the stabilization plan he and Dr. Soong had recommended: " . . . I thought $50 million in the first instance to carry it for a year, but with $25 million more on call." [7] These figures become significant in the light of what transpired when the White plan was put into effect. Young's testimony reveals that greater funds were frittered away in the ineffectual action designed by White:

> . . . this stabilization plan devised by the Treasury . . . proved to be very expensive to China. During the period of about three years, from the middle of 1938 to August, 1941 . . . we had maintained a moderate degree of stability with the expenditure of a little over $40 million. . . .
> Then the Stabilization Board took over in August of 1941 . . . operating an exchange control and that proved to be costly. In about $3\frac{2}{3}$ months from August 18, if I remember correctly, to Pearl Harbor in the early part of December of 1941, their expenditures were about $24 million. In other words, in less than 4 months they had spent a sum of about $24 million compared with the cost that we had been incurring over 3 years of not twice that amount. . . .
> They sold exchange at a fixed rate which I think was fixed too high, and they were unable to buy anything back. It was a one-way proposition, all going out and nothing coming in, whereas on the free market operation we could sometimes buy back, as I mentioned in the case of his (sic) Hankow affair, when we bought back most of the $16 million we had sold, after the market settled down.
> So they had this exchange control. They were giving it all out. In the meantime, the free market rate, which had been steady a number of months, went to pot. It immediately dropped down when there was no support of the free market, and that was a shock and aggravated the prices and made the financial problems more difficult for the Chinese Government, in my opinion.[8]

Documents contained in the nine hundred volumes of the Morgenthau Diaries make clear that a complete nullification of the will of Congress and economic destruction of a valiant ally was accomplished by the establishing of this policy recommended by White. They show that Anna Louise Strong flew from Yenan to Washington, and had interviews with Eleanor Roosevelt and Harry Dexter White in an effort to break up a

---

[6] *Ibid.*, pp. 1958-1959. Exchange control is a system under which the rate is set by the government and artificially maintained by direct controls over demand and supply. Illegal rates, multiple official rates, and disorderly cross-rates often result from exchange controls.

[7] *Ibid.*, p. 1959.

[8] *Ibid.*, p. 1961, p. 1964.

then-pending United States stabilization loan to Chiang Kai-shek, and that White thereafter cut the amount of the loan by 40 per cent and surrounded the remaining 60 per cent with conditions making it virtually useless.

Still earlier, White and Lauchlin Currie had been strenuous advocates of the so-called "Three-Way Loan" under which the United States would have made a loan to the U.S.S.R., which, in turn, would have made a loan to China. The "Three-Way Loan," quite obviously, would have applied an important U.S.S.R. economic pressure against Japan.

The Morgenthau Diaries reveal that subordinates of White were sympathetically dealing with the Chinese Communists, who were dedicated not only to the destruction of our ally, the Nationalist Government, but of our Government as well. The Harry Dexter White story is an important instance of official perversion of our national foreign policy in the Far East.

White and his associates in the Treasury Department played an important part in bringing about the downfall of the Nationalist Government. Frequent letters and memoranda were written by these people. White usually brought them to the attention of Secretary Morgenthau. Morgenthau was almost always persuaded to agree with the White's views. The Senate Internal Security Subcommittee assigns White a major role in the China debacle.

Both Whittaker Chambers and Elizabeth Bentley have stated under oath that White was involved with the Communist underground in government, which furnished secret documents for transmission to the Kremlin. Notes in White's own hand were found in the Chambers "Pumpkin Papers." [9] F.B.I. Director J. Edgar Hoover has stated that the Bentley charges about the White-Treasury apparatus were substantiated from more than thirty sources.[10]

Dr. Arthur N. Young, in his testimony before the Senate Internal Security Subcommittee, told how Congress sought to give our ally, Chiang Kai-shek, desperately needed economic aid. He told how White and his fellow conspirators held back that aid, while secretly communicating with men who became the Red rulers of China. As Young explained it, economic aid to China during the war was at least as important as military aid, if not more important.[11] He cited many documents to substantiate the story he told from his own experience. They boil down to this: China asked for $200 million in gold, in July, 1943, and received approximately $29 million from the time of the loan to July, 1945. Meanwhile her cur-

9 U.S. Congress, Senate, Committee on the Judiciary, Internal Security Subcommittee, *Interlocking Subversion in Government Departments, Final Report,* July 30, 1953, 83rd Cong. 1st Sess. (Washington: Government Printing Office, 1953), p. 19.

10 Testimony of J. Edgar Hoover, November 17, 1953. *Ibid.,* Part 16, pp. 1142-1154.

11 Testimony of Arthur N. Young, *op. cit.,* Part 35, p. 1975. Exhibit No. 329.

rency collapsed in a suffocating inflation, which helped to bring down anti-Communist Chiang Kai-shek and bring up the Chinese Reds.[12]

In July, 1943, Dr. H. H. Kung, Chinese Minister of Finance, wrote proposing that China be allowed to purchase $200,000,000 dollars' worth of gold with the United States loan. The purpose of the loan was to check inflation. He added: "It is earnestly hoped that it can be realized at an early date." They did not want to "lose this good opportunity of checking inflation." [13]

Secretary Morgenthau informed the President that $240 million was being used to back Chinese Government savings certificates and bond issues and that $20 million was being used to purchase gold. The Chinese were urged, however, to "give careful consideration to the best ways of using the gold, particularly because of the great costs, difficulties and dangers inherent in the use of gold as a means of checking inflation under conditions existing in China at present." Treasury officials "especially stressed the fact that the Chinese Government will by this step be sacrificing large amounts of foreign exchange, which could be used in the post-war period to pay for imports needed for reconstruction and rehabilitation." It was suggested that "the gold might be sold to the public in China in small bars of one or two ounces in order to reach the widest possible section of the Chinese public and such bars might have some engraving which might suggest the United States origin of the financial aid, if the Government of China so wished." [14] It was then agreed that $200 million would "be made available from the credit on the books of the Treasury in the name of the Government of the Republic of China for the purchase of gold." [15]

Assistant Secretary White later raised this question and said "we ought to be tough with the Chinese on the question of earmarking $200 million of gold for gold sales which they could not make before the gold could be shipped to them." Morgenthau agreed saying "we ought to be tough in this matter and he told [White] to go ahead and let them have the gold as rapidly as it could be shipped and sold in China." [16]

Insofar as the currency stabilization plan was concerned there were "serious doubts" whether the $50 million Chinese stabilization loan could be renewed since the official dollar-yuan rate was "so much out of line with its real value." White wanted to discuss the matter with Morgen-

---

12 *Ibid.*, pp. 1965-1976, Exhibit No. 329.

13 Message received from the Chinese Minister of Finance (Kung), July 8, 1943. *United States Relations with China*, p. 486.

14 Memorandum to President Roosevelt from Secretary of the Treasury Morgenthau, July 15, 1943. *Ibid.*, pp. 486-487.

15 Secretary of the Treasury Morgenthau to the Chinese Minister of Finance (Kung), July 27, 1943. *Ibid.*, p. 487.

16 Memorandum of a Meeting in the Secretary's Office, by Harry D. White, September 29, 1943. *Scope of Soviet Activity in the United States.* Part 35, p. 1984.

thau since the Chinese were "pressing [them] for a decision," but he and his associates "would like to stall as long as possible." [17] It was this stalling or "foot-dragging on the part of the Treasury," according to Young, which caused China's currency to deteriorate. Finally the shipping delays "proved very embarrassing because the gold began running out and the Chinese Government had no option but to sell for forward delivery which was not nearly as satisfactory as selling spot gold." [18] According to Young this policy had "a serious effect in aggravating the inflation." He explained:

> Whenever gold arrived, when it was shipped from the United States, when it arrived in India, when it arrived in China, each of those stages was reported in the press and had an effect of bolstering confidence, but obviously, when the Chinese Government had no gold deliveries in spite of its commitments, in spite of the feeling that it had a promise from the American Government to send it, there was a feeling of lack of American support and consequently it was one of those intangible things but undoubtedly had an effect in hurting the confidence and in stimulating the financial deterioration that was taking place.[19]

On November 5, 1943, White held a meeting in his office with Hsi Te-mou, Dr. T. V. Soong, and Irving S. Friedman, one of White's close associates in the Treasury Department. Dr. H. H. Kung, Chinese Finance Minister, had not as yet received a reply regarding a proposed visit to China by the Secretary and White. The latter indicated they had not gone on to China from Cairo "because of lack of time and need to return home to attend to urgent business." Apparently this concerned a change in financial policy toward China.

Hsi read a cable which indicated that Kung wished the Treasury to choose whether the 1941 Stabilization Agreement "ought to be terminated or whether it ought to be renewed along the lines suggested by the Chinese."

> Mr. White indicated that the Treasury felt that under present circumstances the 1941 Stabilization Agreement should not be renewed and that Mr. Adler would be asked to resign from the Board. Mr. White pointed out that the Treasury felt that a stabilization agreement should not be entered into on the basis of the present exchange rate which was completely out of line with real conditions. Mr. White also said that furthermore, *it was clear that the Chinese had no need for the financial assistance at this time.* . . .
> Mr. White suggested that if the Chinese felt that it might be in their best interests to give as little publicity as possible to the non-renewal of the 1941 Agreement, the whole question of the status of the 1941 Agreement could, per-

---

17 Harry D. White to Henry Morgenthau, September 22, 1943, *Ibid.*, pp. 1984-1985.

18 Testimony of Dr. Arthur N. Young, *op. cit.*, Part 35, p. 1979.

19 *Ibid.*, p. 1983. White was a brilliant economist and monetary expert. He could not be any more unaware of the psychological factors involved than of the ultimate effects of the policies he followed.

haps, remain in suspense and thus the Agreement could be reactivated at any time with a minimum of fuss. Mr. Hsi indicated that the Chinese would probably prefer this since it might make it unnecessary for the Chinese to pay off their sterling obligations at this time. Mr. White indicated that his suggestion was merely tentative and that it would be best to give further thought to the question of whether the Agreement should be terminated or whether the whole matter should be allowed to lie for the time being.[20]

A Chinese request for transfer of $200 million of gold was also discussed at this meeting. A cable from Kung containing this request was left with White.

Mr. White indicated again, as he had on previous occasions, the reasons why the Treasury was reluctant to make this requested transfer, pointing out that not only would it involve an unnecessary expenditure on the part of the Treasury but that this expenditure would be difficult to explain since it seemed to involve doubting the good faith of this Government. It would be in the best interests of China, as well as of the United States, not to urge the Treasury to make the transfer. The Chinese representatives indicated their personal agreement. Mr. White pointed out that gold was being shipped just as fast as transportation facilities could be arranged. The suggestion was made that the Chinese maintain their gold deposits at the Federal Reserve in New York at a level of $10 million, which gold would be available for shipment to China as shipping facilities became available. The current status of the gold shipments was discussed and difficulties in obtaining shipping facilities pointed out.[21]

When T. V. Soong returned to Chungking early in 1944, he informed Kung that Secretary Hull "was still very friendly to China and realized the need for maintaining the official rate [of exchange]." Solomon Adler, our Treasury attaché at the U. S. Embassy in Chungking, was "sure that T. V. either deliberately or unintentionally misrepresented the Secretary's views, but Kung believes him." President Roosevelt had now endorsed the position of American Government agencies "to procure a more reasonable arrangement" with the Chinese. Roosevelt showed "lack of receptivity to what Americans here call the 'Gimme' which characterizes the Chinese view of the American role."

Adler wrote a series of letters to White. These letters enclosed letters and memoranda written by others. This material featured scathing attacks upon the Nationalist Government. White called Secretary Morgenthau's particular attention to these letters as they were received. Their significance is realized when one considers the fact that Elizabeth Bentley has testified under oath that Adler was "a member of the Silvermaster Group." [22]

---

[20] Memorandum of a Meeting in Mr. White's Office on November 5, 1943 at 12:15 P.M., by I. S. Friedman, *Harry Dexter White Papers*, Princeton University, *MSS*, File II, 24. Italics mine.

[21] *Ibid.*

[22] *Institute of Pacific Relations, Hearings*, Part 2, p. 434. He was also identified by

Adler's correspondence evidences the persistent efforts that were made to undermine the Nationalist Government along the lines favored by the Chinese Communists. On December 15, 1943, Adler sent a very critical memorandum to White. He said that Chiang Kai-shek lost interest in fighting the Japanese because he knows the defeat of the Japanese is inevitable. We ought "to get tough with Chiang if we are to get any results, and that there is no point in eulogizing him to the skies." The Americans in Chungking were able to breathe "a unanimous sigh of relief when they heard that the President had made no financial commitment to Chiang at Cairo." It should be emphasized that "the Central Government is unstable, that its instability is increasing, that it is making no serious attempt to rectify its inherent instability—if anything the contrary, that Chiang no longer fulfills the function of being the main unifying factor in China, and that American policy vis-a-vis China which appears to be postulated on the assumption that the Government is stable and strong should be based on the facts." [23]

President Roosevelt asked Morgenthau to reconsider the possibility of a loan to China. The latter replied it "could not be justified by the results that have been obtained. It is my opinion that a loan is unnecessary at this time and would be undesirable from the point of view of China and the United States." Instead, he recommended that gold shipments be accelerated "to twice the amount we have previously planned to send. It should be possible to raise gold shipments from $6 million a month to about $12 million." He urged the President to keep in mind that "the basic reason for inflation in China is the shortage of goods." [24] Insofar as the request for a billion dollars was concerned, Morgenthau supposed that it was to be used for postwar reconstruction.[25]

The Generalissimo notified the American Ambassador Clarence Gauss

Chambers, *Ibid.*, p. 493. Miss Bentley told the Internal Security Subcommittee that "We were so successful getting information during the war largely because of Harry White's idea to persuade Morgenthau to exchange information. In other words, he would send information over to Navy, and Navy would reciprocate. So there were at least seven or eight agencies trading information with Secretary Morgenthau." p. 422. She said that information from the White House "mostly on the Far East, on China" came from Michael Greenberg, who worked under Lauchlin Currie, executive assistant to the President. *Ibid.*, p. 414, p. 442.

23 Solomon Adler to Harry Dexter White, December 15, 1943. *Scope of Soviet Activity in the United States*, Part 34, p. 1948. On February 14, 1945, Adler wrote: " . . . if the Generalissimo sticks to his present course, and if we stick to our present policy of supporting him unconditionally a la Hurley, we will end up by finding that we are backing a losing horse. The Generalissimo's intransigence is self-defeating. For he is growing weaker while the democratic elements and the Communists are growing stronger. Therefore the longer he defers making concessions to them the greater the concessions he will have to make." Adler to White, February 14, 1945, *Ibid.*, p. 1953.

24 Memorandum for the President by Secretary Morgenthau, December 18, 1943. *Ibid.*, Part 35, pp. 1992-1993; *United States Relations with China*, pp. 488-489.

25 Meeting in the Secretary's Office, December 17, 1943. *Scope of Soviet Activity in the United States,* Part 35, p. 1991.

that the financial situation had been giving himself and Kung "much anxiety" and urged it be made known to Treasury and military authorities that "both the economic and military collapse of China would result from a failure to support the currency of China." The American Ambassador did not favor a loan at this juncture, saying the economic situation "can only be helped by successful military operations on an extensive scale." [26] Chiang again wrote the President on behalf of his earlier request for a billion dollar loan, and added: "I felt keenly when I saw you in Cairo that with your vision and wisdom you completely comprehended the critical situation which now faces this country and that you were eager to extend to our people every means of practical help in order to enable them to march forward shoulder to shoulder with the American people to common victory."

If no loan were forthcoming the Chinese Government "would have no means at its disposal to meet the requirements of United States forces in China and consequently the American Army in China would have to depend upon itself to execute any and all of its projects, for to our great regret we would be placed inevitably in a position in which we could not make any further material or financial contribution, including the construction of works for military use." [27]

In another meeting with Chiang Kai-shek, Ambassador Gauss pointed out that American economists were of the opinion that "no amount of American money to the credit of China in the United States could remedy China's economic and financial situation any more than would be the case if our entire output of machine guns were hypothecated to China but remained in the United States." In substance:

> The Generalissimo replied that American economists know American economy and world economy in general but do not understand Chinese economy or Chinese psychology, the latter having a great deal to do with the situation in China. The Generalissimo said that the exchange rate is absolutely unalterable . . . . that a loan even though the actual cash remained in the United States would be regarded by the Chinese people as a reserve for *fapi*.[28]

The Embassy thereupon informed the State Department concerning "the contemplated magnitude of expenditures and has advised that the matter should be discussed by State, Treasury and War in consultation with the President before any final decision is reached." Dr. Kung had been negotiating with Assistant Secretary of State Dean Acheson concerning a portion of our outlays in China which Kung wanted to be financed

---

[26] Ambassador Gauss to Secretary Hull, December 23, 1943. *United States Relations with China*, pp. 490-491.

[27] Generalissimo Chiang Kai-shek to President Roosevelt, January 16, 1944. *Ibid.*, pp. 492-493.

[28] Ambassador Gauss to Secretary Hull, January 16, 1944. *Ibid.*, pp. 494-495.

by the sale of U. S. Government bonds and "by the sale of gold." The Secretary agreed but was not sure whether "such sales as the Chinese Government makes should be on joint account." Adler said they should be because a Treasury Representative would be able as a member of the Committee determining selling policy, to "ensure both greater efficiency and less 'monkey business.' " [29]

On February 25, 1943, Harry Dexter White was designated by Henry Morgenthau "to take supervision over and assume full responsibility for Treasury's participation in all economic and financial matters (except matters pertaining to depository facilities, transfers of funds, and war expenditures) in connection with the operations of the Army and Navy and the civilian affairs in the foreign areas in which our armed forces are operating or are likely to operate. This will, of course, include general liaison with the State Department, Army and Navy, and other departments or agencies and representatives of foreign governments on these matters." [30] White first proposed what was called the "Bank for Reconstruction and Development of the United and Associated Nations," or, later, the International Fund and Bank, in the summer of 1943. One of the purposes of the Bank as defined by White was "to help strengthen the monetary and credit structures of the member countries." Also: "The Bank shall impose no condition upon an extension of credit or loan as to the particular country in which the proceeds of the loan must be spent." [31]

Later, the Chinese were informed that "the Bank was not designed to provide capital for monetary rehabilitation." They were told "the Bank would provide funds for the purpose of financing imports of capital equipment" but "would not provide funds for the purpose of building up greater reserves for the monetary system of a country." On the other hand, "when funds were provided for the purpose of economic development, however, a country would be helped in its rehabilitation program." [32]

Secretary Morgenthau was desirous of getting control of all foreign aid activities lodged in his department. This desire was quite probably inspired by White and his cohorts, for any such proposals argued for putting White in control. The direction of such aims is indicated in a meeting held in Secretary Morgenthau's office on July 26, 1944:

29 Solomon Adler to Harry Dexter White, February 22, 1944. *Scope of Soviet Activity in the United States,* Part 34, p. 1944.

30 Secretary Morgenthau to Dr. White, February 25, 1943. *Interlocking Subversion in Government Departments,* Part 28, pp. 2317-2318.

31 "Proposal For a Bank For Reconstruction and Development in the United and Associated Nations," August 19, 1943. *Ibid.,* pp. 2320-2321.

32 Memorandum of a Meeting in Mr. Bernstein's Office, by A. Lipsman, May 8, 1944. *Harry Dexter White Papers,* Princeton University. *MSS.,* File I, 24.

MR. GLASSER: "Proposal is that Secretary would ask the President to prepare an Executive Order that would place in a new committee, of which Secretary of Treasury is Chairman, all questions of financial aid to foreign countries or all financial problems relating to foreign countries. This would get all coordination under one single authority—the proper authority." (Mr. Bell added: 'The fiscal branch of the Government'.)

Secretary discussed taking up with the President powers for Treasury relating to Lend-Lease, UNRRA, etc. *Said White should put his brain on this.*[33]

On November 10, 1944, White sent a memorandum to Secretary Morgenthau with the notation: "I think you will be interested in reading this." It contained an excerpt from a conversation of Mao Tse-tung with John Service in which Mao gave advice on how to handle Chiang Kai-shek. The report was sent by Adler to White:

Chiang is stubborn. But fundamentally he is a gangster. That fact must be understood in order to deal with him. We have had to learn it by experience. The only way to handle him is to be hardboiled. You must not give way to his threats and bullying. Do not let him think you are afraid: then he will press his advantage. The United States has handled Chiang very badly. They have let him get away with blackmail. . . . With Chiang you can be friendly only on your own terms. He must give in to constant, strong and unified pressure. Never relax your objectives; keep hammering at him. . . . There is no longer any need or any reason to cultivate, baby or placate Chiang. The United States can tell Chiang what he should do. . . . Visits like Wallace's give good opportunities; there should be more of them. . . .[34]

Eight days later White sent the entire document to Secretary Morgenthau. Apparently Mao Tse-tung's recommended strategy was considered quite important.

On December 3, 1944, White submitted to Secretary Morgenthau a series of memoranda prepared by Irving Friedman who was working for the Treasury Department in China. The reports were oral messages addressed to Secretary Morgenthau. Here, again, we find a singleness of purpose toward undermining the Nationalist Government.

One memorandum is titled: "Interview with General Chou En-lai and His Message to Secretary Morgenthau." General Chou said that with the aid of "our American friends" unity in China would come sooner. China's postwar need "would be foreign capital." To achieve this there would have to be a "peace and security" through democratic reform. He stressed the point that the "Chinese Communists did not feel that the socialization of industry was the proper form of economy for China and that China's industrialization would take place within the framework

---

[33] Some notes for Mr. White's information. Memorandum of a meeting in the Secretary's Office on July 26, 1944, at 9:30, by L. M. Shanahan. *Harry Dexter White Papers*, Princeton University. MSS., File 35, Miscellaneous. (Emphasis in the original.)

[34] Harry Dexter White to Secretary Morgenthau, November 10, 1944. *Scope of Soviet Activity in the United States*, Part 34, p. 1915.

of capitalist economy." [35] Chou's last statement would seem to indicate that he regarded the gullibility of our officials as almost unlimited.

Another memorandum titled "Interview with Madame Sun Yat-Sen" was a continuation of Communist propaganda. She said that the "Chung-king Government was not interested in fighting the war and because of that would not be interested in a coalition government with the Communists who were interested in fighting the war." [36]

At the Conference held at Bretton Woods, New Hampshire, beginning July 1, 1944, Secretary Hull designated Assistant Secretary of the Treasury White, as "head of the American Delegation of the Conference." The Conference was called for the purpose of dealing with monetary and financial matters.[37] A compromise was effected on proposals and plans submitted which resulted in an increase in Russian "prestige and voting power as well as her capacity to receive foreign exchange with which to finance post-war buying." [38]

The Treasury Department was now very actively engaged in formulation of policies leading to a world settlement. The "Morgenthau Plan" was submitted at the Quebec Conference on September 11, 1944.[39] In December of that year White revealed he had some men working "on a similar book on Japan." Meanwhile, the Chinese were pressing for gold.

In a memorandum dated December 9, 1944, White discussed with Secretary Morgenthau one of the many Chinese requests for gold. "We have stalled as much as we have dared," said White, "and have succeeded in limiting gold shipments to 26 million during the past year." [40]

In the meantime, the Chinese Ambassador received another urgent request from Chungking to attempt to secure shipment of U. S. $100,-000,000 in gold coin "at the earliest possible moment so as to stabilize our wartime economy and to further our war effort." [41] The Treasury Department was thereby informed that conditions in China required "the immediate arrival of more gold shipments." [42] While promising "to make available limited quantities of gold for shipment to China," the Secretary was of the opinion the program of "forward sales of gold" should be

---

35 *Ibid.*, pp. 1921-22.

36 *Ibid.*, p. 1923.

37 Cordell Hull to Dr. Harry D. White, June 23, 1944. "The Harry Dexter White Papers," *Interlocking Subversion in Government Departments*, Part 30, p. 2617.

38 "Current Biography," quoted in *Ibid.*, p. 2603.

39 Hull, *Memoirs*, II, 1613-1618. White was author of the original plan. See drafts in *Interlocking Subversion in Government Departments*, Part 30, pp. 2693-2730, and Henry Morgenthau, Jr. to Mrs. Harry Dexter White, August 18, 1948. *Ibid.*, p. 2653.

40 U.S. Congress, Senate, Committee on the Judiciary, *Final Report for the Year, 1956*, 84th Cong., 2d Sess. (Washington: Government Printing Office, 1957), Section V, pp. 71-72.

41 Mr. O. K. Yui, Minister of Finance, to Dr. H. H. Kung, December 30, 1944. *Scope of Soviet Activity in the United States*, Part 35, p. 1995.

42 H. H. Kung, Chinese Ambassador, to Secretary Morgenthau, January 3, 1945. *Ibid.*, p. 1994.

terminated. He deemed the program "ill-advised" due to "difficulties of shipping gold, the limited effects of sales upon price rises in China, the public criticism of such sales and the desirability of using foreign exchange resources to achieve maximum effects." [43] Chinese representatives had "stressed the fact" the previous October "that the cessation of the sale of gold would have very serious effects at this time." [44] Dr. Kung in February, 1945, informed Secretary Morgenthau frankly that gold "shipments to China have been considerably slower than we feel necessary." Urgently, he wrote:

The chief present financial problem of the Chinese Government, as you know, is to finance its large and growing deficit. The Government must handle this deficit in such a way that the inflation does not get out of hand—since if this took place, it would cause most serious consequences to the war effort of China and would be very hurtful to the conduct of American operations against Japan in and from China. Moreover, if inflation should seriously accelerate, this condition would undermine China's economic structure, impair internal stability, make it much harder for China to reoccupy and restore the area now in enemy hands, gravely hamper China's reconstruction and progress in the next few years, and make it much harder for China to play the part in stabilization and peace maintenance in the Far East which its Government and people wish to play and which is desired by the American Government and people.

It is of vital importance, therefore, to reduce in every possible way the deficit financed through increase of note issue. For a little over a year, the Government has been selling gold to realize Chinese currency. . . . The sale of gold has been most helpful, and has definitely prevented the inflation from attaining a higher level which otherwise would have been reached. It helps to check increase of the general price level by diverting to purchase of gold certain funds which otherwise would be used to buy commodities to be held for higher prices.

The American Government, in order to help China, made available U.S. $200 million of gold out of the U.S. $500 million credit. Of this gold, the first installment was U.S. $20 million. . . . Actual shipments to China out of this U.S. $20 million were only U.S. $5,876,118.12. Thus, shipments have fallen far short of what is needed. As a result, the Central Bank was obliged to substitute forward sales for spot sales. . . . Because of lack of gold, the Government has had to print and import more notes than otherwise would have been needed, which adds to the inflation. . . .

Under present conditions it is specially urgent to sell gold actively in China. In the past half-year, the basic budgetary situation has become definitely more critical. . . . Since the first of this year prices have been rising more rapidly and the rising tendency is continuing. . . . It is particularly important, when prices are actively rising, to be in position to sell gold to withdraw money from the

---

43 Memorandum by Secretary of the Treasury Morgenthau to T. V. Soong, May 8, 1945. *United States Relations with China*, p. 505. It is interesting to note they were not prevented from "going ahead with arrangements for increased sales of gold in India." Mr. White to Secretary Morgenthau, December 9, 1944. *Scope of Soviet Activity in the United States*, Part 35, p. 1994.

44 Minutes of a Meeting on Chinese Gold Purchases, in Mr. White's Office, October 2, 1944. *United States Relations with China*, pp. 503-504.

market, thereby lessening the need for increase of circulating notes. The American Government has been concerned about China's inflation and for the present gold sales are the most effective means to combat it. . . .

In view of the urgent need for gold in China, we are most anxious to send forward at once by air the balance of U.S. $12,723,933.28 (say 364,000 ounces) of the U.S. $20 million, which is required at the earliest possible moment to meet near deliveries and to make spot sales. We would, therefore, appreciate your good offices in arranging with the American Army Air Transport Command for such shipment. Also we would like to have a further amount of say 500,000 ounces (U.S. $17,500,000) go forward as soon as practicable by air to enable the Central Bank of China to meet further near deliveries and to make spot sales. In addition, we would like to ship at once 500,000 ounces (U.S. $17,500,-000) by sea to meet later deliveries. Thereafter, shipments should be adapted to needs in order to avoid again running short of gold in China.[45]

In reply Morgenthau said he would consult with military authorities regarding "the possibilities of shipping gold to China during the next few months." [46] A Treasury official, Virginius Frank Coe,[47] recommended that $7 million in gold be shipped to China within three months, but guessed the Secretary would "probably wish to continue the policy of permitting only small shipments of gold to China." [48] Coe recommended that the Treasury "continue to oppose all except minimum shipments of gold" and "should tell the Chinese that we expect them to stop all forms of forward sales of gold immediately." He said "all further gold sent to China should be out of their own funds, and not out of the $500 million loan." Then he charged: "The program of forward sales of gold . . . has been used as a device for enriching a few insiders and has had negligible effects upon the Chinese inflation." He concluded: "The acquisition by China of additional foreign exchange and the sale of gold or any other forms of foreign exchange by China have had no discernible effect in halting the inflation." [49] On April 23, Finance Minister O. K. Yui telegraphed Ambassador Kung: "I feel much concerned and distressed." And five days later, the Central Bank telegraphed the following: "We cannot overemphasize the serious effect in consequence Dr. White's default in meeting its [sic] obligations." [50]

At a meeting of Treasury officials on May 1, Secretary Morgenthau remarked regarding T. V. Soong's request for more shipments of gold,

45 H. H. Kung to Henry Morgenthau, Jr., February 26, 1945. *Scope of Soviet Activity in the United States,* Part 35, pp. 2000-2001.

46 Henry Morgenthau, Jr. to Dr. H. H. Kung, March 3, 1945, *Ibid.,* p. 2002.

47 Coe was named as a Communist by Elizabeth Bentley but refused to divulge any information under questioning. For a summary of Coe's activities, see "Harry Dexter White's Papers," *Interlocking Subversion in Government Departments,* Part 30, pp. xxi-xxvii, p. 2651.

48 Mr. Coe to Secretary Morgenthau, March 2, 1945. *Scope of Soviet Activity in the United States,* Part 35, pp. 1999.

49 Mr. Coe to Secretary Morgenthau, April 27, 1945, *Ibid.,* p. 2011.

50 China and Gold, 1942-45: Memorandum by Arthur N. Young, July 11, 1956. *Ibid.,* p. 1971.

that "we have been in consultation with State and War as to how fast we should feed this thing out, and we've made it just as difficult for the Chinese to get it as possible, that being a sort of joint policy." [51] A week later it was agreed that the Chinese Government be informed of Treasury policy in the matter of gold, and that the following statement be included: "It is most unfortunate that the impression has arisen in the United States that the sale of certificates and the forward sale of gold have to a large extent gone into a few hands, largely for personal aggrandizement, and in this way has failed to be of assistance to the general Chinese economy." Added Morgenthau, carefully: "What I want to do at the end there, just at the end, is this, say 'Listen, T. V., old boy, I'm not saying this is so, but that's the impression.' " Director of Monetary Research, Irving S. Friedman brought up the question of "face" and the Secretary replied: "It's just too darn bad," and added:

Look, this fellow, I know this boy. It just depends on how rough he gets, and if he begins to pound my desk or anything else, they won't have any troops either. Leave it to me, but I just want to throw a little fear into him, see. When he says this impression is wholly false, I'll say, I wouldn't go that far. If you don't mind the sentence, you leave it to me to let him know that I know without saying it. I'll be very oriental. [52]

To Dr. Soong it seemed as if "the country that first got beaten up by the aggressor will be the last to be rescued." [53] Secretary Morgenthau was becoming increasingly agitated over the affair of $200 million in gold which was promised the Chinese in the middle of 1943. He said his assistants ought to be "severely criticised" for putting him in "an absolutely dishonorable position" which was "inexcusable." Coe injected that "we did not say we would not give them the gold." Replied Morgenthau:

That has nothing to do with it. I am facing the Acting President of China, and here I am put in the position that I am bargaining with him about something that I gave my commitment he could have. Now, in this world, and certainly Government to Government, a person's word, and particularly his written word, means something. One of you three should have said, 'Now remember, Mr. Secretary, on July 27, 1943, you told them they could have it. Now, do you want to bargain with them about it?' You are so worried about his face. What about my face? What about the honor of this Government? I think it's inexcusable.

Morgenthau had been receiving reports from Admiral King and others to the effect that the Chinese were "really fighting and moving." They had a dozen "good divisions" to the British six fighting in Burma. "The

---

[51] Meeting in the Treasury Secretary's Office, May 1, 1945. *Ibid.*, p. 2004.

[52] Meeting in the Treasury Secretary's Office, May 8, 1945. *Ibid.*, pp. 2014-2015.

[53] China and Gold, 1942-1945: Memorandum by Arthur N. Young, July 11, 1956. *Ibid.*, p. 1972.

Chinese are really doing it," said Morgenthau, "and here I am acting like a huckster over something which has been settled on the 27th, whatever the month is, 1943. I don't like it." The substance of the conversation follows:

H. M., JR.: Why, in God's name, didn't you bring this letter to my attention, Sol? You knew this existed!

MR. ADLER: I wasn't aware of it explicitly. I had seen it in the file but——

H. M., JR.: You didn't know about it?

MR. ADLER: I knew——

H. M., JR.: You should have—what about you?

MR. FRIEDMAN: Well, Mr. Secretary, if I may say, on this specific thing . . . you expressed to them [the Chinese] that you were considerably doubtful as to this whole idea, and they said to you that the President said to Madame Chiang that they could buy the gold, and you told them and Mr. White told them that you could make the commitment to buy the gold for anti-inflation and for anti-hoarding purposes . . .

H. M., JR.: That's all very nice, but in cold print there it's 'You can have the two hundred million dollars of this money for gold . . .'

H. M., JR.: Did you know about the letter of July 27th?

MR. COE: Yes sir.

H. M., JR.: Well, I certainly think somebody would have said before I went in to this conference, 'Here's this letter. Here's what you said, Mr. Morgenthau.'

MR. COE: The whole basis, as I understood it, of the Treasury giving them limited sums of gold over a longer period had been the original statement that we would, and month by month they were told there is so much transport available.

H. M., JR.: But White told me we were running out of excuses.

MR. COE: . . . The only excuse I ever heard of has been transportation, and we all think that transportation is a thin excuse. . . .

H. M., JR.: . . . Did you know about the letter of July 27th?

MR. BELL: No.

H. M., JR.: Don't you think it puts me in an impossible position?

Mr. Coe said that since the gold transactions were "under attack" the idea was to have the remaining amount of the original $500 million set aside in a stabilization fund. Under Secretary Daniel Bell said he would say to Soong: "All right, you can have the gold, but will you set up a five hundred million dollar stabilization fund out of your other resources?" Coe added: "There is nothing in the proposal you handed him yesterday which contradicts the letter," but, he conceded, "maybe the spirit of it." [54]

That same day, however, Soong rejected the proposal unless the Fund were "established out of new loans." Continued the memorandum: "If Dr. Soong decided not to accept the proposal on the $500 million Fund, the Secretary would obviously be disappointed." The commitment to

---

[54] Meeting in the Treasury Secretary's Office, May 9, 1945. *Ibid.*, pp. 2022-2025. For Morgenthau's proposal to Soong see Memorandum by Secretary of the Treasury Morgenthau, May 8, 1945. *United States Relations with China*, pp. 504-505.

make available $200 million of gold "was not tied up with the fund proposal and the Treasury would study ways of accelerating gold shipments."[55]

A letter addressed to Dr. Soong and dated May 10, read in part: "As I [Morgenthau] informed you yesterday, the Treasury will consider steps to accelerate gold shipments to China." But the Secretary said he didn't like the phrase "accelerate gold" and White then said it could "be taken out." The Secretary reminded him it was a question of "good faith," then White injected the following comments:

I understand you were troubled about the letter of the two hundred million. Mr. Secretary, we have always taken the position we had absolutely no legal grounds for withholding the gold; that what we were doing was skating on thin ice and offering excuses and we were getting away with it as long as we could, and remember because I said we were getting away with it that you better get the President's backing when they begin putting on the heat. It's because I said we have no basis for it. We have been successful over two years in keeping them down to twenty-seven million and we never understood why the Chinese didn't take it in there and do what they are now doing. The whole history is we had no basis for it.

H. M., JR.: I can't remember things that happened, and when he flashed that letter on me it caught me sort of off guard and I didn't remember it.

MR. WHITE: That letter grew out of what you thought the President promised Madame Chiang Kai-shek.

H. M., JR.: They refreshed my memory, but the trouble is that, Harry, I think that the Army and State Departments have advised me very badly on this thing last week and suddenly Will Clayton woke up to that fact himself, entirely on his own, and all the indications are that the Chinese are really going to fight. This man comes here now and he gets a cold shoulder, gets bounced around, he gets nothing. He may get four thousand trucks and this is the money which we have committed ourselves to, and I have sort of come to the decision that I don't know how far I'll go, but I certainly want to loosen up, and I think this is a psychological time for the Treasury to demonstrate we can be a friend to China, when they really need it, with their own money.

MR. WHITE: That isn't the same way I'd say I'd do it. I'll drop that. I do think you need to have now for your own record—and this is wholly for your own record—you need now an exchange of letters from you to the President indicating that this money is being badly used. It will not help inflation and cannot be justified on economic grounds, and that the only basis, for it must be that they feel it is militarily necessary to satisfy his demands. Because, Mr. Secretary, this record—we have advised them against the use of this. It has been badly used and all the rest.[56]

The Secretary agreed and signed the letter to Dr. Soong. Coe then prepared a memorandum for President Roosevelt in which he states:

[55] Minutes of a Meeting on Gold Fund for China in the Treasury Secretary's Office, May 9, 1945. *United States Relations with China,* p. 506.

[56] Meeting in the Treasury Secretary's Office, May 10, 1945. *Scope of Soviet Activity in the United States,* Part 35, pp. 2026-2027.

"(a) we are anxious to give full support to an effective anti-inflationary program for China; (b) the gold sales policy, which was initiated against Treasury advice, is not an effective anti-inflationary device; (c) the history of the Chinese uses of the $240 million which they have so far received from the 1942 $500 million loan would invite requests for additional financial aid probably on a larger scale." It was thereby proposed with the concurrence of the State and War Departments and the FEA that: " (a) the establishment of a $500 million Fund for combatting inflation and stabilizing Chinese currency, to be constituted from the outstanding $240 million of the 1942 $500 million loan and from China's very substantial dollar balances, and (b) the termination of the present gold sales program and the continuation of only limited shipments of gold to China to be financed out of her dollar balances." Coe continues reading the memorandum:

The present Chinese gold sales policy has culminated in a public scandal in China. To make large shipments of gold to China at this time, particularly without making every effort within our commitment to induce the Chinese to withhold their request, would make the Administration vulnerable to criticism at home.

It was implicit in all our arrangements with the Chinese that effective use be made of the funds made available to them from the $500 million financial aid. Dr. Soong advanced no new argument for us to revise our judgment that the sale of gold is not an effective anti-inflationary weapon and that it represents a dissipation of China's foreign exchange assets which she will desperately need to restore financial stability.

The State Department has concurred in the suggestion that I therefore inform Dr. Soong that:

(a) You feel that the Chinese should give most serious consideration to our recommendation for the establishment of a $500 million Fund, and

(b) You agree that it is in the best interests of Chinese-American relations that China withdraw for the time being her request for immediate heavy shipments of gold.

When Coe finished the memorandum, the Secretary stated he wanted the State Department copy of it "immediately withdrawn" saying: "I'm not going to follow this position. It's ridiculous." Secretary Morgenthau explained:

H. M., JR.: . . . You just keep going over the same ground, the same ground, the whole time. This doesn't make it plain to the President of the United States that these people own this gold, that I, over my signature, told them they could have two hundred million dollars in gold.

MR. WHITE: That's where I disagree.

H. M., JR.: I know you do . . .

MR. WHITE: There was behind all these oral discussions, and it implies the fact that any money you gave would be effectively used. There were several discussions which brought out that fact that they were supposed to be using it wisely.

H. M., JR.: Is there anything in writing?

MR. WHITE: And they're not using it wisely.

H. M., JR.: Anything in writing?

MR. WHITE: No. I think that the time to stop that is now. . . .

H. M. JR.: Look, Harry, using your own language, you have told me repeatedly we're skating on very thin ice. You told me that the other day.

MR. WHITE: That's right because we don't have anything down in writing and there are reasons why we don't. . . .

H. M., JR.: We did it because we don't believe it would be helpful to them.

MR. WHITE: It was going down the drain. We'll assume that that was the political situation at that time. Now at this time, you're bringing it to the attention of a new President that they are using this money badly from an economic point of view. Your decision can be overridden but it seems to me important that you make that record and that decision now, because the last few statements are simply to the effect that it's being badly used from an economic point of view. If he can say it, it may be very well, but politically they have to have it—you say okay.

H. M., JR.: I say, as I informed you yesterday, the Treasury will consider statements to accelerate gold shipments to China.

MR. WHITE: That's all right, but that doesn't mean giving two hundred million dollars. We've given them twenty-four million in three years—we'll give them three million a month . . .

H. M., JR.: . . . Here is the situation, the way I see it. I think that the Treasury up to this time, has been correct. And I certainly am part and parcel of this policy of slowing down the shipment of gold just as much as we could, because it wasn't good for them, and looking forward to the day they really need the money. And it's there. If they get it now, we'll have to give them more later on, so we're giving it twice. Now we ask advice all over this town. Other departments are involved and they all tell us to sit tight and thumb our noses at the Chinese. . . . It's unfortunate John Carter Vincent wasn't here . . . or White, because they both have the background, and Coe did the very best he could which was very good, with the assistance of Friedman and Adler. Now, I was going along with these fellows up to a point, and I suddenly made up my mind this was all wrong, and I'm just going to turn a somersault on this thing, and I want to do it; and, particularly when I see that my written word and the promise of Franklin Roosevelt is at stake. Now, I haven't got a leg to stand on. . . .

MR. WHITE: Mr. Secretary, the way I feel about it is this. The Congress turned over five hundred million dollars for the Secretary or the President to use under such terms as they saw fit, for the purpose of combating inflation and stabilizing the economy. In other words, you had a responsibility.

H. M., JR.: That isn't written in the bill. . . .

MR. WHITE: . . . You wrote that letter, and I think there's a way of wriggling out. The wriggling out is justified on the grounds that they are not using this money wisely, and what you're saying, is your responsibility to assume that they are going to use this money well, is that they are not using these funds effectively, and that was the supposed purpose of the grant. Now then, if there are, as you indicate, political reasons or military reasons why you want to give Chiang Kai-shek two hundred million dollars in gold, even if he throws it in the ocean or wants to give it to his friends, I say that should not be your decision in the record. That should be something for the President to say, or the Secretary of State, or the military people, to say that you have an obligation to hold a check on that expenditure so long as it isn't wisely spent, and you ought to tell the

President this isn't being wisely spent, isn't doing any economic good. I don't think it's getting them to fight either, but that's a separate problem.

H. M., JR.: Let me say this. I don't like this memo. I won't have any part of it. I'm prepared to say to him, when I see the President of the United States, that we have given this money, we are lending this money to the Chinese, and I think it's going down a rat hole. . . . I'm going to recommend to him that we do let him have it.

MR. WHITE: I think where we part company is on two things, one, that it would seem to me that the mere fact of having written a two hundred million dollar letter should not commit you to a policy of the rate of speed, because you're going to give it to the Chinese Government. It's not like you were trying to withhold it from the Government. The question is to use it most effectively, and I think you should very definitely state in writing that this money is not being used wisely but badly. . . .

H. M., JR.: The thing I'm objecting to is this memo to the President. Maybe I can get . . . a letter . . . saying "for political or military necessity, let this gold go."

MR. WHITE: If you say at the same time that on economic grounds it's not justified.

H. M., JR.: I'll say that verbally. I don't have to say it in writing. If they write me a letter saying, "For political and military reasons we advise this gold go out," that's good enough for me. We're fighting a war.

MR. WHITE: Well, of course, you make an assumption which has put us on very weak ground. You assume the two hundred million dollars they're getting is going to make Chiang Kai-shek fight, and they are fighting, both of which I question.

H. M., JR.: I think you're wrong. I don't know. How long since you've been there, Adler?

MR. ADLER: I left Chungking on April 7, sir, a little over four weeks ago.

H. M., JR.: Do you feel they're fighting now?

MR. ADLER: Very little.[57]

President Truman and T. V. Soong were duly informed of the Treasury proposals.[58] Dr. Soong stated however that China "must have the nearly $200 million of gold out of the remaining $240 million of the 1942 loan." He had reference to the commitments made in July, 1943, by Secretary Morgenthau and President Roosevelt and, in turn, rejected the Treasury Department's proposal for a $500 million dollar Fund for combatting inflation.

At the suggestion of John Patton Davies, an American Military Observers Mission was sent to the Communist Capital, Yenan. This was not done, however, without months of consultations in Washington, negotiations with Chiang Kai-shek, and pressure from General Stilwell. The

57 Meeting in the Treasury Secretary's Office, May 15, 1945. *Ibid.*, pp. 2027-2032.

58 Henry Morgenthau, Jr. to Dr. T. V. Soong, May 16, 1945. *Ibid.*, pp. 2034-2035. *United States Relations with China*, pp. 507-508. "Despite the promise to accelerate shipments the Treasury continued to send them by sea. Five shipments were made in May and ten shipments in June by sea, the first of which arrived July 17, 1945." *China and Gold*, 1942-45; Memorandum by Arthur N. Young, July 11, 1956. *Scope of Soviet Activity in the United States*, Part 35, p. 1973.

purpose of the mission was primarily to acquire intelligence information in North China—to observe Communist forces, Japanese activity, and Russian operations.

Upon arrival in the Communist capital, the mission received an enthusiastic welcome. Mao Tse-tung remarked to John Service that "any contact you Americans may have with us Communists is good. Of course we are glad to have the Observer Section here because it will help to beat Japan. But there is no use pretending that—up to now at least—the chief importance of your coming is its political effect upon the Kuomintang." [59]

It is significant that on October 16, 1944, Harry Dexter White submitted a memorandum to Secretary Morgenthau titled: "Reports of the American Military Mission to Yenan." The actual text of the mission was not available at the time to the Treasury Department, but the War and State Departments allowed Solomon Adler to read these reports and make copious notes on them. He reported to White that the "Communist political program is moderate in the sphere both of domestic and foreign policy." According to the political expert of the American Military Mission (presumably Service) the interests of the Chinese Communist Party *do not run counter to those of the United States in the foreseeable future and merit a sympathetic and friendly attitude on our part."* [60] The report is exceedingly important in view of its political propaganda.

Their domestic goal is what they call "New Democracy." This includes "extension of internal democracy" and the raising of living standards by "encouraging the growth of progressive capitalism in China." Racial minorities were to be given a "considerable degree of autonomy within a United States of China." It is interesting to note the extreme care the Chinese Reds took to describe all facets of their system in terms pertaining to the American scene. In the field of foreign policy the Communists favor China's adherence to the "Atlantic Charter." [61] This is the type of Communist material White wanted Morgenthau to see.

As a member of the Mission, John Patton Davies wrote: "We are the greatest fear of the Communists because the more aid we give Chiang exclusively the greater the likelihood of this precipitating civil war and the more protracted and costly will be the Communist unification of China. . . . If we continue to reject them and support an unreconstructed Chiang, they see us becoming their enemy. But they would prefer to be friends. Not only because of the help we can give them but also because they recognize that our strategic aims of a strong, independent and democratic China can jibe with their nationalist objectives." [62]

---

[59] As quoted in Lohbeck, *Patrick J. Hurley*, p. 272.

[60] Harry D. White to Secretary Morgenthau, October 16, 1944. *Scope of Soviet Activity in the United States*, Part 34, p. 1924. (Emphasis in the original.)

[61] *Ibid.*, p. 1924, 1925.

[62] *Ibid.*, p. 1933.

In November, 1944, White, Solomon Adler, and John Service were trying to get Secretary Morgenthau to bring Chou En-Lai's views to President Roosevelt. The memorandum stated that the "Chinese Communists believe that civil war is inevitable unless we actively throw our weight against it. *They now regard the American attitude toward them as the decisive factor in the general determination of their policy, and appear to be anxious to cooperate with us.*" [63] The fateful Marshall Mission is foreshadowed in this statement.

Adler, who was part of the Red underground apparatus in the Treasury Department, submitted a memorandum to White on November 18, concerning an interview with Mao Tse-tung, in which he said the hope for preventing civil war in China rests to a great extent on influence of foreign countries. *"Among these, by far the most important, is the United States,* whose growing power in China and in the Far East can be decisive." [64]

Communist influence prevented American gold from reaching China during a crucial period when this gold was essential to avoid collapse of the Chinese currency system. The energetic efforts made by White, while blocking gold shipments to China, to promote a $10 billion postwar loan to Russia, make clear his anti-Chinese Nationalist and pro-Communist dedication.[65]

On May 10, 1945, in the privacy of his own office, White was discussing with his staff the Chinese gold situation. He admitted that there were "absolutely no legal grounds" for delaying shipments. He said: "We have been successful for over two years in keeping them down to 27 million." White's purpose, as he several times stated, was to force the Nationalist Government to agree to a coalition with the Chinese Communists in which the Communists would be equal, and possibly superior, partners. The United States Army and Air Force were then drawing large sums, a third of the entire Chinese budget, from the Central Bank. The important point is that the increase in the Chinese money supply, uncompensated for by payments from the United States Treasury, made inflation unmanageable, and led (together with an almost identical episode in 1947) to the Communist take-over.

Secretary Morgenthau was constantly being hoodwinked by White and his cohorts. On one occasion, January 19, 1944, Secretary Morgenthau was conferring with President Roosevelt by telephone. White was in Morgenthau's office. The President said he remembered we were sending China about 12½ million of gold a month. Morgenthau checked with

---

63 Italics mine. Harry D. White to Secretary Morgenthau, November 18, 1944, *Ibid.*, Part 34, p. 1907.

64 Solomon Adler to Harry D. White, November 18, 1944, *Ibid.*, pp. 1908. (Emphasis in original)

65 *Ibid.*, Part 35, Exhibit #352, pp. 2035-2036.

White, who told him it was "less than that." Actually White knew what Morgenthau obviously did not know: that the President's estimate of what China was getting was about twelve times what it actually got.[66] The Communists were quite willing to ignore President Roosevelt's policies and then lie to him about it. The President probably never did find out about the manner in which these people betrayed his confidence in them.

Dr. Soong in the memorandum of April 20, 1945, to Secretary Stettinius stated that "the continued sale of gold will be the most important single factor in blotting up large issuance of bank notes." He indicated in another memorandum of May 9 to Secretary Morgenthau that the credit of the Chinese Government must be maintained by the immediate delivery of gold to meet its commitments now outstanding. "Such an effective and proven instrument to combat inflation as is represented by our gold sales cannot be abandoned." Dr. Soong concluded his memorandum with the following dire prediction: "Unless the promise made by President Roosevelt and the Treasury to make gold available be fully implemented, a disastrous financial collapse in China is plainly indicated which will inevitably be followed by a military collapse." [67]

On June 26, all sales and deliveries of gold were suspended. This action seemed all the more startling in view of Dr. Soong's frequent assertions in Washington that discontinuance of the sale of gold would bring about financial collapse. Financial collapse did occur, and it is evident that it could have been prevented.

Walter S. Robertson, Assistant Secretary of State for Far Eastern Affairs, gave an interesting view concerning the loss of China to the Communists. In a speech before the National Press Club in Washington, D.C., on June 16, 1959, he said: "We stood by and saw China drift into a state of complete economic collapse. The currency was worthless, they were paying their troops in worthless currency. They had been repudiated by their strongest ally, and then we wonder why there were desertions to the Communist troops and ranks. In Europe we spent 14 billions of dollars to do what? To stabilize the economies, to bring political stability, to prevent the kind of collapse and chaos on which the Communists feed. In France, in Italy, in Turkey, in Greece, we poured out our funds to keep the Communists out. In China, we withheld our funds

---

[66] *Internal Security Annual Report for 1956*, Secretary Morgenthau did not believe that the sales of gold to China would prove "effective in combatting inflation." *Hurley Papers*, File 2106, Document No. 11, *MSS.*, Santa Fe. Hurley was not kept informed of the nature of these gold sales. When he was asked his reaction to the proposed stabilization fund he said he agreed with Morgenthau that "there was little evidence to support" the claims that sales of gold would stop inflation. He went on to say that he could have felt much better about the situation if he had been consulted before the transaction rather than after it had been completed. Ambassador Hurley to Secretary Morgenthau, June 6, 1945, *Hurley Papers*, File 2106, Document No. 12. *MSS.*, Santa Fe.

[67] *Hurley Papers*, File 316, Document No. 9. *MSS.*, Santa Fe.

at the only time, in my opinion, we had a chance to save the situation. To do what? To force the Communists in." [68]

In evaluating our relations with Nationalist China in the postwar period, Congressman Walter Judd, a longtime student of Far Eastern affairs, summed it up this way:

We Americans ought never to forget this one fact, which outweighs every other consideration—namely that when our fleet lay at the bottom of the sea and Japan had carried out in 6 months the single greatest conquest in the history of warfare, only one thing prevented her from completing and organizing her new empire, and turning all her efforts against us. It was this . . . old, so-called backward, corrupt, undemocratic, inefficient China that refused to yield. Chiang could have had peace on very generous terms and saved his people most of the suffering and the economic dislocations and the Communists and the war. Instead he chose to buy for us the precious months and years in which we could rebuild our fleet and capture the islands, one by one, and build the atomic bomb and ultimately bring our superior air power and the bombs to bear upon Japan and give her the final blow. That is a fact that takes precedence over every other in the picture.[69]

---

[68] *U.S. News and World Report*, June 29, 1959, p. 73.
[69] *Congressional Record*, June 19, 1948, p. A4560.

CHAPTER IX

STILWELL'S PERSONAL VENDETTA

From 1941 to 1945 it was the publicly expressed and clearly defined official policy of the United States to aid the Government of Nationalist China. It was also United States policy to keep the armies of that Government fighting the common enemy, Japan. But, during this period there developed a distinct revision of this policy by some of our military men and Foreign Service officers in China. For example, in a memorandum to the War Department, Brigadier General John A. Magruder, Chief of the American military mission to China, said Generalissimo Chiang Kai-shek had received the most military aid for war against Japan and was putting out the least effort.[1] Chiang had been fighting the Japanese for the last four and a half years, had tied down numerous Japanese divisions on the mainland, and had cost the enemy millions of dollars in valuable equipment and supplies. These facts were ignored.

At the request of President Roosevelt, Chiang Kai-shek assumed the post of Supreme Commander of the China Theater early in 1942. The Generalissimo immediately asked the President to appoint an American officer to serve under him.[2] The appointment of General Joseph W. Stilwell was to have a profoundly adverse effect upon the friendship between Chiang and the United States. General Stilwell was a brave soldier and fine commander in the field but he lacked a realistic knowledge of politics or Communism. Because of his intense hatred of Chiang Kai-shek, he was eventually used by our Foreign Service officers to spearhead their attacks upon the Kuomintang, thus serving whatever prejudices they had in favor of the Chinese Communists. Stilwell was instructed to supervise and control all American defense-aid affairs for China, to command under the Generalissimo all American forces in China and such

---

[1] Department of State, *Papers Relating to the Foreign Relations of the United States, China, 1942* (Washington: Government Printing Office, 1956), pp. 13-16.

[2] Charles F. Romanus and Riley Sunderland, *Stilwell's Mission to China* (Washington, D.C.: Office of the Chief of Military History, Department of the Army, 1953), p. 66, 70.

Chinese forces as might be assigned to him, and to improve, maintain and control the Burma Road in China.[3]

General Stilwell arrived in the Far East on February 25, 1942. On March 11 he moved into Burma to take command of those Chinese troops who were opposing the Japanese invasion. The Burma campaign ended in a disaster for the Allied forces. General Stilwell placed the blame for the defeat on Chiang Kai-shek, whom he described as an "ignorant," "arbitrary," and an "unreasonable" man.[4] Stilwell complained of the "endless objections" of members of Chiang's staff to his "suggestions or orders," and of the Generalissimo's "meddling." [5]

The Generalissimo pointed out that China had placed her armies "under American command" and had been ready "to support American policies, sometimes even against our own judgment." He added: "What a contrast this is to the attitude of the British and Russians who, whenever it concerns their own interests, will not make concessions to the general interest, so that to this day they will not concede to the United States the direction and the location of the Supreme Military Council." [6]

After his long trek out of Burma with just a handful of men, Stilwell remarked: "I claim we got a hell of a beating. We got run out of Burma and it is humiliating as hell. I think we ought to find out what caused it, go back and retake it." [7] The results of the futile Burma campaign were far-reaching. Supplies destined for China were diverted into the Burmese "rathole." But Stilwell wanted to erase the humiliation of defeat and advocated the reopening of the Burma Road with thirty divisions. Chiang Kai-shek was skeptical toward any new campaign in Burma and he was supported by General Claire Chennault, the leader of the famous Flying Tigers.[8] The reasons were obvious. There was far greater need for thirty divisions in more important areas than Burma. Secondly, Stilwell's recent disastrous campaign in Burma scarcely recommended a renewal of such a command, drawing new troops to the South. Thirdly, one may wonder why Stilwell did not ask for Red Chinese divisions for the same campaign, and furthermore, one may wonder why they did not make a more active commitment against the Japanese.

Documentary evidence reveals the Reds intended to preserve their

3 *Stilwell Documents*, File No. 2, Section 3-III, *MSS.*, Hoover Institution, Stanford.

4 *Stilwell Black Book*, p. 8, *MSS.*, Hoover Institution, Stanford. *Stilwell Black and White Book*, No. 2, p. 56, *MSS.*, Hoover Institution, Stanford.

5 *Stilwell Diary*, undated, and April 1, 1942, *MSS.*, Hoover Institution, Stanford.

6 Generalissimo Chiang Kai-shek to the Chinese Minister for Foreign Affairs (Soong), April 19, 1942. *Foreign Relations, China, 1942*, pp. 33-34.

7 *The Stilwell Papers*, Edited by Theodore H. White (New York: William Sloane, Associates, Inc., 1948), p. 106.

8 Claire Lee Chennault, *Way of a Fighter* (New York: G. P. Putnam's Sons, 1949), pp. 220-221.

forces for postwar ambitions.[9] The Generalissimo was unwilling to divert thirty divisions from the defense of China to engage in what he considered a futile and useless fight against superior Japanese forces. This difference of strategy, together with Communist influence, made Stilwell hate the Generalissimo.

Stilwell became increasingly bitter toward the British, too, for also opposing his Burma plan.[10] He wrote: "The British never intended to do anything in Burma." Burma was not essential to the defense of China. The idea was to keep China weak and let the U. S. work on Japan. After the war, the British grab for Hong Kong, Shanghai, etc., would be very much facilitated.[11] Some of the sharpest attacks against the British are recorded in his personal diaries. The "limies" and Chinese "will quit," he wrote, ". . . and the god damn Americans can go ahead and fight." Our officials will have to "get tough and nail down the G-mo [Chiang Kai-shek] or he will "get out of hand for good." [12]

As a result of Stilwell's attitude, the Allied war effort was not only hampered, but an entering wedge was formed for vicious anti-Chiang and pro-Communist activity which was destined to change completely our attitude toward Nationalist China. Stilwell frequently complained to his superiors in Washington for not ordering Chiang Kai-shek to "co-operate with him." As the defeat in Burma remained unavenged, Stilwell's bitter and cynical diary began to imply that "everybody is an S.O.B. except Joseph W. Stilwell." [13] The diaries are replete with name-calling for the Generalissimo as revealed by the following entries:

June 22, 1943: "The Peanut's [Chiang Kai-shek] brain is fermenting, I suppose." [14]

July 12, 1943: "Peanut's answer came . . . The little bastard is hooked after 14 months of struggle. Well, by Jesus, that much is accomplished in spite of hell and high water. And what a headache it has been! Insult, delay, obstruction, intrigue, double-cross, bigotry, ignorance, hate, jealousy, corruption and general cussedness. Nobody will ever know what it has meant." [15]

---

9 U.S. Congress, House, Committee on Foreign Affairs. *The Strategy and Tactics of World Communism*, 81st Cong., 1st Sess. (Washington: Government Printing Office, 1949), Supplement III, *Communism* in China, p. 24.

10 Arthur Bryant, *The Turn of the Tide* (New York: Doubleday and Company, 1957), pp. 504-505.

11 *Stilwell Black and White Book*, No. 2, p. 42. *MSS.*, Hoover Institution, Stanford.

12 *Stilwell Black and White Book*, January 8, 1943, p. 168. *MSS.*, Hoover Institution, Stanford.

13 George Creel, *Russia's Race for Asia* (Indianapolis: Bobbs-Merrill Company, 1949), p. 93. "F.D.R. calls me 'Joe,' the double-crossing bastard." *Stilwell Diary*, Book No. 9. Stilwell was also critical of Wedemeyer: "This guy Wedemeyer thinks Wedemeyer is a hell of an important guy." Book No. 9. *MSS.*, Hoover Institution, Stanford.

14 *Stilwell Diary*, Book No. 8. *MSS.*, Hoover Institution, Stanford.

15 *Ibid.*

December 16, 1943: ". . . 4 p. m. Saw the little bastard again. Argued for an hour, but reason does not make a dent in his mind." [16]

September 9, 1944: "What they ought to do is shoot the G-mo [Chiang Kai-shek] and the rest of the gang." [17]

Stilwell's Burma campaign was a series of frustrations. Frequent change of plans by Allied officials and inadequate supply of men and equipment caused the whole operation to become conditional and loose. "This job is a bitch," he wrote in his diary, "We have a few radios; no other means of communications. The usual lack of medical facilities. No medicine. Malaria, scabies, blackwater fever, already appeared." [18] He cursed out Chiang Kai-shek for refusing to support his second Burma campaign and was convinced the Chinese armies were deliberately trying to avoid fighting the Japanese—leaving the job to U. S. forces. "After finding that I would not obey his slightest wish, like the crowd he was accustomed to, he tried to reduce my importance and prestige by ignoring me and anything I was connected with, including his own Army." [19]

After the fall of Burma and the seizure of the southern portion of the Burma Road by the Japanese early in 1942, air transport was the only effective means of getting supplies to China. It became necessary to construct another supply route which would connect the supply lines leading from India with the routes in Burma. The route considered was one from Ledo in northern Assam, India to China. And it was to be an all-weather road. This was a tremendous undertaking—a distance of about 117 miles—rate of construction about three quarters of a mile per day. In January, 1943, when construction started, the rains impeded work on the road; moreover, coolie labor was uncertain. By the end of July, the road reached only fifty miles. Many problems were encountered. Native labor groups had differences in caste, diversity of diet, and language difficulties. Each of India's two hundred dialects was represented.[20] After untold hardships across water-logged mountains and dense jungles, this road, renamed Stilwell Road, was finally opened in 1945.

The Stilwell Road served as the military excuse for Stilwell's Burma campaign. Any realistic appraisal of its logistic value would have revealed it for how worthless it was. By May, four months after the Stilwell Road opened, it delivered only six thousand tons of cargo monthly to China. The American Transport Command was then delivering seventy thousand tons a month over the Hump using six hundred planes and a score of airfields. In a single day—August 1, 1945—ATC delivered five thousand

---

[16] *Ibid.*, Book No. 9.

[17] *Ibid.*, Book No. 13.

[18] *Stilwell Black and White Book*, No. 2, p. 29. *MSS.*, Hoover Institution, Stanford.

[19] *Stillwell Black Book*, p. 52. *MSS.*, Hoover Institution, Stanford.

[20] "SOS-CBI rough draft and reference notes, CBI overall supply—1943." *Stilwell Documents*, File 89. *MSS.*, Hoover Institution, Stanford.

three hundred and twenty-seven tons of cargo to China—nearly equaling the monthly total of the Stilwell Road.[21]

The Generalissimo was greatly impressed by what the U.S. air power could do in China. In January, 1943, he stated that he would not cross the Salween River into Burma, and invited President Roosevelt's attention to what a small air force under General Chennault could do. In April, 1943, the Generalissimo requested that General Chennault receive first priority on all supplies flown to China and have a free hand in his operations.

On the eve of the Trident Conference in May, 1943, Chennault and Stilwell presented their cases to President Roosevelt. Chennault indicated to Secretary Stimson his doubts as to the worth of the Ledo Road. He impressed the President with his argument that "if we received 10,000 tons of supplies monthly my planes would sink and severely damage more than a million tons of shipping." To which the President "banged his fist on the desk" and exclaimed, "if you can sink a million tons, we'll break their back." [22]

Stilwell's presentation of his case to improve the combat efficiency of the Chinese Army was not convincing. The President was for air power and that meant he favored Chennault's program. This was a set-back for Stilwell who expressed the view that Chiang Kai-shek "meant to sit out the war while U. S. power won it for him, at the risk of letting his Army deteriorate beyond redemption." [23] He blamed Roosevelt for being too soft on the Generalissimo who only "needs to yell and we come in." Our air force is actually protecting the Kuomintang in the sense that Chiang is "sucking us to fight the war by ourselves." Moreover, the British want no part of the fight for Burma because "they'll get Burma back at the peace table anyway." [24]

At the Trident Conference it was decided that only the northern part of Burma would be feasible to take. Again this was a disappointment to Stilwell who recorded in his personal diary:

The inevitable conclusion was that Churchill has Roosevelt in his pocket, that they are looking for an easy way, a short cut for England, and no attention must be diverted from the Continent at any cost. The limies are not interested in the

---

21 Chennault, *Way of a Fighter*, pp. 272-273. Joseph Alsop doubts the value of the Stilwell Road. He argues that the vehicles using it barely carried their own gasoline supply. Joseph Alsop, "Why We Lost China," *Saturday Evening Post*, CCXXII (January 7, 1950).

22 Chennault, *Way of a Fighter*, pp. 225-226.

23 *Stilwell's Mission to China*, p. 333. At a meeting of the Combined Chiefs of Staff in Washington in the spring of 1943, President Roosevelt asked Stilwell for a summary of the situation in China. Stilwell rose and belabored the Generalissimo at length. He accused Chiang Kai-shek of being undependable, ungrateful, dishonest, and untruthful. *General Chennault on American Policy in China During World War II* (Washington: Government Printing Office, 1948), p. 7.

24 *Stilwell Black Book*, June 21, 1943, p. 13. MSS., Hoover Institution, Stanford.

war in the Pacific, and with the President hypnotized, they are sitting pretty. Rubberlegs [Roosevelt] wouldn't let me speak my piece. I interrupted twice, but Churchill kept pulling away from the subject and it was impossible.[25]

Despite the slow execution of the Trident plans, Chiang Kai-shek gave his consent and notified the President he hoped U. S. would send more ground units for the operation. Also the British would have to contribute their share of land and naval forces. Stilwell began his diary entry for that particular day: "Red Letter Day," and then recorded, "The answer came from Peanut to the Combined Chiefs of Staff. Saucy proposals. In writing. And signed. After a year of constant struggle, we have finally nailed him down. He is committed in writing to attack Burma." [26] However, hopes for another Burma campaign were short-lived when Chiang Kai-shek was not certain whether he could fulfill his part of the agreement. "Incidentally," wrote Stilwell, "we have carried out our promises to him. He has *not* carried out his to us—we must get on a working basis now. The only way to do it is to get tough. If he reneged [*sic*] on Saucy (the code name for modified Burma operation), tell him 'too bad. It didn't work out. You can go to hell. We are stopping *all* supply to China and putting it where it will do some good.' " [27]

At the first Quebec Conference in August, 1943, the British agreed to an all-out Burma campaign including amphibious landings at Rangoon and an airborne landing by Wingate's Raiders in northern Burma to support Stilwell's Chinese divisions. The U.S. promised three divisions of American troops to strengthen Stilwell's forces, and Generalissimo Chiang Kai-shek agreed to throw in his Salween armies. These plans were scrapped when the British begged off on the Rangoon operations, pleading a shortage of landing craft. Again the Burma campaign was postponed.

As a result of the Cairo Conference in November, 1943, the current plans for the capture of Burma were considerably curtailed. The heavy demand for equipment and personnel in the European and Mediterranean Theaters had so drained the stock piles of Allied forces that tentative commitments to the Burma theater had, of necessity, to be denied. Consequently, upon returning from the Cairo Conference, the planners were faced with the painful necessity of revising the Burma plans on a greatly reduced scale.

At the Teheran Conference in November, 1943, we agreed to mount the cross-channel attack from England to Normandy, and could not spare the equipment previously assigned to BUCCANEER (code name for the Burma campaign.) Stilwell had the unpleasant duty of returning to China with another broken promise. He recorded in his diary: "After

25 *Stilwell Black Book*, p. 15. *MSS.*, Hoover Institution, Stanford.

26 *Stilwell Black Book*, July 12, 1943, p. 32. MSS., Hoover Institution, Stanford.

27 *Stillwell Black Book*, p. 20. *MSS.*, Hoover Institution, Stanford.

Teheran, plans changed. F.D.R. to Chiang Kai-shek. 'Will you accept altered plan?' . . . Chiang Kai-shek came back with squeeze play. 'O.K. if you give me a billion dollars and double the air force and ferry route.' " [28]

Churchill was not in favor of a ground campaign in Burma—nor did he see much value in China's contribution in winning the war against Japan. This attitude conflicted with Stilwell's intense desire to retake Burma. His scorn for the British is rampant throughout his diary—they just did not fight and were only making a show of it. "The limies are our Allies," an entry in his diary read. "We expected them to play fair—and the bastardly hypocrites do their best to cut our throats on all occasions. . . . They get my goat." [29] Nevertheless, he was determined to push his Burma campaign with or without the help of the British Navy. "Burma can be taken," he wrote. "The Japs can be taken. The road can be opened. All we need is pressure on Chiang Kai-shek which I have struggled to get." [30]

The Stilwell controversy remained a thorn in the side of the Sino-American relations. A member of the Institute of Pacific Relations is reported to have told the Generalissimo that Stilwell "was behind a plan to push Peanut aside, put T. V. [Soong] at the head of civil affairs, and Chen Cheng in command of the Army. So that, in effect, [Stilwell] would command the Army. May [Mme. Chiang] had this dope on 9/28 when I saw her. Of course, the Peanut had it too. The effect on the latter may be imagined." [31] Chiang Kai-shek was becoming progressively distrustful of the American general. He told General Brehon Somervell that he wanted Stilwell's removal as soon as possible. When Somervell conveyed this information to Stilwell, the latter became angry and compared the Generalissimo to a rattlesnake: "The rattlesnake was affable as hell. Fifty thousand men? Sure they'll be there. The only thing is to get some gas to move them. Ella [Madame Kung] had told me he was in a jubilant state of mind and ready to be very friendly. Well, if I hadn't heard him rattle his tail, I might have been taken in." [32]

The China-Burma-India Theater was infested with logistic and political problems resulting in a three- or four-cornered contest between the British, General Stilwell, Chiang Kai-shek and General Chennault. Stilwell frequently revealed his gullibility toward the Chinese Communists and his biased attitude toward the Generalissimo. He lacked the diplo-

---

[28] *Stillwell's Black Book*, p. 92. MSS., Hoover Institution, Stanford.

[29] *Stilwell Diary*, August 9, 1944, Book No. 12. Another entry read: "Mountbatten tried to ditch me at Cairo. F.D.R. said No." *Ibid.*, September 4, 1944, Book No. 12. MSS., Hoover Institution, Stanford.

[30] *Stilwell Diary*, Book 10, March 1944, p. 4. MSS., Hoover Institution, Stanford.

[31] *Stilwell Black Book*, September 28, 1943, p. 67. MSS., Hoover Institution, Stanford.

[32] *Stilwell Black Book*, p. 79. MSS., Hoover Institution, Stanford.

matic qualifications so necessary in this area of conflict where the British
and Chinese had their own self-interested plans. "Intrigue, double cross,
under-cutting and skullduggery continue," he wrote.[33] Stilwell used
harsh words to describe his opponents, and at times he found himself so
enmeshed in the intricate politics of China and Asia that he lost some
perspective regarding the purposes of his command. He goaded Chiang
Kai-shek at every turn, castigated the British with great abandon, and
rebuked American officials by a sharp stroke of his pen. His *Black Book*
records his personal feelings:

Hurley talked with Louis [Mountbatten], who is after my scalp. I stood
between him and dominance in China and he wants to get rid of me. . . . What
a sweet gang of crooks we are playing with! The old double cross is going strong.
Louis is playing the . . . game and won't take chances. All he wants is something that can be labelled victory. . . . Louis is working up a 'controversy' between me and Chennault and spoke of it to Hurley. Apparently the idea is to
pre-judge me, take the part of my subordinate, and kick me out. Hurley asked
him right out if he were by any chance following the old British game of
'divide the rule.' [34]

The Chinese Communists stated often that they would like to place
their troops under Stilwell's personal command. The Generalissimo
would have none of this. "The cure of China's trouble," wrote Stilwell,
"is the elimination of Chiang Kai-shek. The only thing that keeps the
country split is his fear of losing control. He hates the Reds and will not
take any chances of giving them a toehold in the government." [35] Sometimes Stilwell's praises for the Chinese Communists went to extremes. For
example, he wrote:

Chiang Kai-shek is confronted with an idea, and that defeats him. He is bewildered by the spread of Communist influence. He can't see that the mass of
Chinese people welcome the Reds as being the only visible hope of relief from
crushing taxation, the abuses of the army and [the terror of] Tai Li's Gestapo.
Under Chiang Kai-shek they now begin to see what they may expect. Greed,
corruption, favoritism, more taxes, a ruined currency, terrible waste of life,
callous disregard of the rights of men.[36]

---

[33] *Stilwell Black and White Book*, No. 2, p. 109. *MSS.*, Hoover Institution, Stanford.
[34] *Ibid.*, p. 8. "The 'feud' between Louis and me is really the conflict of British and
U. S. policy. That's all and when I stand up, I am non-cooperative (and) my own
people smack me down . . ." *Stilwell's Black Book*, June 15, 1944, p. 102. *MSS.*, Hoover
Institution, Stanford.
[35] *The Stilwell Papers*, p. 321. Stilwell refused to attend a luncheon given for the
visiting Senators in China by General Chennault in 1943. He stayed at the airport
while the luncheon was held and a chair was left vacant at his place. *Military Situation in the Far East*, Part 4, p. 2877. According to Wedemeyer, Stilwell accused Chennault of not being loyal to him. *Wedemeyer Reports*, by Albert C. Wedemeyer (New
York: Henry Holt and Company, 1958) , p. 202.
[36] *Stilwell Papers*, p. 317. Stilwell recorded: "Actually, in spite of our Anglo-Saxon
blood, we are closer to the Chinese and the Russians than we are to the British."
Stilwell Black Book, p. 86. *MSS.*, Hoover Institution, Stanford.

It was all too obvious that the relations between Stilwell and Chiang Kai-shek were hardly conducive to proper co-ordination and friendly co-operation. He castigated the Chinese President as being "bigoted and selfish" and suffering from "megalomania." [37]

His obsessive desire to retrieve the disaster he suffered in Burma—in spite of Chiang Kai-shek's determination that any new Burma campaign would be useless—was constantly in the back of his mind. The personal antagonism he had against the Generalissimo did a great deal to strain the relations between their two countries. It became such "a serious nuisance" to Roosevelt, according to Robert Sherwood, Hopkins' biographer, that the President "was on the verge of ordering his recall." [38] Harry Hopkins made a note at the time: "The President indicated his strong dissatisfaction with the way the whole show was running in China. He stated that Stilwell obviously hated the Chinese and that his cablegrams are sarcastic about the Chinese and this feeling is undoubtedly known to . . . the Generalissimo." [39]

Roosevelt decided to bring Stilwell home, but General Marshall, who was responsible for his command appointment, convinced the President that "Vinegar Joe" was the "only high-ranking officer" that the U.S. had who could speak Chinese and that "while obviously he does not like Chinese officialdom, he has a great regard for the Chinese people." [40] Only a vigorous defense by General Marshall dissuaded the President from recalling Stilwell.

It is significant that no criticism of General Marshall ever appeared in Stilwell's personal diaries. He was the one individual Stilwell could lean on for support when the chips were down. Stilwell's diary frequently shows how Marshall intervened on his behalf. "Churchill tried to get me," he wrote; "George C. Marshall prevented it—F.D.R. has gone to his limit. If I can't move Peanut, the jig is up for the season." [41]

During this period there was a strong group of left-wingers in the Far Eastern Division of the Department of State. They used Stilwell's sympathy for the Chinese Communists and his violent antipathy to Chiang Kai-shek as a lever to shift American policy in favor of the Communists. So that General Stilwell might have his own liaison and advisory staff to represent him in dealings with many local political authorities, the De-

---

[37] *Stilwell Black Book,* This entry is titled "Psychoanalysis of Peanut," p. 58. *MSS.,* Hoover Institution, Stanford.

[38] Sherwood, *Roosevelt and Hopkins,* p. 740.

[39] *Ibid.,* p. 739.

[40] *Ibid.*

[41] *Stilwell Diary,* March 26, 1944, Book No. 10½. *MSS.,* Hoover Institution, Stanford. Another entry read: "When the word went around that Peanut was after the Reds again, I squawked to George Marshall, George got after T. V. [Soong]. Within a week Atkinson was told that the Chinese wanted a statement made in U.S. that no forcible measure would be taken against the Reds." *Black Book,* July, 1943, p. 46. *MSS.,* Hoover Institution, Stanford.

partment of State assigned a group of American career diplomats (Foreign Service Officers) to the military headquarters in Chungking. In a memorandum to General Leonard T. Gerow, Stilwell personally requested that the State Department be asked "to attach Mr. John Davies to my staff as liaison agent for the duration of this mission. . . . I am acquainted personally with Mr. Davies and believe that his China background will be of considerable value to me." [42] Davies, in turn, brought with him to Chungking John Stewart Service, Raymond Paul Ludden, and John K. Emmerson, all of whom were to become sympathetic to the Chinese Communists.

Stilwell's obsession with the reconquest of the jungle country of Burma, coupled with his personal hatred and contempt for Chiang Kai-shek, and his natural distaste for administrative work, made it a simple matter for these Foreign Service Officers on his staff soon to dominate the political aspects of our China policy. The reports written by this group of officers had a wide circulation. Copies were sent to the State and War Departments, and a selected few were sent to the White House. From the State Department some were sent to the Treasury, Office of War Information, and Office of Strategic Services. [43]

Since it was still official policy in the summer of 1944 to support the Nationalist Government, "it was a common joke [in Chungking] that Stilwell's headquarters were developing a private foreign policy with John Davies as secretary of state." [44] The Davies-Service clique gained control over out-going military and civilian dispatches. Memoranda berating Chiang Kai-shek and the Nationalist Government were fashioned to the prejudiced mind of General Stilwell. "The information contained in this memorandum," Davies reported, "is derived from two persons close to General Chou En-lai and the Communist headquarters here in Chungking. . . ." "There exists a natural ideological affinity between the regime now in power in China and the Nazis, my informant stated. Within the Central Government there is a pronounced admiration of the Nazis which has been augmented by the conspicious success of German arms. The only Chungking Germans confined to a concentration camp are the German Jews; the Nazi Germans move about freely. . . . " [45]

It was the constant endeavor of these Foreign Service officers in China to assure the Departments of War and State that the Chinese Communists were moderate reformers, simply agrarian in the style of Thomas Jefferson, with no subservience to Moscow.

Agnes Smedley was part of that tightly knit group which was so close

42 Memorandum for General Gerow, *Stilwell Documents,* File 1, Section 3-III. *MSS.,* Hoover Institution, Stanford.

43 Feis, *The China Tangle,* p. 258.

44 Chennault, *Way of a Fighter,* p. 318.

45 Memorandum for General Stilwell by John Davies titled "Conversation with Two Leftists," Chungking, July 10, 1942, *Stilwell Documents,* File 62, *MSS.,* Hoover Institution, Stanford.

to Stilwell. Writers, such as Freda Utley, who visited China, reported the mutual admiration between Smedley and Stilwell,[46] and even Davies referred to her as "one of the pure in heart." [47] Smedley had been exposed by General MacArthur's Intelligence Headquarters as an important cog in a Communist international spy ring which was headed by Richard Sorge who was later convicted of being a Soviet espionage agent and hanged by the Japanese.[48] It is significant to note that when Smedley died she left her estate to the Communist leader, Chu Teh.

A letter which Stilwell wrote to a friend while in China casts much light on his attitude toward the Communists. The letter reads in part as follows: "It makes me itch to throw down my shovel and get over there and shoulder a rifle with Chu Teh." [49] Chu Teh, with whom Stilwell wanted to "shoulder a rifle," was then the Commander-in-Chief of the Chinese Red Armies. He was also in command of the Red Armies that later fought against the United States forces in Korea.

General Chennault describes how Stilwell, in the spring of 1944, sent a mission to his friends in Communist Yenan: "The American mission to Yenan was hardly established," he said, "before Stilwell's Chungking staff began to proclaim loudly the superiority of the Communist regime over the Chungking government. Contents of secret reports from the Yenan mission were freely discussed over Chungking dinner tables by Stilwell's staff. No secret was made of their admiration for the Communists, who, they said, were really only 'agrarian reformers' and more like New Dealers than Communists." [50] The Yenan Communists made a great impression on General Stilwell by "shrewdly letting it be known that they would be delighted to have him command their armies. Stilwell never gave up his hopes of commanding the Chinese Red Armies. . . . " [51] At times he preferred the Communists to the Generalissimo.[52] In a confidential "Marshall-Eyes Only" memorandum, Stilwell made this interesting observation:

"In all negotiations the fact strikes out that CKS [Chiang Kai-shek] and company itch to get control of lend-lease supplies upon delivery in

46 Freda Utley, *The China Story* (Chicago: Henry Regnery Company, 1951), pp. 106-107.

47 *Ibid.*, p. 107.

48 Testimony of Major-General Charles Willoughby, August 9, 1951, *Institute of Pacific Relations, Hearings*, Part 2, pp. 356-362.

49 *Daily Worker*, April 16, 1945. In a conversation with Hurley, Chiang stated that he was convinced Stilwell "was in a conspiracy to overthrow the government." *Hurley Papers*, File 308, Document 121. *MSS.*, Santa Fe.

50 Chennault, *Way of a Fighter*, p. 317.

51 *Ibid.*, p. 318.

52 Joseph Alsop, "Why We Lost China: The Feud Between Stilwell and Chiang." *Saturday Evening Post* (January 7, 1950, p. 47.) Among Whittaker Chambers Pumpkin Papers is a Stilwell intelligence report of this period revealing that even in the 1930's he was already strongly prejudiced against the Chinese Nationalists and in favor of the Chinese Communists. *Ibid.*

China. If they are allowed to distribute these supplies you know who will get them. You also know who will not get them. Somehow we must get arms to the Communists, who will fight. They have communicated with me and will fight under my command, but not under a Chinese commander designated by CKS. If I cannot direct the distribution of this staff, command becomes meaningless, and any group I start to build up may easily be starved for equipment." [53]

When General Patrick J. Hurley, special envoy for President Roosevelt, arrived in Chungking in September, 1944, the clash between Stilwell and the Generalissimo had developed into a serious crisis. As Japanese troops penetrated further into China's Southwest region in August and September, 1944, President Roosevelt again urged the Generalissimo to place Stilwell in command of all Chinese forces. Chiang was willing to agree on condition that the power of distributing lend-lease supplies would remain strictly under his control. But Stilwell confided in his diary: "If the G-mo [Chiang Kai-shek] controls distribution, I am sunk. The Reds will get nothing." [54]

As the Japanese military forces began to encircle the American air base at Kweilin, Stilwell urgently demanded the use of Chiang's divisions that were blocking the Chinese Communists. Stilwell flew to Kweilin, decided the situation was lost, and wrote a sharp report to General Marshall calling the Generalissimo's tactical and strategical conceptions "idiotic." The conversations with Chiang he termed "one and a half hours of crap and nonsense," and referred to the Generalissimo as a "crazy little bastard." [55]

Marshall was attending a conference at Quebec. There, Roosevelt and Churchill were making plans for the destruction and expulsion of all Japanese forces in Burma at the earliest possible date, and for opening the Burma Road by next spring.[56] Marshall was annoyed by Stilwell's telegram because it reported a threat by Chiang to withdraw his forces from Burma. Marshall submitted a blunt message to Chiang with Roosevelt's approval. The Generalissimo was asked (1) to reinforce the Chi-

---

53 *Stilwell Documents* (Undated) File 158. MSS., Hoover Institution, Stanford.

54 *Stilwell Papers*, p. 331. "It made him mad as hell to find that I would not simply pass out lend-lease stuff on his order. . . . He might get sore, but he could get nothing on me, and that was a comforting thought. I could say anything I pleased and go away secure in my own mind that the crowd of yes-men, parasites, idolators, and sycophants around him could not break it down. How could they, if it was true?" *Stilwell's Black Book*, pp. 51-52. MSS., Hoover Institution, Stanford.

55 *Stilwell Diary*, September 15, 1944, Book No. 13. MSS., Hoover Institution, Stanford. When Generalissimo was late to a meeting, Stilwell wrote: "He had been doing his evening prayers which are not to be interrupted by anything. This is a new angle. Are we to add religious bias to political bigotry and military ignorance? Anyway he takes it seriously, whether he is sincere or not. Maybe he is fortifying his intuition by communication with his maker." *Black and White Book*, No. 2, August 4, 1942, p. 95. MSS., Hoover Institution, Stanford.

56 *Report to the Combined Chiefs of Staff* by Vice-Admiral Earl Mountbatten, B Paragraph 260.

nese armies in the Salween area in Burma and to press their offensive in conjunction with the British, and (2) to place Stilwell in "unrestricted command" of all Chinese forces. If he failed to do these things, all efforts —both Chinese and American—to save China would be lost. The Generalissimo must then "be prepared to accept the consequences and to assume the personal responsibility." [57]

The message arrived in Chungking on September 19, 1944, with instructions that Stilwell was to deliver it "in person." [58] Stilwell was full of jubilation; he had waited for this moment to deliver an ultimatum to the Generalissimo. He noted in his diary: "President's message arrived. Hot as a firecracker. 'Get busy, boy, or else.' 'Do it now.' The Peanut will have a red neck on this one." [59]

General Hurley advised Stilwell this was not the time to deliver the President's message. To quote from his later testimony, "I said (to Stilwell) 'You shouldn't now, because of this firm language, pile it on him at a time he has felt compelled to make every concession that we have asked. He has made them; he is ready to go; he is ready to bring troops down from the North to reinforce you in the Salween front; he is going to appoint you commander-in-chief.' " [60] Stilwell would not change his mind. He wanted to humiliate the Generalissimo and said, "I am directed by the President to hand it to him." [61]

Hurley raised the question as to who had the authority to speak for the President, but Stilwell refused to be moved. When Hurley handed the message to Chiang Kai-shek, the Generalissimo read it and Hurley noticed ". . . that he looked like he had been hit in the solar plexus. . . ." Silence followed; no one moved. Then Chiang Kai-shek reached over to his tea cup and put the cover on upside down. Stilwell, in Chinese asked, "That gesture still means, I presume, that the party is over?" Someone in Chiang's staff said, "Yes." Stilwell and Hurley then walked out.[62]

The entry Stilwell made in his notes indicates he was elated. "Got letter translated and took it across the river—5:40 P.M.—handed it to him. The harpoon hit him right in the solar plexus, but although he turned green, he never batted an eye. He just turned to me and said, 'I understand.' What! No teapots? No, just a calm silence. I got out promptly and came home. Pretty sight crossing the river; lights all on in Chiang Kai-shek's." [63]

[57] President Roosevelt to Chiang Kai-shek, September 16, 1944, *Stilwell's Command Problems*, (Office of Chief of Military History, Department of the Army, 1956), pp. 445-446.
[58] *Military Situation in the Far East, Hearings*, Part 4, pp. 2866-2868.
[59] *Stilwell Diary*, September 19, 1944. MSS., Hoover Institution, Stanford.
[60] *Military Situation in the Far East*, Part 4, p. 2868.
[61] *Ibid.*, p. 2866.
[62] Testimony of General Patrick J. Hurley, June 20, 1951, *Ibid.*, Part 4, p. 2868.
[63] *Stilwell's Diary*, September 19, 1944. MSS., Hoover Institution, Stanford. This

Stilwell's lack of tact and his persistent urge to aid and use Communist forces shattered any confidence Chiang Kai-shek had in placing him in command of Chinese armies. He disobeyed the Generalissimo's order during the Burma campaign in 1942; moreover, the request that a foreign officer be placed in command of Chinese armies was difficult for Chiang to accept. John Stewart Service, U. S. foreign service officer in China, had some understanding of the true meaning of the recommendations and what Chiang suspected. "This was, in effect, a proposal that the Chinese Communists be armed," Service later testified, "since it was taken for granted that if General Stilwell was to command all Chinese armies, this would include the Communists and they would therefore be eligible to receive a share of American equipment." [64]

The real meaning of the President's request was also confirmed by John Carter Vincent, head of the Chinese Division of the Department of State, when he testified before the Senate Internal Security Subcommittee investigating the Institute of Pacific Relations:

MR. VINCENT: I recall—and I think it was the War Department—White House matter—that Stilwell was authorized to go over to Chiang and see him and recommend a unified command of all troops in China.
MR. SOURWINE (Committee Counsel): What did that mean?
MR. VINCENT: That meant, so far as I can recollect, that Stilwell was to assume command of all forces in China.
MR. SOURWINE: Didn't that necessarily imply the arming of the Chinese Communists?
MR. VINCENT: If Stilwell was going to take over all command?
MR. SOURWINE: Certainly.
MR. VINCENT: It would imply the arming of them under his command and utilizing them as a unified army.
MR. SOURWINE: That was, then, a proposal for arming the Chinese Communists, wasn't it?
MR. VINCENT: If it had been carried out in the way I understood Stilwell wanted to carry it out, it would.
MR. SOURWINE: It was a proposal for arming the Chinese Communists, whether it was carried out or not, wasn't it?
MR. VINCENT: It was a proposal that Stilwell would take command of all the troops, and I assume it would have followed from that the Chinese Communists would have been utilized.
MR. SOURWINE: It was necessarily implicit, wasn't it?
MR. VINCENT: Yes.[65]

The authority to transfer American aid to the Communists meant eventual destruction of Nationalist China, a government we were committed

---

entry differs from White's book on Stilwell's Papers—apparently White had access to another diary which the authorities at the Hoover Institution inform me they know nothing about.
64 As quoted in Lohbeck, *Patrick J. Hurley*, pp. 275-276; Cf. *Stilwell's Command Problems*, pp. 431-432.
65 *Institute of Pacific Relations, Hearings*, Part 7, pp. 2072-2073.

to support. "If America should arm the Communists, Russia would re-main passive but would also immediately begin to arm them openly. There would then be a grave danger of their overthrowing the Central Government and the Kuomintang Party and China under the control of the Communists, would be united with Russia." These are the words of General Li Tsung-jen, Commander-in-Chief of the Fifth War Area in China.[66]

It is a tragedy we did not accept the repeated warnings of Nationalist leaders and others that the Chinese Communists were part of a Marxist movement for world domination. Perhaps some blame should be placed on the Generalissimo for not selling this point to American officials. He saw the Red threat in the Far East far better than many of our foreign service officials. As a result of our miscalculations, deliberate or other-wise, we are today faced with a formidable threat—Red China. It can be said that the serious menace we face in the Far East was not due to our lack of information. On the contrary, our tragic policy in that area can be mostly attributed to the opposition of U. S. foreign service officers and other American officials to Chiang Kai-shek and the Nationalist Govern-ment. These Americans frustrated attainment of our traditional and an-nounced aims in Asia—preservation of the "territorial and administra-tive" integrity of China.

In his reply to President Roosevelt on September 25, 1944, the Gener-alissimo said he was willing to place an American in command of all Chinese armies and air force and to make such changes in the Chinese army staff and personnel as might be necessary to bring harmony in the relations with the American field commander. But he would not "confer this heavy responsibility upon General Stilwell, and will have to ask for his resignation as Chief of Staff of the China theater and his relief from duty in this area." [67]

The Generalissimo told Roosevelt that "it is with deep regret I come to this decision; my experience has definitely convinced me that 'General Stilwell is unfitted' for this important task. Since his arrival in China 'he showed his disregard for that mutual confidence and respect which are essential to the successful collaboration of all allied forces.'" [68] Stilwell did not like the tone of this *aide-memoire;* in a sharp letter to General Marshall he pointed out that the Generalissimo was simply waiting out the war, and was putting its entire burden on the United States. Further-more, the Generalissimo had "no intention of instituting any real dem-ocratic regime of forming a united front with the Communists." [69]

66 *Hurley Papers,* File 312, Document No. 117. *MSS.,* Santa Fe.

67 Generalissimo Chiang Kai-shek to President Roosevelt, September 25, 1944, *Hurley Papers,* File 325, Document No. 21. *MSS.,* Santa Fe.

68 *Hurley Papers,* File 325, Document No. 18. *MSS.,* Santa Fe.

69 General Stilwell to General Marshall, September 26, 1944, *U.S. Relations with China,* p. 68. "Just the usual walla-walla. To hell with the war. The G-mo thinks it's

Stilwell had been warned on several occasions to tone down his attacks upon the Generalissimo. During General Somervell's visit to China, he was asked to avoid the caustic remarks which so irritated the Chinese leader. Somervell wrote, "I thought it was very unfortunate for you to refer to the Generalissimo in the way you have and to make some other remarks which have caused unnecessary friction." [70]

In Washington, Harry Hopkins and H. H. Kung, Chinese Minister of Finance, discussed the Stilwell affair. Hopkins disclosed to Kung that the President "intended to comply with the Generalissimo's request for the recall of General Stilwell." Kung immediately cabled this information to Chiang Kai-shek.[71] The Generalissimo said he would rather go it alone than permit General Stilwell to become commander-in-chief. In the meantime, General Marshall and Secretary Stimson attempted to defend Stilwell and to force Chiang Kai-shek to give him unrestricted command of all the Chinese forces. Apparently the President was not influenced by this stand and decided to send his own reply instead of a message prepared by Marshall. He sent his reply in a form of a proposal—Stilwell would remain in command, but only as a commander of forces in Burma. He would be relieved from "further responsibility in connection with Lend-Lease matters." [72]

Stilwell's diary entry was sharply critical concerning his resignation:

The G-mo says I must be relieved. The reason is that I have 'lost the confidence of the troops.' He was quite emphatic about it and so I guess that's that. Somervell says the President asked George to relieve me more than once, because I can't get along. Nice backing.

The real reason is hard to guess. It may be that with me out nobody else will push the campaign. Neither the limies nor the Peanut wants to do it, so everything will be jake. Or it may be just the suspicious, jealous oriental mind, listening to lies and thinking that it won't do to let a foreigner gain anymore influence.[73]

Hurley delivered the President's message to the Generalissimo and defended Stilwell as well as he could, but Chiang would not back down on one point—Stilwell must go. In a formal reply to President Roosevelt, Chiang Kai-shek summarized his differences with Stilwell:

So long as I am Head of State and Supreme Commander in China, it seems

almost over anyway. 'Coast boys, the Americans and British will finish it up.' Peanut makes himself President with dictatorial powers. They talk over how they will screw us for dough for reconstruction and how they can liquidate the Communists. They re-align the factions and keep the graft firmly in their possession. They throw a sop to the powers by talking of 'constitutional conventions,' but they don't intend to do a thing but make China safe for gangsters. And we can do the fighting—suckers that we are." *Stilwell Black Book*, p. 56. MSS., Hoover Institution, Stanford.

[70] *Stilwell's Mission to China*, p. 378.

[71] *Stilwell's Command Problems*, p. 456.

[72] *Ibid.*, p. 459.

[73] *Stilwell Black Book*, p. 69. MSS., Hoover Institution, Stanford.

to me that there can be no question as to my right to request the recall of an officer in whom I can no longer repose confidence. . . . I not only have no confidence in General Stilwell, but also lack confidence in his military judgment. . . . General Stilwell and I have never agreed about the Burma campaign. . . . I warned him of the consequences stating specifically that I feared the project would be difficult and costly, and would engage all of China's limited resources at a time when this would be dangerous. He treated my warning lightly. . . . It was not long before my warning was substantiated . . . he consistently refused to release Lend-Lease munitions already available in Yunnan for use in the East China fighting. . . . I am wholly confident that if the President replaces General Stilwell with a qualified American officer, we can work to reverse the present trend and achieve a vital contribution to victory in China.[74]

General Hurley was convinced that the break between the Generalissimo and Stilwell was beyond repair and told the President: " . . . if you sustain Stilwell in this controversy, you will lose Chiang Kai-shek and possibly you will lose China with him." [75] President Roosevelt accepted his view, and recalled Stilwell, even though General Marshall tried to dissuade him.[76]

Lieutenant General Albert C. Wedemeyer was designated to serve as the Generalissimo's chief of staff and the commanding general of the American forces in the China Theater. The question of commanding Chinese forces was dropped. A tragic incident in Chinese-American relations had taken place. Summing up his own conclusions on Stilwell's attitude, General Hurley said: "The record of General Stilwell in China is irrevocably coupled in history with the conspiracy to overthrow the Nationalist Government of China, and to set up in its place a Communist regime—and all this movement was part of, and cannot be separated from, the Communist cell or apparatus that existed at the time in the Government in Washington." [77]

An interesting analysis of the Stilwell affair by Chiang Kai-shek confirms Hurley's point of view. The Generalissimo said:

Stilwell was in a conspiracy with the Communists to overthrow the Government, but if he had succeeded and the Chinese Communists were to seize power, I have evidence that there would have been a Brest-Litovsk with Japan.

---

[74] Chiang Kai-shek to Ambassador Hurley, October 9, 1944, *Hurley Papers*, File 312, Document No. 42. *MSS.*, Santa Fe.

[75] Ambassador Hurley to President Roosevelt, October 13, 1944, *Hurley Papers*, File 312, Document 51. *MSS.*, Santa Fe.

[76] *Forrestal Diaries*, p. 12. Stilwell recorded in his diary titled "The Axe Falls": "Radio from George [Marshall]. I am 'recalled'. Sultan in temporary command. Later C.B.I. to split. Sultan in India. Wedemeyer to command U.S. troops in China and c/c to Peanut. No overall command of Chinese—so Rubberlegs has quit. Everybody is horrified about Wedemeyer. Told White and Atkinson. They also are horrified and disgusted. Atkinson is going home to blow the works." *Stilwell Diary*, October 19, 1944, Book 13, *MSS.*, Hoover Institution, Stanford.

[77] Lohbeck, *Patrick J. Hurley* p. 305.

Nobody realized the implications of the Stilwell matter, certainly not the
dupes of the newspaper correspondents, creatures of Stilwell, Barret, Davies, and
Service. Assuredly not the American public. Had his conspiracy succeeded, the
historic policy of U.S. in the Far East and the Pacific would have received its
death blow.[78]

Following this action by the Chinese Government the President sought
to explain it as the consequence of "a conflict of personalities." There
followed, however, "a flood of stories in the newspapers . . . all emphasizing that Chiang Kai-shek is more interested in perpetuating himself in
power than in fighting the Japanese." William Hassett, the President's
good friend and aide, gives us an inside version of the reaction at that
time:

For months there have been many accusations—some of them by Chinese
patriots and intellectuals—that Chiang is a dictator and anti-democratic, and
was diverting Lend-Lease supplies for use against Chinese rebels rather than
against the common Japanese enemy; and that, like all dictators, he had suppressed freedom of the press. . . . Whether Chiang is anti-democratic and totalitarian or not, his Madame will long be remembered, along with her retinue,
as arrogant and overbearing.[79]

The American press and the Foreign Service Officers continued the
vendetta where Stilwell left off.

[78] Memorandum of conversation between Generalissimo Chiang Kai-shek and Ambassador Hurley, February 16, 1945, *Hurley Papers*, File 313, Document No. 35. *MSS.*,
Santa Fe. In his book *Soviet Russia in China*, Chiang makes this observation: "General
Stilwell was one of those influenced by this Communist propaganda. He had mistakenly
believed that the Chinese Communist forces would obey his command. He asked to
have the Government and Communist troops re-equipped on an equal basis with the
Nationalist forces. . . . He had no idea whatsoever of the Chinese Communists'
schemes. He did not believe that the Communists had tried to sabotage China's
National Revolution upon Moscow's instructions in the past . . . General Stilwell's
subsequent dispute with me was created entirely by the Communists and their
friends." p. 118.
[79] William Hassett, *Off the Record with F.D.R.* (New Jersey: Rutgers University
Press, 1958), pp. 287-288.

CHAPTER X

SOME FOREIGN SERVICE OFFICERS
LOOK TO YENAN

Repeated study of American relations with Nationalist China discloses the painful and irrefutable fact that some American officials and Foreign Service officers sedulously and deliberately usurped the authority to establish U.S. policy towards Nationalist China. In the Russian Communist strategy and tactics for world domination China remained a most important objective. In 1913 Lenin had written short articles about the importance of China and the development throughout Asia of the revolutionary movement that might be expected to follow a revolution in Russia. But his colleagues were too preoccupied with domestic revolution to turn their minds to revolutionary prospects in China. The civil war in Russia itself, the foreign intervention, and the hopes of spreading revolution in Europe employed all their energies within the Russian boundaries. As the situation became more subject to control, their eyes turned toward China. China had launched upon uncharted seas of revolution in 1911, and the inconclusive and troubled eventualities provided welcome opportunity for the Russian masters of world revolution.

During the period of the Soviet Russia-Kuomintang *Entente Cordiale* in the 1920's, the Kuomintang and the Chinese Communist Party co-operated with each other. The Communists promised to support the revolutionary program of the Kuomintang. But it soon became evident to the Kuomintang leaders that the Chinese Communists, egged on by Soviet Russia, were aspiring to turn the revolution into a class war in order to gain supreme control over China. The Kuomintang in 1927 broke with the Chinese Communists and Soviet Russia. The ensuing civil war between the armies of the two parties displayed the bloody excesses characteristic of all class wars.[1]

In 1936 the Chinese Red Army was spared almost certain defeat by acceptance on the part of the Kuomintang of the idea of a united front

---

[1] Committee on Foreign Affairs, *National and International Movements*. Supplement III, *Communism in China* (Washington: Government Printing Office, 1948), pp. 8-13.

with the Communists in defense of their mainland. The united front idea, which applied to Communists in all countries, had been developed in Moscow as a means of safeguarding the Soviet Union against the threat of so-called "fascist aggression" and of expanding the influence of the Communists in "capitalist" democracies.[2] Under the terms of the united front agreement of 1937, the Chinese Communists pledged themselves to cease subversive activities against the Nationalist Government, and to integrate the Chinese Red Army with the Government's Central Army.[3]

This pledge was never kept. Soon after the outbreak of the Sino-Japanese War, the Nationalist Government assigned to the Communists certain defense zones. As a sign of its trust and good will the Government even established a new army composed of Communists, the New Fourth Army, to operate between Nanking and Shanghai.[4]

Obvious differences between the Kuomintang and the Chinese Communists inevitably led to clashes which in turn resulted in a general deterioration of the Chinese defense against Japan.

After the United States entered the war, both the Communists and Kuomintang became more interested in their own status *vis-a-vis* each other than in fighting Japan. The intra-party struggle became of paramount importance. The Chinese believed that America guaranteed victory against Japan, and the fruits of this victory would, in their opinion, obviously go to the party that won in the Kuomintang-Communist struggle for power. In the early stage of the war not only did Communist forces avoid battles with the Japanese, but the latter in turn did not take them seriously and instead concentrated their attack on Nationalist troops.

In its campaign to conquer China, the Soviet Union took steps to cover up the Chinese Communists' direct subordination to Moscow. The International Communists and their fellow travelers no longer referred to the Chinese Communists in their propaganda as an ordinary Communist Party or an instrument of Soviet Russia, but as "a democratic party" of Chinese farmers and "agrarian reformers." The strategy, both of Moscow and the Chinese Communists, was to launch political attacks against the Nationalist Government in order to destroy its effectiveness in the eyes of the world. Central to this propaganda were the operations of the Communist Party in America. Moscow's principal assignment for American Communists and their fellow travelers was two-fold: to damage the Nationalist Government's prestige, and to jeopardize the Sino-American friendly relations. This was to be done by influencing the American Government and American public opinion, and, indirectly, by exaggerating

---

[2] Anatole G. Mazour, *Russia: Past and Present* (Princeton, New Jersey: D. Van Nostrand Company, Inc., 1957), pp. 588-599.

[3] Cheng, *A History of Sino-Russian Relations*, p. 206.

[4] Chiang Kai-shek, *Soviet Russia in China*, pp. 94-95.

the contributions of the Chinese Communists to the war against Japan. The Communist propaganda would build up their strength, their "land reforms," and "New Democracy," portraying "democratic freedoms" and "happiness and progress" in Communist areas in Northern Shensi as if Utopia had become a reality there.

One event which tended to frustrate the efforts of the Nationalist Government was the suggested use of American paratroopers in Communist-held territory. They were to lead Communist bands in guerilla warfare against the Japanese. When Ambassador Hurley first heard of the plan he immediately reported it to President Roosevelt:

While I had some inkling of the plot, I did not know that it had been presented to the Communists until that was made apparent by the Communists applying to Wedemeyer for a conference with you. . . . My directive, of course, was to prevent the collapse of the Nationalist Government; sustain the leadership of Chiang Kai-shek; unify the military forces of China, and, as far as possible, to assist in the liberalization of the government and in bringing about conditions that would promote a free, unified, democratic China. The military plan, as outlined, was, recognition and lend-lease supplies for themselves and destruction of the National Government. . . . They asked Wedemeyer to keep their proposed visit to you secret from the National Government and from me.[5]

There was a quick reaction from the War Department in Washington. General Marshall requested from Wedemeyer an explanation on "the plan to aid the Communists" with recommendations as to "appropriate future action." [6] Wedemeyer made a hasty examination of the subject and replied that "there have been several plans discussed" by officers of his headquarters, but none were known to be revealed to the Communists. He indicated the probable sources of the leak were Dr. Soong and General Chen, and recommended that no further action should be taken. The memorandum ended: "General Hurley has read this message and concurs in my recommendation but does not agree to my statement of facts." [7]

Marshall wanted to know if some of the officers of the Theater Headquarters did actually prepare a plan that would mean "by-passing the Generalissimo regarding the employment of Communist troops?" And "if such a plan was formulated, by whom was it done and by whom was it made known to Mao Tse-tung?" [8]

After a careful investigation by General Wedemeyer, it was discovered

5 Ambassador Hurley to President Roosevelt, January 14, 1945, *Hurley Papers*, File 308, Document No. 87. *MSS.*, Santa Fe.

6 General Marshall to General Wedemeyer, January 15, 1945, *Hurley Papers*, File 308, Document No. 88, *MSS.*, Santa Fe.

7 General Wedemeyer to General Marshall, January 19, 1945, *Hurley Papers*, File 308, Document No. 89. *MSS.*, Santa Fe.

8 General Marshall to General Wedemeyer, January 23, 1945, *Hurley Papers*, File 308, Document No. 95. *MSS.*, Santa Fe.

that a well-considered plan had been organized and made known to the Chinese Communists by three American officers: Major General Robert McClure, Colonel David Barrett, and Lieutenant Colonel Willis Bird of the OSS. General McClure was to command all the Chinese Communist troops and Colonel Barrett was picked to be his chief of staff. The plot was revealed when McClure attempted to arrange passage to Washington for Mao Tse-tung and Chou En-lai.[9] Had they succeeded, it would have jeopardized our official policy towards Nationalist China.

Pressure against Chiang Kai-shek came from other sources too, which eventually benefitted the Chinese Communists. The conditioning of the Department of State toward Communization of China began early in 1942. John Patton Davies, Jr., a career diplomat who was investigated and cleared seven times by State Department loyalty boards and finally discharged by Secretary of State Dulles for lack of judgment, discretion and reliability, maintained a close liaison with Chou En-lai, now premier of China.

As early as 1942, Chou outlined the Communist program for control of China, which was eventually successful. He advised Davies that our government should watch its aid to Nationalist China closely, asserting that Lend-Lease supplies would be hoarded for use after the war to maintain the ruling faction. To encourage further American distrust of Chiang Kai-shek, Chou told Davies that if the Generalissimo would permit, Chou would place Communist troops under his command for a Burma campaign and that he, Chou, would "obey Stilwell's orders." [10]

In a memorandum for Stilwell, March 16, 1943, titled "Conversation with Chou En-lai," Davies said: "Chou reiterated his invitation of last summer for a small group of American officers to set up observers' posts in Shensi . . . " He seemed "particularly anxious that an air officer investigate airfield possibilities in Shensi." [11]

As early as July 22, 1942, John Carter Vincent proposed that the United States should seek to promote a liberal postwar regime in China, asserting "Communists would probably co-operate with it." [12] The actions he wanted included: the use of American influence in the hope of establishing real "democracy" in China, recognition of the Chinese Com-

---

9 Ambassador Hurley to Secretary Stettinius, February 7, 1945, *Hurley Papers*, File 313, Document 30. *MSS.*, Santa Fe. Col. Barrett was for years Assistant Army Attaché in China, a specialist well versed in Chinese language, who had been closely associated with then Colonel Stilwell, an Army Attaché. After the war he was U.S. Army Attaché in Taiwan, but the government there broke with him and he is not allowed by them to return to Taiwan.

10 John Patton Davies (Second Secretary of Embassy in China) to General Stilwell, Chungking, June 29, 1942, *Foreign Relations, China, 1942*, p. 102.

11 Memorandum for General Stilwell by John Davies, March 16, 1943, *Stilwell Documents*, File 67. *MSS.*, Hoover Institution, Stanford.

12 John Carter Vincent (Counselor of Embassy in China) to the Ambassador to China (Gauss), Chungking, July 22, 1942, *Foreign Relations: China, 1942*, p. 226.

munist Army as a participant in the war against Japan, and apportionment to the Communists of a share of American supplies sent to China.[13] In the spring of 1943, after a visit with Chou En-lai, Vincent cabled the State Department from Chungking that the only hope for real democracy in China was a coalition with the Chinese Reds.[14] Gradually the groundwork was being laid for the Marshall Mission.

American Foreign Service Officers in China played a significant part in working for a change in American support from Nationalist China to the Communists. Their reports were very complimentary to the Communists and frequently derogatory of the Nationalist Government. United States policy at this time supported the Nationalist Government under Chiang Kai-shek, but the philosophy of the Foreign Service Officers in China was different. In their reports to the Department of State, they were building up the fiction that the Chinese Communists were the real "nationalistic and democratic" movement in China, which would inevitably dominate the country. To them the Nationalist Government was considered reactionary, corrupt, and oppressive—guilty of hoarding American supplies for a civil war against the Communists instead of fighting Japan. There was no hope for an agreement unless Chiang Kai-shek made concessions to the Communists. The Department of State ended up formulating to a great extent its policy on the basis of what these men wrote. On January 23, 1943, John Stewart Service reported:

In Kuomintang-controlled China the countering of communism is a growing preoccupation of propaganda, of both military and civilian political indoctrination, and of secret police and gendarmerie activity. There is not only a rigorous suppression of anything coming under the ever-widening definition of 'communism' but there appears to be a movement away from even the outward forms of democracy in government. It is now no longer wondered whether civil war can be avoided, but rather whether it can be delayed at least until after a victory over Japan . . . the eventual defeat and withdrawal of the Japanese will leave the Kuomintang still confronted with the Communists solidly entrenched in most of Northern China. In addition, the Communists will be in a position to move into the vacuum created by the Japanese withdrawal from Suiyuan, Jehol, and Manchuria, in all of which areas there is already some Communist activity. In the rest of China they will have the sympathy of elements among the liberals, intellectuals, and students. . . . There is undoubtedly a strong revulsion in the mind of the average, non-party Chinese to the idea of renewed civil war and the Kuomintang may indeed have difficulty with the loyalty and effectiveness of its conscript troops.[15]

General Stilwell's political advisor, John Patton Davies, gave laudatory accounts of the Chinese Communists and bitter criticisms of Chiang Kai-shek's Government. He wrote: "The Chinese Army and Government is

13 *Institute of Pacific Relations, Final Report*, p. 186.
14 *Ibid.*, p. 186, Part 7, pp. 2000 ff.
15 *Institute of Pacific Relations, Hearings*, Part 3, Exhibit #249, pp. 790-793.

ridden by politics and abuses. Any American military man who attempted to compromise and play Chinese politics would promptly find himself enmeshed and rendered useless for the purpose he was sent out." [16] In another memorandum he expressed the view that "As the Chinese Communists moved away from world revolution to nationalism they also moved in the direction of more moderate internal political and economic policy." He wasn't sure these "moves were in compliance with Comintern dictates," but it was "less material than that they were historically and evolutionary sound." He pictured the Kuomintang as being thoroughly corrupt:

> The Kuomintang and Chiang Kai-shek recognizes that the Communists, with the popular support which they enjoy and their reputation for administrative reform and honesty, represent a challenge to the Central Government and its spoils system. The Generalissimo cannot admit the seemingly innocent demands of the Communists that their party be legalized and democratic processes be put into practice. To do so would probably mean the abdication of the Kuomintang and the provincial satraps.[17]

Davies advised Harry Hopkins that the United States "should avoid" making any agreements which would commit us "unalterably to Chiang." We should be ready during or after the war "to adjust ourselves to possible realignments in China." Our policy should be to "avoid finding ourselves at the close of the war backing a coalition of Chiang's Kuomintang and the degenerate puppets against a democratic coalition commanding Russian sympathy." [18]

Davies also advised that we "dispatch immediately" to Communist China "a military and political observers' mission" for the purpose of collecting information on the enemy and assessing the strength of the Communists in China." [19] Since Chiang would probably oppose this move, it was suggested that American authorities compel the Generalissimo to accede to this plan.[20]

The stratagem of the Foreign Service Officers at work in China is clearly shown by their reports, which were generally not favorable to the Nationalist Government. According to Davies, Chiang's refusal to cooperate with the Communists was the basic cause for Chinese disunity. In order to maintain his own position of authority, Chiang was willing to involve the United States in a Chinese Civil War and possible war with the Soviet Union. Davies reported on June 24, 1943:

[16] John P. Davies to Ambassador Gauss, Chungking, March 9, 1943, Department of State, *Papers Relating to the Foreign Relations of the United States, China, 1943* (Washington: Government Printing Office, 1957), p. 29.
[17] Memorandum by John P. Davies, June 24, 1943, *Ibid.*, pp. 258-266.
[18] Memorandum by John P. Davies, December 31, 1943, *Ibid.*, p. 399.
[19] Memorandum by John P. Davies, January 15, 1944, *United States Relations with China*, p. 564.
[20] Lohbeck, *Patrick J. Hurley*, p. 265.

We may anticipate that Chiang Kai-shek will exert every effort and resort to every strategem to involve us in active support of the Central Government. We will probably be told that if fresh American aid is not forthcoming all of China and eventually all of Asia will be swept by Communism. . . . It is therefore not inconceivable that, should Chiang attempt to liquidate the Communists, we would find ourselves entangled not only in a civil war in China, but also drawn into conflict with the Soviet Union.[21]

On April 7, 1944, Service sent another memorandum to the Department of State in which he said: "Chiang's persisting in an active anti-Soviet policy, at a time when his policies (or lack of them) are accelerating economic collapse and increasing internal dissension, can only be characterized as reckless adventurism. The cynical desire to destroy unity among the United Nations is serious. . . . Finally, Russia will be led to believe (if she does not already) that American aims run counter to hers, and that she must therefore protect herself by any means available: in other words, the extension of her direct power or influence." [22] Service continued by stating it was very important, therefore, that the United States have the following aims in its dealings with China, ". . . avoid all appearance of unqualified diplomatic support to China, especially *vis-a-vis* Russia; and limit American aid to China to direct prosecution of the war against Japan. . . . Show a sympathetic interest in the Communist and liberal groups in China. Try to fit the Communists into the war against Japan. . . ." [23]

Serious reflection upon these reports would convince an impartial observer that Service and Davies did recommend a "change in policy." Again on June 20, 1944, Service reported that the National Government under the leadership of Chiang Kai-shek was corrupt and disintegrating: "The government and military structure is being permeated and demoralized from top to bottom by corruption, unprecedented in scale and openness. [and] . . . the policies of the Kuomintang under the impact of hyper-inflation in the presence of obvious signs of internal and external weakness must be described as bankrupt." [24]

Having presented to the Department of State this picture of the China

---

21 *U. S. Relations with China*, p. 571. In a memorandum for General Stilwell, titled "Conversation with Sun Fo", Davies reported: "I . . . gained the impression that he considered the Communists to be a declining factor. The Chinese Communists are drifting from orthodox communism. . . ." *Stilwell Documents*, July 1, 1942, File 62. MSS., Hoover Institution, Stanford. But Davies' comment that we might be "drawn into conflict with the Soviet Union" indicates that he was under no illusions concerning the Moscow ties of the Chinese Communists. His reports to the contrary were obviously nothing more than Communist-line propaganda designed to deceive our government.

22 *Institute of Pacific Relations, Hearings*, Part 3, Exhibit No. 250, pp. 794-795.

23 U.S. Congress, Committee of Foreign Relations, *State Department Employee Loyalty Investigation*, 81st Cong., 1st Sess. (Washington: Government Printing Office, 1952) , Part 2, p. 1978.

24 *U.S. Relations with China*, pp. 567-568.

situation, Service also offered his solution. In June, 1944, he recommended to Washington the following program: (1) Stop building up Chiang; (2) high United States officials should make known the intent of our government as to "democracy and unity in China;" (3) the OWI should point up "the values of democracy in China as a permanent political system and as an aid in waging war against totalitarianism." It should recognize and encourage "liberal and progressive forces," in China; (4) "we should maintain friendly relations with the liberal elements" in China and with the Communists; (5) Madam Sun Yat-sen should be invited to the White House; (6) "we should show an interest in the Chinese Communists . . . and give publicity on the blockade that Chiang was using to contain the Reds;" (7) we should apply pressure on Chiang Kai-shek to dispatch observers to North China; (8) we should train and equip provincial armies to fight the Japanese; and (9) we should "publicize statements by the United States officials . . . such as the Sumner Welles memorandum to Earl Browder, which was disapproved by the Nationalists." [25]

It appears that the first suggestion to establish direct liaison between the United States military mission and the Chinese Communists at Yenan was advanced by John Davies in a memo to General Stilwell. He proposed that an "observers' mission" be sent there to deter, as he put it, "the impulse of the Kuomintang to liquidate the Communists by force." As early as September 1943, Stilwell had recommended that Nationalist and Communist forces be used against the Japanese in the Yangtze area and proposed the Communists "be given sufficient supplies to put it into effect." [26]

During their visit to China, Vice-President Wallace and Vincent pressed the idea of sending Americans as observers to Yenan, and the Generalissimo was finally forced to agree to the scheme.[27] July 22, 1944, was an historic date for the Chinese Communists at Yenan. On that date the military observers arrived, and "a contagious enthusiasm soon prevailed among the American officers and G.I.'s as they got the feel of the Yenan atmosphere." It was "almost too good to be true." Americans in Yenan agreed it was "an invigorating experience, a pleasure second only to going home." Gunther Stein wrote:

The active, natural Yenan atmosphere and those cheerful, warm-hearted, practical Eighth Route Army men seemed to charm all the American officers and G.I.'s. They enjoyed every bit of the Communists' simple, unsophisticated hospitality; the unconventional dinner parties at which famous Chinese generals and their wives—in cotton uniforms and pants, without lipstick and society

25 *Institute of Pacific Relations, Hearings,* Exhibit 254, Part 3, pp. 824-826. For Welles' memorandum see Chap. XII.

26 Based upon Memorandum by Mr. Davies, January 15, 1944, and letter from General Stilwell to the Generalissimo, September 6, 1943. Lohbeck, *op. cit.,* pp. 264-265.

27 Discussions with President Chiang, June 22 and June 23. *United States Relations with China,* pp. 551-558.

manners, but gay and feminine—sat together with young American lieutenants and sergeants, talking with them about their homes and families back in the States; the theatricals in barnlike auditoriums crowded with animated spectators; and especially those rustic Saturday evening dances where everybody, party leader Mao Tse-tung and Commander in Chief Chu Teh, girls and boys from universities and factories, Eighth Route Army men, and, of course, the ever-ready Americans themselves joined in the breath-taking *Yangko* folk dance in waltzes and fox trots. 'Gosh, what a difference from the other side,' they used to say, thinking of the rigid prohibition of all dancing by the New Life Movement in the Chungking territories and of their stuffy, frustrated atmosphere.

The Communists were equally enthusiastic about the eager and natural Americans who seemed all so happy, informal, and young, whatever their age and rank, and who were so keenly devoted to their tasks.[28]

The entry of American newspaper correspondents in Yenan at this time resulted in a flood of pro-Communist and anti-Kuomintang propaganda appearing in the American press.[29] In this connection it is interesting to note the case of Father Raymond J. deJaegher, a Catholic missionary, who witnessed anti-Western slogans everywhere in Red China. However, one day he woke to find a surprise:

. . . he was amazed to find the screaming slogans against America and Great Britain erased from the walls of the city and complimentary posters in English put up in their stead all over town. On inquiry he learned that an American reporter had been invited by the Reds to inspect their anti-Japanese activities in that area. When he arrived a great show was put on for his benefit which undoubtedly left its mark. When he was gone the old signs came up again.[30]

There can be no doubt that the Foreign Service Officers in General Stilwell's staff were determined to destroy the Nationalist Government and remove Chiang Kai-shek as head of State. They were very explicit in their advocacy of this change and argued it repeatedly and forcefully. The Roosevelt Administration formulated its policies largely on the information reported by these men. Now and then Harry Hopkins would call the attention of the President to what they wrote. For example on September 6, 1944, he passed a copy of Service's report of July 28, 1944, with the comment that "Here is Mr. Jack Service's preliminary report on the Communist situation in North China. Service is a member of the State Department staff. He certainly makes some arresting observations." [31]

28 Gunther Stein, *The Challenge of Red China* (New York: Whittlesey House, 1945) , pp. 347-350. Gunther Stein was a member of the Sorge spy ring. According to the Willoughby Report: "His book [*Challenge of Red China*] has been very effective in perpetuating the legend that Chinese Communists are not Communists and are not in any way connected with the Soviet Union. Like Miss (Agnes) Smedley, Gunther Stein was a Soviet agent, and one can be certain that neither of them was publishing the truth about Chinese Communists." Willoughby, *Shanghai Conspiracy*, pp. 76-77.

29 Lohbeck, *op. cit.*, pp. 270-271.

30 Harold Martinson, *Red Dragon Over China* (Minneapolis: Augsburg Publishing Company, 1956), p. 112.

31 Feis, *The China Tangle*, p. 258.

Presumably Hopkins passed to the President the following report by Service of his visit to Communist-held territory:

There is an absence of show and formality in speech and action. Relations of the officials and people toward us, and of the Chinese among themselves, are open, direct and friendly. Mao Tse-tung and other leaders are universally spoken of with respect but these men are approachable and subservience toward them is completely lacking. They mingle freely in groups.

Body guards, gendarmes, and clap-traps of Chungking officialdom are also completely lacking to the casual eye. There are no police in Yenan and very few soldiers are seen. There are no beggars, no signs of desperate poverty. Clothing and living are simple. Almost everyone except the peasants wear the same Chungshan-type of uniform of native cotton cloth. We have no signs of ostentation in dress, living, or entertaining. Women not only wear practically the same clothes (trousers, sandals, or cloth shoes, and often a Russian-type smock), they act and are treated as friendly equals. Their openness and complete lack of self consciousness is at first disconcerting. This does not mean familiarity: the spooning couples seen in parks or quiet street in Chungking would seem as out of place as long gowns, high heels or lipstick . . .

There is everywhere an emphasis on democracy or unlimited relations with the common people. This is shown in their cultured work which is taken very seriously. . . .

There is no tension in the local situation—no guards when one enters the city, no garrisoned blockhouses in the hills. One hears nothing of the banditry or disturbances in the country. Mao has more warmth and magnetism than would be expected from the generally poor pictures of him. . . .

To the skeptical, the general atmosphere at Yenan can be compared to that of a rather small sectarian college—or a religious summer conference. There is a bit of the smugness, self-righteousness, and conscious fellowship.[32]

Service, in his testimony before the Tydings Committee in 1950, tells in detail of the many meetings he had inside and outside the United States government. He said: "I was spending full time being available to officials and others who had a responsible interest in China and wanted recent background, particularly on the Communists. My superiors knew that I was expressing my own personal opinions freely and apparently considered that I had sufficient judgment and discretion." [33]

The influence of these men was probably greatest in the Department of State where their reports, constantly emphasizing the defects of the Kuomintang, were even more convincing and persuasive than their analysis of the Communist regime at Yenan. But they consistently lauded the achievements made by the Mao Tse-tung government, as for example the observation reported by John Davies on August 3, 1944:

The policy of these (Communist) political leaders . . . continues to be: adherence to the United Front; full mobilization to fight Japan; abandonment

---

32 John Stewart Service, "First Informal Impressions of the North Shensi Communist Base," Report No. 1, July 28, 1944, *Stilwell Documents*, File 125. *MSS.*, Hoover Institution, Stanford.

33 *State Department Employee Loyalty Investigations, Hearings*, Part 2, pp. 1971-1972.

of any purely Communist program. . . . This attitude has been clearly expressed by Mao Tse-tung in recent interviews and by Chou En-lai in his talk with me on July 27.

Davies continues with the observation that their brand of Communism "does not mean the immediate overthrow of private capital because there is still almost no capitalism in China." Furthermore, it does not mean the dictatorship of the proletariat because there is as yet no proletariat. It does not even mean the "collectivization of farms because the political education of the peasants has not yet overcome their primitive individualistic desire to till their own land."

It is true that the Chinese Communist Party aims at eventual socialism, Davies reported, but it hopes to arrive at this, not through violent revolution, but through a "long and orderly process of democracy and controlled economic development." This democracy will be "a progressive . . . type." Since the Communists believe in "democracy, they advocate multi-party participation in politics." As a result "they seek compromise with the Kuomintang . . . they refuse to exploit what seems to be a present opportunity to seek the overthrow of the Kuomintang. And for this reason they seek to avoid civil war."

Davies also found the "liberal economic policies" of the Chinese Communists based on "private property." Moreover, they base their policy toward the Kuomintang on a "real desire for democracy" in China. The Communists are desirous of an "orderly economic growth through a stage of private enterprise" and eventually to socialism "without the need of a violent social upheaval and revolution." He concluded:

If this view is correct, it follows that the policies of the Chinese Communist Party *will not run counter to the interests of the United States in China in the foreseeable future.*[34]

Service took note of the fact that the Communists had "not tried to eliminate such groups as the landlords and native capitalists, and they realize that their own advancement and the interest of the country are best served by the co-operation of all groups based on reasonable protection of the interests of all those groups." There was "little aping of Soviet Russia and little evidence of strong ties to Russia." [35] The Communists "exist because the people permit, support, and wholeheartedly fight with them." With their "great popular base" the Reds "cannot be eliminated." Writes Service: that "Kuomintang attempts to do so by force must mean a complete denial of democracy." [36]

---

[34] "Communist Policy Toward the Kuomintang" by Davies, August 3, 1944, Report No. 5. *Stilwell Documents,* File 155. MSS., Hoover Institution, Stanford. Italics mine.

[35] Memorandum by John Stewart Service, September 28, 1944. *Institute of Pacific Relations, Hearings,* Part 14, p. 5422.

[36] Memorandum by John Stewart Service, October 9, 1944. *United States Relations with China,* pp. 566, 572.

On August 23, 1944, Service had an interview with the Communist leader, Mao Tse-tung, who feared America's retreat into isolationism if Roosevelt were not re-elected. Service asked the Red leader how pressure could be exerted upon the Generalissimo to co-operate. Foreign Minister Chou maintained: "The only way to be sure of decisively winning the war in China and avoiding civil war is to give arms to both Kuomintang and Communists." According to Mao, Chiang would have to listen to America because of the economic situation. "Chiang is in a corner." He then summed up his attitudes on the Generalissimo:

Chiang is stubborn. But fundamentally he is a gangster. That fact must be understood in order to deal with him. We have had to learn it by experience. The only way to handle him is to be hardboiled. You must not give way to his threats and bullying. Do not let him think you are afraid; then he will press his advantage. The United States has handled Chiang very badly. They have let him get away with blackmail—for instance, talk of being unable to keep up resistance, of having to make peace, his tactics in getting the 500 million dollar loan, and now Kung's mission to the U.S. and the plea for cloth. Cloth! Are we or are we not fighting the Japanese! Is cloth more important than bullets? We had no cotton here in the Border region and the KMT blockade kept us from getting any from the parts of China that did have it. But we got busy and soon we are going to be self-sufficient. It would be 100 times easier for the KMT, and if they were a government that had an economic policy they would have done it themselves.

With Chiang you can be friendly only on your own terms. He must give in to constant, strong, and unified pressure. Never relax on your objectives; keep hammering at him.

The position of the United States now is entirely different from what it was just after Pearl Harbor. There is no longer any need or any reason to cultivate, baby, or placate Chiang. The United States can tell Chiang what he should do—on his meeting American desires.

On the question of arms aid Mao stated in effect: "For America to give arms only to the Kuomintang will in its effect be interference because it will enable the Kuomintang to continue to oppose the will of the people of China." He did not interpret as "interference" the furtherance of the "true interests of the people of China." The people living in the Communist areas were "free from deadening repression." Said Mao: "The policies of the Chinese Communist Party are merely liberal." On the question of civil war he stated:

One thing certain is that we Communists dread civil war. We abhor it. We will not start it. We will do our best to avoid it—even though we know that as things now are (provided that the KMT does not receive foreign help) we would eventually win. But the Communists are of the people. The people's interests are our interests. The people will not submit for long to the despotic Fascism which is now apparent in Chungking and Sian, and which is foreshadowed even more menacingly in books like Chiang's 'China's Destiny.' If the people fight, the Communists must fight along with them.

On relations with the United States, Mao had this to say:

The United States would find us *more cooperative* than the Kuomintang. We will not be afraid of democratic American influence—we will welcome it. We have no silly ideas of taking *only* Western mechanical techniques. Also we will not be interested in monopolistic, bureaucratic capitalism that stifles the economic development of the country and only enriches the officials. *We will be interested* in the most rapid possible development of the country on constructive and productive lines. First will be the raising of the living standard of the people (see what we have done here with our limited resources). After that we can come to the 'national defense industry' that Chiang talks of in his 'China's Destiny.' We will be interested in the welfare of the Chinese people.

America does not need to fear that we will not be cooperative. We must cooperate and we must have American help. This is why it is so important to us Communists to know what you Americans are thinking and planning. We cannot risk crossing you—cannot risk any conflict with you.[37]

In his report of October 10, 1944, submitted to General Stilwell, Service went to the extreme of frankly suggesting that Chiang Kai-shek be publicly abandoned in favor of Mao Tse-tung. The now famous Report No. 40 is a completely unguarded statement of Service's views. It merits extensive quotation.

. . . Our dealing with Chiang Kai-shek apparently continues on the basis of the unrealistic assumption that he is China and that he is necessary to our cause. It is time, for the sake of the war and also for our future interest in China, that we take a more realistic line. In the present circumstances, the Kuomintang is dependent on American support for survival. But we are in no way dependent on the Kuomintang. We need not fear Kuomintang surrender or opposition. The party and Chiang will stick to us because our victory is certain and is their only hope for continued power . . . We need not fear the collapse of the Kuomintang government. All the other groups in China want to defend themselves and fight Japan. Any new government under any other than the present reactionary control will be more cooperative and better able to mobilize the country . . . We need not support Chiang in the belief that he represents pro-American or democratic China. All the people and all other political groups of importance in China are friendly to the United States and look to it for the salvation of the country, now and after the war. . . . Our policy toward China should be guided by two facts. First, we cannot hope to deal successfully with Chiang without being hardboiled. Second, we cannot hope to solve China's problems (which are now our problems) without consideration of the opposition forces—Communists, provincial, and liberal. We should not be swayed by pleas of the danger of China's collapse. This is an old trick of Chiang's. . . . Public announcement that the President's representative had made a visit to the Communist capital at Yenan would have significance that no Chinese would miss—least of all the Generalissimo. The effect would be great even if it were only a demonstration with no real consultation. But it should be

---

[37] Interview Between Mao Tse-tung and John S. Service, August 23, 1944. *Scope of Soviet Activity in the United States*, Part 34, pp. 1909-1917. Emphasis in Original.

more than a mere demonstration; we must, for instance, plan an eventual use of the Communist armies and this cannot be purely on Kuomintang terms.[38]

When, in 1945, Major General Patrick J. Hurley testified before the Senate Foreign Relations Committee that Service and "the professional Foreign Service men" in China had sabotaged his efforts as Ambassador to China, he was referring specifically to Report No. 40. Although this report was addressed to General Stilwell, Hurley testified that a copy was delivered to the Communist headquarters in Yenan by Service. Hurley complained about this report to Secretary of State James F. Byrnes, whose reply was "that these young men should be encouraged to make reports of this kind to their superiors." [39]

Solomon Adler, Treasury Representative in Chungking, wrote that Service considers Communist *"interests do not run counter to those of the United States in the foreseeable future and merit a sympathetic and friendly attitude on our part."* [40] Under the heading "Highlights of the American Military Mission to Yenan," Adler states: *"The general impression made on the Mission was extremely favorable."* He added: "The Communist political program is moderate in the sphere both of domestic and foreign policy." Further: "The Communist attitude toward the Kuomintang appears on the whole to be fairly conciliatory." [41] According to Service, they use their influence "in a democratic way and to further democratic ends." [42] Davies later added this note:

The Chinese Communists are backsliders. They still acclaim the infallibility of Marxian dogma and call themselves Communists. But they have become in-

---

[38] John Stewart Service to General Stilwell, October 10, 1944, *Hurley Papers.* File 312, Document No. 48. *MSS.*, Santa Fe. On October 9, 1944, Service reported that the Communist government had "improved the economic conditions of peasants by their rent and interest reduction tax reform, and good government. It has given them democratic self-government, political consciousness and a sense of their rights." *U.S. Relations with China,* p. 566.

[39] Testimony of General Patrick J. Hurley, June 20, 1951, *Military Situation in the Far East, Hearings,* Part 4, pp. 2912-2913; Commenting on this report, Congressman Judd of Minnesota, a long time student of Chinese affairs, remarked: "The memorandum illustrates the conniving against highest officials of the Government of China, being carried on even during the war by representatives of our Government. The Chinese Government had the right to expect that the representatives of the United States, its ally, would do their best to help it with its overwhelming problems, which it knew better than anyone else it could not possibly solve without sympathetic understanding and support from us. Instead, officials of the United States were insisting that our Government intervene to coerce the responsible heads of the Chinese Government into so-called cooperation with a Communist rebellion." *Congressional Record,* October 19, 1949, p. 15091.

[40] Solomon Adler to Harry Dexter White, October 12, 1944. *Scope of Soviet Activity in the United States,* Part 34, p. 1929. Emphasis in original. White had several of his men in China at various times and received direct, unofficial reports from them.

[41] *Ibid.,* pp. 1923-1925. Emphasis in original. Adler was identified by Elizabeth Bentley as a member of the Silvermaster group. *Interlocking Subversion in Government Departments,* Part 30.

[42] Lohbeck, *op. cit.,* p. 284.

dulgent of human frailty and confess that China's Communist salvation can be attained only through prolonged evolutionary rather than immediate revolutionary conversion. Like that other eminent backslider, Ramsay MacDonald, they have come to accept the inevitability of gradualness.[43]

Both Service and Davies spent considerable time in China as State Department officials. In their recommendations to Washington both followed the Communist Party line. In discussing the strength of the Chinese Communists, for example, Davies wrote:

The reason for this phenomenal vitality and strength is simple and fundamental. It is mass support, mass participation. The Communist governments and armies are the first governments and armies in modern Chinese history to have positive and wide-spread popular support. They have this support because the governments and armies are genuinely of the people.

He concluded:

The Communists are in China to stay. And China's destiny is not Chiang's but theirs.[44]

In another report Davies then made a plea for U.S. co-operation with the Communists, frankly recognizing that this meant Communist control of China:

The United States is the greatest hope and the greatest fear of the Chinese Communists. They recognize that if they receive American aid, even if only on an equal basis with Chiang, *they can quickly establish control over most if not all of China,* perhaps without civil war. For most of Chiang's troops and bureaucrats are opportunists who will desert the Generalissimo if the Communists appear to be stronger than the Central Government.

We are the greatest fear of the Communists because the more aid we give Chiang exclusively the greater the likelihood of his precipitating civil war and the more protracted and costly will be the Communist unification of China.

So the Chinese Communists watch us with mixed feeling. If we continue to reject them and support an unreconstructed Chiang, they see us becoming their enemy. But they would prefer to be friends. Not only because of the help we can give them but also because they recognize that our strategic aims of a strong, independent and democratic China can jibe with their nationalist objectives.[45]

On November 15, to cite another example, Mr. Davies wrote:

We should not now abandon Chiang Kai-shek. To do so at this juncture would be to lose more than we could gain. We must for the time being con-

[43] "How Red Are the Chinese Communists?" Memorandum by John P. Davies, Jr., November 7, 1944. *Scope of Soviet Activity in the United States,* Part 34, p. 1932; *Institute of Pacific Relations, Hearings,* Part 13, p. 4827.

[44] "Will the Communists Take Over China?" by John P. Davies, Jr., Nov. 7, 1944. *Scope of Soviet Activity in the United States,* Part 34, p. 1931; *Institute of Pacific Relations,* Part 12, p. 4828.

[45] "The Chinese Communists and the Great Powers," by John P. Davies, Jr., Nov. 7, 1944. *Scope of Soviet Activity in the United States,* Part 34, p. 1933. Italics mine.

tinue recognition of Chiang's Government. But we must be realistic. We must not indefinitely underwrite a politically bankrupt regime. . . . A coalition Chinese Government in which the Communist finds a satisfactory place is the solution of this impasse most desirable to us. . . . If Chiang and the Communists are irreconcilable, then we shall have to decide which faction we are going to support. In seeking to determine which faction we should support we must keep in mind these basic considerations: 'Power in China is on the verge of shifting from Chiang to the Communists.'[46]

Lawrence K. Rosinger, an influential publicist and member of the Institute of Pacific Relations, regarded the Communists as harbingers of a "progressive China with which this country could work in harmony," while Chungking was "running an inefficient, reactionary, undemocratic regime whose prestige among the people recently has diminished in unmistakable fashion." [47]

The Communists "recognize that Chiang's position is crumbling, that they may before long receive substantial Russian support, and that if they have patience, they will succeed to authority in at least North China." [48] Adds Davies: "It is time that we unequivocally told Chiang Kai-shek that we will work with and within our discretion, supply whatever Chinese forces we believe can contribute to the war against Japan." Further, "We should tell him that we will not work with or supply any Chinese unit, whether Central Government, Provincial or Communist, which shows any inclination toward precipitating civil conflict." [49]

On November 10, 1944, John K. Emmerson expressed high praise for Communist treatment of Japanese prisoners. "Thirty per cent of prisoners now falling into Eighth Route Army surrendered voluntarily." A Japanese emancipation league had been organized in Communist-held territory. "While much of the indoctrination they received is communistic in nature, no particular pressure is brought upon them to become communists. "The policy of the Eighth Route Army regarding prisoners of war is based on kind and considerate treatment. Japanese prisoners of war are handled expertly and considerately from the moment of capture." [50]

---

[46] *U. S. Relations with China*, p. 574.

[47] Lawrence K. Rosinger, *China's Crisis* (New York: Alfred A. Knopf, 1945), pp. 254, 243. Rosinger was named as a Communist by several witnesses but refused to confirm or deny charge on grounds of the Fifth Amendment, *Institute of Pacific Relations, Final Report*, p. 157.
Professor George Taylor, Director of the Far Eastern Institute of the University of Washington, has written an analysis of *China Crisis*. He concluded that the author's treatment of the subject "followed in a veiled manner the basic concepts outlined by the Sixth World Congress of the Communist International in 1928." See *Ibid.*, Part 1, pp. 349-352.

[48] Memorandum by John P. Davies, Jr., December 9, 1944. *United States Relations with China*, p. 572.

[49] Memorandum by John P. Davies, Jr., December 12, 1944. *Ibid.*, p. 575.

[50] *Stilwell Documents*, File 113. MSS., Hoover Institution, Stanford.

It was United States policy, as stated by the President and the Secretary of State, to support the Nationalist Government of China under the leadership of Chiang Kai-shek. But these career men advised the Communists that General Hurley's "effort in preventing the collapse of the National Government did not represent the policy of the United States." [51] They even recommended that the United States should support the Chinese Communist faction which they believed was getting stronger. General Hurley opposed the idea of dealing independently with the Communists. When, in January, 1945, the Communist military leader Chu Teh made a request for a loan, Hurley recommended that no American arms or equipment should be sent to any authority in China other than the Nationalist Government.

From these differing views a conflict grew between the Foreign Service Officers and General Hurley who had been appointed personal representative of the President to China on August 18, 1944. He had been instructed to support the Nationalist Government. However, the Service-Davies clique was violently opposed to both the Nationalist Government and the Generalissimo.

On January 4, 1945, Davies made some significant political comments in a report titled "China and the Kremlin." It was classified by Davies as unofficial because the views were personal ones. In other words, he doubted the advisability of trying to make this an official commentary "as I do not believe that it would receive the official approval of the Ambassador." In the report Davies made the following comments:

The Russians see the anti-Soviet Government of Chiang Kai-shek decaying—militarily, politically and economically. They observe the Chinese Communists consolidating in North China, expanding southward in the wake of Chiang's military debacles and now preparing for the formal establishment of a separatist administration . . .
A rejuvenated Chiang, Moscow probably recognizes, means an increased likelihood of civil war. . . [52]

On January 5, Davies reported, "If there is no civil war and no coalition, there will be two Chinas. A unified and peaceful Communist North China, and a South China torn by semi-feudal rivalries and strife." [53]

Service regarded the "theories of the Chinese Communists" as "dissimilar to those of the Russian Communists." The Chinese Communists had been "very helpful in making available information . . . in contrast to the difficulties frequently encountered . . . in dealings with the Central Government of Generalissimo Chiang Kai-shek." [54]

---

[51] Hurley's letter of resignation to President Truman, November 26, 1945, *Hurley Papers*. File 315, Document No. 81. *MSS.*, Santa Fe.

[52] *Hurley Papers*, File 326, Document No. 6. *MSS.*, Santa Fe.

[53] *Hurley Papers*, File 400. *MSS.*, Santa Fe.

[54] Major Paul Umbarger to Colonel Stevenson, May 12, 1945, *Hurley Papers*, File 2106, Document No. 1. *MSS.*, Santa Fe.

The Service-Davies reports were building the fiction that the Communists were doing most of the fighting against the Japanese. General Albert Wedemeyer, who was the Commander of all American forces in China, testified before the Senate Internal Security Subcommittee that this was not true, and as far as the Communists were concerned, they did very little fighting against the Japanese.[55] When the subcommittee inquired about the political reporting of his advisors, Davies, Service, and Ludden, who were also advisors to General Wedemeyer's predecessor, General Stilwell, General Wedemeyer said that the reports of these officers played up the "shortcomings, maladministration and unscrupulousness of the Nationalist leaders" and "the orderliness or the potentialities of the Chinese Communist forces in Yenan. . . . If I had followed their advice, Communism would have run rampant over China much more rapidly than it did." [56] The recommendations that Service and Davies made to Washington clearly coincided with the request made previously by the Communist leader Chou En-lai.

The idea that the Chinese Communists were "peaceful agrarian reformers" was peddled everywhere. In Washington, it became increasingly popular in certain sections of the Department of State. The American press carried the "agrarian" theme far and wide. Everybody who was "in the know" was ready to say that the Chinese Communists were entirely different from the Communists of Soviet Russia and would be neither anti-American nor puppets of the Kremlin.[57]

The notion that a coalition government would be a workable solution for China was "sold" by respectable authors throughout America. It was favored in some of the most surprising places in the field of public opinion. It was, in particular, a pet theory of the Far Eastern Division of the Department of State, which did about everything the Communists would have wanted that Division to do.

And yet, Mao Tse-tung had stated in a special report "On Coalition Government," made in April, 1945, to the Seventh National Convention of the Chinese Communist Party, that a coalition would lead to the destruction of Chiang Kai-shek and the defeat of "reactionary American imperialism." The "coalition government" line, as a tactic aimed at the United States of America on behalf of Soviet Russia, was clearly emphasized as such in that report. The entire history of Communist tactics throughout the world had been that all "coalition governments" formed with Communists were sabotaged by them and finally conquered for Soviet imperialist purposes.[58]

It is significant that Secretary of State Dean Acheson, in his testimony

---

[55] *Institute of Pacific Relations, Hearings,* Part 3, p. 782.

[56] *Ibid.,* p. 777, 831.

[57] *State Department Employee Loyalty Investigation,* Part 2, p. 1679.

[58] *Ibid.*

during the investigation of the MacArthur ouster, swore that it is simply not true that any State Department employee ever wrote off the Chinese Communists as agrarian reformers. In reply to Senator H. Alexander Smith of New Jersey, the Secretary said: "I do not know of any State Department people, in the sense of our Foreign Service officers or departmental officers who thought that the Communists were merely agrarian reformers." [59] Yet a State Department employee, Raymond P. Ludden, just after he returned from a seven month trip to Red China, had this to say: "The slogan of the Chinese peasants in the Communist area is, 'a full belly, a warm back, and no one kicking us around,' but the so-called Communists are agrarian reformers of a mild democratic stripe more than anything else." [60]

On the witness stand following Acheson, General Hurley, was asked about the Secretary's statement. He answered by producing a letter he wrote to President Truman in November, 1945:

... it is no secret that the American policy in China did not have the support of all the career men in the Department. The professional foreign service men sided with the Chinese Communists' armed party and the imperialist block of nations whose policy it was to keep China divided against herself. Our professional diplomats continuously advised the Communists that my efforts in preventing the collapse of the Nationalist Government did not represent the policy of the United States. These same professionals openly advised the Communist armed party to decline unification of the Chinese Communist Army with the Nationalist Army unless the Chinese Communists were given control.[61]

Hurley added: "I requested the relief of the career men who were opposing the American policy in the Chinese theater of war. These professional diplomats were returned to Washington and placed in the Far Eastern and Chinese divisions of the State Department as my supervisors. Some of these career men whom I relieved have been assigned as advisors to the Supreme Commander in Asia." [62]

Chiang Kai-shek was not naïve on the subject of Communism. He had studied Communist military and political methods in Moscow, as far back as 1923, and he had been fighting their attempt to seize control of China since 1927.[63] He became increasingly alarmed at the Davies-Service clique's attempts to force the formation of a coalition Chinese Government. He emphasized that the American Government should stop trying to force him to agreement with the Communists. Washington officials, he felt, did not understand that the Communists were determined to domi-

[59] Testimony of Secretary of State Dean Acheson, June 4, 1951, *Military Situation in the Far East Hearings*, Part 3, p. 1873.

[60] Interview by Alexander Kendrick: *Philadelphia Inquirer*, March 23, 1945.

[61] Ambassador Hurley to President Truman, November 26, 1945, *Hurley Papers*, File 315, Document No. 81. MSS., Santa Fe.

[62] *Ibid.*

[63] Chiang Kai-shek, *Soviet Russia in China*, pp. 11-57.

nate all China and sovietize it. On the contrary, they came to mistake the Communist's "New Democracy" for genuine democratic ideas. They failed to see that "United Front" and "Coalition Government" were but combat slogans which the Chinese Communists had devised for subversive purposes.

"How is it," wrote Louis Budenz, "that American opinion was drugged in this fashion? It was the outcome of the most skillful and persistent campaign by the Soviet fifth column coupled with an almost incredible amount of naiveté on the part of leading American citizens. I say this out of my own participation in most of the planning on the part of the Reds, which went on at the 12th Street headquarters." [64]

The strategy of the Foreign Service Officers in China is clearly shown by their reports to the Department of State. They were determined to bring about a change of American policy to one of giving support and supplies to the Chinese Communists—and they were prepared to resort to any means to accomplish this. Joseph Alsop writing in the *Saturday Evening Post* of January 7, 1960, sums up the result of reporting by our Foreign Service officials when he said: "Throughout the fateful years in China, the American representatives there actively favored the Chinese Communists. They also contributed to the weakness, both political and military, of the National Government. And in the end they came close to offering China up to the Communists, like a trussed bird on a platter, over four years before the eventual Communist triumph." [65]

On September 2, 1960, William D. Pawley, who was special adviser to the Secretary of State and had considerable experience in China, imputed to the clique of Foreign Service officers prime responsibility for the fall of China:

It is my judgment, and I was in the Department of State at the time, that this whole fiasco, the loss of China and the subsequent difficulties with which the United States has been faced, was the result of mistaken policy of Dean Acheson, Phil Jessup, Lattimore, John Carter Vincent, John Service, John Davies, Jr.— did I mention him?—Clubb, and others.[66]

Officers in the China Section of the Department of State discredited the warnings that the Chinese Communists had any liaison with Soviet Russia. They believed the Communists who contended that they were in no way receiving the support of Russia. They appeared overzealous in their willingness to listen to and report the most long-winded expressions of discontent on the part of the anti-Kuomintang elements, while they rarely

64 *State Department Employee Investigation,* Part 2, p. 1680.

65 *Saturday Evening Post,* January 7, 1950, p. 17.

66 U.S. Senate, Committee on the Judiciary, *Communist Threat to the United States through the Caribbean.* 86th Cong. 2d Sess. (Washington: Government Printing Office, 1960), Part 10, p. 735.

bothered to record any of the Kuomintang's arguments against its opponents.

These officers seemed to believe anything that the Communists told them. As a result our Department of State was persuaded to base American policy largely on the illusion that the Chinese Communists were somehow not quite Communists—that the United States and the Nationalist Government could get along with them very nicely. Those who adhered to these views must be considered the gravediggers of our national policy in the Far East. Their errors have permitted the Communists to add such area, races, and resources to their war potential, that they may sometime feel strong enough to attack us.

CHAPTER XI

NEGOTIATING WITH THE COMMUNISTS

The subject of unity between Chiang Kai-shek's Nationalists and the Chinese Communists can be traced as far back as 1937, when both factions saw eye to eye on the Japanese threat. As far as American policy towards the problem of unity was concerned, it took on increasing importance as Japanese power expanded in the Pacific. The Soviet Ambassador in November, 1940, told Sumner Welles that he could see "no conflict of interest" in the foreign policies of the United States and the Soviet Union toward the Far East. The policy of the Soviets toward China was "identical with that of the United States." [1] Secretary Hull instructed Ambassador Nelson Johnson to express to Chiang Kai-shek the "continuing interest in Chinese unity" on the part of the American Government, which "comprised one of the principal factors in our policy toward China." [2]

Officials in Washington were convinced that both the Chinese Nationalists and the Communists had more to gain by fighting the Japanese than by fighting each other. Chiang Kai-shek, however, could not depend on the Communists to co-operate against the Japanese instead of increasing their army and expanding their areas of control. In the Communist controlled areas, propaganda and organizational work were being carried on; in the interior banditry was increasing, as well as corruption and disorder in some areas. The Generalissimo had to abandon the past policy of compromise—which merely enabled the Communists to grow more powerful—and to pay increasing disregard to the commands of Chungking.

Some pro-Soviet writers in America seized upon this opportunity to criticize the Nationalist Government. Kate Mitchell, who later was arrested

---

[1] Memorandum by Under Secretary Welles, November 27, 1940. *Foreign Relations, 1940*, III, 237.

[2] Secretary Hull to Ambassador Johnson, December 28, 1940. *Foreign Relations, 1940*, IV, 476.

in connection with the *Amerasia* case in 1945,[3] called upon the American Government in 1941 to "do everything in its power to aid in the preservation of Chinese unity," and urged the dispatch of "immediate and extensive material help" to that country. But "above all," she declared,

The American Government should use its influence to support those groups in China which are anxious to maintain the united front against Japan and encourage them to resist the handful of reactionaries who are proposing to abandon the struggle. Unless such immediate action is taken, the American people will lose their best ally in the world struggle against reaction, militarism and aggression, and the American Government will have been an accessory in the destruction of the chief barrier to fascist domination in the Far East.[4]

Secretary Hull sought to impress upon Ambassador Johnson the importance of continuing "to keep before General Chiang and other appropriate officials of the Chinese Government this government's concern over reports of the dissension between the Kuomintang and the Chinese Communist forces." He pointed out that Chinese unity has comprised one of the principal factors in our policy toward China for many years, that this Government's interest in the progressive maintenance of Chinese unity cannot be overestimated at the present serious juncture in world affairs.[5]

A contrary view was voiced by Major James M. McHugh, the American Naval Attache in China: "I doubt if there is a real basis for any compromise since the ultimate aim of the Communists is a completely new Government controlled by them and since they turn every misfortune of the Government into propaganda for their cause." [6] To members of the Far Eastern Affairs Division of the State Department it was "quite. evident" the Chinese Communists had extended their control to "large portions of Shansi, Hopeh and Shantung, and that they have military garrisons and bases in certain areas of central China." They were also reportedly "inactive in a military sense against the Japanese." [7] We must keep in

---

[3] *Institute of Pacific Relations, Final Report*, p. 54; Later, Miss Mitchell was the editor of the *Far East Spotlight*, organ of the Committee for a Democratic Far Eastern Policy which was cited as subversive by Attorney General Clark. See letter to the Loyalty Board, released April 27, 1949. *Ibid.*, Part 13, p. 4611.

[4] Kate Mitchell, "Political Crisis in China," *Amerasia*, IV (February, 1941), No. 12, p. 542.

[5] Secretary Hull to Ambassador Johnson, March 13, 1941. *Foreign Relations, 1941*, V, p. 491.

[6] Memorandum by George Atcheson, Jr. of the Division of Far Eastern Affairs, April 24, 1941. *Ibid.*, p. 494.

[7] Ambassador Gauss to Secretary Hull, May 19, 1941. *Ibid.*, p. 506. This was not the first time such a view had been expressed. As a matter of fact, the previous fall Ambassador Johnson was informed "by a source very close to the Generalissimo" that the Chinese Communists "desire to prolong the Sino-Japanese conflict; but he expressed the opinion that the Communists wish to foster the continuation of hostilities primarily with a view to consolidating their position in China. In other words they are taking advantage of Chiang's preoccupation with the Sino-Japanese conflict to strengthen their own position in various areas of Central and North China. In this connection, it is generally conceded, even in local Communist quarters, that the

mind that Mao Tse-tung, in 1937, outlined the policy the Chinese Communists were to follow in the coming struggle: "Our determined policy is 70 per cent self-development, 20 per cent compromise, and 10 per cent fight the Japanese." [8] The Chinese Communists were probably inactive in a military sense, but they never ceased in plotting their future conquest of China. One of the ways in which they succeeded in extending their control was through the production and sale of narcotics. Agents were sent out to designated points on the mainland to engage in this trade. In this way the Chinese Communists were able to finance their activities.[9]

By late spring in 1942 the situation was changing due to military pressure applied by the Nationalist forces. Chou En-lai informed John Carter Vincent that the quarantine of Communist Armies by Hu Tsung-nan's forces "continued to be very effective." [10] Ambassador Gauss reported to Secretary Hull on July 7, 1942, that "Chou En-lai and Madam Sun were definite in their statements that relations between the two sides had worsened with the tightening of the Central Government's blockade of the Communist area." [11]

With the breakdown of the United Front, the Kuomintang took on a "strong anti-Communist bias." The head of the security police force was characterized as chief of the "Chinese gestapo." Vincent reported that an element of doubt was injected as to China's determination to resist "under the influence of those in government who have little sympathy with western concepts of democratic government, who have a fear of Chinese communists which beclouds their judgment, and who are intent upon conserving the dominant position of the Kuomintang now and after the war." [12]

In the early summer of 1942 there was talk again of an official mission to China for the purpose of encouraging "the garrison until supplies arrive." The President's executive assistant on Chinese matters, Lauchlin

---

Chinese Communists have engaged in little military activity against the Japanese forces in the past 13 months, contenting themselves largely with the establishment of military bases, mobilization of the people and defense measures against Japanese mopping-up campaigns." To Secretary Hull, October 24, 1940. *Foreign Relations, 1940*, IV, pp. 429-430.

8 *The Strategy and Tactics of World Communism.* Supplement III, *Communism in China*, p. 24.

9 *The Illicit Narcotic Trade of the Chinese Communists* (Taipei, Taiwan: Asian People's Anti-Communist League, 1957), pp. 1-2. See Rodney Gilbert, "The Red Opium Conspiracy," *National Review*, II (September 15, 1956), pp. 9-10, 21.

10 Ambassador Gauss to Secretary Hull, May 14, 1942. Memorandum of Conversation, by the Counselor of Embassy in China (Vincent), May 6, 1942. *Foreign Relations, China, 1942*, p. 199.

11 Ambassador Gauss to Secretary Hull, July 7, 1942: Memorandum by the Second Secretary of Embassy in China (Davies) to the Commanding General, American Army Forces in China, Burma, and India (Stilwell) July 5, 1942. *Ibid.*, p. 99.

12 Ambassador Gauss to Secretary Hull, July 9, 1942. Enclosure: Memorandum by the Counselor of Embassy in China (Vincent), June 28, 1942. *Ibid.*, pp. 107-109.

Currie, recommended Harry Hopkins as "unquestionably" the "ideal person for this mission, both in prestige and ability to get things done." If the trip were "too long and too hazardous," then he, Currie, would be willing to go. He was ready to "leave at a moment's notice," having "already had all the necessary vaccinations and inoculations." [13] The President did decide to send Currie who was, in Roosevelt's own words, working "in close co-operation with officers of the Department in various matters relating to China." Currie was "specially versed in matters relating to the extension of lend-lease aid to China." [14] He enjoyed the "complete confidence" of the President, had "access" to him "at all times and has quietly and in the background been active on all phases of Sino-American relations—military, political and economic—since his last visit to China." [15]

When Stilwell received word from the American Embassy in Chungking that Lauchlin Currie was to arrive in China, he wished to know whether Currie would confer with Ambassador Gauss and himself prior to consultation with Chiang. Stilwell personally felt that he should.[16] As soon as the Presidential representative arrived in Chungking, Stilwell hastened to have a "long talk" with him about the "intriguing and lying, etc." [17] Currie, meantime, gave the Ambassador "only a most sketchy account of his conversations" with various officials and Gauss thought he did "not appear to be very cheerful." [18] At a meeting with the Soviet Ambassador, the Soviet Counselor, the Soviet Military Attache, and John Patton Davies, Currie broached the question of the "exchange of information between the Russian and American military officers in Chungking." The Soviet Military Attaché was of the opinion there "was no close co-operation and that the American officers were not inclined to talk frankly." [19]

On August 21, 1942, the President informed the Generalissimo that he was urging Wendell Willkie "to make every effort to visit you in Chung-

[13] Lauchlin Currie to President Roosevelt, June 3, 1942. *Ibid.*, pp. 62-63.

[14] Secretary Hull to Ambassador Gauss, July 3, 1942. *Ibid.*, p. 91.

[15] President Roosevelt to Generalissimo Chiang Kai-shek, July 4, 1942. *Ibid.*, p. 95.

[16] Memorandum of Conversation by Ambassador Gauss, July 11, 1942. *Ibid.*, p. 114.

[17] *The Stilwell Papers*, p. 129. Stilwell recorded this observation: "Currie is a queer little fella. Very important about his mission. Quite astounded to find himself a Big Man here and doesn't realize it's only because they have him figured for a sucker. Can't stick to one subject for thirty seconds; doesn't want to hear what you have to say; always thinking of some smart angle he doped out. Wants to go back with a cut and dry solution and nice 'staff study.' ('Now, Mr. President, here's the way it looks to me.') Sits and squirms and wiggles and ties his legs in knots and puts his feet on the desk and on the drawers; pulls on . . . his moustache, and then jumps from one topic to another without rhyme or reason. Has a bit of gossip on this and that and gives himself away continually in his interference in W.D. (War Department) matters. (T. V. Soong didn't give him the 'welcome to China.' Ain't that awful?) Why do I waste space on this small fry?" *Black and White Book*, June 17, p. 91. MSS., Hoover Institution, Stanford.

[18] Ambassador Gauss to the Chief of the Division of Far Eastern Affairs (Hamilton), August 3, 1942. *Foreign Relations, China, 1942*, p. 120.

[19] Memorandum of Conversation, by the Second Secretary of Embassy in China (Davies), August 4, 1942. *Ibid.*, pp. 123-124.

king on his return to the United States from Moscow." [20] The former
Presidential candidate was to leave by air on his "special mission," accompanied by Joseph Barnes and Gardner Cowles, both of the Office of War
Information.[21] Upon his arrival in China, Willkie was accorded an "enthusiastic reception" and the Generalissimo could only "regret" he was
not able to remain "long enough to permit of his observing conditions
in our central provinces." [22] Dr. Kung wrote: "Never have I seen such
spontaneous and heartfelt welcome accorded to a foreign visitor by our
people of all walks of life as that shown to your personal representative." [23] Little political significance, if any, can properly be accorded
Willkie's mission except in the realm of propaganda. It was he who did
much to fix in the popular mind the conception of the Chinese Communists as simple, rural reformers. At Chungking he talked "at leisure,
alone and uninterrupted, with Chou En-lai." He wrote: "This excellent,
sober, and sincere man won my respect as a man of obvious ability." If
all of the Chinese Reds were like him, "their movement is more a national and agrarian awakening than an international or proletarian
conspiracy." [24]

Following the tour of Willkie, the President wrote to Chiang expressing thanks for the message he conveyed from Madame Chiang, and said
he was looking forward "with pleasure to the day when we can welcome
her to this country, and, I hope, you also." [25] The Generalissimo replied
that Madame Chiang knew his "mind and heart as thoroughly as it is
humanly possible for one person to understand those of another. I hope,
therefore, that you will talk freely and fully with her as you would with
me." [26] When Mrs. Chiang arrived in Washington in February, 1943, she
"outlined her views at great length about the post-war world, the first
burden of which was that we could be sure China would line up with us
at the peace table." Her idea was to have the four Great Powers talk about
post-war affairs, and she further suggested that the President "should be
Chairman of that group." [27]

In the spring of 1943 Alfred Kohlberg, Chairman of the American

---

[20] President Roosevelt to Generalissimo Chiang Kai-shek, August 21, 1942, *Ibid.*,
p. 140.

[21] Secretary Hull to Ambassador Standley, Moscow, August 24, 1942. *Ibid.*, p. 141.

[22] Generalissimo Chiang Kai-shek to President Roosevelt, October 6, 1942, *Ibid.*, p.
160.

[23] The Chinese Minister of Finance (Kung) to President Roosevelt, October 7,
1942, *Ibid.*, p. 161.

[24] Wendell L. Willkie, *One World* (New York: Simon and Schuster, 1943), pp. 137-
138.

[25] President Roosevelt to Generalissimo Chiang Kai-shek, October 26, 1942, *Foreign
Relations, China, 1942*, pp. 171-172.

[26] Generalissimo Chiang Kai-shek to President Roosevelt, November 16, 1942, *Ibid.*,
p. 175.

[27] Sherwood, *Roosevelt and Hopkins*, p. 706.

Bureau of Medical Aid to China, and Edward C. Carter of United China Relief, began receiving "unfavorable reports from their staff men in Chungking about graft and incompetency in the Chinese Army medical services, which we were aiding." Kohlberg decided to go to China to investigate this matter. Lauchlin Currie phoned and asked him to consult with him before his departure. He told Kohlberg "at considerable length of reports being received from China, of incompetence, corruption and the inability and lack of will on the part of the Chinese to fight." Currie advised him to check with Americans in Chungking and then give him his reactions. When Kohlberg arrived he found the local heads of the American Bureau for Medical Aid to China and United China Relief together with some members of the Embassy confirming "the reports of corruption and incompetence." He discovered their conclusions were baseless.

As none of them had been in the field, I asked their sources, which they protested were confidential. I therefore felt it necessary to check in the field, which I did against their advice. After traveling through five provinces by truck, ambulance, rail, air and horseback, including 8 days in the 6th War Area, I found the itemized charges either completely untrue or greatly exaggerated.

On returning to America I complained to Dr. Stanley Hornbeck, Political Advisor to the Secretary of State on the Far East, and Joseph Ballantine, Director, Far Eastern Division of the State Department, in a lengthy interview. I protested that the untruths were making Chinese-American cooperation difficult, if not impossible, with resultant benefit to the Japanese enemy and unnecessary loss of both Chinese and American lives.

They professed to be unable to do anything about it; Dr. Hornbeck saying: *'When I see the people that this department is sending to China, I shake in my shoes.'*[28]

Hornbeck might bemoan the fact, but there was little he could do to change it. Owen Lattimore had been appointed Presidential Advisor to Chiang Kai-shek without his or the Secretary's consent. It was Lauchlin Currie, then President Roosevelt's advisor "on all Far Eastern affairs," who was in the position of authority.

At this point we should take note of the remarks of John C. Caldwell who was the Director of the United States Information Service in the Far East. He testified that the Institute of Pacific Relations "completely controlled all Far Eastern activities of the OWI to the State Department, to the branch chiefs, and later officials who were formerly IPR members." He added: "It was impossible" to be "in the OWI or State Department in

---

[28] Kohlberg's affidavit of April 16, 1952. *Institute of Pacific Relations, Hearings,* Part 14, pp. 4936-4937. Italics are mine. In a letter to Edward C. Carter, dated November 9, 1944, Kohlberg complained of pro-Communist propaganda put out by IPR and circulated by United China Relief.

A portion of UCR's contributions was made available to Indusco for the purpose of creating co-operative societies. George F. Fitch, "Chinese Industrial Cooperatives," *United China Relief Series* (Chungking: China Publishing Company, 1941), No. 17, 6.

that period and not have contact with the IPR." He had this to say regarding overseas positions:

> . . . In 1943 and 1944 when OWI employees for the Far East, particularly for China, were employed we were brought here to Washington from the New York overseas office for orientation, and the orientation consisted of your seeing two people. The two people were Mr. Laughlin [Lauchlin] Currie and Mr. Owen Lattimore, only the two. From those people we were to get our basic philosophy, you might say.[29]

In the spring of 1944 reports concerning China's unwillingness to wage any war against the Japanese were so numerous that President Roosevelt became alarmed. According to Henry A. Wallace, "The President placed great emphasis on solving the problem of inflation and on getting both sides in China to concentrate on fighting the Japanese instead of each other." He urged that "every effort be made to bring about a settlement of pending differences between China and Soviet Russia as soon as possible in order to prevent Soviet Russia from having a pretext for taking over domination of China after the war." [30] A memorandum by Earl Browder, and the reports of Lauchlin Currie in particular, evidently had enough influence on Roosevelt to induce him to dispatch Henry Wallace to the Far Eastern Theater.[31] His mission to China brought pressure on the Nationalist Government by the United States and this pressure coincided with the recommendations of the Chinese Communists.

When Secretary Hull heard that Wallace was going on his mission he sent Joseph Ballantine, member of the Far Eastern Division of the State Department, to try to stop it, but Wallace had already got Roosevelt's nod for the trip.[32]

Wallace was accompanied by John Carter Vincent (head of the Division of Chinese Affairs of the State Department), Owen Lattimore (then an official of the Office of War Information), and John H. Hazard (chief liaison officer of the Division for Soviet supply in the Foreign Economic Administration). Wallace wrote that President Roosevelt urged him to take Owen Lattimore who, the President said, was "one of the

---

29 U.S. Congress, Senate, Committee on Judiciary, *Strategy and Tactics of World Communism, Hearings,* 83rd Cong. 2d Sess. (Washington: Government Printing Office, 1954), Part 2, p. 110.

30 Testimony of Henry A. Wallace, October 17, 1951, *Institute of Pacific Relations, Hearings,* Part 5, pp. 1358-1359.

31 Miss Josephine Truslow Adams who was Browder's representative to the White House visited the President at least thirty-eight to forty times. She had some interesting testimony before the Senate Internal Security Subcommittee concerning a report dated February 20, 1944, which stated that the Nationalist troops were engaged entirely in blocking the Communist Eighth Army, instead of fighting the Japanese. This must have disturbed the President. *Scope of Soviet Activity in the United States,* Part 54, pp. 3590-3599; James Burnham, *Web of Subversion* (New York: The John Day Company, 1954), p. 163. Louis F. Budenz, "How the Communists Hoodwinked FDR," *American Mercury,* October, 1954, pp. 12-13.

32 Hull, *Memoirs,* II, 1586-1587.

world's great experts on the problems involving Chinese-Russian relationships." [33] En route, a brief visit was made to Soviet Central Asia to inspect its agricultural development. The group arrived at Chungking in
the latter part of June, 1944.

In his talks with Chiang Kai-shek, the Vice President was influenced
by Vincent who would direct the conversations toward a settlement with
the Communists. Vincent had Wallace emphasize the desire of the United
States that Chiang make peace with the Communists, and he urged
Wallace to stress the point that aid would not be forthcoming until Chiang
made peace with the Soviet Union.[34] The relations between the Chinese
Communists and the Nationalist Government, and between China and
the Soviet Union, became the main topics of conversations with Chiang
Kai-shek.

Wallace told the Generalissimo that President Roosevelt had indicated
to him that if the Kuomintang and the Communists could not get together
"they might 'call in a friend' and that he [the President] might be that
friend." [35] The Generalissimo asserted that the Chinese Communists were
not "agrarian reformers"; that they followed the orders of the Comintern;
and that they "hoped for the collapse of the Kuomintang prior to the end
of the war because such a collapse would enable them to seize power." He
urged that the United States maintain an attitude of "aloofness" towards
the Communists which would make them more willing to reach a settlement with the Kuomintang.[36]

Not convinced by these remarks, Wallace declared that "if the Chinese Communists were linked with the Union of Soviet Socialist Republics, then there was even greater need for settlement." [37] He added that
"there should be no situation in China which might lead to conflict with
the Union of Soviet Socialist Republics." [38] The Generalissimo then asked
Wallace to convey a message to President Roosevelt to the effect that if
the United States could bring about a meeting between Chinese and
Soviet representatives, he would very much welcome such friendly assistance and "would go more than half way to reach an understanding" with
the Soviet Union.[39]

At one point, Wallace referred to the "patriotic attitude of the Communists in the United States" and said that he could not understand the
attitude of the Chinese Communists as described by President Chiang.

---

[33] Henry A. Wallace, *Soviet Asia Mission* (prepared) with the collaboration of
Andrew J. Steiger (New York: Reynal and Hitchcock, 1946), p. 17.

[34] Testimony of John Carter Vincent, January 31, 1952, *Institute of Pacific Relations, Hearings*, Part 7, pp. 2065-2066.

[35] *United States Relations with China*, p. 549.

[36] *Ibid.*, pp. 553-554.

[37] *Ibid.*

[38] *Ibid.*, p. 556.

[39] *Ibid.*, p. 558.

The Generalissimo said that this difference in the attitude of the American and Chinese Communists might be explained by the fact that there was no possibility of the American Communists seizing power, whereas the Chinese Communists definitely desired to do so in China.[40] Another topic of their discussion was Stilwell's "unco-operative attitude." The Generalissimo said he "lacked confidence in Stilwell's judgment" and hoped that President Roosevelt would send some top ranking emissary to China—someone who could control and correct General Stilwell.[41]

A gullible victim of any left-wing scheme, Henry Wallace was used by the Davies-Service clique while in Chungking. They wired General Marshall, urging him to persuade President Roosevelt to instruct Wallace to discuss with Chiang their proposed formation of an Observers Mission to be sent into Communist-held territory. On June 22, 1944, Wallace and Vincent brought up the subject during a conversation with Chiang Kai-shek. The Generalissimo argued that such an act would give the Communists prestige. Nevertheless, Vincent urged Wallace to stress that the United States was not interested in Chinese opposition to the Communists but was interested in the military intelligence such a representative would yield. However, when on the following day the subject of the military mission was again raised, Chiang unexplainedly reversed his position saying quietly, "That can be done." [42] The only condition was that the mission should be under the auspices of the Chinese National Council, rather than those of the United States Army, and that Chinese officers should accompany the Americans.

The Generalissimo had acted against his own better judgment in order to be co-operative with the United States. He was very cautious because he knew that the long-range struggle in China was not between China and Japan—for that war was won when the Japanese bombed Pearl Harbor—but between Chinese independence and subjugation to the International Communist revolution.

Wallace submitted two reports to President Roosevelt concerning his mission. The first was in the form of a cable from Kunming on June 28, 1944, in which he reported: that Chiang did not have the intelligence to run postwar China; that Chiang was imbued with prejudice against the Communists; that there should be a united front of Communists and Nationalists; and that he had urged on Chiang the necessity of coming to terms with the Soviet Union. In this report Wallace included a suggestion that General Wedemeyer succeed General Stilwell as commander of United States forces in China, either with autonomous status or under General Stilwell's over-all command.[43] In addition to sending the Kun-

---

[40] Ibid., p. 553.
[41] Ibid., p. 552.
[42] Ibid., p. 555.
[43] Institute of Pacific Relations, Hearings, Part 7, 2287-2293.

ming cable, Wallace gave another report of his trip, dated July 10, 1944, in which he recommended the appointment of a personal representative to act as liaison between the Nationalist Government and the Chinese Reds.[44] The Vice President said Chiang's "hatred of Chinese Communists and distrust of the U.S.S.R. cause him to shy away from liberals." Perhaps, if Washington took a firm hand in the matter, current difficulties could be eased. Wrote Wallace:

> At this time there seems to be no alternative to support of Chiang. There is no Chinese leader or group now apparent of sufficient strength to take over the government. We can, however, while supporting Chiang, influence him in every possible way to adopt policies with the guidance of progressive Chinese which will inspire popular support and instill new vitality into China's war effort. At the same time, our attitude should be flexible enough to permit utilization of any other leader or group that might come forward offering greater promise.
>
> Chiang, at best, is a short-term investment. It is not believed that he has the intelligence or political strength to run post-war China. The leaders of post-war China will be brought forward by evolution or revolution, and it now seems more likely the latter.[45]

The President received the Wallace report with "much interest." He was pleased to learn that "only political means" would be employed in dealing with the Chinese Communists and that Chiang desired to improve relations with the U.S.S.R.[46] When conciliating the Communists proved to be impossible the American leadership insisted, nevertheless, that Chiang Kai-shek bear the blame for the disintegration of China. The Wallace Report was not released at the time. In fact, Secretary Acheson actually denied its existence after Congressman Walter Judd had demanded that it be made public. The Report finally came to light on January 18, 1950, when Senator Herbert R. O'Connor, Democrat from Maryland, made public a copy which Wallace had sent to him some weeks before.

The Wallace Report did not become official American policy until after President Roosevelt's death in 1945. It was then that Ambassador Hurley was instructed to use the Report as a guide. The Report is in line with Owen Lattimore's thinking and is thought by some to have been written by him. It paralleled official American policy as put in a Presidential statement on December 15, 1945, and which formed the basis of the instructions to General Marshall on his departure to China. Both the Wallace Report and the President's message urged that Chiang Kai-

---

[44] Vice-President Wallace to President Roosevelt, July 10, 1944, *Ibid.,* Part 7, pp. 2289-2291.

[45] Summary Report of Vice-President Wallace's Visit in China, July 10, 1944. *Institute of Pacific Relations, Hearings,* Part 7, p. 2291.

[46] President Roosevelt to President Chiang Kai-shek, July 14, 1944. *United States Relations with China,* p. 560.

shek be forced to merge his regime and his army with the Communists, and that American aid and influence be used to expedite this process.

After he returned to the United States, Wallace published a book entitled *Soviet Asia Mission,* in which he wrote: "A brilliant new chapter in the historic struggle for the free world has been recorded through the great victories of the glorious Red Army." He declared further that "while our approach to the satisfactions of the common man's need may differ, our ultimate objectives are identical." [47]

This book, even though published in Wallace's name with all the prestige of the office of Vice President behind it, actually was written by one Andrew Steiger, who was identified before the Senate Internal Security Subcommittee as a Communist and a writer for the *Daily Worker.*[48] The former Vice President admitted that he had written only the passages on agriculture and had left the rest of the book, including the political aspects, to Steiger.[49]

In the book, Wallace states that while he and Lattimore were traveling through China, Sergei Godlize, a high Soviet official—President of the Executive Committee of Siberian territory, and an intimate friend of Stalin—toasted Owen Lattimore and John Carter Vincent at a dinner as the men "on whom rests great responsibility for China's future." [50] The former Vice-President declared that the passage in the book which described this toast was written, not by himself, but by Steiger, who found the toast "significant." [51]

At that time, in 1944, the Institute of Pacific Relations, which "disseminated and sought to popularize false information including information originating from Communist and Soviet sources," published a fifty-six page pamphlet, entitled: *"Our Job in the Pacific,* allegedly written by our Vice-President. "The Russians," the author of the pamphlet claimed, "have demonstrated their friendly attitude towards China by their willingness to refrain from intervening in China's internal affairs." [52] Some years later—on October 17, 1951—when testifying before the Senate Internal Security Subcommittee, Wallace found himself compelled to admit: "It begins to look, for the time being at any rate, that my size-up as made in 1944 was incorrect." [53]

Wallace did not realize, during his tour through Soviet Central Asia, the feverish efforts being made by the Soviets to hoodwink him. For example, he visited Magadan, a city in Siberia, which was one of the

47 Wallace, *Soviet Asia Mission,* pp. 147-148.

48 Testimony of Louis Budenz, August 21, 1951, *Institute of Pacific Relations, Hearings,* Part 2, p. 699.

49 Testimony of Henry A. Wallace, October 17, 1951, *Ibid.,* Part 5, p. 1314.

50 Wallace, *Soviet Asia Mission,* p. 172.

51 *Institute of Pacific Relations, Hearings,* Part 5, p. 1329.

52 *Our Job in the Pacific,* (New York: Institute of Pacific Relations, 1946), p. 28.

53 *Institute of Pacific Relations, Hearings,* Part 5, pp. 1302-1306.

Soviet's most notorious slave labor camps. "Nothing I saw at Magadan or anywhere else in Soviet Asia suggested slave labor." Later he learned of the Soviet action: ". . . to pull the wool over our eyes and turn Magadan into a Potemkin village (an ideal show city especially built for visitors) for my inspection. Watch towers were torn down. Prisoners were herded away out of sight. On this basis, what we saw produced a false impression." Wallace then added these important words: ". . . what I did not see was the Soviet determination to enslave the common man morally, mentally and physically for its own imperial purposes." [54]

The Wallace Mission was significant in that it became one of the forces undermining the position of Nationalist China. Our Ambassador to China, Clarence E. Gauss, obviously disturbed by the Wallace Mission and by the pro-Communist attitude of his diplomatic staff, wrote as follows:

> . . . China should receive the entire support and sympathy of the United States Government on the domestic problem of Chinese Communists. Very serious consequences for China may result from our attitude. In urging that China resolve differences with the Communists, our Government's attitude is serving only to intensify the recalcitrance of the Communists. The request that China meet Communist demands is equivalent to asking China's unconditional surrender to a party known to be under a foreign power's influence (the Soviet Union).[55]

Ambassador Gauss was pessimistic over any political settlement with the Chinese Communists. In one of his reports he concluded that the Russians intended to carry on an aggressive policy in China, and that the "Chinese Communists" unquestionably had a background of subservience to the U.S.S.R.[56]

President Roosevelt was also deeply concerned with the critical military situation in China. To Generalissimo Chiang Kai-shek, he recommended that General Joseph W. Stilwell be delegated "the powers to co-ordinate all Allied military resources in China including the Communist forces." [57] The Generalissimo agreed to this proposal in principle, but requested that a high ranking American official well acquainted with the political as well as the military situation be sent to Chungking. On August 18, 1944, Roosevelt appointed Major General Patrick J. Hurley as his per-

---

[54] Henry A. Wallace, "Where I Was Wrong," *This Week* (September 7, 1952); *Congressional Record*, August 22, 1958, p. 17720. The Communist hoax had been exposed earlier by Elinor Lipper, who spent eleven years in the region of Magadan—as a Soviet slave laborer. She has told her story in a book, *Eleven Years in Soviet Prison Camps* (Regnery, 1950). David Dallin, recognized authority on Soviet Siberia, says the Lipper book is the most authoritative account of slave labor in Russia.

[55] Ambassador Gauss to Secretary Hull, Chungking, August 31, 1944, *U. S. Relations with China*, p. 561.

[56] *United States Relations with China*, p. 64.

[57] *Ibid.*, p. 66.

sonal representative to the Generalissimo. Hurley was instructed to promote harmonious relations between Chiang and General Stilwell, and to
perform certain duties in connection with military supplies.[58] Roosevelt
expanded his instruction to explain that it was the policy of the American
Government to support the leadership of Chiang Kai-shek.

Accompanied by Donald Nelson, chairman of the War Production
Board, General Hurley flew to Chungking by way of Moscow in order to
get Soviet opinion of the China question. During Hurley's conversations
with Molotov, on August 31, the Soviet Minister stated that Moscow had
no connections with the Chinese Communists and that it was the policy
of the Soviet Government to support the Nationalists.[59] Of course, this
was mere Russian propaganda, which fact Hurley was to become aware of
before his resignation as Ambassador.

As far as the Soviet Union was concerned, there was no possible immediate threat arising from Nationalist China, even with American assistance. It was to the advantage of the Soviet Union to support the Nationalist Government at this time while that government was engaged in
war against Japan. American forces were gradually destroying Japanese
military potential, the only bulwark against Communism in the Far East.
Any possible threat to arise against Soviet expansionism would come from
the United States and not from Nationalist China. Moreover, any aid
the United States might give to the Chinese Communists would strengthen
that group against the Nationalist forces. This would operate to further
the Soviet program of world conquest.[60]

The recall of Stilwell caused some complaints in the American press.
Brooks Atkinson, for instance, sent a long dispatch to the New York
Times on October 31, 1944, praising the military achievements of the
Chinese Communists, while calling Chiang Kai-shek a "warlord." He
described the Nationalist Government as "a moribund anti-democratic
regime that is more concerned with maintaining its political supremacy
than in driving the Japanese out of China."

When the Stilwell crisis was over, General Hurley took up the task of
mediating the differences between the National Government and the
Chinese Communists. Negotiations had been going on for years but no
progress had been made. Hurley was hopeful that his fresh approach
could co-ordinate and unite all of the armed forces in China under the
authority of the National Government. On November 7, 1944, he flew
to Yenan to talk with the Communist leaders. He was warmly greeted at

---

[58] President Roosevelt to General Hurley, August 18, 1944, *Hurley Papers. MSS.*,
Santa Fe.

[59] *Hurley Papers,* File 326, Document No. 3. *MSS.,* Santa Fe.

[60] As early as August 29, 1944, John Stewart Service was in the Communist Capital
at Yenan. He recommended that the United States should give aid to the Chinese
Reds despite the opposition of our ally Nationalist China. *Hurley Papers,* Report No.
16, File 2006. *MSS.,* Santa Fe.

the Communist capital, and it was not long before he realized he was in for some hard negotiating. He informed the President: "We argued, agreed, disagreed, denied, and admitted in the most strenuous and friendly fashion and pulled and hauled my five points until they were finally revised. . . ." [61] He brought back to Chungking a five-point draft agreement, which embodied the minimum Communist terms for agreement. The draft agreement, signed by Mao Tse-tung and considered as a "practical plan" for a settlement with the Communists, was typical Communist political propaganda for the ultimate destruction of the National Government. It was full of such terms as "democracy," "freedom," "peace" and "progress" which sought and found a ready reception in the democratic nations. It listed a "coalition government" as one of the conditions. [62]

When Hurley submitted the elusive Communist proposal to the Nationalist Government, Chinese Foreign Minister T. V. Soong's comment was short and to the point. "The Communists have sold you a bill of goods. Never will the National Government grant the Communist request." The agreement would mean the eventual control of the government by the Chinese Communists. Chiang Kai-shek was convinced of this if he accepted a coalition government. [63] The Generalissimo would not like to see a situation created in China similar to that existing in Poland and Yugoslavia—where the admission of Communists to a coalition government resulted in the destruction of all democratic anti-Communist groups. [64]

Hurley was certain that Chiang Kai-shek was sincerely desirous of a settlement. As a counter-move, Chiang made a three-point proposal which agreed to recognize the Chinese Communist Party as a legal party. The principles of Dr. Sun Yat-sen were to be pursued, and high ranking Communist officers were to be designated to membership in the Military Affairs Commission on the condition that the Communist forces be reorganized and incorporated in the National Army. [65]

---

[61] Ambassador Hurley to Secretary Stettinius, January 31, 1945, *Military Situation in the Far East Hearings*, Part 5, pp. 3669-3672; Part 4, pp. 2908-2911.

[62] *U. S. Relations with China*, pp. 74-75.

[63] Ambassador Hurley to President Roosevelt, November 16, 1944, *Hurley Papers. MSS.*, Santa Fe. On November 19, President Roosevelt sent Hurley the following instructions: "I wish you would tell the Generalissimo for me in confidence that a working arrangement between the Generalissimo and the North China forces will greatly expedite the objective of throwing the Japanese out of China from my point of view and also that of the Russians. I cannot tell you more at this time, but he, Chiang Kai-shek, will have to take my word for it. You can emphasize the word 'Russians' to him." President Roosevelt to General Hurley, November 19, 1944, *Hurley Papers*, File 312, Document No. 103. *MSS.*, Santa Fe.

[64] Ambassador Hurley to President Roosevelt, January 14, 1945, *Hurley Papers*, File 308, Document No. 87. *MSS.*, Santa Fe. A "coalition government" was also the technique used in Czechoslovakia—Roscoe Drummond in *The Dallas Times Herald*, March 23, 1961.

[65] *U. S. Relations with China*, p. 75.

These two sets of proposals—one from the Communists, one from the Nationalist Government—spelled out the wide differences that separated the two parties.

The Communists were demanding substantial participation in the government at once. They insisted that Chiang and the Kuomintang abdicate their official status and become merely one of the several political parties in the coalition. They further demanded that their troops be accorded equal status with the National Army, and that Communist military leaders be granted equal representation in the National Military Council.

The National Government offered to grant the Communist Party legal status as a recognized political party, as enjoyed by many other parties in China. The Communist troops would be incorporated into the National Army, but *not as a separate force* of a political party. Chiang's Government rejected the idea of a coalition and would not deny its position as the recognized government of China. Thus, an impasse developed which was to continue until the Marshall mission in January, 1946. The Communist demand for a separate armed force meant continued dissension in Kuomintang-Communist relations. It indicated that as long as the National Government maintained itself in power, the Communists would not seek any real unification of China—other than under the red flag of Communism.

Ambassador Hurley tried to persuade both sides to continue negotiations, even though the differences were great. However, Chou En-lai described the government's proposal as "not satisfactory" and returned to Yenan. On December 8, 1944, he informed Hurley that the Communists "find it impossible to see any fundamental common basis" in the proposals made by the Nationalists, and that it would be "useless" for him to return to Chungking to continue the discussion.[66]

In an effort to ease the situation, Ambassador Hurley requested the Communists to return to Chungking to resume the negotiations.[67] In the meantime, he sent a memorandum to Secretary of State Stettinius on December 23, stating that he was having some success in persuading Chiang to "make liberal political concessions to the Communist Party and to give them adequate representation in the National Government." [68]

Hurley's hopes of a success were deflated considerably when, on December 28, Mao Tse-tung communicated that, before further negotiations could take place, the National Government must first carry out four addi-

---

[66] Letter from Chou En-lai to General Hurley, December 8, 1944, *Hurley Papers*, File 312, Document No. 122. *MSS.*, Santa Fe.

[67] Mr. Clarence E. Gauss resigned as Ambassador to China on November 1, 1944, and General Hurley was appointed to the position on November 30, 1944. He presented his credentials on January 8, 1945.

[68] Ambassador Hurley to Secretary Stettinius, December 23, 1944, *Hurley Papers*, File 2106, Document No. 3. *MSS.*, Santa Fe.

tional conditions: (1) release all political prisoners, (2) withdraw all forces that were surrounding the Communist area, (3) abolish all oppressive regulations which restricted the people's freedom, and (4) end all secret police activity.[69]

The National Government regarded these new Communist demands as equivalent to allowing them to carry on their revolution without hindrance. Hurley assured the Communist leaders that Chiang Kai-shek was "sincerely desirous" of making a settlement possible and suggested that a conference be arranged at Yenan.[70] But the Reds charged that the Nationalist Government "shows no sincerity," and insisted upon a National Affairs Conference to be made up of delegates from the Kuomintang, the Communist Party, and the so-called Democratic Federation (a pro-Communist coalition of minor political groups). If these proposals were agreed to in advance, Mao added, Chou En-lai would be sent to Chungking to continue negotiations.[71]

Thus, negotiations reached a crisis until Chiang Kai-shek, in an effort to conciliate the Reds, announced his willingness to call a National Assembly for the purpose of adopting a national constitution "to pass control of the National Government to the people and to abolish the one party rule of the Kuomintang." [72] The conciliatory attitude of Chiang did not placate the Reds, however, who were bent on preventing the unification of China and avoiding of civil war. On January 14, 1945, Hurley summarized Kuomintang-Communist negotiations in a message to President Roosevelt:

Since my arrival in China, in accordance with your policy, I have exerted my utmost to help bring about Chinese national unification. The Generalissimo was at first cold to the plan but after your suggestion has shown himself ready to grant concessions to the Communists far beyond what he had been willing to grant in the past. He is now favorable to unification, reformation and agreement with the Communists.

. . . He agreed that with or without Communist participation he will take immediate steps to liberalize the Government in spite of the war situation. . . . By means of the War Cabinet he intends to start liberalizing and cleansing the government even before the convocation of the National Assembly and the adoption of a constitution, a measure which I consider a substantial step forward in the organization of a stable, unified and democratic government in China.[73]

Here is a good indication of Chiang Kai-shek's willingness to make con-

---

[69] Chou En-lai to Ambassador Hurley, December 28, 1944, *Hurley Papers*, File 308, Document No. 61. *MSS.*, Santa Fe.

[70] Ambassador Hurley to Mao Tse-tung, January 7, 1945, *Hurley Papers*, File 308, Document No. 81. *MSS.*, Santa Fe.

[71] Mao Tse-tung to Ambassador Hurley, January 11, 1945, *Hurley Papers*, File 308, Document No. 85. *MSS.*, Santa Fe.

[72] *U. S. Relations with China*, p. 80.

[73] Ambassador Hurley to President Roosevelt, January 14, 1945, *Hurley Papers*, File 308, Document No. 87. *MSS.*, Santa Fe.

cessions to the Chinese Communists towards unification of China. The underlying obstacle to this possibility was the Communists' unwillingness to continue serious negotiations, their sole aim being to overthrow the recognized government of China.

With an awareness of the obstacles the Communists were placing in the way of peaceful settlement, Chiang Kai-shek attempted to improve China's internal problems by announcing that the National Government was prepared to make three additional concessions for unification: (1) the establishment of a War Cabinet, upon which the Communist Party would be given representation; (2) the Communist troops to be under the overall command of a U.S. Army officer; (3) the appointment of a committee consisting of an American Army officer, one Chinese Army officer and one Chinese Communist officer to make recommendations regarding the unification of the Chinese military forces.[74]

Chou En-lai objected to these new proposals; he would not give up command of Communist troops to the Kuomintang Party; the Army must remain a separate force. The Communist leaders remained stubborn; negotiations reached an impasse which was to have serious consequences for the solution of China's problems.

Meanwhile, just before Hurley and Wedemeyer returned to the United States to report to American officials, the top Communist Commander, General Chu Teh, sent a request directly to Wedemeyer asking for a loan of $20,000,000 for arms for the Communist forces, with the suggestion that Hurley not be told of it.[75] In commenting on this proposal, Ambassador Hurley wrote: "I am of the firm opinion that such help would be identical to supplying arms to the Communist armed party and would therefore, be a dangerous precedent.[76] General Wedemeyer agreed with Hurley, and during a press conference in Chungking on February 15, 1945, he remarked, "My policy is this, that we will not give any assistance to any individual, to any activity, to any organization within the Chinese Theater (except to the Central Government). . . . Obviously we get requests from time to time for assistance from various sources but I am ordered to support the Central Government and I am going to do that to the best of my ability." [77]

In an effort to discredit the National Government, the Chinese Communists turned documents over to General Wedemeyer, giving what was purported to be an account of secret negotiations between the Japanese

---

74 Ambassador Hurley to Secretary Stettinius, February 7, 1945, *Military Situation in the Far East Hearings*, Part 5, p. 3673.

75 Chu Teh to General Wedemeyer, January 23, 1945, *Hurley Papers*, File 313, Document No. 19. *MSS.*, Santa Fe.

76 Ambassador Hurley to Secretary Stettinius, February 17, 1945, *Hurley Papers*, File 313, Document No. 36. *MSS.*, Santa Fe.

77 *Institute of Pacific Relations, Hearings*, Part 7a, p. 2395.

and the National Government for the sellout of American interests. Chou En-lai was quoted as stating specifically that "General Hurley must not get this information as I don't trust his discretion."

After Hurley examined the twenty-two documents submitted to him by Wedemeyer, he made the following statement to Secretary Stettinius:

> . . . I was not impressed by the belief held by certain American diplomatic and military officers that the Generalissimo had made a deal with Japan and that without such a deal his government would collapse. These are stock arguments of Imperialists, the Chinese Communist Party, and other opponents of a United China that do not impress me. . . .[78]

The pro-Communist American diplomats, whose reports were going direct to the Department of State without passing through Hurley's office, deplored General Wedemeyer's and Ambassador Hurley's "incomplete and non-objective" reporting of the China situation.[79] It was the official policy of the United States "to prevent the collapse of the Nationalist Government," and to sustain Chiang Kai-shek as President. While the objectives had the support of President Roosevelt and Secretary Stettinius, it was no secret that the American policy in China did not have the support of all the career men in the Department of State. The professional Foreign Service men sided with the Chinese Communists, and continuously advised them that Hurley's efforts to prevent collapse of the Nationalist Government did not represent the policy of the United States. These same professionals openly advised the Communists to decline unification of the Chinese Communist Army with the National Army unless the Chinese Communists were given control.[80]

Hurley was trying to hold the line against sacrificing our traditional policy towards a free China. He described the situation as follows: "there was no longer any question in my mind and there was no question in the President's mind about the existence of a Communist conspiracy within the United States government at Washington." The purpose of this conspiracy was to "weaken support for the traditional American policy toward China by smearing its defenders. . . ."[81]

Before Hurley left for Washington, on February 18, he sent an interesting memorandum to Secretary Stettinius, in which he said, "I have insisted that the United States will not . . . supply or otherwise aid the Chinese Communists as a political party or as an insurrection against the National Government. Any aid to the Communist Party from the United

[78] Ambassador Hurley to Secretary Stettinius, February 17, 1945, *Military Situation in the Far East Hearings*, Part 5, p. 3675.

[79] *State Department Employee Loyalty Investigation*, Part 2, p. 1974.

[80] Ambassador Hurley to President Truman, November 26, 1945, *Hurley Papers*, File 315, Document 81. *MSS.*, Santa Fe.

[81] Lohbeck, *Patrick J. Hurley*, pp. 350-351.

States must go to the Party through the National Government of China." [82]

Hurley's visit to Washington gave him an opportunity to discuss the weakness of American Far Eastern Policy with Stettinius, Marshall, Stimson and President Roosevelt. He seemed to have had little influence on these officials. Chiang Kai-shek was now under a barrage of criticism as a "Fascist" from various leftist organizations in America, particularly the Institute of Pacific Relations.

In the meantime the announcement was made of the United Nations Conference to be held in San Francisco in April, 1945. Chou En-lai requested in a letter to Hurley that Chinese Communists be included in the China delegation. Hurley replied that "the conference at San Francisco is to be a conference of nations, not of political parties within a nation." The Chinese Communist party is considered one of the political parties of China and the only difference from an ordinary political party is that it is armed. Moreover, Hurley continued, "recognition by the Conference of any armed political party in China other than the National Government would destroy the possibility of unification of China." [83]

Chou was not satisfied with this analysis. He argued that "America and England have both announced that their delegations will consist of representatives from all important political parties." [84] As a result Hurley conveyed the idea to President Roosevelt who recommended to Chiang Kai-shek that the Chinese delegation to San Francisco be broadened to include members of the Communist Party. The Generalissimo agreed and the delegation of ten men was chosen—including a Communist delegate.

The real purpose of the Chinese Communist Party was not the abolition of the one-party rule itself but rather to overthrow control by the Kuomintang Party and to obtain a one-party rule of China by the Chinese Communist Party. The Generalissimo contented that the Chinese Communists aimed to effect a *coup* by which they would take control of the National Government and convert it into a one-party Communist government similar to that of Russia.

It would be a mistaken belief to say our policy makers did not have adequate information about the dangers of Communism in the Far East. Both Hurley and Wedemeyer, who were close to the scene, continually advised support of the Nationalists.

---

82 Ambassador Hurley to Secretary Stettinius, Chungking, January 31, 1945. *Hurley Papers*, File 312, Document 140; January 16, 1945, File 2106, Document No. 5. *MSS.*, Santa Fe.

83 Ambassador Hurley to Chou En-lai, February 19, 1945, *Hurley Papers*, File 308, Document No. 131. *MSS.*, Santa Fe.

84 Chou En-lai to Ambassador Hurley, February 18, 1945, *Hurley Papers*, File 308, Document No. 130. *MSS.*, Santa Fe.

Of course, Chiang's government was not perfect. There were elements in it which could not be defended and which Chiang himself did not defend. But it must be remembered that the Generalissimo remained our ally despite China's years of suffering, and not once did he compromise with the Japanese; whereas the Chinese Communists had as one of their objectives the destruction of American interests in the Far East. After all, Chiang was trying to lead a vast nation, most of it in the grip of an age-old feudalism, toward a measure of republican government. As Nelson Johnson, former Ambassador to China, expressed it: "We owe a debt of gratitude to Chiang Kai-shek and to his Chinese armies that they choose to oppose the Japanese. . . . They could have joined them, and we would have been in a very bad position indeed if they had, and I for one wonder how we would have found it in our hearts to blame them. Where is France after seventeen days of fighting: Where is Denmark, Norway? And the world fails to note that in spite of everything, with all these troubles, Chiang is governing the country with the same personnel that he started out with twelve years ago." [85]

The choice for the United States was between Chiang's government, which was friendly, and Mao Tse-tung's Red revolutionary army, which was a puppet of Stalin. Every interest of Stalin was wrapped up in Red China and the project of forcing Chiang to take Reds into his government. The Generalissimo was the only top-flight Asiatic leader who was a Christian and anti-Communist. He had fought nearly thirty years of civil war in China and eight years against Japan, part of it as our ally. "In all my negotiations with him," says Ambassador Hurley, "he never once broke his word." [86]

[85] Nelson Johnson to Colonel David B. Barrett, Camberra, April 29, 1944, *Stilwell Documents*, MSS., Hoover Institution, Stanford.

[86] Testimony of Ambassador Hurley, June 20, 1951, *Military Situation in the Far East Hearings*, Part 4, p. 2920.

CHAPTER XII

ABOUT FACE IN THE STATE DEPARTMENT

Throughout Soviet history China has been one of its main considerations. That was dinned in the ears of the Communists over and over again—the importance of China with its great reservoir of manpower. In 1932, Sergei Ivanovitch Gussev, who had served as Comintern agent and Stalin's personal representative in the United States, "commanded the Communists in the United States to take up four tasks." Two of them were the defense of the Soviet Union, and the "furtherance of Red conquest of China." [1] In 1933 the notorious Gerhert Eisler "was secretly sent into the United States by Moscow to make sure these orders were carried out." [2]

In 1935, Georgi Dimitrov was General Secretary of the Comintern. At the 15th Anniversary of the Communist Party of China he laid down the Communist line to the followers:

. . . as a real Bolshevik Party, the Communist Party of China realizes that however great the successes it has achieved, they are only the first serious steps on the road to the liberation of the Chinese people. . . .

The Party . . . is faced with the task of carrying on a systematic struggle to establish a united national front with the Kuomintang. . . .

It is necessary that energetic measures be taken to exert pressure on public opinion and the governments, first and foremost in England, France, and the U.S.A. [3]

The Soviet Union properly evaluated the importance of the United States in any Communist scheme for conquest of China. The American government was to influence Chinese events in a decisive manner. In 1939 Lauchlin Currie was appointed "Administrative Assistant to the Presi-

---

[1] Louis F. Budenz, *The Techniques of Communism*, (Chicago: Henry Regnery & Co., 1954), pp. 162-163.

[2] *Ibid.*

[3] China: The March toward Unity, address "The 15th Anniversary of the Communist Party of China" by Georgi Dimitrov, pp. 83-87. Italics mine.

dent." [4] He was empowered to co-ordinate "the work of the various departments in their relations to the Executive." [5] For this purpose he was located in the offices of the White House, "on the White House telephone." [6]

Shortly before he embarked on his China mission early in 1941, Currie called on Dr. Stanley K. Hornbeck at the State Department. He informed him that Chiang Kai-shek had requested that President Roosevelt select an American advisor for him. The President had decided to nominate Owen Lattimore. When Hornbeck discovered that Secretary Hull had not been consulted on this matter he "expressed doubt whether an assumption by the President of responsibility for such a nomination was a wise procedure and whether the nomination of Lattimore was a suitable nomination." He asked who had suggested Lattimore to the President. Currie replied that he had, whereupon Hornbeck answered: "It should be an easy matter to effect a reconsideration." Unmoved, Currie was confident it was a "suitable nomination, and that, in any event, there could be no reconsideration inasmuch as the nomination had already been sent to Chiang Kai-shek." [7] After his return from Chungking, Currie urged that "before taking any action" the President should seek to obtain Lattimore's confidence. This was "most important." [8]

President Roosevelt was favorable to the choice of Owen Lattimore as his advisor to the Generalissimo. Now it remained for him to obtain the concurrence of his Secretary of State for Currie's recommendation. "It sounds good to me," Roosevelt wrote to Hull, who was obviously annoyed at not having been consulted on the selection.[9] Hull replied curtly that he had "no objection." [10] Later Currie informed Chiang Kai-shek that Lattimore was "a person admirably equipped for the post." [11]

The fact that Lattimore would be going to China as an American advisor to Chiang must have been information of first importance to the Soviet Union. Even before there was any public announcement of the appointment, Lattimore had a two-hour luncheon meeting with Soviet Ambassador, Constantine Oumansky on June 18th. The meeting was

---

[4] Testimony of Lauchlin Currie, August 13, 1948. *Hearings Regarding Communist Espionage in the United States Government.* Hearings before the Committee on Un-American Activities. U.S. Congress, House, 80th Cong. 2d Sess. (Washington: Government Printing Office, 1948), Part I, p. 852.

[5] *New York Times,* July 23, 1939.

[6] Testimony of Edward C. Carter, July 25, 1951. *Institute of Pacific Relations, Hearings,* Part 1, p. 133.

[7] Testimony of Stanley K. Hornbeck, February 15, 1952. *Ibid.,* Part 9, pp. 3209-10.

[8] Mr. Lauchlin Currie to President Roosevelt, May 6, 1941. *Foreign Relations, 1941,* Vol. V, 644.

[9] President Roosevelt to Secretary Hull, May 19, 1941. *Ibid.,* p. 644n.

[10] Secretary Hull to President Roosevelt, May 21, 1941. *Ibid.,* p. 648.

[11] Secretary Hull to Ambassador Gauss, May 29, 1941. *Ibid.,* p. 651.

arranged by Dr. Edward C. Carter, Secretary General of the Institute of
Pacific Relations, who explained: "I was fortunate in getting Lattimore
over from Baltimore, as I thought it was pretty important for him to have
a long talk with Oumansky, in view of his job and the evolving world
situation. It was a most illuminating two-hours." [12] Lattimore could not
give a reasonable explanation to the Senate Internal Security Subcommittee as to why he should confer with the Soviet Ambassador before taking
up his new job in China. Finally, President Roosevelt notified Chiang
Kai-shek of his complete confidence in his new advisor. "I have the highest
opinion of his capabilities and I know he is intimate with and in complete
accord with my basic political attitudes." [13]

Lattimore had spent many years in China. During the late thirties he
is reported to have frequently expressed "his warm admiration for the
Chinese Communists." They constituted for him the wave of the future
and "represented the real people." [14] He advocated general support for
Soviet foreign policy, but opposed "using their slogans" or giving anyone
"an impression of subservience." [15] Lattimore was spoken of as one of
"our men" by General Berzin, then with the Soviet Army in Western
China. He was one of the two Americans suggested as a prospective
candidate for Soviet intelligence.[16] Louis Budenz testified that Lattimore
had been hand-picked "to change the thinking here in Washington and in
America on the Communist activities in China and its relations to the
Soviet Union." Lattimore was thought to be a man "who could put out
propaganda and conceal the Communist activity, but still have it carry
out the policy of the Communists." According to Budenz, "the weight of

12 Edward C. Carter to Philip C. Jessup, June 23, 1941. *Institute of Pacific Relations, Hearings*, Part 9, p. 3264.

On June 20, Dr. Carter wrote Lattimore apropos the luncheon with Oumansky: "If you have time while in San Francisco you and Bill Holland may want to arrange a private talk with Col. Philip R. Faymonville whose present address is Headquarters of the Fourth Army, Presidio of San Francisco, Calif.

"He would, I think, have been thoroughly at home and at ease if he had lunched with us at the Mayflower on Wednesday, I think you get the idea." *Ibid.*, p. 3263.

Colonel, later General, Faymonville long had an interest in Russia. He was ordnance officer to General Graves. He was senior military aide to President Roosevelt in 1933 and 1934. From 1934 to 1939 he was United States Military Attache in Moscow. He shared Ambassador Davies' view concerning the Moscow trials. He said the Soviet Union has "no desire" to conquer other nations. Communist Parties created in non-Soviet areas "have nothing to do with the Russians." He said: "The Soviet Union is completely sincere in backing global cooperation. Its leaders want an organized and peaceful world." Ralph Izard, "A General Looks at the Soviet Union," *Our Times, People's Daily World* (February 18, 1949) 12, No. 35, Section 2; *Institute of Pacific Relations, Hearings*, Part 10, pp. 3700-3703.

13 President Roosevelt to Generalissimo Chiang Kai-shek, June 23, 1941. *Foreign Relations, 1941*, V, 668.

14 Testimony of William Montgomery McGovern, September 28, 1951. *Institute of Pacific Relations, Hearings*, Part 4, pp. 1010-1011.

15 Owen Lattimore to E. C. Carter, July 10, 1938. *Ibid.*, Part 1, p. 40.

16 Testimony of Alexander Barmine, July 31, 1951. *Ibid.*, Part 1, pp. 199-200.

his discussions was always along the lines of the Soviet policy," but the language employed "was non-Soviet in character." [17]

The appointment of Owen Lattimore as "a special political advisor to the Chinese Government" was announced in the *New York Times* on June 29, 1941.[18] The news was warmly received in China and not merely by the Nationalists. Chou En-lai "was pleased to learn of Mr. Lattimore's selection." It was "obvious," he believed, that Lattimore "might have a sympathetic attitude toward the Chinese Communists." [19] Lattimore arrived in San Francisco to address members of the Institute of Pacific Relations a week later. He had only words of praise for the leader of China. "Among the handful of great world leaders, Generalissimo Chiang Kai-shek is conspicuous for the fact that he is not only a great leader but a leader who has steadily grown in strength commensurate with that of the country itself." It was a speech which "rang with faith and confidence in the China he is to serve." [20] Soon after his arrival in Chungking, Lattimore began sending dispatches which demanded a greater effort on America's part on behalf of China. He lamented the fact that "after four years strenuous resistance China . . . has not won a single ally and the nation feels politically isolated." He suggested President Roosevelt either propose to Britain and Russia an alliance with China or that China participate in conferences of the Pacific powers regarding the defense of that area. In Lattimore's opinion "either proposal, if initiated by the President, can safeguard China's equal footing among anti-aggression peoples and remove stigma of discrimination." [21] On this latter point Lauchlin Currie wrote:

China's feeling that the democracies regard her as inferior and not being worthy of being considered an ally is one I encountered. It is deep and persistent and should not, I think, be ignored. Chiang, himself, feels very strongly in this matter.

Currie commented favorably upon Lattimore's recommendations, but added:

If you should decide to communicate the substance of these requests back to Gauss, I trust that he fully understands that he should not disclose his knowledge of them to the Generalissimo.

Pending action on these requests, I propose, if agreeable to you merely to

---

17 Testimony of Louis Francis Budenz, August 22, 1951. *Ibid.*, Part 2, pp. 522-523.

18 *Ibid.*, Part 9, p. 3265.

19 Memorandum of Conversation, by the Second Secretary of Embassy in China (Drumright) , June 30, 1941. *Foreign Relations, 1941*, V, 520.

20 *San Francisco Chronicle*, July 8, 1941.

21 Cable to Lauchlin Currie from Owen Lattimore, August 2, 1941. *Foreign Relations, 1941*, IV, 362. The message was transmitted by Currie to the President on August 4, 1941.

acknowledge receipt and say that the President has the matter under advisement.[22]

While the President was considering plans to strengthen China's position in the Far East, the Communists in America were campaigning for a change of U. S. policy. Speaking before a second front rally of the Young Communist League in New York, Earl Browder unleashed a torrent of abuse upon the officials of the Department of State whose "powerful appeasement forces" were "deliberately withholding 1,000,000 of the most effective soldiers in Asia, keeping them out of the fight against the Japanese, and thereby releasing that many Japanese soldiers for action against our boys in the South Pacific." He charged that "reactionary officials" in the Department were urging Chiang to keep "his best armies out of the war." He was referring to the blockade of the Eighth Route Army by General Hu Chung-han's forces and also the New Fourth Army under General Tang En-po. He charged:

> These two Chinese armies, the best equipped and trained in all China, totaling almost a million men, are being confined to blockading the Chinese Communist armies and territories, because the State Department in Washington has informed Chungking's representatives that our Government would be displeased if complete unity was established in China between the Kuomintang and the Communists. These officials continue the old policy of 'war against the Communists' in China; they tell Chungking it must continue to fight the Communists if it wishes United States friendship, and they thereby accept responsibility for withdrawing a million Chinese troops from the war against Japan, and keep China back from full unity in this war.[23]

The American Government promptly denied the charge, stating that "at no time" had it "entertained a policy of 'war against the Communists' in China. In fact, this Government has repeatedly expressed skepticism regarding alarmist accounts of the serious menace of 'Communism' in China." [24] Thus Browder had succeeded in evoking the desired reply. Browder's statement which "had been prepared by arrangement with Lauchlin Currie," was designed "to smoke out the anti-Soviet elements in the State Department." It had been shown to Louis Budenz, then editor of the *Daily Worker,* who "looked it over and made a few changes." Later is was printed in the *Sunday Worker.* Following publication of the Communist policy statement, a meeting was arranged between Browder, Robert Minor, who was "technically second in command to Browder," Lauchlin Currie, Administrative Assistant to the President on Chinese

---

22 Mr. Lauchlin Currie, Administrative Assistant to President Roosevelt, to the Acting Secretary of State, August 3, 1941. *Ibid.,* p. 361.

23 *The Worker,* New York, October 4, 1942; *Institute of Pacific Relations, Hearings,* Part 2, 596.

24 Memorandum prepared in the Department of State, October 3, 1942. *Foreign Relations, China, 1942,* p. 244.

Affairs, and Under Secretary of State Sumner Welles.[25] Welles later handed the Communist Party Chief a memorandum which satisfied him that his "charges had been made on the basis of incomplete information. . . . I am therefore more than happy," remarked Browder, "to retract those charges without reservation." In this important foreign policy statement, the American Government replied:

With regard to the specific 'charge that it is on the advice of reactionary officials in the State Department that Chiang Kai-shek is keeping his best armies out of the war'; the simple fact is that the nearest approach to 'advice' given by any officials in the Department of State in this context has been an expression of an opinion that civil strife in China, at all times unfortunate, would be especially unfortunate at a time when China is engaged in a desperate struggle of self-defense against an armed invader. The implication of the expression of opinion was that the Chinese Government should try to maintain peace by processes of conciliation between and among all groups and factions in China. And, the course which Chiang Kai-shek has been pursuing is *not* 'keeping his best armies out of the war.' Both the armies of the National Government and the 'Communist' armies are fighting the Japanese. No Chinese armies are actively engaged in large-scale offensive operations against the Japanese—for the reason, principally, that there is lacking to all Chinese armies types and amounts of equipment which are essential to such operations; but this situation is one which both the Chinese Government and the American Government are endeavoring to remedy as soon as equipment becomes available.

With regard to the specific charge that 'the State Department in Washington has informed Chungking's representatives that our Government would be *displeased* if complete unity was established in China between the Kuomintang and the Communists,' what this statement alleges is the exact opposite of the fact. The State Department in Washington has at all times taken the position, both in diplomatic contexts and publicly, that the United States favors 'complete unity' among the Chinese people and all groups or organizations thereof.

With regard to the specific charge that 'these officials continue the old policy of war against the Communists' in China, this government has had no such policy, either 'old' or new. This government has in fact viewed with skepticism many alarmist accounts of the 'serious menace' of 'Communism' in China. We have, for instance, as is publicly and well known, declined to be moved by Japanese contentions that presence and maintenance of Japanese armed forces in China were and would be desirable for the purpose of 'combatting Communism.'

With regard to the specific charge that officials of this Goverment 'tell Chungking it must continue to fight the Communists if it wishes United States friendship,' the simple fact is that no officials of this Government ever have told Chungking either that it must fight or that it must continue to fight the 'Communists'; this Government holds no such brief; this Government desires Chinese unity and deprecates civil strife in China; this Government treats the Government of China as an equal; it does not dictate to the Government of China; it does not make United States friendship contingent; it regards unity within China, unity within the United States, unity within each of the countries of the

---

[25] Testimony of Louis Francis Budenz, August 23, 1941. *Institute of Pacific Relations, Hearings,* Part 2, pp. 593-595.

United Nations group, and unity among the United Nations as utterly desirable toward effectively carrying on war against the Axis Powers and toward creation and maintenance of conditions of just peace when the United Nations shall have gained the victory which is to be theirs.[26]

This statement amounted to a pledge that the "policy of the State Department was not against the Communists in China and that there was to be no distinction made between the Communists and Chiang Kai-shek." This assurance "was used throughout the country as an indication that American policy was seeing eye to eye with Soviet policy in the Far East." Stated Budenz: "As a matter of fact, in a subsequent meeting of the Politburo which I attended, Browder said it was as important as an agreement between nations and that we should emphasize it throughout the country as something very fundamental, representing what he considered to be a great gain for the Communist cause." [27] Dr. Stanley K. Hornbeck, at that time Advisor on Political Relations to the State Department, has stated that the text of the agreement as stated in the *Worker* was "substantially accurate." [28]

The entire memorandum was printed in the *Daily Worker* of October 16, 1942, and was used extensively by the Communists all over the world to give prestige to the Chinese Communists.[29] On October 18, John Stewart Service asked that more such letters be issued by the U.S. Government.[30]

In his own sworn statement before the Tydings' Committee in April, 1950, a statement never repudiated and never challenged, but confirmed by press dispatches, Earl Browder said ". . . in 1942 I did receive information about a change in American policy toward China. . . . This change in policy was given to me as a matter of information by the Under Secretary of State . . . in his office, in the State Department, where I visited on his written invitation to receive that statement. . . . I had received from Mr. Welles, and my own declaration on it, and I simultaneously transmitted that statement of United States government policy on China to Madame Sun Yat sen, in Chungking, by cable."

---

26 Memorandum by Under-Secretary of State Sumner Welles, October 12, 1942. *Foreign Relations, China, 1942*, pp. 248-249. *Institute of Pacific Relations, Hearings*, Part 2, p. 599.

27 Testimony of Louis Francis Budenz, August 23, 1951, *Institute of Pacific Relations, Hearings*, Part 2, p. 600.

28 "Looking at the text of the memorandum as copied from *The Worker* of October 18, 1942, I can say: In that memorandum, dealing with and refuting assertations and charges which had been made by Mr. Browder, there was given an objective account of developments in and regarding China and an honest review of what had been and was the official position of the United States with regard to the question of 'civil strife' in China." Stanley K. Hornbeck to the Assistant Secretary of State (Rusk), June 7, 1950. *Ibid.*, Part 14, 4928.

29 *Daily Worker*, October 16, 1942.

30 *Institute of Pacific Relations, Hearings*, Part 3, p. 826.

". . . I also had occasion, without publicity," Browder continued, "to see that information that I received from Mao Tse-tung in China, regarding the diversion of forces away from the anti-Japanese front, that this information was placed in the hands of the President. . . ." [31]

The influence of the Communists in America on our Far Eastern Policy was confirmed by Browder:

SENATOR HICKENLOOPER: Now then, you have testified here, as I understand your testimony . . . that you worked ceaselessly over a period of years, perhaps beginning in the thirties . . . and continuing up until at least 1942, for the adoption of a definite policy on the part of the United States toward China, and the Chinese Communists.

MR. BROWDER: That is correct.

SENATOR HICKENLOOPER: And you were working on that policy as a Communist policy, were you not? That was the policy of the Communists that you were working on.

MR. BROWDER: That was the policy of the Communist Party.

SENATOR HICKENLOOPER: Then I believe you said that in 1942, that policy upon which you had been working on was adopted as the policy of the United States toward China.

MR. BROWDER: . . . I would say that the central points of that policy . . . [were] identical with the policy of the Communist Party.

SENATOR HICKENLOOPER: . . . the substance of the important views advocated by the Communist Party up to 1942, were in fact adopted by the State Department, toward the Communists in China at about 1942—is that correct?

MR. BROWDER: In October, 1942.

SENATOR HICKENLOOPER: So, to that extent, regardless of the necessities of the situation or the explanations you were successful or success met your efforts in getting that policy established?

MR. BROWDER: The policy which we have advocated was substantially incorporated into the policy of the United States Government.[32]

Under Secretary of State Sumner Welles should have recognized that the pledge he gave Browder must lead to a Communist victory in China. The Department of State would scarcely have failed to be aware of George Dimitrov's statement defining the "united front" as a "Trojan horse policy." That stratagem was no secret. It received considerable publicity in this country, and had been particularly emphasized by the House Committee on Un-American Activities.

The agreement Welles made with Browder gave the Chinese Communists needed prestige. It was easy after that to propagandize Americans into the belief that Mao Tse-tung and his followers were merely "agrarian reformers." This Communist-launched campaign provided a springboard for the "coalition government" idea, adopted by the Department of State, which ultimately led to such tragedy in the Far East.[33]

[31] Testimony of Earl R. Browder, April 27, 1950, *State Department Employee Loyalty Investigation, Hearings,* Part I, pp. 675-683.

[32] *Ibid.*, pp. 686-687, 682, 704-705.

[33] Louis F. Budenz, *The Cry Is Peace*, (Chicago: Henry Regnery, 1952), pp. 26-28.

At a meeting of the American Politbureau in 1943, at which Browder was present, there was a change of line on Chiang Kai-shek. The new line was to attack him. An article by T. A. Bisson declaring that Nationalist China was feudal and Red China democratic, was to be the start. From that time on the Communists were directed to go after Chiang Kai-shek and peddle the idea of a coalition government.[34]

As a tactical move, Browder dissolved the Communist Party and formed the Communist Political Association in 1944. He did this under instructions from Moscow in order to make America believe that Communism was ceasing as a factor on the scene. This move would help obtain American acquiescence in the communizing of China. Louis Budenz, former editor of the *Daily Worker,* testified that Browder "brought home to us . . . that we must achieve the moral disarmament of America so that it would permit the Red conquest of China . . . to bring about the idea that the Chinese Communists were not Communists at all; that they were merely agrarian reformers." [35]

Infiltration of the federal government by the pro-Soviet sympathizers is now a matter of record. Franz Borkenau describes the strategy: "From 1941 onwards the Communists were assigned tasks such as infiltrating the center into the policy-making bodies and intelligence services of America and Britain. Even during the Popular Front phase, the Communists had learnt to conceal their basic political aims. Now—and this was the decisive novelty—they proceeded to conceal, as far as possible, the political identity of their personnel. It was the last consequence of Leninism, of the theory that a closely selected party must lead the country without allowing the masses a share in deciding upon the course to be taken." [36]

In 1945, the Bureau of the Budget conceived a plan that provided that the personnel of wartime agencies be consolidated and infused into the Department of State. This included such notoriously infiltrated outfits as the OWI. J. Anthony Panuch, the State Department Deputy Assistant Secretary, was designated by Secretary of State Byrnes to supervise this consolidation. Panuch testified, on June 25, 1953, that it was this transfer of personnel, involving as it did vast numbers of what he termed "unscreened personnel," that changed the entire complexion of all the Department of State and still was having an adverse effect, security-wise, on the present Department of State.

SENATOR WELKER: Mr. Panuch, a moment ago we referred to Mr. Acheson and his pro-Russian group in the State Department. I will ask you whether or

---

34 *State Department Employee Loyalty Investigation,* Part 1, p. 492.

35 Testimony of Louis F. Budenz, June 9, 1949, U. S. Congress, Senate, Committee on Judiciary, *Communist Activities Among Aliens and National Groups, Hearings,* 81st Cong., 1st Sess. (Washington: Government Printing Office, 1949), Part 1, pp. 228-229.

36 Franz Borkenau, *European Communism* (New York: Harper & Brothers, 1953), p. 280.

not, in your opinion, that Acheson-Hiss pro-Russian group in the State Department contributed to the infiltration of Communists or Communist sympathizers within the State Department?

MR. PANUCH: It is almost impossible to answer that, sir, responsibly. I would say that the biggest single thing that contributed to the infiltration of the State Department was the merger of 1945. The effects of that are still being felt, in my judgment.[37]

In June, 1947, a Senate appropriations subcommittee addressed a memorandum to General Marshall, then Secretary of State:

It becomes necessary due to the gravity of the situation to call your attention to a condition that developed and still flourishes in the State Department under the administration of Dean Acheson. It is evident that there is a deliberate, calculated program being carried out not only to protect Communist personnel in high places but to reduce security and intelligence protection to a nullity. On file in the department is a copy of preliminary report of the FBI on Soviet espionage activities in the United States which involves a large number of State Department employees, some in high official positions. This report has been challenged and ignored by those charged with the responsibility of administering the department with the apparent tacit approval of Mr. Acheson. Should this case break before the State Department acts, it will be a national disgrace. Voluminous files are on hand in the department proving connections of the State Department employees and officials of the Soviet espionage ring.[38]

Congressman Walter Judd, as an acknowledged Far East expert, testified before the Senate Internal Security Subcommittee. He said that top officials in the Department of State were strongly anti-Communist but must depend upon subordinate officials for background material upon which to base decisions. "It is in this paper work that the damage is done," he said. "An assistant secretary of state may find two memoranda lying on his desk, providing the background for a policy decision. If both come from subordinates sympathetic to communist objectives, the official has little liberty of choice." [39]

Judd was summoned by Chief Counsel Robert Morris as an expert to testify about policy decisions in the Far East which lead to Communist

---

[37] Testimony of J. Anthony Panuch, June 25, 1953, U. S. Congress, Senate Committee on the Judiciary, *Interlocking Subversion in Government Departments*, 83rd Cong. 1st Sess. (Washington: Government Printing Office, 1953), Part 13, p. 899. In a memorandum to the Tydings Committee, the State Department listed some of its difficulties: "Thus, as to one of these agencies (the OWI), it was determined that of the entire staff of 7,482 transferred to the Department, only 2,687 had been cleared by the Civil Service Commission. Investigations were discontinued before completion in 1,113 cases and were pending in 262 cases when the transfers were made. Thus, there were thousands of cases of employees in this and other agencies transferred to the Department who had apparently never been fully investigated . . ." As quoted in Wm. F. Buckley, Jr. & L. Brent Bozell, *McCarthy and His Enemies: The Record and Its Meaning* (Chicago: Henry Regnery Co., 1954), p. 12.

[38] Felix Wittmer, "Freedom's Case Against Dean Acheson, *"American Mercury"* (April, 1952), pp. 14-15.

[39] *Chicago Tribune*, June 1, 1956.

victories there. He described the difficulties he had against pro-Communist influences in the Far East Division of the Department of State:

MR. JUDD: Let me say this. I, myself, think in our country there has been a little too much emphasis on the cloak and dagger work of the Communists. We think we have to get somebody who stole documents or wrote something in code to the Soviet Union. I don't think those are the dangerous ones. Those are the little fellows. The really dangerous ones are the ones nobody ever suspected. I remember when John Peurifoy was chairman of security or head of security in the Department in 1947 and 1948, and I was on the sub-committe of the Committee on Government Operations in the House that investigated the Department. We got rid of 131 unsuitable people, *about half of whom were Communists or Communist suspects,* and we didn't have a headline.[40] But he said to me one day, 'Walter, what worries me is how many more there are like Hiss, whom I never even suspected. I used to lunch with Hiss, once in a while. It makes me wonder if the fellow I have my lunch with now is one.'

If you go down through their history and watch what they have recommended over the years, you find it turned out to be favorable to the Soviet Union. I am sure they will never be found to be carrying Communist cards. They would be fools to have meetings in the back end of an alley or a restaurant somewhere. They are clever, and their real danger is their ability, at the lower echelons, to write position papers, which come up to their superiors and become policy papers. Then those policy papers go to the action agencies, like the State Department, the Pentagon, and the National Security Council. If you allow me to write the papers on which my superiors make their decisions, I think I could have a good deal to say about what my superiors will think.[41]

CHAIRMAN EASTLAND: Then you think some of these people that are pro-communist are still in the State Department, and still in the Pentagon?

MR. JUDD: Why yes, I don't mean pro-Communists in the sense that they are in the Party, but they advocate policies that work to the good of the Party. On the law of averages, a mere moron once in a while would make a decision that would be favorable to the United States. When policies are advocated by any group which consistently work out to the Communists' advantage, that couldn't be happenstance.[42]

---

40 (Emphasis by editor.) The problem of blackmail is a continuing one in our government. Soviet agents take advantage of this whenever they can. Robert C. Hill, former Ambassador to Mexico, testified that he was told by the officer responsible for conducting investigations of homosexuals "about 1,400 had been severed from the State Department." *Communist Threat to the United States Through the Caribbean,* Part 12, p. 822.

41 Emmanuel S. Larsen, former employee of the Department of State wrote: "In the Spring of 1945 . . . I worked largely on postwar problems of Manchuria and Korea. . . . When we met on the policy committee, however, we were seated around a conference table with foreign service members of the Japanese and Chinese sections of the Far East Division. We wrote papers on policy, submitted them to the committee for discussion, made changes in conformity with motions that were voted on, and finally filed our completed papers with the higher authorities. In general the system was good and problems were well handled. However, it happened fairly frequently, especially with papers concerning postwar policy toward China, that the China group of foreign service officers fought stubbornly against anything that favored the Kuomintang in the slightest." *State Department Employee Loyalty Investigation,* Part 2, p. 1746.

42 Forrestal says the same thing in his diaries.

CHAIRMAN EASTLAND: Do I understand you to think that the recommendations of these individuals have influence with the real policymakers in the State Department and in the Pentagon?

MR. JUDD: Oh, there is no slightest doubt about it.

MR. MORRIS: You think, Congressman, that influencing our policy to our disadvantage would come from the bottom and not from the top?

MR. JUDD: Oh, I am sure it is not from the top. You talk to some of those people at the top and they are distressed themselves at the miscarriage of orders that are supposed to be against the Communists and yet it doesn't work out. As John Peurifoy said, some of these people are not on our side. . . .[43]

The *New York Times* quoted John Foster Dulles on July 26, 1950, as acknowledging to a group of Republican Senators that he was well aware of the existence of a group of Communists in the Department of State who were working to betray China, and incidentally the U.S. to the Soviets. He said: ". . . I do admit that at one time there was a group that felt a dose of Communism would do some Asiatic countries some good." [44]

The realities of the China situation were completely obscured by the pro-Soviet elements in the Department of State. The Chinese Communists were not "peaceful agrarian reformers," as reported by some of our foreign service officers and certain elements of our press. They were a part of the international Communist conspiracy. Their military strategy, diplomatic orientation, and propaganda policies followed those of the Soviet Union. These were adapted to fit the Communist environment in China, but all high policy was derived from international Communist policy emanating from Moscow. Throughout their history, the Chinese Reds had loyally supported and followed the policies of Soviet Russia and had accepted the whole content of Marxism-Leninism-Stalinism.

Contrary to widely advertised reports of their sympathizers, the Chinese Reds fought the Japanese far less than did the Nationalist Government. Our enemy in Asia and throughout the world should have been identified as Soviet Communism. A policy of supporting the Republic of China should have been a firm and continuing one on the part of our policymakers.

When Ambassador Hurley arrived in China, he found himself surrounded by State Department field officers who had come to admire the

---

43 U.S. Congress, Senate, Committee on the Judiciary, *Internal Security Annual Report for 1956.* 85th Cong. 1st Sess. (Washington: Government Printing Office, 1957), pp. 187-189. Italics mine. A parallel can be made with Cuba. Former Ambassador to Cuba, Earl Smith, stated, "I believe that the policies are determined in the lower echelon, and by the time the higher echelon receives them, policies have already been made, and they have to live by them." *Communist Threat to the United States through the Caribbean*, Part 9, p. 688.

44 Emmanuel S. Larsen, testified that in 1945 "there was a group in the State Department that slanted their reports and their policy rather strongly in favor of the Chinese Communists, who were our allies at that time, and they were exceedingly anti-Chiang . . ." *State Department Employee Loyalty Investigation*, Part 1, p. 1117.

Chinese Communists and who resented the intrusion of a noncareer man. In the course of their relations with, and their interviewing of Communist leaders, they showed sympathy with the Red cause in China by listening attentively to all the anti-Kuomintang gripes and reporting them faithfully and painstakingly to the Department, with personal assurances that the information was reliable.

Hurley's strenuous attempts at mediation were made of no avail—in fact they were willfully sabotaged. And back in the Department of State, his reports were discredited by John Carter Vincent and his advisors. These men often expressed their hatred of Hurley and discussed means of getting him out of the ambassadorship. Hurley became suspicious of the maneuverings in the Department of State regarding our policy towards China. In one of his reports to Roosevelt he requested that it be sent directly to him because as he concluded: ". . . we have been reading and hearing so much about the reorganization of the State Department and the leaks that have been and are occurring that I thought best to send this to you so that it would enjoy the protection that my messages have always received from the White House." [45]

Shortly after the arrival of Ambassador Hurley in Washington for consultations, the question of shipping arms and military equipment to the Chinese Communist forces was raised by American Charge d'Affaires George Atcheson. He prepared a memorandum with John Stewart Service and Raymond Ludden summarizing their recommendations for the Chinese area. It was sent to the Department of State on February 28, 1945, suggesting that the President "inform Chiang Kai-shek in definte terms that we are required by military necessity to co-operate with and supply the Communist and other suitable groups who can aid in this war against the Japanese, and that to accomplish this end, we are taking direct steps . . ." [46] The Generalissimo was to be made to understand clearly that if he refused to accept this proposal the American Government would then publicly express a China policy such as that made by Churchill with respect to Yugoslavia.[47]

It was a matter of record that the Chinese Communists had devoted their main efforts toward trying to overthrow the Nationalist Government, rather than against the Japanese. In effect, Atcheson was recommending that the United States support the Communists in their efforts to overthrow our ally, the Nationalist Government, which Ambassador Hurley was directed to uphold.[48] This meant a complete reversal of the

45 Ambassador Hurley to President Roosevelt, January 14, 1945. *Hurley Papers*, File 308. Document 87. *MSS.*, Santa Fe.

46 Charge d'Affairs Atcheson to Secretary Stettinius, February 28, 1945. *Hurley Papers*, File 2106, Document No. 8. *MSS.*, Santa Fe.

47 *Ibid.*

48 See Hurley's letter of resignation to President Truman in *Hurley Papers*, File 315, Document 81. *MSS.*, Santa Fe.

Roosevelt-Hull-Stettinius policy. The last sentence in the Atcheson message reveals those who were engaged in the effort to overthrow our ally and recognize the Communist regime in China: "This telegram has been drafted with the assistance and agreement of all the political officials of the staff of this embassy." [49] Every political official in the American Embassy at Chungking on the date of that document was attempting to undermine the American policy in China and endeavoring to promote the Communist conquest of China.[50]

This recommendation was made in the absence of Ambassador Hurley. It unquestionably would have weakened the government we were pledged to support. Secretary of State James F. Byrnes, in answer to a question by Senator Arthur H. Vandenberg of Michigan before the Committee on Foreign Relations, stated that the Atcheson memorandum ". . . made a recommendation that would have involved a change . . ." [51]

The Chinese Division of the Department of State upheld the recommendation made in the Atcheson letter to supply Lend-Lease arms and equipment to the Communist armed party in China. Hurley opposed that part of the Atcheson recommendation. Vincent advised Hurley that the Division upheld Atcheson's recommendation and opposed the then existing United States policy in China.

Hurley immediately appealed to President Roosevelt. He conferred with him personally, and the result was Roosevelt's unequivocal approval of Hurley's position and the existing policy in China in regard to the arming of the Chinese Communist party. In the words of a Department of State document:

General Hurley strongly opposed the course of action recommended above, and it remained the policy of the United States to supply military material and financial support only to the recognized Chinese National Government.[52]

Hurley demanded the dismissal of these pro-Communist and disloyal staff members. The Department of State merely transferred them to other areas.

When Hurley appeared before the Senate Committee on Foreign Relations on December 5, 1945, he described Atcheson's letter in this manner: "I immediately contended that if the Atcheson letter constituted the policy of the United States Government, it was a departure from the purpose for which I had been sent to China, and I wished they would

---

[49] Document No. 8, op. cit. See Hurley's letter to the editor of Atlantic Monthly, September 28, 1950.

[50] Ibid.

[51] U.S. Senate Committee on Foreign Relations, Investigation of Far Eastern Policy, December 5, 6, 10, 1945, (Unpublished), p. 212.

[52] U.S. Relations in China, p. 92.

leave Mr. Atcheson in charge and let me stay at home. The result was that, after many days of argument, Mr. Atcheson was recalled." [53]

The Davies-Service clique disagreed with Hurley. Service, in his testimony before the Tydings Committee in 1950, said: ". . . the only way we could attack the question of the use of the Communist armies if Generalissimo Chiang wouldn't agree is simply tell the Generalissimo, as we did in the case of Yugoslavia, we are going to arm any forces that are in a position to actively engage and resist the Japanese." [54] Davies was of the opinion that the U.S. had it within her own discretion the supplying of whatever force we felt was helping in the war against Japan regardless of what Chiang said. Moreover, we ought to tell the Generalissimo that we would not supply any force that was precipitating a civil war. Chiang, who was dependent on the U.S. for supplies, would have very little choice in the matter.[55] Davies could hardly have been unaware of the fixed purpose of the Chinese Communists to conquer China. His remarks about not helping any unit "precipitating civil conflict" would seem to be just so much window dressing.

Hurley received information that a member of the Chinese Communist Party in Chungking, as representative of Mao Tse-tung, had been given a secret document by an official of the Department of State. It was discovered that John Stewart Service returned to China from Washington with a special message to be delivered to Mao Tse-tung in Yenan. At the time, Hurley and Wedemeyer were in the United States. The message contained information concerning secret plans that had been drawn to prepare for a landing on the China coast and "to arm any Chinese forces which . . . can be effectively employed against the Japanese . . . to utilize our influence to bring about . . . the unification of China . . . not necessarily . . . under Chiang Kai-shek. . . ." [56]

This plan was an official American Policy toward China. It was prepared within the Department of State and then forwarded to the War Department with the request that it be sent to General Wedemeyer. The War Department sent the document to Wedemeyer with the following accompanying letter:

Attached for your guidance is a paper stating the United States short and long range objectives in China which has been received from the State Department. This policy should be made known only to key American Staff officers who require the knowledge in the discharge of their duties. The State Department requests that the personnel to whom this information is distributed should also be advised that it represents the current State Department position and is subject to revision in the light of further developments.[57]

[53] Lohbeck, *Patrick J. Hurley*, p. 441.

[54] *State Department Employee Investigation*, Part 2, p. 1991.

[55] *U.S. Relations with China*, pp. 574-575.

[56] *Military Situation in the Far East, Hearings*, Part 4, pp. 2929-2930.

[57] Lohbeck, *Patrick J. Hurley*, p. 340.

According to the State Department plan, we would co-operate with and arm whatever forces we found on the China coast when and if we landed. A movement of Chinese Communist troops towards the coast was observed. The Communists thought that we were going to land, and they were determined to get to the area. Although this secret document "had never come to me as Ambassador," remarked Hurley, it was "made available to the Communists at Yenan." [58]

On March 5, 1945, Ambassador Hurley was called to appear before the Chinese Affairs Division of the Department of State where, in his own words, "I was called on the carpet, with a full array of the pro-Communists of the State Department as my judges and questioners, to defend the American policy in China against 'every official of the American Embassy in China.'" [59] The Chinese Affairs Division was headed by John Carter Vincent, who together with Service and Davies commented: "I have read Atcheson's telegram of February 28th and feel it should receive the most serious consideration." [60] Hurley demanded the dismissal of these pro-Communist and disloyal staff members; instead the Department of State promoted them to supervisory capacities in Washington or transferred them to other posts. [61]

On September 19, 1945, Chiang Kai-shek submitted a memorandum to Ambassador Hurley that stated: "Recent reports appearing in the press indicated that the United States Government is establishing a political advisory board for General MacArthur to assist in determining United States policy in the Far East. Mr. George Atcheson and Mr. John Stewart Service among others are included in the advisory group." The memorandum continued:

Mr. Atcheson and Mr. Service are generally accepted in China as men of strong convictions that a coalition between the Communists and Kuomintang Parties *should be arbitrarily imposed.* They both have expressed views that are definitely unfriendly to the Central Government of China and clearly reveal their support of the policies of the Communist Party. [62]

There is much more in the memorandum that indicates that Atcheson,

---

[58] *Military Situation in the Far East Hearings,* Part 4, p. 2928. The FBI obtained a recording disc of a conversation between John Stewart Service and Philip Jaffe, a Communist. Service notified Jaffe about this plan. See below.

[59] *Military Situation in the Far East Hearings,* Part 5, p. 3256. In testimony given to the Internal Security Subcommittee of the United States Senate, August 29, 1956, former Ambassador Angus Ward said that in January, 1945, he had warned the State Department that Russian plans were "expansionist." A State Department official, Ward says, "said he was astounded that I could so speak of one of our allies and that in so speaking I was a disloyal American." *Scope of Soviet Activity in the United States,* Part 36, pp. 2042-2043.

[60] Feis, *The China Tangle,* p. 272n.

[61] *U.S. Relations in China,* p. 582.

[62] See Hurley's letter to the editor of *Atlantic Monthly* magazine dated September 28, 1950. Italics mine.

Service, and other State Department career men had been undermining American policy in China. For this reason Hurley had them recalled. Now they were being sent back on an advisory commission. The Communists were aware of that fact and believed they had won the battle to overthrow the National Government and to procure America's recognition of the Communist Armed Party in China. Chiang's memorandum commented on this. "The Communists are now placing great stress on this fact. They know that Mr. Atcheson and Mr. Service are sympathetic, and they interpret the above-referred to appointments as indicative of the change in United States policy." [63]

Throughout this period the career diplomats continued to permit leaks that were published in certain papers in the United States and throughout Asia, condemning and undermining American policy in China.[64] John P. Davies became a member—representing the Far East— in the top Planning Board of the Department of State, which drafts over-all policy. John Stewart Service and George Atcheson were actually sent to Japan to advise General MacArthur.

MacArthur flatly refused to have Service, so he was brought back home and—after Dean Acheson succeeded George Marshall as Secretary of State—was put in charge of placements and promotions in the Department. Astonishingly, this took place after Service had been arrested by the F.B.I. in the famous *Amerasia* Case, which involved the theft of hundreds of secret and other classified documents found in the office of the Communist magazine, *Amerasia*. Service admitted giving secret government documents to Philip Jaffe, the editor of the magazine. Jaffe has been named by a government witness as a Soviet agent.[65]

During the course of long months of investigating by the F.B.I. before any arrests were made, Service was found having a conference in a hotel room in Washington with Jaffe. The F.B.I. took a dictaphone record of one of the Jaffe-Service conferences. The following conversation took place:

SERVICE: The reason . . . I had the same idea out in China before I came home, that the President might be playing that sort of a game and was playing a very deep game in not revealing his hand to the Chungking Government, but when I got home and found out the violence and bitterness of the argument going on here, I dropped it. I mean, if so, there wasn't any reason for the

---

63 *Ibid*. Cf. also the draft prepared by Ambassador Hurley for Chiang Kai-shek to Truman regarding George Atcheson and John Stewart Service, September 16, 1945, *Hurley Papers*, File 315, Document 66. *MSS.*, Santa Fe.

64 Major General Patrick J. Hurley, "Why I Resigned as Ambassador to China," *Washington News Digest*, March, 1946, p. 21.

65 *State Department Employee Investigation*, Part 1, p. 1283; see also *Congressional Record*, January 5, 1950, p. 1973. Identified by Budenz, *Institute of Pacific Relations, Hearings*, Part 2, p. 653.

State Department to be smacked down, more or less. There wasn't any reason for Hurley to be kept in the dark.

JAFFE: Well, I'll tell you what I think happened, Jack. I've been thinking about that very hard. I think that Roosevelt recognized after he appointed Hurley, that it was a mistake to appoint him, but once Hurley did his dirty work, there was nothing . . . would have to take time. I think that of the three big nations we are the only one in which the individual plays such a big role. It is inconceivable that a Soviet ambassador would operate as an individual but here it happens frequently. And I think Hurley put Roosevelt and the whole country on the spot, and Roosevelt was trying to find a way of getting out . . . sending Hurley to some very important area where there was some difficulty. So I can't imagine that Roosevelt changed his ideas about China overnight, and he would have been delighted if he could have found some excuse for firing the guy, but of course Hurley put us in such a terrible spot, and has still got us on the spot, where we can't move any longer without openly defying Chungking.

SERVICE: Well, what I said about the military plans is, of course, very secret.

JAFFE: Yes, well, that was talked around about . . .

SERVICE: That plan was made up by Wedemeyer's staff in his absence, they got orders to make some recommendations as to what we should do if we landed in Communist territory. They had several . . .

JAFFE: To co-operate with them?

SERVICE: Well, yes, that's what we planned, and they showed me the plans they had drawn up if we co-operated with Chungking troops—if we in recovering territory, in other words, when we were in Chungking territory, we would have to go on co-operating with them. Those were the orders. But if we landed in the territory where the Communists were, without any question they'd be the dominant force.

JAFFE: Why would they have to co-operate with the Communists?

SERVICE: Chungking, of course, has been putting pressure on us, trying to get us to agree to take in Kuomintang officials, government officials, whenever we land. As far as we know we have not been given any power to do that. But if you get Hurley there, for Hurley to be consistent, why you'd get Hurley putting his influence, probably behind . . . Hurley has all the way down the line only recognized Chiang Kai-shek, and our job is to strengthen Chiang Kai-shek, and to support him, and to bring all the force in China under Chiang Kai-shek's control. If he says all this publicly, he's going to be just sitting there laughing. And he's going to have a hard time refusing to take in Chungking officials.[66]

You will note that Service told Jaffe in the above transcribed record that ". . . what I said about the military plans is, of course, very secret." That plan was made up by Wedemeyer's staff in his absence, and Service

---

[66] *State Department Employee Investigation*, Part 1, p. 1404. Larsen said: "I found that all the government agencies in Washington that handle Far Eastern affairs subscribed to *Amerasia* and took its comments and opinions quite seriously. I was several times called upon to give my own opinion to superior officers regarding *Amerasia* articles that interested them; at times I found that the general picture presented by Jaffe corresponded pretty accurately with that given us by our naval and military attaches in China; however, it generally resembled much closer that of our State Department's field representatives in China." *Ibid.*, Part 2, p. 1743.

was passing it to Communist Jaffe. Service was not even indicted, and the whole affair ended in a whitewash.[67]

Secretary Brynes defended the conduct of Service, and Service was shielded by the Department of State. Brynes wrote the following letter:[68]

My dear Mr. Service:

I am advised that the Grand Jury, after hearing the testimony of witnesses, has found nothing to warrant an indictment against you.

One of the fundamentals of our democratic system is the investigation by a Grand Jury of criminal charges. By that process you have been cleared.

I am advised that at the time of your arrest you were placed on leave of absence without pay. I am happy to approve the recommendation of the personnel board that you be returned to active duty. You have now been reassigned to duty in the Department for important work in connection with Far Eastern Affairs.

I congratulate you on this happy termination of your ordeal and predict for you a continuance of the splendid record I am advised you have maintained since first you entered the Foreign Service.

With all good wishes.

Sincerely yours,
(s) JAMES F. BYRNES

When Service was finally discharged some six years and eight months after Hurley relieved him in China, he was able to say that he had been acquitted by six commissions or other forms of security establishments set up by the Department of State and other departments of the Government.

In a letter to Orlando Ward, Chief of Military History, Hurley described the situation in the Department of State:

In my . . . conference with President Roosevelt in the White House I told him for the first time I was convinced there were more pro-Imperialists and pro-Communists in our State Department than there were pro-Americans. Only a few of our diplomats would uphold the principle of individual liberty, regulated free enterprise, self-government and justice. In other words, I became convinced . . . that the Imperialists and the Communist factions were, even at that early date, dominating America's foreign policy . . .

There were of course men in the State Department dedicated to the principles that have made America the greatest nation on earth and opposed to Imperialism and Communism. But these American diplomats were finally defeated by the pro-Imperialists and pro-Communists in the State Department who are the authors of the give-away policy helpful to the Imperialists and the Communists and detrimental to the American system of liberty.[69]

Just how much influence the pro-Soviet group in the Department had

67 *Institute of Pacific Relations, Hearings,* Part 13, p. 4842; see also *Final Report,* p. 71.

68 *Investigation of Far Eastern Policy,* December 6, 1945, pp. 122-123.

69 General Hurley to General Orlando Ward, January 11, 1952.

during this period is difficult to determine, but according to the testimony of Louis Budenz, former editor of the *Daily Worker* and former member of the American Communists' national committee, the Communist Party mapped out a campaign in 1942 which "began with the attack on Adolph Berle . . . to clean the State Department of all anti-Soviet elements." [70] Berle at that time was the official in charge of security matters in the department.

According to Budenz' testimony, word was sent out through the *Daily Worker* to all loyal Party members to attack and demand the resignation of "those who were considered to be against Soviet policy in the Far East." [71] As a result, there was unloosed a barrage of insidious smear attacks and an all-out attempt to discredit the anti-Communists in the Department of State. This was done through Communist front organizations and by those "liberal" elements of press and radio who customarily promote the key Soviet objectives while pretending to oppose "Communism."

The Communist Party, according to the testimony, used men in the Department of State to weaken the work of the anti-Communists. "The Communists relied very strongly on Service and John Carter Vincent," says Budenz, "in a campaign against Ambassador Hurley." [72]

Our postwar policy toward Japan came under severe criticism by the Communists and their sympathizers. In June, 1944, *Amerasia* came out with a sharp attack on Under Secretary Joseph C. Grew, who was opposed to the proposed bombing of Emperor Hirohito's palace and who was in favor of retention of the monarchy after the defeat of Japan as a stabilizing element in the Far East. Grew's idea, which General MacArthur later put into effect, was a challenge to the pro-Soviet group in the China Section, whose objective seemed to be to foster an internal revolution in Japan.

The national board of the Communist Political Association approved, on June 20, 1945, a resolution to purge the "reactionaries" and "fascists" from the Department of State. In the July issue of *Political Affairs*—the official Communist Party theoretical organ—was the following implicit order to all Party members, both open and hidden:

---

[70] Testimony of Louis Budenz, August 23, 1951, *Institute of Pacific Relations, Hearings*, Part 2, p. 602.

[71] *Ibid.*

[72] *Ibid.*, p. 624. In the *Daily Worker* dated November 28, 1945, Hurley comes under an attack. The article reads: "It is well known that liberal elements like John Carter Vincent and John S. Service in the State Department have opposed Hurley's reappointment. The former Ambassador continually sought to bypass them in his one-man rule of the Embassy in China. It is a significant reflection of his mentality that all his critics are called Communists. . . . Hurley's inflammatory 1,500-word statement was essentially the voice of those American imperialists who are openly anti-Soviet and call everything democratic in Europe and Asia a manifestion of 'Communist imperialism.'"

This growing reactionary opposition to a truly democratic and anti-Fascist Europe in which the people will have the right to freely choose their own forms of government and social systems has been reflected in many of the recent actions of the State Department. This explains why . . . they bolster up the reactionary, incompetent Chiang Kai-shek regime and why they harbor the idea of coming to terms with the Mikado in the hope of maintaining Japan as a reactionary bulwark in the Far East. . . .

In the vital struggles to crush feudal-Fascist-militarist Japan, it is necessary that American labor collaborate in the prosecution of the Anti-Japanese war with all democratic forces who favor and support victory over Japanese imperialism . . . some in the State Department, who are seeking a compromise peace will preserve the power of the Mikado after the war at the expense of China and the other Far East peoples, and directed against the Soviet Union . . .

In the opinion of the Communist Policy Association, such a program should be based on the following slogans of action . . . Remove from the State Department all pro-Fascist and reactionary officials.[73]

Asked what anti-Communist officials in addition to Berle were slated for removal by the Communist Party, Budenz replied:

Joseph C. Grew, Under Secretary of State; Lt. Gen. Albert Wedemeyer, not technically with the State Department but connected at least diplomatically with the State Department relations; Eugene Dooman, who was head of the Far Eastern Division, if I remember correctly, at least he was in control of the details of the Far Eastern policy; and Gen. Patrick Hurley, Ambassador to China, who particularly was under attack from the Communists.[74]

It is interesting to note that *in all cases the men singled out by the Communists were removed.* In effect, the hiring and firing of our State Department personnel was done by Moscow!

According to Freda Utley, author of numerous books and articles on the Far East, "so long as Grew was in charge of the Far Eastern affairs at the State Department, the Communists had comparatively little influence there." [75] But Grew was under pressure to resign as a result of his urging the immediate arrest of two men involved in the *Amerasia* Case. The *Washington Daily News* reported that Grew insisted on the arrests because he was under the "certain impression at that time that the case against the six persons arrested was so air tight as to make convictions all but assured." [76]

In a pamphlet prepared for the Scripps-Howard newspaper chain, Frederick Woltman, a Pulitzer Prize Winner and careful student of the Communist movement, wrote:

Many observers believe this case—one of the weirdest in the history of American criminal jurisprudence—is the key to America's postwar diplomatic debacle

73 *Political Affairs* (July, 1945), pp. 580-584.
74 *Institute of Pacific Relations, Hearings*, Part 2, p. 604.
75 Utley, *The China Story*, pp. 117-118.
76 *Washington Daily News*, June 7, 1950, p. 3.

in Asia. Many believe that if its prosecution had been pursued honestly and vigorously, the pro-Communists in the Far Eastern division of the State Department would have been cleaned out. That Chiang Kai-shek, instead of being hurled back to the island of Formosa, might have driven the Chinese Red Army deep into Siberia. And that China's mainland, with its 450,000,000 people, might today be ruled by a government friendly to the United States, instead of by a Soviet satellite.[77]

Those who attacked Grew were really attacking both his Far Eastern policies and his opposition to Soviet expansionism in Asia. Publication of *The Forrestal Diaries* and the testimony of Eugene Dooman, veteran Far East diplomat and a close associate and supporter of Grew, have made this abundantly clear. Grew's policies were anathema to the Communists, to the New York and Washington "pinko-liberal" politicos, and to the small but vociferous group of policy-influencers who clamored in defense of "our gallant ally," Soviet Russia.[78]

From the earliest days of the war, this coalition had urged the Department of State to oust the "reactionaries" (for "reactionary" read "anti-Communist"). It had called for "unconditional surrender" in the Far East—no matter how many lives it might cost us at the hands of a Japanese nation driven to a last-ditch defense of its religion and its Emperor. The cry that the Mikado must go had been long and determined. As President Truman fumbled and stumbled, he was an easy target for a few men in key places whose ideologies, if not loyalties, were hardly stable.

Grew was the obstacle. So it was decreed that Grew must go. Ironically, the *Amerasia* case became the historical instrument that toppled him. The hubbub over the "persecuted" *Amerasia* victims had, however, died down many weeks before. In August, Grew was forced to resign. On the twenty-fifth of that month, Dean Acheson succeeded him as Under Secretary of State—a post he did not accept until he had exacted from the President a promise of a free hand on all personnel questions.

The day after Dean Acheson replaced Under Secretary of State Grew, he announced he was replacing Eugene Dooman, long-time Far Eastern expert, with John Carter Vincent. It was little wonder, for Dooman— another anti-Communist official slated for removal by the Communist Party—had opposed Acheson's vigorous attempts to inject Owen Lattimore's line for a harsh postwar policy toward Japan.

This occurred during a meeting of the powerful interdepartmental committee representing the State, War and Navy Departments—known as SWINK. Dooman, who was chairman of the Far Eastern subcommittee of SWINK, had just made his report on the proposed postwar policy

[77] Fred Woltman, "The Shocking Story of the Amerasia Case," (Pamphlet, Scripps-Howard, 1950).

[78] For a whole series of articles attacking Mr. Grew in the *Daily Worker* see *Institute of Pacific Relations, Hearings*, Part 2, p. 610.

toward Japan. It spelled out exactly what the United States proposed to
do with our defeated enemy. At the end of that report, according to
Dooman's testimony before the Senate Internal Security Subcommittee
investigating the Institute of Pacific Relations, McCloy, chairman of the
full committee, turned to Dean Acheson and said: "Dean, you are a great
authority on Far Eastern matters. What do you think of what we have
just heard?"

Acheson's answer was: "I have discovered that Far Eastern experts are
a penny a dozen. And you can find some experts who will support any
point of view that you care to have. And I, myself, do not go along with
what we have just heard. I prefer to be guided by experts who think
more along my point of view." Dooman testified that Acheson from
then on " . . . quoted virtually textually from *Solution in Asia* by Owen
Lattimore." [79] Lattimore in his book had advocated the straight Communist Party line on Japan, namely, that we should force a "hard" peace
on Japan—remove the emperor, destroy all successful business, confiscate
all private property, in short, reduce Japan to a weak state which would
be ripe for Communist conquest.

Once Vincent replaced Dooman and became chairman of the Far Eastern Subcommittee of SWINK, he immediately set out to inaugurate policies for Japan which, according to the testimony of Dooman, were the
same as those Russia dictated for satellite countries." [80] Vincent's first act,
according to Dooman's testimony, was to alter an official program entitled:
"U.S. Initial Post Surrender Policy for Japan"—a program which had
already been officially adopted by the government and telegraphed to
General MacArthur "as firm United States Policy for Japan." [81]

The testimony was that the major surgery which Vincent performed
on that already adopted policy was to inject into it the Communist Party
objective of destroying and eliminating the capitalist class in Japan. Following are some excerpts from Dooman's testimony in which he explains
the changes made by Vincent:

DOOMAN: The first thing that was done, and this was in 1946, was to levy
a capital tax of from 60 to 90 percent on all property in excess of $1,000 . . .
That almost at one stroke wiped out the capitalist class . . . The next thing
was to appropriate all land in excess of 5 acres held by any one owner.
SENATOR EASTLAND: That was Communist system, was it not? . . . they were
following now the Communist system, were they not?
DOOMAN: Yes . . . Then all holdings by any one individual in any large
cooperation in excess of 3 per cent were confiscated. . . . They were transferred
to a government pool. And then the Japanese Government was ordered to sell
those shares . . . (and) ordered to disregard any relationship between the price

[79] Testimony of Eugene Dooman, September 14, 1951, *Ibid.*, Part 3, p. 723.
[80] *Ibid.,* p. 716.
[81] *Ibid.,* Part 3, p. 717.

offered and the real value . . . Practically the whole white-collar element in Japanese big business was removed at one stroke. Not because there was any record against them, but because they occupied certain positions. . . . It was an attempt to destroy and eliminate the brains of Japanese business.

. . . The net result was to destroy the previously existing capitalist class. . . . Their places have been taken by hordes of black marketeers and . . . thugs of various kinds who have been engaged in illicit trade of various kinds and have then amassed this enormous fortune. The net result was to replace people who had property with those black marketeers and thugs and blackguards of various kinds.[82]

In this connection, the views of John Stewart Service regarding Japan should be recalled. One of the State Department documents found by the F.B.I. in the *Amerasia* offices was an official report on Japan by Service. Following is an excerpt from that report:

The Japanese Communist Party is still small (Mr. Okano himself does not claim more than 'a few thousand members'), but it has the advantages of strong organization and loyal, politically experienced membership. If its policies as claimed, seek to achieve our own hopes of a democratic, non-militaristic Japan, we may wish to consider the adoption toward it of an attitude of sympathetic support.[83]

General Douglas MacArthur vigorously opposed the State Department's plans for the communization of Japan. He was viciously attacked by both Vincent and Acheson. Vincent accused MacArthur of violating State Department directives to use Japan for "building a bridge of friendship to the Soviet Union." The *New York Times* of September 20, 1945, printed the following story of Acheson's rebuke of MacArthur: "The State Department revealed today a decision for a social and economic revolution in Japan and emphasized that it would be carried out regardless of what might be said about slashing the American army of occupation. Secretary Acheson said that the United States government and not General MacArthur was determining American policy toward Japan." [84]

The Soviet sympathizers in the Department of State came close to victory and their policies came close to fruition in Japan, but General MacArthur was the stumbling block. Acheson never forgave him for it.

In China, they won hands down. We are reaping the fruits of that victory today—in Korea, in Indochina, in Malaya. Certainly, the men who inadvertently gave Acheson and Vincent the lever with which to eliminate Grew and Dooman must have been well satisfied. When their *Amerasia* "trials" were over, Jaffe said to Emmanuel Larsen, a research associate, "Well, we've suffered a lot—but anyhow, we got Grew out." [85]

---

82 *Ibid.*, Part 3, pp. 718-720.
83 *State Department Employee Loyalty Investigation*, Part 1, p. 1328.
84 *New York Times*, September 20, 1945.
85 de Toledano, *Spies, Dupes, and Diplomats*, p. 169.

William D. Pawley, former Special Assistant to Secretary Acheson, was correct when he said that those in the Department of State "who advocated—from as early as 1942—that the National Government of China be scuttled have succeeded in their campaign. I, as an American citizen quite familiar with the Far Eastern problem, am deeply moved by the failure of the Department of State to energetically pursue the same type of anti-Communist expansion program in China and in the Far East as has been carried out by the United States in Europe." [86]

Pawley told of his own experience with the anti-Chiang group in the Department of State. Six months before the Korean conflict he went to see President Truman and told him that "if we do not take a strong hand now and support with tremendous effort the Nationalist movement in China in which Chinese will fight for their own freedom and own independence, China will be lost and you will have a war on your hands in Burma, Indochina, or Korea within one year and you will either commit America or you will lose Asia . . . " [87]

In February, 1951, Pawley was sworn in as Special Assistant to Secretary Acheson. He knew there were officials in the Department that did not like his views. After Pawley was sworn in, Under Secretary of State James Webb asked him to lunch. Webb remarked: "Bill, you and I have been friends a long time and I don't want to make you feel badly, but at a meeting in the Secretary's office this morning, to which we purposely did not invite you, it has been decided that you are to see no document dealing with the Far East, you are to participate in no conference that is held in the Department of State or anywhere else in Government dealing with this matter, and as a favor to the Secretary just don't discuss Far East matters."

Pawley replied, "Jim, am I considered a subversive?"

Webb said, "No, let's say reactionary. We have our views on what ought to be done, and they do not coincide with yours and therefore we don't want any trouble."

Pawley answered, "Jim, when we get to a position in the Department of State in which a man with the years of experience in the Far East that I have had—where you have had none, the Secretary has had none, and no member of the Cabinet that I know, and they are all my friends, has had—and the Secretary rules me out as a devil's advocate, then I think we are in real trouble." [88] Immediately, Pawley saw General Marshall, Secretary of Defense, and told him the story. Marshall wanted to carry it to President Truman but Pawley asked him not to do so because he

86 William D. Pawley, to Under Secretary of State Webb, December 18, 1949. *Communist Threat to the United States Through the Caribbean, Hearings,* Part 10, pp. 730-731.

87 *Ibid.,* p. 727.

88 *Ibid.,* p. 728.

feared it might create differences between Dean Acheson and General Marshall.

An examination of the step by step abandonment of Nationalist China, of the blantant deception visited upon the American people by the Department of State, of the distortion and concealments practiced by its Far Eastern Division, of the high-handed tactics by important United States diplomatic officials to force the Chinese Communists into a dominant position in the Chiang Kai-shek government—all this is a shocking picture of our policy in the Far East.

The betrayal of Asia to world Communism was no accident. It was accomplished by means of complete mobilization of all echelons of Communist infiltration into every important area of American life. It is not surprising that confused American officials and a lethargic public were no match for a disciplined, highly organized force of experts in subversion and political warfare.

Our Department of State has been guilty of colossal and abysmal failures in the field of international relations since 1945. Some of these failures were due to gross miscalculation of the intentions and the capabilities of the Soviet Union. In spite of the fact that the Soviet leaders have frequently and definitely declared that they were actively working for the communization of the whole world, our leaders refused to believe them. The inability of our leaders to understand the intentions and capabilities of the Communists in the Far East is especially noteworthy. For several years the dominant clique in the Far Eastern Section of our Department of State refused to admit that the Chinese Communists were really Communists.

Not only were Soviet agents and sympathizers so located in key spots in the United States Government that they had virtually complete control of our foreign policy. Even this could not have engineered the Far East betrayal in the face of a hostile press. But, throughout the most influential elements of the American press, pro-Soviet control was nearly as complete as in the Department of State. A befuddled American public and a loyal, but bewildered, Washington officialdom caved in under the all-out propaganda deluge.

CHAPTER XIII

CONGRESS LOOKS THE OTHER WAY

Important hearings regarding the situation in the Far East were held before the Senate Foreign Relations Committee in December, 1945. The star witness was Major General Patrick J. Hurley, former Ambassador to China.

The significance of these hearings comes to light after practices disclosed by Hurley were later proved to be contributing factors in the Communist conquest of China. Shady activities of our foreign service officials in China and an anti-Chiang attitude on the part of our China Division indicated a serious weakness in our Department of State in executing the established policy of the United States.

If a thorough investigation of Hurley's charges had been carried out—the supposed purpose of the hearings—the loss of China to the Reds might have been prevented. Unfortunately, the hearings ended in a complete whitewash.

On November 28, 1945, Hurley addressed the National Press Club in Washington, D. C. He said our over-all policy to preserve the administrative and territorial integrity of China was *"weakened by the fact that some of our career men in the State Department were supporting the Communist armed party. Others were supporting the imperialist bloc. Both at that time were following a policy designed to keep China divided against itself."* [1]

When Hurley released this scathing attack on the Department of State, charging sabotage of American policy in China, he had hoped exposure of the misconduct would force an investigation and cleansing of the Department. He charged that the Department of State "was covered with a veil of secrecy which prevents our people from getting the facts." In

---

[1] All material, unless otherwise specified, is derived from 3 volumes of unpublished testimony. United States Senate, Committee on Foreign Relations, *Investigation of United States Far Eastern Policy,* December 1945 5, 6, 10 (Unpublished). All italics in this chapter are my own.

tendering his resignation, Hurley attributed the failure of American foreign policy in Asia to the "weakness and opposition of the United States Foreign Service." He stated that he was directed by President Roosevelt to prevent the collapse of the Government of Chiang Kai-shek. But this objective "did not have the support of all the career men" in the Department of State. Our professional diplomats sided with the Chinese Communists and continually advised them that Ambassador Hurley's views "did not represent the policy of the United States."

Hurley did not charge all the officials of the Embassy with disloyalty to the United States. He did make specific charges against John Paton Davies, Jr., John Stewart Service and John Carter Vincent. He criticized John Emmerson, Raymond Ludden and others, but made no specific charges against them. Those against whom he made specific charges were dismissed from the service years after his resignation, for substantially the same reasons he had stated when he requested that two of them be released from duty in China.

It is significant that Hurley did not charge that these officials were disloyal to him as Ambassador. His charges were that these three officials above-named were disloyal to the United States and were favorable to some kind of collectivism or dictatorship. He did not charge that the officials he criticized were Communists. Such a charge would be hard to prove even if the officials stood alone; but if they had the backing of a great organization schooled in propaganda and falsehood, conviction would be well nigh impossible.

Senator Kenneth Wherry, Republican of Nebraska, introduced in the Senate a resolution calling for a full investigation of the Department of State. The Senate Foreign Relations Committee headed by Senator Tom Connally, Democrat from Texas, held sessions, December 5, 6, 10 to determine whether to reject or report that resolution.

At the first session General Hurley clashed with several members of the Committee in a turbulent three-hour session. At issue were his basic reasons for his sudden resignation as Ambassador and his charges that Department of State career officials were sabotaging the foreign policy of the President and the Secretary of State. He stated that an investigation of the conduct of American foreign policy could be constructive only if handled on a non-partisan basis, with all political considerations set aside, and only the interests of the nation as a whole considered.

Hurley declared again and again that, while he had the support of Presidents Roosevelt and Truman, and their successive Secretaries of State, Hull, Stettinius, and Byrnes, they would not give him a public statement of United States policy on China. Their silence made it possible for a few foreign service officers to attempt to undermine his work by asserting that the policy he was following was his own, and not that of this government.

Chairman Connally asked Hurley if the Secretary of State had not communicated with him from time to time regarding American policy in China and had not Hurley stated publicly a few days ago that he was in entire agreement and support of the Secretary of State's policy and that of the President toward China? Hurley answered:

Yes sir; I did; but those statements were made to me privately, sir, and were not announced as a public policy, and if they had been I would not have been defeated by the gentlemen of the State Department who claim that I was not upholding the policy of my country, that it was a policy evolved by me and not by the United States; and that is the issue, sir. That is the trouble we have been having.

Hurley pointed out that during the war John Stewart Service sent a memorandum to the Department of State on October 10, 1944 (sometimes called Report No. 40) in which he described how we should let the Nationalist Government fall. The report was circulated among the Chinese Communists. Hurley had obtained a copy of this report from a representative of the Communist apparatus. Service was serving under General Stilwell at the time. As a result, Hurley stated, "I could not control him."

Hurley reviewed for the Committee the differences between himself and some of the foreign service officers regarding our policy toward China. Another major difference concerned whether Lend-Lease assistance should have been given to the Chinese Communist armies to help them fight the Japanese. He remarked: *"Career men continuously told the Communist armed party and the world that America was betting on the wrong horse, that the American policy which I was upholding in China did not have the support of the United States Government."*

Hurley realized that more than verbal charges against the foreign service officers would be required to convince the Committee that an investigation of the State Department's China policy was in order. He gave the Committee a list of thirteen documents that would prove his charges regarding the activities of our foreign service officers. Among the documents requested was the secret Yalta Agreement. This request was refused despite the fact that the war had been over for months. Chairman Connally hedged on the point whether the requested documents should be released to the public. Since they were top secret material that the Committee would have to look them over in executive session, he questioned whether it would be helpful to put them in the record:

THE CHAIRMAN: I think the State Department is involved in this matter as well as all the rest of us.
GENERAL HURLEY: I had that intimation, sir; and I assure you that I am not going to be aggressive or belligerent. I feel that the issue before us today is not a partisan issue, and I decline to make it one, and I will, if you require, tell the Committee what I am asking for; but remember, sir, that if I read the papers

correctly, most of these documents have been given out by career men in the State Department, and the *only difference between what I am trying to do and what they have done, they have given them to people who were trying to defeat the policy of the United States, and I am trying to give them to the American people.*

Senator Connally's position that it would be detrimental to national security to release the documents requested did not satisfy Hurley. He was denied the use of these reports and letters, some of which were written by himself, and all of which were among the *Amerasia* papers that were given or sold to the Communists. In this instance the Committee decided not to give the American people the facts—a peculiar attitude toward documents already in Communist hands.

At one point in the hearings, Senator Robert M. La Follette, Progressive of Wisconsin, interrupted to say: "I would like to ask General Hurley . . . exactly what it is at issue, here."

Hurley replied:

Senator, I will endeavor to tell you what the issue is. During the war, I went to China as the representative of the President of the United States with a mission in regard to China. At that time it was predicted . . . that nothing short of a miracle would prevent the collapse of the National Government of the Republic of China. My directive was to prevent the collapse. It was publicly stated that the Chinese Army was disintegrating and was in retreat. My directive was to keep the Chinese Army in the war. It was said that we were not having harmonious relations with the Government of China. My directive was to restore harmony.

Hurley remarked that his mission had been accomplished, but not "without the relief or removal of . . . Americans who either could not go along with the American policy or were incompatible with the officials of the Chinese Government with whom we had to deal. If we had failed, if the Government had collapsed, if the Chinese Army had disintegrated, it would have released more than a million, and nearer two million, Japanese soldiers to meet our soldiers and sailors and marines on the beaches." Hurley asserted that George Atcheson, Jr. was the leader of the policy aimed at "destroying" the Chinese National Government; that in January, 1945, Hurley had called in the heads of all American agencies in China and explained to them what he considered American policy—strong support of the National Government with the object of keeping the armies in the war against Japan.

No one dissented, he said, but when he returned to Washington later for conferences he was "confronted" by a letter from Atcheson recommending that Lend-Lease supplies be given to the Chinese Communists. Moreover, Atcheson said he had the support, the acquiescence, of every official member of the American Embassy in Chungking. Senator Alexander Wiley of Wisconsin asked, "What is the date of that letter?"

GENERAL HURLEY: That letter is dated February 28, 1945. That is again while we were still at war.

THE CHAIRMAN: You say you, of course, opposed furnishing arms to a belligerent group to attack the government you were upholding. Did Mr. Atcheson point out that the purpose of furnishing arms to the Communists was to get them to unite in fighting the Japanese, or not?

GENERAL HURLEY: I see that you have read the letter.

THE CHAIRMAN: No, I have not seen it. You are quite in error. I have never seen the letter and would never have thought of it but for your appearance here. I do not know what is in the letter. I am asking you. It is certainly reasonable to suppose that he had some argument or some reason. I am asking you, was that true? I do not know whether it is true or not. You have read the letter and I have not seen it.

GENERAL HURLEY: It is true. My purpose was the purpose stated by Secretary Byrnes in his public release this morning.

THE CHAIRMAN: I am not talking about that. I am talking about the letter that you say Mr. Atcheson wrote, in which he expressed some disagreement with some of your views and in which he suggested that arms and munitions under Lend-Lease be supplied to the Communist forces.

Now, I am asking you what his reasons for that were. Were his reasons that they would aid in fighting the Japanese?

GENERAL HURLEY: They were already fighting the Japanese.

THE CHAIRMAN: What were his reasons?

GENERAL HURLEY: *His reasons were that that would destroy the National Government of the Republic of China, and the John Service report is for that purpose,* and as soon as I left, George Atcheson and everybody attempted what they had been trying to do when the President sent me to China, and that was to destroy the Government of the Republic of China.

THE CHAIRMAN: He said that in the letter?

GENERAL HURLEY: No, he did not, but he did use all of my arguments for unification.

THE CHAIRMAN: I was asking you about the letter, and what was in the letter.

GENERAL HURLEY: Do not tax my memory too much. I have told you about the letter. You can get it, and I am willing for the American people to read it.

THE CHAIRMAN: Oh, yes; I know. The American people are going to find out about this fact, I hope.

GENERAL HURLEY: I think they are.

When Senator La Follette assumed command of questioning, General Hurley became specific in his charge. He continued to explain the recommendations sent to the Department of State by George Atcheson.

SENATOR LA FOLLETTE: General, you had started out on something in the nature of a chronological statement of these events, and then we did not get very far with it. As I understand it, at some time after you got to China you called in the heads of all the missions in China at your office in Chungking, and you there outlined to them the policy as outlined to you in your directives of the United States toward the situation in China. You then came back here to a conference at the State Department, and you found a communication from a Mr. Atcheson in which he took a position diametrically opposite, as I understood it, to the one which you had outlined at this meeting with all of these representatives of the various missions of the United States in Chungking.

What happened after that? Did not that essential conflict bring about some resolution, some determination here at Washington as to whether you or Mr. Atcheson had the policy of the United States correctly interpreted?

GENERAL HURLEY: Yes, sir.

SENATOR LA FOLLETTE: What happened here at the State Department? If you could just give us a chronological statement of these events and what happened, so that at least I could understand what the issues are here, it would be very helpful.

GENERAL HURLEY: Very well.

As Senator Connally has indicated to you, the report of George Atcheson has a lot of the policy that I had outlined for the heads of the American services in China. In fact, I think that is the first time any career man announced that our policy was to assist in the establishment in China in proper ways without interfering in internal affairs of a strong, united, democratic China. It had been said before in my reports, but he came out for that. There are a lot of good things in the Atcheson report with which I do not disagree. In fact, a lot of them are taken from my own statement, and they are reiterated. *But what Atcheson recommended to the State Department, and what he said he had concurrence in with every official in the Embassy, was that we supply Lend-Lease arms and munitions to the armed Communist Party, which was against the government that I was sent to China to uphold.* That is in the letter.

SENATOR LA FOLLETTE: Then what happened while you were here at the State Department? Did you not then have that issue resolved, and was there not some directive given you to settle this matter as between you and Atcheson on this point on which you were in disagreement?

GENERAL HURLEY: *Yes, sir. I immediately contended that if the Atcheson letter constituted the policy of the United States Government, it was a departure from the purpose for which I had been sent to China, and I wished they would leave Mr. Atcheson in charge and let me stay at home. The result was, after many days of argument, that Mr. Atcheson was recalled, because he had shown that in my absence he had advocated a policy that I felt was destructive to unification.*

SENATOR LA FOLLETTE: Then ultimately the top-ranking officials in the State Department resolved the conflict between you and Mr. Atcheson as to policy in China with relation to Lend-Lease and the Communist faction in your favor, and he was relieved of any further activity in China.

GENERAL HURLEY: Yes, sir.

SENATOR LA FOLLETTE: What happened next? Did that not settle the thing?

GENERAL HURLEY: He came to Washington and became my supervisor in the State Department.

SENATOR LA FOLLETTE: And what was the effect of that, if any, upon your activities and your ability to carry out the policy as you understood it to be in China?

GENERAL HURLEY: It was this, sir; at that point both Mr. Service and Mr. Atcheson were in supervisory capacities in the State Department at Washington, and it meant that I had over me men who disapproved of the policy that I was told to make effective in China.

When asked whether he was able to ascertain any change of policy when he returned home, Hurley made this remarkable statement:

. . . About that time I went to the State Department, and Mr. Drumright showed me a letter that had been received from someone exploding the myth of Hurley, showing that it was my policy and not the policy of the United States that I had upheld in China, and the letter was addressed to President Truman. Drumright prepared a reply to the letter in which he told the gentleman who wrote it the truth, that it was not my policy, that it was the policy of the United States that I had advocated, defended and upheld in China. When the letter went out to the Far Eastern Division, in place of defending me against these charges which had been published again and again, and were rife in China and were weakening every effort that I made, the Far Eastern Division—*and I am told it was Mr. John Carter Vincent*—*struck out all the policy and all the defense, and the letter went out, 'Receipt is acknowledged of your letter dated so and so addressed to the President. Yours respectfully.'* No position was taken in the Far Eastern Division.

SENATOR VANDENBERG: There is one thing I do not understand, General Hurley. Who was responsible for putting these men over you, as you put it, in the State Department, after they had been relieved at your request? Who was responsible for giving them these positions?

GENERAL HURLEY: Frankly, Senator, I do not know.

SENATOR VANDENBERG: Who was responsible for sending them as advisers to General MacArthur?

GENERAL HURLEY: I do not know. I just know they were given supervisory capacity over me here, and they were sent as the top advisers to the Supreme Commander of Asia.

SENATOR VANDENBERG: I find it difficult to put together the two propositions, that the President and the Secretary of State were standing behind you all the time, and yet within their jurisdiction things were happening to the contrary. I can not harmonize those two things.

GENERAL HURLEY: Well, Senator, I have complete sympathy with you. Neither could I. I have thought that the high echelon of policy, as I said a while ago, from the beginning of the Atlantic Charter, from the adoption of the Teheran Declaration, from the splendid exemplification of our policy by Cordell Hull, the high echelon on American policy, has been fine. *But the implementation of that policy, the hiatus between the policy and the performance, is what I am endeavoring to call the attention of the public today.*

After this line of questioning there was a clash between General Hurley and Senator Theodore Green, Democrat from Rhode Island, when the Senator sought to get the former Ambassador to name the "career officials" whom he accused of sabotaging the Government's foreign policy and siding with the Communists. Service and Atcheson already had been named by Hurley, and Senator Green asked him to name others. General Hurley said that three others "of his knowledge" were John Paton Davies, former Second Secretary in Chungking; Fulton Freeman, former Third Secretary in Chungking; Arthur Ringwalt, former Second Secretary in Chungking.

After a bitter exchange with Chairman Connally, Hurley named others who were undermining our China policy: John Carter Vincent and John K. Emmerson. Throughout the hearings Hurley complained repeatedly that the Committee had not obtained from the Department of State documents that, he said, "proved his case." He asserted it was unfair to question him further in the absence of these documents. Senator Shipstead of Minnesota inquired: "You mentioned some documents that the State Department has that I understand we are going to have later. You meant to infer that those documents would substantiate your testimony here when these documents are found, so far as they appear in the record?" Hurley replied: *"I mean that the documents would show that I did not have the support of the career service and, in fact, did have its opposition in attempting to make effective the American policy in China."*

Discussing the events leading up to his resignation, General Hurley said that he had first agreed to return to China, but he had changed his mind after he found out that John Carter Vincent, head of the Far Eastern desk in the Department of State, had declined to send out a proposed letter answering criticisms of General Hurley. Also influencing him was an attack upon his policy by Congressman Hugh DeLacy, Democrat of Washington. "I found I was again left naked to my enemies and the enemies of America," he said; "I decided I would commence firing and I did."

Denied access to documents that he believed would have proved his case, Hurley was constantly needled by Chairman Connally to be more specific in his charges. Connally asked Hurley whether the foreign service officers he had criticized had actually advised the Communists that his efforts in preventing the collapse of the National Government did not represent the policy of the United States. "Do you mean that they went directly to the Communists and made these representations from time to time?" Connally asked.

GENERAL HURLEY: I mean they did more than that, Senator, I mean that when the program was prepared for President Roosevelt to go to Yalta that there is a paper dated January 29th on American policy in Asia, and one paragraph of that paper—it is listed among those I wish—provided, if the military, in landing on the coast of China, found the Communists instead of the National Army, they would have the right to arm all forces in such a condition that would assist the American landing forces. With that I was in agreement. But imagine my consternation when I saw a general movement of Communist troops from a territory just described by Senator Austin, all moving toward a certain port in China. Then I read that some Naval officer had been arrested here, and *the Communists not only knew the port but they knew the most secret plan of the United States, and I picked that up, not from our career men, but from the Communist armed party in China, and I have asked for that record in what I have submitted to you.*

THE CHAIRMAN: You say this was a statement or report made up for the use of the President at Yalta. Is that what you said?

GENERAL HURLEY: That is what I think it was. It was sent to the military.

THE CHAIRMAN: Who made it?

GENERAL HURLEY: I do not know.

THE CHAIRMAN: You do not know whether Atcheson wrote it or Service wrote it?

GENERAL HURLEY: I know that Atcheson did not, because he was not here at that time. But understand, Senator, please do not get me wrong on it. I have never contended that in landing you would not use all forces available to you. I believe that that was essential. I am not quarreling with that as policy. I am quarreling with *the fact that it became known to the Communists and started a big movement from their territory in the north and northwest to the seacoast.*

THE CHAIRMAN: You approved the policy that was outlined in the paper, but you did not like the leak, is that it?

GENERAL HURLEY: I do not like to be leaked on.

THE CHAIRMAN: Who leaked? Do you know who it was that gave the leak?

GENERAL HURLEY: No, sir, I know only that it did leak.

Hurley told of returning to Washington in March, 1945, and of having a conference with the President and Secretary of State. President Truman asked him to return to China. Hurley had told them that he was being undermined in China by our own Department of State, and that it was just too great a task for a man to have to carry his own Department of State on his back while meeting the Communist and Kuomintang controversy on the other. They agreed with Hurley that it was not right. Hurley understood that he could fire anyone in China who did not agree with American policy, but countered that this privilege was not sufficient. "If I fire them they come down here and become my bosses, or are sent over as supreme policy makers in Asia, and I make them stronger by firing them." He continued: "I said we ought to have an unequivocal public statement of the policy, so that I would not have to carry both loads."

SENATOR SHIPSTEAD: When you had that understanding, you understood and believed that these attacks upon you, and the leakage out of the Department of State, would cease, did you?

GENERAL HURLEY: That is what I believed I had understood, and then I came up against the fact that it had not stopped.

SENATOR SHIPSTEAD: That came to you as a result of a speech made in the House of Representatives that indicated to you that information had been given to that Congressman (DeLacy) from the State Department?

GENERAL HURLEY: And an immediate result of a letter that had gone to the State Department, and a proper answer had been prepared, and all the proper answer stricken out and just an acknowledgment, leaving all the charges that I had inaugurated and made by own policy in China.

General Hurley was not fighting any particular individual; he was attempting to inform the Committee that problems existed in our Department of State that needed correction; that although policy announcements were made by our top officials, the implementation of that policy was sabotaged by some "career officials." In other words, policy was made in the fourth and not the fifth floor.[2] He answered the Committee:

Today I am a private citizen. This government has a Department of Justice, an F.B.I., a Military Intelligence Service, and I am told that all of these records are already in the hands of the government. I do not think that I should be asked, as a private citizen, to conduct the prosecution of anyone. I think that is an official responsibility.

Senator Styles Bridges resumed the questioning regarding the foreign service officials.

SENATOR BRIDGES: One question, General. What was the first date that your suspicions were aroused, or anything came to your notice whereby agents of the United State Government here in Washington, were undermining the policies of our country or sabotaging your efforts?
GENERAL HURLEY: *The first that came to my attention was the report of Mr. John Service dated October 10, 1944, and numbered 40. That was the first outward evidence I had of a plan not to uphold but to cause the collapse of the Government of the Republic of China.*
SENATOR BRIDGES: And did these reports, or this action by these various representatives of the State Department, interfere seriously with what you were attempting to do in upholding the Chinese Republic and bringing about better relations between the Chinese Republic and the Chinese Communists?
GENERAL HURLEY: They certainly did.
SENATOR BRIDGES: And that, in turn, was a blow against this country, was it not?
GENERAL HURLEY: Yes, sir.

The Service Report came to Hurley through the Chinese Communists. Service was against the Nationalist Government, our ally, that Hurley was directed to uphold. He was in favor of the Communist Party whom Hurley declined to arm. Hurley's complaint was not that Service reported to General Stilwell or the Department of State. Hurley's complaint was that Service was supplying this information to the Communist armed party in China. The Communist who gave the report to Hurley said it had been delivered to the Communist Headquarters at Yenan by John S. Service.

The next session of the Committee's hearing on the investigation of our Far Eastern policy was held December 6, 1945.

General Hurley continued to explain the recommendations sent to the Department of State by George Atcheson. The Atcheson letter stated most of the general policy that the Embassy and the Ambassador were making effective in China. The letter was cleverly written and much of it was above criticism, and certainly could not be criticized by Hurley. The chief item in the Atcheson letter which Hurley opposed was the

2 This is the same criticism as that made by Earl Smith as to how we lost Cuba to the Communists.

recommendation that the United States should supply Lend-Lease arms and equipment to the Communist armed party, whose avowed purpose was the overthrow by force of our ally, the National Government of the Republic of China.[3]

The meeting opened with Chairman Connally asking General Hurley whether there had been a change in policy toward China despite George Atcheson's letter of February 28, 1945. The following exchange took place.

THE CHAIRMAN: After the letter of Mr. Atcheson, I believe it was, was there any change by the Secretary in his policy in China?

GENERAL HURLEY: No, sir. I was in Washington when the Atcheson letter came in, and they held a hearing in the Far Eastern Division on Atcheson's letter, and I appeared in the hearing.

THE CHAIRMAN: There was no change, though, in the policy of the State Department as a result of that letter, was there?

GENERAL HURLEY: The State Department continued, in the higher echelon (that is, Mr. Stettinius) to support the policy that I was upholding in China, but there was no public official statement of that policy.

THE CHAIRMAN: I know about that. But there was no change in the State Department's policy after that letter. It went on just as it had been going, and was in entire agreement with your conduct, was it not?

GENERAL HURLEY: Yes, sir. It went on just the same, *but the rear men continued to try to destroy the American policy in China. There was no stoppage to what they were doing.*

THE CHAIRMAN: I understand. But I am asking you now, was there any stoppage? Were their actions successful? You say there was no change in the policy. It went on just the same after Atcheson's letter as before. Is that correct?

GENERAL HURLEY: Not exactly the same. I received a cablegram from the State Department dated May 15th, setting out the military and political objectives in China that were contrary to the instructions that I had received. I also had received a cable from the State Department telling me not to become a mediator or an adviser in the Chinese situation.

THE CHAIRMAN: This cable, the first cable you mentioned, you say changed from what your instructions had been. In what respect did it change?

GENERAL HURLEY: President Roosevelt—

THE CHAIRMAN: That was in May, '45.

GENERAL HURLEY: Yes, sir. I know when it was, Senator.

THE CHAIRMAN: I am trying to be courteous to you, General. I do not care to be stormed at any more than you do.

GENERAL HURLEY: I am not storming at anybody. I have asked for a document written by Mr. Atcheson and it has not been given me, and that is the best evidence. You can examine me on that document if you wish, but I would like to see the document or I would like to have it said that it is contrary to public policy to make it public.

THE CHAIRMAN: You have testified about it. Is that the one you are testifying about?

GENERAL HURLEY: Yes, sir.

---

[3] Letter from General Patrick J. Hurley to author, February 20, 1961.

THE CHAIRMAN: I will say to you, General, that we are trying to get all the documents that the State Department thinks can be properly used here. We had men working on them last night until midnight, and during the day they will forward them to us, but we can not present them this morning because we do not have them.

GENERAL HURLEY: Then may I ask the Senator, just as one American to another, does he think it is proper to examine me on these documents when they are the best evidence, without the documents being before him? Is that fair to a servant of this nation who had done the work that I have endeavored to do for it? Am I on trial?

THE CHAIRMAN: If you are on trial, you put yourself on trial. I am not putting you on trial. I am asking you; I did not know there was such a document. I asked you if there had been any change in the policy, and then you referred to this document.

GENERAL HURLEY: And I gave you the documents that you can ask for, and you have not brought them.

THE CHAIRMAN: I am trying to bring them.

GENERAL HURLEY: Then, Senator, let us wait until we get them. I am not obstreperous.

THE CHAIRMAN: All right. I did not bring up the documents. You yourself referred to it this morning for the first time, and then I asked you about it.

GENERAL HURLEY: I did not ask for this hearing, sir.

THE CHAIRMAN: We will just pass on the next point.

GENERAL HURLEY: I did not ask for this hearing, sir, but I have asked for the documents that will prove the assertions I have made. I think it is not fair to me to continue to examine me on documents that I have asked for and I have told you what they contain.

THE CHAIRMAN: All right, General. I thought I was examining you and not the documents. I thought I was asking you for your views about the matter. I was asking you if there had been any change in policy. You were out there, and you ought to know.

GENERAL HURLEY: I do know, and I have told you. The documents show it.

THE CHAIRMAN: There was no change in the policy, so far as you know, from the higher echelon, if I may use that word?

GENERAL HURLEY: Senator, I have testified on that quite fully. If you want to examine me on that again, I will be glad to go over it.

THE CHAIRMAN: Oh, no. You have not testified fully, though, because you just mentioned it this morning.

GENERAL HURLEY: If you will put the documents in, sir, I will testify to them.

THE CHAIRMAN: Anybody can read a document. I want to find out what your views are. I want to know if you regard that there was any change in the policy after this George Atcheson letter.

GENERAL HURLEY: There was this change in the policy, that the State Department again assured me verbally that it was upholding my conduct in preventing the collapse of the National Government of the Republic of China. *There was no change in the attitude of the career men who were attempting to bring about a collapse of that government.*

THE CHAIRMAN: All right.

SENATOR BRIDGES: General Hurley, the Chairman has asked you whether or not you approve the policies of Mr. Hull, Mr. Byrnes, and Mr. Truman and Mr. Roosevelt, and I think that you answered in the affirmative. Now I understood from your testimony yesterday that while you approved the general policies, there was one particular policy which they followed which you did not approve, which I think is the meat of this whole issue, and that is their failure to issue a public statement setting forth American foreign policy in China. Is that right?

GENERAL HURLEY: That is true.

SENATOR BRIDGES: When Mr. Service and Mr. Atcheson were removed from China and subsequently sent to Japan to advise General MacArthur on all our Eastern policy, which is the most ridiculous thing I ever heard of, who succeeded them in China?

GENERAL HURLEY: I do not believe that anyone succeeded Service directly; not in his grade. A very fine executive whose name is Ellis Briggs, who is a career man, was sent to me, and he supported the American policy in China completely.

SENATOR BRIDGES: I have been told that a person by the name of Ringwalt and another by the name of Freeman succeeded them.

GENERAL HURLEY: No; they were already in China in the Embassy. They may have, by reason of Service's relief, advanced in position in the Embassy, but they were there from the beginning, from the time I got to China.

SENATOR BRIDGES: Were they the same type of gentlemen that their predecessors were? I mean, did they have the same ideology and were they attempting to undermine the policies of the United States?

GENERAL HURLEY: That is too broad an accusation for me to make against anyone. I will say that they did not support me in the directives that I had received to prevent the collapse of the National Government of China and keep the Chinese Army in the field, and that they did take the side of the armed Communist party in China.

SENATOR BRIDGES: What was their particular work, General Hurley? Do you recall?

GENERAL HURLEY: They were my political advisers.

Senator Bridges brought out the fact that through the press and even the radio the same crowd that sabotaged Hurley's efforts in China were now centering their attacks on General Albert Wedemeyer. He asked Hurley whether Wedemeyer was doing a good job. Hurley replied: "I think that Wedemeyer is among the ablest officers of the United States Army. There is no question about his ability, his integrity, and his patriotism."

Senator Bridges wanted to know what effect the arming of the Chinese Communists would have on our China policy. Hurley answered: "If the Chinese Communists had been armed at that time, if they had been armed by us or by Russia or by Great Britain, it would in my opinion have made the collapse of the National Government inevitable, and the documents I have asked the Senate Committee on Foreign Relations to obtain I think will prove that the object was to arm the belligerents and withdraw support from the Government, which in my opinion was contrary to the American policy."

Hurley went on to point out that the collapse of the Chinese Government and the disintegration of the Chinese Army would have released anywhere from thirty to sixty Japanese divisions against U.S. soldiers. He paid eloquent tribute to Chiang Kai-shek and explained that there was never any wavering on his part. Senator Bridges asked: "General Hurley, to your knowledge it is true that Chiang Kai-shek had on several occasions opportunities to make peace with the Japs, and that he turned those offers down and did loyally maintain his ties to the United States and the other Allies in carrying through and fighting the war with Japan?"

GENERAL HURLEY: Well, of course, the answer to that question, Senator, involves a lot of matters in the State Department.

SENATOR BRIDGES: I do not want to ask you any embarrassing questions.

GENERAL HURLEY: These same gentlemen of whom I have spoken have reported at great length about communications between Chiang Kai-shek and the Japanese. I have asked for their reports. The Senate Committee can get that. But I reported to the State Department, of course, on that subject at the time, and in my report I said to the State Department that of course there were matters that we could criticize about Chiang Kai-shek and his conduct of the war, and we need not approve the character or quality of the men who were around him. Many of them we could not give our approval to, but that Chiang Kai-shek fought the Japanese alone at a time when they were offering him all of the things that our career men said that Japan was now offering.

The hearings took an interesting twist when Senator Bridges introduced into the record an article from the *Atlanta Journal* for November 28, 1945. It was written by Hugh G. Grant, former Ambassador to Thailand. Grant made much the same charges against the Department of State as had General Hurley.[4]

Senator Wiley resumed the questioning:

SENATOR WILEY: My questions will be very brief. I have listened with interest to your testimony the last two days. As I understand your position it is briefly this—that the State Department failed (1) in that it did not, while you were in China, issue a public declaration of policy, which would have aided you tremendously in carrying out that policy. Is that correct?

GENERAL HURLEY: That is true, sir.

---

4 "Whatever the issues of the American-Chinese political situation, Major General Patrick Hurley, who resigned Tuesday as American Ambassador to China, has rendered a distinct public service in revealing the obstructionist tactics of American Foreign Service 'career' officers in the Far East and the State Department. . . . What General Hurley has revealed is not new. This sort of business has been going on a long time in our Foreign Service, but few men who could speak with authority from actual experience in our missions abroad have had the courage to speak out. They have resigned their missions when they have become disgusted or else have been quietly thrown out ('recalled') and kept their mouths shut because any other procedure usually reacts against the man who speaks out, regardless of the facts he may reveal.

"I am of the opinion that General Hurley has done a real service for President Truman and Secretary Byrnes who, I believe, are sincerely desirous of building an effective foreign service which would be capable of handling the great problems confronting this nation during the post-war era.

"Ambassador Hurley is on the right track about the confusion of our foreign policy as a result of the tactics of professional 'career' officers in the lower brackets of the

SENATOR WILEY: (2) That there were in the Department certain individuals that you mentioned; that these individuals were cognizant of the policy laid down by the State Department and by two presidents, but they apparently did not co-operate with you in carrying out that policy; is that correct?

GENERAL HURLEY: That is correct.

SENATOR WILEY: (3) Were these individuals motivated in your judgment by simply a disagreement as to the validity of the policy, or do you think there was back of their motives something else? And if you have any information or facts that would clarify the answer, I would like to have it.

GENERAL HURLEY: I think, Senator, your first question, that these men disagreed with the American policy, is correct, but my contention with them—and understand I assembled them and talked to them and stated the policy. I have asked for the record of my statement of policy, early, after the President appointed me Ambassador, and inasmuch as we were in an active war theater—it was my contention that when the "die is cast," and when the decision is made, when the policy is announced by duly constituted authority, it becomes the duty of every one of us to make that policy effective; and I charge that these gentlemen did not do that. They continued to snipe the policy and tried to defeat it.

SENATOR WILEY: In other words, your position is that the Chief had called the signals, "Play Ball!" and you were playing ball but they were not?

GENERAL HURLEY: That is correct.

SENATOR WILEY: All right. Now, I do not think you answered the other part of my question. Was there anything back of this "inability," to put it that way, on their part, to play ball with you as the American representative, to carry out the President's foreign policy? Was there anything back of it except simply their own stubbornness, their inability to see that it was their obligation to play ball, or were they disloyal, or were they conniving with the Communists, or what was the picture?

GENERAL HURLEY: *They were disloyal to the American policy.* I would not say they were all disloyal to the United States Government. I think possibly some of them were imbued with the crusader spirit, but that they believed it would be best for China to destroy the National Government and the leadership of Chiang Kai-shek, but I tried to tell them that I could not argue, while I could recommend to Chiang Kai-shek and the Government the changes that I thought should take place—which I did, and a lot of changes did take place—that while I might agree with them on a lot of their criticism, our directive, mine and theirs, was to prevent the collapse of the Government and to uphold the leadership of Chiang Kai-shek, and whether I believed in it or not, as soon as the policy was made by my superior it became my duty to make it effective, whatever my own opinion regarding it might have been; and it is only that attitude that we have followed quite largely throughout our national life that has made this a successful nation, especially in war.

SENATOR WILEY: Now your fourth criticism was that a number of Government agencies in China failed to co-operate or clear through you, the representative of this Government, our Ambassador. I understand that this is basic, in

---

service. Under the existing system neither an ambassador nor a minister has any real control over his own mission, since the cases have 'pipe lines' to powerful fellow 'career' officers in the department. These men can absolutely 'break' a chief or mission and they can ignore and circumvent the established foreign policy of the President and the Secretary of State. The whole system needs to be thoroughly cleansed and reorganized if we are to have constructive policies and the rights and the position of the nation are to be maintained abroad."

your judgment. There should have been real cooperation or clearance through you as an Ambassador, to effectuate the foreign policy of this nation.

GENERAL HURLEY: I mean, Senator, that it should have had one directive from Washington.

SENATOR WILEY: And that was not forthcoming?

GENERAL HURLEY: And that did not come, and there wasn't any coordination among these various American agencies, except what I tried to bring about by having the heads meet with me; and I assure you there wasn't any acrimony between us.

SENATOR WILEY: No, I know.

GENERAL HURLEY: We tried to co-operate together, and tried to bring out a unification of America's effort in China.

SENATOR WILEY: Now, may I trouble you with point six? These men were not playing ball with you; you were the Ambassador of the United States; you complained to the State Department that they were not playing ball with you. Now, in your judgment should there not be some remedy in the hands of an Ambassador when his subordinates do not play ball—just simply send them home? I am asking for a constructive suggestion.

GENERAL HURLEY: Well, Senator, you were probably not in here yesterday, I did send them home, but I notice in the press this morning they tell us about these gentlemen being assigned as advisors to General MacArthur. That is a little remote, because he is only Commander of Asia, and therefore above myself, the one who has relieved these gentlemen; but that is not the real gravamen of this situation. When I relieved these gentlemen in Chungking they were brought back to Washington and placed in the State Department in positions where they became my supervisors, and there they attempted to hamstring every thing that I did in carrying into effect my directive; . . .

SENATOR WILEY: Can you place your fingers on the individuals whom you hold responsible for doing what has been done here? (1) After you had called attention to the State Department that these men were not playing ball with you, that they were sabotaging the American policy in China, and then they were brought back and promoted. Who was responsible for the promotion?

GENERAL HURLEY: Well, of course, I do not think they could be promoted without the approval of the Secretary of State.

SENATOR WILEY: Do you know who recommended it to him?

GENERAL HURLEY: No, sir. I have been saying, and I hope it will not grow hackneyed, that I was 13,000 miles away from there, with rather a full hand, and I just could not keep up with what was happening in the State Department; but I did feel that I did not have the support that the 'tops' of the service had always given me in the missions that they gave me to perform.

SENATOR SHIPSTEAD: What was the cause of the difference between Chiang Kai-shek and the Communists? Was it ideological or political?

GENERAL HURLEY: Of course, there were ideological differences between Chiang Kai-shek and the leaders of the Chinese and Communist armed party. But the ideological differences were supplemented also by the fact that the Communists are quite a formidable political party, who are seeking through political means, while maintaining the status of an armed belligerent, to get control of the Government. Now, from our standpoint, if it is political means, there isn't any objection to any party seeking control of the government under which it lives. Our position was that there can be no unification of China as long as there are armed war lords, bands, or political parties who are strong enough to challenge the action of the government, itself; *and on that basis we have declined to arm belligerents against the government which we have been upholding.*

Before the Committee adjourned Hurley made his position very clear.

GENERAL HURLEY: The committee asked me to advise them who are the men who are guilty of the leaks from the State Department, which leaks are designed to defeat the foreign policy of the United States. Personally I have been on the perimeter of America's influence since we entered the war. I therefore could not have intimate or personal knowledge of what has been transpiring in Washington. I do recall that certain career men were arrested on information supplied by the FBI. Usually the FBI does not cause arrests on suspicions. They usually base their arrests on fact.

In addition to the FBI, I call attention to the investigations made by the intelligence services of both the Army and the Navy, the records of which are available to the committee. If the committee would like me to give them confidentially a list of witnesses that they might call upon from the army service I would be glad to supply it.

I also call attention to the fact that this Congress and this Committee have in control sources through which they can ascertain far better than an individual like myself the facts in regard to the inside opposition, whether by career men or others, that is intended to defeat the policy announced by the top echelon of the policy-making authority of the Nation. *My own endeavor in this hearing is to bring the attention of this Committee to the fact that the announced American policy is being defeated, and has been defeated, all over the world, not alone in China.*

The fact is, Mr. Chairman, that the defeat of the principles of the Atlantic Charter, the defeat of the principles of the Iran Declaration,[5] the use of America's power to uphold predatory ideologies contrary to the announced policy of our government *is an inside job.*

Chairman Connally insisted upon pressing Hurley regarding the activities of the Foreign Service officials.

THE CHAIRMAN: Now, you said in your statement the other day in the press that these subordinates, these foreign-service men, had been continually advising the Communists that your views did not represent the views of the government. How did they advise then—in writing, or by personal contact?

GENERAL HURLEY: Well, I asked this Committee to get a certain document.

THE CHAIRMAN: Well, I know, but you are testifying. I want to know what you know about it. You make the statement that they communicated with them. Now, how did they communicate with them?

GENERAL HURLEY: By writing and by talking and by being with them.

THE CHAIRMAN: Can you say what officials of the Communists they contacted and talked with?

---

[5] The Iran Declaration was signed at Teheran on December 1, 1943. The declaration reaffirmed the principles of the Atlantic Charter as the principles and objectives for which the United Nations were fighting. This declaration was signed by Roosevelt, Churchill, and Stalin. However, any such declaration of "principles" was so much window-dressing. The agreements made at Teheran, and later confirmed at Yalta, made a mockery of any lofty statement of principles. Both Stalin and Churchill had declared themselves in positions of conflict with the Atlantic Charter, which the two of them had previously signed.

GENERAL HURLEY: Well, I would not know exactly, I do not think they all contacted the top officials, but they did contact, and I have told you that it is contained in Public Document No. 40.

THE CHAIRMAN: Oh, I know!

GENERAL HURLEY: Signed by John Service, and dated October 10; and you can get it, in writing, sir.

THE CHAIRMAN: That was addressed to the Secretary of State; that was not addressed to the Communists?

GENERAL HURLEY: No, sir; it was addressed to Stilwell.

THE CHAIRMAN: He was not a member of the armed Communists, he was our officer, was he not—Stilwell?

GENERAL HURLEY: That is right, but I say this document that proves that is addressed to him.

THE CHAIRMAN: Yes, I know.

GENERAL HURLEY: And I have told you where you can get the facts, sir, in writing.

THE CHAIRMAN: Yes, but I want to know. You have made the charge, yourself, and I want to know what you have to say about your statement that they were continuously advising the Communists. Now, they would not advise the Communists through the State Department; they would advise them directly, either in writing or personally. Now, which was it? Do you still adhere to the statement that they were advising them continuously that your views did not represent the Government's views?[6]

GENERAL HURLEY: I most certainly do!

THE CHAIRMAN: Well, would you mind telling us whom they were seeing.

GENERAL HURLEY: All right, I will begin again. I will repeat. A telegram sent by George Atcheson on the 28th of last February, in which he said—

THE CHAIRMAN: To whom?

GENERAL HURLEY: To the Secretary of State.

THE CHAIRMAN: Oh, well, I want to know.

GENERAL HURLEY: Well, you know, it is in writing, sir.

THE CHAIRMAN: Why, certainly.

GENERAL HURLEY: And you ask me to prove what is in that, and I have given you a writing.

THE CHAIRMAN: All right. I was asking what communication they had had, not with the State Department but with the Communists. All right, we will not pursue that any further. We have got to go and find it out, ourselves. Now you say, though, you finally wind up with—

'Despite these handicaps, in spite of this sabotaging that these men were carrying on, and despite their continuous contacting the Communists, despite these handicaps we did make progress toward unification of the armed forces of China. We did prevent civil war between the rival factions, at least until after I had left China.'

Now, your whole program, then, was, up to the time you left China, completed. You kept the Chinese Government, you kept the Chinese Army in the field, you were on the way to the unification of the two forces, and you had the leaders of the two parties together in peaceful discussion. That all transpired

---

6 Hurley had already testified that the Service report had been given to him by a Communist who said that Service had delivered it to the Communist Headquarters at Yenan. Senator Connally's brow-beating of the witness at this point was obviously designed only to confuse the issue.

before you left, so that up to the time you left, everything that you had gone out there to accomplish had been accomplished, had it not?

GENERAL HURLEY: No, sir; I had not made effective the long-range American policy which Mr. Churchill and Marshal Stalin had agreed with, namely, to make or put in operation in China the forces that would enable China to establish for herself a strong united, democratic China Government.

THE CHAIRMAN: Well that was long-range?

GENERAL HURLEY: Yes, sir.

THE CHAIRMAN: But so far as your immediate objectives, you accomplished them all?

GENERAL HURLEY: No.

THE CHAIRMAN: In spite of these handicaps?

GENERAL HURLEY: Now, Senator, you have me in a position where they will begin to debate about. You see one of my objectives was a unification of the armed forces of China.

THE CHAIRMAN: I understand that, and you said you had it improved, and you progressing, you had not accomplished it.

GENERAL HURLEY: Yes.

THE CHAIRMAN: In addition, we undertook the reconstruction of the Burma Road, did we not?

GENERAL HURLEY: That is correct.

THE CHAIRMAN: The Ledo Road?

GENERAL HURLEY: Yes, sir.

THE CHAIRMAN: So you would not say, with those things, that we failed to support the China Government, would you?

GENERAL HURLEY: Oh, no; on the contrary, that is what I was in favor of; but what I am saying is that these men who wanted to arm an armed belligerent against that government were not aiding the Chiang Kai-shek Government but were for its downfall.

THE CHAIRMAN: In other words, your position is that these men were not trying to arm the Communists to fight Japan in connection with Chiang Kai-shek, but were working for the purpose of fighting Chiang Kai-shek and destroying his government, is that correct?

GENERAL HURLEY: Well, that is a little strained, Senator. I would not like to just admit, Yes or No, on that question; but I will say that the effect of arming a belligerent of China, where you had a government that was on the verge of collapse, would have caused the collapse of the Chiang Kai-shek Government.

THE CHAIRMAN: If you had succeeded in your unification program, you would have been willing to arm the Communists, then, would you not?

GENERAL HURLEY: Oh, yes.

THE CHAIRMAN: If they were going to fight with you?

GENERAL HURLEY: Oh, yes, yes.

THE CHAIRMAN: Yes.

GENERAL HURLEY: Through their own government.

THE CHAIRMAN: Why, certainly, certainly.

GENERAL HURLEY: I certainly was willing to arm them through their own government. Any time the National Government wished to arm the Communists I would have been in favor of it, but I was not in favor of arming a belligerent against the government that we were committed to uphold.

The next session of the Committee was held on December 10, 1945.

Theodore H. White, war correspondent for *Time* magazine in China, appeared as a witness. A letter was inserted in the record written by Theodore White, Richard Watts, Jr., Eric Sevareid, Annalee Jacoby, and Jack Belden. The letter read:

Dear Senator Connally:

We realize that it would be presumptuous on our part to stress to you and the members of your committee the extraordinary gravity of the charges made by former Ambassador to China, Patrick J. Hurley. As American newspapermen, whose collective experience extends over eight years of war in the Far East, we feel it our duty to offer whatever assistance or testimony is within our power concerning Mr. Hurley's charges.

We feel that the gravest danger to the work of your investigation is that it may easily bog down in the clash of personalities which Mr. Hurley highlighted and that by so doing it may lose sight of the larger issues of American policy in the Orient.

We should like, as American newspapermen, to go on record as testifying to the complete integrity and conscientious devotion of American interests of the career diplomats whom Mr. Hurley so indiscriminately attacks. It was our job over a number of years to cover the war in China, and the activities of our representatives; our judgments were not ideological but based upon the simple day-by-day standards of their honesty and ability.

The men accused are unable to speak for themselves. We feel, therefore, that as witnesses sent to China by the American press we should announce our belief that the American Embassy in Chungking, upon Ambassador Hurley's assumption of office, was staffed by a good, honest cross-section of Americans. Some were liberals, others, conservatives. They had in common only one quality—that all were reporting the truth to the American Government as they saw it.

As journalists, we should indeed be interested in seeing the publication of the dispatches of our trained specialists, side by side with Mr. Hurley's official reporting in the past year.

The men whom Mr. Hurley attacks are people who have endured years of hardship in China, in pestilence and bombing, serving America's interests. We have met these men in famine areas, in air-raid shelters, at the war fronts. They served as nobly and disinterestedly in the cause of our Republic as any soldier in uniform.

Mr. Hurley disagreed with them, and he got rid of them. By so doing he deprived himself and the State Department of American sources of information that his predecessors had found both valuable and objective.

In justice not only to the men involved and Mr. Hurley, but also the American and Chinese people, we hope that both General Stilwell and former Ambassador Gauss will be called to give evidence at what should be, after all, an examination not of defenseless State Department servants, as Hurley would have it, but an examination before Congress, of United States policy in the Far East.

Respectfully yours,

/s/ THEODORE H. WHITE

/s/ RICHARD WATTS, JR.

/s/ ERIC SEVAREID

/s/ ANNALEE JACOBY

/s/ JACK BELDEN

White's testimony defended the activities of Service and Atcheson all
the way. Here is his testimony:

THE CHAIRMAN: Do you know Mr. George Atcheson? I believe his name is
George.
MR. WHITE: Yes, sir; I do.
THE CHAIRMAN: He was a foreign-service officer out there.
MR. WHITE: I am very proud to know him, sir.
THE CHAIRMAN: Do you know Mr. John Service?
MR. WHITE: I do.
THE CHAIRMAN: It has been testified here by General Hurley that these two
gentlemen, who were career men, were engaged in sabotaging the U.S. policies
and efforts in China. Do you know anything about that?
MR. WHITE: I know of no attempt whatsoever to sabotage General Hurley's
policies in China by any career officer of the State Department; and if you will
permit me, sir, I would like to say a few words.
THE CHAIRMAN: Just go ahead in your own way.
SENATOR VANDENBERG: How would you know whether they were sabotaging
it, or not?
MR. WHITE: Senator Vandenberg, we newspapermen in Chungking lived in
a very. rough situation. I met these men in the field. When you bivouac with
people you know what they think. I have had no access to any embassy documents, but you cannot live with men day and night and be with them in dis-
comfort and danger and not know what they think.
The American policy as laid down by Secretary Byrnes, as I understand it,
was for the creation of a united, democratic China; at least that was the testimony given here last week. I know that those men zealously fought to achieve
that, just by living with them. I do not think it would be possible for any
member of the press in Chungking to be unaware of any conspiracy or of any
attempt to sabotage Ambassador Hurley.
SENATOR VANDERBERG: Well, it might not be a conspiracy. It might be a difference, a very fundamental difference of opinion as to whether or not you
should or should not, let us say, arm the Communist forces in the north. I do not
quite see how you would qualify as a witness to determine whether or not that
was their own point of view, and whether or not they were encouraging their
own point of view.

Mr. White continued his testimony in defense of the foreign service
officers. "Now, I realize," remarked White, "that the main difference of
opinion between General Hurley and Mr. Service was as to the use, the
power, and the value of the Communist arms to the American policy;
but it was Mr. Service's duty to report these things. Sir, I do not believe
it would be possible in Chungking for a man to attempt to conspire with
the 'Communist armed party' as General Hurley calls it, in an attempt
to overthrow the Government of Chiang Kai-shek, without the press corps
knowing it. Having known Service so well, having lived with him in
places like that, he would be guilty of monumental duplicity in every
hour of his daily life if he were actually conspiring. You cannot talk with
a man in the field for so long and not realize what he is doing. I am

absolutely sure he was not conspiring with anybody to overthrow our Government. He was reporting the facts as he saw them."

Documents revealed since the testimony of White show otherwise. The Foreign Service officers were working behind Hurley's back for the downfall of Chiang Kai-shek. Hurley was our Ambassador to China; he had access to official reports. He would not have charged our Foreign Service officers in China with willfully working against our established policy unless he was certain their actions were not in the interest of the United States.

On December 7, 1945, Secretary of State James F. Byrnes appeared before the Committee. He defended the activities of the Department of State. He was asked about the Atcheson letter of February 28, which Hurley has criticized so vigorously.

SENATOR VANDENBERG: Can I ask you in a general way, then, whether the telegram did represent a recommendation of a sharp and distinct change in our Chinese policy?

SECRETARY BYRNES: Yes. As I have stated, while it analyzed the conditions, *it made a recommendation that would have involved a change.*

SENATOR VANDENBERG: The policy which General Hurley had been pursuing in China was the policy of the Government and the State Department, was it not?

SECRETARY BYRNES: Yes. And may I say this. I am glad that you asked it. I thought of it when the General was talking to me, and told him on every occasion, he would readily admit, that if there was any difference in the views of any official and General Hurley, the Department has stood by Hurley.

SENATOR VANDENBERG: And the views submitted by Atcheson in his wire were contrary to the American policy?

SECRETARY BYRNES: It was providing a change.

SENATOR VANDENBERG: That is what I mean.

SECRETARY BYRNES: It was suggesting a change in policy; not that something had been done that was contrary to the policy.

SENATOR VANDENBERG: And you think it was perfectly appropriate for Mr. Atcheson, in his temporary assumption of top authority, to take advantage of the opportunity to send this report to the Department?

SECRETARY BYRNES: I think that the man in charge of an Embassy owes it to the Department, if he believes there is a change in conditions that should be brought to the attention of the Department, to send it.

I think of it this way. Since September the General has not been back, and the official in charge must be free to send to the Department his views with reference to conditions.

SENATOR VANDENBERG: Mr. Atcheson subsequently was withdrawn from China, was he not?

SECRETARY BYRNES: Yes.

Secretary of State Byrnes defended State Department career officials against charges that they had been undermining American policy in China. As to General Hurley's reiterated complaint that his work in China had been handicapped by the failure of Presidents Roosevelt and

Truman and Secretaries of State Hull, Stettinius, and Byrnes to make public announcement of American policy in China, Byrnes said that Hurley had not asked President Truman or him to make such a statement. This was contrary to Hurley's testimony.

Discussing differences between General Hurley and the two State Department officials in China, George Atcheson, Jr. and John S. Service, Byrnes stated that the two had a duty to submit their reports to the Department of State urging a shift in policy. He added that there was no indication that Atcheson or Service had failed to adhere to the American policy and that there was nothing to support the charge that either had been guilty of "the slightest disloyalty to his superior officers." He continued: "If his reports and recommendations are to be useful, it is clear that they must reflect his free and honest judgment."[7] And in describing the report which John Stewart Service had sent from Yenan, on October 10, 1944 (another of the thirteen documents), Secretary Byrnes admitted, "The memorandum itself embodied recommendations for a basic change in United States policy toward the Central Government of China. It was written in forceful language and the conclusions which it drew were rather drastic."

Discussing General Hurley's charges that some officials advised someone associated with the Communist forces that the Ambassador did not accurately represent American policy, Secretary Byrnes said the former Ambassador did not furnish any specific evidence. Republican Senators Arthur Vandenberg and Styles Bridges asked Secretary Byrnes if he was aware of any "intercepted" communications of Service and Atcheson with the Chinese Communists. The Secretary of State replied he was not.

Senator Bridges also reviewed the criminal case involving Service on a charge of disclosing secret State Department documents, an alleged offense for which he was arrested by the F.B.I. agents but was cleared by a Federal grand jury and reinstated in the post by Secretary Byrnes.

Senator Bridges asked if the Secretary was aware of a telephone call from "someone very high up in the Federal Government," advising the Justice Department "to lay off the Service case." Secretary Byrnes replied that he was not aware of such a telephone call, and that if Senator Bridges had any information concerning such a call he should reveal the name of the official responsible. Senator Bridges admitted he had no evidence to support the charge.

Referring to Secretary Byrnes' activities in reinstating Service after he had been cleared of the charges against him, Senator Bridges referred to the letter written by the Secretary expressing gratification that Service could resume his work. He asked Secretary Byrnes: "How can you by

---

[7] "Yes," Hurley said, "but he is not supposed to attempt to defeat the established policy by giving his arguments to the armed Communists and secretly siding with them against his own government."—Hand written marginal note by General Hurley.

any stretch of imagination justify such a letter?" Secretary Byrnes responded tartly that he did not need to stretch his imagination to justify the letter. He explained to Senator Bridges that under the American system of government and justice innocent persons falsely accused of crimes were not subject to continuing punishment in the form of having their former jobs denied to them.

One of the major complaints by General Hurley was the veil of secrecy which surrounded the Department of State. Byrnes attended the Yalta Conference, and according to his memoirs he didn't learn about the secret Yalta Accord until shortly after his departure. It is difficult to believe that Byrnes as Secretary of State did not have knowledge of the agreement, eleven months after it occurred. He was, at the least, evasive in his testimony.

SENATOR BRIDGES: Now Mr. Secretary, at Yalta was there any deal made involving China?

SECRETARY BYRNES: I do not know what you refer to, Senator, as a 'deal.'

SENATOR BRIDGES: Was there any agreement reached relative to China, at Yalta?

SECRETARY BYRNES: I would have to search my mind. A communique was issued which carried a statement as to the various agreements arrived at. If you would indicate what you have in mind, it would bring it back to my mind.

SENATOR BRIDGES: I mean, I was not there, Mr. Secretary, and I understood that you were.

SECRETARY BYRNES: I was there; not—

SENATOR BRIDGES: At least, you were accompanying President Roosevelt, at the time.

SECRETARY BYRNES: Yes; yes.

SENATOR BRIDGES: And I assume that if there was something as important as an agreement made involving China, you would be aware of it.

SECRETARY BYRNES: Without having the communique, I would not like to make a statement. I will get a copy of the communique, which gave all of the agreements arrived at by the three heads of government, and see that a copy is submitted to you.[8]

SENATOR BRIDGES: I think that, involved here in the case, the question this committee has under consideration, it is very important to know whether there was an agreement made at Yalta relative to China, and whether that agreement was made at Yalta between the heads of the three great Governments, the strong, large Governments, the United States, Great Britain, and Russia, without the knowledge of China, at that time, until later.

SECRETARY BYRNES: Any agreement arrived at at Yalta was made by the three heads of government. China was not represented there, that is certainly true, and any agreement was arrived at in the absence of a representative of China.

SENATOR BRIDGES: Would it not be rather peculiar that you should make some agreement involving the life or death or seriously affecting China without a representative of the Chinese Government being present?

SECRETARY BYRNES: I do not know of any agreement of the character that

---

[8] The communique did *not* give "all the agreements arrived at."

you refer to that was made, and unless you specify, Senator, what you have in mind, I would not know; and even if that were done—

SENATOR BRIDGES: I think that is a fair question, Mr. Secretary, as to whether or not there was any agreement made at Yalta involving China. Now, if you do not want to answer it, that is perfectly all right.

SECRETARY BYRNES: Oh, I have answered it, that I do not recall the various agreements. It is entirely possible that some of the agreements arrived at, at Yalta affected China in some way or other, and I have told you that I would gladly furnish you the communique and then you can determine whether or not they affected China. If they were made they certainly were made by the heads of government, and certainly only the three Governments were represented there.[9]

SENATOR BRIDGES: Since you have been Secretary of State, have you fired anyone in the State Department for disloyalty to the United States?

SECRETARY BYRNES: No.

SENATOR BRIDGES: Have you investigated, or have you ordered an investigation?

SECRETARY BYRNES: I am not aware. Of course, I would say that I am not aware of its being done, though, again, the time that I have been Secretary and have been out of the country about fifty percent of the time, it is entirely possible that you might show some instance that I had not been advised of.

SENATOR BRIDGES: I realize that. I am not trying to embarrass you.

SECRETARY BYRNES: I just say I am not aware of it, Senator.

SENATOR BRIDGES: I realize that since you have been Secretary you have been obliged to be out of the country, more or less.

SECRETARY BYRNES: Yes.

SENATOR BRIDGES: And perhaps some of these things you have not had the time to act on, and I am not pressing you.

SECRETARY BYRNES: I am not aware, but if you will tell me the case, I will find out and advise you.

Among the documents requested by General Hurley and refused by the Committee was the secret Yalta Agreement. Secretary Byrnes and Senator Vandenberg and others were about to go to Moscow for a conference. Vandenberg told Hurley that "you are really cutting the ground from under Byrnes and the rest of us in this conference. Why don't you wait until it is over and you will be given an opportunity to say everything you want to say." Hurley did wait and his opportunity did not come until five years later when he appeared before the MacArthur Hearings. He told Vandenberg during the Hearings in December, 1945, that he had no desire of doing anything that would injure his country.

Secretary Byrnes read a statement to the effect that the foreign service officials whom Hurley had sent home from China and whom he charged with sabotaging the American policy on China, were nice boys who had reported to their superiors. He was implying that Hurley's complaint accused them of insubordination and of going over his head.

Hurley didn't make such a charge, but he was never permitted to an-

---

[9] One entire session of the Yalta Conference dealt with China and the Far East. See Chapter IV.

swer Secretary Byrnes. Hurley's main charge was that these men were favorable to a Communist armed party and against the policy of the United States in China, and that is very different from being insubordinate to Hurley in reporting to his superiors over his head.

After the session, Chairman Tom Connally announced that no further hearings would be held. He said he had turned down a direct appeal by General Hurley for permission to testify in another open session. Senator Connally also served notice that as far as his committee was concerned, there would be no action on requests for a "top to bottom" investigation of the State Department practices and personnel. Referring to a resolution by Senator Kenneth S. Wherry to set up a five-man committee for that purpose, he said: "It is lying calmly on my desk. It shows no signs of life, although we have not put a pulmotor on it." [10]

Here the matter rested until Soviet-backed Chinese Communists had conquered China and we had become involved in a bloody war with them in Korea. Then the Senate Subcommittee on Internal Security, under the able direction of Senator Pat McCarran, reopened the case with exhaustive hearings on the Institute of Pacific Relations. Too late was the massive Communist infiltration of our government and media of information proved to the hilt.

The Senate Foreign Relations Committee gave the Department of State a clean bill of health on its conduct of foreign affairs. Senator Bridges held that Hurley's charges warranted a full investigation of our foreign policy. Here was an opportunity to do a thorough house-cleaning in the Department of State. If it had been done in December, 1945, it might have prevented the fall of China and later Cuba to the Communists. Chairman Connally did everything he could to cover up—to refute the charges made by General Hurley. A thorough investigation of the Department of State in 1945 might have prevented an appeasement of Soviet Russia during the crucial period between 1945 and 1950 when we had a monopoly of the atomic bomb. It would surely have prevented the costly and tragic war in Korea. The opportunity was there to do a thorough job which would have been good for our country. It was not done, and we have suffered repeated reverses as a result.

10 *New York Times,* December 12, 1945.

PART THREE

Coup De Grace

CHAPTER XIV

MARSHALL MAKES MATTERS WORSE

In the year 1945 the United States was the dominant military power in the Pacific. We had crushed the military might of the Japanese Empire only to find ourselves faced by 1950 with another menace—Red China. Our military position at the end of the war was unchallenged, and our diplomats were in a most excellent situation to prevent the expansion of Communism in Asia. Our Chinese allies on the mainland in 1945 had begun to hammer at the Communist forces in the civil war within their own land. They were making considerable headway late in 1946 in defeating this armed revolutionary movement when General George C. Marshall intervened and helped destroy the balance of power that had long favored the Nationalist forces. In fourteen months he helped wreck what had been the basic U. S. policy since 1900—to preserve the "territorial and administrative integrity" of China.

When the Japanese surrendered in August, 1945, the Chinese Communists occupied only a small portion of China. A few months later, a significant race began for the control of cities, strategic areas, communications, air and rail lines previously held by the Japanese. The Communist Commander Chu Teh immediately directed his officers to accept the surrender of Japanese armies in adjacent areas. Thereafter, Generalissimo Chiang Kai-shek, in compliance with instructions by the Supreme Allied Command under General MacArthur, issued a directive to the Communist forces to remain at their posts and wait for orders. This order was ignored. On August 16, Chu Teh sent a memorandum to the American, British and Soviet Embassies in Chungking, demanding the right to participate in the Japanese surrender to the Allies. He especially called upon the United States "to stop lend-lease to the Kuomintang Government immediately." In a telegram to the Generalissimo he said: "The Chinese people are dissatisfied with you and your government which cannot represent the broad masses." [1]

---

[1] Dallin, *Soviet Russia and the Far East*, pp. 233-234.

The immediate objective of the Chinese Communists was the control of Manchuria. There must have been some prior communication with the Soviet Union because it was no time at all before the Chinese Reds were pouring into Manchuria and receiving Japanese arms that had been turned over to the Soviet armies in that area. The collapse of Japan found the Nationalist armies still in South and West China, far from the vital ports and industrial centers held by the Japanese. Chinese Communist armies, in contrast, lay along the lower Yangtze Valley and near all the major centers of North China. But in this race to gain possession of captured Japanese arms, the United States provided an air-lift that enabled the Generalissimo's armies to leapfrog Communist forces in their path and occupy the key cities and lines of communications. Navy transports later moved other Chinese divisions to Manchurian ports to begin occupation of the vital area.

To his credit General Albert Wedemeyer, who was in charge of the Chinese Theater, diagnosed the situation accurately and acted with promptness and decision to avert this initial Communist crisis and prevent the Chinese Communists from taking control of China's key areas from the Japanese. He was concerned with Russian policy in that area and requested the United States War Department to send seven American divisions to China "in order to create a barrier through North China and Manchuria." The Joint Chiefs replied that the divisions were "not available." [2]

The Japanese resistance in Manchuria was practically nil, contrary to the belief that Russian forces were necessary in the Pacific War to accept their surrender. General Wedemeyer testified in the MacArthur Hearings that " . . . The Japanese were completely co-operative as soon as they got their order to lay down their arms. We had no trouble with them whatsoever. . . . It wasn't necessary—one person would go and take charge of thousands of them. There was no resistance whatsoever; they became docile and co-operative." [3]

Strategically, Manchuria was the key area of conflict, and an especially complicated one because of the presence of Soviet forces. These had engaged the Japanese Manchurian army for less than a week after the Soviet declaration of war on Japan in August, 1945. In the winter of 1945-46, several Chinese-Soviet disputes developed, as differences emerged over the status of the Dairen-Port Arthur area and it became known that the U.S.S.R. had removed an important segment of Japanese industrial machinery from Manchuria as "war booty." In addition, Soviet forces occupied various nontreaty areas in Manchuria for some weeks beyond the originally scheduled date of withdrawal, December 3, 1945. This had

2 Wedemeyer, *Wedemeyer Reports*, p. 348.

3 *Military Situation in the Far East*, Part 3, p. 2493.

been postponed until February 1, 1946, in accordance with an agreement between the Chinese and Soviet Government.

The Chinese Communists undoubtedly benefitted from the presence of the Russians in Manchuria, for the Kuomintang was hampered by the timing of Soviet withdrawals and by Moscow's refusal, under its interpretation of the August, 1945, treaty, to allow Nationalist troops to enter the region by way of Dairen. The Russians also played a part in the acquisition of surrendered Japanese military equipment which was turned over to the Chinese Reds. In order to obtain their logistic supplies from certain bases, Nationalist troops had to keep the lines open, which resulted in skirmishes between them and the Chinese Communists. As the Communists made sneak attacks on Chiang's troops whenever there was a chance, fighting began to spread to various parts of China.

What had been feared by the American Government—a civil war in China after the Second World War—was now actually happening, and it worried some United States officials. General Patrick J. Hurley, who was then (September 1945) in Washington for consultation, was urged by President Truman and Secretary of State James Byrnes to go back to Chungking to continue his mediation between the Chinese Government and the Communists. Towards the end of November, 1945, Hurley had planned to return to Chungking and then suddenly resigned as Ambassador to China on the ground that career men in the Department of State were sabotaging American policy towards China and siding with the Chinese Communists.[4]

Until late in 1945, it was the official policy of the United States to support the Chinese Nationalist Government. We were determined to keep their armies in the field to fight the Japanese. Officially, we took no hand in China's internal strife, but in 1945 our policy changed to one of intervention; and thereafter our intervention was in aid of the Chinese Communists and in opposition to Chiang Kai-shek. This change of policy which continued from 1945 until 1949 was the result of an anti-Chiang faction within the Department of State, in the press, and in public debates. Dr. Stanley K. Hornbeck, a Far East expert who played an important role in matters during most of the years from 1918 to 1944, remarked:

It was then, in the year 1945—and not before then—that the government of the United States, first having taken action inconsistent with tradition and commitment in regard to China, embarked upon what became a course of intervention in regard to the civil conflict, the conflict between the National Government and the Communists in China. It was then that words and action of the Govern-

---

4 See Ambassador Hurley's letter of resignation to President Truman, November 26, 1945, *United States Relations with China*, pp. 581-584.

ment of the United States began to be expressive of an 'against' and a 'for' attitude; then and thereafter that the Government of the United States brought to bear pressures, pressures upon the National Government, pressures which were not 'against' the Communists but were on their behalf, pressures not to the disadvantage of the Communists, but, in effect, to the disadvantage of the National Government.[5]

The Senate Internal Security Subcommittee had found in its investigation that John Carter Vincent, head of the China Desk in the Department of State, was a close friend and associate of Owen Lattimore who was "from some time beginning in the 1930's, a conscious articulate instrument of the Soviet conspiracy." [6] On June 10, 1945, Lattimore wrote a letter to President Truman expressing his fear that the United States policy of aiding the Chinese Nationalist Government would establish a precedent for Soviet aid to the Chinese Communists, thus causing division in China. Lattimore urged a revision of the existing United States policy of aiding Chiang.[7] He followed up his letter to the President with a visit to the White House on July 3, at which time he left with the President a memorandum stating that China should be unified under a coalition government with the Chinese Communists having real power within the coalition.[8]

Lattimore's views clearly reflected the position of the left-wing, anti-Chiang group that United States policy toward exclusive support of the National Government in China should be halted. Coincidentally, a change of policy was also recommended by the U.S. Communist Party in one of their resolutions which declared that reactionaries in the United States were pursuing a dangerous policy of preventing a "strong, united, and democratic China," and were bolstering the reactionary, incompetent Chiang Kai-shek regime. They also charged that these "reactionaries" were supporting the idea of coming to terms with the Mikado in the hope of maintaining Japan as a reactionary bulwark in the Far East.[9]

The resolution of June 20, 1945, further charged that substantial influential forces in the Department of State were "seeking a compromise peace which will preserve the power of the Mikado after the war at the expense of China and other far eastern peoples and directed against the Soviet Union." It was also charged that forces in the United States Government "plan using the coming defeat of Japan for imperialistic aims, for maintaining a reactionary puppet Kuomintang regime in China, for obtaining American imperialist domination in the Far East." [10] The

[5] *Institute of Pacific Relations, Final Report*, pp. 202-203.

[6] *Ibid.*, p. 224.

[7] Owen Lattimore to President Truman, June 10, 1945, *Institute of Pacific Relations, Hearings*, Exhibit No. 473, Part 9, p. 3087.

[8] *Ibid.*, Exhibit No. 530-D, Part 10, p. 3387.

[9] *Political Affairs* (July 1945), p. 581.

[10] *Ibid.*, p. 583.

Communists demanded that we "remove from the State Department all pro-Fascist and reactionary officials," and also called for "full military aid to the Chinese guerillas led by the heroic Eighth and Fourth Armies." [11] In the same manner, the Seventh National Congress of the Chinese Communist Party meeting in Yenan on May 1, 1945, issued a report calling on the Chinese people "to set up an independent, free, democratic, unified, strong, and prosperous new China." [12] A resolution clearly stated what the party's objective was—a coalition government.

These two Communist pronouncements and the Lattimore letter and memorandum to President Truman were significant. Both Lattimore and the Communists were calling for a "strong, united, democratic" China, and for curtailing rather than augmenting United States support of China's Nationalist Government. They wanted military supplies diverted to the Chinese Communists. Both wanted changes in the Department of State. Perhaps the parallel would not seem important except for the fact that Owen Lattimore was trying to impress President Truman with these views.

In the Department of State at this time the persons most responsible for our Far Eastern policy were Joseph C. Grew, Joseph W. Ballantine, and Eugene Dooman. All three had many years of experience in Japan. Within four months, from the time of the Communist Party resolution, they were removed from the Department of State and were replaced by officers who either had little Far Eastern experience, or who were pro-Communist. The position of Director of the Office of Far Eastern Affairs passed from Ballantine, who was Japanese-trained and had experience in China continuously from 1919 to 1945, to John Carter Vincent, a sympathizer with Chinese Communism.[13] A change of personnel in the Department led to a change of policy toward Nationalist China, which ultimately played into the hands of the Chinese Communists.

On November 10, 1945, the Joint Chiefs of Staff issued a directive to General Wedemeyer which declared "American military aid to China will cease immediately if evidence compels the United States Government to believe that any Chinese troops receiving such aid are using it to support any government which the United States cannot accept, to conduct civil war, or for aggressive or coercive purposes." [14] The implications drawn from this directive is that Chiang Kai-shek was told that the United States would continue aid but it was not to be used to fight a

---

11 *Ibid.*, p. 584.

12 *Institute of Pacific Relations, Hearings*, Part 3, p. 812.

13 *Institute of Pacific Relations, Hearings*, Part 2, pp. 614, 617, Exhibit Nos. 170 and 172; see also Part 10, p. 3377, and *Biographical Registry of Department of State*, September 1, 1944, p. 9.

14 *Military Situation in the Far East*, Part 3, p. 2460.

civil war. Gradually, under pro-Communist pressure, United States policy
was being revised to one of including the Communists in a coalition
government.

On November 27, the Secretaries of War, State, and Navy met "to
define a new policy" for China. During the course of this meeting Secretary Byrnes said that "taking everything into account, perhaps the wise
course would be to try to force the Chinese Government and the Chinese
Communists to get together on a compromise basis, perhaps telling Generalissimo Chiang Kai-shek that we will stop the aid to his government
unless he goes along with this. . . ." Toward the end of the meeting, Dean
Acheson summed up the elements of the program that was then being
shaped up by the Department of State, and which included "to continue
to try to bring about a political settlement under Chiang Kai-shek with
Communist participation, *with pressure on Chiang Kai-shek to be pliable
in this matter.*" [15]

On November 28, 1945, Vincent outlined a new United States course
in China when he recommended that the United States persuade the Chinese Nationalists to include other political elements in the Government.
The Nationalist Government was a one-party government, and the United
States could not support that government by "military intervention in an
internecine struggle." He called for a declaration of truce between the
Nationalists and the Chinese Communists, to be backed by the United
States, Britain, and Soviet Russia.[16] This policy was echoed by Secretary
of State Byrnes who, in a memorandum of December 9, said: "Our
longer-range goal" was the development of a "strong, united and democratic China." The memorandum then urged that the Central Government of China and the various "dissident elements" come to a compromise, and that Chiang's Government be broadened to include "groups
who are now without voice in the Government of China." The memorandum further stated that the United States would exert its influence
"in such a way as to encourage concessions by the Central Government,
by the so-called [sic] Communists and by the other factions." [17]

This reference to the "so-called Communists" shows how completely
Byrnes and Truman had been misled by their advisers in the Department
of State. In another significant paragraph of the memo, Byrnes said:
"Pending the outcome of General Marshall's discussions with Chinese
leaders in Chungking . . . *further transportation of Chinese troops to
North China will be held in abeyance.*[18]

The implication that the Chinese Reds were not really Communists,
but something of a different nature, was a tragic mistake. The fact that

---

15 *The Forrestal Diaries,* p. 123. Feis, *The China Tangle,* p. 404. Italics mine.

16 *Institute of Pacific Relations, Hearings,* Part 7, p. 2207.

17 *Military Situation in the Far East,* Part 5, p. 3184. Italics mine.

18 *Ibid.,* p. 3185.

Russia had an overwhelming influence in Communist China had been long known, or should have been known. For instance, Army Intelligence in 1945 drew up a documented report which demonstrated this influence and domination. A persistent and disturbing factor has been the reluctance of some State Department officials to accept this report as authoritative evidence. Instead the pro-Communist views of our Foreign Service officers prevailed. At the time (1945) that Army Intelligence drafted their report, Raymond Ludden, a Foreign Service officer of the Department of State, upon his return from an extended trip into Red-controlled portions of China, told an American journalist that "the so-called Communists are agrarian reformers of a mild, democratic stripe more than anything else." [19]

When President Truman announced the acceptance of Hurley's resignation on November 27, 1945, he appointed General George C. Marshall, at the suggestion of Clinton P. Anderson, then Secretary of Agriculture, as his special representative in China to continue the work previously begun by Hurley.[20] The Marshall Mission to China was one of the major factors contributing to the Red conquest of that nation. It was unfortunate, according to General Wedemeyer, that Marshall had never had either the time or inclination or "opportunity to study the methods of Communism; and he had implicitly believed the reports of his old friend, General Stilwell, who ascribed all ills of China to the government of Chiang Kai-shek. . . . Moreover, by the time he arrived in China on his fatal mission, George Marshall was physically and mentally too worn out to appraise the situation correctly." [21] His mission in China was to carry out a policy set for him by the Department of State that was utterly impossible to execute. The failure of Marshall's China mission had its roots in the dubious instructions which were given to him.

As one reads the directive for Marshall as announced officially by President Truman on December 15, 1945, it is quite apparent why we lost China to the Communists. In his statement the President advocated a coalition government for China: "The United States is cognizant that the present National Government of China is a 'one-party' government and believes that peace, unity, and democratic reform in China will be furthered if the basis of this government is broadened to include other political elements in the country." To Chinese ears this naturally sounded like a vote of nonconfidence in the Generalissimo and a demand that power be shared with the Communists. Another phrase read: "The existence of autonomous armies, such as that of the Communist army, is inconsistent with, and actually makes impossible, political unity in China. With the institution of a broadly representative government, autonomous

[19] Congressional Record, June 5, 1951, p. 6142.

[20] U. S. Relations with China, p. 132

[21] Wedemeyer Reports, p. 370

armies should be eliminated as such, and all armed forces in China integrated effectively into the Chinese Nationalist Army." [22] Chiang Kai-shek had said on several occasions, let the Communists lay down their arms first, and then we will take them into the government. But the Marshall directive said, take them in first, and then let them lay down their arms.

Perhaps the last paragraph in the directive is the most important one in outlining United States policy: "As China moves toward peace and unity *along the lines described above,* the United States would be prepared to assist the National Government in every reasonable way to rehabilitate the country, improve the agrarian and industrial economy, and establish a military organization capable of discharging China's national and international responsibilities for the maintenance of peace and order." [23]

One becomes immediately suspicious of the directive because of the phrase "peace and unity" as a condition of our assistance.[24] Some months before the "peace and unity" line gained official status, it appeared in the usual leftist circles around the country. For example, it appeared in an article by Lawrence K. Rosinger who later took the fifth amendment before the Senate Internal Security Subcommittee.[25] Henry Wallace had made three or four speeches, always demanding "peace and unity" in China. The phrase became sort of a watchword, and then showed up in the President's directive.

In analyzing the Marshall directive, we may ask the question, how do you get unity in a country where there is an armed rebellion? Of course, one way is to put it down by force, but in the Marshall directive we said to Chiang Kai-shek, you cannot do that because first we must have "peace and unity." The only way you get that is to yield to the Reds. This the Generalissimo was unwilling to do. Admiral Leahy, who was present when Marshall received his directive, emphatically admonished Marshall that his China instructions were wholly at variance with President Roosevelt's attitude toward China and the Far East. The discussion became acrimonious and resulted in a permanent breach of friendship between Leahy and Marshall. Jonathan Daniels quoted Leahy as saying: "I was present when Marshall was going to China. He said he was going to tell Chiang that he had to get on with the Communists or without help from us. He said the same thing when he got back. I thought he was wrong

---

22 *U. S. Relations with China,* p. 608.

23 *Ibid.,* p. 609.

24 For a critical evaluation of the Marshall directive see Testimony of General Wedemeyer, *Military Situation in the Far East,* Part 3, pp. 2323-2324. According to Secretary of State Byrnes, Marshall was told not in writing but verbally by President Truman that regardless of success or failure of his efforts for a coalition, the "Chinese Nationalists were not to be left entirely without help." Byrnes, *All in One Lifetime,* p. 330.

25 *Foreign Policy Bulletin* October 24, 1945.

both times." [26] General Wedemeyer even told Marshall when shown his directive that in his judgment "it would be impossible to bring those two divergent groups [Nationalist and Communists] together." [27]

The United States policy in China, as enunciated by President Truman and implemented by General Marshall, was based on the assumption that the civil war in China was strictly an internal matter and had no connection with Soviet Russia's policy of expansion by revolution. This view received enthusiastic support from various United States publicists. A good example of the type of material is a pamphlet written by Eleanor Lattimore. She said:

> When we speak of the Chinese Communists, we should remember that they stand for something rather different from what is ordinarily meant by the word, 'Communist.' They are not advocating the Russian system for China, and, unlike the Russians, they maintain the rights of private property and enterprise in the areas under their control. Because their chief interest at the moment is in improving the economic conditions of the Chinese farmer and in increasing the number of people capable of taking part in political life, they are often described as a peasant party. They have established a system of popular elections in the regions under their control; they favor extending the vote to the people of the rest of the country; and they have long declared that they would support a democratic republic in which not only they themselves but all other Chinese political parties would be represented.[28]

Maxwell S. Stewart, an editor of *The Nation,* in a pamphlet written for the Institute of Pacific Relations, observed: "As China is not like any other country, so Chinese communism has no parallel elsewhere. You can find in its resemblances to Communist movements in other countries and you can also find resemblances to the grass-roots populist movements that have figured in American history. . . ." [29] Raymond Gram Swing, popular radio commentator with a large audience, described the Chinese Communists as "agrarian radicals trying to establish democratic processes." [30]

The question that baffles some historians is the authorship of the instructions for the Marshall Mission. Senator H. Alexander Smith of New Jersey, in questioning Marshall during the MacArthur Hearings, referred to a report General MacArthur made in 1945 in which he evaluated the armed forces in China. The final paragraph of the report reads as follows: "General Marshall was appointed on December 11, 1945, sat down with Dean Acheson to write out the instructions President Truman was

---

[26] Jonathan Daniels. *The Man from Independence* (Philadelphia: J. B. Lippincott Company, 1950), p. 317.

[27] *Military Situation in the Far East,* Part 3, p. 2326.

[28] Eleanor Lattimore, "China Yesterday and Today," *Institute of Pacific Relations, Final Report,* pp. 208-209.

[29] Maxwell S. Stewart, "Wartime China", *Ibid.,* Part 11, p. 3798.

[30] *Ibid.,* See also *Amerasia,* September, 1943, p. 282.

to give him." [31] When Marshall appeared before the committee, he denied writing the directive. "In the first place I have not a recollection," he said, "of the reference in there that I sat down in the State Department and drew up this policy. *I did not.*" [32] Senator Smith had previously asked: "Do you recall who had a hand in the preparation of the directive that sent you to China?" To which Marshall replied: "At that time, Senator, Mr. Byrnes was Secretary of State, and I presume he had a hand in it; Mr. Acheson was Under Secretary of State, and I presume he had a hand in it; John Carter Vincent was the head of the China group in the State Department, certainly he had a hand in it. I do not know what others did." [33] James F. Byrnes, who was Secretary of State at the time of the Mission gave a different version. He said: "The President made no change in that policy except upon the recommendation of General Marshall or with his approval." [34]

When Secretary of State Acheson testified on this subject, he supplied the senators with his version of the Marshall instructions:

At the end of November 1945, Secretary Byrnes and General Marshall met. This was after Marshall was asked to go to China. Secretary Byrnes read him a memorandum suggesting an outline of instructions for him. General Marshall did not approve of it. General Marshall said that he would wish to try his own hand, assisted by some of his associates, in drafting the instructions. This he did; and a draft was prepared by him, in conjunction with four generals who were working very closely with General Marshall. This was submitted to Secretary Byrnes. On the 8th of December Secretary Byrnes made his suggestions to General Marshall, that is, suggestions of changes of alterations, or additions to the draft prepared by General Marshall. General Marshall's draft, with Secretary Byrnes' suggestions, was discussed at a meeting in Secretary Byrnes' office on Sunday morning, December 9, 1945, by Secretary Byrnes, General Marshall, Mr. John Carter Vincent, General Hull, and myself. I was then Under Secretary of State. Those of us went over the instructions. General Marshall approved the suggestions made by Secretary Byrnes and we had a completely agreed draft.[35]

The testimony of the various Cabinet officers is obviously contradictory. It is the reflection of the confused policy that cost us our Chinese allies, and of the lack of candor that has beclouded the whole issue.

According to the Senate Internal Security Subcommittee which went into the matter carefully, the directive was originally drafted by John Carter Vincent, director of the Far Eastern Office of the Department of State, who was under the influence of Owen Lattimore. Despite the

---

31 *Military Situation in the Far East,* Part 1, pp. 466-467.

32 Testimony of General George C. Marshall, May 9, 1951, *Ibid.,* Part 1, p. 467.

33 *Ibid.,* p. 459.

34 Byrnes, *Speaking Frankly,* p. 226.

35 Testimony of Dean Acheson, June 4, 1951, *Military Situation in the Far East,* Part 3, p. 1848.

abundant evidence that the Chinese Communists were an integral part of a world Communist movement, the myth that they were not became official United States policy under Vincent. In a memorandum dated December 10, 1945, Vincent said: "The President has asked General Marshall to go to China . . . for the purpose of bringing to bear . . . the influence of the United States. . . . Specifically, General Marshall will endeavor to influence the Chinese government to call a national conference of representatives of the major political elements, to bring about the unification of China, and concurrently, effect a cessation of hostilities particularly in North China." [36] The Internal Security Subcommittee unanimously concluded:

> . . . demand for the support of the idea of a coalition government in China, made in May, 1945, by Mao Tse-tung, taken up by the American Communist Party, and recommended to the President by Owen Lattimore in his memorandum of July 3, 1945, was adopted and sponsored by Vincent; memoranda elaborating upon the idea were drafted by Vincent and were affirmed by the Secretary of State; these became the basis of the policy in relations to China which was announced by President Truman on December 15, 1945, and in pursuance of that policy General Marshall was sent to China to bring to bear upon the Chinese National Government the pressure of United States influence.[37]

As to the main possibilities and probabilities concerning what authorship was involved in Marshall's instructions, it must be kept in mind that Marshall himself knew exactly what he wanted ever since the Stilwell debacle. As a prominent military officer in China told Professor David N. Rowe in 1948, in Peiping, "Trying to brief General Marshall was like trying to teach an old bald eagle how to fly." [38]

When Marshall arrived in China at the end of 1945, according to the State Department's own *White Paper*, the Nationalist Government "possessed an estimated five to one superiority in combat troops and in rifles, a practical monopoly of heavy equipment and transport, and an unopposed air arm." [39] Chiang's divisions were chasing the Communists northward, and the prospect of a Nationalist victory was at its highest.

General Marshall arrived in Chungking on December 20. Following an interview between Marshall and Chiang, an American general asked the Generalissimo what he thought of the future prospects of peace talks now that Marshall had come to China as mediator. Chiang replied: "The key to this question is in the hands of Soviet Russia. You have to

---

[36] *Institute of Pacific Relations, Hearings*, Part 7, pp. 2201-2202; *Memoirs* by Harry S. Truman, *Years of Trial and Hope* (New York: Doubleday and Company Inc., 1956), II, p. 72.

[37] *Institute of Pacific Relations, Final Report*, p. 202; Morris, *No Wonder We Are Losing*, pp. 91-92.

[38] Letter to author, February 3, 1961.

[39] *U.S. Relations with China*, p. 311.

get your answer from Moscow." [40] Marshall seemed to be successful in the initial stages. On the day of his arrival, Chou En-lai announced that the Communists would work for an immediate truce to end the civil war and seek negotiations for a coalition government. This offer was sweet to Marshall's ears. From the start, Marshall, long under the influence of General Stilwell, appeared to have been captivated by Chou En-lai who represented the Communists as "agrarian reformers" and the Chungking government as being "despotic" and "reactionary."

At the beginning of 1946, General Marshall arranged a truce between the Communists and Nationalist forces, effective January 13. It provided for a Committee of Three to be set up, consisting of a representative of the Nationalist Government, one from the Communists, and an American. It would undertake to enforce truces between the then winning Nationalists and the losing Communists. An executive headquarters was to be set up in Peiping for the purpose of carrying out these cease-fire agreements.[41] The existing position of the two warring Chinese elements was to be "frozen." However, this truce included a proviso that the Nationalist forces were permitted to move into Manchuria and take it over from the Russians as provided for by the Sino-Russian Treaty of August, 1945.[42] The truce teams were flown in American planes to areas of conflict or threatening conflict to halt or prevent hostilities. Each representative had equal powers of decision, and all questions had to be settled back in headquarters by the unanimous consent of the Committee of Three.[43]

A Political Consultation Conference had been arranged earlier, to begin on January 10, 1946. Represented were eight Kuomintang members, seven Communists, five members of the China Youth Party, nine delegates from the four parties of the Democratic League and nine independents. The delegates agreed to try to form a coalition government. After a transitional period, the coalition was to be replaced by a constitutional regime. The latter was to be formed through the actions of a National Assembly to be convened on May 5, 1946. One of the most important matters agreed upon was the integration of the Chinese Red Armies with the Nationalist forces. While Japan was the main enemy, it would appear sensible to integrate the armies to defeat her. But once Imperial Japan surrendered, the move was a tragic mistake. The Generalissimo had seen how callously the Reds had disregarded a similar integration agreement in 1937 when he formed a united front with them, in their common war against Japan. He was willing to try it again, however, in view of Marshall's belief that a coalition government could be

40 Chiang Kai-shek, *Soviet Russia in China*, pp. 155-156.

41 *U.S. Relations with China*, pp. 609-610.

42 *Ibid.*, p. 137.

43 *Ibid.*, p. 609.

achieved with the Communists, and that the United States considered such an end not only desirable but imperative.

The military reorganization provided that during the first period of twelve months Government troops would be reduced from 354 divisions to ninety divisions. During the same period the Chinese Communists could retain eighteen divisions. During the second period of six months the Government could keep fifty divisions and the Chinese Communists ten divisions. Government troops would maintain a ratio of five to one vis-à-vis the Communist troops. The Nationalist Government and the Chinese Communist Party were both required to submit to the Military Sub-Committee within three weeks of the agreement, a list of ninety and eighteen divisions to be retained.[44] Of a Nationalist Army of twenty divisions, six would be composed of mixed Government and Communist forces. Although the plans for military reorganization and integration were to the advantage of the Communists, actually the integration of the Communist forces into the National Army would be as difficult to achieve as "to negotiate with the tiger for its skin." [45] But the agreements showed that the Nationalist Government was willing to make important concessions. Had they been faithfully carried out by the Reds, China would certainly have made a long stride towards national unification.[46]

Following the cease-fire order and the conclusion of agreements on the reorganization and integration of Communist forces into the National Army, and the agreements reached at the Political Consultative Conference, it was generally thought that China could begin a peaceful reconstruction at last. General Marshall, too, thought the one phase of his mediation mission had come to an end. Soon afterward he returned to Washington to report to President Truman.

Before he left, he talked to a group of news correspondents of a fantastic plan of establishing a "little West Point" for training Communist officers in Kalgan, a city some 124 miles west of Peiping at the Great Wall, the gateway to Mongolia. The American officers would not only teach American military staff methods to higher-echelon Communist officers, but they would also instruct them in the use of American weapons. Obviously, the Communists would have to be furnished with such weapons if they were to learn how to use them.[47] For some reason, however, the "little West Point" for the Communists was never set up, although the American colonels who were to staff the academy began arriving every day in Peiping, until, by early summer there were at least thirty of them installed in a wing of Executive Headquarters.

[44] Ibid., p. 141.

[45] Chiang Kai-shek, Soviet Russia in China, p. 162.

[46] Cheng, A History of Sino-Russian Relations, p. 287.

[47] Raymond J. de Jaegher and Irene Corbally Kuhn, The Enemy Within (New York: Doubleday and Company, Inc., 1952), pp. 271-272.

After Marshall had left for the United States in March, 1946, the Communists tore up the cease-fire agreement by pouring troops into Manchuria, thus setting at naught the cease-fire agreement and extending the area of their rebellion. The Nationalists naturally felt justified in any form of retaliation after this flagrant disregard of the truce terms.[48] On April 15, 1946, the day after the withdrawal of Russian troops from Changchun, the Chinese Communist forces attacked the city, occupying it on April 18. The action was a violation of the cessation of hostilities order and an act which was to have serious consequences. It made the victorious Chinese Communist generals in Manchuria overconfident and less amenable to compromise, but even more disastrous was the effect upon the Nationalist Government. It greatly strengthened the hand of the ultra-reactionary groups in the Government, which were then in a position to say that the Communists had demonstrated that they never intended to carry out their agreements.[49] On April 18, the same day Marshall returned to Chungking, fighting spread to Manchuria. With the help of American forces, seven more government divisions were transported to that area. After bloody fighting, government forces occupied Szepingkai on May 19 and pushed toward Changchun. Four days later the Generalissimo flew to Mukden personally to control the situation.[50]

After seizing Changchun, government forces continued to advance towards Harbin to the north and Kirin to the east. General Marshall then asked for a truce and the Generalissimo complied with this request. The truce sponsored and pushed by Marshall, with all the diplomatic resources of the United States at his disposal, forced the Generalissimo to halt his anti-Communist offensive at a time when it was on the verge of wiping out large bodies of Chinese Communist troops. This was a crucial moment because the advantage lay with the forces of the Nationalists. The Reds had not yet been able to train their conscripts with new weapons handed them by the Russians.

The truce was effected on June 7, and a formal agreement was signed on June 26, for the cessation of hostilities in Manchuria, freezing the situation there as of June 7.[51] But again the truce did not last long, with the blame put upon the Nationalist Government. Madam Sun Yat-sen, speaking for the Communists denounced the "reactionary" policies of the Kuomintang, deplored its decision to achieve a "solution by force," and accused the United States of supporting a government not "truly representative" of the Chinese people.[52] Nathaniel Peffer in the New York

---

48 John Leighton Stuart, "How the Communists Got China," *U.S. News and World Report*, October 1, 1954, pp. 41-42.

49 *U.S. Relations with China*, p. 149.

50 *Ibid.*, pp. 154-155.

51 *Ibid.*, p. 158, 162.

52 *New York Times*, July 23, 1946.

Times weekly magazine section said that the "Nationalists had scuttled the truce."[53] This was untrue in view of the fact that, when the truce was ordered, the Communists had taken advantage of it to expand their area of control.

This truce, which ended the Nationalist offensive in Manchuria, enabled the Communists to regroup and receive further Soviet assistance. A year later, the Red armies were able to launch an offensive which ultimately gave them all of the mainland of China. Christopher Rand, an American correspondent, reported from Mukden in 1947: "Last summer the government had nine armies here totalling perhaps 200,000 regular troops and including some of the best American-trained and American equipped units in China. The Communists were no match for them, as had been proved at the pitched battle of Szepingkai in the preceding spring. . . . Most observers think they could easily have taken the Communists' Manchurian capital of Harbin. They were prevented from doing so by the truce imposed during General George C. Marshall's attempt to mediate the civil war." [54]

As a consequence of the Marshall truce, fighting continued to spread to many areas. The Soviet press violently attacked American policy towards China for encouraging the civil war, and the Chinese Communist Party issued a declaration on July 7 echoing this sentiment. The Communists began to make trouble for American Marines in China. On July 29, 1946, a United States Marine convoy of trucks moving supplies from Tientsen to Peiping was ambushed by about 600 Communists. Four Americans were killed, including the officer in command.[55] Obviously, the purpose of this attack was to create an incident to support the propaganda then being conducted by the international Communists for the withdrawal of American forces in China. It was a tragic mistake for the United States to stop a supply of arms to the Nationalists at the very moment when the Communists began their anti-American activities. Early in April, following the Chinese Communists' breach of the cease-fire agreement, the American Government had stopped its $500,000,000 loan to the Nationalist Government.[56] At the same time no action whatever was taken against the Chinese Communists, despite their violations of the cease-fire agreement. In fact, United States officials did not adopt any measures to prevent Soviet Russia's arming of the Chinese Communists in Manchuria with Japanese weapons. This inertia dealt a severe blow to the anti-Communist forces and constituted a great boost to neutralism.

As hopes of peace swiftly disappeared, Washington began again to

---

[53] *New York Times Sunday Magazine*, May 1, 1949.

[54] *New York Herald Tribune*, June 13, 1947.

[55] Testimony of Admiral Charles Maynard Cooke, October 19, 1951, *Institute of Pacific Relations, Hearings*, Part 5, p. 1495.

[56] *Institute of Pacific Relations, Hearings*, Part 10, p. 3709.

reconsider policy and returned to more normal diplomatic practices. Dr. J. Leighton Stuart, a renowned Chinese missionary-educator, was appointed American Ambassador on July 11, 1946, as Hurley's successor and Marshall's collaborator.[57] On July 23, Edwin Pauley reported that the Russians had incapacitated Manchuria's industrial plant by their confiscations,[58] and Washington reaffirmed its determination to keep the Marines in China. Stuart and Marshall, on August 10, issued a joint statement designed to direct world attention to the gravity of the situation. The American mediators pointed out that China was verging on economic catastrophe and that, although the public wanted a peaceful solution, the fighting "threatens to engulf the country and pass beyond the control of those responsible." [59] On the same day President Truman dispatched a note to Chiang Kai-shek, expressing his concern over the deteriorating situation and over the recalcitrance of the extremists in both parties. Implicit in this statement was the suggestion that America might have to redefine its policy towards China unless substantial progress could be observed in the achievement of a peaceful solution.[60]

Several days later, Chiang issued a statement blaming the Communists for the breakdown in negotiations. He stipulated that for the maintenance of peace the Communists would have to "give up their policy to use armed force to seize political power, to overthrow the Government and to install a totalitarian regime." [61] In another message to the Generalissimo at the end of the month, President Truman expressed the hope that the prompt end of the threat of wide-spread civil war in China would make it "feasible for the United States to plan for assisting in its industrial economy and rehabilitation of its agrarian reforms." [62]

General Claire Chennault has indicated the significance of the truces demanded by Marshall:

North of Hankow some 200,000 government troops had surrounded 70,000 Communist troops and were beginning a methodical job of extermination. The Communists appealed to Marshall on the basis of his truce proposal, and arrangements were made for fighting to cease while the Communists marched out of the trap and on to Shantung Province, where a large Communist offensive began about a year later. On the East River near Canton some 100,000 Communist troops were trapped by government forces. The truce teams effected their release and allowed the Communists to march unmolested to Bias Bay where they boarded junks and sailed to Shantung.

---

57 This appointment was urged by Chou En-lai.

58 *U.S. Relations with China*, pp. 596-604.

59 Text in *Ibid.*, pp. 648-649.

60 President Truman to Chiang Kai-shek, August 10, 1946, *Ibid.*, p. 652. *Truman Memoirs*, II, 82.

61 *Truman Memoirs*, II, 84.

62 President Truman to Chiang Kai-shek, August 31, 1946, *U.S. Relations with China*, p. 654.

The worst fiasco was at Kalgan Pass. This gap in the North China Mountains is a historic gateway between China and Manchuria. At the end of the war there were no organized Communists in Manchuria. Chinese Communists flocked from their base in northwest China through the Kalgan Pass to join the Russian troops in Manchuria. When the Chinese government troops occupied Manchuria they found the great industrial centers stripped bare of machinery and the tremendous arsenals of the famed Japanese Kwantung Army empty. There was no trace of either the Kwantung Army or its equipment.[63]

As a result of pressure from General Marshall, Chiang Kai-shek had agreed in June, 1946, to let the Communists retain Kalgan, which they had held since shortly after VJ day. On September 30, 1946, the Nationalist Government announced that it had begun operations for the capture of Kalgan. Chiang gave to Ambassador Stuart a reply to Marshall's anticipated objection: ". . . it was absolutely essential to the national welfare that the Government gain control of Kalgan, and that the occupation of this city by the Government would do much to prevent further military action by the Chinese Communists." The result was that Marshall became almost convinced that the time had come for his recall. He was convinced that Chiang was pursuing a policy of force under the cover of protracted negotiations.[64] That this, precisely, had been a standard tactic of the Communists appears to have been a little less clear to the General.

On October 10, the Nationalists captured Kalgan. Chiang, on October 16, agreed to issue a new basis for negotiations—an eight point proposal reiterating the government's desire for a peaceful solution. Quite naturally, these eight points were not acceptable to the Communists.[65] On November 8, just before the convening of the National Assembly, Chiang Kai-shek issued another statement in which he declared: "As further evidence of the sincere desire of the Government to achieve a lasting peace and political stability for the country, orders have been issued for all Government troops in China proper and the Northeast [Manchuria] to cease firing except as may be necessary to defend their present positions." [66] However, even this statement did not convince the Communists who stubbornly refused to participate in the National Assembly held on November 16. They wanted no part of any democratic institutions unless they had full control and could subvert them to totalitarian purposes. Chou En-lai came to call on Marshall on November 16 to ask for an American airplane ride to Yenan. At the same time he expressed the fear that the National Government would undertake offensive oper-

[63] Chennault, *Way of a Fighter*, pp. xiii-xiv, *Institute of Pacific Relations, Hearings*, Part 10, pp. 3709-3710.

[64] *U.S. Relations with China*, p. 190.

[65] *U.S. Relations with China*, pp. 674-675.

[66] *Ibid.*, pp. 677-678.

ations against Yenan and said that if this occurred "it would mean the end of all hope for a negotiated peace." [67]

General Marshall hastened to offer United States Army transportation for all Red personnel in China, adding, with a tender touch of solicitude: " . . . while he had had no information of National Government plans for an attack on Yenan, he would deplore such action and oppose it strongly." He also said that if "such an attack occurred he would consider that it terminated his mission." [68] In summing up his impressions of the breach in negotiations represented by Chou's departure for Yenan, Marshall thought the Nationalists obdurate because, they "were thoroughly convinced that the Communists would not carry out any agreement reached . . . and that the Communists would merely disrupt any government in which they participated." [69] Marshall later explained the refusal of the Communists to make a single concession toward accord and peace in very innocent terms: "The Communist Party had . . . defeated itself through its own suspicions." [70]

From the very beginning of Marshall's Mission the Communists were never sincere in working out any kind of a coalition government. It was all or nothing at all. Ambassador John Leighton Stuart after his experience with the Communists said: "Whatever their motives, the evidence seemed to me convincing that the Communists wanted a coalition but only on their terms. The Kuomintang were more hesitant or skeptical. But never in my experience with human beings have I encountered anything like the suspicions on both sides, especially among the Communists." [71] This supports a conclusion made by Congressman Walter H. Judd, who had spent many years in China, and who re-visited China during the latter part of 1945: "They (the Communists) do not want unity. What they want is all the advantages of appearing to want unity so they can get arms and sympathy and support from abroad, while at the same time having all the advantages of complete independence." [72]

Despite the stubborn attitude of the Reds, Marshall continued with his efforts for a coalition. On December 1, 1946, he firmly warned Chiang Kai-shek that the Nationalists could not expect to subdue the Communists because they were too strong, and that, therefore, it was imperative that "efforts be made to bring them into the Government." [73] On December 4, Chou En-lai sent a message to Marshall setting forth the Communist terms for reopening negotiations. They called for the dissolution

---

67 *Ibid.*, p. 208.

68 *Ibid.*

69 *Ibid.*, p. 209.

70 *Ibid.*, p. 210.

71 Stuart, "How the Communists Got China," *U.S. News and World Report* (October 1, 1954), p. 44.

72 *Institute of Pacific Relations, Hearings,* Part 7a, p. 2397.

73 *U.S. Relations with China,* p. 212.

of the National Assembly; the relocating of all Chinese troops to where they stood on January 13, 1946, when the Reds had certain advantages. The National Assembly which convened on November 16, 1946, was in session forty days. After a lengthy debate, a democratic constitution was actually adopted on Christmas day. This was no small feat to accomplish with an Assembly which was composed of 2,045 members of diverse political opinions and from all over China. It may be worthwhile to quote General Marshall's own words in his personal statement issued on January 7, 1947: "In fact, the National Assembly had adopted a democratic Constitution which in all major respects is in accordance with the principles laid down by the all-party Political Consultative Conference of last January. It is unfortunate that the Communists did not see fit to participate in the Assembly, since the constitution that has been adopted seems to include every major point that they wanted." [74]

Meanwhile, President Truman issued a "hands-off" statement of American policy on China on December 18. On January 6, 1947, he announced that General Marshall had terminated his mission.[75] Marshall was named to the Secretaryship of State the following day, as James F. Byrnes resigned. He left China on January 8; his mission, which lasted more than a year, ended in complete failure despite the untiring efforts of himself and his subordinates. The mission to China was based on a total misconception of the Chinese Communists and undoubtedly weakened the Nationalist Government of China and gave substantial assistance to the Communists in preparing for their ultimate conquest.

Prior to his departure, General Marshall issued a lengthy statement in which he equated reaction with distrust of Communism. He said: "On the side of the National Government . . . . there is a dominant group of reactionaries who have been opposed . . . to almost every effort I have made to influence the formation of genuine coalition government. . . . They were quite frank in publicly stating their belief that cooperation by the Chinese Communist Party in the government was inconceivable and that only a policy of force could definitely settle the issue" [76]

Although General Marshall, as Secretary of State, learned in his negotiations with Molotov that it was impossible for a democratic statesman like himself to collaborate with Communists, he had never seen fit to repudiate or retract his statement prior to his departure.

He showed that he never quite understood the nature of Communism, when he said in the same statement: "On the side of the Chinese Communist Party there are, I believe, liberals as well as radicals . . . . it has

---

[74] Stuart, "How the Communists Got China," *U.S. News and World Report*, pp. 44-45. For comment on the constitution see George Mallory, "China's New Constitution," *Foreign Affairs*, XXVI (1948), pp. 390-392.

[75] *U. S. Relations with China*, pp. 689-694; 217.

[76] *Ibid.*, p. 687.

appeared to me that there is a definite liberal group among the Communists . . . who would put the interests of the Chinese people above ruthless measures to establish a Communist ideology. . . . " [77]

Marshall also severely condemned Communist propaganda by saying "In the deliberate misrepresentation and abuse of the action, policies and purposes of our Government this propaganda has been without regard for the truth, without any regard whatsoever for the facts, and has given plain evidence of a determined purpose to mislead the Chinese people and the world and to arouse a bitter hatred of Americans." [78]

Responses to the Marshall report were immediate, and frequently they were sharp. Chiang referred to it as "friendly and constructive." [79] But Chen Li-fu, one of the right-wing leaders in the Kuomintang, complained that "if . . . he (Marshall) could have devoted a little more time in contact with members who take a leading part in the Kuomintang his appraisal of the Chinese situation in its proper breadth and depth might have been more enlightening." [80] In his reply to Marshall's statement, Chou En-lai deplored Marshall's failure to "point out that Chiang Kai-shek is the supreme leader of the reactionary clique in the (Kuomintang)," and that "it is too much for General Marshall to think that a bad government will become a good government under the leadership of the same Chiang Kai-shek. . . . " Chou castigated the American mediator for trying to conclude a truce while American goods and troops were being used by the Kuomintang for attacks upon the Communists. According to Chou, "this proves that the American government is intentionally supporting Chiang Kai-shek in the waging of large-scale civil war." [81] Of course, Chou En-lai did not mention aid—material and psychological—given to the Chinese Reds by Soviet Russia.

In certain quarters in the United States, Marshall's statement was viewed as favorable to the Communists, and arguments were advanced that the Washington officials should support the Kuomintang as a vital bulwark in the world-wide struggle against the advance of Communism. It was asserted that the Chinese Communists were receiving support from Soviet Russia, and that Americans should increase their aid to the Nationalist Government to prevent China from being reduced to a mere satellite in the Soviet orbit. It was also feared that the defeat of the Kuomintang would break the dikes and release the full flood-tide of Communism to spread rapidly to other parts of Asia. [82] Among others in the United States, the Marshall report was applauded as a sound and fair presen-

---

[77] *Ibid.*
[78] *Ibid.*
[79] *New York Times*, January 12, 1947.
[80] Harley Farnsworth MacNair and Donald F. Lach, *Modern Far Eastern International Relations* (New York: D. Van Nostrand Company, Inc., 1955), p. 538.
[81] *Ibid.*
[82] Dallin, *Soviet Russia and the Far East*, pp. 323-331.

tation. The view was advanced that no amount of American aid could possibly save the corrupt Kuomintang, and that the Chinese Communist movement enjoyed the support of the rank and file of Chinese people. The future of China lay in the hands of the Chinese.[83]

General Marshall was primarily a military man who had little knowledge of the nature of international Communism. He became an easy victim to the "crypto-Communists, or Communist-sympathizing sycophants, who played on his vanity to accomplish their own ends." "Otherwise," says General Wedemeyer, "he would never have believed that he could mix oil and water by reconciling the basically antagonistic aims of the Chinese Nationalists and the Moscow-supported Chinese Communists." [84]

At a press interview at Honolulu on January 11, 1947, General Marshall told the reporters that "he knew of no evidence that the Chinese Communists were being supported by Russia." [85] But either this assertion was made by the Secretary of State-designate in order not to offend the Soviet Union, or General Marshall changed his mind later, for in his statement regarding aid to China, given to the Committee on Foreign Relations of the Senate and the Committee on Foreign Affairs of the House of Representatives in executive session in February, 1948, he clearly declared: "The Chinese Communists obtained large quantities of Japanese arms in Manchuria, through direct or indirect Soviet connivance; the number of surrendering Japanese troops in Manchuria is estimated at 700,000." [86] This is an interesting commentary in view of the fact that Marshall, in his efforts to force Chiang Kai-shek to share power with the Communists, embargoed American supplies of arms and ammunition to China. The embargo, which prevented the anti-Communist forces in China from buying, much less being given, American arms and ammunition, was maintained from August, 1946, to July, 1947.

During all this period the Nationalist Government was unable to obtain arms or ammunition from us, while the Russians were supplying the Communists with unlimited supplies from Japanese stocks they had captured in Manchuria and from American Lend-Lease supplies delivered across the Pacific to Siberia after Germany's defeat, for Russia's use in a war against Japan which she never fought.

---

83 The best description of this viewpoint is John K. Fairbank, *The United States and China* (Cambridge: Harvard University Press, 1948).

84 *Wedemeyer Reports*, p. 370.

85 *New York Times*, January 12, 1947; General Marshall stated on February 20, 1948, that "in China we have no concrete evidence that it (the Communist effort) is supported by Communists from the outside." U.S. Congress, Committee of Foreign Affairs, *Hearings on United States Foreign Policy for a Post-War Recovery Program*, 80th Cong. 2d Sess. (Washington: Government Printing Office, 1947), Part II, 1555. The same view was reported by Ambassador J. Leighton Stuart to Marshall in October 1947. He said there was "little if any evidence of material assistance from Moscow." *United States Relations with China*, p. 832.

86 *U.S. Relations with China*, p. 381.

When an agreement was signed between the Nationalist and American governments on August 30, 1946, for the sale of American surplus property located in India, China and on seventeen Pacific islands, with an estimated procurement value of $900,000,000, the Chinese Communists became vehement in their denunciation of American aid to the Nationalists. They attacked Marshall for presuming to mediate between two Chinese parties while the United States furnished war supplies on a grand scale to one of the parties. Marshall himself recognized how untenable this made his position. He took pains to explain to Chou En-lai that the surplus property did not contain military materials, but consisted mainly of machinery, vehicles and communications equipment which would be of use to recovery of the Chinese economy. The Communists simply ignored this explanation. In order to prove his impartiality towards both sides, General Marshall advised the American government to stop the issuing of licenses for the export to China of military equipment. In late September, shipments of combat items from the Pacific Area to China were halted.[87]

Those were crucial years. China's plight was so bad that even the *New York Times* reported on June 22, 1947, that the guns of the Nationalists' armies were so worn and burned that "bullets fell through them to the ground." [88] The Communists, on the other hand, were well supplied by the Soviet Union. Admiral Charles Maynard Cooke, who commanded the United States Seventh Fleet in China waters in 1945-46, has so testified before the Senate Internal Security Sub-Committee:

SENATOR FERGUSON: What effect would the arming of the Nationalists have had as far as the Communists were concerned?
ADMIRAL COOKE: Of course, the Communists were being very well supplied in Manchuria by the Russians from arsenals and from captured Japanese guns and ammunition. We were practically certain that was going on, and of course, in our White Paper reported from our diplomatic representatives in Moscow that it was going on.
SENATOR FERGUSON: So we knew that the Communists were getting arms and ammunition and also it was our policy . . . to put an embargo on the Nationalists?
ADMIRAL COOKE: That is right.[89]

Continuing his testimony, Admiral Cooke stated that the Nationalists had a number of divisions equipped with American arms. When the flow of American ammunition was stopped, these divisions lost their power and were defeated. "The Nationalist defeat was due to so many things. One of them was due to the fact that when they about had the Commu-

---

[87] *Ibid.*, p. 181.
[88] *New York Times*, June 22, 1947.
[89] Testimony of Admiral Charles Maynard Cooke, October 19, 1951, *Institute of Pacific Relations, Hearings*, Part 5, p. 1496.

nists licked, *a truce* took place one way or another because the Commies would say, 'Well, we are going to play ball now.' " [90] Even after the Eightieth Congress appropriated $125,000,000 in April, 1948, for aid to the Chinese Nationalists, shipments were delayed, and, when the guns finally reached their troops in North China, they were without bolts and therefore useless.[91] General Claire Chennault, one of the most experienced and courageous "China hands," testified before the Senate Internal Security Sub-Committee on May 29, 1952, that the first shipment of American arms after the embargo did not arrive in Shanghai until December, 1948. By this time, it was too late.[92]

An official compilation prepared by the Department of Defense showed that from June 31, 1946, the approximate time when the embargo went into effect, there was no appreciable assignment of arms to China until the authorization by the Eightieth Congress in April, 1948, for arms aid of $125,000,000. This report shows that only $17,900,000 in Lend-Lease aid was supplied between June 30, 1946, and the time the China Aid Act of 1948 became effective, many months after its enactment. In addition the value of certain ammunition left behind by the Marines, and which was picked up by the Chinese, was given as $4,300,000.[93] The effect of the embargo was unquestionably devastating to the spirit and morale of the Nationalist forces. Admiral Cooke said that Marshall told him personally in August or September of 1946 that "with the embargo we had in effect first armed the Chinese Nationalists and then disarmed them." [94]

Marshall's entire mission was one of convenience to the Reds. Before he went to China, the Communists occupied a very small portion of China. Their Army numbered less than 300,000 badly equipped troops. When Marshall returned from China to be rewarded by Truman with an appointment as Secretary of State, the Communist-controlled area had greatly increased. The Communist Army had grown from 300,000 badly equipped troops to an Army of over 2,000,000 relatively well-equipped soldiers.

The testimony of General Marshall corroborates the conclusion that an arms embargo was used in an attempt to force Generalissimo Chiang Kai-shek to admit Communist elements into the Government.[95] This action played into the hands of the Communists as witnessed by a remark made

---

90 *Ibid.*, p. 1502. Italics mine.

91 *Ibid.*, p. 1504.

92 Testimony of General Claire Lee Chennault, May 29, 1952, *Institute of Pacific Relations, Hearings,* Part 13, pp. 4769-4770.

93 *Ibid.*, Part 5, p. 1504; Part 10, p. 3711. *Final Report,* p. 205.

94 U.S. Congress, Senate, Committee on the Judiciary, *Report on Internal Security for the Year 1956,* 84th Cong. 2nd Sess., Section XI (Washington: Government Printing Office, 1957), pp. 196-197.

95 *Military Situation in the Far East,* Part 1, p. 555. Sumner Welles, in *Seven Decisions that Shaped History,* remarks that Marshall attempted to "brow-beat Chiang Kai-shek" into bringing Communists into his government." p. 217.

by General Wedemeyer in the MacArthur Hearings. The Marshall Mission, he said, "was just like mixing oil and water. . . . I explained to him [Marshall] that from my observations . . . the Nationalist forces . . . at war's end controlled the largest area and the most people in China. They had the most power and they were determined not to relinquish any of that power." Wedemeyer continued: "The Chinese Communists had an army. The Nationalist Government had an Army, and in my judgment they would never give up their military forces because that was the source of their strength, and I tried to convey to my friend . . . General Marshall, my innermost thoughts in expressing to him my concern that it was impossible for him to bring about this coalition." [96] Marshall reacted angrily and said: "I am going to accomplish my mission and you are going to help me." [97]

Furthermore, in July 1946, Marshall gave his clearest manifestation of subservience to the Reds when, in obedience to the wishes of Chou En-lai, he vetoed the appointment of General Wedemeyer as Ambassador to China. Wedemeyer's appointment was on Truman's desk. Wedemeyer was awaiting his commission when Under Secretary of State Dean Acheson sent for him to say that his appointment had been cancelled. He read Wedemeyer a telegram from Marshall saying, "The Communists are protesting violently." [98] General Wedemeyer told Acheson that "he did not like the idea that the Communists had the power to determine who might be appointed to positions of responsibility within the United States Government." [99]

At the request of Secretary of Defense Forrestal, General Wedemeyer wrote an interesting memorandum as follows:

> General Marshall . . . had 'tried to get a quick solution to the China problem.' Now he was pessimistic. Some people, perhaps in responsible positions . . . might feel that China would be regenerated by first permitting the destruction of the old order, after which a new and better order would arise. This, I pointed out, was the Marxian doctrine which had been applied in Russia. A better solution in consonance with American interests and those of the whole free world was to recognize that China would be in trouble for a long time to come; that Soviet Communism would be 'the force moving into the vacuum created by the fall of the Nationalist Government;' and that the United States therefore had 'no other resource but to support Chiang Kai-shek and his government.'[100]

The morale and strength of the Nationalist Government, which was the foundation of Chiang Kai-shek's tenacious leadership in the war against Japan, was weakened because of the military and diplomatic mis-

---

96 *Military Situation in the Far East*, Part 3, p. 2305, 2463.

97 *Wedemeyer Reports*, p. 363.

98 *Military Situation in the Far East*, Part 3, pp. 2311-2312.

99 *Wedemeyer Reports*, p. 366.

100 *Ibid.*, p. 368.

takes committed by the Marshall Mission. Contributing to this weakness was the thread of misunderstanding and ineptness on the part of our officials, running through the whole postwar period and deriving from a belief that somehow we could get along with the Communists. Some of our officials didn't thoroughly understand Communist strategy and tactics, and they were of the opinion that a new "democratic" force was rising in China compatible with our interests. Nothing was farther from the truth.[101]

On several occasions General Marshall stated that he was never in the dark about Chinese Communism—that he knew he was dealing with Marxists and knew what their aims and nature were. "There was never any doubt in my mind," he remarked, "and never any thought there was any misunderstanding about it." [102] Yet Marshall persisted in pushing for a coalition policy. His efforts to achieve unification of China revolved around an insistence upon an alliance of the Nationalists with forces committed to their destruction, the Chinese Communists. General Wedemeyer has stated that it was unfortunate that General Marshall did not have available "the clear and forceful studies on the Russian situation which have been prepared at the request of President Truman." [103]

The tragedy of the Marshall Mission was that many of the policy makers either deliberately or unconsciously regarded the Chinese Communists as true "liberals" and "agrarian reformers" interested only in bringing "democracy" to China. Marshall from the very first apparently never understood the true nature and dualism of Communist leaders, like Chou En-lai, who could assume at will whatever intellectual posture the exigencies of the moment demanded. When Father de Jaegher sought to see Marshall at his headquarters in China in order to give a full account of his six years in Communist-controlled areas in China, he was obstructed by one of Marshall's own private secretaries who happened to be a Chinese Communist.[104]

The Marshall Mission to China came at a crucial time when the United States was at the peak of her military strength in the Pacific and the Nationalist Government was beginning an offensive to assert its own

---

101 In the fall of 1947, former Ambassador to Soviet Russia William C. Bullitt, on his return from his visit to China, reported that "the so-called mission sent to aid Chiang Kai-shek" had been instructed "not to advise him" with regard to the operation of his forces. He further stated that nearly half of the 1,500-man military mission was composed of fellow-travelers and Communist sympathizers." Utley, *The China Story*, pp. 41-42.

102 *Military Situation in the Far East*, Part 1, pp. 377-378. *Memoirs by Harry S. Truman*, II, pp. 90-91. Yet, in the early spring of 1946, the then Under Secretary of State Dean Acheson was pressing the House Foreign Affairs Committee to provide funds for Marshall's plan to arm 10 Chinese Red divisions, and authority to assign U.S. Army officers to train them.

103 *Wedemeyer Reports*, p. 368.

104 de Jaegher and Kuhn, *The Enemy Within*, pp. 274-276.

sovereignty over Manchuria and North China. Unquestionably, victory would have come to Chiang Kai-shek had Marshall given all-out military support. The balance of power was with the Nationalists against the Communists, and remained so until at least June, 1946. Chiang's divisions were chasing the Reds northward, with the prospect of victory at its highest, when Marshall undertook to bring about a coalition government and commenced to bring pressure on Chiang in order to force his compliance.[105]

We applied pressure upon the Nationalist Government and not upon the Communist. It would seem that we could have exerted pressure upon the Communist regime by letting it be known to Mao Tse-tung and Chou En-lai that unless they recognized the supremacy of the government of the republic, the United States would supply Chiang Kai-shek with such aid as he needed, and with no restrictions. But "we were insisting," says General Wedemeyer, "that Chiang both institute democratic reforms and collaborate with the Communists. We said we wanted a strong and independent China but refused the Nationalist Government the material and political aid and support without which it could not crush the Communists." [106]

Congressman Walter Judd made a cogent comparison. He said that when we aided the anti-Communist forces in Greece we didn't go into that country and say, "Listen, you ought to arrange a coalition with the Communists. You mustn't have a civil war. You mustn't have bloodshed. You must have a truce." Instead, we said, "We will help you only if you resist a coalition with the Communists and fight them instead." And we helped them build up their forces for that purpose. Even so, we did not make much headway until, six months later, we sent over General Van Fleet and authorized him to "advise and train at all levels." [107] It is interesting to note that the policy established by President Truman—known as the "Truman Doctrine"—saved Greece. But it was soon perverted to the "Marshall Plan"—an ambitious program of aid to friends and Communist foes alike.

In Greece, we said, "You must win the civil war." In China we said, "You must not win the civil war; you must have a coalition." Our policy in Greece was right. It succeeded. Our policy in China was wrong. It failed.

American policy in China was based on the assumption that it was both possible and necessary to co-operate with the Reds. During the period of the Marshall Mission, this utterly mistaken notion guided

---

105 *U.S. Relations with China,* pp. 312-314, p. 155ff. Testimony of John Carter Vincent, January 31, 1952, *Institute of Pacific Relations, Hearings,* Part 7, pp. 2215-2217.

106 *Wedemeyer Reports,* p. 377.

107 Statement by Walter Judd.

American policy, and China suffered the most serious consequences. General Marshall had had neither time, inclination, nor opportunity to study the methods of Communism. He had before him the conflicting testimony of two of his close personal friends—Stilwell and Wedemeyer. Unfortunately, he accepted Stilwell's personally prejudiced version of the situation in China.

The net result of Marshall's fifteen month mission to China is appropriately summed up in a sober epitaph written by General Chennault: "The trend of a gradually stronger central government was reversed and the military balance shifted again in favor of the Chinese Communists." [108]

---

[108] Chennault, *Way of a Fighter:* p. xii.

CHAPTER XV

THE IPR: TRANSMISSION BELT FOR
SOVIET PROPAGANDA

Foundation activity has an impact in the field of foreign affairs that is undeniable. It has influenced public opinion and has largely given direction to the international policy goals of our country. An outstanding example is the Institute of Pacific Relations which probably, more than any other single factor, conditioned our people to abandon the mainland of China to the Communists.

The IPR was originally developed in the early 1920's by a group of Hawaiian businessmen who were interested in the social and economic problems of the Pacific. The first conference was held in 1925 when delegates from Korea, China, Japan, Australia, New Zealand, the Philippines, and the United States came to form this important organization. The next conference was held in 1927. Britain and later India had joined. Soviet Russia did not officially become a member until July, 1934, when Edward C. Carter, who became the chief administrator, "welcomed the USSR as a new member of the International Institute for Pacific Relations." [1] Foreign Commissar Litvinov was "extremely gratified that the Soviet Union was to participate fully in the work of the IPR." [2]

In structure, the IPR was a loose federation of national organizations, each with a national council. These were under an international board, called the Pacific Council, and an International Secretariat. The Pacific Council was largely honorary. The principal purposes of the International Secretariat were to prepare the international conferences which were held at intervals of approximately two years, and to publish various books and pamphlets. The American branch of the IPR grew rapidly and prospered, boasting over 1,000 members including businessmen, scholars, teachers, journalists, government officials, community leaders, and others.

---

[1] *Institute of Pacific Relations, Hearings,* Part 1, p. 190.

[2] "Interview with Litvinov at the Commissariat for Foreign Affairs," December 29, 1934. *Ibid.,* Part 13, p. 4506.

The bulk of the members of the IPR, as well as the members of the board of trustees, were inactive and "passive," generally without any influence over the organization and its affairs. There was a relatively small core of active members who carried the main burden of IPR activities and who, most of the time at any rate, directed its administration and policies. The board of trustees of the Institute was studded with personalities of such respectability, and of such pre-eminence in capitalistic achievement, that the very presence of their names on a letterhead might have put at rest all suspicion of intrigue or subversive influence.

No problem of financial assistance existed, because money flowed from such Americans as Thomas Lamont, Henry Luce, Jerome Greene, Brooks Emeny, Juan Trippe, and Gerard Swope. The Rockefeller and Carnegie foundations contributed millions of dollars. A number of prominent business corporations made donations, including International Business Machines, J. P. Morgan and Co., Shell Oil, *Reader's Digest*, Matson Steamship, American and Foreign Power, the British Lever Brothers, and many others.[3]

In its literature and in the words of its officials, the Institute of Pacific Relations has presented itself as an organization engaged in and devoted exclusively to the interest of objective, nonpartisan scholarship and research concerning the Far East.[4] It is upon the basis of this definition of aim that the IPR recommended itself to persons interested in the problems of the Pacific areas—to foundations, corporations, and individuals who might, and in many cases did, contribute funds for various activities.

The evidence before the Senate Internal Security Subcommittee, which vigorously investigated the IPR, discloses that this was not truly a scholarly research organization devoted exclusively to the interest of the Far East. On the contrary, the IPR has been an organization whose chief function has been to influence United States public opinion on Far Eastern matters. The Senate Subcommittee has concluded that the IPR has been "neither objective nor nonpartisan," and that "since the mid-1930's, the net effect of the IPR activities on United States public opinion has been pro-Communist and pro-Soviet, and has frequently and repeatedly been such as to serve international Communist, Chinese Communist, and Soviet interests, and to subvert the interest of the United States."[5]

"As the hearings unfolded, the Committee discovered that scores of important Communist agents had been attracted to the Institute of Pacific Relations, and that these agents had had an effect on our Far Eastern policy."[6] It is shocking to note that fifty-four persons connected in various ways with IPR were identified by witnesses as participants in the

---

3 *Ibid.*, Part 4, p. 1217.

4 *Ibid.*, p. 1215.

5 *Ibid.*, *Final Report*, p. 84.

6 Morris, *No Wonder We Are Losing*, p. 121.

Communist world conspiracy.[7] IPR officials refused to admit that there
was any pro-Communist influence whatsoever—a display of supine ignorance and incredible naiveté. It is their contention that the IPR was
always "objective and nonpartisan" and that its publications advocated
no policy or "line." IPR spokesmen have appealed to the commentator
opinions of "specialists" and Far Eastern experts with no Communist
affiliations.

No matter how many non-Communists were associated with the IPR,
its main over-all political weight and influence were under Communist
control. In political effect the IPR functioned as an instrument of Soviet
policy. This is the contention of five leading Far Eastern scholars, all of
them thoroughly familiar with the history and activities of the IPR.
They testified unequivocally that the IPR and its publications have been
neither objective nor nonpartisan.

Kenneth Colegrove, Professor of Political Science at Northwestern University and a Far Eastern scholar, a former member of the IPR, has characterized that organization as a " . . . propaganda organization supporting a line . . . a Communist line." [8] Professor David N. Rowe of Yale
University, former member of the board of trustees and a Far Eastern
scholar, has denied that the IPR is " . . . a straight scholarly organization with the interest of promoting research and study. . . . " He added
that the IPR's claim of "no propaganda, no point of view" was "completely irreconcilable" with what happened at an IPR international conference he had attended.[9]

Major General Charles A. Willoughby, chief of intelligence for the Far
East and United Nations Command, declared, "the conclusion could be
arrived at" that the Japanese branch of IPR was "used as a spy ring for
Russian Communists and the Russian Red Army." [10] Alexander Barmine, chief of the Russian unit in the State Department's "Voice of America," and once a brigadier-general in the Red Army, said he had been
told by Soviet Intelligence officers that the IPR was "a cover shop for
military intelligence work in the Pacific area." [11] Professor William Mc-
Govern of Northwestern University asserted that he found "very clear
evidence" that IPR's quarterly, *Pacific Affairs*, "was trying to advocate
the Stalinist approach." [12]

Raymond Dennett, once secretary of the IPR's American Council, said:

---

7 *Institute of Pacific Relations, Final Report*, pp. 147-148.

8 Testimony of Kenneth Colegrove, September 14, 1951, *Institute of Pacific Relations, Hearings*, Part 3, p. 916.

9 Testimony of David N. Rowe, March 27, 1952, *Ibid.*, Part 11, p. 4011; 3974.

10 Testimony of Major General Charles A. Willoughby, August 9, 1951, *Ibid.*, Part 2, p. 364.

11 Testimony of Alexander Barmine, July 31, 1951, *Ibid.*, Part 1, p. 202.

12 Testimony of William M. McGovern, September 28, 1951, *Ibid.*, Part 4, p. 1013.

" . . . I do not think it was an objective research organization." [13] There were others, although not members of the IPR, who were in a position to know the activities of that organization. Elizabeth T. Bentley, a former operator in the underground movement of the American Communist Party, mentioned that her superior, Jacob Golos, referred to the IPR as " . . . red as a rose . . . " [14] Igor Bogolepov, former colonel in the general staff of the Red Army and assistant to the chief of the League of Nations Division of the Soviet Foreign Office, referred to the IPR as a "double-way track," furnishing information from America to the Soviet military intelligence and, on the other hand, sending propaganda "to implant in American minds . . . the aims of Soviet Foreign policy." He said: "If you learned the wrong things about the Soviet Union, your thoughts are also wrong." [15] The Senate Internal Security Subcommittee commented on this statement:

> . . . with these words, Mr. Bogolepov may have put his finger on the spinal nerve of recent world history. If it is true that the Western World learned the wrong things about the Soviet Union, then it is certainly true that its thoughts were also wrong. If its thoughts were wrong, the action it took in dealing with the Soviet Union, the agreements it signed, the compromises it agreed to, the concessions it allowed, were wrong too.[16]

It is no longer debatable that at Cairo, Teheran, Yalta, Potsdam, and elsewhere the Western World took the wrong actions in its wartime and postwar dealings with the U.S.S.R. The Red lava flow released by these actions has since engulfed the seven hundred million inhabitants of Poland, East Germany, Hungary, Rumania, Bulgaria, Czechoslovakia, mainland China, North Korea, and part of Indochina. These wrong actions gained wide acceptability, if not outright approval, by a controlling percentage of policy-makers, scholars, writers, and other molders of policy and opinion. They had the "wrong thoughts" about the Soviet Union and Communist China.

Unfortunately, the people of the United States accepted grave misconceptions about these two countries. This question inevitably arises: How did so many Americans learn so many mistaken things about the Soviet Union and Communist China that they approved so many illogical actions which erupted in such volcanic disaster? Bogolepov offered one of many explanations to be found in the hearings. "In the Foreign Office," he said, "we have had a special, I think you call it joint committee, where representatives of different branches of the administration were present. . . . This important body was responsible directly to the political commission of the Politburo for carrying out the infiltration of ideas

---

13 Testimony of Raymond Dennett, September 26, 1951, *Ibid.*, Part 4, p. 966.

14 Testimony of Elizabeth T. Bentley, August 14, *Ibid.*, Part 2, p. 437.

15 Testimony of Igor Bogolepov, April 7, 1952, *Ibid.*, Part 13, p. 4491; 4496; 4512.

16 *Ibid., Final Report*, p. 31.

and men through the Iron Curtain to the Western countries. . . . It was a very big business of ours. . . . " [17]

Bogolepov described this "very big business" in detail. It involved, he said, "the creation of fellow travelers, inducing the Western intelligentsia, to write books and articles which were favorable to the Soviet Union." [18] A large part of the subcommittee's investigation of IPR amounted to an examination of this "very big business." The investigators found overwhelming proof that Communists and pro-Communists had seized control of the Institute—which supposedly was devoted to scholarly research —and transformed it into a Soviet propaganda apparatus.

The Senate Internal Security Subcommittee learned that the members of IPR's inner circle established a direct connection with the Communist International in Moscow as early as 1934. An IPR member went to the Comintern's Far Eastern chief himself for instructions on "editing the vocabulary in left and Soviet articles." The active group in the IPR wrote books, articles, and pamphlets, not only for the IPR itself, but also for an interlocking group of other organizations. It was chiefly through these organs that America learned "the wrong things about the Soviet Union" in the Far East, and it was chiefly because of them also that the actions America took in dealing with the Far East were wrong.

The main strategic use of the IPR was one of blocking effective resistance by the Western powers—particularly by the United States—to the Communist conquest of China. This objective entailed a massive psychological, or propaganda, campaign. Public opinion in the United States and in Europe had to be molded in the shape of ideas and attitudes which would hide the nature of Communist Far Eastern strategy, maintain ignorance of how it could be countered, and weaken the will to resist it. Professor David Rowe, in his testimony before the Reece Committee investigating subversion in foundations, had this to say:

The area of ignorance in the United States about the Far Eastern matters was so great that here was the strategic place in which to strike at the security of the United States by people interested in imperiling our security and fostering the aims of world Communism. They would naturally not pick an area in which we have the greatest intellectual capacities . . . for defense. They would pick the area of greatest public ignorance, with the greatest difficulty of defending against tactics of their attack, and so these people naturally poured into Far Eastern studies and exploited this area as the area in which they would promote the interests of world Communism most successfully in the general ignorance and blindness of the American people.[19]

The Institute of Pacific Relations maintained a near monopoly on

---

17 *Ibid.,* pp. 31-32.

18 *Ibid.,* p. 32.

19 Rene A. Wormser, *Foundations: Their Power and Influence* (New York: The Devin-Adair Company, 1958) , p. 176.

public presentation of material dealing with the Far East. In university circles, this meant that teachers, scholars, or students who were or became interested in the problems of the Pacific naturally depended on the IPR and became unwitting supporters and propagandists for Soviet aims in the Far East.

In the forming of public opinion, no area is of more crucial importance than the school system. This area was heavily and continuously cultivated by the IPR. It would be only natural and inevitable that a self-styled "research" organization dealing with the Pacific countries should establish close links with the universities, the principal home of scholars in modern society. The voice of the IPR reached a much more fundamental level in the American school system and was heard far below the university level.

One reason for the extraordinary influence of the IPR was brought out in the questioning of Owen Lattimore before the Senate Internal Security Subcommittee. Senator Arthur V. Watkins of Utah inquired:

... We had a witness ... who said that they went to the Institute of Pacific Relations publications to get information because there were very few other sources from which they could get information on the Far East. Do you care to comment on that, since you are a student on the Far East?

Lattimore replied:

There were very few in that period. There were very few publications devoted exclusively to the Far East. . . . I believe that in those years, to the best of my recollection, the publications of the Institute of Pacific Relations were the only ones that not only specialized on the Far East but were confined to the Far East.[20]

For the schools below the university level, the IPR had an ambitious and vigorous program. Pamphlets and other study materials, by the hundreds of thousands, were published and distributed in the schools. According to an IPR special report, covering 1943, prepared by Harriet Moore as acting secretary:

The American Council's school program is meeting an evermore enthusiastic response both from school teachers and from educational organizations. . . . Two more pamphlets, the sixth and seventh of the Webster series of unit tests for high school classroom use, are now appearing. . . . The gross income from sales of the first five titles amounted to $45,000 in 1943. A second series designed for the elementary school is now in preparation. . . . In an attempt to focus the attention of the individual school teacher on this area of study, the American Council in cooperation with the American Observer, a school magazine reaching 450,000 children, conducted a test on the Far East . . . [21]

20 Testimony of Owen Lattimore, February 26, 1952, *Institute of Pacific Relations, Hearings,* Part 9, p. 2917.
21 *Ibid.,* Part 8, Exhibit No. 407, p. 2579, p. 2581. The IPR report covering the years 1944-45 states that 1,105,598 copies of the school pamphlets were sold in that two year period. *Ibid., Final Report,* p. 78, fn. no. 9.

In conjunction with the American Council on Education and the Foreign Policy Association, the IPR developed an elaborate program for distributing to the schools what were called Resource Packets.[22] The 1944-46 official IPR report, *Windows on the Pacific,* states of the series of school texts prepared in conjunction with the Webster Publishing Company, that "over a million copies have been sold in the three and a half years . . . and the pamphlets have been placed on the 'adopted' list of reading materials in more than thirteen hundred school systems in various parts of the United States." [23]

The general publishing program of the IPR was varied in kind, range, and type of audience. According to William L. Holland, an official with the IPR since 1929, about two hundred major volumes were brought out from 1925-1951.[24] The official IPR report for 1944-1946 states that 977,-000 popular pamphlets were printed and sold in that two-year period. A quarterly magazine, *Pacific Affairs,* was published regularly under the auspices of the International Secretariat of the IPR. The biweekly journal, *Far Eastern Survey,* was issued as an organ of the American Council. Both of these publications disseminated Communist propaganda cannily and persistently.

The years 1934-1940—the time during which Owen Lattimore was sole editor of *Pacific Affairs* and Frederick Vanderbilt Field was executive secretary of the American Council of the IPR—were apparently those years when Communist influence became entrenched in the two periodicals. At least thirty per cent of all the items that have appeared in the *Far Eastern Survey* have come from pro-Communist sources. During the Field-Lattimore period (1934-1940) almost half the material came from such sources. Pro-Communist contributions in *Pacific Affairs* have been considerably less. They amounted to one-sixth. However, during his term as editor, Lattimore managed to raise the share contributed by such sources to nearly one-fourth of the total.[25]

Another phase of IPR publishing was the supplying of material to Government personnel and agencies, particularly the armed services, during the Second World War. In a letter dated Febrary 2, 1942, W. L. Holland comments: "Elisabeth is greatly excited at the colossal orders we continue to get from the War Department for our pamphlets." [26] Among

---

22 *Ibid.,* Part 8, Exhibit No. 408, p. 2584.

23 *Ibid., Final Report,* p. 78.

24 *Ibid.,* Part 4, Exhibit No. 331, p. 1221.

25 *Ibid., Final Report,* pp. 104-105. During the years 1934-1940, a small clique of twelve persons contributed a total of over 485 items to the two magazines, 357 to the *Far Eastern Survey* and 128 to *Pacific Affairs.* None of the members of that clique contributed less than twenty items, and their average contribution per head during the period named was 40.16, or 5.74 per year. The members of this clique were: Joseph Barnes, Kathleen Barnes, Chen Han-seng, Miriam Farley, Irving S. Friedman, F. V. Field, Andrew Grajdanzev, Owen Lattimore, W. W. Lockwood, Catherine Porter, Lawrence Rosinger, and Virginia Thompson. *Ibid.,* p. 104.

26 *Ibid.,* Part 2, Exhibit No. 193, p. 660.

other things, the Troop Training Orientation Program, designed for instructors, contained a list of thirty-nine books which were recommended for troops as basic training. Twenty-two of the thirty-nine were published by the Institute of Pacific Relations. Two hundred and thirty thousand copies of these IPR volumes were purchased by the Army for distribution at installations throughout the world.[27]

Raymond Dennett, referring to the period when he was Secretary of the American Council, remarked: "The Educational and Information Branch of the Army and the equivalent in the Navy purchased somewhere in the vicinity of several hundred thousand total of pamphlets issued by the American Council for use in the orientation programs on the Far East." [28]

The 1944-1946 official IPR report states that "during the course of the war, over three-quarters of a million IPR pamphlets were purchased by the Government and sent to American troops in Asia and the Pacific area." [29] Other IPR services to the Armed Forces are also mentioned, in particular the supplying of lectures, documents, books, and research materials. It would be logical to conclude that the principal source, direct or indirect, of the indoctrination of the members of the armed forces on the Far East was the IPR. Since the wartime army was a mass citizen army, most members of which returned to civilian status after the war, this meant the exerting of a major influence on general public opinion.

The Department of State also had its share of influence from the IPR. Dr. Edna Fluegel, who was a member of the Postwar Planning Staff of the Department of State, stated that the publications of the Institute of Pacific Relations were almost the only material on the Far East coming into the department. They were in ample supply in the State Department reference rooms.[30]

In estimating the influence of the IPR in the general field of United States publications, attention cannot be limited to books, magazines, and pamphlets which appeared under IPR imprint. The IPR was not a single unit but a complex of interlocking activities. Organizations such as the China Aid Council and the American-Russian Institute were closely tied in. There were looser associations with groups such as the Foreign Policy Association, various magazines, and the trade departments of certain publishers. The thinner, but functioning lines of the IPR stretched very far indeed.

Wherever there was, or could be roused, a call for a review or article

27 U.S. Congress, Senate, Committee on the Judiciary, *Report for the Year 1954*, 83rd Cong., 2d Sess. (Washington D. C., Government Printing Office, January 3, 1955), p. 47.

28 Testimony of Raymond Dennett, *Institute of Pacific Relations, Hearings*, Part 4, p. 959.

29 *Ibid., Final Report*, pp. 78-79.

30 Testimony of Edna R. Fluegel, February 20, 1952, *Ibid.*, Part 8, pp. 2865-2866.

or memorandum on the Far East, the voice of the IPR was ninety per cent certain to be heard. "There was a tendency on the part of the staff," remarked Raymond Dennett, secretary, "to pick people as authors and to submit their manuscript to other writers for critical comment who by and large tended to agree with the point of view of the staff prior to the selection of either the authors or the readers of the manuscript, and this tended over the whole period to give less than a complete objective picture." [31] The IPR functioned as a sort of a "Boosters and Knockers Club." That is to say, they would boost each other's books, and knock anyone, even another IPR member, who was outside, or stepped partly outside, their ideological circle.

It was obligatory on members of the IPR to give mutual and public praise of each other's work—in short, building each other up in public esteem. For example, Israel Epstein wrote a book called *Unfinished Revolution in China*, which was violently biased on the side of the Communists. When Edward C. Carter, Secretary-General of the IPR, read it he was delighted. He sought to use this book to influence the leaders of the Department of State and Congress. He wrote to the publisher that it was "of utmost importance" that he get it read "by Secretary of State George Marshall, Senators Vandenberg, Morse and Ives, John Foster Dulles and John Carter Vincent of the State Department." [32] The *New York Times* asked Owen Lattimore to review the book, and he was delighted with the material. He wrote that Epstein had established himself in the distinguished company of Edgar Snow and Theodore White.[33] Through repeated testimony and many documents, the IPR Hearings established Epstein's long Communist history.[34] On March 3, 1951, his assignment presumably finished and a Senate investigation shortly to begin, Epstein sailed away from our hospitable shores on the same Polish ship "Batory" by which Gerhardt Eisler jumped bail.

It was during World War II and the three years following the war that the IPR went through its major period of development and effectiveness. The extent of IPR activities during this period was described by Edward C. Carter in a letter to G. E. Hubbard of the British Political Intelligence Department, dated January 5, 1942:

In spite of the war, or rather because of it, the IPR is busier than ever. We have had to let some of our staff go to various Government jobs but have managed to fill all vacancies so that on balance both the American Council and the Pacific

---

31 Testimony of Raymond Dennett, *Ibid.*, Part 4, p. 948.

32 *Ibid.*, Part 11, pp. 3738-3739.

33 *New York Times*, June 22, 1947.

34 Testimony of Louis Budenz, August 22, 1951, *Institute of Pacific Relations, Hearings*, Part 2, p. 590. It is significant that Epstein has been in Communist China for years and turned up at the Korean peace negotiations as a representative of the official Communist China press.

Council Staffs are stronger than ever. Lattimore is of course an asset in Chung-king, though he is not technically on the IPR staff. Michael Greenberg and Mrs. Dobbs are carrying on *Pacific Affairs* well within the Lattimore tradition. Chao-ting Chi is secretary-general of the ABC [American-British-Chinese] sta-bilization fund in China. . . . Friedman . . . is now in the Treasury in Wash-ington. Rosinger is in the office of the India Government Trade Commission-er. . . . Shiman has gone to the Tariff Commission, and Miss Ellen de Jong, to Military Intelligence.[35]

The wartime activities of the IPR even penetrated the White House when Lauchlin Currie became executive assistant to the President and special adviser on Far Eastern affairs. From his vantage point in the White House, Currie was acting in the role of a high adviser to the IPR. Carter frequently conferred with him in Washington.[36]

A letter from Carter to Dr. Chao-ting Chi, dated February 18, 1941, shows that the Institute of Pacific Relations was trying to shape policy through Currie. Carter asked Chi, who has been identified as a Com-munist, whether it would be advisable to send a cable to Currie, then in China, suggesting that if the "press could report" that Currie, the President's representative in China, "had visited Chou En-lai," the Com-munist leader, that fact would help public opinion in view of the "pre-sent crop of ugly rumors" concerning the split of the Chinese unified resistance.[37] Currie was responsible for setting up a conference in Wash-ington, on October 12, 1942, between himself, Sumner Welles, then Under Secretary of State, and Earl Browder and Robert Miner, then officials of the Communist Party.[38] Professor George Taylor, of the Uni versity of Washington, relates a story of how Currie was very friendly to him and invited him to his office every Wednesday until Taylor wrote a memorandum saying that the hope of the Kuomintang-Communist co-operation was negligible and that the United States should provide arms to Chiang Kai-shek to fight the Communists. After this incident Taylor was never invited to come back, and he never again saw Currie.[39]

One of the most interesting incidents concerning the IPR was the Washington visit of Vladimir Rogoff, a former *Tass* correspondent, who was one of the most important Soviet intelligence agents in the Far East. Through the good offices of the IPR, Rogoff was closeted with top policy-makers in 1944, a year of many important decisions. Interesting roles in the episode were played by Alger Hiss and by Lauchlin Currie, whom Elizabeth Bentley testified was involved in Soviet Military Intelligence.

---

[35] *Ibid.*, Part 2, Exhibit No. 130, p. 481.

[36] *Ibid.*, Part 2, Exhibit No. 107, p. 428.

[37] Edward C. Carter to Dr. Chao-ting Chi, February 18, 1941, *Ibid.*, Part 2, Exhibit No. 105, p. 426. Chi now works for the Chinese Peoples Republic.

[38] *Ibid.*, Part 2, p. 598 ff.

[39] Testimony of George Edward Taylor, August 7, 1951, *Ibid.*, Part 1, p. 348.

Rogoff was a Soviet intelligence agent who specialized on China. In August, 1943, he wrote the authoritative article in *War and Working Class* which signaled a change in Communist policy toward China. In 1944, he was in the United States and had the credentials of a *Tass* correspondent. The available evidence on this visit indicates that Edward C. Carter, then Secretary General of the IPR, was in New York and was visited by Rogoff. On January 17, 1944, Carter wired Alger Hiss and Lauchlin Currie that his "friend" Rogoff was enroute from Moscow to London and would be in Washington for three days. Carter urged them to see him. Carter also wrote Rose Yardumian, secretary of the Washington IPR office, and enclosed the telegram to Hiss and Currie. He asked Miss Yardumian to call Hiss and Currie and to urge them to talk with Rogoff.[40]

Miss Yardumian's reply to Carter on January 20 proved to be most revealing. She had, as instructed, called Alger Hiss, who told her he had received Carter's wire and was sure "that Carter would understand that he could not make the first advance in arranging a private talk with Rogoff." [41] Hiss mentioned Rogoff's articles in *War and Working Class* and "that Rogoff's materials had caused considerable controversy in circles here." [42] The letter also indicated that Currie had seen Rogoff at noon that day but that Rogoff had expressed the opinion that "he thought it would be unwise" for the IPR to hold a meeting with Rogoff present. The letter revealed that William C. Johnstone, of the Washington Office of the IPR, Carl Remer, head of the Far Eastern Division of OWI, and John Carter Vincent, head of the China desk of the Department of State, had a two and a half hour conversation with Rogoff.[43]

While testifying before the Senate Internal Security Subcommittee, Vincent would not tell the members what took place at the meeting. In further testimony, *Vincent stated that he had not been aware until after World War II that Communism was a menace.*[44] An abysmal confession of ignorance on the part of one of our Far Eastern policy-makers, concerning strategy and tactics of Communism! The fact of the matter is that the Communist movement has existed throughout the world since 1917, has held at least ten world congresses under the name of Communist International or its camouflaged modern version of the Cominform, and has published tons of literature in all principal languages.

---

40 *Ibid.*, Part 1, Exhibit No. 16, pp. 128-131; Part 2, p. 530; Part 1, pp. 140-145. Miss Yardumian ended up behind the Bamboo Curtain as a staff member of Powell's *China Monthly.*

41 *Ibid.*, Part 1, p. 145.

42 *Ibid.*, p. 146.

43 *Ibid.*, Exhibit No. 26, p. 161.

44 Testimony of John Carter Vincent, January 24, 1952, *Ibid.*, Part 6, p. 1949. Italics **mine.**

Perhaps it was the truth when Owen Lattimore declared under oath that he was never a Communist, and when Edward Carter and John Carter Vincent swore that they never had an inkling of any Communists at all in the IPR, except for a tiny suspicion that Frederick Field was "fairly left-wing." But this does not alter in any way the pro-Soviet facts of IPR history. Nor does it negate the role which these gentlemen played in the loss of the China mainland to the Communists. As David N. Rowe said before the Reece Committee investigating subversion in foundations:

In much of the activity that has to do with identification of Communist activity in the United States, it has seemed to me that we are going off on the wrong track when we limit ourselves to efforts to identify overt Communists, or let us say organizational Communists, people who carry a card or who can be positively identified as members of an organization subject to organized discipline. For every one of those that you fail to identify, and it seems to me we even fail to identify most of those, there are a thousand people who could not possibly be identified as such, because they have never had any kind of organizational affiliation, *but among those people are many people who advance the interests of world communism, in spite of the fact that they are not subject to discipline and do not belong to any organization.*[45]

One of the most important documents revealed by the Senate Internal Security Subcommittee was a letter dated July 10, 1938, wherein Owen Lattimore had a most interesting suggestion which he gave to Carter concerning IPR activities. He said: "I think you are pretty cagey in turning over so much of the China section of the inquiry to Asiaticus, Hanseng and Chi. *They will bring out the absolutely essential radical aspects, but can be depended on to do it with the right touch. . . .* "[46] The "China section" referred to by Lattimore was indeed in competent hands. "Asiaticus" was the pseudonym of Hans Moeller who had been a Comintern operative since the 1920's; Chen Han-seng, whose best-known pseudonym was Raymond D. Brooke, had a long clear record of publication in Communist-front magazines and has been identified by Karl Wittfogel as a party member. Chao-ting has also been identified as a Communist before the Senate Internal Security Subcommittee.[47]

The IPR was like a specialized political flypaper in its attractive power for Communists. According to the evidence before the Subcommittee, a remarkably large number of Communists and pro-Communists showed up in publications, conferences, offices, and institutions of the IPR, or were mentioned in the letters of IPR members. Lawrence Rosinger was identified as a member of the Communist Party during the IPR hearings. When questioned about this accusation, he invoked the fifth

45 Wormser, *Foundations: Their Power and Influence*, p. 175. Italics mine.
46 *Institute of Pacific Relations, Hearings*, Part 1, Exhibit No. 4, p. 40.
47 *Ibid., Final Report*, p. 119. Moeller is dead. Chen Han-seng is now an editor of "China Reconstructs," a Peking propaganda publication of world-wide importance.

amendment against self-incrimination.[48] *China Wartime Policies*, written by Rosinger was among the recommended readings in the Army. His activities were by no means confined to writing. In October, 1949, the Department of State paid him as a consultant to participate in a round-table discussion of American policy towards China. Evidence in the transcript indicates that Lattimore and Rosinger were the most active and frequent exponents of the pro-Communist views that prevailed.[49] In the winter of 1949-1950, the Rockefeller Foundation paid Rosinger $2,000 to attend a special New Delhi IPR conference.[50] This foundation also granted "$6,000 or $9,000" to Rosinger to write a book under the title, *The State of Asia*, directed by the American IPR in the spring of 1951.[51]

It is tragic that the IPR was offered access to the minds of eight million American soldiers during World War II. Through the War Department's Information and Education Division, IPR books were recommended to the troops as basic reading. For example, *Wartime China* by Maxwell Stewart was employed for the troop training orientation program in which the author "knowingly and deliberately" used language for "pro-Communist" or "pro-Soviet" purposes.[52] Even with this captive audience, it is uncertain just how many American service men IPR propaganda reached.

Frederick V. Field, one of the most important influences in the IPR throughout its most influential years, was identified as a Communist Party member. He was also a writer for the *Daily Worker*, official organ of the party. He was a registered agent of China's Communist government. In answer to all questions about his Communist activities, he invoked the fifth amendment.[53] Field instigated an IPR pamphlet, *Our Job in the Pacific*, which was drafted by Eleanor Lattimore, though it was published under the signature of Vice-President Henry A. Wallace. The pamphlet was one more of those used by the troop training orientation program.

The influence of the Institute of Pacific Relations spread far and wide in American thinking on Far Eastern matters. Its members were always willing to give advice to editors or writers for magazines, to graduate students, libraries, etc. William Lockwood, who was a member of the research staff of the American Council from 1935 to 1940 and executive secretary of the Council from 1941 to 1943, stated that editors, radio commentators, business firms, teachers, and students, called on the institute daily for library and information services.[54]

---

48 *Ibid.*, p. 157; Part 8, p. 2475.
49 *Ibid.*, Part 5, p. 1551 ff.
50 *Ibid.*, Part 4, p. 1237.
51 *Ibid.*, Part 4, p. 1167.
52 *Ibid.*, *Final Report*, p. 225.
53 *Ibid.*, pp. 153-154.
54 *Ibid.*, Part 11, p. 3880, Exhibit No. 572-A.

Another function of the IPR was to hold international conferences concerning Far Eastern problems. During the 1941-1945 period, the IPR held two such international meetings. The first of these was held at Mont Tremblant, Canada, in December, 1942. Attending this conference were many leaders of the Department of State whom the Institute of Pacific Relations wished to influence in shaping United States policy on China. The American delegation, which numbered twenty-six, included seven persons who were identified during the hearings on the IPR as Communists. Five of the seven were hand-picked, and the IPR persons on the inside closely controlled the program arrangements.[55]

Department of State policy-makers who attended the conference had no organizational role. According to the record, Lauchlin Currie, Alger Hiss, Joseph Barnes, and Philip Jessup, along with E. C. Carter, made the selections of the conferees.[56] The meeting was carefully planned with many influential government officials attending. Mr. William W. Lockwood, the Secretary of the American Council, conferred with Currie regarding the conference, and Currie's recommendations were very significant. They constituted a combination of persons who held key positions and persons who were strong supporters of a change of policy on China.[57]

Around September 25, 1943, the Institute held a round-table discussion on Chinese postwar reconstruction. At this session, the roster of persons in attendance showed the familiar pattern of individuals with evidence of Communist activity and persons influential in the Department of State and other policy agencies. On this occasion the chairman was Harry Dexter White, a man identified by J. Edgar Hoover as a Soviet agent.

The ninth triennial conference of the Institute took place at Hot Springs, Virginia, in January, 1945. Like the Mont Tremblant conference it was a carefully manipulated assemblage. According to Raymond Dennett, who was at the time Secretary of the IPR American Council, recommendations for delegates came from Philip Jessup and Lauchlin Currie.[58] Of approximately thirty recommendations ten were identified by witnesses before the Senate Internal Security Subcommittee as being associated with the Communist Party.[59]

The American delegation caucused before the conference to determine what position it should take *vis-à-vis* other delegations. A report of the caucus meeting showed that it considered the question of taking a position of intervention in the internal affairs of the Chinese Government. Jessup presided at the caucus, and Lattimore was the most vocal and

---

55 Frank Coe, Lauchlin Currie, Len DeCaux, Frederick Vanderbilt Field, Benjamin H. Kizer, Owen Lattimore, Harriet L. Moore. *Ibid.*, Part 2, pp. 425-426; see also *Ibid.*, *Final Report*, p. 183.

56 *Ibid.*, Part 14, Exhibit Nos. 785, 787, 788, pp. 4973-4976.

57 *Ibid.*, Part 2, Exhibit No. 110, pp. 432-433.

58 *Ibid.*, Part 4, pp. 979-980.

59 *Ibid.*, *Final Report*, p. 194.

dominant conferee.[60] The conferees, who included Frederick V. Field, Len De Caux, Frank Coe, and Miriam S. Farley, agreed that their position should be one of pressing for changes in the internal situation of the Chinese Government.[61] John Carter Vincent, then head of the Chinese Division in the Department of State, recommended that a series of dinners for Far Eastern specialists among the delegates be held during the course of the conference. The purpose of this was to bring together some of the technical people for informal discussions of matters on the agenda. Both Hiss and Vincent thought the IPR could be helpful at the Conference.[62]

The conference discussion developed resentment on the part of the British, French, and Dutch delegates at the bitter attacks on colonialism uttered by Lattimore, Andrew Grajdanzev, and T. A. Bisson.[63] The latter two were members of the Secretariat and not delegates and were, under the rules, speaking out of order. Dennett quoted Lattimore as having said that "the world could not exist half slave and half free until the metropolitan countries had freed their colonial territories." [64] Lattimore urged that postwar plans for Japan ignore the Japanese Emperor. Two months after the conference, Alger Hiss recommended that copies of the report of the conference be made available to each of the delegations to the U.N. Conference.[65]

The Institute of Pacific Relations was also very active in postwar planning. Alger Hiss became head of the postwar planning staff for the Department of State, and unfortunately had access to practically every document, paper, and secret of the United States Government.[66] During the war period, the association of Alger Hiss with the IPR often manifested itself. Edward C. Carter wrote to Hiss on February 5, 1947, "You have done so much for the IPR in cooperation and wise advice that I am hoping this fine relationship can continue in your new post." [67] Hiss was then leaving the Department of State to be President of the Carnegie Endowment for International Peace. In 1947 he became a trustee of the IPR.[68] "We have seen many Communists and fellow-travelers recommended by foundation executives for government posts," the House Committee on Tax-Exempt Foundations reported. "In the case of the recommendations to the government made by the Institute of Pacific Relations . . . for experts to be used by our occupation forces in Germany and

---

60 *Ibid.*, Part 4, Exhibit No. 293 ff. pp. 991-994.
61 *Ibid.*
62 *Ibid.*, Part 7A, Exhibit No. 384, pp. 2138-2141.
63 *Ibid.*, Part 4, p. 994.
64 *Ibid.*
65 *Ibid.*, Part 7A, Exhibit No. 384, p. 2138.
66 *Ibid.*, Part 8, p. 2838.
67 Edward C. Carter to Alger Hiss, February 5, 1947, *Ibid.*, Part 1, p. 134.
68 Testimony of Edward C. Carter, July 25, 1951, *Ibid.*, Part 1, p. 134.

Japan, the lists were heavily [infiltrated] with Communists and their supporters." [69]

Professor Kenneth Colgrove, former Secretary of the American Political Science Association, related his experience concerning the selection of civilian advisers for Japan. "I was shocked when I saw the list . . . ," he said. "I wanted to find out where the list came from, and I was told that the list had come from the Institute of Pacific Relations." [70]

If the Communists were to conquer China, effective interference by the Western powers, and in particular by the United States, had to be prevented. Moscow used the IPR as an effective instrument to weaken the West, particularly the United States. The IPR functioned as an instrument of Soviet policy in the sense that the effect of the predominant IPR "line" was such as to aid Soviet interests, and almost never to oppose her advantage. From the Soviet point of view, the IPR fulfilled its mission. According to Igor Bogolopev, former counselor of the Soviet Foreign Office, the IPR was used as "media of propaganda infiltration of general ideas favorable to the Soviet Union." The policy was to implant in American minds views sympathetic to the aims of "Soviet foreign policy in the Far East." [71] The IPR was a "brainwashing" apparatus in the truest sense of the word.

From the early 1930's, the IPR gave favorable, sympathetic and friendly publicity to the Chinese Communists. After the Japanese invaded Manchuria in 1931, but particularly when they moved into China proper in 1937, the IPR started a vigorous campaign to discredit that nation. The theme called for resistance in China of such a sort that the Soviet position in Siberia, and the Communist strongholds in China, would not be endangered. From 1937 to 1944, in keeping with Communist policy and also in response to the increase of the Japanese threat to the Soviet position, Communist propaganda and the prevailing policy of the IPR publications called for a united front between the Communists and the Nationalists against the Japanese.

After American military power crushed Japanese resistance until Japan was no longer a threat, a potent propaganda campaign was started by Communists and their fellow travellers to discredit the Nationalist Government on the one hand and to praise the Chinese Communists on the other. The anti-Chiang crowd was setting the stage for a shift in policy. Chinese Communists were rechristened for temporary and tactical purposes as "agrarians," not genuine Communists, and said to be independent of Moscow.

69 U.S. Congress, House of Representatives, Special Committee to Investigate Tax-Exempt Foundations and Comparable Organizations, *Tax-Exempt Foundations Report*, 83rd Cong., 2d Sess. (Washington: Government Printing Office, 1954), p. 57.

70 *Tax-Exempt Foundations, Hearings*, Part 1, p. 561.

71 *Institute of Pacific Relations, Hearings*, Part 13, pp. 4492-96.

In the July 14, 1943, issue of *Far Eastern Survey*, T. A. Bisson, a lin-
guistically trained member of the IPR family, published a very important
article entitled, "China's Part in a Coalition War," which foreshadowed
a change in the Communist line on China. He stated that there were
two Chinas. One, Kuomintang China, might be called feudal China; the
other, Communist China, might be called Democratic China. After claim-
ing economic and political reforms for Communist China, he wrote:

Over wide areas of this new China, elected councils—village, town and district—and elected executive officials have completely supplanted the old autocratic system of feudal agrarian China. . . . It is this democratic process, finally,
which permits a large measure of free competition to operate over the whole
of the economy. Bureaucratic price controls are not attempted. . . . No landlord or merchant, with the watchful eyes of his neighbors upon him, can engage
in hoarding or speculation. Within limits set mainly by local democratic checks,
the individual landlord or entrepreneur is free, and is even encouraged, to expand his operations, and many are doing so. By no stretch of the imagination
can this be termed 'communism'; it is, in fact, the essence of *bourgeois* democracy applied mainly to agrarian conditions.[72]

Many of the IPR writers followed this common theme sympathetic to
the Chinese Reds and it eventually caused irreparable damage to our
position in the Far East. These views were totally false in that they
claimed that the Chinese Communists are not "really" Communists—at
least not like Russian Communists—but liberals, populists, agrarian reformers, "native radicals," patriots, and so on. Chinese Communism
"springs out of the Chinese soil and Chinese history." The Chinese Communists are honest, efficient. They liberate the peasants. The true and
genuine Chinese revolution is the movement led by the Communists and
this movement is good, democratic, progressive. All anti-Communist
movements are stranglers of the revolution, reactionary, fascist-minded,
and bad. Chiang and his associates are grafters, reactionaries, agents of
foreign powers, oppressors, hated by all the people. The Communists are
the wave of the future: They are inevitably going to win, and Chiang is
through as a leader. These were perennial themes of the books, articles,
reviews, lectures and conversations of the IPR activists.

In a letter to Edward C. Carter, editor of *Pacific Affairs*, dated May 4,
1945, John B. Powell, who spent many years in China as a correspondent, sums up the position of the IPR in this manner:

. . . I have read a great many publications of the Institute of Pacific Relations,
but I have never seen one single criticism of the dictatorial Communist Party in
Russia. According to Sun Fo, who has always been friendly toward the U.S.S.R.,
. . . there isn't the slightest chance of a democratic development in Russia within
fifty years, and possibly it will take a hundred. Why do you ignore the situation

---

[72] *Ibid.*, Part 2, Exhibit No. 134, p. 534.

in Russia while concentrating all the Institute's criticism on China and the Kuomintang? Since practically all the attacks on the Kuomintang and Generalissimo Chiang Kai-shek can be traced back to Chinese Communist and Russian sources, it seems to be that the whole thing is a build-up for a further grab of Chinese territory, this time by the U.S.S.R. All through World War I we appeased Japan; now we seem to be following a similar policy with respect to the Soviet Union and the Communist Party.[73]

The hearings on the Institute of Pacific Relations were among the longest and most vigorous carried out by one congressional committee. They lasted almost a year from July, 1951, until June, 1952. In all, sixty-six witnesses were heard, and two thousand documents were examined and entered in the printed record, which came to six thousand pages. After all this the Senate Internal Security Subcommittee came to the following conclusions:

The Institute of Pacific Relations has not maintained the character of an objective, scholarly, and research organization. The IPR has been considered by the American Communist Party and by Soviet officials as an instrument of Communist policy, propaganda and military intelligence. The IPR disseminated and sought to popularize false information including information originating from Soviet and Communist sources. A small core of officials and staff members carried the main burden of IPR activities and directed its administration and policies. Members of the small core of officials and staff members who controlled IPR were either Communist or pro-Communist. There is no evidence that the large majority of its members supported the IPR for any reason except to advance the professed research and scholarly purposes of the organization. Most members of the IPR, and most members of its Board of Trustees, were inactive and obviously without any influence over the policies of the organization and the conduct of its affairs. IPR activities were made possible largely through the financial support of American industrialists, corporations, and foundations, the majority of whom were not familiar with the inner workings of the organization. The effective leadership of the IPR often sought to deceive IPR contributors and supporters as to the true character and activities of the organization. Neither the IPR nor any substantial body of those associated with it as executive officers, trustees or major financial contributors, has ever made any serious and objective investigation of the charges that the IPR was infiltrated by Communists and was used for pro-Communist and pro-Soviet purposes. The names of eminent individuals were by design used as a respectable and impressive screen for the activities of the IPR inner core, and as a defense when such activities came under scrutiny. . . . [74]

If the Communists did not conquer China by means of the IPR, it is doubtful that they would have conquered without the IPR. The IPR immobilized the sole force that could have blocked the process. For this achievement, which has no real parallel in its field, the Communist manipulations of the IPR must be acknowledged a political masterpiece.

---

[73] *Ibid.*, Part 14, pp. 5297-5298.
[74] *Ibid.*, *Final Report*, p. 223.

Even though the organization has now been exposed and discredited, much of its influence still persists in American thinking and governmental policy. For several years after the IPR had been cited on the Attorney General's list as a subversive organization, it continued to enjoy tax-exempt status with the Treasury Department. Finally, the tax-exempt privilege was removed, only to be restored in 1960.[75]

---

75 Tax-exempt philanthropic foundations clearly have become one principal source of Communist infiltration and subversion in the United States. The House Committee on Tax-Exempt Foundations reports there are 7,000 foundations in the United States today. Their combined trust funds aggregate $7½ billion, with total annual income approximating $675 million. Some 500 of the larger foundations—those holding more than $10 million each—control roughly 56 per cent of the total endowments and collect approximately 32 per cent of all foundation income. Some fifty foundations were named in the hearings as supporters of studies and programs contributing to Communist purposes in the United States. A considerable number of tax-exempt foundations and organizations (i.e., the League for Industrial Democracy) have as their purpose the establishment of socialism in the United States—an objective of the Communists, of course. Congressman Carroll Reece, "Tax Exempt Subversion." *American Mercury* (July, 1957), pp. 56-57.

CHAPTER XVI

SUBVERSION ALONG THE LINOTYPE FRONT: REVIEWERS AT WORK

One of the most important aspects of the China story is the propaganda-writing of a school of Far Eastern experts. Blindly or deliberately, these professional writers misled our country by revoking the traditional Open Door Policy. This resulted in the betrayal of Nationalist China. Through their writings and book reviews, they were able to condition the American people for the loss of the China mainland to the Communists.

As one reads through the numerous books and articles on the Far East between the years 1937 and 1950, the Communist propaganda is apparent. Few people read outright Communist publications except party members; as a result these have little propaganda value as far as the mass of American readers is concerned. But one pro-Communist book or article by an important writer is worth a truckload of *Daily Workers* in advancing international Communism.

Many authors who supported the Chinese Reds were left unchallenged because the American people knew little about the conditions in the Far East. Most people believe that pro-Communist and pro-Soviet propaganda is always written in what might be called Communist jargon. They expect to find an open defense of the Communist program and Soviet interest with words like "revolution," "class struggle," "proletariat," "civil war," "imperialism," etc. This belief is altogether mistaken. The truth of the matter is that even the public Communist press employs scant Communist phraseology. The language is carefully and systematically camouflaged, the purpose being to hide from the untrained reader the true origin and aim of the writing. Communist sympathizers give careful attention to the linguistics, as is abundantly illustrated by many writers on the Far East.[1]

---

[1] For an excellent analysis of manipulation of Communist language see the testimony of Dr. Stefan T. Possony, March 2, 1959, U.S. House of Representatives, Committee on Un-American Activities, *Language As a Communist Weapon*, 86th Cong., 1st Sess. (Washington: Government Printing Office, 1959), pp. 1-5.

After taking power in 1917, the Russian Bolsheviks at first seldom wrote for the non-Communist press. This rule was sharply changed in 1931, the year Molotov prepared a memorandum on the problem:

Who reads the Communist papers? Only a few people who are already Communists. We don't need to propagandize them. What is our object? Who do we have to influence? We have to influence non-Communists if we want to make them Communists or if we want to fool them. So, we have to try to infiltrate in the big press. . . . [2]

David N. Rowe, Professor of Political Science at Yale University, was asked by the members of the Senate Internal Security Subcommittee about the resultant difficulty in detecting the Communist line. He replied: " . . . you have to study it constantly to know what the words and phrases are, the way in which they are used at the moment in order to know what people are talking about. That is why it is so easy for an uninitiated person or group to be hoodwinked." [3]

Chinese Communists and their collection of partisans were able to put their version of events across with little or no opposition. Stories glorifying the Chinese Reds began to circulate shortly after the outbreak of war in Europe and increased until Pearl Harbor. Then the Communists shifted their support to Chiang Kai-shek for a short period before resuming the attack in late 1942. In a circular distributed by the American Committee for Non-Participation in Japanese Aggression we find the following excerpt from a radio broadcast by Raymond Gram Swing dated January 11, 1940. On that date he declared over the air:

It needs to be understood that the Communist movement in China, the one identified with the Eighth Route Army, has about as much to do with the orthodox Communism as do the Social Democrats of Finland, who are a large element of the Government now at war with the Soviet Union. In China they are called Communists, but the programme of Mao Tse-Tung, the Eighth Route leader, calls for only limited socialism. He wants state control of banks, transportation and mines. He wants democratic elections, consumers and producers cooperatives, and encouragement to private enterprise. The correct label for such a program is right-wing social democracy, which is anathema to true Communists, anywhere outside of China. . . . Mao Tse-Tung wants China to be ruled like a democracy with a two party system the Kuomintant (sic!) as one party, the Communists the other.[4]

There appear to have been a number of causes for the sudden popularity of Mao's minions. A year later, our Ambassador dispatched to the Department a lengthy report in which he summarized the efforts

---

[2] *Institute of Pacific Relations, Hearings,* Part 13, p. 4511; See also testimony of Igor Bogolopev, who was once counselor of the Russian Foreign Office, *Ibid.,* p. 4575.

[3] Testimony of David N. Rowe, March 27, 1952, *Ibid.,* Part 10, p. 3990.

[4] American Committee for Non-Participation in Japanese Aggression. *MS,* Stanford University.

made by the Reds in their attempt to secure a following. The methods utilized appear to have been highly successful. Ambassador Johnson wrote:

The Department will, of course, be aware that the Chinese communists have hitherto had and still appear to have a good press abroad. They have exercised much subtlety and skill in their relations with foreign press correspondents, especially Americans. Perhaps the one American who has done more than any other to portray and to explain the Chinese Communists and their principles and objectives in a favorable light has been Edgar Snow, author of *Red Star Over China*. Through the agency of that book alone the Chinese Communists were colorfully dramatized and made known to millions of Americans and Europeans. Other American journalists and writers such as Randall Gould, Anna Louise Strong, Agnes Smedley and Major E. F. Carlson have perseveringly and sympathetically explained the role that the Communists have played and continue to play in China. . . . It seems not unlikely that the favorable foreign press which the Chinese Communists enjoy is ascribable to a variety of reasons: the Communists encourage contact; they utilize propaganda skillfully; they are adept in seeing that their versions of incidents and problems are promptly placed before correspondents and other third-power nationals of consequence. Moreover they are in a sense the 'underdog'; as the chief opposition party they are often recipients of sympathy. They are poor, young, enthusiastic. More important, they have a definite program and they are adroit in describing it.[5]

John P. Davies, Jr., however, sharply dissented from this thesis. Appended to the Ambassador's report was a memorandum which put forth the view that the Central Government lacked "foreign partisan advocates" which the Chinese Communists had "because of such larger factors as the obvious failings of and corruption within the Central Government and the crusading appeal of the Communist movement." [6]

Since 1924, the Kremlin's agents have been spreading lies about Chiang Kai-shek so industriously throughout the world that their efforts have constituted a campaign unequalled in history. It was not until after the year 1937, however, that the bumper crop of books on China and the Far East appeared, most if not all reviewed in a way that must have been highly pleasing to Moscow. Who are some of these authors and reviewers? What were their views on China? It is not within the scope of this volume to name all of them, but only the ones who had a profound effect upon American thinking towards Asia.

By far the most important author dealing with Far Eastern matters was Owen Lattimore, who is a linguistic master of Communist propaganda. Perhaps Lattimore was not the "architect of our Far Eastern policy," as declared by the late Senator Joseph McCarthy, but at the very least he was its chief propagandist. He was recommended by Lauchlin

---

[5] Ambassador Johnson to Secretary Hull, January 23, 1941. *Foreign Relations, 1941*, Vol. V, pp. 469-470.

[6] Memorandum by John P. Davies, Jr., Feb. 19, 1941. *Ibid.* p. 473n.

Currie as a political adviser to Chiang Kai-shek and held a special position in that regard. "Normally messages should go through embassies," Currie wrote, but "special messages may continue to be routed through me." [7] Lattimore has the distinction of having written eleven books and over forty articles. As a book reviewer, he was in a position to exercise his influence on the success of books on the Far East. Let any reader who has the slightest doubt about his ability as a propagandist read Lattimore's books and settle the matter for himself. As you go through his books, you come constantly upon accounts and views which reveal a very marked tolerance for Russian aims in Asia. Professor William M. McGovern, of Northwestern University, traced the Communist language practice as far back as Karl Marx. During the hearings on the Institute of Pacific Relations, he commented on a letter from Lattimore to E. C. Carter: "There is very clear evidence that he was trying to advocate the Stalinist approach." [8] David Rowe, another scholar on the Far East, made the following interesting remark about Lattimore:

... as of today, among Far Eastern specialists in the United States, Lattimore is probably the principal agent of Stalinism. ... I am talking about ideologies and ideas and that he is promoting these ideas and ideologies. ... He is a specialized operator within the field of Far Eastern studies, Asiatic studies, and particularly, of Chinese studies, and in this field I consider him principal agent for the advocacy of Stalinist ideas.[9]

Others paid tribute to Lattimore's special gift, as witnessed by the testimony of Karl Wittfogel, an eminent scholar of Marxist theory and practice, and one of the greatest living experts on China:

Mr. Morris (Chief Counsel): Doctor, have you found in Owen Lattimore's writings any terminology that would demonstrate his intrinsic devotion to Communist interpretation?
Dr. Wittfogel: Generally speaking, he has avoided the jargon. ...
Senator Ferguson: What is your comment ... ? You were talking about jargon' and the use of language.
Dr. Wittfogel: It would show obviously how somebody tries to proceed along certain political lines without showing himself. There would be a technical term for it. Proceeding in a pro-Communist way without 'exposing yourself' .... it is the method which would be used by those elements of the periphery who are really closely coordinated and integrated into the movement, but who try to promote the advantages of the movement without exposing themselves. As a matter of fact, I remember that once Owen [Lattimore] said to me: 'You know, Karl August, I never read Marx, because if I don't read the stuff nobody can ever accuse me of using the Marxist jargon when saying anything pro-Soviet.'[10]

[7] Currie to Lattimore, July 30, 1941, *Ibid.*, p. 687n.
[8] Testimony of William M. McGovern, September 28, 1951, *Institute of Pacific Relations, Hearings,* Part 4, p. 1013.
[9] Testimony of David Rowe, *Ibid.*, Part 10, pp. 3984-3985.
[10] Testimony of Karl August Wittfogel, August 7, 1951, *Ibid.*, Part 1, p. 333.

Even Lattimore's friend and protégé, John Stewart Service, assailed Lattimore's scholarship during his testimony before the Tydings Committee: "I don't think that Mr. Lattimore is a profound scholar. I think he is rather superficial in his views. He has a very active mind, but his views are apt to shift a bit. I don't think his views on current affairs and China in general are particularly noteworthy." [11]

Strangely enough, Lattimore holds no academic degrees, and until recently he was director of Walter Hines Page School of International Relations, editor of the IPR quarterly *Pacific Affairs*, a special consultant to the Department of State, adviser to Chiang Kai-shek, Pacific Coast director of OWI during the war years, and adviser to Vice-President Wallace on his trip to China. He spent three or four months with the Pauley mission and helped draft a report on that mission. In October, 1949, he was a dominant figure among consultants called in by the Department of State to advise on policy. He was a close friend and intimate associate of John Carter Vincent, State Department Director of Far Eastern Affairs, and Lauchlin Currie, presidential executive assistant in charge of Far Eastern matters. [12] Lattimore had a wide opportunity to implement his blueprint for building up the Chinese Communists and undermining the prestige of Chiang's government. He was considered paramount among experts and had a wide influence on the American people through his numerous books, articles, and book reviews.

In his book *Situation in Asia*, Lattimore proceeded on the premise that China already had fallen and that a new direction was to be given to policy. [13] He wrote that the Communists had conquered China; that one of the factors in this conquest was the spirit of revolutionary nationalism —a surge toward independence that the people of colonial Asia were inevitably experiencing; that the resulting government could not be a "Communist" government; that it would have to be a coalition government; that this coalition, unlike the one sought by General Marshall when the balance of power was on the non-Communist side, would be one with the balance of power on the Communist side. [14]

Lattimore also postulated that, if the new China obtained its supply of capital goods, its capital, and its technicians from America, the Communists would slow down their revolutionary consolidation to an evolutionary pace. He wrote:

---

[11] *State Department Employee Loyalty Investigation, Hearings,* Part 2, p. 2052.

[12] *Institute of Pacific Relations, Final Report,* p. 215-216. See also *The Lattimore Story* by John T. Flynn (New York: Devin-Adair Co., 1953) for an interesting account of his power and influence, and Lattimore's, *Ordeal by Slander* (Boston: Little, Brown and Co., 1950), pp. 66-67.

[13] Owen Lattimore, *The Situation in Asia* (Boston: Little Brown and Company, 1949), p. 151.

[14] *Ibid.,* p. 152.

There is a tendency to assume that China's relations with Russia will be determined by the fact that the Chinese Communists are a junior Marxist Party which will unquestionably accept the decisions of Moscow. The truth is that in China devotion to nationalism and national interests is more powerful among more people than devotion to Marxism and Russian interest. Attempts by the Russians to make the Russian interest override the Chinese interest could easily bring into being a Chinese Titoism. . . . The present top leadership of the Chinese Communists consists of men, who, however closely they may study the Moscow line . . . have built their political machine . . . and are not going to turn to foreigners. . . . [15]

He then went on to advocate, as a United States policy, that we should encourage acceptance of opportunities for American enterprises in China without imposing any conditions or reservation based on internal policies of the new Chinese Government. He urged: "That we abandon the stubbornly lingering delusion that we can maintain footholds [in Asia] by supporting rump territories or rump governments. . . . " [16]

On the question of recognition of the Communist government and its admission to the United Nations, Lattimore wrote that the new government would "claim China's Big Five position in the United Nations, including the right to veto. By the use of our own veto, we could delay China in moving into this position—but only by some such *reductio ad absurdum* as pretending that the island of Formosa is China." [17]

Of Mongolia, Lattimore wrote that it lay between Communist-ruled Russia and Communist-ruled China; that it would be to America's interest to recognize that there is a country between Russia and China; and that we would benefit by granting Mongolia a seat in the United Nations.[18] After the Communist victories in China, Lattimore had this to say:

Throughout Asia today there prevails an atmosphere of hope, not of despair. There is not a single country in Asia in which people feel that we are entering on an age of chaos. What they see opening out before them is a limitless horizon of hope—the hope of peaceful constructive activity in free countries and peaceful cooperation among free peoples. There will be disillusionments along the way as these hopes unfold. They should not come from America, or as a result of American policy. A great part of Asia's hopes, however, will be fulfilled and

---

15 *Ibid.*, pp. 163-166. According to the testimony of Prof. William McGovern, Lattimore was advocating in 1944 or 1945 that United States build its China policy on "the forward-looking people in Yenan," referring to the Communists, *Institute of Pacific Relations, Hearings*, Part 4, p. 1021. Prof. Kenneth A. Colegrove testified that, in December 1943, Lattimore in a conversation with him went so far as to say that "Chinese Communists under Mao Tse-tung were real democrats and that they were really agrarian reformers and had no connection with Soviet Russia." Testimony of Kenneth Colegrove, September 25, 1951, *Ibid.*, Part 3, p. 913; Lattimore denied both of these statements, see *Ibid.*, Part 10, p. 3577.

16 *The Situation in Asia*, pp. 178-179.

17 *Ibid.*, p. 180.

18 *Ibid.*, p. 226.

should be fulfilled, with American cooperation. We have everything to gain by being on the side of hope.[19]

In an earlier book, *Solution in Asia*, Lattimore writes, "Finally, we should enlarge our acceptance of a freedom bloc in Asia to include Outer Mongolia. We need take no initiative in identifying ourselves either with the Chinese claim that Outer Mongolia is Chinese territory or with the Russian policy of recognizing Outer Mongolia as independent. The important facts for us are that Outer Mongolia has long been independent in fact. . . ." [20]

Certain passages regarding Outer Mongolia, which were from Lattimore's book, *Solution in Asia*, are very interesting indeed:

> In Asia the most important example of the Soviet power of attraction beyond Soviet frontiers is in Outer Mongolia. It is here that we should look for evidence of the kind of attraction that Russia might offer to Korea in the future. Outer Mongolia may be called a satellite of Russia in the good sense; that is to say, the Mongols have gravitated into the Russian orbit of their own accord (and partly out of fear of Japan and China); they have neither been subjected to a military conquest nor sold to Russians by traitors among their own people. They have gone through their own revolution. They have taken away the titles, revenues, and powers of hereditary princes, and aristocrats; but the sons and daughters of these aristocrats are full citizens with full equality of opportunity, including government service. . . .
> Soviet policy in Outer Mongolia cannot be fairly called Red imperialism. It certainly establishes a standard with which other nations must compete if they wish to practice a policy of attraction in Asia. Russo-Mongol relations in Asia, like Russo-Czechoslovak relations in Europe, deserve careful and respectful study.[21]

This book was promptly praised by the *New York Herald Tribune*,[22] the *Nation*,[23] the *New Republic*,[24] and *Saturday Review of Literature*,[25] and in the *New York Times* Edgar Snow found the book "penetrating and comprehensive, yet succinct and logical in analysis and exposition of the main dilemmas which face us." [26]

William C. Bullitt, former Ambassador in Moscow, declared that, in 1936, Lattimore urged him to wire President Roosevelt recommending the immediate recognition of the independence of the Mongolian Peoples Republic.[27] Lattimore had insisted that there was no Soviet control of

---

19 *Ibid.*, p. 238.

20 Owen Lattimore, *Solution in Asia* (Boston: Little, Brown and Co., 1945) p. 177.

21 *Ibid.*, pp. 141-144.

22 February 25, 1945.

23 March 17, 1945.

24 February 26, 1945.

25 March 10, 1945.

26 *New York Times Book Section*, February 25, 1945, p. 3.

27 Testimony of William C. Bullitt, April 8, 1952, *Institute of Pacific Relations, Hearings*, Part 13, p. 4523.

the territory. Bullitt was particularly shocked by this incident because, in 1934, Soviet Assistant Vice Commissar for Foreign Affairs Karakhan had described to him in detail how Outer Mongolia was terrorized by the Soviet secret police.[28]

Referring to Lattimore's writings on Outer Mongolia, Nicholas Poppe, who was once head of the Mongolian Department of the Soviet Academy of Science, calls them "either superficial, or a distortion of the truth." He contested Lattimore's views by testifying before the IPR hearings that:

Mongolia was completely wild, a nomadic country in 1919. The new revolutionary people's government established by the Soviets and supported by the Soviets and getting orders from Moscow has achieved, of course, some positive achievement, such as, they established schools, hospitals, and so on. And no matter who establishes schools or hospitals in my opinion, does a good job. If there were no schools or hospitals before. But this is not the end of this story. The deportation of the population of the Mongolian Buddhists, Lamaseries, the destruction and the annihilation of the Mongolian Government, the execution of the Mongolian ministers, forced collectivization, the deportation of many people to the Soviet Union, and so on, are rather negative phenomena, I would say.

Therefore, I cannot call such a system a democratic one. . . . In 1932 the entire population revolted against the Soviets. The Red Mongolian Army and many members of the Mongolian People's Army took the side of the revolters, and this rebellion was suppressed by the Red Army, tanks and aircraft were rushed from Russia to Mongolia.[29]

Corroborative testimony on this point comes from a former Soviet General, Alexander Barmine, who explained that Lattimore's book, *Solution in Asia*, is Communist propaganda. He observed that this book was presented "in a very slick and smooth manner, in very devious ways. It never would be the direct statement of the author . . . but in fact it was telling the straight Communist line, camouflaged, I would say, very skilled." [30] In a review of *Solution in Asia*, General Barmine had written:

Lattimore presents a picture of Soviet Russia which corresponds accurately with his picture of Communist China. As usual, he begins cautiously with what in his opinion the Soviet Union represents to Asiatic peoples. 'In their eyes . . . the Soviet Union stands for strategic security, economic prosperity, technological progress, miraculous medicine, free education, equality of opportunity, and democracy; a powerful combination.' And then Lattimore adds his own opinion: 'The fact that the Soviet Union also stands for democracy is not to be overlooked. It stands for democracy because it stands for all the other things.'[31]

---

28 *Ibid.*, p. 4524.

29 Testimony of Nicholas Poppe, February 12, 1952, *Ibid.*, Part 8, p. 2724. By way of another example, Poppe cited Lattimore's article in *Amerasia* for March-August 1938, to the effect that "Soviet policy in Outer Mongolia cannot be fairly called Red Imperialism." *Ibid.*, pp. 2724-2725.

30 *Ibid*, Part 1, p. 215.

31 *New Leader*, April 7, 1945. An advertisement appeared in the Communist publication, *Daily People's World*, June 1945, showing that the Communist book stores in San Francisco advertised the Lattimore book. *Institute of Pacific Relations, Hearings*, Part 9, p. 3073.

When testifying during the IPR hearings, Lattimore contended that Outer Mongolia was independent until after World War II. Yet the record shows conclusively that he knew in 1936 that Outer Mongolia was Soviet-controlled, and that he repeatedly sought from Soviet authorities permission to visit it.[32] "The indisputable fact that Lattimore knew Outer Mongolia was Soviet-controlled at a time when he was representing it as free and independent," concluded the Senate committee, "was one of many facts which demonstrated to the subcommittee in sharp outline that Lattimore's many misrepresentations were not proceeding from ignorance or confused thinking." [33]

It is significant that, during the hearings on the Institute of Pacific Relations the subcommittee questioned Lattimore extensively and came to the conclusion that he "was, from some time beginning in the 1930's, a conscious articulate instrument of the Soviet conspiracy." [34]

Next to Owen Lattimore, the most effective propagandist on matters dealing with the Far East was Edgar Snow. He was the one American who has done more than any other to portray and to explain the Chinese Communists, their principles, and objectives in a favorable light. When the Chinese Reds made their heroic "long march" to Northwest China where they set up their headquarters, Snow was the first American correspondent to visit its capital, Yenan. He gave brilliant and appealing sketches of the Red leaders—Mao Tse-tung, Chou En-lai, and Chu Teh.

In his *Red Star Over China*, Snow gives an exultant account of life among the Chinese guerrillas and of the exploits of the Communist Eighth Route Army. The book, acclaimed as a best seller, may be said to be the opening gun in what subsequently became a tremendous effort to impress the general public with the virtue, courage, bravery, and humanity of the Chinese Communists. In the first edition of the book, Snow described the Chinese Communists as genuine Communists.[35] This description did not hold favor in some leftist circles. For example, the June, 1938, issue of *Pacific Affairs* carried a criticism of the book by Asiaticus, identified in the IPR hearings as the Comintern member Hans Moeller (or Mueller). Asiaticus laid down the official Comintern line of the period:

The policy of the Chinese Communists makes it quite unmistakable that their only immediate aim was to carry through the Chinese revolution which was actually going on, which was not a Socialist but a Nationalist revolution aimed at eradicating the powerful feudal remnants in rural China, and getting rid of the patriarchal, absolutist recationaries. . . . It is a mistake to suggest, as Snow does (p. 212), that the Chinese Communists used land redistribution merely as

---

32 *Ibid.*, Part 10, p. 3300; 3311; 3318-19; 3635; Part 13, p. 4562.
33 *Ibid.*, *Final Report*, p. 216; Part 13, pp. 4518-4519.
34 *Ibid.*, *Final Report*, p. 224.
35 Edgar Snow, *Red Star Over China* (New York; Random House, 1938), p. 374.

a maneuver to gain power. . . . The liberation of the Chinese peasantry was an aim in itself. . . . The Chinese Communists today represent not only the workers and peasants of China but the entire nation in their fight for national liberation; and, therefore, they stand for democratic freedom as a whole. . . .[36]

It is significant to note that in the second edition of his book, Snow eliminated a number of passages unsatisfactory to Moscow.[37]

To the reader of the *Saturday Evening Post*, Snow would sometimes present the Chinese Communists both as real Communists and as harmless "agrarian reformers" in the same article. In his article "Sixty Million Lost Allies," he says that the Chinese Communists "won its following chiefly among the peasants, by working out a program of agrarian democracy with Socialism as an ultimate, but, admittedly quite distant goal." They should not be called Communist at all, and furthermore "there has never been any Communism in China"; that the old Communist Army is now defunct and it ceased to have any contact with Moscow. Snow quoted Colonel Evans Carlson as describing Chu Teh as a man who had the "kindliness of Robert E. Lee, the tenacity of Grant and the humility of Lincoln."[38]

In the February 17, 1945, issue of the *Nation,* Snow wrote that the Chinese Communists "happened to have renounced years ago now, any intention of establishing Communism in China in the near future."[39] In *People on Our Side,* he praised Soviet Russia while damning Chiang Kai-shek. It enjoyed the distinction of being published in a special edition for the United States Armed Forces. Of course, "the people on our side" included the Chinese Communists who later were shooting at our soldiers in Korea.

In another article, Snow displayed the Chinese Communist propaganda line. He first urged that we ought to abandon Chiang Kai-shek in order to secure friendly relations with Russia, and he stated:

Among the 800,000 puppet troops working for Japan, nine-tenths of them are former Kuomintang troops whose generals are now 'serving as quislings'. . . . [The Kuomintang] is diverting the best equipped . . . troops to blockade the 'heroic and patriotic' 8th Route and New 4th Route. . . . Communist troops in North China, rather than fight the Japanese. . . . By opposing unification . . . and the formation of a coalition, Kuomintang officials are sabotaging the war effort. . . . [The Chinese Communists] have won an astonishing increment of power and territory . . . without any help from any government . . . including . . . Moscow and Washington.[40]

---

36 *Pacific Affairs* (June 1938), Vol. XI, No. 11.

37 See testimony of Louis Budenz, August 23, 1951, *Institute of Pacific Relations, Hearings*, Part 2, p. 680.

38 Edgar Snow, "Sixty Million Lost Allies," *Saturday Evening Post* (June 10, 1944), pp. 44-46.

39 Edgar Snow, "China to Lin Yutang," *Nation,* February 17, 1945, p. 180.

40 Edgar Snow, "Must China Go Red?", *Saturday Evening Post,* May 12, 1945, pp. 9-10.

Snow was made associate editor of the *Saturday Evening Post*. In this position, he exercised some influence in the choice of articles on the subject of China. He wrote from July, 1943, to December, 1950, when his name disappeared as an editor from the *Post*. From 1943 to April, 1950, there were sixty-one articles in the *Post* by Snow about China, Asia, Russia, and some about Europe.[41] But, in justice to the *Saturday Evening Post*, it must be noted that its editorials consistently opposed the views expounded by Edgar Snow.

Twenty days before the death of President Roosevelt, Snow went to see him regarding U.S. policy towards China. Roosevelt significantly remarked that although he intended to continue to support the Nationalist Government, the policy of his administration would be to utilize the Chinese Communists "if and when it were practicable." [42]

There were many other writers on the Far East worth mentioning because of the influence they had on the reading public—writers such as Miriam S. Farley, William Mandel, Andrew Roth, Lawrence Salisbury, Dirk Bodde. The common interest of all was a fascination for the Chinese Communists and a growing hatred for the government of Chiang Kai-shek. In 1945, Gunther Stein published *The Challenge of Red China*, which was a violently pro-Communist book. He described the beautiful free air of the Red capital of Yenan compared to the stagnant, corrupt capital of Chiang at Chungking.

Probably the most interesting account of the relationship between the Chinese Communists and the Soviet Union appears in a conversation between Mao Tse-tung and Gunther Stein. Mao's words, as quoted in *The Challenge of Red China*, are stated here at length:

> I do not believe for one moment that conflict between the capitalist world and the Union of Soviet Socialist Republics is inevitable. On the contrary, we Chinese Communists—who are making a success of the New Democracy which brings all social strata in our areas into close cooperation—are convinced that the capitalistic world and the Union of Soviet Socialist Republics can and will learn to cooperate closely in peace as in war, in spite of occasional difficulties. . . .
>
> China can and must be one of the bridges between the two camps, instead of hoping to win foreign support as one of the zones of friction. China's progress depends upon real world peace, and the international role of our country can be enhanced only by sincere cooperation with all countries and by helping them overcome their differences.[43]

An outstanding example of the favorable publicity afforded pro-Communist writers is the treatment of Stein's book by Nathaniel Peffer,

---

[41] John T. Flynn, *While You Slept: Our Tragedy in Asia and Who Made It* (New York: The Devin-Adair Company, 1951), p. 85.

[42] *State Department Employee Investigation*, Part 1, p. 1155.

[43] Gunther Stein, *The Challenge of Red China* (New York: Whittlesey House, McGraw Hill Book Co., 1945) , p. 68.

who went all-out in the *New York Times Book Review* to support the author's enthusiastic eulogy of Communist China:

The distinguishing characteristic of Communist China is not ideological, political or economical but psychological. There is something in Communist China that captures the imagination. . . . Emotional radicals, objective intellectuals, neutral correspondents, diplomatic officials, military officers. . . . They all come away from Yenan ardent defenders if not enthusiasts.[44]

Stein was accused by General MacArthur's intelligence service of being a Soviet agent, and in 1950 he was expelled from France for espionage.[45] He was a member of the Committee for a Democratic Far Eastern Policy, which is mentioned on the Attorney General's list; he wrote for a pro-Communist magazine, *Amerasia;* and he was identified as a Communist by at least three witnesses before the Senate Internal Security Subcommittee.[46]

During the Second World War, Lawrence K. Rosinger wrote two books, *China's Crisis* and *China's Wartime Politics, 1937-1944.* An evaluation of these books was made by Professor George Taylor, of University of Washington, long active in Far Eastern affairs:

In the discussion of the role of the Communists in China and of their Russian background, there are endeavors to present both sides of a possible argument. However, the objectivity is apparent rather than real. The books of 1944 and 1945 both show him in a number of critical instances either disregarding the obvious connection with the U.S.S.R. or directly denying such connection when factual evidence to the contrary exists and must have been known to him.[47]

The manuscript of *China's Wartime Politics, 1937-1944* was sent to John Carter Vincent, Alger Hiss, and John K. Fairbank for comment and criticism. Fairbank's reply, bearing the return address of Lauchlin Currie, The White House, said of the manuscript: "It seems like a very good job indeed. Can't something be done to send Rosinger to China sometime? The Government will not be happy about this but it is so well done they can hardly call it propaganda."[48]

When Rosinger was asked by the Senate Internal Security Subcommittee whether there was a Communist caucus preceeding the 1949 IPR conference of New Delhi, India, he claimed his privilege under the Fifth

---

44 October 28, 1945.

45 Testimony of General Charles A. Willoughby, August 9, 1951, *Institute of Pacific Relations, Hearings,* Part 2, pp. 355ff; 400.

46 General Willoughby, *Ibid.,* pp. 370-377; 384; Testimony of Mitsuasada Yoshikawa, August 20, 1951, *Ibid.,* Part 2, pp. 499-506; Testimony of Hede Massing, August 2, 1951, *Ibid.,* Part 1, p. 267.

47 *Ibid.,* Part 1, p. 349.

48 *Ibid.,* Part 2, pp. 478; 480-482.

Amendment.[49] He also pleaded the Fifth Amendment when asked whether he was a member of the Communist Party.[50]

One of the strongest apologists for everything Communist was Agnes Smedley. As a correspondent for the Manchester *Guardian* in Hankow, she traveled with the Communist Eighth Route Army and used to broadcast in English for the Reds in Siam. Later, in America in 1943, she wrote a glowing eulogy of the Chinese Communists in her book, *Battle Hymn of China,* in which she compared the Kuomintang with the Nazis in Germany. Major General Charles A. Willoughby, MacArthur's intelligence chief, identified her as a member of the celebrated spy ring headed by Richard Sorge, executed by the Japanese in 1944.[51] She wrote to President Truman and asked him to force MacArthur to apologize or waive immunity so that she could sue for libel. What happened was very mysterious. So far as is publicly known, General MacArthur neither apologized nor waived immunity, but the Army in Washington did a strange thing. It issued what was in effect, a retraction and said it had no proof to back up the charges that Agnes Smedley had been a member of the alleged spy ring. This whole episode is another puzzling chapter in our China policy.[52]

When Miss Smedley died, she left her estate to the Communist leader Chu Teh, requesting in her will that her ashes be buried in Peiping.[53]

American correspondents who traveled to Yenan, headquarters of the Chinese Communists, praised their industrial and agricultural achievements, and applauded the fighting spirit and military achievements of Communist troops. Harrison Forman, in the *New York Herald Tribune,* described the refreshing, informal atmosphere of Yenan, declaring: "No one bothers about ceremony, styles of clothing or time. Everything is open and above board, with absolutely no control or restrictions on movements, discussion, interviews, visits or photographs, while every one, from high government officials to lowest peasant workers, sincerely asks for criticism and advice for betterment of himself and working conditions."[54] Gunther Stein, in *The Christian Science Monitor,* declared that

---

49 Testimony of Lawrence K. Rosinger, January 29, 1952, *Ibid.,* Part 8, p. 2497.

50 *Ibid.,* p. 2475; Called a Communist by at least three witnesses: (Karl Wittfogel, *Ibid.,* Part 1, p. 313) , (William Canning, *Ibid.,* Part 2, p. 467), (Louis Budenz, *Ibid.,* Part 4, p. 1077) ; he was also affiliated with the pro-Communist *Amerasia* and China Aid Council, *Ibid.,* Part 5, p. 1513.

51 *Ibid.,* Part 2, p. 384; Testimony of Mitsuasada Yoshikawa, *Ibid.,* Part 2, p. 507. See also General Willoughby, *Shanghai Conspiracy.*

52 *New York Times,* February 11, 1949, p. 1; February 12, 1949, p. 4; February 19, 1949, p. 1. She was affiliated with the Pro-Communist magazine, *Amerasia,* and was a member of the Committee for a Democratic Far Eastern Policy, cited as subversive by the Attorney-General. *Institute of Pacific Relations, Final Report,* p. 157.

53 *Ibid.,* Part 2, p. 384; Geraldine Fitch, *Formosa Beachhead* (Chicago: Henry Regnery Co., 1953), p. 126.

54 June 23, 1944.

any Allied Commander "would be proud to command those tough well-fed, hardened troops whose exercises show both high skill and spirit."[55]

A writer like Harrison Forman could say in his book, *Report from Red China* that he saw "not the slightest tangible connection with Russia" among the Chinese Communists. He could even tell us that "occasionally I saw portraits of Marx and Lenin; but these seemed the relics of a revolutionary past."[56] And these were the words of a man who was accepted by the American people as one of the leading authorities on China as late as 1945. What he wrote could be refuted by every fundamental document issued by the Chinese Communists and their leaders when they were writing for themselves and not giving interviews to Americans.

Had Forman and other leading American "authorities" familiarized themselves with the Chinese Communist programs, they would know that repeatedly these Communists stated their adherence to the revolutionary doctrines of Marx, Engels, Lenin, and Stalin. When Mao Tse-tung told Forman that they were no longer Communists in the Russian sense of the word, the latter had the naïveté to advise Mao to change the name—"change it to 'Neo-Democracy' or 'Democratism' or some such—anything but 'Communism.' Mao shook his head. 'It doesn't matter to us or to our consciences what we or others call our system. And if we were to change suddenly to some other name, there are those in China today—and abroad, too—who would make capital of it, would accuse us of trying to cover up something. No—we cannot, we must not, change the name. . . . It is the content and the practice that are important—not the label!' "[57]

The *Daily Worker* gave its support to Forman's book when Samuel Sillen wrote: "Interest in China as the pivot in the war against Japan has been registered during the past year in a number of stimulating books by Harrison Forman, Owen Lattimore, Edgar Snow, and other American observers. These authors, riddling the heavy fog of Kuomintang censorship, have played an important part in enlightening the American reading public on the Far East. They have persuasively refuted the lies of Lin Yutang regarding the Chinese Communists. They have urged consistent American policy of encouragement to the democratic, unifying forces in China as the key to quick victory in the Pacific."[58]

Thunder Out of China by Theodore White and Annalee Jacoby was an all-out attack on Chiang Kai-shek and the Nationalist Government

[55] June 27, 1944.

[56] Harrison Forman, *Report from Red China* (New York: Henry Holt Co., 1945), pp. 176-177.

[57] *Ibid.*, pp. 179-180.

[58] *Daily Worker*, August 3, 1945, p. 11; According to the testimony of Louis Budenz, Forman's book was required reading for all Communists and also should be pushed forward in non-Communists organizations. *Institute of Pacific Relations, Hearings*, Part 2, pp. 654-655.

and a big victory for Communist propaganda. Through almost 300 of its 325 pages runs the red streak of bias. In 1946, as a result of its selection by the Book-of-the-Month Club, *Thunder Out of China*, attained very wide circulation.

One of the leading exponents of the theory that Communist China should "more accurately be called democratic" was T. A. Bisson. A frequent contributor to articles in *Amerasia* and *China Today*, he was one of the four hundred "intellectuals" who, in August, 1939, signed the famous letter whitewashing the Soviet Union a few days before the Stalin-Hitler Pact. Bisson acted as the main link between the Foreign Policy Association and the Institute of Pacific Relations. In 1942 he became a member of the International Secretariat of the IPR, and in 1945 he was appointed adviser to General MacArthur in Japan, where he proved to be a hindrance in the implementation of liberal anti-Communist policy.[59]

In 1947, Israel Epstein, a Communist, wrote a book called, *Unfinished Revolution in China*. Edward Carter, Secretary of the IPR, liked it so much he wrote to the publishers that it was of the utmost importance that he get it read "by Secretary of State Marshall, Senators Vandenberg and Morse, and Ives; John Foster Dulles and John Carter Vincent [head of the Far Eastern Division of the Department of State]." He added: "Lattimore was asked by the *New York Times* to review the book. I hope other publishers will make as wise a choice."[60] Lattimore did review the book and wrote that Epstein, the author, had established himself in the distinguished company of Edgar Snow and Theodore White.[61] The *New York Herald Tribune*[62] and the *New Republic*[63] agreed heartily with Lattimore's views.

Epstein wrote for Communist publications and was identified as a member of the Communist Party. During the hearings on the Institute of Pacific Relations, he was out of the country and unavailable for subpoena. He was also subject to action by immigration authorities on grounds involving loyalty and national security.[64]

---

[59] *State Department Employee Loyalty Investigation, Hearings*, Part 2, p. 1921. Bisson was on the editorial board of the pro-Communist magazine, *Amerasia*, as well as associate editor of *Pacific Affairs*. He was affiliated with Friends of Chinese Democracy, a Communist organization, as well as the following Red organizations: American Committee in Aid of Chinese Industrial Cooperatives, Committee For a Democratic Far Eastern Policy. He was also a signer of a statement attacking the United States for "suppressing the Chinese masses and fomenting civil war among them." See *Institute of Pacific Relations, Hearings*, Part 2, p. 622; Part 11, p. 3793; Part 12, p. 4272; Part 8, p. 2789; and *Final Report*, p. 151.

[60] *Ibid.*, Part 2, p. 452; 465.

[61] *New York Times*, June 22, 1947.

[62] June 29, 1947.

[63] June 23, 1947.

[64] Testimony of Elizabeth Bentley, *Institute of Pacific Relations, Hearings*, Part 2, p. 435; also Testimony of Louis Budenz, *Ibid.*, Part 2, p. 590; 634. Epstein was affiliated with the following Communist publications and organizations: *Allied Labor*

Maxwell Stewart, who had extensive Communist associations, wrote a pamphlet in 1944 for the Institute of Pacific Relations, called *Wartime China,* which praised the Chinese Communists. He argued that they were agrarian reformers, and painted resemblances in the Chinese Communists to the grass roots Populist movements in American history.[65] The Army troop training orientation program used this pamphlet to acquaint our soldiers with conditions in China.

China was the key to Soviet domination of Asia. It is ironical that America's path in China paralleled that of Soviet Russia, and that the whole idea of "coalition government" which American officials adopted resulted in victory for Communism in the Far East. According to the record, the Communist Party in America campaigned for a "coalition government" in their official publications, speeches, etc. Then, oddly enough, this policy became the patent medicine of the Far Eastern Division of the Department of State.[66]

No hoax has been more complete and convincing than that which deluded the American people from coast to coast into the belief that the Chinese Communists were a mild edition of agrarian reformers. The books on China during the period from 1937 to 1950 had a profound effect on American thinking. Pro-Communist oriental "experts" had a virtual monopoly on the book reviewing in the most influential publications. They must be assigned considerable responsibility for "engineering" American consent in the sell-out of Nationalist China.

John T. Flynn made a study of thirty books dealing with the political conditions of China. He found that twenty-three of these books were pro-Communist, seven were anti-Communist. He explains the whole subject with this interesting statement: "Every one of the 23 pro-Communist books, where reviewed, received glowing approval in the literary reviews . . . that is, in the *New York Times,* the *Herald Tribune,* the *Nation,* the *New Republic* and the *Saturday Review of Literature.* And every one of the anti-Communist books was either roundly condemned or ignored in these same reviews."[67]

Far Eastern publications offered little criticism of Communist China

---

News, *Amerasia,* Friends of Chinese Democracy, China Aid Council, and Committee for a Democratic Far Eastern Policy, *Ibid., Final Report,* p. 153.

65 *Ibid.,* Part 2, Exhibit No. 140, pp. 564-565; p. 629. Stewart was affiliated with the following: *Amerasia,* American Committee in Aid of Chinese Industrial Cooperatives, American Friends of the Chinese People, Committee for a Democratic Far Eastern Policy, signer of a statement attacking the United States for "suppressing the Chinese masses and fomenting civil war among them," and signer of a statement defending the Soviet Union as "a consistent bulwark against war and aggression." *Ibid., Final Report,* p. 158.

66 *Ibid., Final Report,* pp. 186-187.

67 Flynn, *While You Slept,* p. 73. Flynn made at least one mistake, admitted later in writing. He included in his list of pro-Communist books David Nelson Rowe's *China Among the Powers, 1945.* This book received critical reviews in the *New York Times* (Eleanor Lattimore), and the *Herald Tribune* (Edgar Snow).

or the Soviet Union, but were severely critical of the Nationalist Government. Many of the writers had no real claim of scholarship in the fields they covered. The same names appeared over and over in the most influential review sections of our important journals. For a period of only five years, from 1945-1950, the following authors wrote a total of 162 book reviews: Richard Watts, Jr.—40; Owen Lattimore—26; John K. Fairbank—20; T. A. Bisson—18; Nathaniel Peffer—15; Eleanor Lattimore—13; Lawrence K. Rosinger—9; Annalee Jacoby—9; Gunther Stein—7; Theodore White—3. All of these people were good friends and associates, all propagandists for Mao Tse-tung's "agrarian reformers." A mutual admiration society was established of such an extent as to arouse immediate suspicion. So completely were the book reviews of the leading newspapers taken over by the pro-Chinese Communist aggregation that one could almost predict in advance the fate of an anti-Communist book on China.

The outpouring of books, articles, and book reviews made a terrific impact upon United States opinion, largely setting the tenor in the academic and journalistic fields. As Owen Lattimore put it in the *New York Times* on June 22, 1947.

From Edgar Snow's *Red Star Over China* to Theodore White and Annalee Jacoby's *Thunder Out of China* the list of names is distinguished. . . . It is noteworthy that the recent and current trend of good books about China, well documented and well written, has been well to the left of center.[68]

Lattimore was quite right. The list was more than noteworthy. In general, though not in every detail, these books assumed a common pattern arguing three fundamental points: First, the Chinese Communists "are not Communists," not according to the Russian definition of the term; second, the Chinese Communists are fighting the Japanese, and the Chinese National Army is not; third, Chiang Kai-shek is a Fascist, and his totalitarian regime is preventing the Communists from establishing democracy.

The authors of these books endorsed each other's publications with remarkable success. Their praise was glowing, but a spoonful of criticism was often put in to give the right tint of impartiality. The few authors and journalists who tried to warn the Americans of the Communist peril in the Far East were subject to severe criticism. For example, in the *Saturday Review of Literature*, Edgar Snow lambasted George Creel, President Wilson's Public Information Officer during World War I and an uncompromising enemy of Communism. Of Creel's *Russia's Race for Asia*, Snow said with a forthrightness that would lose him no lecture dates, "nearly every page . . . is distinguished by errors of fact, judgment, and understanding."[69]

---

[68] *New York Times,* June 22, 1947.
[69] April 9, 1949; p. 11.

Creel took the matter up with the *Saturday Review of Literature* and the editors printed a letter of his which is sharply critical:

Edgar Snow, in what purported to be a review of my book, *Russia's Race for Asia,* started off with an ugly sneer at my conduct of the Committee on Public Information in the First World War, and then proceeded to berate me for 'errors of fact, judgment and understanding,' the use of quotations out of context and other dishonesties.' . . . I have always assumed it was the right of the author to have his work reviewed objectively or, at least, with some reasonable degree of impartiality and dispassion. . . . When you handed *Russia's Race for Asia* over to Mr. Snow, you cannot have been unaware that for years, both in books and articles, he has specialized in presenting a favorable picture of the Chinese Communists. . . . It could have been no secret to you that he would particularly resent my denunciation of 'those credulous liberals and fellow-travelers' who have labored so faithfully to persuade American opinion that the Chinese Communist party is a purely native movement, led by agrarian reformers and born of a people's spontaneous revolt against corruption and oppression. All propaganda that I branded as the Ultimate Lie.[70]

Creel had another sample of this when the *New York Times* turned his *Russia's Race for Asia* over for review to Nathaniel Peffer of Columbia University, a frequent contributor to the *Times Sunday Magazine Section* and its *Sunday Book Section.* Peffer has been an unremitting foe of Nationalist China and Chiang Kai-shek in virtually everything he has written since the Japanese surrender in 1945. Peffer found it "a foolish book." Creel was not to be taken seriously because "he fears Russia and does not like or trust the Chinese Communists."[71]

Whenever a book came out that was critical of the Chinese Communists, the entire anti-Nationalist crowd would marshal their efforts to kill it. For example, Lattimore attacked Harold Issacs' anti-Stalinist book on the Chinese revolution, *No Peace in Asia.* He remarked: "Mr. Issacs, referring to China, writes of 'the cold embrace of Communist totalitarianism'; but it appears from other accounts that it is in these areas that there really is a beacon of hope. . . ."[72]

Another example of what happens to authors who wrote anti-Chinese Communist material occurred in June, 1945. *Reader's Digest* published an article by Max Eastman and J. B. Powell, sharply attacking the Chinese Communists and the position of Owen Lattimore on China. At once the anti-Chiang group was roused to action. Owen Lattimore, Edward C. Carter, T. A. Bisson and their friend, Corliss Lamont, were busily engaged formenting a scheme. Lattimore drafted a letter to the *New York Times.* The text was not merely a defense, but a counter-attack, calling in effect for a shift of United States support toward the Chinese Communists. It was desired to do something more adroit than

---

[70] Letter to the Editor, May 21, 1949, p. 24.

[71] *New York Times,* March 13, 1949, p. 10.

[72] *New York Herald Tribune,* June 22, 1947, p. 10.

a public letter signed by one of their own professional names. With Corliss Lamont's help, the plan was to get his father, the well-known partner of J. P. Morgan Co., Thomas W. Lamont, to sign the text which they had prepared. Thomas Lamont, however, in a letter dated July 5, 1945, declined: "In effect I think you are suggesting that I write to the *Times* a letter urging our Government to alter its apparent present policy, and to make available lend-lease supplies to the so-called Communist armies."[73]

When Lin Yutang exposed the brutality of the Chinese Reds in *Vigil of a Nation,* he suddenly saw his great popularity with the American people vanish. Among the architects of this rejection was Harrison Forman, who made good use of the opportunity, panning the book mercilessly in *Saturday Review of Literature.* To write of China and her politics, he stated, was beyond Lin Yutang's "first hand knowledge."[74] In the *Saturday Review of Literature,* Forman was rewarded for attacking Doctor Lin. Forman's *Report from Red China* was given to Richard Watts, Jr., a leading light of the Communist-front Committee for a Democratic Far Eastern Policy, for review. Watts was moved by Forman's evidence that the "Chinese Communists form a free and independent body without subservience to Moscow and are interested not in . . . collectivizing China, but in bringing about a unified democratic nation."[75]

Annalee Jacoby appeared in the *New York Times Sunday Book Section* on December 16, 1946, as the reviewer of *My Twenty-Five Years in China* by John B. Powell, an American of unquestioned integrity, who lost both of his feet in a Japanese prison. Here she takes sharp issue with Powell, who persists in calling the Chinese Communists "bandits." Mrs. Jacoby berates the author as an old fashioned "reactionary" and insists that peace in China's Civil War depends on "progress of negotiations between the Kuomintang and the Communists." She is especially contemptuous of Powell's suggestion that there is a "red menace."[76]

Anyone who wishes to examine the evidence will find confirmation of a virtual monopoly in book reviewing by the anti-Nationalist faction. We find, in the *New York Herald Tribune,* that when Mrs. Edgar Snow writes a book, Mrs. Owen Lattimore reviews it in highly favorable terms. Later, the favor is returned when Mrs. Snow favorably reviews a book by Mrs. Lattimore. *The Chinese Labor Movement,* by Nym Wales (Mrs.

---

[73] *Institute of Pacific Relations, Hearings,* Part 1, pp. 169-170.

[74] February 3, 1945, p. 10.

[75] March 10, 1945, pp. 9-10; Richard Watts Jr., who during the war was head of the News Division of the Office of War Information in Chungking, subsequently became a member of the Board of Directors of the "Committee for a Democratic Far Eastern Policy," which has been designated by the Attorney General as a Communist front. *Institute of Pacific Relations, Hearings,* Part 1, p. 55, Part 3, p. 771, Part 3, p. 1017. He is listed as pro-Communist by the Senate Internal Security Subcommittee, *Ibid., Final Report,* p. 100; Affiliated with the American-Russian Institute, *Final Report,* p. 159.

[76] *New York Times,* December 16, 1945, p. 7.

Edgar Snow), was reviewed by Eleanor Lattimore on April 8, 1945. *The Situation in Asia,* by Owen Lattimore, was reviewed by Edgar Snow on April 10, 1949. Both reviews appeared in the *New York Herald Tribune Weekly Book Review.*

The Challenge of Red China by Gunther Stein, who was named a Soviet agent in a SCAP intelligence report, was favorably reviewed in the *New York Times* by Nathaniel Peffer and in the *New York Herald Tribune* by Lattimore. Said Peffer: "The leaders of the Communists . . . are exceptionally . . . straight-forward, simple, of unquestionable integrity. . . . They have paternal concern for the people over whom they rule."[77] Said Lattimore: "The most up-to-date hand book amazingly complete."[78]

Thunder Out of China, by Theodore White and Annalee Jacoby, was chosen by the Book-of-the-Month Club, giving it a double stamp of respectability. But to ensure its success, the top-flight reviewers of the pro-Chinese Communist aggregation were on hand to give it a rousing send-off. Edgar Snow in the *Saturday Review of Literature,*[79] John K. Fairbank in the *Times,*[80] and Richard Watts Jr. in the *Tribune* gave it the highest praise.[81] Fairbank wrote that if China were to go Communist, it would be because "Chinese Communist Democracy" has succeeded in appealing to the people more effectively than the Kuomintang. He was in agreement with the authors that the issue was not one of Communism, but merely of good government. "Readers who believe that Communism is an uncalled-for conspiratorial subversion," Fairbank wrote, "will have apoplexy from *Thunder Out of China.*" We have let our fears of Russia and of Communism, on which the right-Kuomintang plays so skillfully, drive the Chinese revolution further into dependence upon Russia and upon Communism."[82]

When Fairbank wrote *The United States and China,* Annalee Jacoby recalled Fairbank's words about *Thunder Out of China* and wrote in the *Times* that she could not "remember another volume which holds . . . as much scholarly information about a single subject."[83] Furthermore, on the jacket of Professor Fairbank's book was Theodore White's assertion that this was "the best one-volume job on China I've ever read." [84]

When Richard Lauterbach wrote *Danger From the East,* Mark Gayn, in the *Saturday Review of Literature,* called it "one of the most brilliant reporting jobs done since the end of the war."[85] When Gayn published

77 October 28, 1945, p. 4.
78 October 14, 1945, p. 3.
79 October 26, 1946, p. 12.
80 October 27, 1947, p. 1.
81 October 27, 1946, p. 1.
82 *New York Times,* October 27, 1946, p. 43.
83 July 11, 1948, p. 1.
84 Published by Harvard University Press, 1948.
85 November 29, 1947, p. 11.

Japan Diary, Lauterbach, in the *Tribune,* returned the favor with "in the richest tradition of American journalism."[86]

When Owen Lattimore wrote his *Ordeal by Slander,* his friend John Fairbank managed to write a front-page review in the *New York Herald Tribune,* in which he concealed the fact that he was one of the participants in organizing the Lattimore defense publicity campaign.[87] To such depths had academic integrity declined.

The tally is almost endless. Bit by bit, and shamelessly, the pro-Communist clique created the myth that Mao Tse-tung's forces in Asia were merely "agrarian reformers"; that they fought the Japanese single-handed, "blockaded" by vicious Chiang Kai-shek; that they were independent and could be won over to America. Steadily, this propaganda undercut the only armies in the field—the Nationalists—which blocked the spread of Communism in Asia. This was the period during which the champions of the Chinese Communist cause masterfully bolstered the tragic State Department policy which led inevitably to Red control of the mainland.

The record shows that numerous authors deluded the American people about China from 1937 to 1950. Books on the Far East became among the most effective avenues for insidious propaganda which affected our attitude toward the Nationalist Chinese in favor of the Reds. The book reviewer played a significant role because he stood between the public and the publisher's products.

The bookseller, the librarian, and the general reading public are largely influenced by what the critic says. The importance of the reviewer is evident by the fact that the only news the public sometimes gets of a book is through its reviews. Paid advertising, more often than not, depends on the amount, kind, and quality of the reviews. If the reviews are poor, the publisher will not put money into paid advertising. He cannot afford to. And the extent of the sales effort expended on the book depends considerably upon the reviews it receives.

Books on the Far East during the period of 1937-1950 colored the news and opinions in the American press and in pulpits, classrooms, and political organizations all over the country. The general theme was that the Chinese Communists were not real Communists but mere "agrarian reformers" independent of Moscow.

We know today that all the resources of the Cominform were thrown into the battle for China—a battle that was waged with effective propaganda that blanketed the truth and captured the American mind. The anti-Communist mind, whenever it showed, was smothered by every means of opposition. As one looks backwards at China now from the tragically

[86] November 28, 1948, p. 2.
[87] July 30, 1950.

clear perspective of hindsight, it is apparent that the battle of books was won by the anti-Nationalists through their power and influence. The American people had no real knowledge of China. The Communist sympathizers filled the vacuum with their own books, reviewed favorably by each other. They derided and denounced all others who had a kind word to say for the Nationalist Government. These people were able to exercise an incredibly effective censorship over what the American people should be allowed to read, know and think about Far Eastern affairs.

CHAPTER XVII

TOO LITTLE, TOO LATE:
AID TO NATIONALIST CHINA

As a result of the surrender of Japan in 1945, a vacuum developed in the Far East. Chinese and American officials were deeply concerned. The Chinese Communists were more strategically settled in North China than were the Nationalist forces at war's end. The main drive of the Reds was directed toward control of the important cities. This effort, if successful, would mean virtual domination of areas essential to China's economy. General Albert C. Wedemeyer, commander of U. S. forces in China, realized the imperative need for stationing the Chinese Nationalist troops in the areas to be vacated by the defeated Japanese. On November 20, 1945, he was instructed that "while the State Department wanted to help the Nationalists under Chiang Kai-shek to get the Japanese out of China, *'it does not wish to support the National Government directly against the Communists.'* "[1]

This foreshadowed an irresolute State Department policy toward Nationalist China in the postwar period. James F. Forrestal, Secretary of the Navy, recorded the following in his dairy: "But the State Department, impressed by the backwardness, corruption and unpopularity of the Nationalists under Chiang Kai-shek, convinced that Mao's Communists represented an important popular movement and that the United States could not openly combat it without suffering disastrously under the charge of 'imperialist meddling,' wished to stay clear of the struggle between Chiang and Mao."[2] The charges feared by the State Department constituted a central theme of the Communist *Daily Worker*.

Whatever the implications of the State Department's decision not to transport any more Chinese Nationalist troops to Manchuria and not to "support the National government *vis-à-vis* the Communist except in so far as necessary to get the Japanese disarmed and out of China,"[3] the

---

[1] *The Forrestal Diaries*, p. 109. Italics mine.
[2] *Ibid.*
[3] *The Forrestal Diaries*, p. 109.

Chinese Communists were able to consolidate their position in North China and Manchuria.

When Wedemeyer requested the War Department "to send seven American divisions to China in order to create a barrier through North China and Manchuria against Soviet Russia,"[4] there was still time to check Communist expansion in China because Communist troops were neither well organized nor sufficiently equipped to provide serious resistance. But, because of differences of American opinion as to what action should be taken, the Nationalist cause was seriously weakened.

On November 26, 1945, the Navy and War Departments completed a long memorandum for Secretary of State James F. Byrnes, recommending their policy for China. It stated that "it was impossible to support Chiang against the Japanese without also supporting him against the Chinese Communists." The memorandum "firmly elected to accept the risks of the latter course."[5] This was a direct confirmation from the diary of Secretary Forrestal, who was head of the Navy Department. After extended consideration, he and Secretary Robert Patterson of the War Department had agreed that the policy of supporting Chiang Kai-shek against the Chinese Communists should be adopted. American military authorities had settled upon a realistic course designed to preserve the fruits of our victory in the war.

The recommendations contained in the Patterson-Forrestal memorandum for aid to Chiang Kai-shek against the Chinese Communists were rejected by the Department of State, with Dean Acheson, then Under Secretary of State, taking an active part.[6] Instead, the State Department conducted direct consultations with the Soviet Union regarding China. Subsequently, General Marshall made his fateful mission to China with instructions to try to force Chiang Kai-shek to accept the Chinese Communists into his government.

Marshall's embargo on the shipment of all aid to the anti-Communist forces seriously weakened the Nationalist military strength. The embargo lasted from August, 1946, to May, 1947—a period of approximately ten months, during which time no material was sent except 130,000,000 rounds of ammunition that was especially made for the so-called "Generalissimo rifle" and could not be obtained elsewhere.[7] During the same period, there were no Russian restrictions on arms to the Chinese Communists.

According to a statement made by the Chinese Delegation before the

---

4 *Wedemeyer Reports,* p. 348.

5 *The Forrestal Diaries,* p. 112.

6 Testimony of Harold Stassen, October 8, 1951, U.S. Congress, Senate Subcommittee on Foreign Relations, *Nomination of Philip C. Jessup, Hearings,* 82nd Cong., 1st Sess. (Washington: Government Printing Office, 1951), pp. 694-695.

7 *Military Situation in the Far East, Hearings,* Part 3, pp. 1948-1949.

Political Committee of the 6th Session of the United Nations General Assembly, the Soviet army in Manchuria, between August 9 and September 9, 1945, took 594,000 Japanese prisoners of war and captured 925 airplanes, 369 tanks, 35 armored cars, 1,226 artillery pieces, 4,836 machine guns, 300,000 rifles, 133 radio sets, 2,300 motor vehicles, 125 tractors, and 17,497 horses and mules.

In addition to the above, the Japanese surrendered all stocks in depots and warehouses, including 1,436 artillery pieces, 8,989 machine guns, 11,052 hand grenades, 3,078 trucks, 104,777 horses, 21,084 supply cars, 815 special vehicles, and 287 command cars.[8]

The Soviet government also supplied the Chinese Communists in Manchuria with some 2,000 trained workers, composed of Soviet citizens and Japanese prisoners of war. Furthermore, some 600 shiploads of Lend-Lease supplies were sent by the United States across the Pacific to Vladivostok and Siberian ports for the Russians to use against Japan. Almost none of it was used for that purpose by the Russians in their six days of fighting. The balance was given by them to the Chinese Communists. Most of the American material paraded by the Chinese Communists under the guise of having been obtained from Nationalist soldiers was Lend-Lease material we had sent to Russia. But this fact did not impair the propaganda in the American press to the effect that Nationalist soldiers were surrendering their arms to the Communists.

Once the struggle for Manchuria was resumed, many Americans demanded a re-evaluation of our China policy. It was at this juncture that President Truman sent Lieutenant General Albert C. Wedemeyer to China on a fact-finding mission. He was instructed to make "an appraisal of the political, economic, psychological and military situations," and to inform Chinese officials that "the United States Government can consider assistance in a program of rehabilitation only if the Chinese Government presents satisfactory evidence of effective measures looking towards Chinese recovery." He was to advise China that "any aid which may be made available shall be subject to the supervision of representatives of the United States Government."[9]

The Nationalist Government expressed the hope that this mission would result in economic and military aid, while the Communist reaction was bitterly hostile. General Wedemeyer arrived in Nanking with a group of experts and, during a month's stay in China, visited the principal centers of the country, talking with a large number of Chinese people and American officials. On August 22, 1947, he was invited by Chiang Kai-shek to address a joint meeting of the State Council and all the Ministers of the National Government. In his speech, Wedemeyer

---

[8] *China Handbook* (1952-53), pp. 391-393.
[9] *United States Relations with China*, pp. 255-256.

severely criticized the National Government for its corruption and inefficiency and asserted that: "the Central Government cannot defeat the
Chinese Communists by the employment of force, but can only win the
loyal, enthusiastic and realistic support of the people by improving the
political and economic situation immediately." [10]

These remarks were immediately challenged by Nationalist Premier
Chang Chun, who, in an interview on September 2, told the United Press
correspondents at Shanghai that he recognized the good intentions of
General Wedemeyer, "but as a representative of the President of the
United States Wedemeyer's statement caused a lot of criticism among the
Chinese people." Chang also said: "General Wedemeyer paid more attention to people outside the government than in it. . . . There were many
people who wanted to see Wedemeyer and could not. And there were
many things not known to the General." [11] On the other hand, a Communist broadcast on August 28 called General Wedemeyer a "blood-
thirsty butcher" and a "hypocrite" and declared: "It is very possible that
he will urge Washington for further aid to Chiang to prop up the
Kuomintang government from imminent collapse. Chiang Kai-shek will
also exert all his effort for a final struggle and American imperialists will
rush aid to Chiang." [12]

Prior to his departure, the National Government gave General Wedemeyer a memorandum explaining its determination to check inflation,
carry out necessary political reform, and build up a democratic constitutional government. With regard to the Communist problem, the memorandum stated: "the Communists as an armed political party must be
suppressed. . . . The government fully realizes that the success or failure
of this fight against the Communist peril will not only decide its own
fate but also the life and death of China as a sovereign power." [13]

After returning to Washington, Wedemeyer submitted to President
Truman, on September 19, a report which was not made public until two
years later. This report cannot be commended too highly for its objectivity and for its sound realization that Russia was on the march in Asia
to the destruction of our Far Eastern policy. The document is worthy of
extensive quotation. Its recommendations, if implemented, might have
set up a barrier against the Red tide. Wedemeyer analyzed Russia's
position in the Far East with this observation:

Events of the past two years demonstrate the futility of appeasement based
on the hope that the strongly consolidated forces of the Soviet Union will adopt
either a conciliatory or a cooperative attitude except as tactical expedients.

10 *Ibid.*, p. 759.
11 *Ibid.*, p. 815.
12 *Ibid.*, pp. 816-817.
13 *Ibid.*, pp. 817-822.

Soviet practice in the countries already occupied or dominated completes the mosaic of aggressive expansion . . . far exceeding that of Nazism in its ambitious scope and dangerous implications.

Therefore in attempting a solution to the problem presented in the Far East . . . every possible opportunity must be used to seize the initiative in order to create and maintain bulwarks of freedom.[14]

Our difficulties, Wedemeyer continued, arose in the Far East because we "facilitated the Soviet program in the Far East by agreeing at the Yalta Conference to Russian re-entry into Manchuria and later by withholding aid from the National Government." [15] Moreover, it was also through our mediation effort and embargo that advantage was given to the Chinese Communists. And, in spite of the Sino-Soviet Treaty of 1945, the Soviet Union "has hindered the efforts of the Chinese Government to restore its control over Manchuria." Instead, the Soviet Union "assisted the Chinese Communists in Manchuria by the timing of the withdrawal of Soviet troops and by making available, either directly or indirectly, large quantities of surrendered Japanese military equipment." [16]

As to the importance of China to the American position in the Far East, Wedemeyer stated:

Any further spread of Soviet influence and power would be inimical to the United States strategic interests. In time of war the existence of an unfriendly China would result in denying us important air bases for use as staging areas for bombing attacks as well as important naval bases along the Asiatic coast. Its control by the Soviet Union or a regime friendly to the Soviet Union would make available for hostile use a number of warm-water ports and air bases. Our own air and naval bases in Japan [the] Ryukyus and the Philippines would be subject to relatively short range neutralizing air attacks. Furthermore, industrial and military development of Siberia east of Lake Baikal would probably make the Manchurian area more or less self-sufficient.

On the other hand, a unified China friendly or allied to the United States would not only provide important air and naval bases, but also from the standpoint of its size and manpower, be an important ally to the United States.[17]

As one reads through this report, it is quite obvious that the Communist menace gave General Wedemeyer grave concern. He pointed out clearly that the military situation had reached a point where "prompt action is necessary to prevent Manchuria from becoming a Soviet satellite." [18] Moreover, "the present industrial potential of China is inadequate to support military forces effectively. Hence outside aid in the form of munitions (most urgently ammunition) and technical assistance are

---

[14] *Report to the President* submitted by Lt. Gen. A. C. Wedemeyer, September 1947 (Washington: Government Printing Office, 1951), p. 1.

[15] *Ibid.*, p. 2.

[16] *U.S. Relations with China*, p. 777.

[17] *Ibid.*, pp. 809-810.

[18] *Ibid.*, p. 808.

essential before any plans of operations can be undertaken with reasonable prospect of success." [19]

To bolster China in its civil war against the Reds, Wedemeyer had
some positive recommendations. First, China had 16,000 motor vehicles—
chiefly trucks—which it could not use because of lack of spare parts which
we had agreed to supply but had not. "The United States," he said, "is
morally obligated to complete this program." Secondly, the United States
should enable the Chinese to buy military equipment owing to the fact
that:

> Since completion of the 39 division program nearly two years ago, very little
> has been supplied. Thus, there are many shortages in military equipment which
> react to the disadvantage of Nationalist military efforts. Credits should be
> established for China to purchase the necessary military equipment needed to
> effect a supervised revitalization of her ground and air forces. Without such aid,
> American equipment purchased during and subsequent to the war is, or soon
> will be, valueless since maintenance parts will not be available to continue the
> equipment in use.[20]

Wedemeyer also had some cautious advice bearing upon the future of
the civil war in China. The Nationalist armies had consistently complained of "shortages of ammunition of all types and calibers." Unless
replenished in the "near future," the shortages would become severe.
The United States had a "moral obligation to assist the Chinese Government to obtain ammunition." [21]

The Wedemeyer Report was not made public until 1949—two years
later. The suppression of this report led members of the press, as well
as radio commentators, members of Congress and officials in the Pentagon, to attempt to elicit some information. "I felt that at least top officials
in the Pentagon and certainly members of the Senate and House Foreign
Relations Committee," said Wedemeyer, "should have full access to it
and to members of the mission if explanation or amplification were
required." [22]

When General Marshall wanted Wedemeyer to "delete certain specific
portions," he refused. So the report was suppressed. Pressures were
brought to bear on other members of Wedemeyer's mission, who were
warned not to divulge the contents.

"It dawned upon me," remarked Wedemeyer, "that all my work had
been to no purpose, and the recommendations I had made with such
high hopes were being quietly ignored." [23]

---

[19] *Ibid.*, p. 810.

[20] *Ibid.*, p. 811.

[21] *Ibid.*, p. 812.

[22] *Wedemeyer Reports*, p. 396.

[23] *Ibid.*, p. 397. It is significant that Louis Budenz, former editor of the *Daily
Worker*, testified that General Wedemeyer was on the Communists' blacklist and was
scheduled to be removed from the scene: ". . . the Communists viewed General

The *China White Paper* states that the Wedemeyer Report was not made public because it contained a recommendation that the United Nations place Manchuria under a guardianship of five powers, including the Soviet Union, and if this were made public at that time, it would be highly offensive to the Chinese susceptibilities as an infringement of Chinese sovereignty.[24] This explanation by the Department of State is hardly justified. Since the turn of the century, it had been U. S. policy to protect the "territorial and administrative integrity" of China. The Wedemeyer report contained some wise recommendations which, if implemented, might have accomplished this objective by saving China from Red domination. It is more likely that we were still imagining we could and should get along with our Russian ally, and that General Marshall and other officials were afraid the release of the report might irritate our relations with the Soviet Union. The report, in almost every detail, repudiated the Marshall Mission to China. General Wedemeyer summed up the controversy this way:

I knew that the delay in implementing my recommendations for immediate moral and material support to the Chinese Nationalist Government was serving the purpose of the Communists. The State Department knew as well as I that the situation was deteriorating rapidly, yet the hands-off attitude prevailed. I asked myself with increasing anxiety why I had been sent to China. Had General Marshall simply wanted me to reinforce his own views by submitting a report completely confirming his existing do-nothing policy? Had he wanted me to join the host of sycophants whom he had despised in the earlier years when he told me that he valued most those who frankly expressed their honest convictions? . . . *I feel positive today that the publication of my report would not have caused embarrassment to my Government and to the Chinese or the Koreans.* If I am wrong, then it would appear that the subsequent publication of my report in the White Paper in 1949 was a serious mistake in diplomacy.[25]

When General Wedemeyer appeared before the Senate Committee on Appropriations on December 17, 1947, he was asked if he had his report with him. He replied that Secretary Marshall "admonished" him and asked him "to insure that the members of my mission would maintain security with reference to the report." [26] Marshall was asked before the Senate Armed Services Committee, "Why did you join in the suppression of the Wedemeyer report on China?" He curtly replied: "I did not join in the suppression of the report. *I personally suppressed it.*" [27]

Wedemeyer as the enemy of the Soviet interests in the Far East." *Institute of Pacific Relations, Hearings,* Part 2, p. 623.

[24] *U.S. Relations with China,* p. 260. Joseph Alsop, "The Foredoomed Mission of General Marshall," *Saturday Evening Post,* January 21, 1950, p. 114.

[25] *Wedemeyer Reports,* pp. 397-398. Italics mine.

[26] *Military Situation in the Far East, Hearings,* Part 1, p. 546.

[27] U.S. Congress, Senate, Committee on Armed Services, *Nomination of General of the Army George C. Marshall to be Secretary of Defense, Hearings,* 82d Cong., 2d Sess. (Washington: Government Printing Office, 1950), p. 22. Italics mine.

The dubious performance of General Marshall in the China story is an open record to all ardent historians. It is unfortunate that he did not live up to any real military leadership at such a crucial time in our history. Had he been less amateurish in his outlook and more experienced in the tactics of international Communism, there might have been a chance of preventing China from falling into the Moscow orbit.

The recommendations by General Wedemeyer, while drastic in scope, would have checked Communist advances in China, had they been fully carried out. But, as President Truman and Secretary of State Marshall were inclined towards a hands-off policy, the report was shelved and no action whatever was taken by the American Government. This decision served no other purpose than to promote the Communist conquest of China.

On August 18, 1946, Truman issued an executive order to the effect that China was not to be allowed to acquire any "surplus" American weapons "which could be used in fighting a civil war," meaning a war with the Communists. Thus Nationalist forces had to rely on the dwindling supply of their own arsenals. These were soon proved wholly inadequate to match the vast quantities of Japanese munitions which came into Chinese Communist hands in Manchuria.

It is evident that, as the Communist military successes began to mount in the Far East, pressure for aid to the Kuomintang became greater in Washington. The Republicans, in particular, charged that the Democratic administration was permitting China to fall into the hands of the Communists and eventually into the waiting arms of Russia, and that it was impossible to fight Communism successfully in Europe alone. Secretary Forrestal took up the cry, holding out for more and more aid, while Secretary of Labor Lewis B. Schwellenbach—in agreement with several other Cabinet members—argued that "he saw no reason why we should continue to interfere in the affairs of China; [if] they wanted to have a civil war they should have it, but that we should not be in the position of trying to impose any form of government on any nation." [28]

Repeated warning came from our Ambassador to China, Dr. John Leighton Stuart, who wrote frequently of the critical situation of the Nationalist forces and their desperate need of ammunition. Here are a few examples. On July 1, 1947: "Persons in direct contact with the Nationalist troops in rural areas state there are insufficient small arms and ammunition to arm all combatant troops now in the field." [29] On September 20, 1947: "The political, military and economic position of the Cen-

---

28 *The Forrestal Diaries*, p. 190.

29 Ambassador Stuart to Secretary Marshall, Nanking, July 1, 1947, *U.S. Relations with China*, p. 733. During the MacArthur Hearings, Senator Brewster of Maine asked General Wedemeyer the following questions:

SENATOR BREWSTER: We have heard a great many stories about equipment and matériel but would it be true that if they lacked the ammunition, all the guns in the

tral Government has continued to deteriorate within recent months in accordance with previous expectations. Currently, the cumulative effect of the absence of substantial financial and military assistance expected from the Wedemeyer Mission and renewed Communist military activity are intensifying the Chinese tendency to panic in times of crisis." [30]

On February 5, 1948, Ambassador Stuart made this observation:

> The situation is very definitely one to cause pessimism. If American aid should materialize in adequate measure and palatable form, the tide may turn quickly in our favor . . . . if our plans are deemed to be insufficient or unpalatable, or unlikely to be effective, it is more than likely that disaffection of some elements now in the government may ensue. Such disaffection may well result in the replacement of present dominant elements with the group desirous of effecting union with the Communists through the good offices of the Soviet Union.[31]

On March 31, 1948, Stuart wrote: "The Chinese people do not want to become Communists yet they see the tide of Communism running irresistibly onward. In the midst of this chaos and inaction the Generalissimo stands out as the only moral force capable of action." [32]

In his widely circulated "Report on China" printed in *Life* for October 13, 1947, William C. Bullitt recommended the sending of American military advisers in training and operations, the immediate release of certain stocks of munitions by the U.S., to be rushed to Manchuria, and that the American military should have direct military control of all supplies to the Nationalists. The cost would be about $200 million a year for three years.[33] The Department of State preferred a policy of watchful waiting. Marshall told the Senate Committee on Foreign Relations in November that the Department contemplated a $300 million aid program in 1948 to help China fight inflation.[34] When the President called a special session of Congress to deal with the critical situation in Europe, some Republi-

---

world and all the motors (*sic?*) in the world and all the tanks in the world would be utterly useless—?

GENERAL WEDEMEYER: Yes, sir.

SENATOR BREWSTER: (continuing). If they did not have the ammunition?

GENERAL WEDEMEYER: Yes, sir.

SENATOR BREWSTER: And that was one of the great problems which the Chinese Nationalists faced?

GENERAL WEDEMEYER: Yes, sir. *Military Situation in the Far East, Hearings*, Part 3, p. 2512.

[30] Ambassador Stuart to Secretary Marshall, Nanking, September 20, 1947. *U.S. Relations with China*, p. 830.

[31] Ambassador John L. Stuart to Secretary Marshall, Nanking, February 5, 1948. *Ibid.*, pp. 842-843.

[32] Ambassador Stuart to Secretary Marshall, Nanking, March 31, 1948. *Ibid.*, p. 845.

[33] William C. Bullitt, "A Report to the American People on China," *Life* (October 13, 1947), pp. 152-154.

[34] U.S. Senate, Committee on Foreign Relations, *Interim Aid for Europe, Hearings*, 80th Cong. 1st Sess. (Washington: Government Printing Office, 1947), p. 43.

can leaders, notably Senator Bridges and Representative Judd, attempted to add $60 million for China to the sum appropriated for Europe.[35]

As Congress debated the Marshall Plan, pleas for aid to China continued. On February 18, 1948, President Truman asked Congress to appropriate $570 million for fifteen months of economic assistance to China. Congressional supporters of Nationalist China did not, however, accept the idea of limiting the China program to economic aid. They wanted to "transform some of the economic aid into military aid and then to have it administered in a manner somewhat like the Greek-Turk program." [36]

A demand for placing all requests in one omnibus bill came from the House of Representatives. A majority of the Congressmen viewed aid to Chiang Kai-shek as equally important as aid to Western Europe to fight Communism. Finally, the 80th Congress added a provision in the Marshall Plan Act, setting up a program of economic and military aid to China. The bill was signed by the President on April 3, 1948, providing for the sum of $463,000,000 as aid to China. However, only $125,000,000 of this could be used for arms and military equipment.[37] Portions of the bill which the President had requested for use in Europe were promptly put into action. Not a bullet or anything else moved in the direction of China until early November. "I doubt it would have moved then," says Congressman Walter Judd, "if the pressures in the campaign had not forced Truman just before election to order that something be 'got going' on the China program." [38]

It seems probable that the morale and effectiveness of the Nationalist troops would have improved, enabling them to hold back the Red tide in the Far East, had the shipment of arms been expedited more efficiently. But months passed before anything was available at a critical stage in the China campaign. The Chinese Ambassador to the United States had been pleading in vain for implementation. On June 2, Senator Styles Bridges of New Hampshire sent a strong note to the White House concerning this delay.

It was not until July 28, four months after the passing of the China Aid Bill, that the Defense Department was empowered to issue material from its own stocks. Even then, the first ship loaded with ammunition did not sail for China until November 9. On the West Coast, Harry Bridges maneuvered a shipping strike to delay further effective aid to the embattled Nationalists. China was finally lost during these months. When

---

[35] *Congressional Record,* December 15, 1947, p. 11346, also December 19, 1947, pp. 11679-80.

[36] H. Bradford Westerfield, *Forein Policy and Party Politics: From Pearl Harbor to Korea* (New Haven: Yale University Press, 1955), p. 264.

[37] "China Aid Act of 1948," Public Law 472, Title IV, 80th Cong., 2d Sess., pp. 25-26.

[38] Letter to the author, September 7, 1959.

the arms did arrive in Shanghai, the Communists had already overrun Manchuria and North China and were knocking at the gates of Nanking. "For some reason or other," said Vice Admiral Russell S. Berkey on May 5, 1950, "it took nine months to get specific items to China. Somewhere in the United States somebody slipped up, bogged down, or was interfered with. It has never been made plain why this material did not arrive in time." [39]

After the loss of Manchuria to the Communists, the situation required our serious attention if China was to be saved. On November 9, 1948, Chiang Kai-shek wrote to President Truman, asking for more immediate military aid and requesting a high-ranking military officer to help plan operations.[40] In his reply on November 12, President Truman did not make any commitments beyond the amount of aid already prescribed by Congress.[41] In the meantime, Madame Chiang Kai-shek arrived in Washington on December 1 and made a personal appeal to Secretary Marshall to stop the conquest of China by the Communists and to prevent the Sovietization of the Far East. This was followed by another urgent request, made directly to the United States Congress on December 15 by the Nationalist Government.[42]

Ignoring these frantic efforts by the Nationalist Government proved disastrous. What little postwar aid we actually granted China was not only woefully inadequate, but also too late to save that country from Red domination. This was clearly pointed out by William C. Bullitt, before the Committee on Foreign Affairs, on March 2, 1948:

The American Government has not delivered to China a single combat plane or a single bomber since General Marshall in August, 1946, by unilateral action, broke the promise of the American Government to the Chinese Government and suspended all deliveries of planes under the 8⅓ group program. . . . In August, 1946, as a means of pressure to compel Generalissimo Chiang Kai-shek to take Communists into the Chinese Government, General Marshall stopped all fulfillment of this program and dishonored the pledge of the United States.[43]

In this connection, General Claire Chennault remarked: "After more than 30 months since the date of the agreement [China Aid Act 1948] we

<hr>

[39] Utley, *The China Story*, p. 45. Within two weeks after Acheson became Secretary of State, the National Security Council recommended that Truman halt shipment of $60 million of military material which still remained out of the Eightieth Congress' $125 million "additional aid" fund for China. This advice was approved by Acheson. Westerfield, *Foreign Policy and Party Politics*, p. 346.

[40] *U.S. Relations with China*, pp. 888-889.

[41] *Ibid.*, pp. 889-890.

[42] *New York Times*, December 15, 1948, p. 1.

[43] Testimony of William C. Bullitt, March 2, 1948, U.S. Congress, House of Representatives, Committee on Foreign Affairs, *United States Foreign Policy for a Post-War Recovery Program*, 82d Cong., 2d Sess. (Washington: Government Printing Office, 1948) Part 2, p. 1899.

still owe China 35% of the total number of planes promised. . . . We have supplied only about 10% of the ammunition, bombs, and other explosives included in the agreement." [44]

Why did our government in Washington drag its feet? Roosevelt had ordered a survey taken of the surplus rifles and ammunition we had in the United States, to replace what the British had lost at Dunkerque. In eight days they were being loaded into boats at Perth Amboy to go to England. In contrast, the Congress in 1948 passed a law which the President signed on April 3, authorizing economic and military aid to the hard-pressed Republic of China. But it was eight months before a single rifle moved.

Many questions should be asked with reference to our aid to Nationalist China. For example, why was it that, following Japan's surrender, shipments of Lend-Lease to China from India were stopped? Why were large quantities of munitions and equipment intended for China either destroyed or dumped into the Indian Ocean? Who was responsible for this action? Why was Michael Lee, an employee in the Department of Commerce, permitted to hold up Chinese gasoline permits from July 1 until September 20, 1948?[45] Was he merely following the general policy of the Executive Branch at that time? Why was there a shift in our policy after the surrender of Japan from one of supporting our ally Nationalist China to one of constant pressure for coalition government with the Chinese Communists? Moreover, why did American officials place an embargo on all supplies to Nationalist China when they had knowledge the Russians were at the same time aiding the Communists?

These are perplexing questions that have added confusion to our China policy. As Admiral William Leahy, who served so long and brilliantly under President Roosevelt, remarked: "Our postwar attitude toward the Government of China is completely beyond understanding. . . ." [46] But the Communists were not confused. In the Sunday edition of the *Daily Worker* for December 2, 1945, is the blueprint for World Communism. In this issue, instructions from the Kremlin were given by William Z. Foster, head of the Communist Party in this country, to the national committee of the party at its meeting on November 18, 1945, shortly after VJ-Day. It read: "On the international scale, the key task as emphasized in Comrade Dennis' report, is to stop American intervention in China." In other words, stop American assistance to China.

---

44 Testimony of General Claire Chennault, March 10, 1948, *Ibid.*, p. 2215.

45 *Congressional Record*, February 17, 1950, pp. 1891-1892, and May 25, 1950, pp. 7740, 7444-7447. *Nomination of Philip C. Jessup*, p. 707. William Remington, who occupied a key position in the Department of Commerce, was able to hold up export licenses for the delivery of supplies to the Republic of China.

46 *Congressional Record*, July 27, 1959, pp. A6482-A6483.

Why should the Soviets think that the most important thing for American Communists to do, right after the defeat of Japan, was to stop American assistance to China? Because they knew, as everyone knew, that, without the right kind of outside assistance, the Chinese Government could not possibly survive. Sovietization of China was one of their primary objectives.

Chiang Kai-shek was not too corrupt as long as he was fighting the Japanese, but as soon as he turned against the Communists, he was held to be inefficient, a Fascist, and a dictator. This change of attitude was one of the significant shifts in the Communist Party line.

Senator Pat McCarran tried to improve the situation by introducing a bill, on February 25, 1949, providing for a $1.5 billion loan for economic and military aid to the Republic of China. In a letter to Senator Connally on March 14, Secretary Acheson discussed Senator McCarran's $1.5 billion aid to China bill (S. 1063). The Secretary stated that aid to China since VJ-Day reached a point "aggregating over $2 billion," that the "national government does not have the military capability of maintaining a foothold in South China against a determined Communist advance," that "the Chinese Communists have captured the major portion of military supplies, exclusive of ammunition, furnished the Chinese Government by the United States since VJ-Day," and that "there is no evidence that furnishing of additional military material would alter the pattern of current developments in China." [47]

On April 15, 1949, Senator McCarran issued a release to the papers in which he charged that the Acheson letter was both "misleading and false" and that the State Department Division of Far Eastern Affairs was "definitely soft to Communist Russia." The Senator presented an elaborate analysis of China aid figures, concluding that realistic analysis shows that post VJ-Day effective military aid totaled "only $110,000,000"—not the two billion dollars implied in the Secretary's letter.[48]

It is apparent that the figure of two billion dollars is not an accurate sum when one breaks down the items as to their actual employment. A case in point are those figures released by the White Paper which included $335,817,910 charged as "aid to China" for disarming and repatriating Japanese troops.[49] This questionable entry, alone, amounted to three times our actual postwar military aid to the Nationalist Government. The Chinese Government contended it had received vital arms and ammunition of a value of only $110,000,000 and had documented proof to that effect.[50]

---

47 *Congressional Record*, April 22, 1949, p. 4914.

48 *New York Times*, April 17, 1949, p. 25.

49 *U.S. Relations with China*, p. 1051.

50 *Congressional Record*, August 22, 1949, p. A5452.

The White Paper runs the total grants up to a misleading $1,596,-000,000. But it does this by including purely nonmilitary ECA aid and $474,000,000 in UNRRA grants.[51] Not only were the UNRRA payments nonmilitary, but also they were shared impartially between the Government and Communist-controlled areas. Since the areas under the Communists were primarily food-producing, the Communists' needs were largely for clothing and medical supplies. Fifty-two thousand tons were delivered to the Communist areas.[52]

A substantial amount of the material sent to the Nationalist forces, moreover, was unusable for actual combat. It is understood that, due to the tropical weather in areas where the material was abandoned, a great portion of it was in various stages of deterioration. As an example, in the sales agreement a truck was defined as a vehicle "with less than 20 percent of its parts missing." Approximately one-third of the total of Pacific surplus was represented by vehicles of all kinds.[53]

It is unfortunate that there has never been the same amount of effort by the State Department on behalf of Asiatic matters as there has been toward those of Europe. As a matter of fact, official government reports show that since VJ-Day our former enemy countries, Japan, Germany, and Italy, have each received more United States aid and assistance than our wartime ally and historic friend the Republic of China.[54] In the postwar period we gave to our former enemy country, Japan, $1,720,-000,000; to Germany, a former enemy country, $3,089,000,000; to Italy, a former enemy country, $2,046,000,000.[55]

In a report to the American Congress on December 18, 1946, President Truman made the following statement:

Assistance took the form of goods and equipment and of services. Almost half the total made available to China consisted of services, such as those involved in air and water transportation of troops. According to the latest figures reported, lend-lease assistance to China up to VJ-Day totalled approximately $870,0000,000. From V-J Day to the end of February, shortly after General Marshall's arrival, the total was approximately $600,000,000—mostly in transportation costs. Thereafter the program was reduced to the fulfillment of outstanding commitments, much of which was later suspended. . . . China agreed to buy all surplus property owned by the United States in China and on seventeen Pacific Islands and bases with certain exceptions. Six months of negotiations preceded the agreements finally signed in August. It was imperative that this matter be concluded in the Pacific as had already been done in Europe,

51 *U.S. Relations with China,* pp. 1042-1043.

52 *Congressional Record,* August 22, 1949, p. A5452.

53 *Ibid.*

54 U.S. Congress, Senate, Joint Committee on Armed Services and Foreign Relations, Individual Views of Certain Members, *Military Situation in the Far East* (Washington: Government Printing Office, 1951), p. 37.

55 *Military Situation in the Far East,* Part 2, pp. 1126-1127.

especially in view of the rapid deterioration of the material in open storage under tropical conditions and the urgent need for the partial alleviation of the acute economic distress of the Chinese people which it was hoped this transaction would permit . . . . *all non-demilitarized combat material, and fixed installations outside of China were excluded. Thus, no weapons which could be used in fighting a civil war were made available through this agreement.*[56]

By the statement of the President of the United States himself, these so-called surplus sales, which were included in the over-all figure, did not include any which could be used in combat in the Chinese Civil War. General Marshall even made assurances to the Communists that the surplus property contained no combat matériel.[57]

There is another factor in this grave Far Eastern equation. The State Department's "wait and see," or "let the dust settle," China policy contributed to the fall of the mainland to the Chinese Communists. The Chinese people became so disheartened and demoralized by our attitude that they finally ceased to resist the Communists. T. F. Tsiang, the Chinese delegate to the United Nations, was given a mild rebuke when he appealed to Secretary of State Marshall for help while the latter was in Paris. Tsiang begged for munitions and asked Marshall "as to the advisability of Chinese appeal to the United Nations because of Soviet training and equipping of Japanese military and also the Koreans." [58] Marshall "did not offer encouragement." He rejected the Chinese proposal to appeal to the United Nations, saying, "I thought it an inadvisable procedure and discussed possible Soviet moves to take advantage of rather than to counter such a move." [59]

The policy of supporting the Republic of China should have been the firm and continuing policy of the United States. President Chiang Kai-shek had consistently opposed Communism and had made our task less costly in lives and time in the Pacific War by containing over a million Japanese soldiers. The evidence is clear that one of the main reasons for the fall of his government was lack of sufficient support, both moral and material, by the Truman Administration.

The importance of moral support in the civil war was emphasized by General Wedemeyer when he testified that it was the key to the downfall of the Nationalist Government.[60] Confirmation of this lack of moral support can be found in the frequent attacks leveled by administration supporters, both in and out of government, against Chiang Kai-shek and all those who wanted to support him in his twenty-five years of struggle against Communism. He was depicted as an "unscrupulous dictator,"

---

56 *U.S. Relations with China*, pp. 691-692. Italics mine.

57 *Ibid.*, p. 180.

58 Secretary Marshall to Undersecretary Lovett, Paris, November 6, 1948, *Ibid.*, p. 887.

59 *Ibid.*

60 *Military Situation in the Far East*, Part 3, pp. 2317-2318.

says General Wedemeyer, "whereas actually the man was trying to bring order out of chaos and still follow democratic procedures." [61]

Long before many of us here in the United States awoke to the threat of Communism, Chiang Kai-shek was fighting it without compromising. His record, in the face of tremendous difficulties, was pointed to in a report by the Senate Foreign Relations Committee, in 1948, on the China Aid Bill:

> In the judgment of the committee, the Nationalist Government of China, led for 20 years through tremendous difficulties by the selfless patriotism of General-issimo Chiang Kai-shek, represents our common contest against threats to international peace and security and against Communist aggression and deserves support within our resources as proposed in this act.[62]

Early in 1948, there were in China three high American officials who felt the need for immediate action if China was to continue free of Communist domination. These officials—Ambassador Leighton Stuart, ECA Mission Chief Roger Lapham, and Vice Admiral Oscar Badger—journeyed to the north of China to see for themselves what could be done to stall the Communist advance and place the initiative in the hands of the Nationalist forces. They were impressed with the appearance, actions, and spirit of the armies of General Fu Tso-yi as well as by the military stature of General Fu.

General Fu told the United States officials that "he could do little more than to keep the Communists out of the area with his equipped armies and that he was constantly employing them on a defensive basis to meet Communist thrusts from various directions." But the General went on to say that "if he could obtain equipment for the four additional trained armies he would then be able to set up an offensive to the northeast stabilizing the Chinhuangtao-Hulutao corridor and for eventual relief of Mukden." He explained that "in relieving Mukden he would reopen a channel of supply for about 300,000 of the best troops in China (many of them American-trained and equipped) which were cut off there and were very lacking in American munitions." [63]

Immediately after this conference with General Fu Tso-yi, a recommendation was sent to the Joint Chiefs of Staff, specifically listing the equipment required, with the total cost estimated at $16 million. It was approved in July, 1948, but no specific action was taken to implement the decision. There was a lag between time of need and any deliveries on our part. In November, 1948, when Admiral Badger was notified that a

---

61 U.S. Congress, House of Representatives, Committee on Un-American Activities, *The Communist Program for World Conquest*, 85th Cong. 2d Sess. (Washington: Government Printing Office, 1958), p. 21.

62 *Congressional Record*, August 22, 1949, p. A5453.

63 Testimony of Admiral Oscar Badger, June 19, 1951, *Military Situation in the Far East*, Part 4, p. 2746.

ship was about to enter Tientsin with approximately ten per cent of the recommended equipment on board, he remarked, "Well, that's pretty bad. It's too bad that it isn't the full business, but maybe it will still have a morale effect." [64]

After the cargo was unloaded, Admiral Badger received a communication from General Fu reporting the deficiencies of the weapons. Of the total number, 480 of the machine guns lacked spare parts, tripod mounts, etc. Thompson machine guns had no magazine or clips. There were no loading machines for the loading of ammunition belts. Only a thousand of the light machine guns had mounts, and there with only a thousand clips for the 2,280 light machine guns. General Fu's commentary on this deplorable situation was, according to Admiral Oscar Badger, along the following lines: "The above-mentioned weapons are not in good condition, and for the most part cannot be used. I do not know how or why these weapons were forwarded in an incomplete state."[65] As a result of the arrival of this long anticipated shipment of arms in such an unusable condition, General Fu's plan for an offensive collapsed. The troops were completely demoralized. In Admiral Badger's judgment this action "was the straw that broke the camel's back." [66]

General George E. Stratemeyer relates a similar story about shortages of equipment. He testified before the Senate Internal Security Subcommittee that he flew 90,000 Chinese troops north into the Tientsin-Peiping area from Canton. We promised we would supply them, but the troops were left there, stranded, at the mercy of the Communists. "They had no ammunition, they had no spare parts, they couldn't fight. They had to live, so the Communists took them over, and those they didn't kill, I think they forced into their services." [67]

Admiral Badger described how he had personally witnessed a lamentable situation in North China where some unequipped Chinese divisions that were going up to take the places of others in the front actually lined up and received from outgoing divisions their rifles and other equipment so that they could go up with a reasonable complement of arms. He also stated that there were cases in which the Chinese troops were asked to go up on an operation with as few as three or four cartridges per man.[68]

On February 5, 1949, at a White House Conference, Secretary Acheson and Philip Jessup, Ambassador at Large, proposed to the President that

---

[64] *Ibid.*, p. 2747.

[65] *Ibid.*

[66] *Ibid.*, p. 2748.

[67] Testimony of General Edward Stratemeyer, August 25, 1954. U. S. Congress, Senate, Committee on the Judiciary, *Interlocking Subversion in Government Departments*, 83rd Cong. 2d Sess. (Washington: Government Printing Office, 1954), Part 22, pp. 1711-1715.

[68] *Military Situation in the Far East*, Part 4, p. 2745.

"the supplies which were then being loaded in ships in Hawaii and San Francisco for the Chiang Kai-shek government be dramatically stopped as a move toward world peace." [69] This meant that all armaments would be immediately cut off from the Chinese Nationalists and that the ships that were then on the way and then being loaded—about five—should all be stopped. Senator Arthur H. Vandenberg, chairman of the Foreign Relations Committee, attended this meeting and clearly pointed out in his diary that:

> . . . if, at the very moment when Chiang's Nationalists are desperately trying to negotiate some kind of peace with the Communists, we suspend all military shipments to the Nationalists, we certainly shall make any hope of negotiated peace impossible. We shall thus virtually notify the Communists that they can consider the war ended and themselves as victors. We virtually withdrew our recognition of the Nationalist Government. We seal China's doom. Regardless of the justification of previous charges that our American policy has been largely responsible for China's fate, if we take *this* step at *this* fatefully inept moment, we shall never be able to shake the charge that *we* are the ones who gave poor China the final push into disaster. . . .[70]

As a matter of fact, President Truman did gradually cut off aid to the Nationalists after the surrender of Peiping, acting in a manner that was intended to avoid the shock of any sudden cessation of American support of Chiang Kai-shek.

Senator Vandenberg may have at times sounded like a staunch defender of the National cause, but his compromising attitude toward the appeasement forces in and out of the government had some effect on the China crisis. According to Bradford Westerfield, "By 1948 Vandenberg and Dulles had been privately won over to the State Department's view of the hopelessness of American intervention on behalf of Chiang Kai-shek in China, far more than had other leading Republicans who were supporting the Greek-Turk program and the Marshall Plan in Europe." [71]

When Dean Acheson testified before the House Foreign Affairs Committee on March 20, 1947, concerning Greek-Turkish aid legislation, Congressman Walter Judd asked a pertinent question: "Mr. Secretary, a great many Americans obviously are confused by what seems to be a contradiction in our foreign policy with respect to the governments which become Communist-dominated. If it is a wise policy for us to urge, for example, the Government of China to unite with organized Communist minorities there, why is it a wise policy to assist the Greek Government to fight against the same sort of armed Communist minori-

---

69 *Nomination of Philip C. Jessup*, pp. 696-697. Jessup is now the United States Justice on the World Court, to which we are being asked to surrender a significant part of our sovereignty.

70 *The Private Papers of Senator Vandenberg*, p. 531. (Emphasis in original)

71 Westerfield, *Foreign Policy and Party Politics*, p. 248.

ties in Greece?" Acheson replied that the Greek Government and economy had collapsed. He added, "The Chinese Government is not in the position at the present time that the Greek Government is in. It is not approaching collapse. *It is not threatened by defeat by the Communists. The War with the Communists is going on much as it has for the past 20 years."* [72]

Actually there were many similarities between the civil war in China and the one in Greece, except when you compare the American aid and moral support given the two. Greece was given much more. According to a declaration by Dr. T. F. Tsiang, China's representative in the General Assembly of the United Nations, during the period from August, 1947, to March, 1949, United States aid to China was $125,000,000, less than half the amount given to Greece during the same period.[73]

When a civil war involving Communists started in Greece, our officials adopted an entirely different attitude from that toward the conflict in China. With reference to the civil war in Greece, the President enunciated the so-called Truman Doctrine.[74] Greece is a much smaller nation than China, but we sent a mission under General Van Fleet, with officers and enlisted men, for the purpose of supervising the training of Greek Government troops to resist the Communists. While we did not have soldiers actually firing upon the enemy in Greece, we did enable our officers to go down to battalion level to give advice to the Greek officers and men.[75] We did not pull out, and we did not endeavor to avoid a civil war. Our policy was to help the Greek Government, our ally, to *win* the civil war. Tragically, this is what our Government *never* seriously tried to do in China.

Our aid and support in Greece was far more effective than in China, where it was not supervised. In China, we prohibited United States officers and men from going down to the levels where they might actually come into contact with the Communists. Our military advisory group was directed to forbid the sending of air or ground or naval officers into areas of combat or into disputed areas held by the Communists or the Nationalists.[76] This was a grave mistake.

[72] U.S. Congress, House, Committee on Foreign Affairs, *Assistance to Greece and Turkey*, 80th Cong. 1st Sess. (Washington: Government Printing Office, 1947), pp. 16-17. Italics mine.

[73] Chinese Delegation to the United Nations, *China Presents Her Case to the United Nations* (New York, 1949), p. 38.

[74] The "Truman Doctrine" was initiated while Secretary Marshall was out of the country. President Truman's purpose was one of helping weak countries in opposing Communist domination. Aid to any Communist country was specifically excluded. Secretary Marshall, upon his return, succeeded in corrupting the "Truman Doctrine" into the "Marshall Plan." Under the terms of the latter, aid was to be dispensed to Communist countries also. President Truman's anti-Communist effort was short-lived.

[75] *Military Situation in the Far East*, Part 1, p. 558.

[76] *Ibid.*, Part 3, pp. 2358-2359.

The myth that the Republic of China fell because Chiang's troops refused to fight is refuted by the evidence, despite the fact that Secretary Acheson stated in his letter of transmittal: "A large proportion of the military supplies . . . since V-J Day has, however, fallen into the hands of the Chinese Communists through the military ineptitude of the Nationalist leaders, their defections and surrenders, and the absence among their forces of the will to fight." [77] No one can dispute that there was ineptitude, corruption, and maladministration in the Nationalist Government. But, in evaluating and assessing those characteristics of the Government, we forget the contributions those people made, plus the terrific dislocation caused by years of war. The Nationalists stuck by us despite many opportunities to make favorable peace terms with the Japanese. This would have released about 1,200,000 Japanese for possible employment against us in the Pacific. We owe them a debt of gratitude.

When asked by Senator Brian McMahon of Connecticut whether he thought Chiang's government was corrupt and inefficient, General Wedemeyer answered, "Yes sir. . . . But . . . I think it is dangerous to overemphasize . . . because we find corruption in our own Government—and it was inevitable with a government that was down and out economically." [78]

The contention that the administration consistently and firmly supported the Chinese Republic is simply not true. Dr. Leighton Stuart, who lived in China for fifty years and who was the last American Ambassador on the mainland stated: "The aberrant and contradictory policies of the United States Government during the period between the end of World War II and the beginning of the Communist attack in Korea in 1950 served to weaken rather than strengthen the National Government at a time when it desperately needed sympathetic understanding and assistance." [79] Again,

We Americans mainly saw the good things about the Chinese Communists, while not noticing carefully the intolerance, bigotry, deception, disregard for human life and other evils which seem to be inherent in any totalitarian system. We kept Communist meanings for such objectives as progressive, democratic, liberal, also bourgeois, reactionary, imperialist, as they intended we should do . . . therefore, we cannot escape a part of the responsibility of the great catastrophe—not only for China but also for America and the free world—the loss of the Chinese mainland.[80]

A great deal of emphasis has been placed upon the quantity of material aid that we have given to Nationalist China. In his letter of trans-

77 *U.S. Relations with China*, p. xv.
78 *Military Situation in the Far East*, Part 3, p. 2354.
79 Stuart, *Fifty Years in China*, p. 272.
80 *Ibid.*, pp. 237-238.

mittal for the presentation of the *White Paper* to President Truman on
July 30, 1949, Secretary of State Acheson stated:

> Since VJ-Day, the United States Government has authorized aid to Nationalist
> China in the form of grants and credits totaling approximately 2 billion dol-
> lars. . . . In addition to these grants and credits, the United States Government
> has sold the Chinese Government large quantities of military and civilian war
> surplus property with a total procurement cost of over 1 billion dollars.[81]

The average reader would immediately get the impression that we gave
Nationalist China an enormous amount of aid and that, therefore,
nothing else could be done to save the situation. However, if you take
the actual value of the material to the Chinese when they got it, there
was little more than scrap iron. "A lot of it," said General Wedemeyer,
"was equipment that they were not capable of using. . . ."[82] Such military equipment as the Nationalists received in the critical days of the
war against the Communist regime has been described as "moldy, broken,
lacking parts," etc. One shipment of automatic weapons arrived without
magazines, in such shape the guns were of no "more value than broom-
sticks."[83]

In an important speech in Washington on April 11, 1950, Colonel L. B.
Moody, now retired, who served with Donald Nelson's mission to China,
stated that the inevitable defeat of the Nationalist Army was due to their
deficit in the items of infantry equipment, especially ammunition. He
explained that what the Nationalists really needed were small arms and
ammunition, but these were exactly what America denied. What we really
sent were ". . . billions of moldy cigarettes, blown-up guns and junk bombs
and disabled vehicles from the Pacific islands, which have been totaled
up with other real or alleged aid in various State Department, Communist
and leftist statements to create the impression that we have furnished the
Nationalist Government with hundreds of millions or even billions of
dollars worth of useful fighting equipment."[84]

In mid-November, 1948, General David Barr, who was head of the
U. S. military mission to China, reported to the Department of the

---

81 *U.S. Relations with China*, p. xv.

82 *Military Situation in the Far East*, Part 3, p. 2330.

83 *Military Situation in the Far East; Individual Views of Certain Members*, p. 37.

84 *Military Situation in the Far East*, Part 3, p. 1951. In the MacArthur Hearings,
Senator Brewster of Maine asked General Wedemeyer: "This emphasis on the shortages of ammunition is a matter which has been quite thoroughly discussed. There
has been quite a little discussion about it here. Do you feel that was an important
factor in the difficulties which the Chinese Nationalist Government experienced?"
Wedemeyer replied: "Yes, sir. The availability of ammunition would have, of course,
enabled the Chinese Nationalists to operate against the Communists effectively, again
provided American advisers were present. . . ." *Ibid.*, Part 3, p. 2512. In the later stages
of the Korean War, ammunition was withheld from our own troops to prevent their
going on the offensive. The same technique was used to install Castro in Cuba. It
appears to be a standard method used to insure Communist victory—part of the *modus
operandi* of pro-Communist elements in our government.

Army that "No battle has been lost since my arrival due to lack of ammunition or equipment." [85] This statement has been used frequently by the anti-Chiang group to prove that we had given sufficient aid to the Nationalist Government. However, Admiral Badger pointed out in the MacArthur Hearings that there

> . . . is a difference between the arithmetic of saying that no battle was lost due to lack of ammunition—I know that in the battle of Weihsien the defenders lost about 50 percent of their troops, and when the Communists overwhelmed them by their attack on that town, the defenders were not only throwing rocks, bottles and bricks at them, but they were dropping homemade bombs out of small planes made of bottles with powder in them and ordinary caps. They just ran out of ammunition at Weihsien, and that is all there was to it. It was a tough fight.[86]

When appraising the causes of the fall of the Nationalist Government of China, there is no single or simple interpretation. Since this catastrophe is a matter of recent history, all the evidence has not been made available to historians. Secretary Acheson tried to put all the blame on Chiang Kai-shek's Government for the defeat on the mainland and admitted no mistake in American policy. "Nothing that this country did or could have done," wrote Acheson, "within the reasonable limits of its capabilities could have changed that result; nothing that was left undone by this country has contributed to it. It was the product of internal Chinese forces, forces which this country tried to influence but could not." [87]

According to Acheson's statement, the reader would almost get the impression that we did everything we could to save the Nationalists. But to Congressman Judd, Acheson's assertion does not tell the whole story. In a letter to the author, Judd explained it this way:

> You will note that Acheson says, 'nothing that was left *undone* by this country has contributed to it.' He does not state 'nothing that was *done* by this country has contributed to it.'. . . Yet this is the statement that describes the situation. There was a multitude of things that this country did which contributed decisively to the loss of China. The big four were: (1) The Yalta decision giving the Russians effective control of Manchuria, thereby destroying what the Chinese, under Chiang, had fought eight years against Japan to try to regain and which had been promised to the Chinese by us at Cairo; (2) The four ceasefires into which we forced the Chinese Government at times when they had the upper hand during 1946, thereby destroying the confidence in us of the Chinese and weakening decisively the morale of the armed forces; (3) The 1946-47 embargo on 30-caliber ammunition; and (4) the 'deactivation' of about 180 of

---

85 *Ibid.*, Part 3, p. 1856.

86 *Ibid.*, Part 4, p. 3003.

87 *U.S. Relations with China*, p. xvi. This is still the standard line among the more questionable elements in the liberal press.

Chiang's 300 divisions, throwing their officers and men into the street, in effect leaving them little alternative except to go over to the Communists and of course demoralizing the 120 divisions left. It told them that the same fate would come to them. They might better go over to the Communists. It was not the individual Chinese soldiers who defected; it was whole units which were taken over to Communists by their officers, when they saw how other officers who had fought loyally under Chiang for eight years were treated, at the insistence of General Marshall. Doubtless, the latter thought he was helping Chiang get a stream-lined army but to use that method at that time served only to destroy the army he did have, as Marshall was warned would be the case by those in China who understood the score.[88]

When asked what he thought of this statement by Secretary Acheson, Professor Kenneth Colegrove, of the Political Science Department at Northwestern University, said that Acheson's "letter of transmittal was thoroughly dishonest, especially the paragraph of the letter which says that . . . the United States had left nothing undone that might have saved him [Chiang Kai-shek] and kept the Communists from winning the victory. . . . That obviously was a lie." [89] As for Secretary Acheson's attempt to explain the fall of China in the *White Paper*, Colegrove testified that it "was one of the most false documents ever published by any country." [90]

General Stratemeyer was asked by the Senate Internal Security Subcommittee what he thought were the main causes for the fall of Nationalist China. He replied: "Well, I would say two things. The Marshall Mission, in which we tried to associate Communists and Nationalists together and make it work. . . .the other cause was that we, the United States Government, did not keep its promise to the Generalissimo, and that was to maintain the equipment that we left there and give him sufficient spare parts, ammunition, et cetera, to continue his occupation of North China and to fight the Communists." [91]

Aid to China was one of the most perplexing and controversial problems confronting the United States in the postwar period. In general, our policy had long been one of deep interest in maintaining the integrity and independence of China. We regarded her as essential to peace and stability in the Far East. However, there were people in and out of government who had little use for Chiang Kai-shek and his Nationalist government. Our policy became one based on the mistaken belief that the Chinese Communists would bring a new surge of democracy to China. As late as March 11, 1948, General Marshall, as Secretary of State, told a press conference that "The United States . . . still favors

---

88 Letter to author, July 6, 1960.

89 Testimony of Kenneth Colegrove, September 25, 1951, *Institute of Pacific Relations, Hearings*, Part 3, p. 923.

90 *Ibid.*, p. 922.

91 Testimony of General Stratemeyer, *op. cit.*, Part 22, pp. 1711-1714.

a broadening of the base of the Chinese Government to include the Communists." [92] Eleven months later, as the Communists' armies swept toward victory in China, fifty-one Republican members of the House addressed a letter to President Truman on February 7, 1949, inquiring, "What is our policy toward China?" Secretary of State Dean Acheson told them in a private session, on February 24, 1949, that it was the intention "to wait until the dust settles" before deciding upon a policy.[93] But the dust had already settled over unfortunate China—a Red dust.

Both the Chinese people and their leaders had the will to resist the Communists, but what we gave them in the form of aid and moral support was the difference between a hopeless and effective resistance. What amount we did give them in terms of actual aid was "too little and too late" to be of any real use. As a result, Chiang Kai-shek, under the impact of continued Communist military pressure, was forced to surrender one position after another.

Regarding aid to Nationalist China, General MacArthur's testimony is quite pertinent:

SENATOR WILEY: . . . What would you have done—what would you have advised, under the circumstances that existed back there in 1945—what would you have done?

GENERAL MACARTHUR: I would have given such assistance to the conservative Government of China as to have checked the growing tide of Communism.

A very little help and assistance in my belief, at that time would have accomplished that purpose.

SENATOR WILEY: For a good many years you have been acquainted, I take it, with the Russians and with the Communist infiltration.

Would you have sought to have gotten those two forces together?

GENERAL MACARTHUR: I did not catch the question.

SENATOR WILEY: Would you have sought to have amalgamated the Commies and Nationalists—have gotten them together?

GENERAL MACARTHUR: Just about as much chance of getting them together as that oil and water will mix.[94]

In that colloquy lies the whole story of the greatest mistake of a century. Time alone can show how damaging, how devastating, have been the errors of Teheran and Yalta.

In summarizing the problem of aid to Nationalist China, we should keep certain factors firmly in mind. From the time the China Aid bill was signed by the President on April 3, 1948, to the actual time of delivery, there was a seven months delay, at which time the Communists began their first major successful drive in North China. Those seven months delay were of crucial importance.

[92] New York Times, March 11, 1948, p. 6.

[93] Background to Korea (Washington, D. C.: Republican National Committee), pp. 9-10. Acheson's explanation of the remark can be found in Military Situation in the Far East, Part 3, pp. 1765-1766.

[94] Miltary Situation in the Far East, Part 1, p. 32.

The apologists for the strategy of defeat which prevailed at that time talk about how much in dollars was the value of our aid to China. But they do not tell you how much of what was delivered, to whom, when, where, and in what condition. And they do not mention the intangibles, such as moral support and effective training. They have led the public to believe that we gave enormous amounts of aid to China, that it was all wasted, that we did everything we could, that the Chinese Government never took our advice, that the Chinese soldiers had no will to fight—in short, that the Government of China was so bad that there was nothing we could have done that could have saved it. All of these assertions have been proven to be absolutely untrue.

The charge that we did everything we could is refuted by the plain fact that from VJ-Day until Eisenhower's inaugural address in 1953, very few words of *moral* support from the American Government can be discovered—nothing but public and private vilification. Furthermore, our Government steadfastly refused to give to our military advisors in China the same authority that it gave to Van Fleet in Greece to "advise and train at all levels"—without which authority he could not possibly have succeeded there, any more than without it, our "advisors" could have succeeded in China.

Aid that arrives too late, no matter how much its dollar value, is not real aid. Lend-lease aid that was dumped into the Bay of Bengal was not aid to China, no matter how many hundreds of millions of dollars it figures in the tables of alleged "aid to China." The equipping of Chiang's best thirty-three divisions with American 30-caliber rifles, and then putting an embargo on 30-caliber ammunition—as General Marshall did from the summer of 1946 until at least May, 1947—is not aid, no matter how much the value in dollars of the rifles. The total operation had the net result of effectively *disarming* Chiang's best troops instead of arming them as Americans have been led to believe was the case.

When 30-caliber ammunition finally was released for China, it was charged against the funds provided by Congress at the rate of replacement costs of $85 per 1,000 rounds, instead of its actual cost to us, on original manufacture, of $46 per 1,000 rounds. But ammunition sent from the same dumps to the Greeks was charged at a "surplus price" of $4.60 per 1,000 rounds. So State Department accounting methods lacked something in the way of honesty.

Refusal to let Chiang get, either by purchase or by grant, aviation gasoline for the planes and air force Chennault had built is not effective aid, no matter how many dollars show up in the tables as the cost of the planes!

Most important of all was the refusal to let our military mission in China give real advice and training to the Chinese armed forces at all levels and in the field. It would be virtually impossible to train any army with a thousand advisers compelled to sit in Nanking working on tables of organization.[95] And, still worse, the refusal to give one word of moral support and encouragement during those long, dreary years did much to bring about the defeat of the Nationalist Government on the mainland. There is no other case in American history where a supposed ally spent several years in vicious vilification of a friend it was posing before the world as trying to help.

In short, what China needed was *proper aid* even more than more aid. *Proper aid* was what our Government systematically, and with apparently malicious forethought, refused to give. If we had treated Greece, Italy, France, or even England the way we treated the Government of China, they probably would have gone down too. It is the sorriest chapter in the history of America's relations with other countries.

The result—sovietization of China and Manchuria—could be the only logical outcome of postwar United States policy toward China. The utter consistency of our policy in serving Soviet ends leave no conclusion other than that pro-Communist elements in our government and press "planned it that way." But top American officials who sought to buy Soviet co-operation at any price must bear the final responsibility.

---

95 Stefan Possony put it cogently: "At no time did the U.S. find it advisable to deploy strong military forces into China. The American government did not make a decision to oppose the Chinese Communists by military strength." *A Century of Conflict* (Chicago: Henry Regnery Co., 1953), p. 327.

CHAPTER XVIII

FALL OF THE MAINLAND

Deprived of moral and material support from the United States, the Nationalist forces were compelled to give up the ancient capital of Peiping in January, 1949. Successive Communist military victories encouraged some United States columnists, writers, scholars, and political leaders to pin their hopes on the presumption that Mao Tse-tung would become a second Tito and break away from the Soviet Union. Judging from subsequent events, we must say this assumption was based on unrealistic thinking, since Red China's military forces were "hopelessly tied to Soviet Russia by the umbilical cord of supply." [1]

The *New York Times* printed a series of articles by C. L. Sulzberger, in which the Tito theme was apparent. On February 14, 1949, for example, Sulzberger wrote:

> The United States, clearly recognizing the possibility that while Mr. Mao is a devout Marxist he may also be a 'Titoite' heretic, cannot crystallize its own Chinese policy until the political photograph is clarified. . . . There is no question about the sincerity with which Mr. Mao regards himself a Marxist. However, possibly ideology is the only tie between Mr. Mao and the Kremlin. It may alone keep him the abject political tool of Moscow. It may not. For this reason Washington policy makers must watch and wait.[2]

James Reston, in an article on April 23, described the failure to defeat the Chinese Communists as not the fault "of the United States, but of the Chinese Nationalists who have lost the confidence of their people." Some officials in the Department of State believed "Mao Tse-tung and the other Communist leaders will rapidly show signs of Titoism once they are in control." [3]

---

[1] Hollington K. Tong, "Why Red China Won't Break with Russia," *Readers Digest* (July, 1957), p. 98.

[2] *New York Times*, February 14, 1949.

[3] *Congressional Record*, April 28, 1949, p. 5, 241; *New York Times*, April 23, 1949.

In his book, *Situation in Asia,* Owen Lattimore put forward the idea that if the "New China," as he called the Communist Government, secured its capital from the United States, it would slow its revolution. In China, devotion to "nationalism and national interests is more powerful among more people than devotion to Marxism and Russian interests. Attempts by the Russians to make the Russian interest override the Chinese interest could easily bring into being a Chinese Titoism." [4] Interest in the Tito theory was also expressed in the Chinese language broadcasts beamed out of San Francisco daily by the "Voice of America." Marshal Tito of Yugoslavia figured largely in those broadcasts, being "cited again and again as an example Chinese Communists might follow." [5]

There is no substantial evidence that Mao Tse-tung would be a Tito if he could. He has always been committed to the program of Marxism-Leninism. Through twenty years of defeats he never seriously wavered; now that he had won one of the greatest victories of all history, he would hardly desert the side which had been winning in Asia, to join our side which had been losing.

The "Titoism" line was scarcely realistic. Ignored or concealed was the fact that Tito's breach was with Stalin and not with the tenets of Marxism-Leninism, which demanded the violent overthrow of all Capitalist governments—including that of the United States. Any thought of Tito as a sort of ally of the United States *vis à vis* the Soviet Union was foolish.

On July 1, 1949, Mao Tse-tung issued a manifesto commemorating the 28th anniversary of the birth of the Chinese Communist Party. The text failed to reveal any signs of Titoism, and its appeal to Communists and their fellow-travelers everywhere was significant. It said: "To unite in the common struggle with the countries of the world which regard us as an equal nation, and with the peoples of all countries. This means alliance with the U.S.S.R. . . . Internationally we belong to the anti-imperialist front headed by the Soviet Union, and for genuine friendly aid we must look to this front and not to the imperialist front." [6]

While the Tito argument was getting press coverage in the United

---

4 Lattimore, *The Situation in Asia,* p. 163. Lattimore's endorsement of the "Titoism" line should be sufficient to indicate its phony nature.

5 *San Francisco Chronicle,* March 14, 1949. For a critical evaluation of the schism between Soviet Russia and Red China see Suzanne Labin and Christopher Emmett: "Is There A Sino-Soviet Split," *Orbis* (Spring 1960), pp. 28-38.

6 *Congressional Record,* July 13, 1949, pp. 9396-47. The American White Paper, *U.S. Relations with China,* in the letter of transmittal stated: "The Communist leaders have forsworn their Chinese heritage and have publicly announced their subservience to a foreign power." p. xvi. On February 14, Chou En-lai signed a "Treaty of Friendship, Alliance, and Mutual Assistance" with the U.S.S.R. Max Beloff, *Soviet Policy in the Far East, 1944-1951* (London: Oxford University Press, 1953), p. 260.

States, the Nationalist cause in China was weakening under constant Communist military pressure. Shanghai fell on May 27, 1949. Shortly afterward, Generalissimo Chiang Kai-shek prepared to withdraw his forces to Formosa, though he told Clyde Farnsworth of the Scripps papers that he had no intention of giving up his leadership of China.[7] Following the fall of Shanghai, the Communist armies renewed their offensive. By the end of July, they were converging upon Changsha with its direct rail line leading to Canton. These military successes of the Communists caused some apprehension along the corridors of the Department of State. But the Chinese specialists in the Department were really not much disturbed by the prospect of Chiang's collapse. They were working to promote "Titoism" in China. On July 27, Secretary of State Acheson announced that our entire Far Eastern policy would be reviewed "with the aid of non-governmental counsel."[8] This counsel was to consist of Philip Jessup, Deputy Chief of the United States delegation to the United Nations, Raymond Fosdick, and President Everett Case of Colgate University. They were assisted by such Department of State officials as George Kennan, Walton Butterworth, and others.[9] Invitations were also extended to many Far Eastern specialists to participate in the conference, scheduled for October. The announcement led Senator Arthur Vandenberg publicly to express a hope that any review of our policy would not overlook ways and means of bolstering anti-Communist forces in Asia.[10]

On August 5, the Department of State issued a White Paper on China, edited by Jessup. The timing of this document was extremely damaging. It jarred the morale of the Chinese Nationalists. It was determined upon by the Department of State despite warnings that such publication would only aid the Communist conquest of China.[11] Jessup rejected a strong plea from General Chennault, who argued that release of the White Paper would only undermine the National Government at a critical time in her struggle against the Chinese Communists.[12] The contents evoked a strong protest from William C. Bullitt, former Ambassador to Russia. In a letter to Jessup, dated August 28, 1949, Bullitt stated that the Administration's version of how China was conquered by the Communists is "proof of the lengths to which our government officials will go to protect their vested interest in their own mistakes. To publish an inquest on a faithful ally—not yet dead but fighting in despair to preserve its national independence—is incompatible with any standard of decent con-

[7] *New York Times*, July 6, 1949.

[8] *New York Times*, July 28, 1949, *Institute of Pacific Relations, Hearings*, Part 4, p. 1049.

[9] *Institute of Pacific Relations, Hearings*, Part 3, p. 917, 924; Part 4, p. 1128.

[10] *Institute of Pacific Relations, Hearings*, Part 4, p. 1039, 1041, 1049.

[11] *Ibid., Final Report*, p. 211; Part 4, p. 1041, 1049.

[12] Testimony of General Claire L. Chennault, May 29, 1952, *Ibid.*, Part 13, p. 4770.

duct. And our Department of State has done this not to serve a national American interest but to serve domestic political expediency." [13]

John Leighton Stuart, who spent a lifetime in China, was just as critical:

The White Book served to inform the world that the Nationalists in the opinion of the United States Government, had lost the 'civil war.' Without admitting any mistakes in United States policy, it tried to place all the blame upon the Nationalist Government of China. United States policy, it claimed, had been in no way responsible for the 'ominous result.' By implication it announced that the United States support of the National Government and the efforts of the United States toward survival of that government were at an end.[14]

It was apparent to some political observers that the Administration was attempting to wash its hands of any guilt for the downfall of Chiang Kai-shek. Robert Aura Smith, editorial writer on the *New York Times*, noticed that "this document was designed to justify President Truman's declaration that we should 'give no further aid and advice' to Nationalist China." [15] Owen Lattimore's later explanation to Communist and pro-Communist readers of the *New York Compass*, a left-wing New York publication, gave the lie to the Department of State pretensions: "As it became more and more obvious that Chiang Kai-shek and the Kuomintang were doomed, the conduct of American policy became increasingly delicate. *The problem was how to allow them* [China] *to fall without making it look as if the United States had pushed them.*" [16]

While people were debating the reasons for the loss of the mainland, Mao Tse-tung consolidated his newly won military victories. He proclaimed establishment of the Central People's Government of China on October 1, 1949, and declared it to be the "sole legal government representing all the people." He served notice that his government was ready to establish diplomatic relations "with any foreign government willing to

13 William C. Bullitt to Philip Jessup, August 28, 1949, *Institute of Pacific Relations, Hearings*, Part 13, Exhibit No. 752, p. 4533.

14 John Leighton Stuart, "How the Communists Got China," *U. S. News and World Report*, October 1, 1954, p. 124. For further comment on the White Paper see *Congressional Record*, p. A5223, A5391, A5148. The China Section of the Department of State, as early as November, 1948, recommended "going to the American public to explain the inadequacies of the Chiang Kai-shek government." Secretary Marshall, with Truman's approval, rejected this extreme measure. Forrestal noted that Marshall "felt that this would administer the final *coup de grace* of Chiang's government, and this, he felt, we could not do." *Forrestal Diaries*, p. 534. Defense Secretary Johnson said "I raised the question of its accuracy, and said that I think the files of the Defense Department contained things that conflicted with proposed things in the then draft." He continued: "I again raised the question of the political advisability of the document." Testimony of Louis A. Johnson, June 14, 1951, *Military Situation in the Far East, Hearings*, Part 4, pp. 2668-2669.

15 *Foreign Policy Association Bulletin*, December, 1952.

16 *Compass*, New York, July 17, 1949. Lattimore continued: "The thing to do, therefore, is to let South Korea fall—but not to let it look as though we pushed it." Italics mine.

observe the principles of equality, mutual benefit, and mutual respect of territory and sovereignty." [17] The day after Mao's proclamation, the Soviet Union extended recognition to the Red regime and severed diplomatic relations with the National Government, calling it a "provincial government." Within a short time, the other Communist-controlled countries followed suit.

From the outset, Great Britain, the Netherlands, and some of the Commonwealth powers, particularly those which were neighbors of China, leaned toward establishing relations with the new Communist Government. Apparently the Department of State harbored a desire to do the same, but the Communist regime began mistreating American citizens. Benjamin Welles, an American correspondent, reported from London on May 17, 1949, that "the United States and British Governments have agreed to coordinate their policies toward eventual recognition of the Chinese Communist regime. . . . " [18] The Department of State did not announce recognition because undue restrictions were placed on the American consulates to the point where they could not fulfill their official duties.

In July, 1949, the American Vice-Consul in Shanghai, William M. Olive, was arrested and subjected to humiliating treatment.[19] Communist soldiers invaded the bedroom of Ambassador Stuart in the American Embassy at Nanking. Our consular offices at Peiping were deliberately seized. The most flagrant violation of accepted international practice, however, was the treatment of Angus Ward, the American Consul General at Mukden. He and his staff were detained under house arrest.[20] In addition to these humiliations, a campaign of anti-American propaganda became more vitriolic day by day. The allegiance of Mao Tse-tung to the Soviet Union became increasingly evident. As a result of Communist perfidy, such a wave of popular resentment was produced in the United States that "official action affirmatively favorable to the Communists was precluded." [21]

It is of interest to note and report the treatment of the United States in 1946 by the Russians who established a 12-mile zone outside Dairen. When Admiral Charles M. Cooke sent a ship up there to give supplies to the predecessor of Angus Ward, the Russian commander gave the ship officer and the one who was delivering supplies to the Consul General an ultimatum to leave the port within an hour or two. The United

---

17 *Keesing's Contemporary Archives*, 1948-1950, p. 10441.

18 *Time*, October 15, 1951.

19 *Department of State Bulletin*, December 13, 1949, p. 908. January 23, 1950, p. 119.

20 U. S. Congress, Senate, Committee on the Judiciary, *Policy Perversion*, 84th Cong., 2d Sess. (for the year 1956), Section XI (Washington: Government Printing Office, 1957), p. 189; also *Department of State Bulletin*, December 26, 1949, p. 955.

21 Stuart, *Fifty Years in China*, p. 274.

States government refused to take any proper action against the Russians at that time. The so-called (by the State Department) Agrarian Reformers not only followed their Russian preceptors, but they were guided by these preceptors stationed in great numbers at Peiping at the time.[22]

In the meantime, early in October, 1949, a very important three-day conference on the Far East was held under the auspices of the Department of State and presided over by Philip Jessup. The tone of this meeting was set by Owen Lattimore in a significant memorandum submitted to Jessup several months before the conference convened:

The type of policy represented by support of Chiang Kai-shek does more harm than good to the interests of the United States, and no modification of this policy seems promising. Chiang Kai-shek was a unique figure in Asia. He is now fading into a kind of eclipse that is regrettably damaging to the prestige of the United States, because the United States supported him. His eclipse does not even leave behind the moral prestige of a good but losing fight in defense of a weak cause . . .

As a first step, the United States should accept the list of countries recommended for admission to the United Nations by Mr. Trygve Lie, Secretary General of the United Nations [one of them is Communist China] . . . . it would at this time be a good move for the United States to accept with good will an initiative from the Secretariat of the United Nations. . . .[23]

The memorandum covered many of the recommendations Lattimore brought up at the conference. In attendance were twenty-five persons selected by the Department of State. Most of them expressed their views on our Far Eastern policy. Also present were several State Department officials.

In the first session on October 6, Ernest McNaughton of the First National Bank of Portland made this pessimistic observation: "Presently I think we are all washed up in China." His proposal for withdrawal of our forces from China gave a very dismal beginning to the discussion.[24] Kenneth Colegrove, Professor of Political Science at Northwestern University, took exception to this view. He said, "Dr. Fosdick [who was presiding], I would not agree at all that we are so-called 'washed up in China.'" Colegrove pointed out that there were still bright spots of resistance in China which should be considered in our evaluation. His views were rather warmly criticized by some members.[25]

On the third day of the conference, Jessup, presiding as chairman, remarked, " . . . I would like to suggest that we might have a few minutes

---

[22] Letter from Admiral Cooke to author, August 12, 1960.

[23] *Institute of Pacific Relations, Hearings*, Part 3, Exhibit No. 280-B, pp. 928-931.

[24] Department of State, *Transcript of Proceedings: Conference on Problems of United States Policy in China* (Division of Central Services, Washington, D. C., October 6, 1949), p. 99.

[25] *Ibid.*, pp. 101-102.

taking up the question of the recognition of the Communist Government in China. . . . " [26] Since there was a strong sentiment against recognition throughout the country, some members expressed the belief that the question of timing would be important. For example, Nathaniel Peffer, professor at Columbia University, took up the argument: "I would also make it [recognition] a matter of timing. . . . I would wait . . . five or six weeks. I don't know when the Communists will get to Canton, but I would guess not over six or seven weeks. The only other Chinese regime will be in Formosa, which is, at least technically, not Chinese territory. It is still Japanese." Besides, "is not the burden of proving on those who don't want to recognize? The Communists are there. They are going to take twenty, thirty, forty years. Who knows? What do you lose by recognizing? What do you gain by not recognizing?" Moreover, "there is no real argument against real recognition except that a lot of people are going to blow up. If this country—the most powerful in the world at the most dangerous time in the world—is at a stage in which the government is hog-tied against its better judgment because some people are going to blow up, then God alone help the Republic. That is all." [27]

Following Peffer's remarks there was an applause which is rare—in fact, almost unheard of—in this kind of a conference with thirty men sitting around the table.

Owen Lattimore, also, urged recognition. "Overhaste in recognizing the new situation [Communist] China might indicate panic," he said, but . . . "on the other hand, too much delay might have a deteriorating effect on our prestige in Asia that in the long run would be more damaging to us. . . . " He continued: "as Mr. Peffer cogently pointed out, that doesn't really alter the mechanics of how we handle things in the United Nations; for instance, the veto ratio is changed but the veto situation is not changed. . . . " [28] The Lattimore line was that, after all, Russia had one veto now, therefore, what if you did give the Communists two vetoes? Two vetoes would not do them any more good than one, as we still had one veto.

Lawrence K. Rosinger commented, "I'd like to associate myself with the view frequently expressed around this table that we should extend recognition. My own personal feeling is that the recognition should come as early as possible." He continued: "I think, though, that in terms of preparing American public opinion for recognition, there is a process of disentanglement from the Chinese Nationalists, which can be carried out

26 *Ibid.*, p. 416.

27 *Ibid.*, pp. 425-428. Peffer states that Formosa was not, at least technically, Chinese territory, in spite of the fact that it was turned over to the Chinese government in 1945 and a local Chinese government established and maintained there for four years before Peffer made this statement. Japan had seized Formosa from China in the treaty of Shimonoeski, April 17, 1895.

28 *Ibid.*, pp. 434-435.

in the weeks ahead and I think to the extent that we disentangle ourselves from the Chinese Nationalists, we lay the basis for recognition." [29]

Benjamin Kizer, formerly Director of the China Office, UNRRA, remarked, "I should like to follow Mr. Lattimore with the suggestion to
go on trading before recognition." [30] This meant, of course, continuing
American trade with Communist China in the period of weeks before
recognizing them. Dr. Arthur Holcombe, of Harvard, suggested that before we recognize the Communists we ought to insist on some reforms,
some assurance that the minority parties in China will have a chance
and not be liquidated because of political differences. To this Kizer remarked, "I couldn't go as far as Dr. Holcombe's suggestion that they
reform their government by recognizing various parties. That is a matter of scuttling recognition and introducing conflict where we should introduce agreement." [31] Kizer did not want to introduce a conflict with
the Chinese Communists by insisting that they have some minority party
representation. The erstwhile sauce for the Nationalist goose was not for
the Communist gander.

As a prelude to recognition, McNaughton urged trade: "We will never
get this world going unless we start trade, and I would start trade with
the Communists in China until I found out they were impossible to do
business with." [32] J. Morden Murphy, a trustee of the American Branch of
the Institute of Pacific Relations, commented, "I feel that if we don't
trade with the Communists in China it is pretty obvious that since they
have a very crying need for goods it simply amounts to forcing them to
trade with Russia on Russia's terms." [33] William R. Herod, President of
International General Electric Company, did not favor immediate recognition but advised recognizing if and when the Communists attained the
position of having complete control of the machinery of State, "unless in
the meantime there has been some other factor." [34]

It is interesting to note that the panel did not discuss *whether* the
Communist Government should be given American recognition, but
when such recognition should be granted. However, Harold Stassen did
point out that recognition would not bring the blessings which so many
people fondly expected to accrue from such recognition; that Communist
countries do not subscribe to the underlying principle of our international
society, namely, sanctity of treaties and good faith in observing agreements. Recognition "would be a very sad mistake in our world policy."
It would not only mean that we must withdraw recognition of the Na-

29 *Ibid.*, pp. 442-444.
30 *Ibid.*, p. 455.
31 *Ibid.*
32 *Ibid.*, p. 331.
33 *Ibid.*
34 *Ibid.*, pp. 421-422.

tionalist Government but we would have to "join in an affirmative action to throw the Nationalist Government out of the United Nations. There are no half-way measures on this. . . . " [35]

The conference had a brief discussion on the question of ships that were taking military supplies to the Chinese Communists through a blockade or port closure which the Chinese Nationalists were enforcing. Kizer suggested that "we should make a public disavowal" of the blockade established by Chiang Kai-shek, then follow this up with a withdrawal of recognition of the Kuomintang.[36]

On the question of Formosa, John K. Fairbank of Harvard made a proposal that we abandon that island. "To try to hold Formosa with troops," he said, "would give such ideological ammunition to the Chinese Communists that it would unite China more readily against us." Moreover, "to hold Formosa would defeat our ends by a miscalculation of the response in China, just as our military support of Chiang Kai-shek defeated our ends because we couldn't foresee his inefficiency. . . . " [37] Many of our top military officials have repeatedly stressed the strategic importance of this island to our Pacific defense. One would think General Marshall, who sat through the sessions and was the only member with any military experience, would have objected to giving up that island to a militant satellite of the Soviet Union. He had no apparent objection to the proposal.

However, judging from Marshall's past performances, there are several reasons why one should not think that General Marshall might object. First, General Marshall helped Communist activities in many ways in his efforts to force the Nationalist government to give in to them. Knowing that Soviet Communists were rearming, reorganizing, giving operation advice to the Communists, he stopped all aid from the United States to the Nationalists. He put mild pressure on Admiral Cooke not to help establish a Nationalist Navy, in spite of the Congressional resolution to do precisely that. When Admiral Cooke pointed out the fact, Marshall kept silent. Further, strategy affecting sea control and islands in the seas is a Navy problem. During World War II when we were set to take Formosa, General Marshall opposed; he favored MacArthur's desire to go to the Philippines first. MacArthur, however, fully appreciated the vital importance of Formosa to the United States. He has told Admiral Cooke often during the last ten years how much he learned about naval strategy in conducting operations in the South Pacific during the war.[38]

35 *Ibid.*, p. 459.
36 *Ibid.*, p. 456.
37 *Ibid.*, pp. 138-139.
38 Letter from Admiral Cooke to author, August 12, 1960. *Time* Magazine for August 7, 1950 wrote that Secretary of State Acheson had persuaded the United States Joint Chiefs of Staff, against the advice of General MacArthur, that the United States

Throughout the three-day conference the Lattimore-Rosinger group stayed close together and never differed essentially with one another on any important point. Rosinger, when given an opportunity before a Senate committee to deny allegations of Communist membership by at least three credible witnesses, pleaded the Fifth Amendment.[39] At the conference he recommended that U. S. aid be withheld from the Chinese Nationalist Government; that the U. S. shun economic and military intervention in Formosa; that Formosa be turned over to the Chinese Communists; that no impediments to normal trade with Red China be imposed; that any action that would tend to prolong what he called the Nationalist blockade be avoided; that normal trade be established between Japan and Red China; and that *de jure* recognition be accorded to the "Chinese Peoples' Republic." [40] This was a precise summary of the current Communist line.

Lattimore's recommendations coincided with Rosinger's in almost every respect. He urged withdrawal of support from Chiang Kai-shek and from the "scattering of little Chiang Kai-sheks in Asia"; avoidance of cutting off trade with Communist China; encouraging Japan to come to terms with Red China; discontinuance of efforts to keep South Korea alive; and the admission into the United Nations of Red China and the Mongolian Peoples' Republic.[41] The "prevailing views" at the conference can be summed up as follows: recognition of the Chinese Communist Government, establishment of normal trade relations between Communist China and the United States, and the breaking of what the conference called the Nationalist blockade.[42] The "views" which would be held by Jessup, Lattimore, and Rosinger were easily predictable. It should be obvious that these were the views the Department of State intended to follow. The conference itself was just window-dressing to lend an aura of deliberation to policy already decided upon by the dominant clique in the Department of State.

Harold Stassen testified before the Senate Internal Security Subcommittee that Jessup told him "the greater logic" was on the side of giving

---

should not intervene in Formosa. He advanced the argument that if Russia had its way in Asia, the Communists would eventually become highly unpopular among Asian people and the United States would gain popularity for its nonintervention.

39 He was identified by Dr. Wittfogel, *Institute of Pacific Relations, Hearings,* Part 1, p. 313; William Martin Canning, *Ibid.,* Part 2, p. 467; Louis Budenz, *Ibid.,* Part 4, p. 1077. For Rosinger's Fifth Amendment pleas see Part 8, p. 2475.

40 Morris, *No Wonder We Are Losing,* p. 96. See Rosinger's memorandum to Philip Jessup, September 22, 1949. *Institute of Pacific Relations, Hearings,* Part 9, Exhibit No. 354, pp. 2500-2503.

41 *Ibid.,* pp. 96-97; see text of Lattimore's memorandum in *New York Times,* April 4, 1950.

42 *Institute of Pacific Relations, Hearings,* Part 4, p. 1045. Jessup states that eleven members were for recognition and five were opposed. *Nomination of Philip C. Jessup,* p. 610.

diplomatic recognition to the Chinese Communist Government. He explained the following before the Committee:

THE CHAIRMAN: Was it to Lattimore or Jessup that you expressed your hope that the policy put out by the Lattimore group would not be carried out? . . .

MR. STASSEN: No, it was to Dr. Jessup that I said that; I pleaded with him not to implement the Lattimore policy. This, you understand, was at the recess of the third day when I saw the way the discussion was going, and when I felt strongly as to the tragic implications of it for our country.

THE CHAIRMAN: He expressed himself contrary to your views?

MR. STASSEN: He said he felt the greater logic was on the position advanced by the Lattimore group.[43]

Another account of the conference—similar to that given by Stassen— may be found in the testimony of Professor Colegrove. According to his version, "One group was very obviously pro-American in its thinking, put America first, that is, foreign policy must serve the national interest of the American people," while another group "tended to be sympathetic to Communistic China and very considerate of the Kremlin." In answer to a question by Senator Ferguson whether this latter group "were favoring, in your opinion, the Communist line rather than the good interest of the United States of America?" Colegrove replied: "That was my impression." The testimony continued:

SENATOR FERGUSON: From what was said?

MR. COLEGROVE: Yes.

SENATOR EASTLAND: Did they advocate economic aid to Communist China?

MR. COLEGROVE: Yes, very, very strongly.

SENATOR FERGUSON: And recognition of Communist China?

MR. COLEGROVE: Immediate recognition of Communist China, and were very much opposed to a Pacific pact.[44]

In another appearance before the same committee, Colegrove made this remark: " . . . One thing that amazed me at this conference which was on China, there was little reference to the traditional American policy in Asia. That traditional policy was the Open Door Policy." Furthermore, "I was rather surprised when I came to Washington to attend this conference to find so many members of the conference who had been among the group who were partly responsible for the fall of Chiang Kai-shek and the victory of the Communists." [45] The following analysis was given:

SENATOR SMITH [of New Jersey]: All right. Now, did you feel that that conference was rigged, so as to have that type or that group predominate? Was that your feeling at the time?

---

[43] *Institute of Pacific Relations, Hearings,* Part 4, p. 1063.

[44] Testimony of Mr. Kenneth Colegrove, September 25, 1951, *Ibid.,* Part 3, pp. 919-921.

[45] *Ibid.,* Part 5, pp. 1290-1291.

MR. COLEGROVE: Definitely, Senator, that was my feeling. I thought the conference should have included quite a number of men who were left out but who were, you might say, in favor of the Chiang Kai-shek government. . . . I expected to see a more even balance.

SENATOR SMITH: Did you have the feeling at that time that those men or those types of men had been purposely left out so as not to have a full argument on the other side?

MR. COLEGROVE: Definitely so.

SENATOR SMITH: Now, did you have any specific evidence that would justify you other than just the general feeling.

MR. COLEGROVE: Well, the only evidence would be the number of pro-Communist experts invited to the conference and the smallness of the number of anti-Communist experts on the other side.[46]

Former Ambassador to China John Leighton Stuart was also very critical of the recommendations made at this conference. "What I heard was disconcerting," he said. "Relatively little was said about China's difficulties within and without, and all the onus for the National Government's collapse was placed upon that government itself." [47]

Subsequent events affecting our policy toward Nationalist China indicated the strong influence of the Lattimore-Rosinger group. Just six weeks after the conference, on November 16, 1949, Secretary Acheson protested the Nationalist firing on the *Flying Cloud* which was running the Nationalist blockade in bringing war supplies to the Chinese Communists. On December 3, Acheson said that the United States did not recognize the legality of the Nationalist blockade, and he protested the shelling of the United States ship. These decisions were in line with the prevailing Lattimore-Rosinger group.[48]

On December 23, the Department of State sent a significant memorandum to its foreign personnel all over the world, playing down the importance of Formosa and, in effect, writing it off by saying that "its control by the Communist forces would not imperil our position in the Far East." [49] The implications of this memorandum are exceedingly important. It not only served as a guidance directive for our overseas personnel, but it revealed the defeatist attitude of the Department of State.

Pressed by Senator Knowland, Secretary Acheson admitted to the Senate Committee on Foreign Relations, on January 10, 1950, that he was responsible for this secret directive. He stated it was issued for the purpose of propaganda in minimizing the importance of Formosa in the event that that island fell into Communist hands.[50] This explanation, however, does not alter the real meaning of the directive, which resulted

---

46 *Ibid.*, General Wedemeyer was invited but could not attend.
47 Stuart, "How the Communists Got China," *op. cit.*, p. 124.
48 *Institute of Pacific Relations, Hearings*, Part 4, p. 1067.
49 *Military Situation in the Far East*, Part 5, p. 3589.
50 *Ibid.*, Part 3, p. 1671 ff.

in bringing "all embassy women and children and non-essential personnel home from Formosa." [51] In December, 1949, Acheson told a *Time* correspondent, "What we must do now is to shake loose from the Chinese Nationalists. It will be harder to make that necessary break with them if we go to Formosa." [52]

Formosa was one of the topics discussed at the State Department conference of October 9, and the prevailing view was to abandon that island. When Admiral Charles Joy met Jessup in Tokyo, it was his distinct impression that Jessup attempted to persuade him that Formosa was of no importance strategically to the defense of the Pacific. [53] Similarly, Jessup "attempted over and over to convince" General Stratemeyer that "Formosa was not needed in our periphery defense." [54] Top military officials have repeatedly stated that it would be detrimental to the United States to let Formosa fall into enemy hands. [55] General Wedemeyer pointed this out definitely when he was asked to comment on the Acheson directive abandoning Formosa, "I would never have accepted that as a correct interpretation of my recommendation to minimize the loss of the fall of Formosa, because all the military men recognize that Formosa does have strategic significance. It is an important segment of a line of defense along the Asiatic mainland there." [56]

In the meantime, on December 22, 1949, the Joint Chiefs of Staff drafted a memorandum to the National Security Council, urging that a military mission be sent to Formosa to assess defensive and operational needs. This recommendation was rejected by President Truman on December 30, when he announced that United States occupation of Formosa was not advisable. [57] Again on January 5, 1950, the President stated categorically: " . . . The United States Government will not pursue a course which will lead to involvement in the civil conflict in China. Similarly, the United States Government will not provide military aid or advice to Chinese forces on Formosa." [58] The announcement came only thirteen days after Acheson issued his directive to abandon Formosa and just three months after the State Department conference on revising American policy.

Apparently Acheson influenced the President in his decision. Criticism was quickly voiced in Congress. After his return from a visit to the

---

[51] Fitch, *Formosa Beachead*, p. 238.

[52] *Time*, October 15, 1951, p. 23.

[53] *Interlocking Subversion in Government Departments*, Part 26, p. 2130.

[54] Testimony of General George E. Stratemeyer, August 25, 1954. *Ibid.*, Part 22, p. 1717.

[55] *Military Situation in the Far East*, Part 3, p. 1677.

[56] *Ibid.*, Part 3, p. 2425.

[57] *Time*, January 2, 1950, pp. 11-12 and January 9, 1950, pp. 9-10.

[58] *A Decade of American Foreign Policy, 1941-1949*, p. 728.

island of Formosa, Senator Knowland was sharply critical of the administration's inept policy: "Munich should have taught us," he said, "that appeasement, then as now, is but surrender on the installment plan." [59]

Secretary Acheson made another installment when, in a speech at the Press Club in Washington on January 12, 1950, he omitted Formosa and Korea from our strategic line of defense in the Pacific.[60] It is little wonder that the American people and Asian diplomats and officials were confused as to the intention of our government. Acheson's omission of Formosa and Korea from a list of areas vital to our security in the Pacific became a fiery controversial point when the Korean War broke out. Critics of Acheson asserted that his speech had invited the Communists to take over South Korea—quite probable, in view of Lattimore's earlier comment. Some Congressional members called for Acheson's resignation and the adoption of a policy more favorable to Nationalist China.

It is difficult to believe that our officials in the Department of State, having access to intelligence reports and expert consultants, could fail to realize that the Communist movement constituted a threat to our national security in the Pacific. None of the representatives of the three intelligence agencies, or four, if we include the Air Force Intelligence Agency, was permitted to go into Formosa in 1949 and 1950, and all reports made by the Naval and Military attachés had to fit into State Department policy. One of the Army attachés (Captain Manning), knowing that reports derived from a Communist underground provided the information for the United States diplomatic reports sent to Washington, made his own report to the Department of the Army. He was summarily detached. The State Department knew that reports being received, and being disseminated through the military departments, were distorted and false. The State Department did nothing about this in the way of corrective action.[61]

The course of action the State Department followed led to the scrapping of our traditional Open Door Policy towards China. In its place was formulated what appeared as a do-nothing policy, but what was really a sell-out China policy. The late Senator Arthur Vandenberg remarked on the floor of the Senate, on April 16, 1947: "What the policy of the State Department is, I am unable to testify. There is a considerable amount of misunderstanding about the so-called bipartisan foreign policy of this country." [62] Ambassador Stuart, with long experience in China, was just as critical: "I found the attitude of the Department of

59 *Time,* January 16, 1950, p. 15.

60 Text of the address, entitled "Crisis in Asia," is published in U. S. *Department of State Bulletin* (January 23, 1950), pp. 111-118.

61 Letter from Admiral Cooke to Author, August 12, 1960.

62 *Congressional Record,* April 16, 1947, p. 3474.

State on the whole subject of China essentially one of frustrated unsympathetic defeatism." [63]

Whatever their motives, our officials cannot be absolved from responsibility for the decisions in the China situation. Blindly or deliberately they misled our country on China. The fact that Soviet Russia had an overwhelming influence in organizing the Communist Party in China had long been known to Washington officials. Army Intelligence submitted a documented report which described this influence and domination, but the disturbing factor has been the reluctance of some officials to accept it as authoritative.

Since 1922, moreover, successive Communist International Party Congresses had announced to the world their determination to destroy all capitalistic countries, including America. Repeated warnings of the Communist threat came from individuals in the Far East with first hand experience. Entries in the *Forrestal Diaries* bear this out: "Robertson [American Commissioner in China] forecast that if Americans withdrew from China, the Russians would surge in. . . . General Pfeiffer of the Marines confirmed . . . [that] American withdrawal would mean Communist domination of all Manchuria and China." [64] Small room had been left for misunderstanding of the situation.

Various statements and actions by responsible American officials indicated that at least some officials in our Department of State intentionally aided the Communist movement in the Far East. Others were completely subservient to the British Foreign Office; still others were motivated by visions of "one world," bought by unlimited appeasement of international Communism, and made possible only by the erection of Marxist regimes everywhere. Together, they prevailed. Had it not been for mistreatment of American personnel following the surrender of Japan and then the Communist aggression in Korea, the Department of State probably would have recognized the Peiping regime. At least a number of incidents indicated this possibility. Brigadier General Louis Fortier, intelligence officer of the United States Far Eastern Command, was greatly concerned over the Communist threat to our security. Recognition of the New People's Republic would give the Communists increased moral and political support necessary for consolidation of their position. On January 6, 1950, Jessup told General Fortier in Japan that

---

[63] Stuart, *Fifty Years in China*, p. 273. "My purpose in testifying here," Eugene Dooman told the McCarran Committee, "was to indicate in general that policies put forward by the left-wing press, from the *Daily Worker* right down through the line, were in effect substantially translated into U.S. policies, and to indicate from personal knowledge how that operation was carried out." *Institute of Pacific Relations, Hearings*, Part 3, p. 754.

[64] *The Forrestal Diaries*, July 8, 1946, p. 175.

the United States would recognize Red China in a period of about two or three weeks.[65]

Senator Alexander Smith made the following diary notation on November 23, 1949: "Went up to Assembly at Flushing. Lunch with Philip Jessup and Ray Fosdick. They are leaning towards the British who want to recognize Communist China. Also, they do not see the danger of the Formosa situation." [66] Senator Tom Connally, Chairman of the Foreign Relations Committee, told a group of reporters that "while the United States' recognition of Communist China would not be accomplished 'in a hurry' it was on its way." [67]

On about November 30, 1949, Admiral Cooke learned that Jessup would head a mission going to Bangkok to make arrangements for the future actions of the United States in the Southeastern Asia area. He made arrangements to go to New York to talk to Jessup, because he (Admiral Cooke) knew quite a bit about Southeast Asia, and had read the report sent in by the Lapham Committee, which made recommendations with which he disagreed. Admiral Cooke had never met Jessup before, and knew little about him. But in a conversation he soon learned that Jessup was hostile to Chiang Kai-shek and the Nationalist Government.[68]

In September, 1960, William D. Pawley testified that General Marshall stopped Jessup "from bringing back from China a recommendation [in December, 1949] to recognize Red China." He continued:

It was general knowledge in the Department of State that we were about to recommend recognition of Red China, and the way it was planned was for Jessup to represent Acheson at a meeting of U.S. Ambassadors in the Far East and get from that meeting a recommendation to recognize Red China, and bring them into the U.N.

I met with Jessup on December 10, 1949, and made a tremendous effort to dissuade him from this policy. After my hour and a half meeting with Jessup convinced me that he was going to carry out this policy in spite of my pleas against it—although he, of course, did not directly admit it—I so informed General Marshall, then president of the Red Cross. At Marshall's request I arranged a meeting for the next day between Marshall, Jessup, and myself at Marshall's apartment. General Marshall's impression of Jessup's intentions was so similar to my own that he stated to Jessup that if the Department of State did pursue a plan of recognition of Red China that he personally would take it up with the President, in order that this serious mistake not be made. After Jessup left,

---

65 Testimony of General L. Joseph Fortier, September 29, 1951, *Institute of Pacific Relations, Hearings,* Part 3, pp. 844-845; Part 4, p. 1062. Jessup denied this—see Hearings on the *Nomination of Philip C. Jessup before the Senate Foreign Relations Committee,* p. 618.

66 *Institute of Pacific Relations, Hearings,* Part 14, Exhibit No. 1407, p. 5643.

67 *New York Times,* January 11, 1950.

68 Letter from Admiral Cooke to author, August 12, 1960.

General Marshall told me that he intended to discuss this matter with President Truman.

SENATOR McCLELLAN: That is who?

MR. PAWLEY: Phil Jessup, Special Assistant to the Secretary of State.

SENATOR HRUSKA: Was he acting on his own or was that a policy decision of the Department?

MR. PAWLEY: It was a policy of the Secretary at that time.[69]

Yet Ambassador Jessup, under oath, told the Foreign Relations Committee considering his appointment to the U. N. General Assembly in October, 1951, that the Department of State had at no time "considered" the possibility of recognizing Red China.[70]

If the Administration had shown more energy during the critical days of the China situation, something might have been accomplished toward preventing Red conquest of the mainland. But, while Acheson and our government waited "for the dust to settle" in the Pacific area, the Communists in China continued to win one victory after another. With the fall of Chungking in December, 1949, all effective resistance on the mainland ceased, and the Nationalist government was forced to Formosa.

This uneasy situation in the Far East gave Admiral Cooke, Commander of the U. S. 7th Fleet, deep concern. He was particularly anxious to prevent Formosa, the last remaining stronghold, from falling to the Chinese Communists. He had an opportunity to observe the conduct of our diplomats on Formosa and discovered their action to be contrary to our China policy. He tried in vain to warn American officials of the serious consequences which would result from recognition of the Red regime. The story of his experiences was told before the Senate Subcommittee on Internal Security:

When the Communist government was set up in Peiping, I knew that it was being done largely by the Soviet Communists. This was confirmed by the recognition of the Chinese Communist government by the U.S.S.R. two days later on October 3, 1949.

I felt that this might likely lead to the recognition of Communist China by the United States Government, which in turn would lead to the loss of Formosa

---

[69] *Communist Threat to the United States Through the Caribbean,* Part 10, p. 734.

[70] *Nomination of Philip C. Jessup,* p. 614, 930, ff. Secretary of Defense Louis Johnson gave his views on the Administration's plans for recognition:

SENATOR SALTONSTALL: . . . What is not clear to me is the attitude of the State Department toward Chiang's government, say, from the time of Marshall's return in 1947 to June 25, 1950. Did it always support that government but with varying degrees of intensity, but it had changed from one of nonsupport to support in 1950 after Korea? Would you be willing to try to help me clear up that?

MR. JOHNSON: Generally speaking, it seemed to me that the State Department was critical of and did not support the government we recognized. Personally, *I was extremely fearful* that we were going to recognize Communist China in the indirect way of permitting it to become a member of the United Nations. It was my understanding that we would not use the veto in the Security Council to keep them out. *Military Situation in the Far East, Hearings,* Part 4, p. 2640; p. 2663. Italics mine.

to the Communists. I considered that if we recognized Red China we would soon lose Formosa, and if we lose Formosa we would certainly recognize Red China, and that both or either were very serious disasters to United States security and world freedom.

I therefore went to Washington and spent about two months in the Washington area, working in large degree with Mr. William Pawley, ex-Ambassador to Brazil, in an effort to set up a group of ex-United States naval and military officers and retired officers to go to Formosa to assist the Nationalist government in preventing the fall of Formosa to Communism.

I made formal recommendations to the State Department and informal recommendations to the President himself, through his aide, that this be carried out, but I never received any action one way or the other on these recommendations; no red light, no green light.

Finally, about the 1st of December of 1949, I discontinued my efforts and returned to Sonoma, California.[71]

Admiral Cooke did not remain at his home very long. President Truman and Secretary Acheson issued their statements abandoning the island of Formosa and indicating that Korea was not included in the United States strategic defense perimeter. Admiral Cooke telephoned Pawley in Washington to express his grave disappointment. He impressed upon Pawley that "this could be very disastrous to the United States, and every effort should be made to modify the Government's decision." He continued: "I proceeded that night to Washington and talked to a number of Senators, all of whom agreed, but none of them could do anything about it. So I returned to my home at Sonoma, California." [72]

In the course of his personal efforts to avert disaster, Admiral Cooke made some revealing discoveries at firsthand. While in Washington, during the period of October, and November, 1949, he saw reports which had been sent by the United States Consul General in Taipei, Formosa, stating in effect that Formosa would fall to the Communists within a period of one or two weeks from the time of the reports. "I knew that we did not at that time have any naval intelligence representatives in Formosa," he said, "and I felt that these reports were not well founded. In fact, I was sure that they were not correct." [73] The Communists were obviously incapable of an immediate amphibious assault on Formosa.

Robert Morris, Chief Counsel of the Senate Internal Security Subcommittee, questioned Admiral Cooke about the significance of these reports:

MR. MORRIS: Well, Admiral, were these reports, in your opinion, causing damage?

ADMIRAL COOKE: Yes, I considered that they were causing a very serious adverse effect on the United States policy and action. I found that many of the

---

[71] *Internal Security Report for 1956*, p. 197. Italics mine.

[72] *Ibid.*, pp. 197-198.

[73] *Ibid.*, p. 198.

people in the Government to whom I presented the idea that we should help the Formosa Nationalist Government hold on to Formosa against Communist attack were undoubtedly influenced by these reports of a debacle in Formosa that would be forthcoming in the very early future.[74]

Morris then asked whether the warning by Secretary Acheson to all our diplomatic personnel around the world to be ready to explain the fall of Formosa had any adverse effect. Admiral Cooke replied, "Yes, I considered that it did in a very high degree, because the Nationalist Government, just having been driven off the mainland, was in somewhat of a precarious position in Formosa, with particular regard to its relationship with all the countries in the world, some of which would be ready to recognize Communist China without delay." "In other words," said Admiral Cooke, "if this warning of the State Department was supported by certain things going badly in Formosa, there was a great chance that the recognition of Red China at this time might become fairly worldwide." [75]

With no support forthcoming from our officials in Washington, Admiral Cooke decided to go to Formosa to see the situation at firsthand, and to determine what could be done about "helping to hold this island." When he arrived on Formosa, he did not find that conditions coincided with the reports submitted by the Consul-General. "I did not find anything in Formosa," he said, "which supported the reports made in October and November of 1949, setting forth as they did, the imminence of the fall of Formosa to Communism within a period of two or three weeks." [76]

At the beginning of 1950, Great Britain recognized the Communist regime. Norway, Finland, Sweden, Switzerland, and the Netherlands soon followed suit. The Department of State would have openly advocated recognition if it had not been for the humiliation suffered by our government at the hands of the Chinese Communists. In January, 1950, American consular property in Peiping was seized in violation of treaty rights and "the most elementary standards of international usage and conduct." [77]

The Department of State then announced it was recalling all American official personnel from Communist China, as it had notified the Chinese Communist authorities it would do if these threats did not stop. Later Secretary Acheson stated:

. . . as old friends of the Chinese people, we say to them that the representatives of our country are leaving them not by any wish of ours. They are leaving

---

[74] *Ibid.*, p. 198.
[75] *Ibid.*, pp. 198-199.
[76] *Ibid.*, p. 200.
[77] *Department of State Bulletin,* January 23, 1950, p. 119.

because the normal and accepted standards of international conduct have not been observed by the Chinese Communist authorities in their treatment of our representatives and because they have, in effect, even been summarily ejected from their offices in Peiping. Under such conditions our representatives could not fulfill their normal functions. We regret this leaving of our people, but our Chinese friends will understand again where the responsibility lies.[78]

Segments of the public and Congress became intensely opposed to any step which might weaken the Chiang Kai-shek government. The problem of recognition of Communist China and her admission to the United Nations aroused a serious debate in the press, on public platforms, and in Congress. On May 10, 1950, thirty-five senators wrote to President Truman, asking for clear assurances that the United States Government did not intend to recognize the Communist regime in China or to give support to the movement to admit that regime to the United Nations.[79] Ex-President Herbert Hoover, when asked for his views on the China situation by Senator Knowland, asserted that the United States should not only continue to recognize the Nationalist Government, but should continue to support it, giving naval protection if necessary.[80] Congressman Judd and others expressed similar views on the subject.

There were still some individuals who were opposed to upholding the Chiang Kai-shek government on Formosa, and who advocated recognition of Red China and its admission to the United Nations. Without a doubt, one of the strongest critics of the Nationalist Government has been Owen Lattimore, who has written numerous books and articles sympathetic to Communism. His views were fairly representative of a segment of the press and officialdom still advocating recognition of the Communist Regime at Peiping. In the January, 1950 issue of *Atlantic Magazine*, Lattimore proposed a backdoor approach to recognition of Red China. "For the problem of the recognition of the new government of China," he said, "the United Nations offers the ideal avenue to a solution. If, with no pressure against China from the United States, a majority of non-Communist countries in Europe, Latin America and Asia should vote to seat new Chinese representatives to the United Nations, the United States should not vote against the verdict." [81] This approach found considerable favor among "liberal" pundits—and still does.

---

78 Speech to the Commonwealth Club at San Francisco, March 5, 1950, *Department of State Bulletin* (March 27, 1950), p. 469.

79 See "The China Lobby," *Congressional Record*, 82nd Cong., 2d Sess. (June 6, 1952), p. 16. The phrase "China Lobby" originated in the West Coast Communist newspaper, *People's Daily World*. The term quickly became a standard smear device in the "liberal" press.

80 *Time*, January 16, 1950, p. 15.

81 Owen Lattimore, "Rebuilding Our Policy in Asia," *Atlantic Magazine* (January 1950) , p. 23. The Lattimore approach was used, in 1961, in the Case of Outer Mongolia.

On April 15, 1950, Lattimore spoke to members of the American Academy of Political and Social Science, in Philadelphia:

The United States should disavow approval and support of the old Government of China. . . . This can be done by allowing those members of the United Nations who wish to do so to vote to unseat the old Chinese delegations to the United Nations and seat a new one. Direct relations between Washington and the new Government of China can wait. They should wait until the Chinese Government is willing to make dignified and honorable relations possible. If, in Chinese domestic politics, there is a foreign nation that deals with and favors one political party rather than the entire nation and people, let that be Russia. America should be willing to show friendliness not toward individuals and not toward any one party, but toward the nation and the people.[82]

Dr. Karl A. Wittfogel, director of a Chinese history project co-sponsored by the University of Washington and Columbia University in New York, testified before the House Committee on Un-American Activities, on December 7, 1950, that he first became acquainted with Lattimore in 1935 in China. They were good friends, he said, until late in 1944 when Lattimore defended the Russian purge trials as "democratic" and voiced his contempt for "ex-Communists." "He was sympathetic to a number of things," remarked Dr. Wittfogel, "no doubt about it. . . . The sum total of his writings makes a friendly case for Chinese Communists. I talked with him in 1944 about the future of Korea. He thought it was not a bad thing if Korea would be turned over to the Russians. Then both of us blew up." [83]

After the outbreak of hostilities in Korea and the subsequent entrance of Chinese Communist forces into the conflict against the United States, recognition of the Communist government in China was set aside. Our government once more was forced to reverse its policy toward China. In his statement on June 27, 1950, President Truman castigated the Communists in no uncertain terms and made it clear that any attack upon Formosa would be a direct threat to the security of the United States. This change of attitude on the part of the President was in marked contrast to his earlier statement abandoning that island. Formosa now became strategic to our war in Korea; American aid to the Chiang Kai-shek government in Formosa decidedly increased. Both the House and Senate unanimously passed resolutions stating that the Communist Chinese Government should not be admitted to the United Nations. The Department of State evinced a willingness to use the veto, if necessary, in the Security Council to keep the Chinese Communists out of that organization.[84]

---

[82] Owen Lattimore, "Point Four and the Third Countries," *The Annals of The American Academy of Political and Social Science* (July 1950), p. 6.

[83] *Washington Times-Herald*, December 8, 1950.

[84] On February 1, 1951, the U. N. General Assembly, in a resolution, condemned the

In December, 1950, British Prime Minister Clement R. Attlee made a visit to Washington and discussed the Korean conflict with President Truman. The British leader was in a pacifying mood, for he proposed to compromise with the Chinese Communists by offering them a seat in the United Nations so that a Korean cease-fire could be obtained. This proposal was rejected by the President.[85]

There have been few issues of foreign policy which have been so widely supported as our recent policy in China. Congress has passed five unanimous resolutions opposing the admission of Communist China to the United Nations or recognition of Peiping by the United States; both political parties included planks to this effect in their 1956 national platforms, and every major Communist-free American organization has adopted similar expressions from time to time. This overwhelming support is ignored by the forces which favor appeasement of Red China. The opposition to recognition was based on the ruthless record of Red China, which included repudiation of international obligations, torture and murder of prisoners, execution of numerous missionaries, and seizure of American property.[86]

President Truman ordered the United States Seventh Fleet to prevent any attack on Formosa and called on the Nationalists to cease all operations against the mainland. One of the first official acts of President Eisenhower upon assuming office was to issue instructions that "the Seventh Fleet no longer be employed to shield Communist China." [87] However, this did not change the policy of using it to defend Formosa.

The cessation of hostilities in Korea in mid-1953 did not alter United States policy toward recognition of Communist China. Moreover, the United States took precautions that any contact with representatives of the Communist regime necessary to settle the Korean problem should not be interpreted as conferring recognition. At the Berlin Conference in early 1954, when the United States agreed to participate in a later conference at Geneva, with representatives of the Chinese Peoples' Republic present, we insisted that the following assertion be written into the official communique of the conference: "It is understood that neither the invitation to, nor the holding of, the above-mentioned conference shall

Peiping regime as an aggressor and, on May 18, in another resolution, recommended that member states immediately prohibit shipment to Communist China and North Korea of arms, ammunition, strategic materials, etc. MacNair and Lach, *Modern Far Eastern International Relations*, p. 638, 642.

[85] *Memoirs by Harry S. Truman*, II, 396-399. *As It Happened: The Autobiography of Clement R. Attlee* (New York: The Viking Press, 1954), p. 282.

[86] For an excellent account of Red China's record of criminal acts, see *Invasion Alert!: Red China Drives on the UN*, by Joseph C. Grew, (Baltimore: Maran Publishers, 1956). The butchery of people in China has exceeded even the "liquidation" practiced by the Soviets.

[87] *State of the Union Message*, February 2, 1953.

be deemed to imply diplomatic recognition in any case where it has not already been accorded." [88]

Until the stark object lesson in Korea, pro-Communist elements in the United States had it all their way. The evidence shows the terrific impact of the propaganda campaign against the Chinese Nationalist Government, originated by forces both within and without the United States. The constant attacks upon the leadership of Chiang Kai-shek and the repeated assaults upon the alleged corruption and graft of his associates softened the fiber of Nationalist resistance, especially since many of these attacks originated within a nation which claimed to be aiding and supporting the Republic of China.

It cannot be denied that there were valid grounds for criticism of the Nationalist Government of China, or, for that matter, of any other government that has ever existed. But, for the most part, the motive behind the criticism was evidenced in the venomous nature of the attacks. While it cannot be denied that irregularities and incompetence on the part of certain officials contributed to the fall of the Chinese government, they were not a major factor in the opinion of many qualified and objective observers.

"Squeeze" was an old and accepted practice in China as in most Eastern countries, but it was not until a runaway inflation had made the value of salaries almost meaningless that irregularities became a menace.

It was then that certain government officials, no longer able to subsist on their salaries, succumbed to temptation and resorted to graft.

At a press conference in Shanghai, General Wedemeyer said he very much doubted he would be incorruptible if he had to live on the salary of a Chinese General. Even the White Paper testifies that "the men at the very top are of high integrity and continue to struggle bravely against terrific difficulties." [89]

In a lecture given at the National War College on November 18, 1946, General Wedemeyer had this to say: "Although the National Government of China was frequently and derisively described as authoritarian or totalitarian, there was a basic difference between it and its Communist enemies, since the Kuomintang's ultimate aim was the establishment of a constitutional republic, whereas the Communists want to establish a totalitarian dictatorship on the Soviet pattern. In my two years of close contact with Chiang Kai-shek, I had become convinced that he personally was a straightforward, selfless leader, keenly interested in the welfare of his people, and desirous of establishing a constitutional government according to the precepts of Sun Yat-sen. This was obviously impossible

---

[88] *Department of State Bulletin*, March 1, 1954, p. 318.
[89] Utley, *The China Story*, p. 61.

so long as China was fighting first the Japanese and then the Communists backed by Soviet Russia." [90]

Wedemeyer pointed out that the revenues of the National Government shrank instead of increasing when peace came after V-J Day. "More and more appropriations had to be made for the repair of railways, mines and industries, and military expenditures were swollen to ever greater proportions. Hence the demoralizing inflation, resulting corruption and a general decline of morale greater than during the long years of holding out against Japan."

"The reforms we kept urging the Nationalists to institute," General Wedemeyer said, "would have been hard enough to carry out in peacetime even with United States aid, and were totally impossible in the midst of the civil war, which was in fact a Sino-Russian war."

In General Wedemeyer's opinion, to call Chiang Kai-shek a Fascist dictator was a ridiculous reversal of the truth. "The powers of the Chinese National Government," he said, "far from being totalitarian, were much too limited. It interfered with the individual too little, not too much. Its sins of omission, not of commission, were the cause of its eventual downfall." [91]

In his preamble to *Report to the President,* General Wedemeyer wrote: "Unlike other powers since V-J Day, China has never been free to devote full attention to internal problems that were greatly confounded by eight years of war. The current civil war has imposed an overwhelming financial and economic burdens at a time when resources and energies have been dissipated and when, in any event, they would have been strained to the utmost to meet the problems of recovery." [92]

Despite the fact that the majority of knowledgeable American people are opposed to recognition of Communist China, there is still a quiet but persistent effort to begin diplomatic relations with Red China, and to admit that regime to the United Nations. President Truman's intervention in Korea, after that nation had been scheduled for liquidation, upset the applecart for the pro-Reds. It became necessary to let the American people "cool off" before placing the United States stamp of approval on the Communist conquest of China.

Recognition of Communist China or its admission to the United Nations would greatly enhance the prestige and power of that state, harm many of our allies, make a greater farce of United Nations, and certainly would not serve the national interest of the United States. Numerous articles have been written, speeches made and debates held on this sub-

---

90 *Wedemeyer Reports,* p. 373.
91 *Ibid.,* p. 377.
92 *Report to the President,* p. 3.

ject.[93] In view of Red China's zeal for murdering Christian missionaries, it is astounding that one of the most influential sources of propaganda in behalf of the regime consists of American church organizations and publications.

In summarizing the defeat and collapse of the Nationalist Government on the mainland, certain factors must be kept in mind. Up until 1944, our policy was one of firm support of the government of Chiang Kai-shek. After the Japanese Empire began to show definite signs of defeat, the Generalissimo became a villain who was no longer useful to our Far Eastern policy. The only alternative to support of Nationalist China was acceptance of a Communist menace far more dangerous to our national security.

Certainly, one of the more important causes for the downfall of the Nationalists on the mainland was the eight-year Sino-Japanese War; it ruined China financially, economically, and morally. Other causes, perhaps more important, may be attributed to the mistakes committed by our government. The Communist sympathies of our Foreign Service Officers and Treasury Officials, the Yalta Agreement, the Marshall Mission, the embargo on arms to China, the release of the State Department White Paper at a crucial moment—all of these events played into the hands of the Soviet Union and the Chinese Communists.

To be more specific, William Pawley stated: "It is my judgment, and I was in the Department of State at the time, that this whole fiasco, the loss of China and the subsequent difficulties with which the United States had been faced, was the result of mistaken policy of Dean Acheson, Phil Jessup, Lattimore, John Carter Vincent, John Service, John Davies, Jr., . . . Clubb, and others." In answer to a question by Senator McClellan, "Do you think those mistakes were all sincere mistakes of judgment, or what?" Pawley replied: "No, I don't, Senator." [94]

The menace of Russia, curiously enough, had been accurately forecast by Commodore M. C. Perry about a century ago. Speaking before the American Geographical and Statistical Society of Massachusetts on March 6, 1856, after just returning from Japan, Commodore Perry said:

. . . . it seems to me that the people of America will, in some form or other, extend their domination and their power, until they shall have . . . placed the Saxon race upon the eastern shores of Asia, and I think too, that eastward and southward will her great rival in future aggrandizement (Russia) stretch forth her power to the coasts of China and Siam; and thus the Saxon and the Cossack will meet. . . . Will it be in friendship? I fear not! The antagonistic exponents of freedom and absolution must thus meet at last, and then will be

---

[93] See J. Weston Walch, *Complete Handbook on Recognition of Communist China,* (Portland, Maine: J. Weston Walch, Publisher, 1954).

[94] *Communist Threat to the United States Through the Carribbean,* Part 10, p. 735.

fought the mighty battle on which the world will look with breathless interest; for on its issue will depend the freedom or the slavery of the world; . . . I think I see in the distance the giants that are growing up for that fierce and final encounter; in the progress of events that battle must sooner or later be fought. . . ."

General MacArthur summarized the results accurately when he said that the greatest mistake in 100 years of American diplomacy was allowing the Communists to gain power in China. It happened because those who wanted it that way were able to gain the upper hand in our government and our media of information.

PART FOUR

Post Mortem

CHAPTER XIX

RETROSPECT AND PROSPECT

In the Introduction to his *Philosophy of History* Georg Wilhelm Friedrich Hegel wrote, "Peoples and governments never have learned anything from history, or acted on principles derived from it."

Indeed, the exceptions are few. A notable one appears in the founding of our own government as a constitutional republic with severely limited federal powers. In this remarkable instance, men of sound historical perspective deliberately set out to establish a government designed to avoid repetition of the errors of the past. The liberal ideal, sought by men of conscience throughout the ages, became for the first time concrete—a truly revolutionary force in the world. The years that followed were golden ones of startling growth and of transcendent influence for good.

Recent decades have been characterized by retreat from the liberal ideal of the freedom of man. Retreat to the debilitating habit of the ages—magnification of the State and a consequent shrinking of man—has been all too evident. This reactionary reversal of the most promising social and political endeavor in history has characterized itself by the customary devices of oppression: private affairs of citizens encompassed by mounting taxes, controls, and interference; military conscription; perpetual involvement in foreign interventionism and war. Precisely such conditions impelled a hardy people of European stock to settle the New World and to establish therein a government denied the powers to reinstitute the baneful practices from which these people had fled.

The doctrines of "collective security" and "indivisible peace" are those of Soviet Foreign Commissar Maxim Litvinov. These entangling doctrines are antithetical to the ideas of Washington, Madison, Jefferson, and Monroe, which permitted flexibility in the matter of national conduct and enabled the dictates of peaceableness, honor, and principled reason to be followed. Committed to a libertarian and pacific course, America's conduct among the nations of the world could, consistent with

439

her liberal ideal, command unsought respect and influence. Conversely, today's hollow preachments, belied by our practice, garner the type of respect and influence customarily enjoyed by a wealthy hypocrite.

Of even more serious—and possibly fatal—import is America's regression to the posture described by Hegel. Subtly involved is elevation of ignorance to a status of positive good. It is the primitivism of anti-knowledge that drags civilizations from their pinnacles and looses the rapine instincts of the savage.

The force of Hegel's observation lies in the nature of the error itself. Rational activity is self-correcting to a high degree. In fields of science, business, and many others where men progress by virtue of rationality, mistakes are cognized and analyzed. Men are instructed by their mistakes, and the prudent man seeks to avoid repetition of his miscalculations. Paradoxically, in the broad realm of politics, men incline to adopt a policy of anti-knowledge, building instead an elaborate body of false knowledge.

Perhaps Alexander Pope put his finger on the point of weakness when he wrote, "Party is the madness of many for the gain of the few." Be that as it may, anti-knowledge by definition rules out self-correction. It is ultimately fatal for any civilization that indulges it. Anti-knowledge is the implicit element in Hegel's observation. Apparently it is a customary failing of advanced civilizations. It must represent some latent uncivilized tendency toward regression to the primitive. Thousands of years of political history reveal repeated manifestations of a tendency among men to retreat to despotism—to endless reinstitution of the stultifying governmental forms of the past. But this is not rational conduct; knowledge and history would forbid it. Degeneration of a free civilization must, therefore, evidence irrationality. It finds expression in George Orwell's slogans of *1984*: "War is Peace; Freedom is Slavery; Ignorance is Strength."

Our American civilization, and world civilization with it, stands at the brink of fulfillment of Hegel's observation. The conditions for our survival as a free civilized people involve knowledge of our history and willingness to take rational action based upon the best and most accurate knowledge we can obtain. Man distinguishes himself from the brute by his reasoning capacity and by his rational application of knowledge. And thereby he establishes civilization—or, failing, destroys it.

A work of history is, first, a search for knowledge for its own sake. But knowledge is not static. It is the beginning, not the end. Acquisition of knowledge by man implies the drawing of conclusions, the passing of rational judgments, the determination of courses of action. False knowledge leads to false conclusions, irrational judgments, and wrong courses of action. No knowledge—ignorance—casts a weight into the scales of regression.

In the foregoing pages, an attempt has been made to trace the sequence of events involved in one of the most complex and disastrous periods of American diplomacy. Conclusions have been drawn, and judgments have been ventured. The period was unquestionably one of determined ignoring of historical facts, of repetition of grave mistakes, of service to ulterior purposes that were often extreme to the point of fanaticism, and of incredible susceptibility to the influence of obviously subversive elements.

An historical work can rarely be considered final, and one dealing with recent and contemporary events can never be so considered. Barring complete descent of an anti-knowledge curtain, it is anticipated that further data will become available in the future. It seems reasonable to assume that additional evidence will only contribute further to an indictment of our war and postwar foreign policy. Otherwise there would be no conceivable reason for its continued suppression. An expurgated collection of the Teheran documents has finally been published. A large portion of the most important material is still being suppressed. We may never get complete, uncensored editions of the Teheran and Yalta documents.

It is anticipated that this book will be vigorously contested. If so, let there be presentation of additional evidence and documentation. We need knowledge—all the knowledge we can get. But we can afford no more of the anti-knowledge of the intellectual barbarians. That is already leading to our destruction.

The author is not motivated by a desire to indulge in uncharitable criticism of men. But he insists upon close scrutiny of the official policies and acts of men, with due attention to the deleterious consequences of such policies and acts. The life of a civilization is far more important than the political reputations of men. Any notion otherwise simply repeats the vanity of the absolute monarchs of early times. They had their "court historians." We, unfortunately, have ours.

There has never been an infallible government on the face of the earth, nor a President of the United States who has not made mistakes. Complexity of the situation enhances the making of mistakes. Seriousness of situations enlarges their consequences. Mistakes in policy lead to multitudes of mistakes in application. A President of the United States may be very much at the mercy of the folly or disloyalty of his subordinates and advisers. Bad policy decisions derive from bad advice and from faulty or deliberately false information. Men, particularly in times of war, become elevated to positions of responsibility beyond their capabilities. Our government is today faced with immense responsibilities of terrible potential import. The least it can be expected to do is to learn something from experience. This it has largely failed to do, under the administration of three postwar presidents.

Our prime concern in the world today lies in the existence of a totally depraved criminal conspiracy openly determined upon our destruction as a free people. It is bent upon imposing on us an economic system that is destructive of individual freedom and reactionary in the extreme. The conspirators intend to make it stick by subjecting us to a ruthless political world dictatorship. The thing we face is a criminal conspiracy, and it must be combated as such. Although there is a threat of military force, that is not the primary or even the eventual means. The so-called war we are losing is of a different sort.

Why and how has this conspiracy been succeeding? The question is rational and extremely important. Careful scrutiny of the *modus operandi*—the method of operation—plays an important part in the detection and prevention of crime. It is vital to success in combating the sort of criminal conspiracy with which we have to deal. The Communist conspiracy has been succeeding largely on the basis of our mistakes and of the ability of their agents to procure such mistakes on our part.

An exacting clinical study of our mistakes is in order. The disaster of United States diplomacy in Asia, if scrutinized, reveals many damaging mistakes that we can avoid repeating. This sequence of events permits us, also, to sketch in exacting detail the *modus operandi* of the enemy.

Perhaps the key mistake, leading to many of the others, was an incredibly blind ignoring of Soviet intentions. There never was any reason for doubt on that score. Unless we assume that our government was staffed exclusively with idiots, we can take it for granted that there was, among governmental officials and advisers, some passing acquaintance with the writings of Lenin and Stalin. Theses and programs of the Communist International were readily available. Dispatches of our Ambassador in Moscow, William C. Bullitt, were highly instructive. The most conclusive evidence concerning Soviet intentions was blithely ignored. We proceeded to destroy completely the balance of power in Europe and in the Pacific.

President Franklin Roosevelt's desire for personal diplomacy—carried to the point of keeping his own Secretary of State in the dark—was another source of mistakes. The President's knowledge was general rather than specific and detailed. Preferring to "shoot from the hip" and to lean toward intuitive judgment, President Roosevelt consistently failed to avail himself of extremely valuable information. Or, as Arthur M. Schlesinger, Jr. has commented, Roosevelt "played by ear" in politics and, especially, in foreign affairs. The President was a consummate politician—an unexcelled "vote-getter." He was impelled to a vain assumption that his political appeal would work with calculating Josef Stalin as it had worked with a most uncalculating American electorate.

Another source of mistakes is to be found in the lack of clearly defined postwar political objectives, as distinguished from the military objective of winning the war. On this score, Captain Russell Grenfell takes Prime

Minister Winston Churchill severely to task. The criticism may apply in even greater degree to President Roosevelt. To the degree that President Roosevelt and some of his associates did have postwar political objectives, they were secret and visionary ones conducive of graver mistakes than would have been the case had there been no objectives at all. Actually, any searching inqury into reasons for our deleterious wartime and postwar diplomacy must distinguish between effects of no objectives and of those which were ill-advised.

Our wartime military objective amounted to complete destruction of the balance of power at both ends of the Eurasian Continent. The nature of the postwar power situation this would present was, apparently, hardly considered. As in World War I, we fought in service to slogans rather than with a cognizance of the realities of global power politics. Infatuation with schemes for rather visionary international organizations for peace finds appropriate description in Charles A. Beard's term for America's twentieth century adventurism: "perpetual war for perpetual peace." No other words can better describe America's only consistently distinguishable objective in two incredibly destructive wars.

Hand in hand with the use of American military might to destroy the balance of power was our lavish dispensing of Lend Lease aid to the Soviet Union. Once maneuvered into the war, the United States could, understandably, supply arms to any nation fighting the common enemy. But expenditure of billions of dollars to build up the Soviet Union into a formidable postwar power has no rational explanation in terms of American interest. Ironically, this was not even conducive to securing Soviet co-operation in President Roosevelt's vision of international organization. However, there was one purpose that could be served. The extreme internationalists were painfully aware of Woodrow Wilson's inability to sell the League of Nations to the American people. Existence of a powerful and threatening external "enemy" would be the only lever strong enough to convince Americans that they should relinquish their national sovereignty. It was also the only rationale for perpetuation of wartime taxes and regimentation.

Extensive Communist infiltration of key positions in our governmental departments—particularly during World War II—has been massively documented. Considerable infiltration and influence were also achieved by Communists throughout the broad spectrum of the institutions of our society. A large influence was thereby exerted upon the thinking of public officials and private citizens alike. President Roosevelt was warned by Representative Martin Dies, long before World War II, of Communist infiltration of our government. The President simply regarded this as no cause for concern. As a matter of fact, the more socialistic of the early New Deal agencies could provide a congenial atmosphere for Communists as well as for other socialists. More radical, perhaps, but the

Communists were neither unsympathetic nor unco-operative with the early New Deal.

The movement of the Communists to the wartime agencies was a natural one from their standpoint. It could have been prevented only by realistic appraisal of official Soviet objectives. Instead, the Burns memorandum very nearly made pro-Communism a requirement for anyone dealing in any way with Soviet-American relations—an extremely broad field when Soviet Russia was our ally in war.

The "Cold War" followed closely on the heels of World War II. Any delusions concerning the desirability of having Soviet agents in our own governmental departments should have been dispelled. To some degree, at least, the Communists had become well enough entrenched in government and in the media of information to defend their positions quite skillfully. In many cases, they were in positions to influence or even control the information and advice given to the President and Secretary of State. It is interesting to note, for instance, that Treasury Department advisers at important conferences were almost invariably Soviet agents. This was also sometimes the case with State Department advisers.

President Truman did little or nothing to eliminate or reduce the often decisive Communist influence in our government. He inherited a task of trying to learn the details of President Roosevelt's highly secretive personal diplomacy. In addition, President Truman was faced with the task of conducting American diplomacy during a most critical period, with many damaging moves having already been made. His additional inheritance of an infiltrated government was something with which he failed to cope. And this led to his diplomatic failure in China.

President Truman's failure to cope with Communist infiltration can be attributed partially to his intensely partisan outlook. His first reaction seemed to be to regard any criticism as a partisan attack, calling for blind, instinctive defense of his administration. An accompanying reaction was one of covering up anything likely to be politically embarrassing—a failing he shared with most professional politicians. It was a luxury that neither the United States nor President Truman could afford in such a critical and dangerous area.

It seems evident that President Truman's refusal to credit the fact of Communist infiltration brought him a harvest of false information and bad advice. In a considerable degree it eventually proved to be his political undoing. Left to himself, he seemed to have a sound inclination to move in the direction of American interest. A case in point was his opposition, as a Senator, to American involvement in a war between two ruthless dictators. Another was his realistic and highly effective policy in Greece and Turkey. But the President was quickly overwhelmed by his office and his advisers. Bad advice caused him to throw away victory in Korea.

Perhaps the key figure in the China debacle was General George C. Marshall. His embargo on munitions and equipment for the Chinese Nationalists turned imminent Nationalist victory into eventual Communist conquest. The proximate cause of Communist military victory in China was virtual disarming of Nationalist forces by the cutting off of their supplies of small arms, automatic weapons and, especially, ammunition. In later stages of the Korean War ammunition was supplied in limited quantities to the combat troops—especially the South Koreans—to prevent their mounting an offensive against the Communist armies. In the case of Cuba, the State Department embargo on arms and ammunitions effectively disarmed the Batista forces. But the embargo, naturally, did not halt Castro's receipt of munitions from Communist and other sources, including secretive shipments from United States ports. In fact, the embargo, as it pertained to American citizens, appears to have been somewhat selectively enforced—in favor of the Communists. The devastating method involving interruption or curtailment of vital military supplies for opponents of Communist military forces has been thrice evidenced—four times, if we count the withholding of air support promised the anti-Castro forces which landed on the Cuban coast. However, this latest event is more analogous to the way in which the Soviet Union contrived the destruction of the Polish patriotic underground in Warsaw. The obvious lesson is simply the fact that these mistakes, or methods, or whatever they are, have been repeated too many times to be mere coincidence. They obviously form a part of the *modus operandi*.

Another technique which aided the Communist forces in China was the use of "truce talks" to save their military forces from threatened destruction. General Marshall obligingly fell for the fraud each time. The technique was used again in the Korean War, and with equal effectiveness. Something similar was used by the Soviets to set the Budapest revolutionaries up for destruction.

The "agrarian reformer" propaganda line, too late, became so thoroughly discredited as to be something of a joke. But a similar propaganda line, built up in the American press, enjoyed equal success in the case of Castro and Cuba—despite the fact that Castro had been a leader in the bloody Communist uprising in Bogotá, Colombia, in 1948.

It is incredible that so many obvious techniques can be successfully repeated time and again. Indeed, if we may assume that our purpose has been that of defending freedom and resisting Communist conquest, the only appropriate comment must be in the words of Solomon: "As a dog returneth to his vomit, so a fool returneth to his folly."

But it is obviously ridiculous to stipulate that so many top officials of four successive American administrations have been fools. Yet this would be the inevitable conclusion if we are to assume that our foreign policy has been what it has been officially advertised to be. If the so-called

"Cold War" were entirely genuine, and if our determined policy were defense of the so-called "free world," as advertised, the more obvious mistakes of the China debacle would hardly have been repeated on more recent occasions. It would simply not make sense. Nor would our conduct to help the Soviet Union at the time of the East German riots in 1953 have made sense.

In fact, we may observe our government officials from the President on down, today, proclaiming that "aid to the underdeveloped countries" is absolutely vital to the fight against Communist aggression. But we find, also, that one of the main points in the Program of the Communist Party, U.S.A., for 1961 is "aid to the underdeveloped countries." This does not make sense.

A key document, in regard to this whole question, was published by the Foreign Policy Association in 1948. It was written by a knowledgeable "liberal" internationalist, Joseph C. Harsch. The title of this *Headline Series* pamphlet was, appropriately, "Does Our Foreign Policy Make Sense?" [1] Harsch found that our foreign policy did not make sense if taken in the context of the traditional American policy of national independence. But he found that the Roosevelt foreign policy did, indeed, make sense if that policy was designed to move the United States into a world government. Regretted was the incidence of the "Cold War" to slow our progress toward that goal which, Harsch intimated, was the basic objective of the Roosevelt administration. Regretted, also, was President Truman's failure to grasp the full import of the foreign policy he inherited. Early removal of some of the domestic wartime controls was another impediment to our progress toward world government.

A former OWI assistant to Elmer Davis, Tris Coffin, has written more explicitly concerning President Roosevelt's primary foreign policy goal: "The United Nations became the great passion of his life. Perhaps it was his pride, the idea of succeeding where others had failed. Perhaps it was a challenge to his imagination, *the radical idea of bringing all the nations of the world together in a federation.*" [2]

If Harsch and Coffin are, indeed, correct in this estimate of President Roosevelt's basic foreign policy goal, the President's far-reaching concessions at Teheran and Yalta become, at least, explainable. The President, we know, was most eager to secure Marshal Stalin's agreement to the founding of a United Nations organization. The price paid, in Europe and in Asia, was an extremely high one. Coffin concedes, explicitly, that Soviet expansion represented the paying of a price: "Mr. Roosevelt was willing to gamble that he could soften the harshness of Soviet Commu-

1 Joseph C. Harsch, "Does Our Foreign Policy Make Sense?", *Headline Series* No. 69, May 20, 1948, (New York: Foreign Policy Association).

2 Tris Coffin, *Missouri Compromise* (Boston: Little, Brown and Company, 1947), p. 9. Emphasis mine.

nism and its imperialism. Part of the formula was to quiet Russian fears for its own security. *The price was expansion to the west."* [3]

It is obvious to any rational person that any sort of world government can be achieved only on Soviet terms. Indeed, that is precisely the long-range Soviet objective. A basic condition would have to be a socialist—or Communist—world economic system. This is the price that must be paid, by all peoples of the world, including those of the United States. This, too, Coffin concedes: "But basically, *Roosevelt planned to pool and reallocate all the basic wealth of the world.* He wanted nations to share their ports and lines of communication and transportation. One program was for pooling the world's shipping and reallocating it by percentages. No one nation, then, would be dependent upon another to carry its goods." [4]

Throughout the administrations which have followed that of President Roosevelt, there has been a considerable degree of continuity in the federal bureaucracy. Continuity of a world government objective has, quite evidently, been maintained by a number of highly influential individuals. The "Cold War" has produced a shift of emphasis toward the idea of regional federation within the framework of NATO. But this can hardly be the end-point for the self-appointed One World planners.

If our government is secretly pursuing a long-range foreign policy goal of world government, success can be achieved only by making vital concessions to the Communist bloc. Accommodation can be gained by no lesser means. Such acts are disastrous ones in terms of American national interest. But if American national interest has already been forfeited in the framing of the goal, then we can see how repeated payments of very expensive installments can be lightly regarded. The sequence of disastrous "mistakes" in the China episode could be regarded as small payment, merely foreshadowing the final payment here at home.

This is all quite fantastic. It would be difficult to credit, were it not for a too-often observed failing of human nature. Fanatics have always, in order to get what they want, been willing and demanding that others pay any price for it. To the degree that these world government advocates enjoy control or influence in our government—and it is only a question of degree—their actions will militate against American national interest and our free enterprise system. In fact, their actions will be difficult to distinguish from those of Soviet agents, so closely parallel are their objectives. The only genuine contest is over who shall rule it, hardly over what it shall be.

Before we can evaluate what has been happening since the close of

---

3 *Ibid.,* p. 273. Emphasis mine.
4 *Ibid.,* p. 272. Emphasis mine.

World War II, we must recognize that the most fanatical sort of extremists have enjoyed a large measure of influence in Washington for more than two decades. Sensible and realistic internationalism is one thing. But this sort of irrational extremism is something else. It is, at the least, potentially suicidal. It is also sacrificial in a most callous sort of way, as millions of people in Eastern Europe and in China could testify.

Ironically, these extremists have long posed as "peace advocates," and undoubtedly they do want peace. They want to build it, personally, on their own terms—and they have been willing to indulge in any amount of war to get it. America's involvement in two tragic world wars in this century—wars made immeasurably more destructive by America's industrial might—has been largely an exercise of these same peace advocates. The art of organizing others for "peace" is the art of conquest. For obvious reasons it usually ends up as war. Imperialism may wear new semantic clothes and be supranational in character, but it is still imperialism.

It should be clearly evident that the Communists cannot gain the world unless our own government helps them to do it. Soviet agents cannot run the United States government, but their purposes can be accomplished by extremists who are willing to seek accommodation at every turn, and if the aim is the formation of a world "coalition government." The China debacle was not achieved by Communists alone, nor could it have been. The Communist conquest of China was secured by non-Communists who had their own reasons for doing what they did. But it does seem reasonable to suppose that a fanatical extremism equalled only by that of the Communists themselves was at least partially responsible.

The details of the China debacle have been recorded with a fair degree of completeness. As a case study, this episode is of extreme value and significance. As an exposure of the *modus operandi* of Soviet conquest, it can hardly be equalled. The lessons we can learn are vital ones on which our future as a free people could depend. In the case of China, we junked our traditional policy which insisted upon the territorial and administrative integrity of China. There is no doubt on that point.

If our present objective is maintenance of the territorial and administrative integrity of the *United States*, careful study of the China episode and application of its lessons can be of great usefulness. The serving of such an end is one purpose the author has in writing this book.

But, even as General Hurley repeatedly and unsuccessfully called for a clear official pronouncement of our China policy, so must we, today, seek some definition of our United States policy. Is it the policy of men of basic peaceableness, of moderation, and of genuine belief in individual freedom as a way of life? Or is it the policy of extremists who blanch neither at war nor at Communist tyranny, if these will further their plans for the world?

Careful study of the sequence of events in China and in Washington shows what to do or what not to do, depending upon the goal to be sought. If our basic policy is maintenance of the territorial and administrative integrity of the United States, then the mistakes made in China should be repeated no more. But if our basic policy is destruction of the territorial and administrative integrity of the United States—that is, world government—the methods used in China are appropriate for the preparatory Fabian communization of the world.

Was American diplomacy in China the debacle we have assumed it to be? Or was it a howling success?

BIBLIOGRAPHY

I. PRIVATE PAPERS

General Joseph S. Stilwell, *MSS.*, Hoover Institution, Stanford

General Patrick J. Hurley, *MSS.*, Santa Fe

Harry Dexter White, *MSS.*, Princeton University

II. PRINTED SOURCES

Official Documents

U. S. Congress:

The Congressional Record, 1941-1949.
Joint Committee on the Investigation of the Pearl Harbor Attack. *Hearings before the Joint Committee on the Investigation of the Pearl Harbor Attack.* 39 parts, 79 Cong., 2d Sess., Washington: Government Printing Office, 1946.
Report of the Joint Committee on Atomic Energy.

Department of State:

Conference At Cairo and Teheran, 1943. Washington: Government Printing Office, 1961.
The Conference of Malta and Yalta, 1945. Washington: Government Printing Office, 1955.
United States Relations with China. Washington: Government Printing Office, 1949.
A Decade of American Foreign Policy, 1941-1949 Washington: Government Printing Office, 1950.
Bulletins, 1945-1950.
Papers Relating to the Foreign Relations of the United States, China, 1942. Washington: Government Printing Office, 1956.
Peace and War: United States Foreign Policy, 1931-1941. Washington: Government Printing Office, 1943.

Papers Relating to the Foreign Relations of the United States, Japan, 1931-1941, 2 vols. Washington: Government Printing Office, 1943.

Papers Relating to the Foreign Relations of the United States, 1943. Washington: Government Printing Office, 1956.

Papers Relating to the Foreign Relations of the United States: The Soviet Union, 1933-1939. Washington: Government Printing Office, 1952.

Transcript of Proceedings: Conference on Problems of United States Policy in China. Division of Central Services, Washington; 1949.

Papers Relating to the Foreign Relations of the United States: Conference of Berlin (Potsdam). 2 vols. Washington: Government Printing Office, 1960.

International Military Tribunal for the Far East:

Record of Proceedings. Alexandria, Virginia: Federal Records Building, 1946-1948. (Mimeographed).

Navy Department:

U.S. Strategic Bombing Survey, Naval Analysis Division, *Japan's Struggle to End the War.* Washington: Government Printing Office, 1946.

U.S. Strategic Bombing Survey, Naval Analysis Division, *Interrogation of Japanese Officials.* 2 vols. Washington: Government Printing Office, 1945.

U.S. Strategic Bombing Survey, Naval Analysis Division, *The Summary Report of the Pacific War.* Washington: Government Printing Office, 1946.

U.S. Strategic Bombing Survey, *The Effects of Strategic Bombing on Japan's War Economy.* Washington: Government Printing Office, 1946.

U.S. Strategic Bombing Survey, *The Effects of Atomic Bombs on Health and Medical Services in Hiroshima and Nagasaki.* Washington: Government Printing Office, 1947.

U.S. Strategic Bombing Survey, *Air Campaigns of the Pacific War.* Washington: Government Printing Office, 1947.

U.S. Strategic Bombing Survey, *The Campaigns of the Pacific War.* Washington: Government Printing Office, 1946.

Department of Defense:

The Entry of the Soviet Union into the War Against Japan: Military Plans, 1941-1945. Washington: Department of Defense, Office of Public Information, 1955.

Department of the Army:

Cline, Ray S. *Washington Command Post: The Operations Division in the United States Army in World War II.* Washington: Office of the Chief of Military History, 1951.

Wedemeyer, Lt. Gen. A. C., *Report to the President.* Submitted September, 1947, Washington: Government Printing Office, 1951.

Stilwell's Command Problems. Washington: Office of the Chief of Military History, 1956.

Romanus, Charles F. and Riley Sunderland, *Stilwell's Mission to China.* Washington: Office of the Chief of Military History, 1953.

U. S. Congress, Senate:

Committee on the Judiciary, *Communist Threat to the United States Through the Caribbean.* 12 parts, 86th Cong., 2d Sess. Washington: Government Printing Office, 1960.

Committee on the Judiciary, *Strategy and Tactics of World Communism, Hearings.* 22 parts, 83d Cong., 2d Sess. Washington: Government Printing Office, 1954-56.

Committee on the Judiciary, *Internal Security Annual Report for 1956.* 17 parts, 85th Cong. 1st Sess. Washington: Government Printing Office, 1957.

Committee on Foreign Relations, *Investigation of United States Far Eastern Policy,* 3 vols.; December, 1945.

Committee on the Judiciary, *Report for the Year 1954.* 83d Cong. 2d Sess. Washington: Government Printing Office, 1955.

Committee on the Judiciary, *Report on Internal Security for the Year 1956.* 84th Cong. 2d Sess. Washington: Government Printing Office, 1957.

Subcommittee on Foreign Relations, *Nomination of Philip C. Jessup, Hearings.* 82d Cong., 1st Sess. Washington: Government Printing Office, 1951.

Committee on Armed Services, *Nomination of General of the Army, George C. Marshall to be Secretary of Defense, Hearings.* 82d Cong. 2d Sess. Washington: Government Printing Office, 1950.

Committee on the Judiciary, *Policy Perversion.* 84th Cong. 2d Sess. Washington: Government Printing Office, 1957.

Committee on the Judiciary, *Interlocking Subversion in Government Departments, Hearings.* 30 parts, 83d Cong. 1st Sess. Washington: Government Printing Office, 1953.

Committee on Armed Forces and the Committee on Foreign Relations, *Military Situation in the Far East, Hearings.* 5 parts, 82d Cong. 1st Sess. Washington: Government Printing Office, 1951.

Committee on the Judiciary, Internal Security Subcommittee, *Institute of Pacific Relations, Hearings,* 15 parts, 82d Cong. 1st Sess. Washington: Government Printing Office, 1951.

Committee on Foreign Relations, *State Department Loyalty Investigation,* 2 parts, 81st Cong. 2d Sess. Washington: Government Printing Office, 1950.

Committee on Foreign Relations, *Interim Aid For Europe, Hearings,* 80th Cong. 1st Sess. Washington: Government Printing Office, 1947.

Committee on the Judiciary, Internal Security Subcommittee, *Scope of Soviet Activity in the United States.* 90 parts, 85th Cong. 1st Sess. Washington: Government Printing Office, 1957.

Committee on the Judiciary, Internal Security Subcommittee, *Interlocking Subversion in Government Departments, Final Report.* 83d Cong. 1st Sess. Washington: Government Printing Office, 1953.

Committee on Foreign Relations, *A Decade of American Foreign Policy: Basic Documents, 1941-1949.* Washington: Government Printing Office, 1950.

Committee on Foreign Relations, *The Nomination of Charles E. Bohlen to be United States Ambassador Extraordinary and Plenipotentiary to the Union of Soviet Socialist Republics, Hearings.* 83d Cong. 1st Sess. Washington: Government Printing Office, 1953.

Committee on the Judiciary, *Final Report for the Year, 1956.* 84th Cong. 2d Sess. Washington: Government Printing Office, 1957.

U. S. Congress, House of Representatives:

Committee on Foreign Affairs, *National and International Movements,* Supplement III, *Communism in China.* Washington: Government Printing Office, 1948.

Committee on Un-American Activities, *Language As A Communist Weapon.* 86th Cong. 1st Sess. Washington: Government Printing Office, 1956.

Committee on Un-American Activities, *Hearings on American Aspects of the Richard Sorge Spy Case.* 82d Cong. 1st Sess. Washington: Government Printing Office, 1951.

Committee on Un-American Activities, *Hearings Regarding Communist Espionage in the United States Government.* 80th Cong. 2d Sess. Washington: Government Printing Office, 1948.

Committee on Un-American Activities, *Hearings Regarding Shipment of Atomic Material to the Soviet Union during World War II.* 81st Cong. 2d Sess. Washington: Government Printing Office, 1950.

Select Committee, *The Katyn Forest Massacre, Hearings.* 7 parts, 82d Cong. 1st Sess. Washington: Government Printing Office, 1949.

Special Committee to Investigate Tax-Exempt Foundations and Comparable Organizations, *Tax-Exempt Foundations, Report.* 83d Cong. 2d Sess. Washington: Government Printing Office, 1954.

Committee on Un-American Activities, *International Communism: Consultation with Major General Claire Lee Chennault.* 85th Cong. 2d Sess. Washington: Government Printing Office, 1949.

Committee on Foreign Affairs, *United States Foreign Policy for a Post-War Recovery Program.* 82d Cong. 2d Sess. Washington: Government Printing Office, 1948.

Committee on Un-American Activities, *The Communist Program for World Conquest.* 85th Cong. 2d Sess. Washington: Government Printing Office, 1958.

Committee on Foreign Affairs, *Assistance to Greece and Turkey,* 80th Cong. 1st Sess. Washington: Government Printing Office, 1947.

Unofficial Collections of Documents, Letters, Speeches

China Presents Her Case to the United Nations, Chinese Delegation to the United Nations, New York: 1949.

Documents on International Affairs, Royal Institute of International Affairs, United Nations Documents, 1946.

Jones, S. Shepard and Denys P. Myers, *Documents on American Foreign Relations, 1941.* Boston: World Peace Foundation.

Roosevelt, Elliott, (ed) *F.D.R., His Personal Letters, 1928-1945.* 2 vols. New York: Duell, Sloane, and Pearce, 1948.

Rosenman, Samuel I. (ed) *Public Papers and Addresses of Franklin D. Roosevelt.* 13 vols. New York: 1938, 1941, 1950.

Stalin's Correspondence with Churchill, Atlee, Roosevelt, and Truman, 1941-1945. 2 vols. London: Lawrence and Wishart, 1958.
Wartime Correspondence by President Roosevelt and Pope Pius XII. New York: Macmillan Company, 1947.

III. NEWSPAPERS AND PERIODICALS

Newspapers

Chicago Tribune
Daily Worker
Dallas Morning News
Dallas Times Herald
Des Moines Register and Tribune
New York Herald Tribune
New York Journal-American
New York Times

New York Times Book Section
New York Times Sunday Magazine
Philadelphia Inquirer
San Francisco Chronicle
Sunday Compass
Washington Daily News
Washington Evening Star
Washington Post

PERIODICALS

Amerasia
American Journal of International Law
American Magazine
American Mercury
Annals of the American Academy of Political and Social Science
Atlantic Monthly
Christian Century
Collier's
Confidential
Facts Forum News
Far Eastern Quarterly
Far Eastern Survey
Foreign Affairs
Foreign Policy Association Bulletin
Fortune
Harper's
Human Events
Life
Look

Mississippi Valley Historical Review
Nation
National Review
New Leader
New Republic
New Yorker
Orbis
Our Times, People's Daily World
Plain Talk
Political Affairs
Public Affairs
Public Opinion Quarterly
Readers Digest
Reporter
Saturday Evening Post
Saturday Review of Literature
The Spectator
This Week
United Nations World
U. S. Naval Institute Proceedings
U. S. News and World Report
Washington News Digest

IV. DIARIES, MEMOIRS, MISCELLANEOUS

Arnold, H. H., *Global Mission*, New York: Harper and Brothers, 1949.
Attlee, Clement R., *The Autobiography of Clement R. Attlee.* New York: The Viking Press, 1954.

Barmine, Alexander, *One Who Survived*. New York: G. P. Putman's Sons, 1945.

Bryan, Arthur, *Turn of the Tide: Diaries of Field Marshal Lord Alanbrooke, Chief of the General Staff*. New York: Doubleday and Company, 1957.

Byrnes, James F., *All in One Lifetime*. New York: Harper and Brothers, 1958.

Byrnes, James F., *Speaking Frankly*. New York: Harper and Brothers, 1947.

Chambers, Whittaker, *Witness*. New York: Random House, 1952.

Chennault, Claire Lee, *Way of a Fighter*. New York: G. P. Putman's Sons, 1949.

Churchill, Winston, *Hinge of Fate*, vol. 4, Boston: Houghton-Mifflin Company, 1950.

——————————, *The Grand Alliance*, vol. 3, Boston: Houghton-Mifflin Company, 1950.

——————————, *Triumph and Tragedy*, vol. 6, Boston; Houghton-Mifflin Company, 1953.

Deane, John R., *The Strange Alliance*. New York: The Viking Press, 1946.

Dimitroff, Georgi, *China: The March toward Unity*, address "The 15th Anniversary of the Communist Party of China."

Eisenhower, Dwight D., *Crusade in Europe*. New York: Doubleday and Company, Inc., 1948.

Farley, James F., *Jim Farley's Story: The Roosevelt Years*. New York: Whittlesey House, 1948.

Gitlow, Benjamin, *I Confess*. New York: F. P. Dutton, Inc., 1940.

Grew, Joseph C., *Ten Years In Japan: A Contemporary Record Drawn from His Diaries and Private and Official Papers, 1932-1942*. New York: Simon and Schuster, 1944.

——————————, *Turbulent Era: A Diplomatic Record of Forty Years, 1904-1945*, 2 vols. Cambridge: Riverside Press, 1952.

Halsey, William F., *Admiral Halsey's Story*. New York: Whittlesey House, 1947.

Harry Dexter White Papers in *Interlocking Subversion in Government Departments*, Parts 28, 30.

Hassett, William, *Off the Record with F.D.R.* New Jersey: Rutgers University Press, 1958.

Hull, Cordell, *The Memoirs of Cordell Hull*, 2 vols, New York: The Macmillan Co., 1948.

Ickes, Harold, *The Secret Diary of Harold L. Ickes*. 3 vols., New York: Simon and Schuster, 1954.

Jones, Jessie, *Fifty Billion Dollars*. New York: The Macmillan Company, 1951.

Jordan, George Racey, *From Major Jordan's Diaries*. New York: Harcourt, Brace and Company, 1952.

Kai-shek, Chiang, *Soviet Russia in China*. New York: Farrar, Straus and Cudahy, 1957.

Kase, Toshikazu, *Journey to the "Missouri"*. New Haven: Yale University Press, 1950.

Kenney, George, *General Kenney Reports*. New York: Duell, Sloan and Pearce, 1949.

"Kido's Diary" in *International Military Tribunal for the Far East*, Document 1632.

Kimmel, Husband E., *Admiral Kimmel's Story*. Chicago: Henry Regnery Company, 1955.

King, Ernest J., and Whitehill, Walter Muir, *Fleet Admiral King: A Naval Record*. New York: Norton and Company, 1952.

Kravchenko, V., *I Choose Freedom*. New York: Charles Scribner and Sons, 1950.

Lane, Arthur Bliss, *I Saw Poland Betrayed*. Indianapolis: Bobbs-Merrill Company, 1948.

Leahy, William, *I Was There*. New York: McGraw-Hill Book Company, Inc., 1950.

Lipper, Elinor, *Eleven Years in Soviet Prison Camps*. Chicago: Henry Regnery Company, 1950.

Millis, Walter, (ed) *The Forrestal Diaries*. New York: The Viking Press, 1951.

Morgenthau Diaries in *Interlocking Subversion in Government Departments*, Parts 29, 30.

Mountbatten, Earl, *Report to the Combined Chiefs of Staff*.

Perkins, Frances, *The Roosevelt I Knew*. New York: The Viking Press, 1947.

Roosevelt, Elliot, *As He Saw It*. New York: Duell, Sloan, and Pearce, 1948.

Roseman, Samuel I., *Working with Roosevelt*. New York: Harper and Brothers, 1952.

Shigemitsu, Mamoru, *Japan and Her Destiny: My Struggle for Peace*. New York: E. P. Dutton and Company, Inc., 1958.

Standley, William and Ageton, Arthur A., *Admiral Ambassador to Russia*. Chicago: Henry Regnery Company, 1955.

Stettinius, Edward R., Jr., *Roosevelt and the Russians: The Yalta Conference*. New York: Doubleday and Company, 1949.

Stilwell Papers, Ed. by Theodore H. White. New York: William Sloane Associates, Inc., 1948.

Stimson, Henry L., *Diary* (November-December 1941) in *Pearl Harbor Attack*, Part II.

————————— *Diary* in *Potsdam Papers*.

Stimson, Henry L. and Bundy McGeorge, *On Active Service in Peace and War*. New York: Harper and Brothers, 1947.

Stuart, John Leighton, *Fifty Years in China*. New York: Random House, 1954.

Truman, Harry S., *Memoirs: Year of Decision*. Vol. 1, Garden City: Doubleday and Company, 1955.

————————— Memoirs: *Years of Trial and Hope*. Vol. 2, New York: Doubleday and Company, Inc., 1956.

Vandenberg, Arthur H., Jr. (Ed.) *The Private Papers of Senator Vandenberg*. Boston: Houghton-Mifflin Company, 1952.

Wallace, Henry A., *Soviet Asia Mission*. New York: Reynal and Hitchcock, 1946.

Wedemeyer, Albert C., *Wedemeyer Reports!* New York: Henry Holt and Company, 1958.

Willoughby, Charles A., *Shanghai Conspiracy: The Sorge Spy Ring*. New York: E. P. Dutton and Company, Inc., 1952.

Wilson, Hugh, *Diplomat Between Wars*. New York: Longmans, Green and Company, 1941.

V. ARTICLES

Alsop, Joseph, "The Foredoomed Mission of General Marshall," *Saturday Evening Post*, January 21, 1950, 114.

——————, "Why We Lost China: The Feud Between Stilwell and Chiang," *Saturday Evening Post*, January 7, 1950, 471.

Barnes, Harry Elmer, "Hiroshima: Assault on a Beaten Foe," *National Review*, May 10, 1958, 441.

Baruch, Bernard M., "A Few Kind Words for Uncle Sam," *The Saturday Evening Post*, June 12, 1948, 16.

Batsman, Herman E., "Observations on President Roosevelt's Health During World War II," *The Mississippi Valley Historical Review*, June 1956, 97.

Beatty, Frank E., "Another Version of What Started the War with Japan," *U.S. News and World Report*, May 28, 1954, 48.

Budenz, Louis, "How the Communists Hoodwinked FDR," *American Mercury*, October 1954, 12-13.

Bullitt, William C., "A Report to the American People on China," *Life*, October 13, 1947, 152-154.

——————, "How We Won the War and Lost the Peace," *Life*, August 30, 1948, 94.

——————, "Can Truman Avoid World War III?" *American Mercury*, June 1947, 646.

Byrnes, James F., "Yalta and Hiss and the Atom Bomb," *Look*, October 14, 1958, 79.

Chamberlain, John, "The Man Who Pushed Pearl Harbor," *Life*, April 1, 1946, 85.

Chamberlain, William Henry, "Hindsight, Foresight, and Blind Sight," *Human Events*, July 23, 1955.

Coughlin, W. J., "The Great *Mokusatsu* Mistake," *Harper's*, March 1953.

Cousins, Norman and Finletter, Thomas K., "A Beginning for Sanity," *Saturday Review of Literature*, vol. 29, no. 24, 78.

Curran, Charles, "Stalin Merely Smiled," *The Spectator*, September 18, 1959.

Current, Richard, "How Stimson Meant to 'Maneuver' the Japanese," *Mississippi Valley Historical Review*, June 1953, 74.

Davis, Elmer, "The Crusade Against Acheson," *Harper's*, March 1951, 28.

Deane, John R., "From Washington to Moscow," *American Mercury*, December 1952, 107.

Earle, George H., "FDR's Tragic Mistake," *Confidential*, August 1958, 57-58.

Fishel, Wesley R., "A Japanese Peace Maneuver in 1944," *The Far Eastern Quarterly*, VIII, 1949, 387-97.

Fluegel, Edna R., "Are We Ready for the Summit?" *Free World Forum*, May, 1959.

Gilbert, Rodney, "The Red Opium Conspiracy," *National Review*, September 15, 1956, 9-10, 21.

Grey, Hilary, "In Memoriam: James V. Forrestal, American Patriot," *American Mercury*, June 1959, 12-13.

Harsch, Joseph C., "Does Our Foreign Policy Make Sense?" *Headline Series* No. 69, May 20, 1948.

Hopkins, Harry, "The Inside Story of My Meeting with Stalin," *American Magazine*, CXXXXII, December 1941.

Hurley, Patrick J., "Why I Resigned as Ambassador to China," *Washington News Digest*, March 1946, 21.

Izard, Ralph, "A General Looks at the Soviet Union," Our Times, *People's Daily World*, February 18, 1949, XII, 35.

Kittredge, T. B., "The Muddle Before Pearl Harbor," *U.S. News and World Report*, December 3, 1954, 137.

Knebel, Fletcher and Bailey, Charles W. II, "Hiroshima: The Decision that Changed the World," *Look*, June 7, 1960, 26-27.

Kubek, Anthony, "How We Lost the Pacific War," *Human Events*, December 1958.

Labin, Suzanne and Emmett, Christopher, "Is There a Sino-Soviet Split?" *Orbis*, Spring 1960, 28-38.

Latourette, Kenneth Scott, "A Church-Made War with China?" *Christian Century*, LVII, 5, January 31, 1940, 140-142.

Lattimore, Owen, "Point Four and the Third Countries," *The Annals of the American Academy of Political and Social Science*, July 1950, 6.

——————, "Rebuilding Our Policy in Asia," *Atlantic Magazine*, January 1950, 23.

——————, "South Korea—Another China," *Sunday Compass*, July 17, 1949.

Law, Daniel S., "Manchurian Booty and International Law," *American Journal of International Law*, 40, July 6, 1946.

Levine, Isaac Don, "Stalin's Spy Ring in the U.S.A.," *Plain Talk*, December 1947, 3.

Mallory, George, "China's New Constitution," *Foreign Affairs*, XXVI, 1948, 390-392.

Minot, Peter, "Harriman: New Deal Reshuffled," *National Review*, December 14, 1955, 14.

Mitchell, Kate, "Political Crisis in China," *Amerasia*, IV, February 1941, 542.

Moorehead, Alan, "Traitor—Klaus Fuchs," *Saturday Evening Post*, May 31, 1952.

Morrison, Samuel Eliot, "Why Japan Surrendered," *The Atlantic Monthly*, October 1960. 44.

Morton, Louis, "The Japanese Decision for War," *U.S. Naval Institute Proceedings*, vol. 80. no. 12, December 1954, 1328.

Nomura, Kichisaburo, "Stepping-Stones to War," *United States Naval Institute Proceedings*, LXXVII, September 1951, 930.

Norton, Louis, "The Military Background of the Yalta Agreement," *The Reporter*, April 1945, 20.

Puleston, "Blunders of World War II," *U.S. News and World Report*, February 4, 1955, 121-123.

Reece, Carroll, "Tax-Exempt Subversion," *American Mercury*, July 1957, 56-57.

Sherwood, Robert, "The Secret Papers of Harry L. Hopkins," *Colliers*, July 17, 1948, 23.

Snow, Edgar, "China to Lin Yutang," *Nation*, February 17, 1945, 180.

—————, "Must China Go Red?" *Saturday Evening Post*, May 12, 1945, 9.

—————, "Sixty Million Lost Allies," *Saturday Evening Post*, June 10, 1944, 44.

Stimson, Henry L., "The Decision to Use the Atomic Bomb," *Harpers*, February 1947, 105.

Stokes, Richard L., "A Tragic Tale of Lend-Lease," *Human Events*, April 1, 1953.

Stuart, John Leighton, "How the Communists Got China," *U.S. News and World Report*, October 1, 1954, 41-42.

"The Story Marshall Told Me," *U.S. News and World Report*, November 2, 1959, 50-56.

Wallace, Henry, "Where I Was Wrong," *This Week*, September 7, 1952.

White, Patrick J., "New Light on Yalta," *Far Eastern Survey*, XIX, 1950, 105-112.

Wittmer, Felix, "Freedom's Case Against Dean Acheson," *American Mercury*.

Woltman, Fred, "The Shocking Story of the Amerasia Case," (Phamphlet) Scripps-Howard, 1950.

Wylie, J. C., Jr., "Reflections on the War in the Pacific," *United States Naval Proceedings*, 78, April 1952, 352.

Zacharias, Ellis, "How We Bungled the Japanese Surrender," *Look*, May 23, 1950, 13-21.

—————, "The Bomb Was Not Needed," *United Nations World*, August 1949.

—————, "The Inside Story of Yalta," *United Nations World*, January 1949, 16.

VI. BIOGRAPHIES, HISTORIES, SPECIAL STUDIES

Alsop, Joseph and Catledge, Turner, *The 168 Days*. New York: Charles Scribner's Sons, Inc., 1938.

Armine, Michael, *The Great Decision: The Secret History of the Atom Bomb*. New York: G. P. Putman's Sons, 1949.

Background to Korea. Washington: Republican National Committee. (Pamphlet)

Bailey, T. A., *A Diplomatic History of the American People*. New York: Appleton-Century-Crofts, 1958.

—————, *The Man in the Street*. New York: Macmillan, 1948.

Bakewell, Paul, Jr., *What Are We Using for Money*. New York: D. Van Nostrand, Inc., 1952.

Baldwin, Hanson, *Great Mistakes of the War*. New York: Harper and Brothers, 1950.

Barnes, Harry Elmer, (Ed.) *Perpetual War for Perpetual Peace*. Caldwell, Idaho: Caxton Printers, 1953.

Barron, Bryton, *Inside the State Department*. New York: Comet Press, 1956.

Beard, Charles, *President Roosevelt and the Coming of the War, 1941*. New Haven: Yale University Press, 1948.

Beloff, Max, *Soviet Policy in the Far East, 1944-1951*. London: Oxford University Press, 1953.

Borg, Dorothy, *American Policy and the Chinese Revolution, 1925-1928*. New York: The Macmillan Company, 1947.

Borkenau, Franz, *European Communism*. New York: Harper and Brothers, 1953.

Brown, Elizabeth C., *The Enemy at His Back*. New York: The Bookmailer, 1956.

Buckley, William F. and Bozell, L. Brent, *McCarthy and His Enemies: The Record and Its Meaning*. Chicago: Henry Regnery, 1954.

Budenz, Louis F., *The Cry of Peace*. Chicago: Henry Regnery, 1952.

——————————, *The Techniques of Communism*. Chicago: Henry Regnery, 1954.

Burnham, James, *Web of Subversion*. New York: John Day Company, 1954.

Butow, Robert, *Japan's Decision to Surrender*. Stanford: Stanford University Press, 1954.

Chamberlain, William Henry, *America's Second Crusade*. Chicago: Henry Regnery, 1950.

Chang, Carsun, *The Third Force in China*. New York: Bookman Associates, 1953.

Cheng, Tien-fong, *A History of Sino-Russian Relations*. Washington: Public Affairs Press, 1957.

Chennault, Claire Lee, *General Chennault on American Policy in China during World War II*. Washington: Government Printing Office, 1948.

China Handbook (1952-1953).

Ciechanowski, Jan, *Defeat in Victory*. New York: Doubleday and Company, 1947.

Coffin, Tris, *Missouri Compromise*. Boston: Little, Brown and Company, 1947.

Creel, George, *Russia's Race for Asia*. Indianpolis: Bobbs-Merrill Company, 1949.

Crocker, George N., *Roosevelt's Road to Russia*. Chicago: Henry Regnery, 1959.

Crofts, Alfred and Buchanan, Percy, *A History of the Far East*. New York: Longmans, Green and Company, Inc., 1958.

Current, Richard, *Secretary Stimson: A Study in Statecraft*. New Jersey: Rutgers University Press, 1954.

d'Albas, Andrieu, *Death of a Navy: Japanese Naval Action in World War II*. New York: The Devin-Adair Company, 1957.

Dallin, David, *Soviet Russia and the Far East*. New Haven: Yale University Press, 1948.

——————————, *The Rise of Russia in Asia*. New Haven: Yale University Press, 1949.

Daniels, Jonathan, *The Man from Independence*. Philadelphia: J. B. Lippincott Company, 1950.

Dawson, Raymond, *The Decision to Aid Russia, 1941*. Chapel Hill: University of North Carolina Press, 1959.

Deconde, Alexander, *Isolation and Security*. Durham: Duke University Press, 1957.

Drummond, Donald F., *The Passing of American Neutrality, 1937-1941*. Ann Arbor: University of Michigan Press, 1955.

Dulles, Allan, *Germany's Underground*. New York: The Macmillan Company, 1947.

Fairbank, John K., *The United States and China*. Cambridge: Harvard University Press, 1948.

Field, James A., Jr., *The Japanese at Leyte Gulf*. Princeton University Press, 1947.

Feis, Herbert, *Between War and Peace: The Potsdam Conference*. Princeton University Press, 1960.

——————, *Churchill, Roosevelt, and Stalin*. Princeton University Press, 1957.

——————, *The China Tangle*. Princeton University Press, 1953.

——————, *The Road to Pearl Harbor*. Princeton University Press, 1950.

Fitch, Geraldine, *Formosa Beachhead*. Chicago: Henry Regnery, 1953.

Flynn, John T., *The Lattimore Story*. New York: Devin-Adair Company, 1953.

——————, *While You Slept: Our Tragedy in Asia and Who Made It*. New York: The Devin-Adair Company, 1951.

Grew, Joseph C., *Invasion Alert!: Red China Drives on the U.N.* Baltimore: Maran Publishers, 1956.

Gunther, John, *Roosevelt in Retrospect: A Profile in History*. New York: Harper and Brothers, 1950.

Hankey, Lord, *Politics: Trials and Errors*. Chicago: Henry Regnery, 1950.

Hillman, William, *Mr. President*. New York: Farrar, Straus, and Young, 1952.

Hunt, Frazier, *The Untold Story of Douglas MacArthur*. New York: The Devin-Adair Company, 1954.

Illicit Narcotic Trade of the Chinese Communists. Taipei, Taiwan: Asian People's Anti-Communist League, 1957.

Isaacs, Harold, *The Tragedy of the Chinese Revolution*. Stanford: Stanford University Press, 1951.

Jones, F. C., *Japan's New Order in East Asia: Its Rise and Fall, 1937-1945*. London: Oxford University Press, 1954.

Kecskemeti, Paul, *Strategic Surrender*. Stanford: Stanford University Press, 1958.

Langer, William L. and Gleason, S. Everett, *The Undeclared War, 1940-1941*. New York: Harper and Brothers, 1953.

Lattimore, Owen, *Ordeal by Slander*. Boston: Little, Brown and Company, 1950.

——————, *Solution in Asia*. Boston: Little, Brown and Company, 1945.

——————, *The Situation in Asia*. Boston: Little, Brown and Company, 1949.

Levi, Werner, *Modern China's Foreign Policy*. Minneapolis: University of Minnesota Press, 1953.

Lohbeck, Don, *Patrick J. Hurley*. Chicago: Henry Regnery, 1956.

MacNair, Harley Farnsworth and Lach, Donald F., *Modern Far Eastern International Relations*. New York: D. Van Nostrand, 1955.

McCarthy, Joseph R., *America's Retreat from Victory: The Story of George Catlett Marshall*. New York: Devin-Adair Company, 1951.

McIntire, Ross T., *White House Physician*. New York: G. P. Putnam's Sons, 1946.

Martinson, Harold, *Red Dragon over China*. Minneapolis: Augsburg Publishing Company, 1956.

Mazour, Anatole G., *Russia: Past, and Present*. Princeton: D. Van Nostrand Company, Inc., 1957.

Mikoljczk, Stanislaw, *The Rape of Poland: Pattern of Soviet Aggression*. New York: Whittlesey House, McGraw-Hill Book Company, Inc., 1948.

Moorad, George, *Lost Peace in China*. New York: E. P. Dutton and Company, 1949.

Morgenstern, George, *Pearl Harbor: The Story of the Secret War*. New York: Devin-Adair Company, 1947.

Morris, Robert, *No Wonder We Are Losing*. New York: The Bookmailer, 1958.

Pollard, Robert T., *China's Foreign Relations, 1917-1931*. New York: The Macmillan Company, 1933.

Possony, Stefan, *A Century of Conflict*. Chicago: Henry Regnery Company, 1953.

Puleston, W. D., *The Influence of Force in Foreign Relations*, New York: D. Van Nostrand Company, 1955.

Rauch, Basil, *Roosevelt from Munich to Pearl Harbor*. New York: Creative Age, 1950.

Rosinger, Lawrence K., *China's Crisis*. New York: Alfred A. Knopf, 1945.

Schroeder, Paul W., *The Axis Alliance and Japanese-American Relations, 1941*. Ithaca, New York: Cornell University Press, 1958.

Sherwood, Robert, *Roosevelt and Hopkins: An Intimate History*. New York: Harper and Brothers, 1948.

Smith, Merriman, *Thank You, Mr. President*. New York: Harper and Brothers, 1946.

Snell, John L., *The Meaning of Yalta: Big Three Diplomacy and the New Balance of Power*. Baton Rouge: Louisiana State University, 1956.

Snow, Edgar, *Red Star Over China*. New York: Random House, 1938.

Spykman, Nicholas J., *America's Strategy in World Politics: The United States and the Balance of Power*. New York: Harcourt, Brace and Company, 1942.

Stein, Gunther, *The Challenge of Red China*. New York: Whittlesey House, McGraw-Hill Book Company, 1945.

Stettinius, Edward R., Jr., *Lend-Lease*. New York: The Macmillan Company, 1944.

Survey of International Affairs, 1939-1946: America, Britain, and Russia, Their Cooperation and Conflict: 1941-1946. London: Oxford University Press, 1953.

Tansill, Charles C., *Back Door to War*. Chicago: Henry Regnery Company, 1952.

Toledano, Ralph de, *Spies, Dupes and Diplomats*. New York: Duell, Sloan and Pearce, 1952.

Walch, J. Weston, *Complete Handbook on Recognition of Communist China*. Portland, Maine: J. Weston Walch, Publisher, 1954.

Wallace, Henry A., *Our Job in the Pacific*. New York: Institute of Pacific Relations, 1946.

Welles, Sumner, *Where Are We Heading*. New York: Harper and Brothers, 1946.

——————————, *Seven Decisions That Shaped History*. New York: Harper and Brothers, 1950.

Westerfield, H. Bradford, *Foreign Policy and Party Politics: From Pearl Harbor to Korea*. New Haven: Yale University Press, 1955.

White, Theodore and Jacoby, A., *Thunder Out of China.* New York: William Sloane Associates, Inc., 1946.

Whitiny, Allen S., *Soviet Policies in China.* New York: Columbia University Press, 1954.

Whitney, Courtney, *MacArthur: His Rendezvous with History.* New York: Alfred A. Knopf Publishers, 1956.

Wilbur, Ray L. and Hyde, Arthur M., *The Hoover Policies.* New York: Charles Scribner's Sons, 1937.

Willkie, Wendell L., *One World.* New York: Simon and Schuster, 1943.

Willoughby, Charles A., *MacArthur: 1941-1951.* New York: McGraw-Hill Book Company, 1954.

Wilmot, Chester, *The Struggle for Europe.* New York: Harper and Brothers, 1952.

Wu, Aitchen K., *China and the Soviet Union.* London: Methuen Company, 1950.

Zacharias, Ellis, *Behind Closed Doors.* New York: Putnam and Company, 1950.

—————————, *Secret Missions,* New York: G. P. Putnam's Sons, 1946.

INDEX

Acheson, Dean, 126, 136, 187, 240, 325, 386; opposition to Grews's plan, 125; opposition to imperial system in Japan, 135-36; denial of 'agrarian reformer' Designation, 239; and Wallace report, 251; protection of Communist personnel by, 271; removal of Dooman by, 283; policy of for postwar Japan, 283, 284; influence of Lattimore on, 284; attack on MacArthur, 285; urges cooperation with Communists, 322; and Marshall instructions, 326; cancellation of Wedemeyer appointment by, 340; opposition to McCarran bill, 397; and aid to Nationalist China, 401-02; criticism of Nationalist China, 404; and cause of fall of China, 406; 'wait till the dust settles' policy, 408, 427; review of Far Eastern policy by, 413; opposed to Nationalist blockade, 422; secret directive by, 422, 429; influence on President Truman, 423; and recall of personnel from China, 429-30

Adams, Josephine Truslow: Browder's representative to White House, 248n

Adler, Solomon, 188: member of Silvermaster Group (Communist cell), 185; criticized by Chiang Kai-Shek, 186; report by on mission to Communist China, 199; approval by of Chinese Communists, 234 and n

Alanbrooke, Field Marshal Lord, adviser to Churchill: comment on Russian attitude, 59

Alsop, Joseph, 207n, 240

Amerasia Case, 278; 282: attack on Ambassador Grew, 281; documents given to Communists in, 291

American Circular Note, x

American Military Mission: welcome to by Mao Tse-tung, 199

American Observer: schoolpaper used by Institute of Pacific Relations (IPR), 349

American Press: pro-Communist bias of, 229, 287; address by General Hurley to, 288; defense of career men by, 307

American Transport Command: results of air lift by into China, 206-07

Anderson, Clinton P., 323

Anti-Comintern Pact: signed by Japan, 10

"Anvil": operation in Southern France, 79

Army Intelligence: report of on influence of Russia on Chinese communism, 323

Army Operations Division: plans of for end of war, 139

Army Signal Corps: Japanese diplomatic code broken by, 26

Arnold, General H. H., 62, 119, 131

"Asiaticus" (pen name of Hans Moeller): criticism of Snow by, 371-72

Atcheson, George, 292-93, 299, 395; recommended aid to Chinese Communists, 274, 391; effect of recommendations by, 274-275; recall of, 276; defended by General Hurley, 291, 297-98; by Byrnes, 310

Atkinson, Brooks: praise of Communists, 254; attack on Nationalist Government by, 254

Atlantic Charter, 12, 43, 63, 95, 160, 304

Atom Bomb: discussion of at Yalta, 101-102; test of, 143; Great Britain on the use of, 151; second dropped, 152; objections by scientist to use of, 154-55; affect of on surrender of Japan, 155; use of justified by President Truman, 157

Attlee, Clement, Prime Minister of Great Britain, 147, 432

Austin, Senator, 295

Badgar, Vice Admiral Oscar C., 400, 406: on Soviet weakness in the East, 122; report by on condition of weapons, 401

Bagge, Widar, Swedish Minister to Japan: opposed "unconditional surrender" plan, 118

well, 219-20; mission of to China, 214;
American paratroopers in China, 223;
efforts of sabotage by American pro-
Communists, 234, 237, 239, 259, 274, 277,
280, 289, 294-95; use of Wallace Report
by, 251; personal representative to
Chiang Kai-shek, 253-54; agreement
secured from Communists, 255; negotiation between Nationalists and Communists, 256, 257; opposition of to aid for
Communists, 259-60; tribute to Chiang
Kai-shek, 261, 301; resignation of, 289;
objective of mission by, 289; support of
Presidents and Secretaries of State, 289;
no statement of policy made, 289, 296;
request for use of documents, 290-91;
urged recall of Atcheson and Service,
293; answers to La Follette, 293; on
Communist knowledge of secret documents, 295; conference with President
Truman, 296; praise of Wedemeyer by,
300; work of appraised, 301n; statement of position of, 304; exchange with
Byrnes, 312-13; resignation of, 319

Ickes, Harold L., 24n, 41
India: discussed by Roosevelt and Stalin,
85
Indochina: France and, 85
Inner Mongolia: occupation by Japan, x;
defense against Russia, 3
Interim Committee; advisory to Truman
on use of atomic bombs, 153 and n,
154 and n
International Fund and Bank, 188
Institute of Pacific Relations (IPR): Far
Eastern activities assigned to, 247-48;
pro Communist bias of, 247n, 252, 345-
346, 355; history and structure of, 344;
purposes of, 344-45; membership of, 345;
political effect of, 346; on aid to Communist China, 348; production of
printed material by, 348-49; influence of
on schools, 349; and Troop Training
Programs, 351; interlocking activities of,
351-52; aid of to Rogoff, 353; Communist connections of, 355, 358, 359; International Conferences sponsored by, 357;
effect of on fall of Nationalist China,
360-62; cited as subversive, 362; Lattimore editor for, 367; hearings on Mongolia by, 370-71
Iran Declaration: principles of defeated,
304
Issacs, Harold, author, No Peace in Asia,
380
Iwo Jima, conquest of, 162

Jacoby, Annalee, 379: defense of career
men by, 307; book review by 381; joint
author of Thunder Out of China, 382
Jaffe, Philip, 285
Japan: export market for United States,
ix; threat to of Communism in China,
3, 7-8; withdrawal from League of Nations, 3; effect of embargo on, 4; cancellation of commercial treaty, 4; new policy of, 5; advance into Indochina
planned, 9; commitment in China, 25;
plan for war against, 80; defeat of certain, 91; surrender terms offered, 91-92;
secret offers of surrender, 92, 129, 137,
138, 145; economic condition after Leyte,
116; and Potsdam Declaration, 146, 148;
dominance of Army in, 149; conditional
offer of surrender, 152; acceptance of
peace terms, 152-53; effect of war with,
158
Japanese Planning Board: estimate of
country's resources by, 6
Jarsky, American prisoner in Russia, 34
Jessup, Philip, 240, 357, 401, 413, 425-26:
present position of, 402n; recognition of
Red China suggested by, 417
Joffe, Adolf, 1
Johnson, Colonel Dana: report by on Japanese readiness for peace, 123
Johnson, Herschel V., American Ambassa-
dor to Sweden: peace plan reported to,
118
Johnson, Louis: on admission of Commu-
nist China to United Nations, 427n
Johnson, Nelson, American Ambassador to
China,: orders to promote Chinese unity,
242; on United States obligation to Na-
tionalist China, 261; on defense of Chi-
nese Communists, 365
Johnstone, William C.: correction of with
Rogoff, 354
Jordan, Major George R.: connection of
with closing Newark airfield, 44
Joy, Admiral Charles, 423
Judd, Congressman Walter: on relations of
United States and China, 202, 234n;
Wallace Report demanded by, 251; on
Communists in State Department, 271-
273; on Communist motives, 334; com-
parison of China and Greece, 342, 402-
403; on aid to China, 394, 406-07

Karakhan, Leo, Russian agent in Far East,
1, 370
Kase, Toshikazu: peace bid after Saipan,
115; on acceptance of ultimatum, 148
Kawabe, Lieutenant General Ija,: on Manchuria, 117-18